THE DARTNELL

ADVERTISING

MANAGER'S

HANDBOOK

DARTNELL is a publisher serving the world of business with business books, business manuals, business newsletters and bulletins, training materials for business executives, managers, supervisors, salesmen, financial officials, personnel executives and office employees. In addition, Dartnell produces management and sales training films and cassettes, publishes many useful business forms, conducts scores of management seminars for business men and women and has many of its materials and films available in languages other than English. Dartnell, established in 1917, serves the world's whole business community. For details, catalogs, and product information, address: DARTNELL, 4660 N. Ravenswood Avenue, Chicago, Illinois 60640, USA—or phone (312) 561-4000.

Second Edition
"Second Printing, April, 1979"

Copyright 1969, 1977
in the United States, Canada, and Great Britain by
THE DARTNELL CORPORATION

All rights reserved

Library of Congress Catalog Card Number 68-21480

International Standard Book Number 0-85013-084-0

Printed in the United States of America by Dartnell Press, Chicago, Illinois 60640

THE DARTNELL
ADVERTISING
MANAGER'S
HANDBOOK

by
Richard H. Stansfield

THE DARTNELL CORPORATION
CHICAGO and LONDON

INTRODUCTION

THERE are not many 1,500-page handbooks these days, publishing costs being what they are. This one runs to slightly over that many pages. But the subject—the complex art-science-trade of advertising—requires a lot of elbow room for definitive treatment of all its aspects.

Given the elbow room by his publisher, The Dartnell Corporation, Richard H. Stansfield has come up with what I consider the first truly definitive handbook on the subject. His work will be treasured as a reference book by many different kinds of people in the field—from ad managers to copywriters to agency chairmen of the board. It is truly a panoramic view of the good practitioners at work.

Every aspect of modern advertising is treated in depth in this big handbook—campaign planning, agency selection, prospect identification, copywriting, headlines, media, research, surveys, source material, corporate image-building. All of this, and more, is easily available to the reader through the extensive index.

The text abounds in case histories—and not only of the good ads and successful campaigns. Dick Stansfield makes use of the "what not to do" training technique with many inclusions he labels Horrible Examples. The author not only tells his reader *how* something should be handled—he also tells him *why*, which is something many of us have forgotten.

For the beginner in advertising, this handbook is as good as 10 years in the business. For the seasoned advertising man, it is a treasure of reference. As someone has said, we read not so much to be informed as to review what we already know. And the veteran of the advertising wars will find much here to convince him that he stands with the elderly farmer who told the university agricultural extension professor, "I already know how to farm better than I'm farming now." Any one of us now toiling in the advertising field could benefit from a review of Dick Stansfield's work.

Richard H. Stansfield has sat on both sides of the advertising desk. He has worked for top-flight agencies serving large industrial clients, and he has dealt with agencies as manager of advertising for large industrial clients. He knows the strengths and the weaknesses of each, and how one should work with the other to accomplish the most for client and company.

While this handbook may seem oriented entirely toward industrial advertising, there actually is much here that can be fruitfully applied to consumer advertising, particularly in these days of overstress on the "hot little creative shops." While industrial advertising has displayed plenty of creativity, the "hot little shops" could learn much from the hard-working, dollar-conscious objectivity of the good industrial ad manager and agency.

This is a "gutsy" handbook. Dick Stansfield doesn't believe in sacred cows. But he's realistic enough to know there are a few around, and tells you where they might be hiding. He warns the advertising manager of the prejudices and the myths which top-management people cherish about advertising—and he offers the kind of arguments designed to overcome such obstacles. Here are the fact-packed answers to the vice-presidents and sales managers and engineers who think their company advertises only "because everyone else does."

This is not an *opinionated* handbook. Dick Stansfield knows his research, and when he's discussing the pros and cons of one ad method over another, one position over another, a choice of media or which technique, he takes a firm stand. But he offers proof from the findings of established advertising studies on the question. Dick Stansfield rests his case only upon the available evidence.

It will be a wise top-management man who sees to it that a copy of this handbook is on the desk of every hand in the ad department. He can trust his people to the mind of Dick Stansfield, who is cost-conscious on every page. Stansfield sees advertising as the handmaiden of sales, not as a direct source of sales, and he likes to see every dollar spent on advertising earn its way. Short cuts, dollar-savers, and timesavers abound in the text.

There are nearly 500 illustrations in *The Advertising Manager's Handbook* and many helpful charts and tables.

Altogether it's a prime investment for anyone concerned with advertising, from the company president who okays the budget down to the neophyte just starting or the student who's planning a career in the most fascinating business in the world.

ZENON C. R. HANSEN
Former Chairman of the Board and President,
Mack Trucks, Inc.
One of the Signal Companies

CONTENTS

CONTENTS

Page

CONTENTS

ACKNOWLEDGEMENTS

MORE THAN 300 persons in industrial advertising and the agency field helped make this book. They contributed case histories or other data, and were responsible for most of the illustrations. To their generous and unselfish help, the author and the publisher are deeply grateful. The names of the men and women who contributed follow, in two groups divided as to whether they are agency-media or industry people.

AGENCY AND MEDIA PERSONNEL

R. B. AMAND, Account Supervisor, Northlich, Stolley, Inc.

AMERICAN BUSINESS PRESS, INC.

DON BALDWIN, Account Executive, Batten, Barton, Durstine & Osborn, Inc.

The Late W. STORRS BALDWIN, Vice-President, Diamond T Motor Truck Co.

LEE BARTLETT, Former Vice-President, Marsteller Inc.

GENE BEAUDET, Editor-in-Chief, *Iron Age*

JOHN F. BELCHER, Account Executive, Cunningham & Walsh Inc.

JACK E. BERGREN, Regional Business Manager, *Iron Age*

GRADY C. BOLES, Vice-President, Edward H. Weiss and Company

CHARLES BOWES, President, The Bowes Company (Retired)

THOMAS R. BRAMSON, President and Publisher, *Production*

HALE CAREY, District Manager, *Dun's Review*

RICHARD C. CHRISTIAN, President, Marsteller Inc.

BRUCE COLE, Vice-President, General Manager, Marsteller Inc. (Chicago office)

WILLIAM CONDIT, President, Condit Corporation

WALTER G. CRUICE, Vice-President, Pohlman Studios, Inc.

VAN CUNNINGHAM, Vice-President, Fuller & Smith & Ross Inc.

JOHN DAGHLIAN, Reader Feedback Project Manager, McGraw-Hill Publications

RICHARD DIERCKS, Account Executive, Campbell-Mithun, Inc.

WILLIAM J. DWYER, District Manager, *Research/Development*

EUGENE ELDRIDGE, District Manager, *Analytical Chemistry*

THOMAS FALLON, Regional Vice-President, Chilton Company

GEORGE JOEL FINE, Promotion Manager, Visual Panographics, Inc.

JOHN T. FOSDICK, President, John T. Fosdick Associates, Inc.

MISS LINDA F. FRIEDMAN, Account Supervisor, Universal Public Relations, Inc.

ACKNOWLEDGEMENTS

JOHN A. FROST, Account Executive, Howard H. Monk and Associates, Inc.

C. A. GODING, Account Supervisor, Marsteller Inc.

KENNETH W. GOOD, Account Executive, Associated Techdata Inc.

J. J. GRAHAM, Managing Editor, *Advertising Age*

RICHARD H. GROVES, Executive Vice-President, Chilton Company

J. SANDERS HAAS, N. W. Ayer & Son

JASON HAILEY, Photographer

HENRY L. HAYDEN, Vice-President, Vernet/Hayden, Inc.

JOHN B. HOLMES, District Manager, *Product Design & Development*

JAMES J. HUGHES, Managing Editor, *Steelways*

PAT HURLEY, Public Relations Department, Gray & Rogers, Inc.

EUGENE H. JACOBS, Publisher, *Automotive Industries*

ALFRED J. JAFFE, Editor, *Marketing Forum*

JEFFERSON ADVERTISING AGENCY, creator of the Norplex ad, "It Can't Be Done."

MISS BARBARA H. KAPLAN, N. W. Ayer & Son, Inc.

MICHAEL J. KELLY, Vice-President, *Production*

ROBERT E. KENYON, JR., Executive Vice-President, Magazine Publishers Association, Inc.

ELAINE KORTAS, Media Director, Marsteller Inc.

RICHARD H. LABONTE, Director of Promotion, McGraw-Hill Publications

JOHN K. LEE, Assistant Director, Marketing Communications Research Center

ROBERT LETWIN, Editor, *Sales Meetings*

The Late T. J. LOPATKA, Vice-President, Diamond T Motor Truck Company

J. BRADLEY MacKIMM, District Manager, *Electronics*

RICHARD MANVILLE, Richard Manville Research Inc.

JAMES B. MARINE, President, The Bowes Company

ROBERT McCANN, Traffic Manager, Papert, Koenig, Lois, Inc. Advertising

ROBERT G. MERRICK, Hal Lawrence Incorporated

CHARLES S. MILES, Assistant Publications Manager, Thomas Micro-Catalogs, Thomas Publishing Company

DAVID H. MURRAY, Account Executive, Chirurg & Cairns, Inc.

DOROTHY M. NEWMAN, Editorial Assistant, *Industrial Marketing*

MELVIN B. NYLUND, District Manager, *Construction Methods & Equipment*

DON "Antelope" OLSON, friend, hunting partner, and provider of moral support; he assured me a wise old buck was growing a pair of huge, 18-inch horns while I was writing this book, and that I would surely cut his trail when the next season rolls around in Wyoming.

WILLARD D. PEASE, President, Images West

WILLIAM A. PHAIR, Publisher, *Product Design & Development*

FRANK M. PHILLIPPS, Phillipps Associates, Inc.

FRED C. POPPE, President, Complan Inc.

CHARLES B. RAWSON, Editor, *Commercial Car Journal* (Retired)

G. BRUCE RICHARDSON, General Manager, Marsteller Inc. (Pittsburgh office)

M. R. Robinson, Director, Cahners Audit, Cahners Publishing Company Inc.

Frank Rock, Jr., Vice-President, Busch and Schmitt, Inc.

Richard L. Scheidker, Senior Vice-President, American Association of Advertising Agencies

Harold Scott, District Manager, *Successful Farming*

J. J. Smiley, Jr., Vice-President, Graphic Service

Smith-Klitten Advertising (agency for Genisco)

Stanley B. Stewart, President, Stewart, Price, Tomlin, Inc.

Howard A. Stone, President, Daniel Starch and Staff

Carroll Swan, Editor, *Media/scope*

Gilbert Thayer, Publisher, *Research/Development* (Retired)

Frank W. White, Account Executive, Harris D. McKinney, Inc.

E. C. Wiegand, Jahn & Ollier Engraving Company

Roland Werth, Regional Vice-President, Chilton Company

Jerome S. Wilford, Vice-President, *Production*

Dave Wilson, Account Executive, Marsteller Inc.

John Wilson, Vice-President, Batten, Barton, Durstine & Osborn, Inc.

Spencer Zogg, Vice-President, Pohlman Studios, Inc.

INDUSTRY PERSONNEL

Kay Ackermann, Secretary, Lindberg Hevi-Duty

W. Scott Allan, Assistant Vice-President and Manager of Public Relations, Liberty Mutual Insurance Company

J. W. Ament, Vice-President, Transue & Williams Steel Forging Division of Standard Alliance Industries, Inc.

Richard J. Andersen, Manager, Advertising and Sales Promotion, The Ingersoll Milling Machine Company

B. E. Anderson, Director of Advertising and Public Relations, Bliss & Laughlin Industries

R. F. Anderson, Manager, Advertising, Centralab Electronics Division Globe-Union Inc.

Robert S. Atcheson, Manager, Advertising and Public Relations, Marbon Chemical Division of Borg-Warner Corporation

J. W. Atkinson, Sales Promotion and Advertising Manager, A. B. Dick Company

Jon Avrigean, Director of Advertising, Wheeling Steel Corporation

J. R. Barlow, Manager—Advertising and Sales Promotion, Chrysler Motors Corporation

Albert M. Battis, Vice-President, DeJur-Amsco Corporation

Ben S. Beall, III, President, Lindberg Hevi-Duty Division of Sola Basic Industries, Inc.

Ross T. Beirne, Advertising Manager, Giddings & Lewis Machine Tool Co.

Howard Bersted, Director, Advertising and Sales Promotion, Automatic Electric Company, Subsidiary of General Telephone & Electronics

P. A. Binney, Manager, Public Relations, Norton Company

D. A. Blanchard, Director of Advertising and Public Relations, Royal Typewriter Company, Inc. A Division of Litton Industries

D. E. Bockover, Advertising & Sales Promotion Manager, Carrier Air Conditioning Company

Richard M. Boden, Promotion Group Supervisor, Advertising & Sales Promotion, The Babcock & Wilcox Company

M. W. Bolster, Manager, Commercial Products Advertising and Sales Promotion Department, Shell Oil Company

Francis L. Bria, Manager, Product Promotions, Motorola Semiconductor Products Inc.

J. S. Brown, Advertising Manager, Reichold Chemicals, Inc.

Ted Burke, Director, Public Relations and Advertising, The Garrett Corporation

Ted Busch, Sales Manager, Shooting Equipment, Inc.

M. V. Buzzi, Media Manager, The Firestone Tire & Rubber Company

A. W. Cameron, Advertising Manager, ITT Semiconductors

Alec Cameron, Manager, Marketing Services, ITT Semiconductors

Richard H. Campbell, Manager, Advertising and Sales Promotion, Millers Falls Company

Wayne E. Chambers, Jr., Advertising Coordinator, Aluminum Company of America

Darden Chambliss, Director of Communications, The Aluminum Association

John M. Clampitt, Director of Advertising, United Air Lines

Arthur P. Clark, Director of Communications, Basic Incorporated

R. W. Clark, Sales Manager, Detrex Chemical Industries, Inc.

H. Walton Cloke, Vice-President, Corporate Public Relations and Advertising, American Can Company

J. W. Cohoe, Advertising Manager, Corporate Staff, Ex-Cell-O Corporation

Conrad H. Collier, Director, Advertising and Public Relations, Tenneco, Inc.

Miss Barbara Conway, Manager, Special Advertising Programs, Eastern Air Lines Incorporated

J. T. D. Cornwell, Jr., Advertising and Sales Promotion Manager, Celanese Chemical Company, A Division of Celanese Corporation

D. Gregg Cummings, Advertising Manager, Electro-Motive Division, General Motors Corporation

John Cunin, Bearings, Inc.

Wes Curry, Sales Promotion Supervisor, Packard Instrument Company, Inc.

Wm. B. Daub, Advertising Manager, Industrial Products, Sun Oil Company

Frank E. Davis, Jr., Director of Advertising, Koppers Company, Inc.

James Dean, Advertising Manager, McGregor Division, Brunswick Corporation

John L. DeFazio, Marketing Communications Representative, Electronic Components and Specialty Products, Westinghouse Electric Corporation

E. A. Dehner, Advertising and Sales Promotion Manager, Exide Industrial Marketing Division, ESB Incorporated

James R. Derose, Advertising Manager, Soabar Company

Morris D. Dettman, Director, Advertising and Merchandising, Honeywell Inc.

JERRY DORFMAN, President, Protective Lining Corporation

WILLIAM T. DYER, Advertising Manager, Corning Electronics Products Division, Corning Glass Works

A. E. EGGERS, Advertising Manager, Residential Lighting Division, Thomas Industries Inc.

J. DAVID EHLERS, Advertising Manager, Mallory Battery Company, A Division of P. R. Mallory & Co., Inc.

RICHARD EHRLICH, Advertising Director, Hertz System, Inc.

JAMES ELDER, Sales Promotion Assistant, Holo-Krome Company

HERBERT H. FEINGOLD, Director, Corporate Planning, Servo Corporation of America

J. O. FERCH, Sales Department, Modern Equipment Company

G. D. FERREE, Chief, Product Information and Advertising, Chandler Evans Inc. Colt Industries

ROBERT D. FRENCH, Advertising Manager, Potlatch Forests, Inc.

B. T. FULLERTON, Director of Marketing, The Warner & Swasey Company

D. F. GAINES, Advertising Manager, The National Cash Register Company

S. M. GATES, Assistant Director of Advertising, Republic Steel Corporation

DONALD GAY, Vice-President—Sales, The Bristol Brass Corporation

MEYER GOLDBERG, General Sales Manager, Wide World Photos, Inc.

C. R. GRAHAM, Advertising Manager, Industrial Products, The Goodyear Tire & Rubber Company

JAMES W. GRAHAM, Manager Marketing Services, Brush Instruments Division, Clevite Corporation

DONALD G. HANSEN, Pitney-Bowes, Inc.

DON HARGRAVE, Advertising Manager, Siliconix Incorporated

J. E. HARTMAN, Assistant to the Director, Marketing Communications, Westinghouse Electric Corporation

HOWARD H. HAVEMEYER, Thomson Industries, Inc.

W. H. HELFRICK, Advertising Manager, Landis Machine Company

W. H. HENDERSON, JR., Director of Corporate Relations, North American Car Corporation

EDWARD D. HENDRICKSON, President, Hendrickson Manufacturing Company

DONALD F. HENRY, Marketing Services Manager, Anaconda Aluminum Company

M. M. HERRICK, Sales Promotion & Advertising Manager, Johnson Service Co.

F. LEROY HESS, Vice-President, Editorial Division, Standard Rate & Data Service, Inc.

J. R. HIGHT, Director, Public Relations and Advertising, Jones & Laughlin Steel Corporation

J. F. HOBBINS, Advertising Manager, The Anaconda Company

L. GREGORY HOOPER, Chicago Rawhide Manufacturing Company

JAMES J. HUBBARD, Account Executive, Marsteller Inc.

THOMAS G. HUBER, Director, Jeolco, Inc.

DAVID P. HUGHES, JR., Advertising Manager, E. F. Houghton Company

(Continued on page 1447)

Chapter 1

DEPARTMENT ORGANIZATION AND FUNCTIONS

A TTEMPTING to draw up a nice, neat organizational chart for the typical industrial advertising department is something like trying to describe the average sunset. It can't be done because there isn't any such thing.

Advertising departments are like the companies they serve. They vary widely in size and organizational complexity. This is due to differences in the number of product lines manufactured, the number of markets in which these products are sold, distribution channels, company marketing objectives, advertising objectives, the competitive climate and, of course, the size of the company.

Assume for a moment that there is such a thing as a typical advertising department in a typical company which sells a typical product through typical distribution channels to typical customers. Makeup of this department is, unfortunately for the typical company, the archaic one-man-and-a-girl operation common in industry since the birth of advertising. This one-man department almost invariably reports to the sales manager. His work load is heavy, and consists of a mixture of space ads, product literature and direct-mail pieces; thrown at him from time to time are requests to "write a nice speech for the president to give at the local lodge," and similar odds and ends. After all, he is the company's communications specialist.

Change in the Wind

Happily for industry, this casual attitude toward—and reluctance to provide sufficient funds for—a key staff function is fast becoming a thing of the past.

This is not due to a spontaneous burst of philanthropic generosity on corporate management's part, however. Rather, it is the result of the realization that, in an increasingly competitive economy something *must* be done to reduce the cost of sales and at the same time increase total sales volume.

Making generalizations is usually a time-wasting exercise, although occasionally a valid one crops up. One is that in the overwhelming majority of small- and medium-sized industrial companies the level of marketing sophistication is low when compared to the industrial giants, and even more so when compared to leading manufacturers of consumer products.

In the modest-sized industrial firms advertising is still regarded strictly as a tool "to help sell the product." And, incredible as it may seem, attitude studies consistently show that almost half of the presidents of these companies have either a negative attitude toward advertising, or have serious mental reservations as to its true effectiveness. It is inconceivable to these business executives that advertising can solve other communications problems for their companies.

This naiveté, this failure to exploit fully marketing's most versatile tool, is reflected in a simple organizational structure. The advertising manager, who is not really a member of the marketing team, generally reports to the director of sales, or, if the title exists, to the director of marketing. Advertising, such a potent and productive force when used properly, makes a minimum contribution to the sales success of such firms because it is not permitted to do otherwise. The straight-line organizational chart common in this type firm is illustrated here.

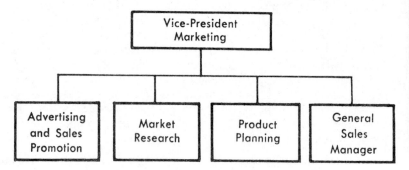

Attitudes within the company affect the organization of the advertising department and its place within the company's structure. Whether a company is marketing oriented, or product oriented, whether it is aggressive or complacent, whether it is growth minded or content to drift, are but a few of the factors affecting advertising's importance in the corporate scheme of things. They also affect how the advertising department is organized, and determine to a large extent how good a job advertising is allowed to do.

Large companies with a history of success have a large and effective marketing arm. The advertising department in such companies is highly competent and is departmentalized for maximum efficiency, as shown on page 20. It is in such surroundings, where advertising is recognized as perhaps the most important marketing service, that it makes such a significant contribution. It is here that it is permitted to.

House-Agency Advertising

Hybrid advertising departments, so called because they actually are a combination advertising department and advertising agency, are on the wane. Few really large ones exist in industry now, although they attained a considerable degree of acceptance 20 years or so ago.

The 150-man-plus department of Deere & Company, a leading manufacturer of farm equipment and construction machinery, is a good example of the house-agency type of operation.

Administrative and supervisory personnel normally found in any industrial advertising department are present, and function in similar capacities at Deere. In addition, Deere has on the company payroll personnel encountered at no other place except in a recognized agency. Copywriters, art directors, media directors, production men, traffic, all are represented.

Deere also has a large, lavishly equipped photographic department. Its staff is able to produce top-quality illustrative photos, either in the studio or on some far-flung location, in black and white or color. Few advertising departments can say as much, for this is a far cry from the average ad man's ability to grab the company Speed Graphic and shoot a plant picture to save calling in an expensive commercial photographer.

Just as input, in terms of talent, is high at Deere, output of the advertising department is of a very high caliber. Space ads and collateral material are as thoroughly professional as any produced by the best Madison Avenue shop.

Oddly, Deere space is placed by a recognized 4A advertising agency in return for market-research assistance. The agency, of course, receives the commission on the space expenditure.

The decline and fall from favor of the hybrid department is due to a number of things. High on the list, although not necessarily at the top, is the staggering cost. Competent creative people com-

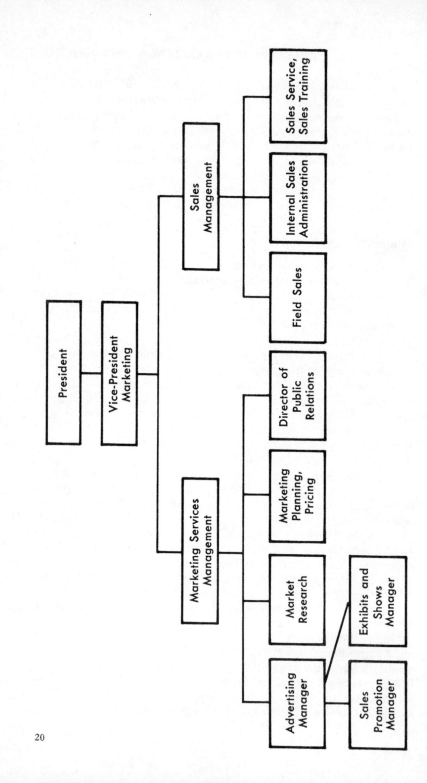

mand excellent salaries, as do those in associated advertising functions. Add salaries to the fringe costs customary in industry, and the result is a cost so high few companies can, or will, bear it. This cost would not have to be tacked onto the normal cost of the department if the company went the usual route and retained an advertising agency to create and produce its material.

Even more important, however, is the lack of fresh thinking. Most companies which have tried and rejected the house-agency concept did so on this score. There's a tendency, apparently an inexorable one, for house-agency personnel to go stale. The creative people tend to take the same tack, to use the same "tried and proved" approach to different problems year after year. Ultimately the unspoken goal of some house shops seems to be to achieve a medium grade of mediocrity, to produce ads and literature that are neither good nor bad, material that cannot be faulted on any specific point. They achieve this, but also achieve a communications program with a deadly-dull sameness to it; it is certainly far from exciting and vital and alive.

Geographical locations share the blame, too. Isolation breeds stagnation. If the creative advertising man is a distance from a large metropolitan center, there is little opportunity to talk shop with fellow professionals—excepting those with whom he works. And in the house agency there is no constant infusion of new blood and new ideas as the result of personnel turnover which is accepted as normal in the agency field; in the house agency, advertising men become imbued with the company attitude in all things, including that of long tenure. In any event, lack of frequent contact with others in the field outside the company contributes an intangible something, perhaps a frame of mind, that makes the creative spark sputter.

How Du Pont Keeps on Top

One of the largest, one of the most efficient, and almost certainly one of the most organizationally complex advertising departments in industry is that of E. I. Du Pont de Nemours & Company. Du Pont is a household name almost as familiar as your next door neighbor's. The company is near the top of *Fortune's 500*.

At Du Pont the advertising department is one of 13 staff departments that provide top management—and the company's 12 industrial departments—with a wide range of advertising and promotion services essential to the functioning of the company.

Advertising for 10 of the 12 industrial departments, all of which have a high degree of autonomy, is handled by the central advertising department at company headquarters in Wilmington, Delaware.

Advertising and promotional activities for Du Pont's textile fibers department are managed by a separate staff attached to that organization; this deviation from the Du Pont pattern is due to particular problems and needs unique to that operation.

The chart shows the structure of this efficient department.

Efficient it must be, for Du Pont's industrial departments are responsible for the manufacture and sale of some 1,250 different product lines! Advertising is behind 90 percent of all Du Pont product lines—not 90 percent of all products, but all product lines.

Of interest is the fact that when an industrial department's sales organization is organized along product lines, the ad managers function similarly. But when the sales setup is in terms of market composition, rather than product identity, their ad managers gear their programs with this objective.

Each year the department handles a work load that is enough to stagger the imagination of the average advertising manager. Du Pont's ad department prepares not one but 79 separate product ad budgets and seven institutional and nonproduct budgets. Annually the advertising group produces more than 2,300 new advertisements which appear in more than 2,000 different magazines and newspapers for a total of more than 14,500 insertions.

Contrary to the impression which the chart might convey, Du Pont's advertising department is not overorganized. At the huge chemical company there is no place in the scheme of things for organization for organization's sake. As *Industrial Marketing* said, a free-wheeling flexibility permeates the advertising operation so that individual units can function along organizational lines dictated by individual marketing situations. Such situations can and do change frequently.

Heading this huge department is a director and an assistant director. Next in line are seven division managers. These managers are responsible for all activities of the department, including consulting with and counseling other departments and management on product and nonproduct advertising.

Reporting to the division managers are 24 advertising managers. Immediately under them are 68 advertising assistants.

Also in the department, reporting to the assistant director of advertising, are a personnel manager and a technical advisor. In addition, there are eight different staff service units in the ad depart-

DEPARTMENT ORGANIZATION AND FUNCTIONS

ORGANIZATION CHART

ADVERTISING DEPARTMENT — E. I. DU PONT DE NEMOURS AND COMPANY

ADVERTISING
AGENCIES

DIRECTOR — H. LLOYD TAYLOR

DIVISION MANAGER — A. W. BALLENTINE
- INDUSTRIAL CHEMICALS DEPARTMENT — ADVERTISING & PROMOTION MANAGER — R. E. HUTTER, SR. — — — AYER
- PLASTIC PRODUCTS AND RESINS DEPARTMENT
  - INDUSTRIAL FILMS, PACKAGING FILMS & SPECIALTY MARKETS DIVISIONS —
    - ADVERTISING & PROMOTION MANAGER — C. K. JOHNSON — — — — — — — — — — — — — — — — AYER
- POLYMER INTERMEDIATES DEPARTMENT — ADVERTISING & PROMOTION MANAGER — R. T. ELDRIDGE — — — AYER
- EMPLOYEE RELATIONS DEPARTMENT — ADVERTISING & PROMOTION SUPERVISOR — J. C. DILTS — — — — — AYER
- SPECIAL PROJECTS — ADVERTISING & PROMOTION MANAGER — D. C. MC SORLEY
- PIGMENTS DEPARTMENT — RT&E

DIVISION MANAGER — C. E. CROWLEY
- BIOCHEMICALS DEPARTMENT
  - AGRICHEMICALS MARKETING DIVISION — ADVERTISING & PROMOTION MANAGER — S. P. BLISH — — — — R–H
- PLASTIC PRODUCTS AND RESINS DEPARTMENT
  - COMMERCIAL RESINS AND FLUOROCARBONS DIVISIONS —
    - ADVERTISING & PROMOTION MANAGER — W. W. CARTY — — — — — — — — — — — — — — — — AYER
  - PLASTIC PRODUCTS DIVISION — ADVERTISING & PROMOTION MANAGER — J. P. SWAN — — — — — — — AYER
  - POLYMER PRODUCTS AND POLYOLEFINS DIVISIONS —
    - ADVERTISING & PROMOTION MANAGER — J. L. JENEMANN — — — — — — — — — — — — — — — AYER
- GENERAL COMPANY — CORPORATE ADVERTISING — BBDO
- TEXTILE FIBERS DEPARTMENT — AYER & BBDO

DIVISION MANAGER — H. E. DAVIS
- ORGANIC CHEMICALS DEPARTMENT — ADVERTISING & PROMOTION MANAGER — E. J. O'BRIEN
  - DYES & CHEMICALS, "FREON" PRODUCTS AND PETROLEUM CHEMICALS DIV. — — — — — — — — — — AYER
  - "ZEPEL" — BBDO
- AUDIO-VISUAL SECTION — MANAGER — W. D. DAVIS
- CONTROL SECTION — MANAGER — A. B. BAKER
- DU PONT MAGAZINE — EDITOR — W. C. HALLEY
- PROCUREMENT, OFFICE SERVICES AND EXHIBITS — MANAGER — C. P. PALMER
  - OFFICE MANAGER — E. M. MERRILL
- PRODUCTION/GRAPHICS — MANAGER — T. J. NIEMKIEWICZ

DIVISION MANAGER — R. M. DE GRAFF
- FABRICS & FINISHES DEPARTMENT
  - AUTOMOTIVE PRODUCTS — ADVERTISING MANAGER — R. J. ALFANO — — — — — — — — — — — — — BBDO
  - CONSUMER PAINTS & "REACH" TOOTHBRUSH — ADVERTISING MANAGER — J. B. BOYER — — — — — AYER, R–H
  - "CORIAN" PRODUCTS, EXPORT, REFINISH & MAINTENANCE FINISHES
    - ADVERTISING & PROMOTION MANAGER — J. K. GOUNDIE, JR. — — — — — — — — — — — — — AYER
  - "TEFLON", INDUSTRIAL FINISHES, INDUSTRIAL PRODUCTS & APPLIED TECHNOLOGY
    - ADVERTISING & PROMOTION MANAGER — J. E. SLY — — — — — — — — — — — — — — — — AYER
- CENTRAL ADVERTISING DEPARTMENT — EUROPE — MANAGER — R. S. IREDALE
- PHOTO PRODUCTS (FRANKFURT) — ADVERTISING MANAGER — A. E. ROBINSON
- DU PONT OF CANADA — ADVERTISING DIVISION MANAGER — C. D. CLARANCE
- REMINGTON ARMS COMPANY — ADVERTISING DIRECTOR — J. D. MITCHELL — — — — — — — — — — BBDO, R–H
- HOTEL DU PONT — J. K. GOUNDIE, JR. — RT&E

DIVISION MANAGER — D. J. GLUCK
- MARKETING RESEARCH — MANAGER — I. GROSS
  - MARKETING SCIENCES — MANAGER — J. B. FREY
  - COMMUNICATIONS RESEARCH — MANAGER — R. C. GRASS
  - F & F MARKETING RESEARCH — MANAGER — E. S. ERICKSON, JR.
  - INDUSTRIAL MARKETING RESEARCH — MANAGER — J. A. THATCHER
- ELASTOMER CHEMICALS DEPARTMENT — ADVERTISING & PROMOTION MANAGER — H. B. HORNING — — — — AYER
- PHOTO PRODUCTS DEPARTMENT
  - ELECTRONIC PRODUCTS, EXPORT, INDUSTRIAL, PRINTING & X-RAY SALES DIVISIONS
    - ADVERTISING & PROMOTION MANAGER — A. SHILLING — — — — — — — — — — — — — — — — AYER
  - INSTRUMENT PRODUCTS DIVISION — ADVERTISING & PROMOTION MANAGER — C. W. HOEFTMAN — — — AYER

PERSONNEL MANAGER — E. M. CARLETON

KEY TO ADVERTISING AGENCIES

AYER — N. W. AYER ABH INTERNATIONAL
BBDO — BATTEN, BARTON, DURSTINE & OSBORN, INC.
R–H — RUMRILL–HOYT, INC.
RT&E — REESE, TOMASES & ELLICK, INC.

The advertising department of E. I. Du Pont de Nemours & Company is large but not overstaffed in relation to its many responsibilities.

ment, separate and distinct from the product and corporate advertising groups. They are as follows:

Advertising budget-control section—responsible for the accounting of all advertising expense, maintaining budget controls, and preparing advertising-expense statements. Using electronic processing equipment, this section supplies data grouped by individual projects, with monthly information on altered budget figures vs. original plans, committed expenditures, and expended budget dollars.

This section also checks invoices from Du Pont's advertising agencies and suppliers of advertising materials and services. In addition, it maintains statistical information, both current and historical, concerning Du Pont advertising.

Advertising research section—functions fall into two categories: Services to ad managers requesting them, and original research and/or evaluation of advertising research done by others.

In the area of original research this section designs experiments to be performed by outside agencies, analyzes data available in reports published by others, develops new statistical procedures and computer applications, and performs fundamental research in the general area of psychological measurement.

Research services to departmental personnel include, in addition to advice and counsel, the preparation of a bimonthly digest of new and important developments in any phase of advertising research.

The section is composed of a manager who is an experimental psychologist, an additional experimental psychologist, three operations-research specialists, a former chemical engineer, a statistician, two statistical clerks and four secretaries.

Audiovisual section—responsible for the production, maintenance, and distribution of films, and for producing presentation materials varying from those appropriate for an audience of one up to those needed for presentation to a large group in an auditorium.

This section provides assistance in selection of film producers, script and storyboard development, location and studio shooting, and similar specialized aids. Ad managers must notify this section when they are considering a new motion picture or strip film.

Graphics and exhibits section. Divided into two groups, this section provides graphic-design services and display-planning and handling services.

The graphics group consists of designers who not only create designs but also direct the work of outside artists, and then work with the printing division of Du Pont's general services department to assure prompt completion of the job. Their work ranges from the layout of booklet covers to package design.

The exhibits group is responsible for providing all display services—from initial planning through design, construction, installation, dismantling, transportation, storage, and maintenance. Coordinators from this group get information about particular shows, advise Du Pont participation (or nonparticipation), select space, process space contracts, and other details of trade-show exhibition.

Each exhibits coordinator is assigned to work with ad managers whose budgets include a provision for exhibits participation. Operating expenses are recovered by a percentage levied against each exhibits budget, as determined by the ratio of total operating expenses to total exhibit budgets each year.

Du Pont participates in almost 200 exhibits each year.

Office-management and procurement section. This unit provides administrative services incidental to running an office, including acquisition of operating supplies, office relocations, and other housekeeping functions.

Personnel section—responsible for recruiting advertising personnel and for the ad department's "training and development" program, which involves every facet of stimulating professional growth of Du Pont advertising personnel. Included are individual performance reviews, public speaking courses, group discussions, workshops, management courses, and other educational opportunities up to courses directed toward a graduate degree. Du Pont pays tuition for such courses in a number of nearby colleges and universities.

Printing-production control section. Formed several years ago, this section consists of a printing specialist, an assistant, and a secretary. The section is responsible for developing methods and procedures for making estimates more accurate, for setting standards in pricing, and for reducing costs through better use of mechanical methods. One Du Pont spokesman reports that this section has saved the company several hundred thousand dollars per year, and that "there is promise of still greater efficiency."

Technical advisor's office. Maintains a wide variety of technical and historical data needed to produce factual, technically correct ads and printed literature. Other functions of this office include assistance in the production of booklets, scripts, technical films; servicing all requests from directory and catalog publishers for information about Du Pont trademarks, both active and inactive; clearance of all technical statements in radio and television scripts, pictures for corporate advertising, review of all toxicity statements about new products, and new statements about old products.

Television section—primarily responsible for all phases of Du Pont's television shows, including regularly sponsored programs as well as the superb documentaries which Du Pont presents from time to time. Although not strictly a staff service unit, this section is available for counsel and assistance to ad managers whose budgets include an allocation for TV commercials.

Corporate print advertising—responsible for periodic advertising —such as community ads—placed in newspapers and various specialized publications.

Du Pont magazine. This section produces the Du Pont external house organ directed primarily to customers and prospects. Published six times a year, the circulation is around the 250,000 mark.

Employee relations and Du Pont Hotel. This section handles the advertising requirements for the college recruitment program of Du Pont's employee relations department, and for the commercial hotel owned by the company.

College-recruitment activities involve placement of ads in various college engineering magazines, placement of educational exhibits at selected universities, and similar programs designed to make known Du Pont's desirability as an employer. Advertising programs relative to the Du Pont Hotel are similar to those which would be used by any organization promoting a commercial hotel.

International Advertising

The method of handling Du Pont international advertising is determined primarily by the function and location of foreign subsidiaries and distributors.

Except for the textile fibers department, export advertising is part of the responsibility of the domestic-advertising sections headquartered in the central ad department in Wilmington. Ad managers work with export sales managers in the industrial departments they serve, and develop prototype advertising primarily for overseas distributors in markets not served by Du Pont affiliated companies.

Du Pont International, in Geneva, Switzerland, has within it an advertising activity consisting of a dozen or more specialists. Working under a marketing director, they service Europe in much the same manner that the central ad department in Wilmington services the industrial departments in the United States.

Under the direction of advertising people in Du Pont, International, S. A., are more than 20 different advertising agencies—all foreign. Agency selection is the responsibility of Du Pont International, with advertising and marketing people having the authority to select the agencies for the product lines they handle.

Latin American subsidiaries have no counterpart of the Geneva marketing organization. In countries where market size warrants it, individual subsidiaries have their own ad managers and agencies, with liaison maintained with Wilmington product ad managers.

Flexibility Is Important

In concept and in practice, the most distinctive characteristic of Du Pont's overall advertising organization is that of flexibility.

Today's volatile marketplace and expanding economy dictate that Du Pont ad managers have the freedom they need to move rapidly to capitalize on any unique marketing opportunities which may arise. It is policy that they have considerable latitude in autonomous operations, with, however, an overall integration of company-wide effort.

As individual market conditions change, or new sales opportunities become apparent, the inherent flexibility of Du Pont's departmental advertising organization makes it possible to get a fast, effective start on market developments.

After all, producing more than 2,300 new ads a year, placing them in some 2,000 publications for an insertion total of over 14,500, directing advertising for a world-wide marketing effort, requires a dedicated team of knowledgeable professionals. They must have room to move, to improvise, to realize their full potential. Du Pont's ad department gives them just that.

Du Pont has these advertising career men, to the tune of 273 people in the advertising department. Of course, this includes secretarial, stenographic, and clerical personnel.

In addition, the five advertising agencies retained by Du Pont have assigned 148 people to work on Du Pont advertising, making a grand total of 421 highly talented individuals with one prime concern—planning and developing the most effective, most productive advertising they can for Du Pont.

In large advertising departments, Du Pont's for example, which are well organized and where management runs a tight ship, proper delegation of authority and assignment of various functions to the right individual are assured. Wasted effort, wheel spinning, and time squandered on nonadvertising projects are practically nil.

This situation does not always exist in small to medium-sized industrial companies, however. Frequently just the opposite situation is found. Many companies harbor a cruel trap into which many an unwary advertising manager falls—that of diluting his effectiveness by becoming the company whipping boy, the agreeable character upon whom every cat-and-dog job is shoved. The insidious thing is, this happens before the ad manager realizes it. It happens because an advertising man is essentially a salesman with a salesman's psychological makeup. He finds it almost impossible to say "no." But by not doing so, by tackling every miscellaneous assignment that comes along, he endangers his professional status and, at the same time, shortchanges his company by not devoting his time to his primary responsibility.

Functions of the advertising department have changed as advertising—and business itself—have become more complex and marketing strategy has grown infinitely more sophisticated.

Back before the century turned, advertising was a lusty infant with no idea of what its grown-up occupation would be. Its one and only function was to help sell goods and services. There were no advertising agencies then, nor were there advertising managers. Instead, the "agency" end of the business was a hard-sell broker of newspaper space whose office was in his hat. This enterprising individual bought space wholesale and sold it at retail, thus making a profit for himself. Even then, though, there was competition. The space broker soon came to the conclusion that he had to offer more services if he was to continue to sell space and to increase his sales volume.

So, the broker branched out. He opened an office. He wrote copy and laid out ads for his advertisers. Soon he hired others to perform these services for him to save his selling time. Needing more product to sell—more space, that is—the broker induced magazines to take a step that was a genuine milestone in the business world. He persuaded class publications to accept advertising, something that until then was too crassly commercial for them to consider. Quality media for mass communications were available for the first time.

The Full-Service Agency

By the early 1900's the full-service ad agency had arrived. As population grew, business grew. Advertising kept pace. Not only did advertising volume expand, but advertising was called upon to accept more tasks and to solve more and more business communications problems. Business growth accelerated, as did the investment in advertising, for one simple reason: advertising paid an outstanding return on the investment. That is why—the realization that advertising is not an expense, but is an investment that returns a profit—today's investment in advertising in the United States is more than $7 billion. This investment is larger than the gross *combined* sales of R. J. Reynolds, W. R. Grace, McDonnell Aircraft, Minnesota Mining & Manufacturing, Eastman Kodak and Caterpillar Tractor, all nice solvent enterprises.

Cynics and fast-buck misanthropic exposé artists to the contrary, one thing is certain: Advertising can legitimately claim the major share of the credit for making more goods available to more people at lower cost, for building our brand-name system, for playing a key role in creating a continuing demand for newer and better products, and for exerting a powerful influence toward development of a mass production, mass distribution, mass consumption economy. It is nothing short of sheer tragedy that there is no possible way to measure the incalculable contribution advertising has made to the growth of our economy during the last half-century. If such data could, by some magical means, be developed, advertising's detractors would be effectively and quickly silenced. It is no exaggeration to say that without advertising the world's most dynamic, most productive economy would not exist.

Signs for the Formal Gardens

Exactly what functions legitimately belong in the advertising department is a touchy subject. It is a real bone of contention in many companies, with the ad manager insisting his department is unjustly charged with chores and costs not rightly a part of the advertising program. If the problem is analyzed objectively, it is immediately apparent in most instances that his complaint is well justified.

An example which may well become a classic throughout advertising concerns the flora-fancying wife of the president of a prosperous midwestern manufacturer. This charming lady's all-consuming passion was several immaculate acres of formal gardens of flowers of all descriptions on the family acreage in rural suburbia. The flowers were fed and watered and fertilized with tender loving care by two full-time gardeners, but they were as close to the lady's heart as if she had pollinated them herself.

It's a bit difficult to detect the common denominator of formal flower gardens and an industrial-advertising program. But the advertising manager of the lady's husband's firm found it, and upon doing so he grew into a fervid flower hater. Each year before the lady entertained (catered, of course) the local garden club, new identifying signs had to be made for each blooming species throughout the estate. Nice, neat little printed signs protected by cellophane made by the gardeners looked bourgeois. No class. They clashed with quality surroundings. So the problem fell upon the broad shoulders of the husband's company's advertising manager, as obviously it should because he was a graphic arts expert. After all, he knew all about catalogs and signs for buildings and trade shows and that sort of thing.

This hapless chap decided that only the best was good enough for the wife of the boss. That meant type. So, after wasting most of a day getting the correct spellings (English and Latin) for the flowers from the gardeners—then checking *them* against library versions—the ad manager had type set. In a burst of pure inspiration he had the typographer pull etch proofs on the shop's proof press, using choice textured enamel stock. Then he had the paper laminated onto wood and the entire assembly coated with liquid plastic, transparent and colorless and waterproof. Appropriate rustproof-brass hardware was bought and put on by a master mechanic in the toolroom. The proud ad manager hand delivered the job to the president's wife, which took only two-thirds of a day.

Cost of the entire operation, not counting the ad manager's time, the toolroom charge, and mileage on the car, was a bit short of $2,000. What transformed an otherwise normal advertising manager into a man with the unique idiosyncrasy of detesting flowers, all flowers, was what happened when he gave the bill to the president. He was told that it should be paid out of the advertising budget. Rationale was that the company "would receive much favorable publicity from the local newspapers as the result of the impression made by the flower gardens." Try as he might, the ad manager found it a bit difficult to judge just how much this would influence industrial purchasers of his company's products—particularly those a thousand miles away.

Admittedly, this case is unusual. But it is undisputable that a vast gray area exists when it comes to what should be charged to the advertising department, for there are no hard-and-fast rules as to what is desirable or undesirable, of what is right and what is wrong. Differences of opinion are usually resolved with a liberal dose of that old bromide, company policy. Policy itself is merely precedent set by a number of people over a number of years in a number of different marketing situations. One thing is certain, though. Regardless of whether the ad manager considers his position on legitimate functions and charges tenable or untenable, he might just as well reconcile himself to engaging in a number of skirmishes on this subject every year at budget time, and with relentless regularity throughout the year. Sacred cows die hard and company attitudes don't change overnight.

What the Ad Department Shouldn't Do

Before getting into functions which rightfully fall to the advertising department, let's be negative and take a look at activities which do *not*. These items have been rejected by an overwhelming majority of well-run industrial companies, although there is by no means unanimity of thought on every one. Most are self-explanatory, although some bear discussion. It goes without saying that, while the advertising department should not be charged with many of these functions, a large number of them will be handled by the department because its personnel are the only ones in the company qualified to do the job. Functions not an integral part of advertising as far as the budget is concerned are:

Corporate advertising

Travel expense for nonadvertising personnel

    Annual reports.

    Employee welfare activity.

    Internal house organ.

    Company recreational program.

    Christmas gifts to employees.

    Christmas gifts to dealers, jobbers, or representatives.

    Company Christmas cards.

    Business cards.

    Letterheads and envelopes.

    Entertaining customers and prospects.

    Hospitality suites at conventions, shows, etc.

    Product tests.

Boxes, packages, cartons, and labels.

Premiums, spiffs, "deal" merchandise.

Charitable donations.

Salesmen's samples.

Salesmen's sample cases.

Binders.

Proposal covers.

Price lists.

Price books.

Cost of distribution of literature to field force.

Corporate literature (in multidivision companies).

Signs on factories or office buildings.

Burden (rent, light, heat, maintenance of advertising-department office space).

Telephone and telegraph.

General trade-association memberships.

Reprints of magazine articles.

Showrooms.

Market research.

Office supplies.

Product displays in offices or reception areas.

Production expense of signs for president's wife's formal flower garden.

The Budget

That corporate advertising is a necessity is not disputed in reasonably sophisticated circles. Even corporate presidents, who tend to take a dim view of advertising per se, embrace it wholeheartedly. They are, after all, primarily interested in just two things: Making a profit, and making this fact known to the financial community so there will be greater awareness of the corporation as an aggressive, growing company, thus stimulating demand for the company's stock.

Benefiting the company, the stockholders, and one's self—simultaneously—has undeniable appeal. Doing so by using advertising is a tacit admission that advertising *does* work, which admission is directly opposed to the same gentlemen's scepticism as to advertising's effectiveness in other areas.

In multidivisional companies the corporate advertising program should be handled on the corporate level, not on the divisional level. It is properly the responsibility of the corporate director of advertising, if the position exists, or of the top marketing executive and the president. They customarily work directly with the advertising agency, although divisional ad managers are consulted because of their intimate knowledge of divisional advertising objectives and problems.

One sure way to gut a well-planned divisional-advertising program is to make an arbitrary assessment to provide funds for corporate advertising. When this short-sighted step is taken, the "tax bite" frequently runs around 15 percent of budget—total budget, not merely space cost—of the divisional appropriation. The first time this happens to the industrial advertising manager, he experiences a sense of bewilderment, for he is honestly unable to understand the thinking on the corporate level which led to emasculation of his program.

The traditional pattern is for the bite to continue for two or three years. Then, as the company progresses and matures, and divisional ad managers continue their strenuous protests against taxation without representation, the corporation reevaluates, reconsiders and ultimately adopts the procedure most common throughout industry. This is to earmark a certain percentage of corporate profits for the corporate promotional program, or, alternatively, to assess each division—*not* each divisional advertising appropriation—an amount based on anticipated sales volume. This assessment, as a rule, is somewhat less than $\frac{1}{4}$ of one percent of gross sales.

Although not a function or activity of the advertising department, "travel expense for nonadvertising personnel" has deliberately been included in this list because it is a significant expense item which absolutely does *not* belong in charges allocated to any industrial advertising department.

A definite correlation exists between a company's marketing naiveté and its tendency to charge off every conceivable miscellaneous expense item against advertising. In one well-known company, a potent factor in the marketplace and a leader in its highly specialized field, a cherished tradition of years' standing was for engineering, order department, sales, research and development, administrative and marketing personnel (and even *Personnel* personnel) to journey happily to far distant cities to attend trade shows at which the company exhibited. True, some were needed for their technical knowledge, although product-wise field salesmen from the immediate locality had responsibility for manning the booth. The others "increased their technical knowledge and evaluated competitive equipment." Oddly enough, it invariably required four or five days (depending on the length of the show) to accomplish this. And even more odd, their travel expenses, including the best hotels and (gourmet) meals, were charged to advertising. A new advertising manager stopped this wasteful dilution of promotional funds, though not without opposition. Few care to give up an extra week of vacation and an all-expense-paid trip on another department's expense account.

What the Ad Department Does Do

A complete listing of all functions of the busy industrial advertising department would be boringly long, including as it would activities engaged in infrequently and those which are relatively inconsequential. Instead of such an exhaustive—and exhausting—tally, the six activities of primary importance are shown, along with major breakdowns. In subsequent chapters each topic, and others, will be covered from a how-to-do-it standpoint. Following are the principal functions found in almost every industrial ad department, though not necessarily in order of importance. This would vary with individual companies.

Administration

> Establish policies.
>
> Budgeting.
>
> Appropriations.
>
> Expense control.
>
> Departmental organization.
>
> Administer salaries and departmental personnel records.
>
> Establish efficient inquiry handling procedure.
>
> Evaluate competitive advertising.
>
> Evaluate own ads.
>
> Analyze and interpret readership studies.
>
> Make customer calls to get feel of product(s).

Coordinate advertising with other marketing activities, and with other departments.

Participate in activities of local advertising associations.

Planning

Reflect company policies with an integrated promotional program.

Work with marketing management to establish marketing objectives and incorporate these objectives into a *written* marketing plan.

Establish communications objectives which will help achieve marketing objectives.

Develop a short-range advertising plan.

Develop a long-range advertising plan.

Develop an advertising campaign which will achieve all communications objectives and thus achieve marketing objectives.

Develop a copy platform.

Put on paper a timetable for creation and production of campaign, and for collateral material; use or develop suitable forms to organize this activity.

Demonstrate effectiveness of advertising to management and other key personnel.

Contact field sales personnel for ideas and suggestions; evaluate these carefully.

Marketing

Product analysis and familiarization.

Market research, internal and external.

Break down company markets by S.I.C.

Break down customer list by S.I.C.

Analyze past sales to determine possible trends and to verify if advertising emphasis is correctly directed.

Develop distributor (or jobber, dealer) support program.

Consult with marketing management on special problems as they arise.

Suggest new uses for existing products.

Suggest new products which research, advertising response show are salable.

Media

Analyze all potentially useful media.

Rate media quality and desirability on: editorial policy, editorial content, editorial format, circulation, publication image, readership, market potential, advertiser acceptance, services to advertisers, and space cost.

Develop a schedule of advertising insertions.

Schedule insertions.

Verify insertions through checking copy.

Purchase space (customarily done by agency when an agency is retained).

Sales promotion

Write and produce effective sales literature.

Write and produce salesmen's catalogs.

Produce instruction manuals; technical information and schematic drawings procured from product manager or engineering.

Develop point-of-purchase material for dealers, jobbers, or distributors.

Write and produce direct-mail material supplied to dealers, jobbers, or distributors for their use.

Purchase and supervise product photography, either in plant, in studio, or on location.

Direct creation and production of trade-show exhibit(s).

Direct trade shows, including followup of equipment or items to be exhibited; shipping and erection of booth; scheduling of personnel to man the booth; display of products; tear-down of booth and reshipment of products.

In conjunction with sales department, develop sales contests and incentives for field force.

Direct creation and production of movies and strip films.

Develop effective mail campaigns.

Develop high-quality lists for direct-mail use.

Direct the actual mailing, usually through a lettershop if the list is large.

Merchandise all advertising and new collateral material to management, key personnel, and to the field sales force. This should include dealers, jobbers, distributors, or representatives.

Production

Purchase art.

Purchase photography.

Purchase layout.

Purchase type.

Purchase printing.

Produce mats and electros for field use.

Direct work of outside specialists and suppliers.

Chapter 2

WHY YOU NEED AN ADVERTISING AGENCY— AND HOW TO SELECT IT

APPROXIMATELY 40 percent of all industrial advertising is produced and placed by recognized advertising agencies. The surprising figure is not the 40 percent who do, but the 60 percent who do not use agencies. In this age of sophisticated marketing it is almost inconceivable that any serious advertiser can justify the decision to go the do-it-yourself route.

The fact is, though, that out in the hinterlands the misconception still exists that it is poor business to use the talents and services of an advertising agency. The thinking is that to do so is a needless extravagance and a much more costly way of producing advertising. Exactly the reverse may be true.

And, incredible as it seems, some advertisers—and this includes top executives of otherwise reasonably well-managed companies— firmly believe that no "advertising agent" can be trusted with competitive information or company money. The concept of an agency honestly having its clients' welfare at heart, of an agency basing its business future on the premise that agency growth can come only through client growth—due to the client's increased sales and profits —is so alien that it is summarily rejected. This is all too true in too many instances.

These fallacies, along with the *we-don't-need-those-city-fellers-to-tell-us-how-to-run-our-business* philosophy are, fortunately, becoming anachronous, not so much so from an enlightened desire to reject antediluvian thinking as from realization of its impracticality.

Gradually it has dawned on even those most obdurate in resisting change that competition in the marketplace is too cutthroat and the penalty for failure too severe to accept any handicap, however slight, in competing on an equal basis. So, rather than run the risk of failure, it's been widely though reluctantly decided to accept agencies as a fact of life and hope that a good one might enable the firm to be *more* equal than the competition.

WHY YOU NEED AN ADVERTISING AGENCY

Agencies Today

There are now some 4,500 advertising agencies doing business; no firm figures can be cited at any given time because formation and dissolution of small agencies occur at a rate which must assuredly be the Eighth Wonder of the World. These 4,500 agencies employ more than 70,000 people.

Advertising Age, the trade publication which is the voice of the advertising business, lists 80 agencies which have an annual volume of more than $14 million, progressing from this lower figure on up to the world's largest advertising agency, giant J. Walter Thompson Co., whose billings (sales volume) are well above the *half-billion* mark. Most agencies concentrate on consumer accounts because that's the range where the big budgets roam, although the majority also accept industrial accounts which measure up to their criteria.

Some agencies, however, such as Marsteller Inc., Buchen Advertising, Zimmer, Keller & Calvert, and Robert A. Becker, Inc. concentrate on serving industrial accounts. Agencies of this type, regardless of their size, and assuming only that they are large enough to provide complete agency service, are probably the most fertile hunting ground for an industrial ad manager seeking a productive agency affiliation. If his account is relatively large, however, he should not overlook the large consumer-oriented agencies which actively woo—and produce excellent advertising for—the industrial advertiser. It is interesting to note that huge Batten, Barton, Durstine & Osborn, a consumer agency, has for years led all agencies in volume of industrial advertising placed in the nation's business press. And the Fuller & Smith & Ross's, D'Arcy's and Compton's and many other large, respected shops are home of a happy blend of consumer and industrial accounts, all of which benefit from the best thinking the agency can provide.

Just below the really huge agencies are found a vast number of shops in the $5- $10-million bracket, commonly referred to as "medium size" agencies. It is generally recognized that it is this size agency which feels the financial pressure the greatest; agency management in medium-size agencies know they must provide all of the "extra" services—marketing, merchandising, research and what have you—to compete successfully with the bigs. As a result, the client can often expect to pay more for these ancillary services, and for collateral material, than he would in a larger organization.

Farther down the ladder are newly founded agencies (and many that have been around for years) that are still small, but often staffed with top talent which fled from the regimentation of the larger agencies. Often an industrial advertiser with a modest budget will find a warm welcome and top-flight creative thinking in such an agency.

At the bottom of the heap, and bearing close scrutiny if actively considered as a prospective agency, are the tiny agencies. Many are either the one-man-and-a-girl type operation, or a hybrid setup which is part agency and part art studio; seldom can these marginal operations provide other than the most rudimentary services.

Agencies Compete on an Equal Basis

There is no bargain-basement advertising. That's because agencies, to achieve "agency recognition" by media, and thus qualify for the traditional 15 percent commission on space and time purchased, must measure up to criteria established by each individual medium and/or associations formed by media. Media, incidentally, is the plural of medium. A medium is the vehicle which carries the advertising message—a magazine, newspaper, TV, radio, or even the sky in the case of skywriting.

Recognized agencies are simply those which, in the opinion of media, are equipped to perform the services clients must have, are financially responsible, and meet ethical standards.

To be recognized, an agency must convince media that:

1. The agency is a legitimate business enterprise not owned, influenced, or controlled by either an advertiser or a medium. This is essential if the agency is to be unbiased, and if it is to be able to give candid advice free from coercion or pressure which would be inimical to the best interests of the advertiser.

2. The agency must retain as earned income all commissions received from media on the purchase of space and time. There can be no fee-splitting or rebating of commissions to either advertisers or media. This provision assures advertisers that agencies will have sufficient income so that they can devote the necessary time, talent, and manpower to clients to further client interest. Also, it means that all agencies compete on an equal basis as far as costs are concerned, so there is no necessity for large agencies with large staffs to reduce the amount or quality of the services they provide in an effort to compete with cut-rate competition from less competent agencies.

3. The agency must have the depth of personnel, qualified and experienced in each of the key agency functions, to provide the

necessary counsel and services. This provision obviously aids the able and acts as a hindrance to the incompetent and ill equipped.

4. The agency must provide proof of financial strength to assure its continued solvency and operation, and to assure media it is capable of paying for space and time it purchases. Long established is the principle that the agency—as the buyer—is responsible for paying media. The agency issues space contracts or time contracts in its name to media; these are legal contracts issued by an independent contractor *in its own behalf,* not as an agent of the advertiser. So, if the agency fails to collect from the advertiser, the agency must nonetheless pay media for space and time contracted for. However, if the agency fails to honor its contract with media, media sustain the loss. It is easy to understand why, from media's viewpoint, this provision concerning agency financial strength is so important.

Procedures for Buying Space and Time

These provisions are incorporated in the four Standard Order Blanks developed by the American Association of Advertising Agencies. They are: Order Blank for Publications (on page 42), Contract for Spot Broadcasting, Contract for Spot Telecasting, and Order Blank for Transportation Advertising.

Agency Income

Approximately 65 percent of agency income derives from commission on space and time, although this varies from agency to agency, and is usually higher in agencies with a preponderance of consumer accounts on its roster of clients. The commission is paid not by the client, but by media. The balance of agency income is received directly from clients, generally in the form of fees for special services, such as market research, and as markups on services and materials the agency contracted for as part of producing a product for the client. Photography, typography, art, layout (if done outside), keyline, electros, and narration are examples. The agency quite legitimately marks up its cost of these products and services when it invoices them to the advertiser, for agency personnel have invested their time and knowledge in selecting what their experience dictates is the best to be had at a price that is acceptable. Markup ranges from 17.65 percent on prosaic purchases such as type to 40 percent or more on expensive art commissioned for the client.

Order Blank for Publications
(Copyright October 1956)

(Member of A.A.A.A.)

NAME OF ADVERTISING AGENCY
ADDRESS
CITY   STATE
TELEPHONE NUMBER

☐ IF CHECKED HERE, THIS
IS A SPACE CONTRACT

☐ IF CHECKED HERE, THIS
IS AN INSERTION ORDER

TO PUBLISHER OF   NO.

CITY AND STATE   DATE

PLEASE PUBLISH ADVERTISING OF (advertiser)
FOR (product)

┌─────SPACE─────┐   ┌────TIMES────┐   ┌──────────DATES OF INSERTION──────────┐

POSITION

COPY	KEY	CUTS

ADDITIONAL INSTRUCTIONS

RATE

LESS AGENCY COMMISSION	PER CENT ON GROSS	LESS CASH DISCOUNT	PER CENT ON NET

Subject to conditions stated below and on back hereof:

NAME OF ADVERTISING AGENCY, PER..
CITY

Member of
AMERICAN ASSOCIATION OF ADVERTISING AGENCIES

Order Blank for Publications   Copyright October, 1956   American Association of Advertising Agencies, Inc.   *(OVER)*

Standard order blank for publications designed by the American Association of Advertising Agencies.

While this 40-percent figure might seem exorbitant, net profit for an agency on such art usually is about on a par with other commissionable purchases. One example concerns some meticulously detailed full-color illustrations which were ordered by an agency art director for a manufacturer of huge, extremely costly machine tools. Some of the illustrations were of sufficient complexity that the agency art director and the outside artist engaged for the job had to travel from Chicago to northern Canada, to the Gulf Coast, and to Arizona, as well as three other locations to inspect installations of the advertiser's equipment. They took reference photography before the artist proceeded with the "roughs"—semicomprehensive pencil sketches to give the advertising manager a chance to make any necessary corrections before work in oils took place. Each installation differed so much from the others that it was essential that the artist actually see and absorb the peculiarities of each locale to be able to capture the feeling of the individual locations. True, the artist might have gone alone and cut travel expenses in half. But the agency was responsible for the end result, and the only way it could be sure of art up to its standards was to have the account art director provide direction for the artist—on the spot. In this case the client was billed the cost of the art and an agency markup of 40 percent, plus out-of-pocket expenses incurred by the art director and the artist. The agency's only compensation for the art director's time was in the markup on the artist's invoice.

Not legitimately marked up are internal services. One agency, for example, habitually marks these up—from 17.65 percent to 60 percent or more, apparently capriciously and depending on just one factor— the agency's profit picture for the month. *This is unethical.* The advertising manager has an obligation to his company to lodge a long, loud protest if he encounters this. Agencies are entitled to make a fair charge that produces an acceptable profit on work they do internally—layout, for example—but they are *not* entitled to add a commission on their own internal charges. To do so is like putting a tax upon a tax. Incidentally, clients of this particular agency who complain about this method of milking them invariably have their invoices recalled and reduced by the exact amount of this unjustified commission. Only those ad managers who didn't realize they were being gouged and didn't raise an objection incurred this charge. This practice is not widespread, although the agency which habitually practices this form of invoice padding is still in business at the same old stand and, presumably, continues to overcharge those it can. The time an ad manager spends in carefully checking invoices is not time wasted.

Agency Commission From Media

Agency commission is given voluntarily by media, and almost all business publications allow it. Customary figure is 15 percent of the published space rate, although most media allow an additional 2 percent cash discount for prompt payment. This 2 percent is customarily passed on to the advertiser as an incentive for him to pay the agency invoices promptly; discount period is usually 10 days; although some agencies shorten it to 7, others who are all heart lengthen it to 14.

Methods of Agency Compensation

Three methods of agency compensation prevail in industrial advertising today. They are:

1. *Commission.* On space advertisements, this includes space at gross cost, and 15 percent of the cost of actually producing the ad. Production cost involves photography or art, typography, keyline, engravings, and electros.

2. *Minimum billing agreement.* This includes earned commission and a guaranteed minimum profit to the agency as compensation for handling the company's advertising. Consensus is that this system accounts for all but a tiny fraction of all formal agreements between industrial advertisers and their agencies. The figure most commonly quoted is that 98 percent of all client-agency agreements are of this type.

3. *Agreed fee.* This is arrived at by establishing a program, determining the net cost of media and production, then adding an agreed-upon fee. Other cost-and-fee arrangements have been worked out, but most are arithmetic for arithmetic's sake, or are an elaborate justification for one essential—an acceptable profit margin for the agency.

Industrial Marketing, a highly respected trade publication which every ad manager should subscribe to, recently reported yet another fee arrangement is in use by Paul Klempter & Co., Fuller & Smith & Ross, and other agencies. Under this arrangement, the advertiser guarantees that the agency will make a net profit on its account between 1.5 percent and 2.5 percent on gross billings. Any profit over and above this agreed-upon amount is split equally between agency and advertiser. This is undoubtedly an equitable solution to a problem that has plagued advertising from its inception, and probably will for the foreseeable future.

All of these methods of agency compensation are workable, otherwise they would long since have departed the scene. The advertising manager should think long and carefully before departing from them. He should shy away from—in fact, avoid like the plague—any kind of a cost-plus fee arrangement where an agency's media cost and production cost are added to a fee which is theoretically a specified fraction of actual cost. Arrangements like this, whether they are a cost-plus proposition between a manufacturer of military hardware supervised by a bunch of government bureaucrats, or a cost-plus arrangement with an advertising agency, have one thing in common: they pay a premium for poor performance. The seller has no incentive to effect economies which would do just one thing —reduce profit from the job. Who voluntarily reduces profit?

How Agency Commission Is Derived

Let's take a look at what actually produces commission for the agency—a purchase of space, and since we're interested only in industrial advertising, space in a business publication.

Rates—cost of space—are based on circulation. The average business publication, "trade book" in ad terminology, with a circulation of around 65,000, charges approximately $1,000 for one full page of space. This is for a standard 7" x 10" ad, with "bleed"—an ad printed so that it runs into the gutter and/or to the top and side of the page flush with the edge—carrying an extra price tag of about 10 percent over and above the basic page price. In addition, if the advertiser wants a second color (black and one other standard color), he may specify it for an added charge of about 10 percent. A third color, or full four-color process, is available from many leading publications at a still higher price. Increase in readership with bleed and additional colors is discussed in depth later on.

For the sake of illustration, assume that the agency contracts for one page. Published rate (on the book's rate card) lists the space at $1,000. Agency commission is 15 percent of the gross price, or $150, which is deducted from the amount that is invoiced to the agency by the medium. Thus the agency pays the medium only $850 less, in most cases, the standard 2 percent discount for prompt payment, or another $17. This $17 is not money earned by the agency, however, for it is passed along in turn to the agency's client—the advertiser— as an incentive for him to pay the invoice promptly.

While on the subject of agency commissions, an amusing incident points up advertising's need to communicate better with company management:

The advertising manager of a nationally known company was having a routine discussion of advertising, as it applied to his major product line, with one of the company's marketing managers. To the ad man's amazement, a worried expression crossed the marketing manager's face. He got up, closed the door to his office, sat back down behind his desk and looked the ad manager in the eye. He lowered his voice and asked, in a horror-stricken tone, "Do you realize our agency is getting a kickback from magazines we advertise in?"

The ad manager was stunned, at a loss for words. Finally, he decided the marketing manager was pulling his leg. Questioning proved this was not so, however, so the ad manager proceeded quickly to explain the facts of life as far as agency commissions are concerned. When the explanation was over, the marketing expert looked relieved, and said, "I'm glad to hear that. I thought our agency people were above taking something under the table, but that's what it looked like to me. I thought we paid them to do our advertising."

This is not a fable—it's a verbatim (almost, anyway) record of a conversation. This naïveté is widespread, very much so, and every industrial ad manager will do well to remember it and explain fiscal facts about agency relationships to key people occasionally. Once won't suffice as a rule; mention it at opportune times, such as when budget discussions are being held.

A.A.A.A.

The American Association of Advertising Agencies is the national organization of the advertising agency business. Throughout the advertising world, "A.A.A.A."—or "4A"—is the symbol of able, ethical, and responsible advertising-agency service.

The 355 agencies which are members of 4A place *more than two-thirds* of all advertising in this country, industrial and consumer. They operate 604 offices in 129 cities in 42 states and the District of Columbia, as well as 213 offices in 78 cities in 46 other countries.

The association was formed in 1917 at the suggestion of the advertising media to be the responsible spokesman of the country's agencies. Membership is by application and is open to all agencies who are able to meet the A.A.A.A.'s qualifications. The association has three main aims:

1. To foster, strengthen and improve the advertising agency business.

2. To advance the cause of advertising as a whole.

3. To give service to members—to do things for them which they cannot do for themselves, or which can be done better or less expensively through the association.

A.A.A.A. agency service standards, continuously promoted by the association, are a "delineation of fundamentals" of successful agency operation, adopted in 1918 and continued practically without change until the present time. They are as valid today as when originally adopted.

Service standards were drawn up so that "advertisers and media may know what to demand and agencies may know what may be expected of them in dealing with the problems of advertising."

Under the seven headings, the standards make clear that agency service extends from "a study of the product or service" to "co-operation with the sales work."

Advertising, they state, should be based on a plan. The plan should be based, in turn, on studies of the product or service, the present and potential market, the factors of distribution and sales, and the available media which can profitably be used.

Only after a plan has been developed and approved does the agency proceed to create the campaign and the individual advertisements, order the space or time, supply the messages (copy) in proper form to media, verify the publication or broadcast, audit and bill the client.

Following are agency service standards of the American Association of Advertising Agencies. They were first adopted on October 9, 1918, and were most recently revised on February 15, 1956:

Agency Service consists of interpreting to the public, or to that part of it which it is desired to reach, the advantages of a product or service.

Interpreting to the public the advantages of a product or service are based upon:

1. A study of the product or service in order to determine the advantages and disadvantages inherent in the product itself, and in its relation to competition.

2. An analysis of the present and potential market for which the product or service is adapted:

    As to location

    As to extent of possible sale

    As to season

    As to trade and economic conditions

    As to nature and amount of competition

3. A knowledge of the factors of distribution and sales and their methods of operation.

4. A knowledge of all the available media and means which can

be profitably used to carry the interpretation of the product or service to consumer, wholesaler, dealer, contractor, or other factor.

This knowledge covers:

Character

Influence

Circulation . . . quantity . . . quality . . . location

Physical requirements

Costs

Acting on the study, analysis and knowledge as explained in the preceding paragraphs, recommendations are made and the following procedure ensues:

5. Formulation of a definite plan.

6. Execution of this plan:

   a. Writing, designing, illustrating of advertisements, or other appropriate forms of the message.

   b. Ordering the space, time, or other means of advertising.

   c. The proper incorporation of the message in mechanical form and forwarding it with proper instructions for the fulfillment of the contract.

   d. Checking and verifying the insertions, display, or other means used.

   e. The auditing and billing for the service, space, and preparation.

7. Cooperation with the sales work to ensure the greatest effect from advertising.

Individual agencies are, of course, free to determine with their clients just what services they will perform. Additional services routinely offered by many agencies today include package design, sales research, sales training, creation and production of sales and technical literature, designing of merchandising and point-of-purchase displays, creation and production of movies, slide and strip films, merchandising programs, and creation and production of direct-mail programs.

How much or how little an advertising manager wants his agency to do depends on his internal staff members and their ability to produce necessary material—and on his budget.

The above delineation of the fundamentals serves a useful purpose and shows what types of services should be offered by applicants for membership in the association. The more clearly agency service is understood by those who offer it and by those who receive it, the more adequate and intelligent advertising service will become, and those equipped to render a complete and effective service will be encouraged in doing so.

Qualifications for membership in the 4A are thoroughly defined by the association. The 4A says: "The qualifications are intended as a definition, by agency people themselves, of the kind of agency most likely to develop advertising *which succeeds for the advertisers*. They are based on the premise that the agency should be independent, unbiased and objective; should offer adequate staff and experience; should be ethically operated; and should be soundly financed. Only such an agency can fulfill its obligation to advertisers, to advertising media, and to the public."

Membership in the A.A.A.A. is not necessary for an agency to be good, or for it to be the right agency for your company. Membership *does* mean, however, that an agency *is* good and *is* right for its clients. In this business of intangibles, where the nebulous is weighed carefully, an affiliation such as this is more than a mere indication—it can frequently be taken as a recommendation.

To become a member of the association, individual agencies must apply on a standard form. Applicant agencies are investigated by a regional board—Eastern, East Central, Central, or Western—then voted upon. From time of application to time of final decision requires many months as a rule because the speed with which the application is processed depends entirely upon time voluntarily made available by widely scattered individuals.

Size of the agency is not a determinant. Volume of business is not a factor, although agencies must be adequately equipped to be considered eligible for membership.

To be accepted for A.A.A.A. membership, an agency must have been in the agency business long enough to demonstrate adequate experience and ability to ensure a stable operation. Two years is the minimum.

No agency is eligible unless the persons who control it, whether by ownership or contract, are employees of the agency.

To become a 4A agency, it is mandatory that the agency shall not own any interest in a printing, engraving, or other business supplying material to its clients, to any degree that disqualifies the agency from giving unbiased advice and service. Although ownership of any such interest by one or more of the owners, directors, officers, or employees of the agency is not ownership by the agency, it is recognized that such ownership could lead to bias. Therefore, it is most important that any substantial ownership be disclosed to the association, to the agency's clients and, in case of media interest, to other media.

Character is a quality that's difficult to measure with a yardstick, but it is vitally important. The 4A character investigation will be directed so as to determine the agen y applicant's business record, its policies and principles, its ethical practices, and its reputation for honesty, integrity, and sincerity of purpose. The association aims to bring agency operations into accord with the best ethical standards of business, so it can receive into membership only those who give reasonable assurance of readiness and ability to uphold such standards. A.A.A.A. says: "It is essential to know how an agency operates in relation to certain practices, declared by the association to be unfair practices in the light of the obligation agencies have not only to their clients, but to the media they employ, to the public, and to each other. These practices are stated in the 'Standards of Practice of the American Association of Advertising Agencies'."

Adopted in 1924 and revised in April 1962, the A.A.A.A. Standards of Practice are illustrated nearby.

The Creative Code of the Association of American Advertising Agencies spells out in detail the standards which all member agencies must measure up to if they are to retain their membership in good standing. It is also illustrated.

If accepted for membership, an agency is assessed dues based on its annual volume of business in the association's fiscal year. Dues are payable quarterly and are subject to adjustment at the end of the year if the agency has ended the year in a lower or higher income bracket. An initiation fee is required of all new members amounting to 10 percent of the tentative first year's dues.

For its dues an agency receives many benefits. A.A.A.A. works to advance the cause of advertising as a whole, and with considerable success. Advertising in the United States is more and more gaining recognition as "the institution of abundance."

More and more economists and business leaders are shifting emphasis from production to marketing and consumption. There is a growing awareness that advertising is the counterpart in marketing of the machine in production, and that advertising can and should play an ever larger role in finding customers and educating them to the enjoyment of higher standards of living. A.A.A.A.

STANDARDS *of* PRACTICE *of the*
American Association of Advertising Agencies

FIRST ADOPTED OCTOBER 16, 1924 — MOST RECENTLY REVISED APRIL 28, 1962

WE HOLD THAT a responsibility of advertising agencies is to be a constructive force in business.

We further hold that, to discharge this responsibility, advertising agencies must recognize an obligation, not only to their clients, but to the public, the media they employ, and to each other.

We finally hold that the responsibility will best be discharged if all agencies observe a common set of standards of practice.

To this end, the American Association of Advertising Agencies has adopted the following Standards of Practice as being in the best interests of the public, the advertisers, the media owners, and the agencies themselves.

These standards are voluntary. They are intended to serve as a guide to the kind of agency conduct which experience has shown to be wise, foresighted, and constructive.

It is recognized that advertising is a business and as such must operate within the framework of competition. It is further recognized that keen and vigorous competition, honestly conducted, is necessary to the growth and health of American business generally, of which advertising is a part.

However, *unfair* competitive practices in the advertising agency business lead to financial waste, dilution of service, diversion of manpower, and loss of prestige. Unfair practices tend to weaken public confidence both in advertisements and in the institution of advertising.

1. Creative Code

WE THE MEMBERS of the American Association of Advertising Agencies, in addition to supporting and obeying the laws and legal regulations pertaining to advertising, undertake to extend and broaden the application of high ethical standards. Specifically, we will not knowingly produce advertising which contains:

a. False or misleading statements or exaggerations, visual or verbal.

b. Testimonials which do not reflect the real choice of a competent witness.

c. Price claims which are misleading.

d. Comparisons which unfairly disparage a competitive product or service.

e. Claims insufficiently supported, or which distort the true meaning or practicable application of statements made by professional or scientific authority.

f. Statements, suggestions or pictures offensive to public decency.

We recognize that there are areas which are subject to honestly different interpretations and judgment. Taste is subjective and may even vary from time to time as well as from individual to individual. Frequency of seeing or hearing advertising messages will necessarily vary greatly from person to person.

However, we agree not to recommend to an advertiser and to discourage the use of advertising which is in poor or questionable taste or which is deliberately irritating through content, presentation or excessive repetition.

Clear and willful violations of this Code shall be referred to the Board of Directors of the American Association of Advertising Agencies for appropriate action, including possible annulment of membership as provided by Article IV, Section 5, of the Constitution and By-Laws.

2. Contracts

a. The advertising agency should where feasible enter into written contracts with media in placing advertising. When entered into, the agency should conform to its agreements with media. Failure to do so may result in loss of standing or litigation, either on the contract or for violations of the Clayton or Federal Trade Commission Acts.

b. The advertising agency should not knowingly fail to fulfill all lawful contractual commitments with media.

3. Offering Credit Extension

It is unsound and uneconomic to offer extension of credit or banking service as an inducement in solicitation.

4. Unfair Tactics

The advertising agency should compete on merit and not by depreciating a competitor or his work directly or inferentially, or by circulating harmful rumors about him, or by making unwarranted claims of scientific skill in judging or prejudging advertising copy, or by seeking to obtain an account by hiring a key employee away from the agency in charge in violation of the agency's employment agreements.

These Standards of Practice of the American Association of Advertising Agencies come from the belief that sound practice is good business. Confidence and respect are indispensable to success in a business embracing the many intangibles of agency service and involving relationships so dependent upon good faith. These standards are based on a broad experience of what has been found to be the best advertising practice.

Standards of practice advocated by the American Association of Advertising Agencies are fairly specific about such matters as false or misleading statements, authenticity of testimonials, price claims which can be substantiated, fair comparisons with competitive products, and the avoidance of statements, suggestions, or pictures which are offensive to public decency.

therefore carries on a continuing four-part program for the improvement of advertising, aiming to:

1. Help attract, select, train and handle more high caliber people.
2. Raise ever higher the quality and quantity of advertising research.
3. Improve advertising content.
4. Gain public understanding of advertising and its key role.

Advertising Personnel in Agencies

Each year, the A.A.A.A. estimates, the advertising-agency business needs some 3,000 new people—half of them specialized personnel. Advertising as a whole needs many more, of course.

To help meet this need, A.A.A.A. carries on a continuing program to present advertising as a career to promising young people.

The program is aimed at high-school students through some 9,000 teachers engaged in vocational guidance. It is especially aimed at young men and women on the student publications in nearly 1,000 colleges and over 10,000 accredited high schools, directly and through their faculty advisers. A booklet, *The Advertising Business and Its Career Opportunities,* is regularly offered to the students and teachers.

Closely related to this work is a 4A Plan for Cooperating with Teachers of Advertising. Local committees of A.A.A.A. agency people offer their help—visits by agency executives to the college campuses, guest lectures, invitations to teachers to attend A.A.A.A. meetings, and other planned communications to those in colleges in their areas which provide advertising courses.

Another activity assisting agency management but also benefiting advertising as a whole is the A.A.A.A. continuing study of methods of selecting agency personnel and of agency training methods.

Advertising Research

Research provides the solid floor of facts on which to practice the art of advertising. A.A.A.A. therefore engages in numerous activities to expand the field of scientific advertising knowledge.

Some of these are carried on by the association itself. The *A.A.A.A. Market & Newspaper Statistics,* issued annually since 1933, provides data on cities of 100,000 population and over and their

CREATIVE CODE

American Association of Advertising Agencies

The members of the American Association of Advertising Agencies recognize:

1. That advertising bears a dual responsibility in the American economic system and way of life.

To the public it is a primary way of knowing about the goods and services which are the products of American free enterprise, goods and services which can be freely chosen to suit the desires and needs of the individual. The public is entitled to expect that advertising will be reliable in content and honest in presentation.

To the advertiser it is a primary way of persuading people to buy his goods or services, within the framework of a highly competitive economic system. He is entitled to regard advertising as a dynamic means of building his business and his profits.

2. That advertising enjoys a particularly intimate relationship to the American family. It enters the home as an integral part of television and radio programs, to speak to the individual and often to the entire family. It shares the pages of favorite newspapers and magazines. It presents itself to travelers and to readers of the daily mails. In all these forms, it bears a special responsibility to respect the tastes and self-interest of the public.

3. That advertising is directed to sizable groups or to the public at large, which is made up of many interests and many tastes. As is the case with all public enterprises, ranging from sports to education and even to religion, it is almost impossible to speak without finding someone in disagreement. Nonetheless, advertising people recognize their obligation to operate within the traditional American limitations: to serve the interests of the majority and to respect the rights of the minority.

Therefore we, the members of the American Association of Advertising Agencies, in addition to supporting and obeying the laws and legal regulations pertaining to advertising, undertake to extend and broaden the application of high ethical standards. Specifically, we will not knowingly produce advertising which contains:

a. False or misleading statements or exaggerations, visual or verbal.

b. Testimonials which do not reflect the real choice of a competent witness.

c. Price claims which are misleading.

d. Comparisons which unfairly disparage a competitive product or service.

e. Claims insufficiently supported, or which distort the true meaning or practicable application of statements made by professional or scientific authority.

f. Statements, suggestions or pictures offensive to public decency.

We recognize that there are areas which are subject to honestly different interpretations and judgment. Taste is subjective and may even vary from time to time as well as from individual to individual. Frequency of seeing or hearing advertising messages will necessarily vary greatly from person to person.

However, we agree not to recommend to an advertiser and to discourage the use of advertising which is in poor or questionable taste or which is deliberately irritating through content, presentation or excessive repetition.

Clear and willful violations of this Code shall be referred to the Board of Directors of the American Association of Advertising Agencies for appropriate action, including possible annulment of membership as provided in Article IV, Section 5, of the Constitution and By-Laws.

Conscientious adherence to the letter and the spirit of this Code will strengthen advertising and the free enterprise system of which it is part.   *Adopted April 26, 1962*

Creative code of A.A.A.A. reveals concern with advertising standards.

newspapers—their circulation, rates, advertising lineage, differential between local and national rates, and circulation obtained through special prices, premiums or other inducements. The group also publishes the *A.A.A.A. Newspaper Rate Differentials*—an annual study of changes in general and retail advertising rates.

When research data is to be used by advertisers and media as well as by agencies, however, it is best carried on jointly through tripartite organizations. Agencies, advertisers, and media jointly determine the survey methods so that results are acceptable to all. Media pay all or most of the research cost, since it can be reflected in their rates and thus be shared by all users of the medium in proportion to use. A.A.A.A. cooperates with advertisers and media in two major joint research enterprises—the Advertising Research Foundation and Traffic Audit Bureau.

The Advertising Research Foundation was established by the A.A.A.A. and the Association of National Advertisers in 1936. (It was later reconstituted, in 1951, as a subscription organization to which individual media, agencies, and advertisers may subscribe. A.A.A.A. and A.N.A. continue as founder subscribers.)

Prior to 1951 the foundation worked mainly with media associations on research of print media. It conducted and published more than $1,750,000 worth of media studies which made lasting contributions to research techniques.

Since then the foundation has published some 50 studies, ranging from bibliographies on motivation research to estimates of television households in the U.S. They include a monumental 500-page study called *Printed Advertising Rating Methods;* this is of particular interest to the industrial advertising manager despite a justifiably large portion of the study being devoted to consumer advertising.

The foundation offers a consultation service that is available on a cost basis to prospective sponsors of research at any time during the planning of their projects. For media, this helps to assure acceptance of research findings. On request to subscribers, published media studies of industry-wide significance may also be appraised by the foundation.

The Traffic Audit Bureau, another joint research enterprise, certifies the circulation and space-position values of outdoor-advertising plants throughout the country.

T.A.B. was established in 1933 by the A.A.A.A., A.N.A., and the Outdoor Advertising Association of America to meet the needs of advertisers, advertising agencies, and billboard operators for uniform, reliable, and accurate information on the circulation values of outdoor media. Later the three corresponding Canadian associations joined in sponsorship and support. It is the only source on the continent for information on the outdoor medium validated by agencies and advertisers.

Improving Advertising Content

The association works in two ways to improve advertising content: (1) By *encouraging* the highest standards in the creative output of agency people, and (2) by *discouraging* advertising which is in bad taste or otherwise objectionable.

In the first direction, aiming to stimulate creative activity, papers by outstanding creative leaders are a regular feature of the A.A.A.A. annual meetings and are supplied on request, in thousands of copies, to people in member agencies.

Opportunity is given at the annual meetings to see exhibits of prize-winning advertising art, outstanding film commercials, and so forth. On occasion these are made available to the A.A.A.A. local councils or to individual members.

At the regional conventions—regularly at the Eastern Annual Conference and the Central Region Annual Meeting—specialized workshops, open to all member agency people, are devoted to copy, art, and general subjects. These papers are also offered to members. Local councils from time to time arrange meetings on creative subjects.

In another direction, the association works steadily to reduce the small percentage of advertising which is objectionable to the public and tends to lessen the effectiveness of all advertising by undermining consumer and industry confidence by offending taste.

A.A.A.A. advocates, in its standards of practice, that "The advertising agency should not recommend, and should discourage any advertising of an untruthful, indecent or otherwise objectionable character."

In addition, A.A.A.A. conducts an interchange of opinion among agencies on advertising which is outside the scope of regulatory bodies. When an agency considers an advertisement objectionable for any reason, it may submit the criticism to A.A.A.A. headquarters. Each criticism received is forwarded without identification to each of 16 members of the A.A.A.A. Committee on Improvement of Advertising Content, asking whether they agree or disagree with it. The criticism and the committee's vote and comments are then sent, unidentified as to source, to the responsible agency.

The Interchange, a biennial report of the A.A.A.A., began operations in 1946 under the auspices of a committee of the American

CONFIDENTIAL   DATE: _____

To: Secretary, ANA-AAAA Committee for
    Improvement of Advertising Content
    155 East 44th Street, New York 17, N.Y.

Interchange Case No _____ Advertisement for _____ Medium _____

Description _____

The criticism of the advertisement, as received in the Interchange, is attached for your information. You are asked to give your opinion of the advertisement, however, and not simply your opinion of the criticism.

☐ If for competitive reasons you should not give an opinion on this advertisement, please check here and return form.

1. Do you believe that criticism of this advertisement is in the scope of the ANA-AAAA Interchange?

_____NO.   The problem seems to be entirely one of factual validity, involving facts not available to us.

_____YES. The problem seems to be, at least in part, whether the advertisement is in bad taste or "manifestly misleading" (No. 3 below) or otherwise harmful to advertising.

If "yes" please continue to check below and add any comments which may be helpful to the advertiser and the placing agency.

2. Is there anything in the advertisement in bad taste?

Yes_____ No_____ Don't know _____

If "yes," what?_____

_____

_____

_____

_____

3. Do you question the advertisement as likely to be "manifestly misleading" (i.e., based on internal evidence within the ad, such as visual or verbal trickery)?

Yes_____ No_____ Don't know_____

If "yes," in what way?_____

_____

_____

_____

(Continued on page 2)

Reproduced above and on the opposite page is the form used by members of the Joint Committee to cast their votes on advertisements submitted to the Interchange of the A.A.A.A. and the National Association of Advertisers.

Association of Advertising Agencies. For the first 14 years it worked only indirectly with advertisers, through their agencies. The idea behind the Interchange was simple:

- To invite advertising professionals to register their criticisms when they considered an advertisement harmful to their craft on the ground of taste or opinion.

- To supply expert evaluation of the criticism by a top-ranking committee of advertising experts.

- To give their opinions privately and in confidence to the advertiser and his agency when the committee agreed that an advertisement was harmful to advertising.

–2–

4. Is the advertisement for some other reason likely to be harmful to advertising?

Yes_____ No_____ Don't know_____

If "yes":

a. Is it because of disparagement of competitors?

Yes_____ No_____

Comment:_____

b. Is it because you think the advertisement is unsuited to the medium?

Yes_____ No_____

Comment:_____

c. If other than (a) or (b), what is the reason?

_____

_____

_____

5. Do you regard this advertisement as detrimental to advertising and requiring corrective action by the Committee?

Yes_____

No_____

Additional comments, if any:

NAME_____

Member, ANA-AAAA Committee for
Improvement of Advertising Content

Improvement of Interchange

Early in 1960, the Association of National Advertisers was invited to explore various ways in which *both* the agency and the advertiser might work together on the problem of objectionable advertising. The way was soon found to make the Interchange a truly joint operation and it was agreed that each association would be represented by nine members and its president ex-officio; that there would be two co-chairmen; a third of the committee should be appointed each year and that the two associations would share equally the out-of-pocket expenses for the Interchange operation.

In September of 1960 the combined A.A.A.A.—A.N.A. Interchange came into being.

Ben Wells, president of the Seven-Up Company, summed it up this way: "This is not an assemblage of holier-than-thou do-gooders. All of us are heavily involved in producing advertising that helps to produce sales and profits, and we realize full well that if advertising fails to do this it doesn't make any difference how socially acceptable it is or how impeccably it may be in good taste. At the same time we feel strongly that advertising which offends the canons of good taste and decency, and which deliberately misleads or that appears to smear and besmirch other advertising is not only bad advertising but bad business."

The Interchange is set up to deal with national or regional *agency-placed* advertisements which might prove harmful to advertising as a whole. Sensitive areas include:

- Bad taste
- Suggestiveness
- Statements offensive to public decency
- Pictures or copy offensive on religious, ethnic or political grounds
- Visual trickery
- Weasel wording
- Improper disparagement of other products or industries
- Derogation of the advertising industry

The Interchange deals essentially with questions of taste and opinion. It does *not* deal with the factual validity of claims, since the committee does not have access to the facts and does not have the machinery to develop such facts through investigation, hearings, and research.

In short, the Interchange does not and should not attempt to duplicate the work of government regulatory bodies such as the Federal Trade Commission, or can it deal with problems of deception and deceit such as those covered by the better business bureaus.

The committee does not handle generalized complaints, but only specific objections to specific advertisements, in print, or on the air, if a complaint falls within the scope of the Interchange.

How Complaints Are Handled

The complaint itself, together with a tear sheet, radio script, or TV photocopy of the offending advertisement is sent to all 20 members of the committee together with the voting form shown in two parts. Each member votes individually and confidentially.

If a majority of the committee considers the advertisement detrimental to advertising as a whole, the criticism and the committee votes and comments—not identified by source—are sent concurrently to the advertiser and to the placing agency of record.

If a majority of the committee regards the advertising as seriously objectionable, the advertiser and placing agency are asked to respond and to take corrective action. If they fail to do so within 30 days the committee notifies the board of directors of the A.A.A.A. and A.N.A.

The committee vote is never reported to the complainant, since the committee works in confidence with the advertiser and the placing agency. It must also be emphasized that the source of the complaint is never divulged to the committee or to anyone else; it is seen only by the committee secretary, who serves for three years and who processes all complaints.

The Interchange is not censorship. It is helpful criticism and must, of necessity, rely on voluntary regulation. Nevertheless it has brought about clear-cut improvement in a considerable volume of advertising including campaigns with wide public exposure.

Agencies and advertisers urge their personnel to be alert to questionable advertising by the use of posters such as this one. These posters are part of a series of bulletin-board reminders distributed by the committee over the past two years.

Posters like these appear in agencies and offices throughout the country. They are distributed by the Interchange Committee to remind advertisers and their agencies of the need to police the ad industry for the good of all. The posters inspire many reports of objectionable advertising to the industry's joint committee.

MIND YOUR OWN BUSINESS

Report objectionable advertising to

_____

In print. Clip the advertisement and note where it appeared.
On the air. Make a note of sponsor, message, time and station.

Complaints and their disposition during the committee's fourth and fifth years follow:

	1964	1965
Criticisms received	52	55
Deemed detrimental and requiring committee action	5	5

The experience in later years has followed a similar pattern. Most criticisms were received by Interchange from people in advertising agencies. This is to be expected because agency people are more familiar with the Interchange, since it was operated by A.A.A.A. before coming under joint A.A.A.A.—A.N.A. auspices. Also, agencies often forward criticisms on behalf of clients.

Some criticisms, however, come directly from advertisers. In the past some have come from media. It is still not unusual to read of a medium refusing to accept an advertisement.

A few have come from individuals outside of advertising who have heard about the Interchange. Though not actively solicited, these are welcomed and treated exactly as the others are.

In 1964 and 1965 the experience was typical of current reports:

	1964	1965
From agency people	37	40
From advertisers	4	5
From people outside of advertising	7	5
From associations	4	5
TOTAL	52	55

Of the 52 criticisms received in 1964 and the 55 in 1965, the media breakdown (typical of more recent years) was as follows:

	1964	1965
Newspaper	16	13
Television	10	11
Consumer magazines	15	14
Radio	1	2
Business publications	6	10
Transit	3	3
Direct mail	1	2

If we assume the worst—that all of the direct-mail criticisms were leveled against industrial advertising—and add those to the business-publication advertising for the year 1965, we find that industrial advertising had a total of 12 criticisms out of 55.

On the surface, this seems creditable. But this is almost *one-fourth* of all criticisms when it is remembered that industrial advertising is but a tiny fraction of all advertising. It is obvious that this area could stand a good spring housecleaning.

The committee does not make general pronouncements as to the specific type of criticisms it received, although a subcommittee report stated that advertising directly attacking individual competitors seemed to be on the increase.

They stated that while vigorous competition in advertising should always be encouraged, they recommended that the A.A.A.A. take an even stronger stand against denigration of competitors, that name-calling and even name-naming should be discouraged, and that widespread derogation of competitors, even when technically true, could have a serious effect on the public's confidence in advertising.

It is interesting to note Hertz's abandonment of a particularly strong campaign in the bitterly competitive car-rental industry occurred with amazing speed. Of even more interest is speculation on the reasons why; obviously Hertz was stung enough to lash out at Avis, and from the tone of the ads it initially seemed they would run for an extended period of time.

Some members of the Interchange felt that derogation of competitors was so self-defeating that it would fall of its own weight, while others believed that each derogatory advertisement would invite retaliation, that disparagement would therefore proliferate, and that the total result might bring discredit to advertising as a whole unless a stronger stand were taken.

Subsequently, the A.A.A.A. board of directors adopted a policy statement based on the subcommittee's report.

Advertisements using sex, violence, and "suggestive" copy were the source of numerous complaints to the Interchange. A number of these involved promotion for motion pictures. At its first meeting in 1965, the Interchange took note of this and voted unanimously to commend four newspapers for having tightened their standards for such advertising.

Complaints were also received on advertising which seemed to ridicule or make light of patriotic symbols, religious beliefs, and ethnic characteristics. In those cases deemed serious by a majority of the committee, the advertisements were withdrawn.

This has been the record in all cases judged detrimental to advertising by the committee—further evidence of the stature of the committee on the one hand and of the sense of responsibility by both advertisers and their agencies on the other.

In February 1966, Norman H. Strouse, chairman of the J. Walter Thompson Company, the country's largest advertising agency, responded to the presentation of the Advertising Gold Medal Award with these words:

> "We must continue our climb toward higher standards of practice, greater self-discipline, and greater sensitivity concerning the outer boundaries of public tolerance. These are responsibilities which we cannot shift to someone else. The agency initiates creative ideas—the client approves them—the media accept them in final form. All must accept responsibility for clearing the air of any advertising that offends public taste, irritates sensibilities, intentionally misleads, or denigrates a competitor."

Better Understanding of Advertising

The service that advertising performs as an economic and social force needs wide understanding. Among people engaged in advertising, such insight helps them to see the importance of their jobs to the economy as a whole. Among businessmen, it encourages proper use of advertising as a business tool. Among government officials, educators, and consumer leaders, it helps to assure that advertising is not unfairly criticized or restricted.

A notable joint enterprise in public relations, unique in American business, is *The Advertising Council*. Jointly sponsored by the 4A's, A.N.A., and four leading media groups, The Advertising Council is a continuous demonstration of the use of advertising for the public service.

Through the council, volunteer advertising agencies contribute creative work and media and advertisers donate more than $160,-000,000 per year in space and time toward the support of non-partisan public-service campaigns—for better schools, community chests, forest-fire prevention, the Red Cross, mental health, accident prevention, and many others.

In an average year, it is estimated that some 500 agency people contribute around 25,000 man-hours to prepare the campaigns. A.A.A.A. obtains the volunteer agencies, underwrites the agencies' share of council financing, names agency representatives on the council board, and distributes campaign material to advertising agencies throughout the country.

Continuing since 1941, the council's public-service program is helping to gain proper recognition for advertising among government, business, and public groups.

Another joint enterprise in public relations is the *Committee on Understanding of our Economic System,* cosponsored by A.A.A.A. and A.N.A. The Joint Committee has developed and promoted three programs of far-reaching influence:

> "This Is Our Problem," which stimulated employer-employee programs of economic education in plants throughout the country, leading to the Advertising Council's "Miracle of America" campaign and booklet.

> "The Future of America" which was credited by Dr. Arthur F. Burns, then economic advisor to President Eisenhower, with helping to correct "recession" psychology in 1954 and helping to bring about the economic upturn.

> "Challenge to America," which explained the importance of marketing and advertising in realizing our country's economic opportunities.

In domestic economic affairs, A.A.A.A. is represented on the National Distribution Council of the Department of Commerce.

In international affairs, it sponsored the First International Meeting of Advertising Agency Leaders, attended in 1956 by leaders from more than 35 different countries throughout the world. It is regularly represented at meetings of The International Chamber of Commerce and the ICC's U.S. Council.

Other A.A.A.A. Committees

In addition to committees and functions already discussed, the American Association of Advertising Agencies has 15 active committees which meet either on a scheduled basis, or as necessary. They are committees on:

> Client service
> Agency management
> Government and public relations
> Improving advertising
> Work with students and educators
> Broadcast business affairs
> Broadcast policy
> Business publications
> Consumer magazines
> Direct-mail advertising
> Newspapers
> Out-of-home media
> Print production
> Fiscal control
> Research

A TYPICAL ADVERTISING AGENCY
ORGANIZATION CHART
BY FUNCTIONS

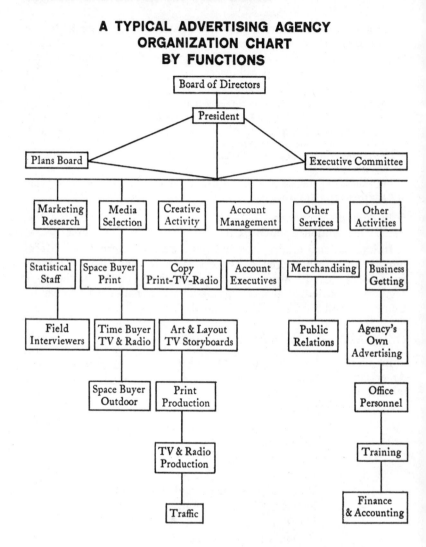

One of the greatest services the group performs for its member agencies—and for advertising in general—is its vigorous campaign to attract the cream of the crop of young people to the business. The A.A.A.A. has a continuous program of presenting advertising as a *desirable activity* to high-ranking young high-school and college graduates, and of testing them to determine their suitability for an advertising career. It has been estimated that the four branches of advertising—media, advertisers, advertising agencies, and suppliers and special services—employ around 100,000 men and women; an additional 100,000 are in related administrative and clerical activities. The four branches of advertising probably need a total of 20,000 newcomers each year, of which advertising agencies will absorb about 7,000, including novices.

What Is an Advertising Agency?

Just what is an advertising agency? How is it organized? What are its primary functions? What can it do for the industrial advertising manager and his company that he cannot do himself?

To put these questions in their proper perspective, let's look at the organizational structure of a typical agency, and glance at the functions it performs. Many of them will be discussed at greater length in the following chapters, of course.

The chart (left), by courtesy of the American Association of Advertising Agencies, shows that a typical agency has the familiar line and staff organization common throughout industry.

Except for the extremely small operation, the average agency is staffed with professionals in every facet of communications. It is a specialized creator of a custom-built, one-of-a-kind product, for each campaign and each ad within the campaign is truly unique in that it can be used by only one advertiser, and, more often than not, at only one specific time.

These skilled professionals within the agency are often multi-talented, although usually they are experts in one specific field—copy, art direction, market research, media, and so on. Each contributes his expertise to the program which the agency produces for each of its clients.

In general, most agencies have 15 areas of specialization:

1. Executive
2. Administrative
3. Client contact
4. Client services
5. Copy
6. Art
7. Radio and TV
8. Direct mail
9. Collateral material
10. Marketing
11. Media
12. Research
13. Production
14. Accounting
15. New business

Agency Organizations Most Prevalent

In most agencies today, again excluding the very small ones, one of three organizational structures and systems are used. An agency using what we shall call System 1 assigns writers, art directors, media specialists, and production and traffic people to a group of accounts. These people work only on these specified accounts and are directed by an account executive or account supervisor. When an agency uses System 1, it usually has a number of such groups of specialists working on groups of accounts. Each account group is much like a small agency in that it performs all of the necessary services for its clients. An advertiser whose agency is so set up is assured that he will have a team working on his account that *knows* his account, his products and his market; there is no question of having his work pushed off onto someone who is not thoroughly familiar with it, or of lacking service because "his" agency people are too busy or are out of the agency engaged in projects for another advertiser.

System 2 is known in the agency field as the "departmental system." It is departmentalized by function and consists simply of having pools of people, all talented specialists, engaging in their specialty for all of the agency's clients. In such a setup, for example, an agency would have a copy department where copy is written for all agency accounts. As a rule, the individual writers would write on the same accounts most of the time, perhaps as many as a dozen or more different accounts, but not necessarily so. Just as business problems tend to be the same in different businesses, so do copy problems. A really good copywriter can, after a brief review of material previously written—and a talk with the account executive to learn the client's desires—write on almost any product or service with equal facility. All layout artists and art directors would similarly be located in an art department, media personnel in a media department, and production specialists in a production department.

This system works well for many agencies and is probably the one most widely used. Advantages claimed for it include having work done in the various departments produced for the approval of the department head, himself a skilled professional in his field. Proponents of the system feel that various department heads are likely to have more knowledge and better judgment of their specialties than any individual account executive. The so-called crosspollination effect resulting from having individuals within the various departments exposed to many advertisers' problems, rather than those of just one advertiser, as found in System 1, is theoretically beneficial. There's no denying that experience broadens.

Furthermore, under System 2 it is somewhat easier to have all work reviewed by a plans board or by the agency's executive in charge of client service. Such review benefits the client by having his problems known to and considered by additional agency personnel. This tends to preclude any possibility of the agency not adopting the one best plan of attack for the client.

System 3 is probably the best of all for the industrial advertiser, particularly if his products are technical. It is the so-called copy-contact system, which is actually System 1 with modifications to transform it into System 3. These changes are slight, however, and involve only the account executive and the copywriter—who is one and the same individual. Many of the biggest and most successful industrial advertising agencies, Marsteller Inc., for example, are structured this way.

Rationale behind this type of organization is that the one person most closely acquainted with the advertiser's products and problems is the one who actually sees the client frequently—the account executive. The account executive gets his direction and information firsthand, right from the advertising manager. When the account executive, "A.E.," as he is commonly called, is the copywriter there is no necessity to transmit instructions and technical information and to explain the ad manager's wishes to a copywriter. Thus there is far less chance of misinterpretation, false starts, and wasted time and money.

How One Firm Went Wrong

One large Chicago-based division of a national corporation recently encountered this problem. Its agency, a sizable System 1 operation, assigned a new account executive to the account at the same time a new ad manager joined the firm. With both men inexperienced, it was almost a case of the blind leading the blind. The agency made the initial mistake, of course, in not providing the necessary continuity for the client. This resulted in a great deal of floundering on the part of both parties—and considerable poor copy, poorly conceived collateral material, and wasted effort. This is a trap into which no ad manager should fall; if new on the job, he should insist that the A.E. familiar with the account stay on it until he is broken in. Sometimes, of course, the situation cannot be helped because coincidentally the A.E. left the agency at an inopportune time and was not available.

Had a copy-contact system been used in this situation, the person who actually called on the advertiser would have known whether or not he had firm and correct direction, and full and factual information. He would have been sure of the course to take. Having an inexperienced account executive relay instructions to a copywriter with whom he wasn't familiar, and an art director who had never met the ad manager (or anyone else from the company) resulted in a costly fiasco.

On the other hand, when the copy-contact man (account executive-copywriter) returns to his agency from a session with the advertising manager, he has his notes and his reference material— *plus a feeling* for what the ad manager wants which can only be gotten by an across-the-desk conference.

With System 3 the A.E.-copywriter has solid backing from a group, just as in System 1. He has his account supervisor who backstops him and substitutes for him as required, the group account supervisor, art director, media director, and production people, all of whom are intimately acquainted with the ad manager's account. These people are a constant, a team built by the agency to service a certain number of accounts. This system works so well that it should surely be an important influence when consideration of an agency is being entertained.

How an agency is structured is, however, of less importance to the advertising manager than whether he gets the quality of service and the quality of people and creative thinking that leads to solutions of his problems. If he gets these, the agency is right for his company. If he doesn't, he should examine himself, his direction of the agency he presently retains, and, finally, the agency itself.

How to Select an Agency

With some 4,500 advertising agencies in this country to choose from, just how does an industrial advertising manager select an agency—either his first, or a new agency if his present one is not satisfactory? What can the advertising manager do to lessen the odds against an unwise choice?

One ad manager, James Dean of the MacGregor Division, Brunswick Corporation, devised a "score sheet." The sheet was given to all members of the company who viewed presentations given by a number of advertising agencies who were interested in acquiring the account. Each member of the MacGregor Division scored each agency, then the score sheets were collected and the results tabulated. The score sheets asked such questions as:

Agency..

Date...

Rated by...

	Par	Score	Remarks

General background — **15**

How long has the agency been in business?

(This question will help indicate whether or not the agency's operation is a stable one.)

How many accounts does the agency have?

In what industries are they?

What companies are they?

What is this agency's record of growth?

How many new accounts has this agency acquired in the last two years? On what dates?

(This question may point up an agency being stretched too thin to handle additional accounts at this time, as far as their personnel are concerned.)

How much agency growth represents new business, and how much is due to increased billing from present clients?

(This question can show whether the agency's clients visibly benefit from agency counsel and services.)

What is the agency's record of account losses in the last five years?

(All agencies lose accounts; this question is valuable because it makes possible an evaluation of the agency's honesty and candor in answering it.)

General attitude — **15**

What kind of people are they?

What is the agency's business philosophy?

Is the agency businesslike in its approach?

	Par	Score	Remarks

Do they show a genuine desire to work with us, or do they seem merely to want more business?

Physical organization   10

Does their agency seem well organized?

(A disorganized agency is the last thing an ad manager needs.)

What is the general experience of the group with whom we talked?

What type of personnel does the agency have?

Is the agency staffed to handle our business?

Who would work on our account? On how many other accounts would these people work?

(Would they have time for us?)

Compatability   10

Do we like these people *as people?*

(If they are not really liked now, while they are selling themselves to us, it is unlikely we will ever warm up to them.)

Would we like doing business with them?

Experience   30

Has this agency solved problems similar to ours?

Can they identify problem areas?

Do they approach problems intelligently and analytically?

(If not, stop wasting time with this agency.)

Has the agency developed any particularly effective business-publication campaigns?

(If not, it is unlikely they will start now.)

Has the agency had experience in our field?

WHY YOU NEED AN ADVERTISING AGENCY

Par	Score	Remarks

(This is a loaded question. Experience in a specific field is not a prerequisite for an agency to do an outstanding job. In fact, a fresh, objective, outside viewpoint may well pay dividends in pinpointing perplexing problems and solving them most effectively.)

Does the agency have a proved formula for effective advertising?

(If it does, steer clear! A formula is an excuse for a failure before it occurs for lack of fresh creative thinking. It presages mediocrity at best, complete and utter failure at worst.)

Does the agency experiment with new communication techniques?

(If not, it has probably gone—or is going—stale.)

Is the agency "arty" or are they marketing oriented?

Do they show a good basic grasp of desirable business practices?

Related abilities   10

Is the agency equipped to handle our public relations?

Product publicity?

Package design?

Market research?

Make market tests?

Solve our marketing problems?

Our sales meetings?

Dealer displays?

(If not, this agency is probably too small and we would have to have additional outside sources for these necessary services.)

Par is 100, a bit high for other than a real dub golfer, but a good score for a top-notch agency to achieve on such a score sheet. According to James Dean, this system of scoring largely eliminates emotional reaction to a presentation and makes it relatively easy for company personnel to evaluate agencies to whom they have talked.

Additional Steps in Agency Selection

Books have been written on the single subject of agency selection. One of the best is *The Critical Partnership—Standards of Advertising Agency Selection and Performance,* by Mark Hanan, managing partner of the management consultant firm, Hanan & Son. Hanan lists six steps in selecting an agency:

1. Screening	4. Decision
2. Interviewing	5. Announcement
3. Presentation (s)	6. Preparation

The author of this work also added that the advertiser is responsible for 80 percent of the planning of an advertising program. He is responsible for 20 percent of the execution, and he has responsibility for a full 50 percent of the control. The agency assumes responsibility for the remaining portions in each category.

This all seems simple, but there are a number of decisions which must be made before consideration is given to talking to the first prospective agency.

First of all, the decision must be made as to who is going to make the decision of which agency will be retained. In small companies, the advertising manager is usually the man who makes the choice. However, in larger companies the trend is to make the decision by committee; the committee is usually made up of the ad manager, the marketing director, the sales manager, the assistant sales manager and, not infrequently, the company or division president.

Agency responsibility must be decided upon. This involves specifying just what the agency is expected to do for the advertiser; this may well include advertising campaigns, market research, public relations, sales promotion, collateral material—or portions of each. This must be clearly defined for the company's sake, as well as to have all agencies competing on an equal basis for the advertiser's business.

Narrowing the List

The list of prospective agencies must be narrowed down. There are simply too many to consider talking to all of them in a geographic area. Factors which enter in here are agencies with experience in products or markets similar to yours; it has long been standard practice to exclude agencies which have competitive products, or even products which are noncompetitive, but which are manufactured and marketed by a company which *does* make competitive products. Recently, however, the American Association of Advertising Agencies suggested that agencies be permitted to handle products even if they currently handle a competitor's noncompeting products. The 4A's feels that the account conflict problem inhibits agencies' growth and limits the number of agencies available to clients. The problem becomes more pressing all of the time due to mergers, company acquisitions, and the huge number of new products introduced annually. A.A.A.A.'s recommendations of this subject are found in a report titled, "The Ideal Client-Agency Policy on Account Conflicts." The Association will send a copy upon request.

Geographic location is usually quite important, although distance in this age of jet aircraft is less of a barrier than it was a few years ago. However, it follows that the agency located close by can logically be expected to provide better service, and to call more frequently than one which is hundreds of miles away. The cost of travel being what it is, it is not profitable for the agency if too much accrues against an account. The answer to that one is to cut the service back to where the account *is* profitable.

The amount the account bills is an important consideration. It is axiomatic in the agency business that an advertiser with a budget large enough to represent a sizable portion of the agency's total business has much "clout." This advertiser is going to get the kind of service he wants. There are many small advertisers who enjoy good service in giant agencies and wouldn't change for the world however, just as there are numbers of advertisers with huge budgets who receive fine service and first-rate thinking from small agencies, and the idea of a change is the farthest thing from their minds. Size isn't everything, but dollars still talk. And more dollars talk louder, particularly in an atmosphere where there isn't too much talking being done.

Initially, consider 25 agencies. Not talk to 25, but consider and evaluate them internally and narrow the choice down to a half-dozen or so. These finalists will be the ones chosen to make presentations to executives.

It is up to the ad manager, as the only individual in the company qualified to do so, to accumulate as much raw data about prospective agencies as possible. Sources for facts include agencies themselves; acquire a list of clients of the agencies under consideration. Evaluate them as to the type of businesses they are, decide whether your company is the same general type, and whether or not your company would feel at home in that atmosphere. Check these clients in reference works such as the Rome Report to determine approximately how large their budgets are as far as space placed through the agency is concerned. An initial evaluation of this type will reveal a number of agencies where the business climate is obviously so foreign that these agencies should be dropped from the roster of possibles.

Once the list of prospects is reduced, information about the remaining agencies should be rounded out to provide a better picture of what each could do for your company. The best advice in the world at this stage is to assume nothing. Naturally, good service, good creative thinking, good problem-solving ability are all desirable and necessary, but not every agency provides—or *can* provide—them. Many agencies stay in business without doing so.

Talk to Other Clients

The best possible way to determine what your company could logically expect to receive from the agencies under consideration is to talk to their clients. It is only common courtesy, however, to request permission to do so; needless to say, the "request" will never be refused.

When talking with the ad manager of a company that is a client of an agency you are considering, explain your situation fully. Ask his opinion of the agency's strong points—and its weak points. All agencies have them in varying degrees. Ask him what he thinks of the agency's creativity—its ability to plan campaigns, to develop communications programs based upon marketing objectives, to produce tight, pithy copy that informs, and layouts that are arresting. Ask about the agency's role in producing collateral material such as sales literature and catalogs—whether it is weak or strong, whether the agency tackles these tasks willingly or accepts them grudgingly, and a general idea of his opinion about agency charges for these services. A frank discussion with *several* ad managers from different companies about *each* agency, with careful note-taking, will result in a very revealing profile of the capabilities of the prospective agencies.

Also, don't overlook past clients of the agency. All agencies lose accounts, of course; relationships are frequently dissolved for reasons beyond the control of either party—such as when a merger occurs, or when a company is purchased by another, for example. In such instances the account invariably goes to an agency already retained by the dominant firm in the consolidation.

Bear in mind, however, that if an agency has a history of high attrition in client relationships, of acquiring clients only to lose them a year or two later, be wary—very wary. Some agencies' major strengths—and efforts—lie in the acquisition of new business. Once an account is in the house the ad manager never again sees the personable, persuasive, hard-sell individuals who initially convinced him that *this* is *the* agency to have. Instead, an entirely different team takes over work associated with his account. They may be capable and efficient, but they are definitely the agency's second team. The first team is saved for new business presentations.

On the other hand, clients sometimes demand too much, are naturally difficult to get along with, or accounts are simply not profitable for the agency. Any of these factors, among others, can cause an agency relationship to be terminated, or cause the agency to resign the account. In fairness to all concerned, the prospective agency should be given the opportunity to rebut adverse comments from former clients.

Space Salesmen Know

Another prime source of information about the agencies being evaluated are representatives of business publications. These space salesmen make more contacts—with advertisers and agencies—in the course of a week than the ad manager makes in six months. Conscientious "reps" will usually give an unbiased and knowledgeable assessment of an agency if assured their remarks will be held in confidence. After all, they sell space to the agencies they are being asked about, so the ad manager must *not* attribute any remarks to them. Since advertising is replete with back-fence gossips to an extent probably unknown in any other business, representatives have picked up information which is strictly closed-door material; much of it is revealing, helpful, interesting—much is useless. Every bit helps round out the picture and makes an informed decision possible.

For a number of years the so-called "questionnaire approach" was considered the last word in sophistication in agency selection. An advertiser in search of a suitable agency developed a questionnaire which was sent to agencies under active consideration, and they were asked to complete it and return it to the advertising manager. Many of these questionnaires had merit and asked pertinent questions in an objective way. Questionnaires of this type showed clearly and concisely what an agency expected to do, and would do, for the advertiser. They are helpful to all concerned and save everybody's time.

Some advertisers, however, in an effort to "trap" agencies into some kind of admission which would be detrimental to their cause, deliberately loaded questionnaires, wording questions in such a way that the agency executive answering them had to be psychic to come up with the "correct" reply—much in the same way that the old "have you stopped beating your wife?" question is a bit difficult to answer. The better agencies were quick to realize this was happening and today many refuse to reply to questionnaires sent to them unsolicited. Thus these advertisers, actually in need of an agency, defeated their own purpose. They put *themselves* out of the running and reduced the field from which they could select.

An alternate and much better approach is to write to the agencies being actively considered. Best make the letter relatively short, not over one page, typed and single-spaced. Ask straightforward, information-seeking questions. The answers, of course, can be either quite short, or very extensive; both types of answers will reveal much of the agency's thinking and should be analyzed thoroughly. For the most part, agencies will reply to a request such as this, whereas they may ignore a questionnaire.

The Final Contenders

By this time most of the agencies in the original list of 25 have been eliminated for one reason or another. It is now time to visit the five or six finalists and get acquainted. Phone or write for an appointment (as you'd expect if the situation were reversed). Be punctual; the agencies undoubtedly will have an array of executives on hand for the meeting and they are tying up an expensive group.

In exploratory meetings such as this, *all* agencies greatly prefer to let their prospective client do most of the talking. It is to their advantage to learn all they can at this crucial stage of the game so that they can gain some edge over their competitors. Resist this temptation; your time to talk will come soon enough. Let the agency people you're visiting carry the conversational ball. Make them sell themselves—and their agency—to you. Make them demonstrate their capabilities by showing you case histories—problem-solving programs they have prepared for other clients. Meet their people. Evaluate them—their competence, business ability, attitude, and their interest in working for you.

Ask to see their "house" ads—the advertisements they have prepared to advertise their agency. Advertising agencies, the good ones, believe in what they're doing. They advertise for the same reason that any company does. Much can be learned about an agency and its philosophy by reading what it writes about itself. Naturally you'll be welcome to take reprints of the ads with you when the meeting is over; analyze them and add comments to the files of the various agencies you've built up.

An agency's ad about itself can be revealing.

The next step is to invite the finalists—excluding any eliminated during your visits to the various agencies, of course—to make a formal presentation in your office. At this time many ad managers prefer to ask the marketing director, the sales manager, or both, to sit in on these meetings. It is now that generalities must be dispensed with and real specifics discussed. Each prospective agency should be asked to state precisely just what it will do for your company; who they will assign to the account and how much service they propose to provide. This is the time to discuss—and agree completely on—all of the details of agency compensation. All parties must understand and concur on every detail, and they must do so *now*. Later is too late. Work out a financial arrangement that is fair to both the company and the agency. Spell it out and *write it out*. When this is done you'll find that disagreements about money—always unpleasant, frequently embarrassing, and occasionally fatal to a good working relationship—almost never crop up. The financial agreement must be discussed with all of the agencies making presentations so that all may be judged fairly and impartially.

Presentations Vary

Presentations run the gamut from full-blown "dog and pony shows" to relaxed, informal talks. Many agencies have audio-visual presentations consisting of a slide show with synchronized, taped commentary, or the comments are made by one of the agency people. Despite the possibility of being dazzled by the elaborate presentation, the ad manager is usually less likely to be talked into an affiliation that is unsuitable than are others in the company who are less familiar with agencies.

An agency presentation, whether flip-chart, show cards, audio-visual, or just conversation, should do one thing—sell the agency to those who see it. There's nothing inherently wrong with being sold, or in doing the selling. After all, it's the agency's business to help sell your product. The personality and the capability of the agency should come through loud and clear in any presentation. That, after all the dust has settled, is what you're buying.

Speculative campaigns, or ads "done on spec," merit little consideration. An agency making a presentation has had so little opportunity to learn your business and familiarize itself with your product or service—and your problems—that it is unfair to expect them to present at this time a campaign worth the artist's board it's mounted on. Any campaigns or individual ads are undoubtedly off target and are undesirable. They are a waste of time for the agency which prepared them and, most ad managers feel, reflect undisciplined thinking in the agency which prepared them.

Assuming your product is technical, and the majority of industrial products are, no agency can come armed to the teeth with knowledge of how this widget actuated that gizmo so that the product performs as promised. Nobody is justified in asking that.

Instead, the knowledgeable ad manager looks for market knowledge which proves to him that the agency understands where the product is sold and used, and how it is sold. Ability to absorb technical knowledge is vitally important, however, and should be demonstrated by agencies during their presentations. It is safe to assume, for example, that if an agency successfully prepares ad copy and collateral copy on diesel engines that it can easily do so for fork-lift trucks. Or, if it writes well on semiconductor production equipment, it can do the same for laboratory test instrumentation. It is wise to point this out to other company members evaluating presentations, for they may be unaware of this.

Score each "contestant" as previously discussed. Then compare and evaluate the scores and the other information accumulated and tabulated during this period. Make a final decision as quickly as possible. Each competing agency is understandably anxious to learn the outcome, and it is decent to notify them without delay. A little tact and thoughtfulness is in order, and the losing agencies should be let down gently and with consideration for their feelings. The courteous thing to do is to write each, thanking them for their time and effort and for considering your company as a client. Tell them what agency was selected.

The Written Agreement

Good business practice is to get together immediately with the new agency and draw up a *written* working agreement. It should state:

1. When the agreement takes effect, and that it will be in effect until terminated. That the agreement may be terminated by either party by written notice, 30 days prior to its taking effect, is a typical stipulation.

2. Specific services the agency is to provide should be listed, as to products or services, market areas, and any limitations are noted specifically.

3. Billing terms should be stated, with a full explanation of how the agency will bill for services and how purchases will be made for the client. A brief statement of how and when the agency pays media, together with billing and discount dates, makes it easy for the accounting department, as well as the ad manager, to handle agency invoices.

4. If for any reason the relationship is terminated by either the client or the agency, the rights and obligations of both should be stated, with particular emphasis placed on how work in process and current contracts with media are to be handled.

It is not negative to talk about termination immediately upon joining forces. It is good business for both the client and the agency to have a written agreement in the files—with both parties hoping that the day it is signed is the last time it is ever seen!

Client and Agency Relationship

It's obvious by now that selecting and appointing an agency is not undertaken lightly or done on the spur of the moment. Many have compared the client-agency relationship with marriage, and the analogy isn't an inappropriate one. Agency selection is made less emotionally and, perhaps, for better reasons, but both relationships are as important as any the ad manager is likely to experience.

A good agency is one that studies and learns the company's products and markets. It is one with a strong desire to have its clients succeed, so that it customarily does more than is expected. It is one that is a real pleasure to work with. Such an agency is a full half of the advertising team. It is far more than a placement service which buys space, issues insertion orders, and ships electros. The agency is a *partner,* and the ad manager fortunate enough to pick one that's really right should provide prompt and proper input for the agency, give it his complete backing—and cherish it.

Much has been written and will be written on the client-agency relationship. Much of it needed to be said, much didn't. The fact is that both the client and the agency have one objective which they share—to make a profit. Far too many people on the corporate side of the desk cheerfully pay lip service to "wanting our agency to make money," but too few, unfortunately, actually understand what is involved. The conscientious ad manager will familiarize himself with agency problems and costs and procedures, so that he can assure himself that his agency is getting a fair shake. Agencies, good ones, do as much or more for their clients.

At first the relationship will be formal. But people are pretty decent whether they're in corporations or agencies, and the ad manager will want to progress to a first-name basis. If all of the factors involved in the selection were evaluated correctly, a firm business friendship will develop over the years. It comes as a surprise to some ad managers—those who have endured an agency relationship that was less than productive and effective—that agencies are, by and large, inhabited by unusually talented individuals who earnestly want to make their clients successful and their ad managers look good.

It's always more pleasant to do business with friends. In the client-agency relationship the ad manager should be businesslike, should properly insist on running a tight ship; but he shouldn't be a martinet. Nobody likes a freeloader, even if he *is* a client; a good advertising manager has an expense account and he should use it. It is not right for the agency to always buy the lunch!

Few Secrets in Business

Trust the agency. Take it into your confidence. There should be no company secrets. The agency has a legitimate interest in such vital statistics as cost of manufacture of the product(s), sales volume, margins, gross profit, selling costs, marketing costs, sales projections, and the current and anticipated competitive conditions. Without this information the agency is working blindfolded.

Some advertisers say they feel this information should be withheld from the agency because it might not always be their agency. This is quite true. But they conveniently ignore the fact that there are very few secrets in business. If an agency resigns, or is terminated, some very confidential information is loose in the business community. But when a key employee resigns, or is enticed away by a competitor, just how secret is this secret information? Some things must be taken on trust.

One major goal of the ad manager as well as the agency is to make the relationship an *enduring* one. On the face of it, it is quite obvious that whether or not it endures is contingent upon the quality of service the agency provides. This would include campaign planning, copy, layout, research, merchandising, media counsel, and agency willingness and ability to become totally involved in the company's communications problems.

In addition, though, there must be an honest desire on the part of both the company and the agency for the relationship to be a long-lived one for this desire to be translated into actuality. If the agency is right for the company (if it isn't, why was it selected?), and the agency is convinced the company is the right client, all concerned should strive consciously from the very beginning to build a solid and satisfactory relationship based on mutual trust, respect for, and need of each other.

Bear in mind that a new agency is much like a new employee— or, for that matter, much like the ad manager himself when he was new on the job. It is illogical in the extreme to choose a new agency, then to expect to receive almost from the start brilliant, compelling advertising that is difficult to improve upon. This is unrealistic. A new agency, like a new ship, requires a shakedown cruise before it is truly ready to take on all that comes its way. The agency needs time to become acclimated, time to learn the products or services, time to learn the people they're involved with and establish a rapport with them. And, most important, time to think. This last is crucial if the agency is to develop a program that will achieve the desired results.

Work with the agency, give it every bit of help possible and refrain from unfavorable evaluation of initial efforts. There's plenty of time later for this sort of thing if it becomes necessary.

That Difficult Second Year

The consensus is that while building an enduring relationship is never easy, the second year is the perilous one. It is in this year that serious misunderstandings—or even a complete break—are most likely to happen. By this time it has become apparent to all that the agency is composed of hard-working, unusually competent people—not super-humans from whom frequently come blinding strokes of sheer brilliance which lay low all the problems of the past, present and future. The ad manager and others in the company have had time to become accustomed to the advertising the agency produces. They may tend to regard it as increasingly plodding and pedestrian, rather than vigorous and vital, interesting and exciting. Sales probably have not surged dramatically, and possibly the cost of selling has not been drastically reduced by advertising, which should do just that. A psychological letdown in such a situation must be guarded against.

Now, before the situation deteriorates further so that there is nothing to be saved, is the time for the advertising manager to remember two things: (1) Breaking in a new agency is an incredibly difficult, time-consuming, and costly proposition which nobody in his right mind wants to have to do any oftener than required, and (2) it is now that the agency needs the help and encouragement of the ad manager.

Show the agency by your actions that they have your complete confidence and respect. Resist at all costs the temptation to make the mistake so many industrial ad managers with little experience make—needling, prodding, attempting to "keep the agency off balance." The ad manager who attempts to manage with such woefully misguided ideas and crude tactics is kidding nobody but himself. He succeeds merely in making himself disliked, in creating a poor impression for his company in the minds of agency personnel, and keeps the agency too busy keeping its skirts clean to do the job the ad manager must have done.

Ignore the siren songs sung by competitive agencies who want your account. There will be some who do at any given time. Talk with one, even informally, and the word inevitably will get back to your agency because the entire advertising business is a tightly knit group. What this will accomplish is to kill off all enthusiasm of your agency, instantly and probably with great finality. Then the A.E. who calls has turned into an on-guard zombie who reflects the feeling of the agency—that they've been stabbed in the back, that the client isn't to be trusted.

From then on, instead of getting the best thinking of which the agency is capable, the ad manager will receive *what the agency thinks he wants to hear—what the agency thinks it can "sell."* This input from the ad manager, polished and rewritten and fleshed out, always lacks the creative spark which distinguishes advertising created by craftsmen who believe in what they're doing from advertising cranked out because an assignment must be completed. Cost to the client is exactly the same.

Chapter 3

LAYING THE GROUNDWORK

INDUSTRY suffers from the Wilbur-and-Orville-Wright syndrome. An incredible percentage of companies whose products are sold to industry are afflicted with this debilitating syndrome, which is nothing more than flying by the seat of the pants when it comes to marketing in general and advertising in particular.

More poor ads are run, more ineffective campaigns are developed, and more money is poured down the drain—absolutely wasted—on industrial advertising that doesn't have a ghost of a chance to do its assigned job because of a dismal lack of adequate planning than for any other reason.

Planning—and the preplanning stage which we'll call laying the groundwork—are neglected much oftener than not. Perhaps it's because this is considered the least interesting activity (or *lack* of activity) the industrial ad manager encounters. But, properly done, it can be one of the most productive.

Many industrial advertising managers routinely perform the fantastically difficult feat of operating in a vacuum. They are uncommonly apt at producing advertising in the most wasteful, most ineffective way ever conceived—without an overall plan. Ads turned out one or two at a time on a hit-or-miss basis, in response to some minor panic, or possibly in reaction to a bit of pressure from sales, are far more likely to miss than to hit. And they'll waste an appalling amount of money in the process.

It's pathetic but true that this is seldom the fault of the advertising manager. He's a victim of circumstances, but there's something he can do about it.

Poor planning, or lack of *any* planning, usually starts at the top of the ladder in the small or medium-sized industrial firm. It is due either to vacillation or naiveté. Companies which don't plan are as familiar as apple pie, the corner drugstore, or the stereotype of the American-boy-makes-good success story.

Many were founded some 40 years ago by an engineering genius who had an Idea. Invariably the Idea was translated into an intricate, highly engineered product that was genuinely superior. It sold steadily because it was like the well-known mousetrap, and the company prospered. As the economy grew, so did the company. Suddenly, though, competition—serious competition—reared its ugly head.

The engineering genius, now a full-fledged business tycoon with a paneled office with private washroom, remained innocently content with simply building a better widget, never doubting for a single minute that his company would get its fair share—or more—of the market. He continued to regard his company as a production organism and continued to place primary emphasis on engineering and production. Marketing and advertising were words almost outside the corporate vocabulary for all practical purposes. What little advertising that was done was done because everybody else did it. Inevitably the company's sales deteriorated, as did its competitive position. Then the engineering genius retired to fish in Florida and control of the firm passed from his hands. As a rule, new management reversed the downtrend with smart marketing and smart advertising. Sound familiar?

The Marketing Concept

When a company is solidly product oriented, rather than embracing the "marketing concept" like a long-lost lover, it finds its position in the marketplace constantly harder to maintain. A product-oriented company thinks in terms of what *it* knows best, of what *it* wants to build, of what *it* wants to sell, of how *it* wants to distribute, of how *it* wants to provide after-sale service—rather than thinking of these basic concepts in terms of the customers' desires, or looking at them through the customers' eyes.

It is incontrovertible that successful companies, those whose performance is head and shoulders above that of their industries as a whole, are adherents to and believers in the marketing concept. Ask IBM, Xerox, Avis, P&G, 3M, or Sears, Roebuck.

The cornerstone of successful marketing strategy and getting the most out of the marketing concept is a *written* marketing plan. It is an absolute essential. This is so vitally important it bears repeating: a written plan is an absolute essential. The following letter, written by an industrial advertising manager to his boss, a vice-president of marketing, spells out just why a written plan is so necessary, what benefits derive from having it, and what happens as a result of doing without. The situation is real, incidentally, as is the letter and the advertising agency. All names have been changed for obvious reasons.

Mr. John M. Wiegand
Vice-President, Marketing
Acme Engineered Products, Inc.
1234 West Boulevard Street
City, State 56789

Dear Jack:

One thing I'll say about a vacation: It lets me do something I don't have time to do at work—some random thinking.

Jack, I think it's imperative that we adopt the marketing concept if Acme is to better its competitive position. Unless we do, we'll be hard put even to retain our present position.

This is elementary, I realize. But I say it because throughout the company much lip service is given to the marketing concept, yet we remain very much product oriented.

As you know, there's nothing esoteric about the marketing concept. It is simply determining exactly what our prospects want, then producing those products and selling them at a profit—preferably a fat one.

However, to realize the full potential for profit inherent in the marketing concept, it is essential that we have a written marketing plan.

Without one, we drift.

Writing a marketing plan isn't the easiest thing in the world, nor is it a terrible task:

But I think it must be done. If you agree, I suggest that you, J. Winston Johnson, and I get our heads together behind a closed door with the phone cut off.

We should discuss Acme's past performance; our position in our various markets; our major strengths; how these strengths were built up; where our weaknesses are; suggestions for overcoming them; major market trends; a rundown on what competition is now doing—and what they are likely to do; dollar volume and profitability requested by management.

Part of the preparatory work on the marketing plan is already completed. Our agency, J. Winston Johnson, has completed an internal audit, as you know.

Your knowledge of products and markets, supplemented with that of our market managers, will provide a relatively objective analysis of our desires —as the manufacturer—as well as those of our prospects.

Once these topics have been discussed and there is complete unanimity of thought, we can put words on paper.

Jack, I think our marketing plan should emphasize four major points:

1. It should describe our present position.

2. It should clearly state management's viewpoint and decisions made on products, new products, research and development, changes in the field

force, changes in or additions to our present channels of distribution, and subjects for and audiences for our external communications.

3. It should establish long-range objectives, preferably five years ahead.

4. It should establish short-term goals and assign specific responsibilities to individuals—with target dates.

Some companies fall short of established goals and objectives, even when there is a written marketing plan—probably due to failure to adhere to point 4 above.

This is understandable and probably inescapable. No management expects marketing people to have extrasensory perception, nor does it expect perfection in prognosticative powers. All managements do, however, expect a good return on the investment and on the sales dollar. They usually get it when the marketing plan is right.

Jack, I know that with the guidance and direction of a good, sound, written marketing plan I can make our advertising and sales promotion do a much more effective job than ever before.

Call me when we can discuss this, will you please?

Cordially,
/s/
Advertising Manager

Less Than 10 Percent Plan Properly

Most companies do not have a written marketing plan. They talk at great length about the total marketing concept and what it can do for them, but they haven't planned for it. A survey made by Cresap, McCormick and Paget, well-known management consultants, disclosed that most companies not only don't have advertising objectives, but they don't have marketing objectives. Supplementary studies made by Marsteller Inc., the country's largest industrial advertising agency, indicate that less than 10 percent of American industry follows formal, written marketing programs geared to marketing objectives.

If no marketing plan exists, the advertising manager is in a unique position to make a significant, recognizable contribution above his assigned responsibilities. It is one that could make a massive contribution to company growth over the years. He is probably the one professional in the company who can poke and prod and guide those in various areas of activity to an agreement. Then he can do something—*write* the plan.

The letter above covers what should be in the plan, and it can serve as a rough outline. Naturally, current and projected sales, profit margins, cost of sales, analyses of individual markets, total sales, and other items peculiar to each company will also be included. Of vital importance is having *complete* agreement of all parties on all points in the plan. To achieve this, disputed passages must be rewritten and restated until they are acceptable, without reservation, by all. Point 3 above should be particularly well thought out so that it states, clearly and concisely, management's objectives for company growth, expansion, and acquisitions. Point 4 above, which makes specific assignments to specific people with target dates, is the action area which management must watch closely. It is here that impending failure to achieve as planned will first be evident.

For the ad manager the written marketing plan is like a road map to the tourist. It helps him find the right route and, once found, helps him stay on it. Furthermore, having the plan to refer to makes it much easier to develop an integrated promotional program that will speed achieving the set objectives. Without a written plan the ad manager is in the untenable position of working blind, of relying on conversations for his direction. Those can easily be misinterpreted and even more easily forgotten.

The Other Side of the Fence

Sometimes the industrial advertising manager comes down with an affliction which closely resembles envy, except that this is a word with a poor image. Still, he looks wistfully at his cousin, ad manager of a company which markets nice simple little products to nice simple little consumers. He reasons with much justification that the consumer ad man has an easier job. For one thing, his products are nontechnical. And his market is so vast it staggers the imagination; after all, everybody's a consumer, so everybody's a prospect. He doesn't have to try to determine who can use his product—and how—then determine the best way to communicate with him. The consumer ad man's story almost tells itself it seems, because all he has to do is come up with an advertising campaign with flair and style, one loaded with sure-fire appeals which trigger the right emotions, as carefully determined beforehand by the researchers and psychologists. Then dazzle 'em with four-color spreads in the mass magazines, complete with expensive art and clever, clever copy. Add appealing point-of-purchase displays, dealer tie-ins, cooperative campaigns and then, for a *coup de grace* if the budget permits (it usually does), turn to TV to beam the message to those who don't, won't, or can't read magazines. It's all very simple.

Unfortunately, the industrial advertising manager doesn't advertise nice simple little products to a mass of nice simple little consumers. His market is highly selective and his products are strictly another breed of cat, falling as they do into four main categories. These are:

1. Items or materials used, or consumed upon the premises of the manufacturer, although not consumed in the manufacturing process itself.

   Examples: sweeping compound, light bulbs, replacement V-belts, saw blades, grinding wheels, air conditioners, floor polishers.

2. Those products consumed in the manufacturing process.

   Examples: industrial adhesives, nails, flux, lacquer thinner, solder, screws, rivets, polishing compound, bolts, escutcheons.

3. Those items incorporated into the end product, either individually, or as a completed subassembly.

   Examples: upholstery fabric, transmissions, cabinet hinges and knobs, semiconductors, piston rings, tires, transistors, bricks, electric motors, window frames, valves, meters, thermocouples, batteries, compressors, radios.

4. Capital equipment used to produce the end product or service.

   Examples: machine tools, conveyors, hoists, kilns, cranes, motor trucks, draglines, heat-treating furnaces, bulldozers, dust collectors, lift trucks, computers, office copying machines, typewriters, trenching machines, diesel-electric locomotives.

Sophisticated Customers

Just as the industrial ad man's product is entirely different from those dangled enticingly before the eager consumer, so is his company different. It depends upon different distribution channels, and upon decisions of a buyer who is a unique species.

To plan an effective promotional program it is necessary to understand how the industrial buyer thinks and how his buying decisions are made. You can start with the premise that he does not buy for his own use. He neither eats, wears, sits on, nor rides in the products he purchases, and he buys with money that is not his. He makes his buying decisions coldly and dispassionately and logically, aware that they influence both his future and that of his company. Impulse purchases are foreign to his nature and, theoretically, at least, he remains emotionally detached from his decisions.

For a number of years now the magic terminology among purchasing agents—and this has, through osmosis, spread outward and upward through countless companies—is "value analysis." There's nothing esoteric about the term or the concept, for it is nothing more than an objective appraisal of a product's merit based on a meticulous analysis of its favorable and unfavorable features; entering in also is consideration of delivery schedule, reputation of the manufacturer, availability of parts and service, and price. When viewed in this light, it becomes obvious that these sophisticated buyers are really looking for *reasons why* they should buy a given item.

This, then, is the key to the thinking of the industrial buyer. He wants reasons why he should, or should not, buy from one source as opposed to another, or why he should buy one brand or make in preference to others. Industrial advertising must give him those reasons why.

From the industrial buyer's viewpoint, perhaps the single most compelling reason why he decides as he does is the "pocketbook reason." If an advertisement presents believable evidence to him that a product will help cut production cost of his product, reduce maintenance expense, or last longer, the ad has done its job even if he doesn't, panting with eagerness, grab the phone and call in an absolutely firm order. This happens so rarely it's akin to science fiction when it does. If the ad has left a favorable impression of the product or service, and of the advertiser, the company's salesmen will find a receptive climate when they call. They will find it easier to close a sale because they can skip several preliminary steps in the creation of a sale because advertising has partially presold the buyer.

Recognize that the purchasing agent cannot be ignored and that the wise policy is to touch all bases. The PA, however, is generally *not* the *key* buying influence. As a rule purchasing is told what to buy, or is presented with three acceptable products and asked to get prices, delivery dates, check warranties, ascertain what after-sale service policy is, and similar information so as to be able to make a reasoned buying recommendation.

Ford and Maytag Policies

Actually, the term "buyer" is a misnomer when a purchase is in the offing that involves a large expenditure. The plural of the word is much more accurate, for one individual almost never makes the decision to buy when the dollar amount is high. Such purchases are a team effort, with the final decision contingent upon recommendations by technical-level personnel to inhabitants of walnut-paneled offices.

Ford Motor Company's transmission plant at Livonia, Michigan, is a good example of multiple buying influences when capital equipment is acquired. This establishment buys new gear-cutting equipment quite frequently. Three buying offices are regularly contacted by salesmen of this equipment, but six other buying influences are involved in most of the purchases, including one or more individuals who decide whether *any* purchase will be made, along with several others who decide on the type of equipment Ford needs. Finally, all nine people are involved in varying degrees when the make of equipment is decided. Only *one-third* of the buying influences were contacted by salesmen in this instance, although this is a higher percentage than usual in a capital-equipment acquisition. Bear in mind that salesmen usually call on those on the technical level, and that *they are not acquainted with and do not have an entree to buying influences in the upper echelons of management.* But advertising does.

Another example of multiple buying influences in industry is the Maytag Company, Newton, Iowa, appliance manufacturer. This firm held weekly meetings for each major manufacturing department in two plants. Topics for the discussions included budget adherence, cost and quality problems, manpower requirements, and production schedules. Solutions to problems often included proposals for process and methods changes—and equipment procurement. These meetings were chaired by the department head, and his "staff" included, among others, the vice-president of manufacturing, the works manager, his plant manager, an industrial-engineering representative, a production engineer, and any specialist who might be called in because of a problem in his area of specialization. Any of these men, of course, might introduce an idea, or propose a solution to the problem under discussion. A purchase was involved as often as not. All of these individuals are buying influences once a course of action is decided upon. It is costly self-delusion for any company hoping to sell to Maytag—or a company its size—to adopt the complacent attitude that their salesmen call upon the decision makers in the company. They don't.

In large organizations, those with 1,000 or more employees, the involvement of less than six people in a major buying decision happens almost as frequently as salesmen walk on water. It is far more likely that the actual number would be from nine to 12, although this depends to a certain extent on just where the line is drawn as to what constitutes an influence. People who will say "yes" or "no" to the final proposal are admittedly few in number, but many times their number affect the nature of the proposal. And when we consider time as a factor—time which may delay a sale or purchase, increasing the risk of an alternate action being taken—the influences are almost countless.

Participants in buying decisions either have the technical background necessary to evaluate products under consideration, or call upon technical experts within the company. Occasionally, when extremely complex capital equipment that has not been used by the company in the past is considered, outside consultants assist in making the buying decision, particularly when an entire process is being changed. And how many salesmen call on *them?*

Urgency and Availability Factors

Time required to make a buying decision is, more often than not, affected by two factors. One of these certainly is the urgency of the need. The other is the availability of answers. These two factors have intereffects or relationships which are rather interesting. For example, a production-engineering and management group may recognize a need to expand capacity, or improve quality, or cut costs. The time required to make a buying decision will be affected by a management-imposed deadline. It can be delayed by the group's interest or willingness to probe for alternate solutions. At the same time, an answer may emerge to a need that has not been recognized. This happens when a better way to do something is made known, even though the present way has apparently been satisfactory.

Most plants did not need automation or computers until they appeared on the scene. At least, they were not actively looking for these solutions to existing problems. In a sense, invention becomes the mother of necessity.

A complete change in the production process invariably involves a lengthy purchase time, such as that which accompanied International Harvester's decision to install a numerically controlled machining line to produce cylinder blocks. This giant step forward in production machining marked a major development in the transition of numerical control from the toolroom, model shop, pilot plant, and defense-industry job to competitive commercial manufacturing.

Installed at IHC's construction equipment division plant outside Chicago, the block machining line involves 14 tape-controlled units—including a tape-controlled transfer machine—out of a total of 43 machine tools. The new automated line gives International the versatility they require, as well as a significant cost reduction. Alternate to the automated line would have involved a total of 65 machines, many so specialized they would have been idle two-thirds of the time. Changeovers for different model runs would have taken a week, compared to 16 hours; floor-space requirements would have doubled, and storage of jigs and fixtures would have created serious problems in an already overloaded plant. These considerations and many more were involved in the buying decision.

According to the works manager, the decision to go the tape-controlled route, that is, to automate, was the result of planning that began *five years* before the purchase was made, when International Harvester engineers were developing a new family of engines. As a guide to setting a course, IHC production-engineering department personnel set up five objectives:

1. No cost penalties must be incurred.
2. Maximum flexibility must be developed.
3. Minimum jigs and fixtures to be required.
4. Minimum setup or changeover time.
5. Minimize obsolescence caused by model changes.

Some free thinking was generated by these objectives, much of it gravitating toward numerically controlled machines which were considered exotic at the time. But the division accumulated experience and data, pursued various ideas, weighed and evaluated, and ultimately made the decision to buy.

The number of buying influences is almost impossible to calculate, although it certainly runs into the hundreds. How could purveyors of this sophisticated new hardware installed at IHC hope to have their salesmen call on all of these buying influences—or even a significant percentage of them—over such a long time span, and to keep in regular contact? It is an impossibility. Continuity of contact in such a situation can be maintained in only one way— through a well-planned, sustained advertising program.

Ordinarily the longer time periods are the result of a radical process change, as at Harvester. However, many companies such as National Cash Register have a policy that is intended to forestall perpetuation of a multiple-unit process where units are replaced one at a time. For example, a battery of six automatic screw machines may have been built up over a period of years, and the natural tendency is to begin replacing them at the rate of their deterioration or obsolescence. Such buying decisions are relatively simple and can easily be made in days or, at most, a few weeks. Where this situation exists, National Cash Register insists that

HARVEY RESEARCH ORGANIZATION, INC.

ORIGINATION OF THE IDEA FOR PURCHASE		JUSTIFYING THE POSSIBLE PURCH.
STAGE 1 INITIAL PROJECT OR MOTIVATION	STAGE 2 BASIC OBJECTIVE	STAGE 3 ANALYZING THE PROBLEM
[Check one]	NOTE: Check one, or number in order of importance	NOTE: Check activities in which you participated
☐ Continuing Cost Reduction or Profit Improvement Effort	☐ CUT COSTS	☐ Process or Methods Comparisons
or		
☐ Model Change or New Product	☐ IMPROVE QUALITY	☐ Production Cost Analysis ☐ Product Design Review
or		
☐ Periodic Review of Equipment/ Tools or Materials	☐ ADD CAPACITY	☐ Parts or Process Quality Analysis ☐ Materials Evaluations
or		
☐ Plant or Process Modernization	☐ NEW PRODUCT LINE	☐ Plant or Dept. Capacity Analysis ☐ Make vs. Buy Review
or		
☐ New Plant	☐ Other_____	☐ Other_____ ☐ Plant Capacity Studies
☐ Other_____		☐ Other_____

The seven stages of a purchase.

each decision to replace "kind for kind" be prefaced by a thorough examination of available alternates to the total process. NCR realizes the wisdom of finding out what is available that will possibly do a better job than the battery of six machines it now owns. Technology changes, and the company which stays tied to the past and its tried-and-proved way of doing things the same old way lags instead of leads.

Salesmen could never reach all of the buying influences at NCR when a process is being evaluated, even if they knew when this evaluation was taking place. Advertising in the right business publication does, though, communicate with all levels.

Diagram of a Purchasing Program

The evolution of a decision to buy, and how that decision was made, is graphically shown in the purchase-process diagram nearby, which is part of an extensive research study made recently for *Production* magazine by Harvey Research Organization, Inc. The

PURCHASE PROCESS DIAGRAM – (WHITE SHEET A)

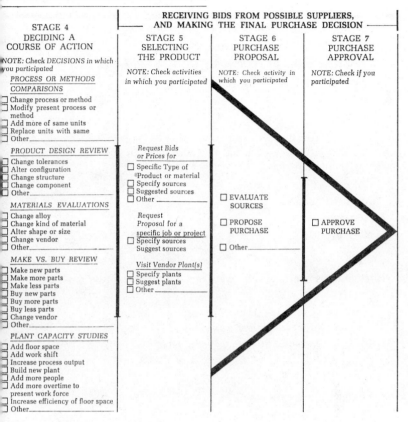

STAGE 4 DECIDING A COURSE OF ACTION	RECEIVING BIDS FROM POSSIBLE SUPPLIERS, AND MAKING THE FINAL PURCHASE DECISION		
	STAGE 5 SELECTING THE PRODUCT	STAGE 6 PURCHASE PROPOSAL	STAGE 7 PURCHASE APPROVAL
NOTE: Check DECISIONS in which you participated	NOTE: Check activities in which you participated	NOTE: Check activity in which you participated	NOTE: Check if you participated

STAGE 4
DECIDING A
COURSE OF ACTION

NOTE: Check DECISIONS in which you participated

PROCESS OR METHODS COMPARISONS
☐ Change process or method
☐ Modify present process or method
☐ Add more of same units
☐ Replace units with same
☐ Other____

PRODUCT DESIGN REVIEW
☐ Change tolerances
☐ Alter configuration
☐ Change structure
☐ Change component
☐ Other____

MATERIALS EVALUATIONS
☐ Change alloy
☐ Change kind of material
☐ Alter shape or size
☐ Change vendor
☐ Other____

MAKE VS. BUY REVIEW
☐ Make new parts
☐ Make more parts
☐ Make less parts
☐ Buy new parts
☐ Buy more parts
☐ Buy less parts
☐ Change vendor
☐ Other____

PLANT CAPACITY STUDIES
☐ Add floor space
☐ Add work shift
☐ Increase process output
☐ Build new plant
☐ Add more people
☐ Add more overtime to present work force
☐ Increase efficiency of floor space
☐ Other____

STAGE 5
SELECTING
THE PRODUCT

NOTE: Check activities in which you participated

Request Bids or Prices for
☐ Specific Type of Product or material
☐ Specify sources
☐ Suggested sources
☐ Other____

Request Proposal for a specific job or project
☐ Specify sources
   Suggest sources

Visit Vendor Plant(s)
☐ Specify plants
☐ Suggest plants
☐ Other____

STAGE 6
PURCHASE
PROPOSAL

NOTE: Check activity in which you participated

☐ EVALUATE SOURCES

☐ PROPOSE PURCHASE

☐ Other____

STAGE 7
PURCHASE
APPROVAL

NOTE: Check if you participated

☐ APPROVE PURCHASE

diagram dissects the entire process, starting at Stage 1 at the time of the initial project or motivation, through Stage 7 and, finally, the issuance of a purchase order.

Since this is the most current major study of this subject, as well as one of the best that has been made to date, we should examine the diagram in detail in order to gain a better understanding of the research results.

According to the diagram, the purchase is broken down into three main increments:

    I. Origination of the idea for purchase.

    II. Justifying the possible purchase.

    III. Receiving bids from possible suppliers, and making the final purchase decision.

In Increment I, Stage 1 consists of initial project or motivation. Only six considerations motivated all buying influences. They are:
Continuing cost reduction or profit improvement effort.
Model change or new product.
Periodic review of equipment, tools or materials.
Plant or process modernization.
New plant.
Other.

Stage 2 is the basic objective of the buying influences. In the research study, each was asked to check one, or number several in order of their importance. Objectives are:
Cut costs.
Improve quality.
Add capacity.
New product line.
Other.

Interviewees were asked in Stage 3, analyzing the problem, to check activities in which they participated. Activities are:
Production cost analysis.
Parts or process quality analysis.
Plant or department capacity analysis.
Other.
Process or methods comparisons.
Product design review.
Materials evaluations.
Make vs. buy review.
Plant capacity studies.
Other.

In deciding a course of action, Stage 4, those questioned were asked to check the *decisions* in which they participated. Listed decisions are:
Process or methods comparisons
Change process or method.
Modify present process or method.
Add more of same units.
Replace units with same.
Other.

Product design review
>Change tolerances.
>Alter configuration.
>Change structure.
>Change component.
>Other.

Materials evaluation
>Change alloy.
>Change kind of material.
>Alter size or shape.
>Change vendor.
>Other.

Make vs. buy review
>Make new parts.
>Make more parts.
>Make less parts.
>Buy new parts.
>Buy more parts.
>Buy less parts.
>Change vendor.
>Other.

Plant capacity studies
>Add floor space.
>Add work shift.
>Increase process output.
>Build new plant.
>Add more people.
>Add more overtime to present work force.
>Increase efficiency of floor space.
>Other.

For Stage 5, selecting the product, those interviewed were asked to check the activities in which they participated. Those were:

Request bids or prices for
>Specific type of product or material.
>Specify sources.
>Suggested sources.
>Other.

Request proposal for a specific job or project
>Specify sources.
>
>Suggest sources.

Visit vendor plant(s)
>Specify plants.
>
>Suggest plants.
>
>Other.

In Stage 6, purchase proposal, those participating in the study were asked to check activities in which they participated from this list:

>Evaluate sources.
>
>Propose purchase.
>
>Other.

The short and crucial stage, Stage 7, lists only one statement to be checked:

>Approve purchase.

Space was provided for entering the respondent's name, title, company, product manufactured, name of purchased item, and its description.

Field work on the project involved visiting 86 plants and interviewing 145 people. Plants were selected at random from *Production's* circulation galleys. This produced a pattern closely approximating market distribution, with 76 percent of the plants in Standard Industrial Classifications 35, 36, and 37. Of these plants, 58 percent employ between 100 and 1,000, 33 percent employ more than 1,000. Of the respondents, 62 percent were in production engineering and management functions, 17 percent in purchasing, 12 percent top management, and 8 percent design engineers.

Each respondent was carefully qualified as having participated within six months in one or more purchases of capital equipment, tools, or materials. Using the diagram and questionnaire, the first contact in each plant was interviewed with respect to a specific purchase. Additional contacts, supplied by the first man, were interviewed with respect to the same purchase to the extent they were available.

Based on the outline of the purchase-process diagram, here are salient points revealed by the study:

I. 96 percent of the respondents stated that the purchase-process diagram represents the evolution of a purchase in their plant.

II. With respect to the successive stages, which are outlined in the following section (III), in no instance did all of the respondents participate in any one stage. A summary of activity shows that 90 percent participated in Stages 1 and 2, 85 percent in 3 and 4, 75 percent in Stage 5, 71 percent in Stage 6, and 51 percent in Stage 7.

Obviously, far more people are active in developing the information and directions upon which proposals and approvals are based than in these final stages.

III. An analysis of the factors affecting, leading to, or determining purchases, based on the purchasing-procedures diagram, follows:

Stage 1. Initial motivation of purchases:

   a. Cost-reduction programs 52%

   b. Model change or new-product development 33%

   c. Plant or process modernization 25%

   d. Periodic equipment, tools, materials review 15%

Note: More than one motivation is involved in many purchases. For example, a cost-reduction program and a model change may be initiating forces behind the same purchase.

Stage 2. The objectives of initial motivations:

   a. Cost reduction 50%

   b. Quality improvement 50%

   c. Added capacity 40%

   d. New-product production 30%

Note: Profit begins to appear to be a more consistent reason for production improvement than new-product tooling or materials specifications.

It is also interesting to see that more than one objective is the target of initial motivations. Scrap, for example, may be the target of both cost reduction and quality improvement. It is also apparent that any of the objectives can be the target of any of the initial motivations. Plant modernization might have the targets of both added capacity and quality improvements.

Stage 3. Analyzing the problem:

   a. Production cost analysis 40%

   b. Part or process quality analysis 40%

   c. Plant or department capacity analysis 40%

The purpose of this analysis is to define or establish the area of attack. Degrees of attention to more detailed analysis are indicated as follows:

   a. Process or methods comparisons 40%

   b. Plant capacity studies 33%

   c. Make-or-buy studies 30%

   d. Product design reviews 25%

Stage 4. Deciding a course of action:

Decisions were made, as a result of problem analysis, to do the following things. Note that more than one decision was made in the evolution toward a single purchase of a piece of equipment, a tool, or material.

a. Change process or method 36%
b. Change product tolerances 27%
c. Change kind of material 20%
d. Make new parts instead of buying them 24%
e. Increase floor-space efficiency 35%

Note: Many other decisions were also made. Those shown above were the most common.

Stage 5. Selecting the product:

Nearly 50 percent of those involved requested bids for a specific type of product as determined by the decisions made in Stage 4. Other activities indicated less certainty about the kind of action that the decisions made in Stage 4 called for. These activities included requests for proposed sources and visits to vendor plants.

Stage 6. Purchase proposal:

a. Evaluating sources 54%
b. Proposing purchase 48%

Stage 7. Approving the purchase:

Of those involved in the evolution of a purchase, 51 percent were also involved in the approval of the equipment, tool, or material which was finally purchased. In several instances, more than one individual's approval was necessary.

IV. *Effect of marketing influences—salesmen, publication advertising, direct mail, trade shows:*

1. The time involved in the various stages of a purchase is pertinent to the marketer's decision on the use of marketing tools. From Stage 1 to Stage 4 involved anywhere from one day to two years. The most frequent intervals ranged between three months and one year. From Stage 4 to Stage 5 took from one day to six weeks, with less than three weeks involved in 40 percent of the cases. Stages 6 and 7 together required less than three weeks in more than one half of the cases. More than three months was required in only 9 percent of the cases.

2. The effect of sales representatives is felt most at Stages 4 and 5 among those buying influences that actually saw a representative. Of all the respondents involved in a purchase, 62 percent talked to a representative of the company from whom a purchase was made. Of this group, 75 percent saw the representative at Stages 4 and 5. In 72 percent of the contacts between a representative and a re-

spondent, the contact was made at the buyer's request. In 18 percent of the cases, the contact was initiated by the salesman.

3. The effect of advertising on buying influences is indicated by a question which asked which source of information is "most useful in keeping informed about equipment, tools and materials used in your industry."

Of the respondents, 49 percent say that industrial and trade publications are the best source of information; 26 percent say that salesmen are most useful, and 16 percent believe catalogs and literature are most useful. Direct mail and trade shows account for the balance.

Conclusions

While detailed conclusions and authoritative commentary depend on careful analysis of the purchasing-procedures study, it is apparent that industrial and trade publication advertising must play a stronger role in developing sales.

It is obvious that in the problem-solving and direction-setting stages of a purchase, salesmen have the least contact with buying influences. Advertising is important at these stages because:

1. Many of the influences do not see salesmen at all, yet they must have some kind of information in order to move from one stage to the next.

2. The greatest amount of time is spent by the buying influences in the early stages, when it would be inefficient and possibly ineffective for salesmen to be involved. Advertising is a relatively low-cost means of searching out buying influences, and of building and sustaining contact with them.

3. The time spent in the latter stages is relatively short. Because most salesmen are seen at the request of the influence, it appears that advertising is important in "bringing the customer into the store." It is also apparent, in view of the short time interval, that advertising may be important in reinforcing the salesman's effort at a time when he is contending with other salesmen. In some instances, it is conceivable that these latter stages may develop so rapidly that advertising may be the main contact in encouraging the customer to request a bid or to visit a vendor's plant.

Seldom does decision making follow a straight, well-marked path. A single decision does not determine if a purchase is to be made, much less *what* is to be bought. Widely accepted is the fact that at least *three* buying decisions are made—feasibility, technical, and administrative.

The feasibility decision is the easiest of the three to make, and it involves less time than the other two. It is made by technical personnel concerned primarily with the economics of the situation. The criterion by which they judge is how will it affect the corporate pocketbook. Management, to whom they report, wants to know if the company can anticipate reduced costs, higher productivity, improved quality, less rejects, use of lower-priced materials, less maintenance, or other economic benefits from the proposed purchase. If the answer to these considerations is a solid affirmative, and if it is backed up with facts, the second decision is then taken up.

The second, technical decision is usually made on a relatively low level of management. It involves choosing between two or more items of the same kind. For example, recently a large manufacturer of earth-moving equipment needed a new overhead 20-ton crane on the main production floor of the plant. Here the technical discussion on the merits of several makes of cranes involved production foremen, superintendents, the general foreman, and the maintenance superintendent responsible for keeping production equipment in good working condition. This group compared all of the pros and cons, feature by feature, of the various makes of cranes with which they were familiar, then recommended the three which they felt best suited their needs. The customary three-bid purchasing procedure followed.

The administrative decision is the last one to be made, and it is made by top management. It differs in that it also includes consideration of whether company funds could be better invested in, say, a new mechanized paint-spray-booth system, a new wing on the office building, additional inventory, or a fleet of trucks. Capital equipment dollars are limited. No company, regardless of size and prominence, ever has enough. It is estimated that outlay for capital equipment in 1967 is around $63.8 billion.

Who Are the Customers?

It is axiomatic that 80 percent of a company's business is secured from 20 percent of its prospects. Scan any company's "customer list" and its record of incoming orders and this quickly becomes apparent. These "cream" accounts provide most of the business booked because they are the firms which do a large volume and have great purchasing power. This is not to say, however, that any company sells to all of the prospects it would like to. Every sales manager has target accounts he just itches to penetrate, but has not been able to. On the whole, the 20 percent figure is a valid one because it does not include the tremendous number of small establishments whose low business volume makes it a marginal proposition to spend much time and money trying to close sales with them.

Questions arise very quickly when developing a promotional program. Just who are our customers? Where are they located? In what businesses are they? What do they buy from us? Who are the key buying influences we must reach? What is our share of the market? From the answers to these questions come data which will influence capital investment, research and development, engineering and production decisions, new product introduction, as well as marketing programs. All of these questions must be answered in order to develop a cohesive communications program. Fortunately, the answers are easy to come by, although they are found in a number of places.

The question, "Whom do we sell to?" is partially—but only partially—answered by the customer list. All companies have one, of course, usually complete with addresses. Mere firm names assigned to smokestacks mean little, however, although this does take care of the "who" and "where" questions for the time being.

"What do they buy from us?" is usually a tough one if the company produces a diversified line of products, or products for several major markets. As a rule, there is no pat answer because customer lists are quite like Topsy—they just grew. New names are added constantly, while few are culled out even if the customers are not active ones, or if they cease doing business. Not one company in a hundred assigns this responsibility to any one individual with instructions to keep the list clean and current. The result is a long list of firm names, usually several thousand, with basic information—model number, specifications, accessories, and other pertinent data noted beside each customer. But this is still raw data, for no *pattern* has emerged. A pattern—a simple, logical arrangement that is easy to analyze—is necessary so that the advertising manager can make use of this mass of statistics.

A question that elicits blank expressions and shoulder shrugging is, "What lines of business are our customers in?" The average company simply does not know, not at company headquarters, although the field salesman or district manager is familiar with the firms on which he calls in his territory. This is of little help, however, to the advertising manager, for if he queried all field men and waited until he received the volume of information he needed, he'd be ready to file for Social Security, despite sending urgent memos requesting this data at the tender age of 31.

How to Get the Job Done

To get the job done, rather than grow senile wishing it was, add four basic reference books to the advertising department's library, and use them.

Largest and perhaps the most useful of these is *Poor's Register of Corporations, Directors, and Executives.* This massive volume (more than 3,100 pages) contains approximately 74,000 names of executives and directors of manufacturing and mining companies, utilities, railroads, banks, savings and loan associations, engineering and insurance companies, financial and investment institutions, and law firms. The reference book includes more than 1,717 pages devoted to a corporation directory, in which are listed the official rosters of some 31,000 leading American and Canadian corporations. A separate geographical index is provided for convenience. The seven main sections of the book are:

Standard Industrial Classification Index
Standard Industrial Classification Codes
Corporation Directory
Directors and Executives Section
New Companies Section
New Individuals Section
Obituary Section

Personnel listed include all officers and directors; other important executive personnel such as sales, advertising, general, production and traffic managers, personnel directors, engineers, and purchasing agents. To indicate company size, the number of employees and approximate sales volume is given for each company. Accuracy is practically a fetish; more than 100,000 major changes are made in the work each year, while the total number of revisions exceed 460,000. Type proofs are sent to each firm listed to verify accuracy, in itself a huge job. The book may be rented or bought outright; purchase price is $135.

A company representative is located in each metropolitan center, or the book may be ordered directly from:

Standard & Poor's Corporation
345 Hudson Street
New York, New York 10014

Poor's Register is kept current throughout the year by quarterly supplements which are automatically mailed to every registered holder of the book.

Other prime sources of information are the reference books published by Dun & Bradstreet. D & B's books provide roughly the same wealth of information that *Poor's Register* does, although arrangement is somewhat different.

Dun & Bradstreet's Middle Market Directory is a huge work which lists nearly 20,000 business enterprises in the United States; all have an indicated worth in the $500,000 to $999,000 range. A companion work is D & B's *Million Dollar Directory,* which identifies corporations with more than $1,000,000 in annual sales. This is the most important group of buyers in the country; they account for the greatest proportion of goods and services consumed each year.

The *Middle Market Directory* does not include any foreign corporations, professional and consulting organizations, engineering services, credit agencies, or financial institutions. D & B arranges the directories in three sections:

Section 1—Businesses alphabetically.

Section 2—Businesses geographically.

Section 3—Businesses by product classification—four-digit SIC. Nearly 900 different codes give a fine breakdown by line of business. A single establishment may be listed under as many as six classifications.

Upon request to D & B, interim information between publishing dates is available on typical concerns which may not yet be listed.

To help the marketer pinpoint his marketing area, and to assist him in reaching it more quickly, selected data from all of the listings in the *Middle Market Directory,* the *Million Dollar Directory,* and the *Metalworking Directory,* are available in the following convenient forms:

> Magnetic tape.
> Punched tabulating cards.
> Pressure-sensitive labels.
> Cheshire labels.
> Direct addressing masters.
> 3x5 cards.
> Tabular listings.
> Printed tabulating cards.

Dun & Bradstreet also publish annually the *Metalworking Directory, State Sales Guide, Apparel Trades Book,* and an exhaustively researched book on a classification system which might possibly supplant SIC sometime in the future—*D-U-N-S Code Book.*

Data Universal Numbering System

According to Dun & Bradstreet, D-U-N-S, which stands for Data Universal Numbering System and also happily abbreviates to the firm's first name, is ideal for the company which uses or expects to use electronic data processing in its operation. In this system, a unique random number known as a D-U-N-S number is assigned to each of the 390,000 establishments in the four DMI market divisions, plus other establishments of significance in commerce, principally larger wholesalers and service organizations, for a total of more than 450,000. The D-U-N-S number is an eight-digit number of which the high order position is, at present, a zero. This provides for expansion when the numbering of other establishments is undertaken at a later date. The check digit—in this case the last digit—allows a computer or other automated data-processing equipment to check whether a given number is valid or contains an error, such as a transposition. It is called a "Mod 10, double-one-double-one check digit." It will detect all but the most exceptional errors.

Benefits to the advertising manager are that the system:

1. Provides an operational universal numbering system.

2. Keeps the system up-to-date through the nationwide reporting facilities of Dun & Bradstreet (maintenance is one of the biggest problems of "private" numbering systems).

3. Makes practical the imprinting of the identification number (D-U-N-S) on a company's documents, thus reducing clerical look-up time.

4. Permits intra or intercompany communication on specific accounts which may be of common interest through the use of a common identification number.

5. Permits interdepartmental consolidation and evaluation of accounts which may represent both customers and suppliers.

6. Offers companies the possibility of drawing upon additional data contained in Dun & Bradstreet's computerized files.

The Data Universal Numbering System, when combined with the marked "identifiers" of DMI, discussed above—tape, tab cards, labels, or whatever form in which information can be most easily handled—provides an information system that is unique in American business. Applications in sales, market research, advertising, and sales promotion are almost limitless because they help the ad man identify his prospects so that he can reach them quicker and at lower cost.

Dun & Bradstreet has offices in principal cities, or you may write directly to:

Dun & Bradstreet, Inc.
P.O. Box 1770
Church Street Station
New York, New York 10008

The fourth text that belongs in every industrial advertising department is *Standard Industrial Classification Manual.* Standard Industrial Classification—SIC, as it's called—is the hub around which all modern industrial marketing programs now revolve. The textbook was prepared by the Technical Committee on Industrial Classification, Office of Statistical Standards of the U.S. Government. It is available in a permanent binding from:

Superintendent of Documents
U.S. Government Printing Office
Washington, D.C. 20425

The price is $2.50, and your order should be accompanied by a bank draft, cashier's check, or money order to conform to government regulations. A paperbound supplement to the SIC Manual, may be ordered at the same time from the same government agency for 30 cents. Again, send the money in such a way that the government will not cast a jaundiced eye on your remittance.

The introduction to the SIC Manual says that SIC was developed "for use in classification of establishments by type of activity in which they are engaged; to facilitate the collection, tabulation, presentation, and analysis of data relating to establishments; and to promote uniformity and comparability in the presentation of statistical data collected by various agencies of the United States Government, state agencies, trade associations, and private research organizations.

"SIC classification covers the entire field of economic activities; agriculture, forestry, and fisheries; mining; construction; manufacturing; transportation, communication, electric, gas, and sanitary services; wholesale and retail trade; finance, insurance, and real estate; services, and government." It is fortunate the last activity is included, for it is fast becoming as large as all of the others combined.

Follows Logical Principles

The following general principles were borne in mind while the classification was developed:

1. The classification should conform to the existing structure of American industry.

2. The reporting units to be classified were establishments rather than legal entities or companies.

3. Each establishment is to be classified according to its major activity.

4. To be recognized as an industry, each group of establishments must have significance from the standpoint of persons employed, volume of business, and other important economic features, such as the number of establishments.

The manual describes an establishment as "an economic unit which produces goods or services—for example, a farm, a mine, a factory, a store. In most instances, the establishment is at a single physical location; and it is engaged in only one, or predominantly one, type of activity for which an industry code is applicable."

Number 3, above, and the manual's definition of an establishment should be noted well. Translating "governmentese" into plain English, it means that any given establishment may have a primary SIC, as well as one or more secondary SIC's. An example would be a large metalworking shop which is classified as, "Machine shops, jobbing, and repair—SIC 3591."

Within this metalworking shop might be a department which produces forgings, although this activity would constitute a small portion of the overall work volume and sales dollar of the establishment. In this case, then, the establishment would also be classified as a producer of "Forgings, iron and steel: light and heavy board drop and steam hammer, upset and press—not made in rolling mills —SIC 3391."

Furthermore, this establishment could also have a small metal-melting operation to produce special castings used in conjunction with some of the machined parts which are its prime product. Even though the foundry is small and might operate sporadically, the establishment would nonetheless acquire yet another secondary classification—SIC 3321, for "Foundries, gray iron and semisteel."

The SIC manual is easy to assimilate. Although a bit heavy-handed, the logic can't be faulted. Establishments engaged in essentially similar functions are arbitrarily lumped together into "Major Groups." An example is Major Group 37—Transportation Equipment. The manual says, "This Major Group includes establishments engaged in the manufacturing of equipment for transporting passengers and cargo by land, air, and water. Important products produced by establishments classified in this Major Group include motor vehicles, aircraft, ships, boats, railroad equipment, and miscellaneous equipment such as motorcycles, bicycles, and horse-drawn vehicles."

Because SIC's have four digits to permit precise classification, the next breakdown after the Major Group is the Group Number. Group Number of "Motor Vehicles and Motor Vehicle Equipment" is 371. Motor vehicles themselves are SIC number 3711. Passenger car bodies are SIC 3712, truck and bus bodies, SIC 3713. Also within Major Group 37 you'll find "Aircraft and Parts," which is Group Number 372. Within this subclassification is found aircraft, SIC 3721, aircraft engines and engine parts, SIC 3722, and so on. "Ship and Boat Building and Repairing" is Group Number 373, with ship building and repairing wearing SIC 3731, boat building and repairing 3732. Group Number 374 covers the railroad industry; locomotives and parts have SIC 3741, railroad and street cars 3742.

When you first consider it, having almost 1,000 SIC's might seem to carry things too far. But in this age of computerized marketing, when memory banks retain billions of digits on a tiny roll of tape and make detailed printouts in minutes, marketing data must be reduced to numbers—the Esperanto of computers.

"SIC-ing" Your Customer List

SIC is a key tool of the industrial advertising manager. He should become intimately familiar with the system, and he can do so easily. A couple of hours with the manual will enable him to take the next important step toward identifying his market—"SIC-ing" his customer list.

This can be done internally, right in the advertising department, if sufficient clerical time is available. SIC-ing the customer list is merely a look-up operation using *Poor's Register* or one of the Dun & Bradstreet books as source material. However, if the time element is important, and it usually is, Dun & Bradstreet will do the entire job for approximately $125 per 1,000 establishments. This includes look-up and key-punching the information into IBM cards. Cost will be increased only slightly to have a separate deck of cards punched showing secondary SIC's of your customers, and this information can be identified by a separate digit preceding the primary SIC, or it can be coded elsewhere on the card. Secondary

SIC can be vitally important information when you're trying to pinpoint a market.

When the deck of cards is returned from D & B it can then be turned over to a convenient data-processing service firm to have a printout made—assuming idle computer time is not available internally. Cards should be sorted by county and state before the final run, as well as by city if you wish; requirements vary with distribution channels and organization of the field sales force.

You will receive the printout from the tab house in six or seven working days as a rule, in the form of a continuous, perforated business form, all neatly separated and bound into a stiff paper binder, complete with two carbon copies. More carbons may be ordered when the printout is made, of course, at nominal extra cost. Cost of having a printout in triplicate of approximately 5,000 firms runs around $125—$200 in most major cities; this is in addition to a standard setup charge of $50 to cover the cost of programming the machine to handle each specific job. Sorting charge, if necessary to have done differently than D & B provides, is relatively low, usually between $35 and $75 for a run of this size.

Once the printout is on hand, you probably have for the first time an orderly analysis of whom your company sells to, with like SIC's grouped for easy tallying on an adding machine. This is far more than a group of numbers with firm names following them, however, because this printout represents the manufacturing plants that have a use for your product. They have a use for it because it solves a problem for them—one, perhaps, that your product alone can do.

This invaluable information can be put to many uses. It can be broken down by sales district or territory because it's already separated by county and state; the information can be forwarded to the district offices by making copies on the office copying machine. It can be used for direct mail. The sales department will want a copy to analyze to determine if the sales force is devoting its time to hunting ducks where the ducks actually are—instead of making useless, or nearly useless calls upon marginal prospects. Marketing will undoubtedly want to evaluate its objectives in relationship to this data, and will probably have sales review it for comment; quite possibly sales will want some district or regional managers to go over the statistics, for memories of past sales tend to be short when new ones are constantly pending. And, finally, the advertising manager will find the SIC'ed customer list a tremendous help in planning his program, particularly when it comes to evaluating media and determining the creative approach he will take.

Since manufacturers with the same SIC make the same product, it naturally follows that those with SIC's found on your customer list printout are your best possible prospects. They obviously encounter the same problems that your present customers do, and *they* have found that your product solves their problem, or they wouldn't be your customer. So, what is needed is a complete list of all establishments with the SIC's which represent the bulk of your profitable business. (Marketing and sales management can assign weights or priorities to miscellaneous categories of establishments, although it can be assumed that the cat-and-dog accounts will be of relatively little importance.)

The Lindberg Hevi-Duty Plan

Compiling a list, possibly of 10,000 companies or more, is a time-consuming task. It should not be attempted manually due to the amount of time involved, and also because of the probability of a high percentage of errors creeping in. Inhuman computers, however, are not error prone and should be relied upon. Dun & Bradstreet can supply any desired breakdown by SIC of any type of establishments you're interested in, all with machine precision. One list used by Lindberg Hevi-Duty, Division of Sola Basic Industries, for its metal-treating market consists of approximately 8,700 metalworking firms which do on-premises heat treating. The company bought this information from D & B in a three-card deck. That is, each establishment is represented in the master deck by three IBM cards. Information about each of these 8,700 firms includes:

> Name of company
> Street address
> City
> State
> Zip Code
> Primary SIC classification
> Secondary SIC classification(s)
> Number of employees
> Annual sales volume
> Names of:
>> President
>> Executive Vice-President
>> Vice-President, Manufacturing
>> Director of Purchasing

This data, also sorted by county and state, was then printed out and the customer list checked against it. A remarkably high percentage of the company's customers were included in the master three-card deck; those who were not were then added. Lindberg Hevi-Duty then knew exactly who their customers were, and who their prospects were—including the name of the key buying influence, the director of manufacturing—for their extensive line of industrial ovens and heat-treating furnaces. The list was supplemented, of course, by names received in response to advertisements, direct mail, publicity, and from field salesmen before being used as the new master list for direct mail.

Baker Division of Otis Elevator Company, manufacturer of Baker fork-lift materials-handling equipment, defined its present market, projected the market potential and identified key buying influences through market research based on SIC. To do so, officials first determined where the company's sales were coming from—according to the SIC of their incoming orders and past sales. Next, the number of employees in customer companies, financial strength and similar information were analyzed to give Baker people a profile of their customers. They then projected their markets by SIC, assuming that all firms with similar SIC's as those of customers on the books were likely suspects to become new customers. The projection was made with the help of another reference volume, also available from the Government Printing Office, *County Business Patterns U.S. Summary;* this book gives the exact counts of each four-digit SIC in the United States.

Using this book, Baker Division's ad manager determined that his company could logically expect about 260,000 companies to be their total market, but they refined this massive number down to around 25,000 firms whose SIC's exactly matched their customers' in every respect, including, to be positive, cross-checking against the customer profile.

Relying on advertising to reach all 260,000 prospects, including the 25,000 target accounts, Baker qualified this smaller group by direct mail, asking each firm to tell them who the buying influences are in their companies for materials-handling equipment. Some 60 percent of the recipients of the mailing responded, giving Baker names of decision makers. These industrial buyers were reached by advertising—and by well-conceived, well-executed direct mail. Dealer salesmen were sold on the program and were given the names of the recipients of Baker's direct mailings. The program was evaluated a year later—and Baker's sales were up 26 percent in the face of an industry decline, proving conclusively that prospect identification by SIC pays! It is actually the only easy, practical way to delineate a market that can run into hundreds of thousands of companies.

The Use of Trade Directories

Trade and professional directories can also provide vital market information, particularly when a company's prospects are in a market that is relatively small and stable.

This method was used by Szabo Food Service, Lyons, Illinois. Szabo sells an industrial "product"—a management service—to five major markets. One, colleges and universities, was growing at a fantastic rate due to an exploding population and a war-baby boom. This national corporation, formed shortly after World War II, achieved an annual sales volume of more than $30 million without the support of advertising or other promotion, but in an increasingly competitive market inevitably found itself on a sales plateau. The company decided to advertise to this one market, on a trial basis, to "see if advertising really works."

To get immediate results and quality sales leads, a three-pronged approach was taken—research, advertising, and merchandising.

First step was to define the market, and identify Szabo's prime prospects. To do this, all of the colleges and universities in the country with 1,000 or more on-campus students (minimum profitable size for Szabo to handle) were identified, using directories such as *College and Private School Directory of U.S. and Canada; College Blue Book; College Guide; Accredited Higher Institutions;* and *American Universities and Colleges.*

Marketing management at Szabo had determined that the business manager of each college and university was the one most important buying influence, although there were many others, including various faculty members, deans, presidents, members of boards of regents, and trustees. The individuals who were going to make the vital decision had to be identified by name and title. To accomplish this, a questionnaire was mailed to each institution's business manager. It was frank and straightforward, telling him that Szabo wanted the names of decision makers interested in student feeding so that they could be kept informed about developments in this field. A return of better than 61 percent from this qualification mailing gave Szabo the names of those pivotal individuals who would participate in making a decision of what food-service-management firm would be retained, if any, or if a change were to take place. The questionnaire is shown on the following page.

Please correct and complete the information below and return to:

> Mr. R. A. Longworth
> President
> SZABO FOOD SERVICE, INC.
> 4242 South First Avenue
> Lyons, Illinois   60534

From _____

_____

	NAME	TITLE

President _____   _____

Deans _____   _____
_____   _____
_____   _____
_____   _____

Executives
Responsible For:

Business Management
_____   _____
_____   _____
_____   _____
_____   _____

Food Service
Policy
_____   _____
_____   _____
_____   _____
_____   _____
_____   _____

From Mr. _____ Title_____

Thank you for your assistance. A stamped, addressed envelope is attached for the return of this form.

This is the questionnaire used by Szabo Food Service to obtain the names and titles of individuals responsible for making food-service decisions.

Next, four ads were written and produced, each scheduled to run twice in the best magazine in the educational field. A typical ad is reproduced here.

The offer of an eight-page illustrated booklet containing a wealth of information essential to an educator on the topic of student nutrition triggered an excellent response. All of the ads pulled inquiries,

116

good ones, which were promptly followed up by the field sales force.

Key to this program, however, was merchandising the ads to the qualified prospects. When an ad ran, a letter from Szabo's president was written, reproduced on a Szabo letterhead by the multilith process, "signed" in blue ink from a signature cut, and then individually addressed to the prospect with a matching fill-in. A reprint of the advertisement was enclosed, and again the booklet was offered. A postage-paid reply card was enclosed, also mentioning the booklet, and containing a small reproduction of the illustration in the ad to remind the prospect of it. A typical letter and reply card are shown.

Response to this low-cost program (under $20,000) was outstanding. Szabo had almost 200 requests for their booklet out of a qualified list of only 800—a return of 25 percent. And many colleges checked a box on the reply card to request a no-charge, detailed survey of their requirements in student feeding, enabling Szabo to submit many more formal proposals than in any similar period in the company's history.

Szabo's sales force was understandably enthused, and management was firmly convinced that advertising *does* work because several colleges signed contracts with the management service firm as the result of this program. Each sale the company makes is substantial; when a college of 15,000 students is acquired, that adds up to 300,000 meals a week on a 20-meal-a-week basis, common in this field.

Note that success of this entire promotional program hinged on one factor—correctly identifying the market and the individual buying influences within it who made the decision of what brand to buy, in this case, what firm to retain. Here, trade directories provided the target establishments, personal knowledge the job function of the one key influence, and a mail questionnaire the names of the secondary influences. Used correctly, they resulted in new sales.

The Iron Age Checklist

Iron Age magazine has an excellent checklist of what to look for in mail questionnaires. It follows:

CHECKLIST FOR INDUSTRIAL MAIL SURVEYS

I. Has the universe (market) for the project been clearly defined in terms of:
   a. Title or function of respondents?
   b. Plants by:
      1. Industry?
      2. Size?
      3. Geographic locations?

II. Will the sample, assuming returns are representative, yield sufficiently large returns to allow classification of data according to the universe (market) description?

III. Has the covering letter been written so as to encourage the respondent to fill out and return the questionnaire?

a. Is it brief and to the point?

b. Is it personal in tone?

c. Does it stress the importance of the survey?

d. Are any benefits to the respondent clearly described?

e. Does it reassure the respondent of the confidential treatment of his reply if such a step is warranted?

IV. Have the questions been properly conceived in order to provide accurate and unbiased answers?

a. Will all questions be clearly understood by all respondents?

b. Are no undue demands made on the memory or knowledge of the respondent?

c. Are the questions few enough in number to avoid aggravation or fatigue on the part of the respondent?

d. Are open-end questions kept to a minimum?

e. Have leading or biasing elements in the questions been eliminated?

V. Has the physical format of the questionnaire been well planned?

a. Do the letter and questions present an uncrowded appearance?

b. Does the questionnaire contain as few pages as possible? (Typeface can be varied to include more data on limited space and provide a change of pace.)

c. Does the address fill-in match the body of the letter?

d. Does the signature appear realistic?

e. Is the stationery of good quality?

VI. Has proper consideration been given to the reply envelope?

a. Where highest response is needed, stamped envelopes are worthwhile (airmail for nonlocal respondents).

VII. Does the nature of the survey indicate a blind letterhead (confidential) or the letterhead of the company conducting the survey?

VIII. Has a premium been considered to increase response?

a. Is the premium of interest to the type of respondent being questioned?

(A summary of the replies is often useful.)

IX. Has provision been made for a possible second mailing to nonrespondents?

a. Are questionnaires keyed so that they can be matched with the original sample?

X. Has the questionnaire been pretested in order to gain some assurance of its success?

a. A limited mailing often uncovers the need for some rephrasing of questions and provides an indication of eventual percentage response.

    b. One or two personal calls with the proposed questionnaire may be helpful?

XI. Are the returns representative of the sample and universe?

    a. Have they been compared with the original universe characteristics?

    b. If utmost accuracy is desired, has a check of nonrespondents been made with reference to key points?

XII. *IF YOU RECEIVED THE QUESTIONNAIRE, WOULD YOU FILL IT OUT AND RETURN IT?*

If questionnaires are well written—and you should judge that by whether or not they are almost conversational in tone, not stilted, not forbiddingly technical, not depressingly dull—they will do an effective job that can otherwise be done only at great cost by personal interview. Throughout this volume other examples are given; note that they adhere strongly to this checklist, that they are as light in tone as possible considering the subject, and that they *communicate* the way most of us think.

The covering letter should also be as good a piece of copy as it's possible to produce. Hone it and whet it—refine it and rewrite it—until the letter reads as if a friend were talking to you across your desk. That's the kind of letter that pulls response in direct mail and it's the only kind to use. Few people write like that; if you can't, you are in good company—with 99 44/100 percent of all industrial advertising managers. If such is the case, face it and go to a specialist in your agency, or to a direct-mail house or sales-promotion studio and pay somebody to write it for you. The cost is less than $100, as a rule, and if the letter makes the difference between a 10 percent return on your questionnaire and a 60 percent return on a mailing to 1,000 names, the cost is inconsequential.

Get the "Inside" on Your Market

Other sources of market information are open to you. For example, all first-class business publications are prime sources for the basic information the advertising manager must have to plan his program. Here's what one such magazine offers to help the advertiser define his market.

Iron Age, published by Chilton, is a leading business book which serves the vast metalworking industry. *Iron Age* has done extensive market research for many years, and has compiled a wealth of meticulously detailed market information. If a company sells only to one specific market such as metalworking, the advertising manager can cut his cost and save considerable time in pinpointing his market by using data the publication will provide. He need have no doubt as to its being authoritative. The really good trade publication knows its market better than any company's entire marketing organization. After all, the publication lives by its market knowledge.

A census of every metalworking plant in the country has been made repeatedly by *Iron Age*. Since the magazine's census must reflect all of the changes that occur, it maintains a comprehensive and continuing roster of all metalworking plants, old and new. Plants are classified by SIC, of course.

All metalworking establishments, in *Iron Age's* breakdown, are in eight two-digit groupings, which are in turn broken down further into 214 four-digit groupings. Most sources provide only four-digit SIC groupings for advertising and marketing activities. The *Iron Age* census, with its six-digit classification, provides the most definitive breakdown available in its industry for market analysis and planning of sales and advertising. The six-digit classification was developed by *Iron Age*.

Information was obtained by mail questionnaires, telephone interviews, and every available authoritative source, including state-development commissions and private plant-finding organizations. Pertinent facts were recorded on tabulating cards, electronically processed and summarized in statistical form. This was a massive job.

The continuing plant census is an essential tool employed by *Iron Age* in its own circulation and editorial planning. In common with other business publications in which a large investment has been made by the publisher, *Iron Age* realized that sound market research and prospect identification is a prerequisite for effective selling and advertising, so makes this information available to companies in metalworking and to those selling to this industry.

The magazine's *Metalworking Data Bank Marketguide* provides a statistical summary of the *Iron Age* census. It details the size and scope of the metalworking market; summarizes the two-digit, four-digit and six-digit census data; gives a state-by-state recap; and includes a state-by-state count of significant metal service centers. The information can be pulled from the *Metalworking Data Bank* by two-, four- and six-digit SIC, with further selections refined by employment size range (e.g., 20 to 99, 100 to 499, over 500); or by State, County or Zip Code selection. This makes it easy to hunt ducks where the ducks are. No wasted time chasing smokestacks.

The *Marketguide* gives specific examples of how to establish sales potentials, how to plan sales territories and prospect for sales.

The book's *Metalworking Data Bank* locates 45,279 plants with 20 or more employees. It identifies corporate headquarters, R&D locations and 1,717 metal service centers.

From time to time, *Iron Age* will take a reading, either statistically or by actual count, of major production operations performed in these plants. They cover such basic operations as:

Abrasive belt grinding	Nonferrous foundry
Adhesive joining	Numerically controlled machining
Anodizing	Painting, spray coating
Automatic bar machining	Phosphatizing
Boring	Pickling
Brazing (induction or furnace)	Planing
Chemical milling	Plastic molding
Die casting	Plate or structural
Drilling	Polishing or buffing
Electrical-discharge machining	Press brake
Electrochemical machining	Riveting
Electroplating	Roll forming
Extruding	Sand or grit blasting
Forge shop	Screw fastening
Galvanizing or tinning	Shaping
Gray-iron foundry	Shearing
Grinding	Stamping
Heat treating (in furnaces)	Steel foundry
Heat treating (induction)	Threading
Induction furnace melting	Tool and die shop
Malleable-iron foundry	Turning
Metal washing and degreasing	Welding on product (arc or gas)
Milling (nonchemical)	Welding (resistance, flash, spot)
Nondestructive testing	

The *Iron Age Master List of U.S. Metalworking Plants* is a two-volume listing that provides current information on the 45,279 plants covered in the census.

Volume I lists all plants alphabetically, by state. Each plant is defined by company name, division name (if applicable), full physical address with Zip Code, county code, six-digit primary and secondary SIC codes, number of employees, and activity codes designating corporate headquarters, divisional headquarters, manufacturing, R&D, and engineering.

Volume II lists these establishments by primary six-digit SIC, alphabetically by states. Provided in this numerical sequence by SIC, Volume II offers an easy way to pinpoint prime prospects. It is quick, accurate and remarkably simple to use.

To ensure accuracy, updated information is issued annually. This is a distinct improvement over the old twice in three years.

All of this information in the *Iron Age Metalworking Data Bank* is stored in a computer. It is available in a variety of forms: microfiche film; magnetic computer tape; master lists (two-volume set, or individual volumes); IBM punch cards; printouts on 3x5 cards, mailing labels or continuous labels. Partial extracts are also available

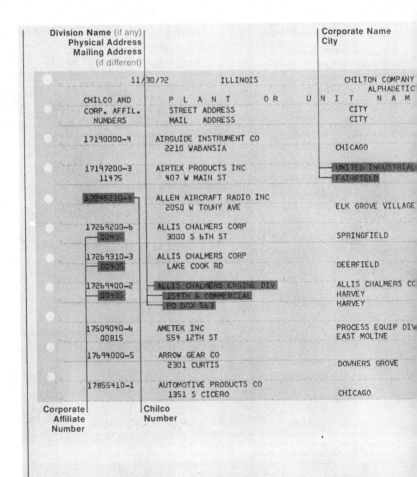

at a base cost of $200 for selection and $80 per thousand for punch cards or $50 per thousand for any of the printout forms.

On these pages is a picture of the total information in the *Iron Age Metalworking Data Bank,* in sample form. It suggests the kind of extracts you can make.

Laying the groundwork is simplicity itself with such precise, current information available in highly usable forms to suit individual needs. It is incredibly valuable when you determine market

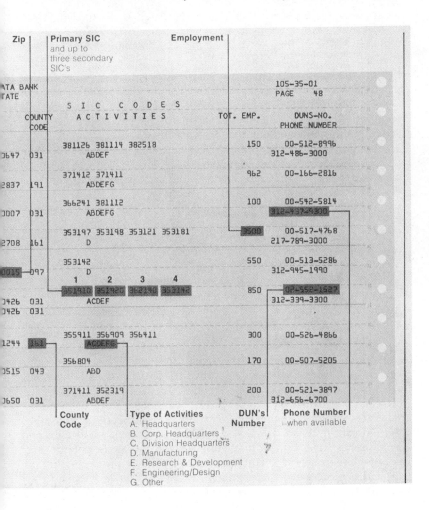

potentials, plan sales territories, locate new prospects and markets, and plan and direct advertising and merchandising programs.

In common with most business publications, *Iron Age* will also handle direct-mail programs, using the *Metalworking Marketguide,* extracting almost any segment or geographical entity desired. The IBM cards may be sorted on a straight national-plant-selection basis, by SIC, or by state, area, or activities code criteria. Charges for addressing, either by typewriter, or by affixing a four-line label, are reasonably structured and probably competitive with local letter shops. Too, the magazine will multigraph letters (on your letterhead, if supplied), insert enclosures, affix postage, sort by Zip Code, tie and deliver the mailing to the Philadelphia post office.

Many publishing companies who have in-house research departments will carry out, on a fee basis, studies to determine market potential for new products. Additionally, they customarily conduct —some of them almost continuously—research to determine just what individuals in companies in the industries they serve are actual buying influences. For a fee, usually relatively nominal, this information is available to the advertising manager, permitting him to be highly selective and go after his decision makers with a rifle approach rather than scattering material with costly abandon.

Pinpointing Influential Prospects

As a rule of thumb, it's safe to assume that the vast majority of calls made by industrial salesmen are made upon the wrong people. This is not to infer that the average salesman, who's a pretty hard working and conscientious member of the marketing team, is incompetent. Instead, it must be recognized that the salesman calls upon buying influences who are too low on the corporate ladder to approve a purchase. The salesman talks with influences who can recommend a purchase, which is a far cry from approving one.

Sales Management magazine made an extensive study of this subject and stated categorically that 64 percent of all industrial sales calls were misdirected in this manner. Not only are they misdirected, but when a purchase of capital equipment is pending, salesmen simply do not have access to those executives who make the ultimate decision. It speaks well for salesmen's persistence and perseverance that, although starting low on the totem pole as they do, they are somehow able to guide many of their proposals through the chain of command and emerge with the order as often as they do. Knowing this enables the ad manager to place as much or as little credence as he finds desirable when considering the field force's recommendations of key buying influences for use in direct mail, merchandising, or what have you.

Many business publications have research data that's free for the asking on specific products, thus eliminating many tedious steps in defining a market and its potential. Admittedly, most of these studies tend to be self-serving in that they emphasize the necessity of advertising in the publication supplying the data to achieve sales success in its market. This is not due to figure juggling or distortion of information, however, but is the inevitable result of making studies from a sampling of the magazine's circulation list. Readers of the magazine are obviously very likely to have read advertisements and editorial matter about a product simply because it is there, and because they read the magazine regularly.

A Study of pH Meters

One illuminating study was recently conducted by *Analytical Chemistry* magazine, a publication of the American Chemical Society, which makes advertising planning for a manufacturer of pH meters and pH electrodes somewhat less of a game of economic Russian roulette.

The study was conducted to determine:

1. The extent to which readers of the magazine use pH meters and pH electrodes.

2. Brand names of the pH meters and pH electrodes in use, and the number of each.

3. Brand names of pH meters to be purchased in the future.

4. Types of pH meters readers intend to buy during the next 12 months, and how much they expect to spend per unit.

5. Information on pH meters and pH electrodes that readers need in order to make a purchasing decision.

A letter and questionnaire were sent to a random sample of 500 readers of *Analytical Chemistry*, with 180 respondents tallied up for a 36 percent return by the time the cutoff date rolled around. Survey highlights show:

1. Of the respondents to the *Analytical Chemistry* survey, 97.78 percent have pH meters. They average 4.3 pH meters per respondent.

2. Nineteen firms were mentioned as suppliers of pH meters. However, seven firms accounted for 89 percent of all pH meters in use: Beckman (55.5 percent), Leeds & Northrup (13.4 percent),

Radiometer (6.2 percent), Corning (6.1 percent), Photovolt, (3.6 percent), Coleman (3.2 percent), and Instrumentation Laboratory (2.1 percent).

3. Of the respondents to the magazine's survey, 83.33 percent intend to buy one or more pH meters during the next 12 months.

4. Of the respondents, 92.78 percent indicated the brands of pH electrodes they use. Sixteen firms were mentioned. However, six of the firms account for nearly 93 percent of all pH electrodes in use: Beckman (65.4 percent), Leeds & Northrup (9.2 percent), Corning (8.0 percent), Fisher Scientific (5.1 percent), Radiometer (2.9 percent), and Coleman (2.2 percent).

Statistical data, carefully tabulated and developed to 2 percentage points, shows that respondents mentioned as many as 22 brands in some questions. Despite this diversity of choice, one conclusion is obvious: The ad manager of a manufacturer of pH meters and pH electrodes, given this data, could analyze the leading competition and come up with some pertinent information.

He'd find it easy to make a meaningful report on buying patterns to the sales department; to sales and engineering for an unbiased product-vs.-product evaluation, with possible needed improvements coming to light; and to marketing to help determine if a basic shift in strategy might enable the company to whittle away at the sales lead of the leader. Particularly pertinent are the answers to the question, "What features do you look for in a pH electrode?" In order of mentions, here are the features given most often by respondents:

1. Ruggedness, durability 98
2. Stability 40
3. Small size 28
4. Sensitivity 27
5. Accuracy 23
6. Temperature and pH range 22
7. Long service life 17
8. Reliability 17
9. Versatility, adaptability 14
10. Reproducibility 14
11. Fast response 11
12. Construction details 10
13. Low cost 9
14. Low sodium error 8

Objective, unbiased, completely honest opinions are frequently almost impossible to come by; salesmen are usually given erroneous answers to similar questions simply because the prospect to whom they talk wish to spare their feelings. When the salesmen, in turn, pass this false information back to their home offices, misconceptions are born, nurtured, reared to maturity, and cherished for decades. A third-party survey turns fallacies into facts—and fast.

Then the ad manager will want to analyze the leader's advertising strategy and his collateral material. Sales literature is easily acquired, either through a friendly dealer or distributor or from a salesman with a penchant for collecting. Possibly the leader leads because—partially, at least—of more effective advertising. If so, the reason why will become apparent and action can be taken to change the communications objectives and creative approach to negate the influence of the competitor's advertising. An advertising program should never be developed, however, merely to counter that of the competition, despite its being obvious that Avis's hurts Hertz.

It is interesting to note that when *Analytical Chemistry* readers were asked in the questionnaire to name the brands of pH meters they have and the numbers of each, the top 10 firms in both categories were also discovered to be regular advertisers of pH meters in *Analytical Chemistry*.

Furthermore, when respondents to the survey were asked to name the firms they would contact to order a pH meter, they again chose those firms advertising pH meters in the magazine as their top 10 brand preferences. This is hardly happenstance. Coincidences do occur, but the odds against this being pure luck are astronomical.

Coincidence may indeed have a long arm, but certainly not long enough to account for the fact that *all* independent surveys, those conducted by professional research organizations, manufacturers, foundations, trade associations, and others with no axe to grind, all state flatly that industrial advertising plays a major role in establishing and maintaining brand recognition, brand acceptance, and brand preference.

Gold Mines of Information

In one respect major publishers are like the Superstition Mountain's fabled Lost Dutchman gold mine: they are the repository of wealth in such quantity as to stagger the imagination. Instead of precious metal, however, they hold a fabulous deposit of information that's readily converted into more effective advertising to lower the cost of selling—precious stuff itself. And instead of being hidden, this deposit of data is easy to find, although it is largely untapped by the average advertising manager who has a kind of thing about asking for outside assistance for what he thinks should be *his* job.

As an example, McGraw-Hill, the General Motors of business publishing, has so much to offer the individual advertiser that the company publishes a 120-page guide to what they *do* offer—a vast number of marketing services. Many of these services are available to advertisers at no cost. Others which entail investment of considerable time by teams of specialists, are charged for on a flat-fee arrangement, agreed to beforehand. McGraw-Hill revenue is derived from sale of space in some 50 magazines, so the company apparently does not consider research and merchandising facilities a profit center.

Of course, the services that are available are concerned primarily with advertising, but they are thought of in terms of marketing problems and are so arranged in the guidebook, *McGraw-Hill Marketing Services.* A glance at the contents pages shows that each McGraw-Hill business publication is analyzed for the benefit of prospective advertisers who may be considering adding it to their schedules.

Business Week, to pick one, has as its main objective the presentation of "business news for management men." This one publication is then discussed for two and one-half pages under the following general headings:

Name of publication.

Founded (date).

Issue date.

Subscription price.

Paid circulation. McGraw-Hill has traditionally favored paid circulation, rather than controlled circulation; controlled circulation is sending a publication to qualified readers at no cost to them. Lately, however, a number of McGraw-Hill books have been converted to controlled circulation.

Market served. Men at management levels in business and industry. Money is returned to those who attempt to subscribe to *Business Week* who do not meet the publication's rigid qualifications as to position held.

Editorial content.

Types of products and services advertised. Almost everything sold to business markets and upper-income male consumers is advertised in this magazine.

Advertising rate per page. This is broken down by the entire book, then by regional editions.

Closing dates for advertising.

Economic indexes. *The Business Week Index of General Business Activity* appears in each issue. It is computed weekly from 11 major indicators which, when properly weighted and adjusted for seasonal variations, together reflect the trend throughout business and industry.

Editorial indexes.

Motion pictures and/or filmstrips. Although primarily promotional for the publication, these audio-visual materials are also sophisticated tools which can help the advertising manager sell his management on both *Business Week* and the desirability of advertising to the influential audience it reaches.

Research data. Several hundred market and research reports are available to advertisers and their agencies through *Business Week* district managers. These reports are classified as follows:

Advertising results
> Results obtained by advertising in *Business Week,* including "before and after" recognition-study results, testimonial letters, etc.

Advertising statistics
> Competitive statistics relative to cost, volume of advertising pages, dollars, and other yardsticks of *Business Week* and books which sell against it.

Circulation
> Presented in a competitive manner.

Editorial
> Letters and comments concerning editorial. Statistics demonstrating editorial effectiveness. Lloyd Hall analysis of editorial content of *Business Week* and other business publications.

Market
> Discussion of markets the book reaches.

Presentations
> General and special presentations for advertising agencies and prospective advertisers.

Readership
> Information about and results of publication-readership studies. Much of this material is very elaborate and thorough and is of real value. Subjects such as teamwork of product and corporate advertising, management buying influences, summaries of publication readership of scores of leading companies, readership of magazines by financial analysts and newspaper business editors, profile of this magazine's

audience, including job responsibilities, income, personal, and business use of specific industrial and consumer goods; company size, position; discussion of the market for corporate stocks.

Research services

Readership-preference studies; Starch Advertising Readership and Starch Reader Impression Studies. Recognition studies.

Merchandising services

These are so numerous that *Business Week* issues a special catalog, yours free.

Publication literature

This explains *BW's* publishing policy, editorial objectives, and circulation standards.

Direct-mail lists

McGraw-Hill has a huge staff of direct-mail specialists who work on a 24-hour-a-day basis keeping the company's direct-mail lists current. The lists are segmented by industry, job function, type of business, and several other classifications; all are broken down geographically by state and alphabetically by cities. All plants are identified by four-digit SIC. McGraw-Hill builds special lists for clients and eliminates duplication for clients who use McGraw-Hill lists in addition to their own. The publishing company offers a complete service in this field, including letter reproduction, filling-in, addressing, and mailing.

Key personnel

Business Week management people are listed by name and job function in the guidebook.

Just *one* McGraw-Hill publication offers all of this to the advertising manager. In addition, the guide to the company's marketing services discusses these topics:

McGraw-Hill census of manufacturing plants.

McGraw-Hill research.

McGraw-Hill Department of Economics, economic indexes.

Industry newsletters.

Editorial services.

Market research visits.

Industrial company conferences.

Press conferences.

Business information service.

Marketing literature reports.

Reference library.

Recognition studies.

Space checking.

Publications checked (annually for advertising space used).

Product classifications checked. The 750 basic product classifications for which advertising space reports are prepared are listed alphabetically, with numerous cross references.

Marketing studies.

Editorial reports.

Company promotion department.

Media selection.

Magazine preference.

Copy planning.

The field photo service.

Training materials and information services.

Measuring readership.

Reader feedback service.

Measuring advertising effectiveness.

Advertising case histories.

Laboratory of advertising performance.

Merchandising services.

Direct-mail division.

Writing for McGraw-Hill publications.

McGraw-Hill books on advertising, marketing, and selling.

Display-advertising sales.

Classified-advertising sales.

Key personnel (on the corporate level).

Regional areas.

Regional area map.

You can mine many a nugget of priceless information from business media with a ridiculously low cost in money and time. A bonus is that this information negates the natural human tendency to think each of our companies is unique, that each has problems the likes of which are outside the experience of mortal man. Business publishers were, perhaps, the first to recognize that this is a fallacy. They long ago established the common denominators of almost all marketing problems, many of which are, contrary to popular opinion, almost ubiquitous. Business publishers are aware of the problems most of us encounter, they've defined them, segregated them, grouped them, and solved them for the most part. They can save much time and many trials and tribulations for the ad manager who asks for their help, and make it easier for him to produce more and better results—in less time.

Another prime source of information about prospects, both companies and people, lies in inquiries received from advertising and editorial exposure in the trade press. Inquiries will be discussed in depth in a later chapter, but it is important to recognize that a careful analysis and tabulation of them always provides enlightening information.

Detective Work on Prospects

Check against the customer list, check the SIC, check the printout of your mailing list; these will tell you if you have a likely prospect whose name should be bucked to the field force, or if you have a literature collector or other "nixie." As a rule, you'll find that most inquiries received via "bingo cards" (order blanks requesting literature) are valid inquiries, with one qualification: Most such inquirers are fairly low on the corporate table of organization. Granted, this is a generality, but it holds true rather consistently, especially when capital equipment is concerned.

This is not to say that inquiries, either from bingo cards or from any other source, are not worthwhile. Most of them have merit and sometimes they disclose an unusual amount of interest in a given item from a number of sources in one company. When this situation exists, it is a loud and unmistakable signal to send the first-string sales team calling *right now*. Markets do differ, and in the scientific, medical, educational, dental, and government areas, to pick some specific examples, returners of bingo cards tend to be in at least the middle echelon on the organizational chart, and frequently are higher.

Another source of information required to build a solid foundation under the communications program involves a bit of intelligence work. Unfortunately, the sleuthing is not as glamorous as that done routinely by the suave superheroes of paperbackdom, since it involves neither high living nor an overly anxious bevy of beauties. You can't have everything, though, and the information is highly important because it concerns one of business life's major worries, the competition.

Competitive information is acquired in a number of ways. Sales management, through the field force, keeps tab on what their opposite numbers say; they easily determine this via feedbacks from friendly prospects and customers. Marketing management has its sources of information. But it frequently falls to the advertising manager to tell management what the competition is officially saying, what story they are telling, what kind of creative approach they are using in their advertising, and what specific selling propositions they are stressing. In addition to keeping management posted on what competitors are doing, it is necessary for the ad manager to have this information to plan his own program.

He does *not* need this information to *react* to competitive advertising, for doing this merely plays right into the competition's hands. Instead, he requires this intelligence so that he can develop a more forceful, more informative program that is different, that separates his company from the herd. Look-alikes are usually also-rans.

This information can be accumulated in a number of ways. Least costly, at least in terms of actual dollar outlay, is the look-up method. All industrial advertisers who use 12 or more full pages in business publications are listed in *Rome Report of Business Publication Advertising*. This reliable reference work lists companies, breaks down divisions of corporations, and then tabulates just how much advertising space they ran in the preceding year, and in what publications. Only a few minutes are required to check up on your competition to see where they appear; then, by going through back issues of applicable publications, you can quickly tear out ads for further study. If you don't have access to back issues, it is probable the public library in any large city has them; you can't tear out pages, of course, for ripping paper breaks the silence libraries love. But you can make copies on the library copying machine. The *Rome Report* is probably in your agency's library, but if you want to own your own, it is available from:

Rome Research
1960 Broadway
New York, New York 10023

The Standard Advertising Red Books provide detailed, current information of this nature, also. *The Standard Directory of Advertisers* published by this company lists 17,000 companies doing national or regional advertising, their advertising agencies, media used, ad budgets, and also lists 80,000 executives by name and title.

The classified edition of this book shows companies in 51 business classifications. It is usually published in April. Several arrangements are offered:

> *Standard Directory of Advertisers* (classified edition) plus nine monthly revisions, each containing all changes since publication of the directory, plus geographical index, has an annual subscription price of $108.

> *Standard Directory of Advertisers* (classified edition) carries a single-copy price of $76.00.

Standard Directory of Advertisers (classified edition) plus three issues of the *Standard Directory of Advertising Agencies* (listing 4,000 agencies, their key personnel and accounts) plus supplements and weekly bulletins, has an annual subscription price of $165.

These useful volumes may be ordered from:

The Standard Advertising Red Books
Skokie, Illinois 60076: 5201 Old Orchard Road
New York 10017: 20 East 46th Street
Chicago 60601: 333 North Michigan Avenue
Los Angeles 90048: 6300 Wilshire Boulevard
Atlanta 30326: 3400 Peachtree Road N.E.

Here are some related sources of advertising information which will help you. Transit Advertising Rates and Data published by Standard Rate and Data Service, Inc. Each issue contains listings arranged in geographic/alphabetical order, includes branch offices, representatives, transit lines, communities served, card requirements, advertising rates, restrictions, circulation, and so forth. Published quarterly, $18.00 a year.

How to Check the Competition

It is an oddity of business life that every company is too busy selling its own products to analyze continuously and accurately what the competition is officially saying in advertisements. The alert ad manager will read and analyze all competitive ads, possibly with the assistance of the marketing director. He will then submit a report, perhaps quarterly, to management on the results of this intelligence operation. Much of value may be gleaned from material that is widely disseminated if it is well analyzed and properly presented. The report should be presented much like a newspaper article— most important facts first, others arranged as to importance in descending order.

If you feel it necessary to keep a month-by-month dossier on the competition but don't have unlimited time, the best way to do it is to use a reliable clipping service.

Bacon's Clipping Bureau, among others, does an outstanding job. This firm is in a position to supply complete reading coverage of the 3,700 business, trade, consumer, and farm magazines, in addition to more than 650 daily newspapers. All of these media are listed in *Bacon's Publicity Checker,* in well-organized format. Bacon's service covers both advertising and editorial material, or it can be limited to one or the other, as the ad manager wishes. Specialized research reading teams at Bacon's carefully read their assigned publications, picking up any articles or ads mentioning the key words relating to the subjects specified. When these readers find an article or an ad covering the subject they've been alerted to spot, they mark it and it is clipped from the publication after the reading is completed. Clippings are sorted, order by order. They are edited by Bacon's editing department to cull items which may contain the right key words, but which are otherwise not pertinent. Only edited material is submitted to the customer, who can be almost certain of getting only what is actually needed—and very close to 100 percent of that.

Bacon's basic rate for subject research is a $30 monthly service charge for the first subject checked, and $10 a month for each additional subject. Over and above this fee is a charge of 18 cents for each clipping. This is a bargain. No ad manager could hope to read —or even scan hurriedly—all of these publications, even if he received them. If he values his time at anything at all, Bacon's modest charge is almost a giveaway. Bacon's may be reached at:

> Bacon's Clipping Bureau
> 14 East Jackson Boulevard
> Chicago, Illinois 60604

One approach to determination of advertising direction is the so-called competitive-oriented approach. It certainly is not the best, but the ad manager must know how his company's advertising effort stacks up with that of the competition.

Many publishers, McGraw-Hill among them, can assist the ad man here. McGraw-Hill offers two services to help advertisers and their agencies with this ever-present problem.

RECOGNITION STUDIES: McGraw-Hill research makes studies for subscribers to determine the standing of a company's products versus those of competition.

It is highly advisable that any one of several types of recognition studies be conducted by either a publisher or an agency before a new advertising campaign starts. Then, after the campaign has been running for some time, an identical campaign can be made over a different but comparable list to measure the change in awareness of readers' attitudes toward the product, the theme of the advertising, or other characteristics being promoted by the campaign. Studies such as these are very useful in ascertaining the extent to which a manufacturer is known in specific fields among specific types of buyers, how that recognition compares with the competitors, the extent of recognition for particular products, and changes in recognition.

ADVERTISING SPACE CHECKS: What are the advertising experiences and practices of leading competitive advertisers? Which publications do they use in their advertising programs? Their advertising records are often the distillation of years of experience, extensive experimentation, and trial-and-error development. Meaningful comparisons of competitive publications in terms of their advertising volume (by product or by advertiser) can often be helpful.

Such an analysis reveals the leading competitive advertisers, the volume and frequency of advertising space they use, the business publications used most heavily, the industrial/commercial markets and job functions reached, and the competitors' approximate dollar investment in business publication advertising space.

McGraw-Hill does a thorough job, for the company continually checks the display advertising appearing in every issue of 211 U.S. business publications and records the following information on magnetic tape so it can talk to you through computers:

> Name of advertiser—company, subsidiary, or division
>
> Name of publication
>
> Products or services advertised
>
> Size of space used (fractions, pages, spreads)
>
> Date of issue
>
> Industry code

Included in the computer programming for this service to advertisers, which McGraw-Hill says is available exclusively through them, are the 750 basic product classifications. Updating of the master tape is done on a six-month cycle; computers used are the IBM 1401, 1402, and 7070; printout is done by an IBM 1403 high-speed printer.

Advertising space reports are available in three basic forms—by product, by company, or in a combination product-company summary. Cost is nominal.

PRODUCT SPACE REPORTS from McGraw-Hill provide the following information:

Names of 20 leading advertisers of specific product.

Total pages of ad space placed by each leading advertiser of this product.

Total pages of advertising space placed by all other advertisers of the product.

Publications used, grouped by fields, or functions.

Pages of advertising space used by each leading advertiser in each publication.

Total pages of space for the product placed in each publication.

Frequency of issue for each publication.

Name of product and its code number.

Cross references to other related products.

Time covered by the analysis.

Advertising page rate for each publication, in dollars, on a six-times, black-and-white basis, unless otherwise noted.

Product space reports can be used to find leading competitors, amount of space used, publications being used, leading publications carrying advertising, industrial fields being cultivated by advertising by each firm, approximate amount of money invested in business publication space, and many other facts.

COMPANY SPACE REPORTS give the advertising manager the following information from the publications checked:

Publications used by a specific company for each product advertised. Pages of advertising space placed in each publication for each product. Time period covered by the analysis. Trends and patterns of advertising for specific companies can be determined if these reports are thoroughly studied.

Again in the case of competitive information from publishers, the ad manager avoids drudgery and wasted time spent in detail work. The information he needs is there, it's in an easy-to-understand tabulation, it's necessary, and acquiring it won't impose a strain on even the most modest budget.

A number of other firms are in the information-gathering business and provide similar information about consumer advertising in all media, including newspapers, radio, and television. They do not concern us, however, for they concentrate exclusively on the frenetic frenzy of curing headaches fast, *fast*, *FAST*—or of hammering home what brand of detergent should be used in washing machines twice as tall as the advertising manager's wife. They don't get into the industrial field . . . where advertising communicates with sensible, rational humans who can think.

Why People Buy Your Product

The final portion of the foundation upon which a good advertising program can be built consists of a piece of information that is always crucially important to the ad manager. It is why people buy —or *don't* buy—your product. One is as important as the other, and never mind the negative connotation.

The thing is, this information is frequently quite difficult to acquire, particularly since it must be thoroughly reliable. Far too many companies suffer from the Ostrich Complex, which is merely burying one's head in the sand and refusing to face facts. These companies blithely gloss over the difficult self-analysis entailed in developing a thoroughly objective critique of the company, its service and its product(s). Some apparently feel it is either an unnecessary waste of time, or, hugging their omnipotence to their corporate breasts, take the attitude that they know all there is to know about their company, service and products. After all, it's *theirs*.

However, product weaknesses, lack of ability to accommodate to changing markets and conditions, and unwillingness to—or inability to—provide direction which will result in a uniformly high level of performance from all hands can all contribute to the reasons why sales are lost. They must be analyzed and corrective action taken before any advertising and communications program—no matter how well conceived—can stand a chance of helping to achieve the objectives.

One of the most hallowed, but still one of the best, methods of establishing attitudes toward a company or product is the survey. Customers and noncustomers should be surveyed to find out why they bought your product or service—and, in the case of prospects who did not become customers, they should be asked exactly why they did *not* buy from you.

Many cogent reasons will be unearthed, although it is extremely difficult for surveys and interviews to be completely dispassionate and objective if done by company personnel. It's far better to have your advertising agency, or a firm which specializes in industrial research, undertake the task. They can handle it without bias, without emotion, and submit a meaningful report. They will let the chips fall where they may. Those who are emotionally involved with a company and its products are generally incapable of doing this. Just a hint of personal feeling, a delicate and subtle shading of a section of the report, or a desire—even a subconscious one—to shift responsibility can obscure or alter the facts and make them worse than no facts at all.

Spotlight on Product Weaknesses

In the course of such a research program actual product weaknesses may be brought to light. Some of these may almost preclude sales to certain markets, while they have little effect in others, depending upon product application. Price structure, or dealer-discount arrangements, may be such that your company operates at a strong competitive disadvantage; often this can be altered slightly to offset the edge the competition enjoys. The product may be such that salesmen have a difficult time discussing all of the user benefits, especially when prospects must keep sales calls short due to a heavy work load. Finally, and no company likes to admit it, prospects may not have heard of your product, or, at best, may be only vaguely familiar with it.

Advertising can counter all of these handicaps which limit sales. If the price cannot be lowered, advertising can present the product so favorably by stressing all of the benefits, the features which are built into it (and, by inference, lacking in competitive products), that price becomes a secondary consideration. John Ruskin remarked that quality is remembered long after price is forgotten, and this sage observation holds as true today as when it was made before the turn of the century.

Advertising has the unique capability of presenting a complex story about a complex product exactly the way you want it done, time after time. It never varies, there's no worry about how a salesman may weaken the presentation. And advertising has as long a time to get the story across as the prospect wishes it to take.

If your product or service happens to be one with which the prospect is not thoroughly familiar, fine! This is advertising's forte. Among all methods of communications, word of mouth, gossip over the backyard fence, a chit carried on a forked stick, drum beats, smoke signals, or what have you, advertising alone can present a selling message about your product to thousands of people who are important to you, and do it simultaneously. Try to do that any other way.

Finally, touch bases with the sales department to verify the validity of your research findings. If the sales manager is a hardheaded realist—as most are—he can lend real support, as well as be a valuable source of information.

Chapter 4

PLANNING A CAMPAIGN

$\mathbf{B}$ACK when all of this was much simpler, common practice was for the industrial ad manager to engage in a considerable amount of soul searching, crystal-ball gazing, pure unadulterated guesswork, add a pinch of hunch, and finally indulge in a profound session with the nearest Ouija board. Then, with various mysterious incantations, unsullied motives, and hopes higher than the Himalayas, he'd bring forth a program which reflected the input he received from the sales department, the marketing people (if any), and top management. As a rule it was more or less on target, even if the target was obscured by the mists of foggy thinking.

Frequently the program was responsible—at least, in part—for sales growth, reduced cost of selling, increased market penetration, or some other goal. *What* part was largely unmeasured and thus open to interpretation. *Whose* interpretation determined how effective the program was. Even today the ad manager should do his own interpreting when he sells his accomplishments to management.

Back then, the imagination usually had to have great elasticity to enable it to stretch enough to consider the program a campaign. A true campaign is a connected series of events or operations—closely related and carefully conceived—designed to bring about desired objectives. This, after all, is all that an advertising campaign is when stripped of excess verbiage—the complete advertising plan developed to achieve objectives spelled out in the marketing plan.

Reviewing the Groundwork

Now that we're ready to think about planning a campaign, let's take a fast look at some of the necessary groundwork which has been laid to make campaign planning possible.

1. Necessity to achieve both short-range goals and long-range objectives, as set forth in the marketing plan, is recognized and the campaign is to be designed to accomplish this. Realistic objectives

which can be measured must be established for the entire communications program before it is completed.

2. Industry's buying procedures are understood, and it can be taken for granted that your company's distribution channels are right for your products and your markets; that dealers and distributors (or representatives) are solvent, aggressive, in the right market locations, and that they devote sufficient time to your product(s).

3. Multiple-buying influences are a part of the scheme of things, and a varying number of individuals influence every purchase in every company, inconsequential items excepted. These buying influences are on different levels of management, but all are important and all must be communicated with.

4. Industrial purchase procedures are made in six stages—six separate increments of time—and they follow one another in sequence as inevitably as invoices arrive or personal income tax falls due. To communicate with the many influences involved in all six steps over a prolonged period of time is a job done most effectively and at lowest cost by space advertising. Advertising gives the influences information they need to move from one stage to another.

5. The market must be defined, customer and prospect companies classified by SIC, addresses and cities, then by sales territory, and the key buying influences located by name and title in each establishment. The campaign must have as one objective reaching these buying influences; this will affect media selection, budgeting, copy platform and a number of other considerations, each of which will be discussed separately.

6. Reviewed what business publishers can contribute, particularly in basic information necessary to build a campaign.

7. Realize how important it is to scout the competition to see what it has done, and what it is likely to do in the future. This can influence the tack you take in planning the advertising program, so your company capitalizes on the weaknesses of competitors and uses it to your advantage. This information influences media, budget, schedule, and creative approach.

8. The truth has been faced up to about why people buy, or don't buy, your product. Benefits people want can be stressed in advertising.

The next step is to develop an advertising campaign based on the above information. The campaign must be coordinated so that bits and pieces mesh together to form a coordinated whole; it must also be carefully integrated into overall marketing strategy so there's every chance it will contribute as much as is expected. Advertising must be the working partner of the field sales force and must complement these efforts, as well as those of distributors, agents and dealers.

Avoid All Generalities

The knowledgeable ad manager will want his advertising plan to be fully as specific as the marketing plan is, with generalities avoided like the plague. All too frequently advertising plans contain such solemn statements of good intention as: "This program is designed to increase sales of . . ." or, and probably even worse, business-style gobbledygook such as: "When maximized, the subsequent plan and interrelated activities are formulated to . . ." The first is akin to a ringing affirmation favoring motherhood, flag, and paying one's bills on time. Such evidence of good citizenship is highly commendable, but it doesn't pay off in sales. Advertising does. The second doesn't even deserve comment.

Nonobjective objectives cost—cost in wasted time and wasted opportunity and wasted dollars. Vague and nonspecific, they offer a haven to the fuzzy thinker who can't or doesn't want to produce. They demand that advertising handle all functions of communications, something it never pretended to be able to do. They espouse the viewpoint and desires of the advertiser, rather than those of the prospect. And, equally important, nonobjective objectives make it impossible to measure advertising effectiveness.

Following is an actual example of such fuzzy thinking. This amazing treatise is not a figment of somebody's disordered imagination. It is an actual memo to the advertising manager of a well-known company, from the marketing manager of a highly technical product line sold to an unusually sophisticated market. It was written in response to a request for marketing objectives at the start of a new fiscal year. *Not one word has been changed except the name of the company. Not one.*

TECHNICAL SALES DEPARTMENT
ADVANCED WIDGET MANUFACTURING COMPANY, INC.
MARKETING OBJECTIVES

It is the purpose of this plan to establish marketing objectives, specific and concrete in form, to firm our position in the marketplace through several media. Our objectives are focused around (1) service, (2) promotion, (3) products, and (4) advertising. A fifth topic could be our future market position, that is, to regain that percentage of the market that has been lost to the competition. However, this topic is related directly to sales activity and our goal is obviously correlated to the entire market. In outline form, some of our marketing objectives are as follows:

A. *Service*

1. To develop a service policy by virtue of a self-sustaining service organization; service personnel located in each key marketing center and manufacturing facility.

2. To supply service engineers with necessary data and information to supplement policy.

3. To provide educational facilities by methods of formalized training programs, manufacturing experience, etc., to supplement such a service organization.

4. To extend to various customers the training facility on a formalized basis to reach the technical level of management.

B. *Promotion*

1. To promote Advanced Widget Manufacturing Company product group by means of trade shows, monthly promotional mailings, PR releases, trade-journal articles, etc.

2. To promote our status with field-sales personnel by virtue of supplemental activities; i.e., gifts for the top salespersons, plaques for achievement, expense-paid trip, etc.

3. Individual customer promotions to increase sales and/or regain as a customer.

4. To develop high morale within organization that is conducive to participation.

C. *Products*

1. To develop new products to keep pace with an ever-changing market requirement.

2. To stay abreast with "state-of-the-art" processes.

3. To substantiate the salability of existing products by research tools and analyzing the market for current needs.

4. To acquire companies that are established for additional products beyond our design capabilities providing the products fit within our present forces.

5. To increase the volume forecasts (securements of market share and profit), by means of present and future promotional activities.

6. To firm our marketing objectives by existing policy on products and present marketing approach.

D. *Advertising*

1. To analyze the market and objectives and justify programs.

2. To reach the buying powers through public relations and advertising media.

3. To promote other activities which comprise the overall marketing plan.

4. To recommend marketing appeals and strategy.

5. To be responsible for advertising matter through bulletins, brochures, and monthly promotions.

6. To be accountable for PR releases.

7. To recommend effective advertising programs and to assist in providing data for promotional activities and service training information.

The information contained herein should enable the advertising department to develop a plan and proposal to management for advertising activities derived from overall marketing objectives.

Insist Upon Realistic Goals

An advertising manager would have to be a genius of the first water to develop a program to help achieve such nonobjectives. Just what could be recommended to "increase the volume forecasts (securements of market share and profit), through present and future promotional activities," for example? Perhaps a saturation skywriting campaign in the six largest cities in the Yukon Territory.

An ad manager faced with such a frustrating situation can, of course, attempt to translate the vague generalities into what he believes are valid marketing objectives, relying on his knowledge of the company, its operation, its product, and its markets.

Chances are he would come quite close. But the fact remains that *the responsibility is not his.* Properly it rests with the marketing director, or, if the company is organized so that these functions are handled by a sales manager, then by that worthy gentleman.

The advertising manager *must* have firm direction, preferably in writing, on the marketing objectives of each product line or for each market to which the company sells. These objectives may be taken directly from the company's marketing plan if one exists, although it is still prudent to check them with the individual with marketing or sales responsibilities. Making a change before a program is actually under way is easy. Afterwards, it's expensive.

The alternative, and the proper course, is to reject such lack of direction as wholly inadequate. Decline to proceed further with the development of an advertising program until legitimate objectives are received. Then, and only then, should work start on the advertising campaign planning.

So that he personally can make a significant contribution to his company's marketing success, the ad manager wants to assure himself that advertising realizes its full potential—and this means that advertising must be assigned specific tasks. However, because the tasks are well defined does not mean that the program need necessarily be narrow or limited. On the contrary, it can be quite broad in scope.

How Du Pont Introduces New Products

Awareness that innovation is synonymous with success in the marketplace literally permeates E. I. du Pont de Nemours & Company. This awareness may well be the single most significant factor in the chemical giant's dominance of its industry.

This holds true in research and development, at which Du Pont excels, as well as in its advertising philosophy. Du Pont advertising thinking is solid and professional. It is built on the bedrock of well-directed research which precludes going off on tangents—at the expense of lost time and money. There's not enough of either.

The company recently introduced a new product, Microfoam, which was unique. Even uniqueness didn't result in that happy, happy situation where competition is nonexistent, however. Microfoam had established competition. Microfoam meets head-on with any number of older packaging materials such as crepe paper wadding and air bubble material, all used to protect various products from shipping damage. Shipping damage, incidentally, is on the increase in all modes of transportation, the result of don't-give-a-damn attitude on the part of rank and file employees.

Du Pont advertising executive William H. Nimtz supplied the rationale for positioning a new product (Microfoam) in the marketplace by use of advertising.

As Mr. Nimtz said, Microfoam joined the ranks of the thousands of products that preceded it, all of which can logically be termed "continuing innovations." Microfoam admittedly does a job that is already being done by a similar product, although not one that's a Du Pont brainchild. Even though Microfoam is a packaging product and most packaging products are paper, the fact still remains that other plastic packaging products were on the market—were, in fact, produced long before Microfoam was even thought of.

Market analysts at Du Pont took a long, hard look at the marketplace and decided to position their new product as a continuing innovation in the booming packaging market. Current theory held by up-to-date advertising practitioners holds that a product must be "positioned" so that prospective purchasers will immediately recognize the product's place in the scheme of things.

As a result, Du Pont's major communications objective was to persuade the end user, when thinking of buying a packaging product, to at least *consider* Microfoam along with others. Not considered, not bought. It's that simple.

Positioning the Product Is Critical

After discussion, the decision was made to face the competition squarely and to show—actually to show—competitive products in each Microfoam advertisement. Purpose, of course, was to position Microfoam in the mind of the reader as a logical alternative to the other packaging product shown in the ad. Du Pont people felt it very important to illustrate clearly to the reader that if he now used the competing product to package his widget, he could also now use Microfoam to do the very same job. And do it better.

Call it positioning, or call it what you will, after reading the ad the reader simply *must* come away with the clear understanding that instead of staying in a rut and using crepe paper wadding or bubble wrap to package his beautiful product, he now had the option of using Microfoam. Times change, improved products appear.

If only this *one* objective were achieved, the ad would have done its assigned task. Microfoam would have been successfully positioned in the mind of the consumer of packaging products. He'd be aware that an alternative to what he used exists.

An additional major role for advertising was recognized by Du Pont, of course. That role was to inform as many potential users of Microfoam as possible of its availability and of the benefits to be derived from using the new product in its various forms.

This effort would create awareness of Microfoam through mass communications and also by the very presence of the product in the marketplace help to persuade Du Pont distributors to put a push behind Microfoam—and to launch advertising and promotional programs of their own in its support. This would enable them to capitalize on the awareness created by Du Pont's advertising so that their efforts would have a synergistic effect.

A secondary role of advertising and promotion was to assist with selective promotion to high potential markets, thus increasing the effectiveness of the Du Pont sales force, as well as convincing distributors and their salesmen that it would be in their own self-interest to spend more time and effort selling Microfoam.

Incidentally, every advertiser large and small—whether of one product in a multi-product company, as well as advertisers with only one product to sell—shares a common problem. He is in direct competition *with every other advertiser* for two things: his share of salesmen's time, and his share of mind all along the channels of distribution. If you don't get your share of those two things, you can forget everything else. Because you're doomed to bomb out.

Du Pont's other objectives were to develop programs aimed at selected markets; to back up its new emphasis on direct sales effort aimed at large volume users; and to generate inquiries for direct sales follow-up in end-user markets. This last would enlist distributor salesmen as valuable allies and stimulate them to greater efforts to develop new business—and, coincidentally, to lay claim to more of the salesmen's selling time for Microfoam.

Specific Markets and Additional Promotional Efforts

The universe with which Du Pont needed to communicate about Microfoam's benefits was broad indeed, consisting as it did of industry as a whole. Specific markets on which the company wanted to concentrate were the furniture market and the government market.

Early and enthusiastic reception of Microfoam by two well-known manufacturers of quality furniture, Thomasville and Futorian, helped substantially in introducing Microfoam to the top 100 furniture manufacturers in the country. The new product was advertised in the following media. Circulation figures correct as of this writing. Frequency and space size shown.

It was anticipated that an expanded space advertising program in 1975 will provide additional distributor support, as well as pound home the fact that Microfoam is a GSA-stocked item. When the General Services Administration approves an item, further government sales accrue as a routine matter.

Various branches of the Federal Government consume incredible amounts of packaging materials and shipments made to and by the

YEAR MARKET	MEDIUM	CIRCULATION	SCHEDULE
1973 General packaging market	Packaging Digest	57,600	6x, b/w page
1973 General packaging market	Purchasing	70,000	4x, b/w page
1973 Electronics market	Electronics Packaging & Production	27,000	4x, b/w page
1974 General packaging market	Packaging Digest	60,000	6x, b/w page
1974 General packaging market	Package Engineering	49,000	4x, b/w page

Armed Forces are so numerous the mind literally boggles when contemplating them. Fortunately we taxpayers have lots of money. And if the dollars happen to run short, there's always an ample supply of the bureaucrats' standby, red ink.

Shown nearby are the first three business publication advertisements for Du Pont Microfoam. They appear in order of insertion in media discussed above.

These are typical Du Pont ads for business books. Strong headline with user benefits, product advantages hammered home, the product clearly positioned. You'll note in the introductory ad how lower cost and better performance on the job—the two criteria by which both Microfoam and competitive products are judged—are hit "fustest with the mostest." Lead from strength, always. Bridge and advertising are no different in that respect.

Following in rapid-fire order are bulleted product superiorities and, in a box, additional benefits realized when the product is actually used. Each is succinct, relevant and persuasive.

These Du Pont ads put the product's best foot forward and never hesitate to tell one and all they're simply not with it if they're not using Microfoam, newest and best packaging product to come down the pike.

Hedge Your Bet With Direct Mail

It's usually a mistake to rely heavily on only one medium, even though that medium is business publication advertising, the best and lowest cost way yet devised to communicate with a specific audience. Du Pont, as a very savvy marketer, realized this fully so it also developed direct mail material to supplement its efforts in the business press, its primary communications vehicle.

MICROFOAM® sheeting: It's the one that protects better and costs less.

1/4" crepe paper wadding   1/8" MICROFOAM sheeting

When you specify your next protective packaging material, keep this comparison in mind: Compared to ¼" crepe paper wadding, ⅛" Du Pont MICROFOAM sheeting gives you all these advantages:

• Costs less for equal or better cushioning
• Stands up better to repeated impact
• Better protection against abrasion of product surfaces
• Sheds water like a duck
• Superior insulation properties
• Snowy white
• Can be printed, die-cut or embossed

And now Du Pont MICROFOAM sheeting is easier to use than ever (see box at right).

Why not send for some samples and work out the savings for your particular application. For samples and more information, write: Du Pont Company, Room 22987-A, Wilmington, DE 19898.

Now available in 6", 12", 18", 24" and 36" perforations.

Now you can get MICROFOAM sheeting in perforated form (6", 12", 18", 24" and 36" perforations) offering these extra advantages.

• No cutting required • Quick, easy, efficient handling • Reduced material waste and less packing room labor • Easy dispensing from overhead or under-the-bench storage • Still available in custom-sliced widths • Standard perforation lengths ideal for uniform packaging of standard-sized products • Standard 6" perforation size can be used in any multiple of 6" size sheets, because perforations *do not* affect cushioning performance.

Note the hard-hitting copy that Du Pont used for its inaugural ad for Microfoam. Du Pont believes in strong headlines with user benefits, with product advantages hammered home.

149

The advertisement on the top was the second in the Du Pont series and the one immediately above was the third. Note the continuing strong headlines.

Shown nearby are three of the direct mail pieces designed to look like and reflect the themes of the three ads previously illustrated. The mailers are cleverly designed to include a postpaid reply card addressed to the distributor over whose name the mailer was sent—in this case, Iroquois Paper Company, Chicago.

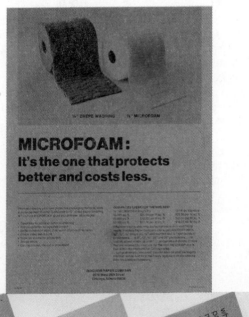

Supplementing the mailing pieces which supplement the space ads are illustrated post cards mailed by business publications. This is an excellent and inexpensive way to get additional exposure and generate a substantial quantity of sales leads. Cost, in 1975, is around $750 to $800 for a postcard mailing. Postcards are usually available only to display advertisers. The publication mails your card in a package along with others to the book's mailing list.

You don't even have to do any printing—merely send the book camera-ready art (keyline and glossy photo) and they proceed to print your postcard. This is a real bargain in these inflationary times because you couldn't begin to print 75,000 or so mailing pieces, pay outgoing postage and handle the thing for anything near the modest cost charged. Incoming postage is an expense, of course, but the number of returns you'll receive is a tiny fraction of the number that were mailed. This cost is inconsequential. And it's bulk rate, at that.

YOU GET A LOT OF EXTRA MICROFOAM FOR YOUR PACKAGING DOLLAR

For the price of 1,543 sq. ft. of 1/8" air bubble material, we'll sell you 1,800 sq. ft. of 1/8" MICROFOAM. That's like getting an extra roll of MICROFOAM with every 6 rolls. You also get superb cushioning performance, excellent void filling and unmatched surface protection from MICROFOAM.

SEND FOR FREE INFORMATION

Name _____ Title _____

Company _____

Address _____

City _____ State _____ Zip _____

Application: _____

DU PONT

microFoam

FIRST CLASS
PERMIT No. 9
WILMINGTON, DEL.

BUSINESS REPLY MAIL
No Postage Stamp Necessary if Mailed in the United States

POSTAGE WILL BE PAID BY

E. I. du Pont de Nemours & Co. (Inc.)
Room 23604
Wilmington, DE 19898

Du Pont used this direct mail promotion to reinforce its ads in the business press.

Final sales tool in Du Pont's well-conceived introduction of its latest example of chemical wizardry is the attractive four-page sales literature shown nearby.

The familiar Du Pont logo appears prominently on the front and second pages of this two-color (black and blue) literature; for some reason that doesn't come to mind, the company was uncharacteristically modest on the other two pages and ignored the distinctive oval logotype.

Illustrations in the literature are conventional black-and-white halftones, along with two duotones on the front page. Duotones are a combination of halftones in black, along with a second color; a duotone is *not* a tint block laid on top of a b/w halftone, however, but has highlights that are clean.

Good judgment was shown in the selection of the illustrations because Microfoam is seen being used, cut, stored, made into pouches and so on—in a variety of different ways. You'll note, too, that names of well-known companies which use Microfoam are casually dropped in for an implied endorsement. Strong stuff, and very effective, too.

And on the last page of the literature Du Pont discusses availability, military specifications and the comparative ratings of both Microfoam and other flexible cushioning materials. This is done in an apparently objective manner and it carries conviction.

Du Pont company policy prohibits disclosure of actual sales volume or percentage of market penetration. However, its advertising executives feel sure that sales targets have been hit and that Microfoam is assured of its rightful place in the sun.

Du Pont the Innovator

Having practically put plastic on the map over the last quarter-century, along with a host of other goodies such as Nylon, Dacron, Teflon and scads of others, Du Pont is not a company to rest on its laurels. Naturally, this delights my stockholder's heart because a tidy share of what the chemical giant ends up with on the bottom line accrues to us who own the company.

Recently the marketing-product, development-research types in Wilmington got their heads together and came to the conclusion that wrapping produce—and even potatoes—in transparent plastic simply wasn't the way to go. It lacked class.

Their additional conclusion was that savvy retailers are right. Every smart retailer has a bedrock belief that the shopper who can fondle, feel, see and smell the merchandise is a shopper who is going to buy that merchandise. And, as every retailer will tell you, that's the name of the game.

Du Pont's innovative people analyzed produce packaging in a number of supermarkets and immediately a number of "musts" were apparent. First of all, the package must hold the produce firmly so it won't open accidentally under the probing fingers of value-conscious female shoppers. They can *really* probe. It must present the produce so it is readily visible. It must be extremely light in weight so that at the checkout counter there won't be vociferous protests against weighing the packaging material. It must be easy to use. And, finally, it must be low in cost.

With these major considerations in mind, Du Pont teams went to work with the objective to produce a truly superior product, one with real class and one that would make a significant penetration of the market in a very short period of time.

Enter Vexar

After a suitable amount of work so that product development wouldn't appear too easy to the powers that be, there emerged an unquestionably superior new product—Vexar. Vexar is a fantastically strong, fine-mesh plastic netting. It is produced in food colors— yellow for grapefruit or lemons, for instance, or red for apples, and so on.

Vexar was a new concept, one that supermarket management was completely unfamiliar with. New concepts aren't always embraced with open arms, people have to be persuaded to accept them.

Because Vexar was a new concept, it called for exceptionally effective advertising if the corporate objective of compressing the time scale between product introduction and product profitability was to be realized.

The new Vexar was assigned to Wim van der Graaf, a solid, well-rounded advertising professional who's an alumnus of Northwestern University and that great training ground for advertising people, Montgomery Ward. The possessor of an unusually keen, analytical mind, Wim van der Graaf has a long list of outstandingly effective campaigns to his credit, along with the customary wall full of awards, plaques and so on that gravitate to topflight advertising people.

To digress for a minute, it has always seemed to me—and this has been borne out by almost three decades of management experience—that exceptional competence in industrial advertising demands an exceptionally active and inquisitive mind, one with wide-ranging interests and activities. This is in addition, of course, to a well-rounded formal education in advertising and marketing plus sufficient dedication to continue to upgrade one's knowledge of the field.

This is certainly borne out in van der Graaf's case. He's a prospector who delights in panning placer gold in rushing mountain streams in the West's high country; a dedicated ghost town buff; a first-rate tennis player; water skiier and Coast Guard-certified small craft skipper; breeder and trainer of purebred dogs; music lover,

New Orleans jazz *aficionado,* tape nut; rock hound and turquois connoisseur; an expert on Indian arts and crafts; skilled woodworker; shooter and handloader; a duck and goose hunter and a sportsman who exults in fair stalk for antelope and deer. All of this, although fun stuff, broadens his outlook and gives him background knowledge in many fields. Combined with his writing of magazine articles these avocations contribute to his continuing informal education; he also continues formal study, of course, as do most professional ad people.

Soon Only Advertising Tigers Will Survive

Contrast van der Graaf with a hypothetical ad man (I've actually known some like him) whom we'll call John Average. Incredibly, this John Average didn't bother to finish high school; he feels that two years of high school are enough. True, this "ad man" may play golf and bowl and pub crawl and memorize the statistics of other people's accomplishments, such as those of professional athletes. This provides just about zero mental growth, of course, but such an "advertising man" sees no need for growth, no need to learn the intricacies of his chosen field. The John Averages are midgets among their peers and they rely on having a top management which knows even less about advertising than they do—or they rely on having a superior carry them because they're too lazy to learn.

With the economy in a state of flux—you'll forgive the understatement—every advertising person owes it to himself, his family and his company to hone his professional skills to a razor edge. He owes it to them to grow through constant learning—on and off the job—if he's ever to be worth his salt. The mid-70's is no time for complacency and laziness.

To digress for just a minute more, the move to certify industrial advertising people as professionally competent—following a comprehensive certification examination—is gaining impetus. Chances are, certification will be done through the Business/Professional Advertising Association (the old Association of Industrial Advertisers). It seems likely that within just a few years industrial advertising people will fall into just two classes: those with their certification as competent professionals, and the lazies like John Average who find it just too much bother to learn the profession they've chosen. This is well and good. Industrial advertising has long been saddled with too many John Averages, well meaning but inept. Come certification day, these incompetents will no longer be able to bluff or con their way because they'll be shown up for what they are—people who can't measure up to professional standards. Needless to say, an ad man in that position will find job opportunities severely limited.

Hunt Ducks Where the Ducks Are

Wim van der Graaf had already established that the primary market for the revolutionary new fine-mesh netting was high-volume supermarkets. Some supermarkets receive their produce in reefer (refrigerated) trailers in bulk. Large burlap bags. Bushel baskets. Cardboard boxes. It's up to the store manager, through his produce manager, to repackage to give the produce as much eye-appeal as possible so that your wife and mine will buy, not pass by.

The new Vexar had to be introduced with a bang so loud the impact would be roughly comparable to that of John Wayne arriving at full gallop just in the knick of time to keep the good cowboys from being slaughtered by the black-hatted guys. It was a range war, of course, over fences and water.

After thorough analysis, it was decided to run a 13X schedule in *Supermarket News,* the leading book read by supermarket managers, their key people and the big brass at the headquarters of the country's supermarket chains.

The schedule was meticulously planned down to the last detail —including the critically important element of timing. Ads showing Vexar-wrapped (or bagged) produce and fruit were scheduled to run just prior to the time the food came into season. That is, when grapefruit was coming into its best time of year, a grapefruit-Vexar ad was run; when apples were ripe for selling, an apple-Vexar ad was inserted, and so on.

We'll look at van der Graaf's Vexar campaign in a minute, but it's only fair to mention that it has won wide acclaim. Among other kudos the campaign received was the gold medal at the Rochester, New York, Art Directors' Show. While we all realize that our primary function as industrial advertising people is to help sell more and more of the product, and to reduce the cost of selling through effective mass communications, winning gold medals is not really important. Yet who can dispute the fact there's always a warm glow around the heart when your efforts are endorsed, approved and judged *numero uno* by your peers? That's just human nature.

Shown nearby are three Vexar ads. Let's examine them and see what makes them tick—and sell.

Back in the initial planning stages of this campaign, van der Graaf realized that black-and-white ads for a packaging product

THE ORANGES IN VEXAR®
GET TWICE THE ACTION FROM SHOPPERS
IN SIDE-BY-SIDE SALES TESTS.

Sold: 407 bags of oranges in Du Pont VEXAR plastic netting...
170 in plastic film. Same oranges. Same price. Side by side on the
same amount of counter space.

That's the result of a carefully controlled supermarket sales
audit over a two-week test period.*

It's no wonder that shoppers show a more than 2 to 1 preference
for oranges in VEXAR. Bags of VEXAR let the natural color and
fresh appeal of the oranges come through. There's no hazy film, no
shiny glare. Shoppers get all the convenience of bagged fruit with
the appearance of bulk display. And oranges look fresher because
they *stay* fresh longer in well-ventilated bags of VEXAR.

So the buying action goes where the VEXAR is. For you that
means faster turnover, more efficient use of precious display space,
less waste and spoilage. More consumer satisfaction and an
enhanced quality look for your entire department.

If you'd like a piece of the extra action, specify citrus and
other produce in bags of fine-mesh VEXAR plastic netting.
*Details of this study on request.

FOR BETTER NET RESULTS—DU PONT VEXAR PLASTIC NETTING

*Half of these oranges is wrapped in plastic and half is wrapped in Vexar. Not
only can you see the fruit better but you can actually smell the oranges.*

enclosing such colorful items as oranges, grapefruit and apples would have all of the strength of wet spaghetti. So he decided the additional investment for four-color was both called for and justified. Four-color ads, you know, get 53 percent greater readership than do black-and-white ads.

The ad nearby that occupies a full page in this book has for its illustration a mouth-watering bin of lush California oranges. Approximately half of the oranges are conventionally wrapped in polyethelene, in the quantity customers ordinarily purchase— or the amount that fits into the supermarket's price structure. Only thing, the oranges in plastic don't really have the visual appeal store management relies on to sell the merchandise. No getting around it, the plastic glares, reflecting back the overhead lights. This distracts. And no matter how you look at it, there is a certain amount of color degradation inherent in looking through any plastic. The vividness, the eye appeal, just don't come through.

On the left side of the illustration we see the same lot of California oranges bagged in Vexar. There's no comparison between the two. Vexar lets you see the oranges in all of their freshness, all of their lush color. And Vexar, unlike plastic, enables shoppers to *smell* the oranges. This is a superspecial subliminal fringe benefit from using Vexar.

Let's take a look at what the ad says.

Like all Du Pont ads, this one is straightforward and to the point with no frills or beating around the bush. It presents Vexar in the most favorable light possible and translates product features into user benefits that supermarket managers can readily translate into extra dollars in their cash registers. The ad reads:

THE ORANGES IN VEXAR®
GET TWICE THE ACTION FROM SHOPPERS
IN SIDE-BY-SIDE SALES TESTS

Sold: 407 bags of oranges in Du Pont VEXAR plastic netting . . . 170 in plastic film. Same oranges. Same price. Side by side on the same amount of counter space.

That's the result of a carefully controlled supermarket sales audit over a two-week test period.*

It's no wonder that shoppers show a more than 2 to 1 preference for oranges in VEXAR. Bags of VEXAR let the natural color and fresh appeal of the oranges come through.

*Details of this study on request.

There's no hazy film, no shiny glare. Shoppers get all the convenience of bagged fruit with the appearance of bulk display. And oranges look fresher because they *stay* fresh longer in well-ventilated bags of VEXAR.

So the buying action goes where the VEXAR is. For you that means faster turnover, more efficient use of precious display space, less waste and spoilage. More consumer satisfaction and an enhanced quality look for your entire department.

If you'd like a piece of the extra action, specify citrus and other produce in bags of fine-mesh VEXAR plastic netting.

FOR BETTER NET RESULTS—DU PONT
VEXAR® PLASTIC NETTING

The other two four-color Du Pont Vexar ads are shown nearby. Again, they stick to the tried-and-proven pocketbook appeal and promise supermarket owners and operators more profit—backing up the claims with irrefutable logic and case history data.

Take the apple ad, for example. The same illustrative technique is employed as in the orange ad—half a bin of plastic-wrapped apples, half a bin of apples bagged in Vexar. And it's again obvious that Vexar wins hands down. It isn't even a contest, it's so one sided. Copy reads:

STORE AUDIT SHOWS
APPLES IN VEXAR® OUTSELL
APPLES IN PLASTIC FILMS BY 3 TO 2 MARGIN

Shoppers prefer packaged apples they can see. And smell. In a carefully-controlled supermarket test, they proved it. Given a choice between apples in bags of Du Pont VEXAR plastic netting and apples in plastic film, they bought 50 percent more of the apples in VEXAR. Same Red Delicious apples. Same price. Same counter space.

Little wonder. With bags of fine-mesh VEXAR, nothing gets between the appeal of the fruit and the shopper. No hazy film. No glare. In follow-up interviews, shoppers said they like the *visibility* of apples in VEXAR (11 to 1 over the look of apples in plastic film). And they recognized that well-ventilated bags of VEXAR keep apples fresher (by 4 to 1).

So the buying action goes where the VEXAR is. For you that means faster turnover, more efficient use of precious display space, more impulse purchases. Less waste and spoilage, more consumer satisfaction and an enhanced quality look for your entire department.

If you'd like a piece of the extra action, specify apples and other produce in bags of fine-mesh VEXAR plastic netting.

FOR BETTER NET RESULTS—DU PONT VEXAR® PLASTIC NETTING

Because one of the real keys to advertising success is repetition of major benefits and features, Du Pont's Wim van der Graaf wisely kept hitting the salient points in each ad, including the grapefruit one.

There's no need to reprint the entire copy of the grapefruit ad, but note that stress is placed on the most important parts of the message. In the headline we find, "shows grapefruit moving 100 percent faster." And in the body copy there's additional food for thought (you'll forgive that one, please), such as "in side-by-side tests, customers preferred grapefruit in Vexar by more than 2 to 1." Also, that during the same period they "bought 153 bags of grapefruit in Vexar vs. only 59 in plastic bags." Then we find the no hazy film, no glare story which emphasizes the natural color of grapefruit in Vexar. And of primary importance in these days when the liberal politicians in Congress are trying their best to destroy the dollar through deficit spending, is the fact that produce in Vexar *stays* fresh due to excellent ventilation. Finally, there's the pocketbook appeal to the storekeeper of faster turnover, more efficient use of counter space, less waste and spoilage, plus more consumer satisfaction. If Du Pont can keep the price of Vexar even close to competitive with plastic film, it will have a real winner.

A Clean Campaign Look

These ads have a superb "campaign" appearance due to use of the same clean, uncluttered layout, fine illustration, and excellent typography. Incidentally, Du Pont advertising people would rather have their ads *read* than run them to impress a dwindling segment of good-hearted but misled types who haven't really done their homework when it comes to typefaces. All of these Du Pont ads, you'll notice, have a strong headline typeface—and all of them are set in a highly readable, attractive serif type face for the body copy. Body copy set in serif type invariably receives higher readership than the same copy set in a sans serif face. Cost is the same, so why penalize yourself by making it hard for the reader to read?

Fortunately, the craze for sans serif body copy type is one that is rapidly departing the scene. For far too long, far too many advertising people rushed lemminglike to join the throng whose main interest was to impress their friends, rather than have their advertisements read. Are we really trying to impress bearded, long-haired Eastern art directors in World War I army blouses and bearskin vests and sandals by using sans serif type—or are we trying to do everything possible to achieve higher readership by using serif type? Think it over.

Not All Begs In One Askit

The attractive four-color space ads we've just looked at launched Vexar with an appropriate bang. But Wim van der Graaf, seasoned old pro that he is, isn't one to put all of his begs in one askit. To rely on only one medium to carry the bulk of the load is to court disaster in the marketplace, or at the very least, to stretch out the time between product introduction and product profitability.

Back when he first developed the communications plan for the new fine-mesh netting, van der Graaf emphasized the importance of using direct mail to augment the introductory push put on by Du Pont's space advertising. Properly, however, he stressed that space ads were the primary communications vehicle because they reach more people at lower cost than any other means of communicating with the universe he had to reach.

Obviously van der Graaf could have taken the easy way out and gone with the hoary "writing them a letter" technique. He could even have carried this one step farther and used the ancient caper of mailing a letter and an ad reprint. And if he chose the ultimate in yesteryear's gambits, he'd have come up with mailing a letter and an ad reprint and a postpaid reply card. This, however, is a weak, wishy-washy and moss-grown approach to direct mail that was in its heyday around the turn of the century.

This isn't to infer that merchandising your ads is less than essential. Just the opposite is true. The smart, dollar-conscious industrial communications man always merchandises ads because it's an effective way of assuring the message's getting the most possible readership in a target universe.

Direct mail has changed, progressed and become both more exciting and more productive in recent years. It has come of age. The dull and the trite no longer achieve their erstwhile purpose of attracting the individual's attenion for a long enough time to get a message across. The average buying influence in industry receives so much direct mail now that only the truly exceptional, truly creative efforts are not consigned to the round file without a second glance.

3-D Was the Key

Knowing this, van der Graaf's conclusion was that only a "3-D" (three-dimensional) mailing would grab the recipient's attention and entice him into reading the enclosed message.

Moreover, there's no better way to dramatize a product, to imbue a strong curiosity about it, than to send an actual sample of it. (Remember all of the direct mail you've received from manufacturers of trousers, each with a swatch of fabric tipped onto descriptive literature?) The swatch *forced* you to read at least part of what the manufacturer had to say.

As good fortune would have it, van der Graaf had an absolute natural for a unique 3-D direct mail campaign that would achieve memorability almost akin to a Louis Armstrong blues record. Like every first-rate idea, van der Graaf's looks deceptively simple—so simple that the natural reaction is to think, "I could have come up with that." But the distinguishing mark of the true professional in this business is that he generates good ideas as they're needed, time after time after time.

Shown nearby is the first Vexar 3-D direct mail piece, this one on grapefruit. Name just one better way, if you can, of promoting Vexar, the fine-mesh netting for bagging produce and citrus fruits, than sending each individual on the mailing list a fresh, juicy grapefruit! My bet is you can't top this. Is there anybody who thinks this mailing wasn't noticed? That it didn't stand out from the rest of the morning mail? That it could be overlooked?

The box used for the bagged fruit was specially designed to withstand the rigors to which it would be subjected by the post office. My box of Vexar-bagged grapefruit arrived in Colorado in perfect condition and was the appetizer for the next morning's breakfast. Naturally, a tastefully done piece of tie-in literature was enclosed in the box with the grapefruit; it, too, is shown nearby.

The Vexar literature enclosed with the grapefruit, neatly bagged in you know what, is also highly professional and in four-color. The model holding the bag of grapefruit is perfect for the job. She looks like the wife of one of your friends, or maybe *your* wife, but she *doesn't* look "modelish."

The headline, WOULD SHE KID YOU? can't be resisted. The supermarket owner-manager who receives this mailing simply *has* to open the mailer. And when he does, there's a beautiful, lifelike four-color illustration of a bag of grapefruit on the left, and a ready-to-eat half grapefruit complete with maraschino cherry.

Copy is conversational, convincing and persuasive. It hits the major selling points for Vexar again, emphasizing visual appeal and no spoilage. It reads:

WELL . . . NOT ABOUT GRAPEFRUIT, SHE WOULDN'T

Give her half a chance and she'll double the action at your grapefruit counter.

Just don't ask her to select her fruit through the haze of plastic film. She wants to see it.

Don't suffocate it in airless film where heat and moisture can build up and lead to spoilage. She wants it fresh.

In other words, she wants grapefruit wrapped in VEXAR,® the fine-mesh plastic netting that lets her see, feel, even smell what she's buying.

We know she does, because we conducted an in-store survey of 528 shoppers, and 55 percent preferred the netting, while only 21 percent selected polyethelene.

Our test was made with oranges. But, if she has this thing about oranges, would she kid you about grapefruit?

FOR BETTER RESULTS—DU PONT VEXAR® PLASTIC NETTING

These fine Du Pont ads and 3-D mailers are both highly creative and exhibit superb craftsmanship. Needless to say, they met the acid test of every campaign—they sold the product.

According to Du Pont's Wim van der Graaf, results so far have "been highly gratifying." That is, no doubt, an understatement because it is Du Pont company policy to refrain from divulging information as to sales.

Du Pont has received a large number of carload orders for Vexar to be used by the growers and marketers to bag citrus fruits and produce. Thus shipped to supermarkets, Vexar will certainly dominate the shelf space because there won't be any other kind of packaging there on display!

This is in addition to sales made directly to supermarkets, of course. And speaking of supermarkets, van der Graaf reports that Du Pont has been very successful in converting a major supermarket chain to 100 percent use of Vexar! Additionally, another large chain has converted at least part of its regions and it's only logical, given Vexar's superiority over plastic wrapping, that the chain will ultimately convert fully.

So satisfactory has Vexar proven in use that one large supermarket chain is contemplating using Vexar to bag lettuce! Every shopper knows, of course, that it is extremely difficult to judge the freshness of lettuce when it's encased in an armor-plating of plastic.

A fringe benefit of primary importance has been realized from van der Graaf's Vexar space ads and direct mailers, too. That is firing up the Du Pont field sales force. Enthusiastic salesmen are productive salesmen. And nothing stimulates a sales force to greater efforts than the feeling that the "home office" is giving them effective support. Advertising that does a preselling job on prospects before the salesman calls is certainly support with an upper-case "S!"

Vexar has been successfully launched. It has achieved widespread acceptance in an incredibly short time, although Du Pont can't yet consider itself in a position to sit back and rest on its laurels. Vexar must be, and no doubt will be, promoted aggressively for some time to come before the promotional push can be reduced. Those prime prospects for Vexar—supermarket managers, produce merchandisers and buyers, along with growers of citrus fruit, potatoes and lettuce— now have awareness of Vexar and what it has to offer them. So, for that matter, do consumers.

Wim van der Graaf's advertising campaign can be credited in large part with having paved the way for near-immediate acceptance on a national basis. Without advertising it is conceivable that the same marketing objectives could have been accomplished—but most decidedly not in the same short span of time, not for the same relatively low cost. The rewarding payoff for this imaginative campaign was that in 1975 it received the coveted Direct Marketing Leader Award of the Direct Mail/Marketing Association.

Nothing has yet been devised, even with all of the technological advances that have taken place in our society, that can either replace or displace advertising.

The Story of Wheeling Steel

Advertising is a far cry from the legendary horseman who blithely leaped aboard his trusty mount and galloped off in all directions simultaneously. Advertising, to be successful, has to be specific and precise; it must have firm direction; it must have carefully planned, concrete objectives laid out point by point. Campaigns we've studied and those that follow make this quite clear.

Another example: Wheeling Steel Corporation, one of the largest producers of steel and corrugated iron. Wheeling Steel assigned a task to advertising of such magnitude that it is no exaggeration to say that the entire future of the company hinged to a large extent on advertising's ability to deliver—to achieve the objectives set for it.

In the industrial field such importance is seldom attached to advertising effectiveness. It's far from the hue and cry and partial insanity surrounding the introduction of a new cake mix, a new or improved detergent, or a new spray that is guaranteed to hold feminine hair so firmly it resists wind—and old-fashioned males who don't believe that woman's crowning glory should have the firmness of structural material.

In Wheeling's case advertising *had* to produce. As Jon Avrigean, Wheeling's director of advertising, put it: "Wheeling had a big hole to crawl out of. The company was in such a fix because lackadaisical past management permitted it to drift into it. Once a major contender among the top eight steel producers, Wheeling didn't invest in modernization programs. It took the usual steel industry ho-hum attitude to customers generally. It was a very product-oriented company, it broke no records for on-time delivery. Profits slipped down and down.

"New management took over two years ago, and started to turn it around. Much investment in new facilities—nearly $200 million—many top management changes, and creation of a new marketing department took place.

"And Wheeling established a marketing policy that said, in effect, 'we're customer-oriented. Customer needs come before anything else.'"

This was a major—and critically important—series of steps in the right direction, of course. But Wheeling still faced the problem of attracting new customers, then of keeping them and retaining the goodwill—and business—of present customers while the new plant was being completed and going through its shakedown cruise.

Something, some force, had to exert a strong effect on the market—in the minds of the buying influences who specify what kind of steel will be bought and from whom it would be bought. Wheeling management assigned to advertising the twin tasks of firmly establishing in the minds of both present and prospective customers two messages:

1. That Wheeling, because of a massive expansion program and greatly expanded production facilities, was a potent new force in the steel industry—one that had grown in strength and ability to serve.

2. That Wheeling *wanted* to serve rather than merely accept orders, that the company was completely committed to the marketing concept; that Wheeling was "dedicated so strongly to needs of customers above all else that the company was willing to break long-standing traditions."

The steel business is no different than any other, in that service —particularly meeting delivery schedules—is near the top of the list of customer gripes when it isn't up to snuff. Wheeling formerly shared a fault that is prevalent throughout the steel industry—taking customers for granted, adopting the attitude that they had to go *some* place for steel and that a satisfactory volume of business would automatically accrue regardless of service.

Wheeling analyzed this situation correctly, then astutely established an advertising objective. It was to build an image of a customer-oriented steel producer, one from which the customer received genuine service—not lip-service about service.

To create this image, Wheeling and its agency developed the now-famous "Hustle" campaign. Robert M. Morris, Wheeling president, credits the campaign with a "major contribution to the continuing task of forging Wheeling Steel into a modern, aggressive, growing, and profitable enterprise."

The ads hustle, no doubt about that. The one shown here can scarcely be confused with a shrinking violet, and it is immediately obvious that it is not an ad run by a Casper Milquetoast company.

In reverse (white on black) it has what has to be one of the shortest possible headlines, followed by single-word, single-idea body copy. It reads: "Expand, innovate, promote, sell, serve, *and* deliver. Have you looked at Wheeling lately?" Short, terse, bold, and brash—and *read*. This ad set the pace and the tone for the campaign, calling attention as it did to Wheeling's activities, its expanded facilities, and its unabashed determination to capture a much larger share of the steel market.

Another Wheeling ad is dominated by an aggressive, dramatic two-word headline in type that's a full 4⅞" high—never mind translating that into "points." Copy reads:

PUSHY

AMBITIOUS

CALL US WHAT YOU WILL

The name of the game is hustle!

So we're hustling. And we're not embarrassed to admit it.

We've got responsibilities to think about.

pushy
ambitious

Call us what you will.

And we aren't just thinking. We're actively doing.

Our basic oxygen furnaces have been fired up. Our brand-new $80 million computerized hot strip mill is raring to go at up to 45 miles per hour. And another little item: 167 percent more hot rolled steel than last year.

What's more, our new 60-inch continuous galvanizing line is hard at it. We've got new coatings, better shape, better flatness. Plus 68 percent more galvanized.

What else could a steel buyer want?

On-time delivery? O.K., on-time delivery. Mill to market scheduling that'll get your order where you want it. When you want it.

You still want more? All right. Our new P.T.O. (price-at-time-of-order) policy guarantees for six months the price you order at—no matter what. Unless prices go down—then your price goes down.

Like we said, call us what you will. But call us.

Have you looked at Wheeling lately?

This ad announced the bombshell that literally caused great wailing and gnashing of teeth as the rest of the steel industry went into a massive flap. Wheeling is the *only* major producer to adopt this customer-first policy. The industry has traditionally accepted orders for steel, quoted a price, and shipped at another if prices happened to go up in the interval between order and fulfillment.

171

As Wheeling's ad director said: "While this may appear to be a small point, think back in recent history. If you placed an order in July of this year for shipment in September (a fairly normal procedure), you would not pay the price you thought you would. Why not? Because the steel industry announced a price increase on the first of August (or just before). It was 15 cents per hundred pounds. Or $3 a ton, which is $15,000 on a 5,000 order. Many major manufacturers use that much per month. Industry screamed, and rightly so."

Would you order a suit for $75 and pay $85 on delivery?

Welcome to the steel industry. That's exactly what steel buyers do—order at one price then pay another (higher)—when the goods are delivered.
Ridiculous?
Yes.

That's why we introduced P.T.O.—our Price-at-Time-of-Order purchase policy—last November.
We decided it was time for the steel industry to join the 20th century.
Wheeling P.T.O. guarantees your price-at-time-of-order for six months—no matter what.
Unless prices go down—then your

price goes down, too.
Sounds tailor-made, doesn't it?
Our new customers say it is.
Have you looked at Wheeling lately?

Wheeling

Here's copy on one of the now-famous ads which Wheeling produced to publicize this precedent-shattering policy. It does so so simply it's tremendously effective, in a way that everybody can grasp instantly. It says:

WOULD YOU ORDER A SUIT FOR $75 AND PAY $85 ON DELIVERY?

Welcome to the steel industry. That's exactly what steel buyers do—order at one price then pay another (higher) —when the goods are delivered.

Ridiculous?

Yes.

That's why we introduced P.T.O.—our Price-at-Time-of-Order purchase policy—last November.

We decided it was time for the steel industry to join the 20th Century.

*Wheeling P.T.O. guarantees your price-at-time-of-order
for six months—no matter what.
Unless prices go down—then your price goes down, too.*
Sounds tailor-made, doesn't it? Our customers say it is.

Have you looked at Wheeling lately?

That ad is well written, crisp, clean, well laid out and well
thought out—and very enticing. It solves a problem that has
plagued purchasing agents and other executives in manufacturing
ever since we've *had* manufacturing. According to Wheeling, "many
customers have applauded our P.T.O. efforts and continue to do so.
The president of the National Association of Purchasing agents has
made it a battle cry—and all of his speeches this year refer to it."

Two More Great Ads

Two other ads in this campaign are memorable; almost impossible to pass up and not read. Copy goes like this:

REMEMBER THE FIRST TIME THE
STEEL INDUSTRY RAISED PRICES . . .
AFTER YOU PLACED AN ORDER?

That policy, which has been penalizing steel buyers since
day one, was simply one of the bleaker facts of life—till
November 1965.
That's when we introduced our revolutionary Price-at-
Time-of-Order (P.T.O.) purchase policy.
*Wheeling P.T.O. guarantees your price-at-time-of-order
for six months—no matter what.
Unless prices go down—then your price goes down, too.*
Wouldn't you rather do business this new, 20th Century
method?
There has to be a first time for everything.
Our number is (304) 233-2200.

Have you looked at Wheeling lately?

A great ad, light, colloquial, and so human you can almost see
the copywriter chortling at his typewriter, certain he's done what
he set out to do—write a great ad. Bet the telephones at (304)
233-2200 got a real workout.

And, then, to prove that a good ad man is a salesman—and a psychologist with a keen insight into human nature—Wheeling then
ran the following copy:

WHY THOSE DIRTY

A lot of people had warm pet names for Wheeling when we introduced our revolutionary Price-at-Time-of-Order (P.T.O.) purchase policy last November.

Remember?

Wheeling guarantees your price-at-time-of-order for six months—no matter what. Unless prices go down—then your price goes down, too.

And a lot of new customers called us to say they liked the P.T.O. idea.

Many old customers called and said, "good show," and instantly signed up for new orders.

Why don't you call us . . . anything you like. But call us.

Have you looked at Wheeling lately?

Why those dirty

The *Wheeling campaign drew many "fans." Thousands wore "Hustle" buttons in their lapels, and thousands more wrote in to request reprints of the ads for their walls. Readership studies of the ads recorded high scores.*

Reaction to this campaign in the business community ranged from benign approbation to highly complimentary to downright admiring. Wheeling said, "Our sales organization was highly complimentary and continues to be." Well and good, for advertising should stimulate the sales force; it's a fringe benefit, but a necessary one.

"Customers wrote in and congratulated us," Wheeling said, "several hundred letters. We've sent out 3,000 to 4,000 reprints to hundreds of people who wanted 'Hustle' for their walls and to stimulate their sales organization or company people. We've handed out 50,000 'Hustle' buttons, are on the second 50,000, and have difficulty keeping them in stock.

"Right now we're just getting readership studies. To date: top readership awards in *Purchasing* and *Purchasing Week,* in *Design News,* and in *Engineering News-Record.* The New York Ad Club saluted us with a brand-name luncheon and testimonial on Wheeling's 'outstanding advertising and marketing program.'"

Wheeling's campaign was also selected as the industrial-advertising campaign of the year by *Industrial Marketing* magazine, and Wheeling's president, Mr. Morris, was chosen Adman-of-the-Year —only the third time a nonadvertising executive was so honored.

Mr. Avrigean, director of advertising, added: "For more substantial evidence of performance: We are averaging 200 inquiries a week, and have for many, many months, from all parts of the ad program (there are roughly a dozen product programs, plus an 'umbrella' program, Hustle). Since the first of the year, we have tabulated approximately 200 new customers—people who hadn't done business with us in the last two years. Their orders amount to $2 million. This is only for the steel company, not for the corrugating company, a division doing roughly ⅓ of our total volume. The guess at corrugating is at least 300 new customers, and another $2 million in sales.

"While advertising can't claim all of this $4 million in additional sales, the ad program, our new P.T.O. policy, and company publicity were the only things that changed in our overall marketing program prior to and during this period.

"Frankly, this program is simply more proof to me that when you run advertising that *says something* and direct it at audiences whose needs you understand, results are inevitable."

Mr. Avrigean summed it up nicely, except to add that Wheeling's success with this campaign is also due to precise and realistic advertising objectives—and to a great campaign!

Why Set Advertising Objectives?

Few quibble with the concept that advertising, if it's to accomplish its objectives, must have objectives. But equally few establish them. Less than 10 percent of all industrial companies have a formal, written marketing plan. It naturally follows that only this same small segment of industry has firm, well-defined marketing objectives, advertising objectives, and advertising strategy. The others don't. They follow, the 10 percent leads.

Most industrial companies are simply not advertising or marketing oriented. They attach such a small importance to the function that management is unwilling to allocate sufficient time to the planning function so that advertising can contribute its full potential.

Vague notions and good intentions suffice, and somehow they muddle through. Others emphasize catchy slogans, cute ideas, and intriguing themes for their campaigns. And because advertising is part art, part science, with many intangibles, occasionally one of these intuitive advertisers hits upon a real gem of an idea and makes it pay off big. Some gamblers do in Las Vegas, also—and just about as often.

Planning Gains Followers

On the whole, however, corporate management during the past few years has become increasingly enthusiastic about introducing the management-by-objective technique into just about every area of business. This applies to many areas where it was formerly thought impossible to realize benefits from application of this scientific-management philosophy, with advertising in particular singled out. As a consequence, advertising professionals in agencies and advertiser companies have been busily examining various methods of improving and measuring advertising effectiveness and efficiency. This is not difficult when advertising is developed and used to achieve specific objectives, nor is it difficult to determine advertising's contribution to the total marketing effort.

Merely having objectives acts as a creative catalyst, for they aid, rather than impede, those who actually create the advertising compaign and the individual advertisements, literature, sales aids, and other promotional material. Furthermore, the advertising manager who has firm objectives is able to evaluate the creative efforts and thinking behind them much more objectively, and to provide proper direction for those in this area more easily.

If ads are pretested one against the other, or if various slogans, themes, headlines, copy approaches, product features, and user benefits are pretested so that the most effective may be used, specific objectives make development of definitive survey questions and subsequent interpretation of results both easier and more valid.

Since objectives either suggest—or actually spell out on occasion —the audiences advertising must communicate with if it is to succeed, media selection is simplified. Merely having objectives does not result automatically in a detailed media analysis and schedule, of course. The final choice cannot be dictated by any plan or set of objectives regardless of how well thought out they are. Selection of media is one of the responsibilities of the advertising manager.

Another important advantage that accrues to the ad manager who has specific objectives is that it is possible to measure, accurately and precisely, the effectiveness of an advertising campaign. If you make a bench-mark study before a campaign breaks, you then have a record of your public's attitude toward, awareness of, and comprehension of your product(s) or service(s). When you're introducing a new product a study is obviously not necessary, but a study after the campaign has run and the product is launched reveals just what it—and you—accomplished. Many ad managers find such studies extremely helpful in selling management on advertising.

How to Set Advertising Objectives

No two companies are alike, nor are their problems and aspirations. Procedures for setting advertising objectives are much the same from one company to another, or from industry to industry, for that matter. Steps usually taken are:

1. Gathering information.

2. Developing tentative objectives.

3. Expressing the objectives.

4. Gaining management approval of objectives.

5. Distributing the approved objectives to proper people within the company and in the advertising agency.

In some highly organized companies the mere setting of objectives has become an objective in itself, complete with elaborate ceremonies and much hue and cry, somewhat akin to fertility rites at the time of a full moon in a pagan society.

Some companies have detailed checklists with a statement pertaining to every conceivable eventuality. They tend to overemphasize the forest and obscure the individual trees. They make too much out of the basic procedure of pairing marketing and advertising objectives, and the statement of how they will be attained. Even some advertising managers have been known to devote their full time and energies to establishing meaningful objectives, so much so that they never got around to doing much advertising.

Let's take each step individually.

Gathering Information

The ad manager bases his decision and builds his programs on a foundation of facts. Getting the facts and putting them together into a logical, usable format takes a bit of doing as a rule. That's because the advertising manager requires far more information than anybody in his company—even the marketing director—realizes. Much of it is available from marketing management, of course, but must be dug up by the advertising manager. Information essential to setting advertising objectives includes:

1. Market potential, in dollars. Your company's share of this market. Distribution pattern. Product features. User benefits. Competitive information. Analysis of previous advertising your company has done, and *its* objectives.

2. Identification of your prospects. Profile of prospect companies. Identification of buying influences by function, title, and name. Where these prospect companies are located, by state, county, and city. What businesses they are in. Their present attitude toward your company. Their present attitude toward, or opinion of, your product. Their need for your product. Why do these prospects buy —or not buy—your product? What advertising can logically be expected to do to influence them to buy from you, if they are not now doing so?

3. Your company's marketing objectives. If your company has no written marketing plan, help write one, or write one for marketing management's approval; lack of marketing objectives makes setting of realistic advertising objectives virtually impossible.

An advertising manager should never try to second-guess product managers and establish their marketing objectives for them. Most product managers—frequently found wearing the title of marketing manager—are unable to set marketing objectives. These individuals are so technically oriented, knowing as they do a complex line of equipment inside-out, that they are die-hard adherents of eyeball-to-eyeball selling. Setting marketing objectives is outside their experience, despite their being charged with responsibility for all marketing activities for their product in specified markets. They neither know nor understand advertising, nor do they believe, deep down, that it is an effective tool for them.

These unsophisticated product managers *are* capable of setting their marketing objectives—*if skillfully led by the advertising manager*. Ask leading questions and you'll probably get answers which will enable you to write explicit marketing objectives *for approval by the director of marketing, the sales manager, or other final-word executive.* Do *not* assume his responsibility in this matter, for to do so puts you in the untenable position of establishing your legitimate advertising objectives based on your illegitimate marketing objectives. Often the director of marketing will be an engineer or other technical man, and he, too, must be led.

4. Full information on the balance of the marketing mix—plans for the field force. Additions to the field force. Contemplated changes in distribution. Additions to the distribution setup. Any changes in price structure or discount arrangements.

Developing Tentative Objectives

With the required background information on hand, sort it out in your mind, then put it down on paper so it's easily referred to. The ad manager of a major manufacturer organized his information in this way:

(INTEROFFICE MEMO FORM)

Date April 21, 19—

TO: J. Smith

SUBJECT: Metalworking-market marketing objectives

At a meeting on April 19, you stated your marketing objectives and a suggested communications needs for the metalworking market for our next fiscal year.

The sequence of your comments has been rearranged so that all marketing-areas' marketing objectives are organized in the same manner. This is for the convenience of management, which reviews all of the marketing areas' objectives collectively and individually.

1. Existing situation

A. *Market*

The total market in metalworking for our Widget line is $260 million; our present share of this market is $56 million.

Industries which constitute our market include, but are not limited to, the following:

Aerospace	Aircraft
Automotive	Ordnance
Farm equipment	Mechanical power transmission
Machine tools	Electrical equipment

Products sold into the metalworking market are as follows:

1. Standard Widgets	$14,000,000
2. Modified Widgets	4,000,000
3. Special Widgets	7,000,000

4. Custom-built Widgets 6,000,000

5. Automated Widget lines 12,000,000

6. Complete Widget systems 11,000,000

7. New products 2,000,000

We are the leader in automated Widget lines and in the controls for them. This market is expanding at the rate of 57 percent a year.

A broad base in metalworking uses our Standard Widgets; this product's sales volume grows almost in step with the economy as a whole.

The total market for Modified Widgets is approximately $90 million; we have a bit less than a $4 million share. This is a fertile field for us.

The market for Special Widgets is probably the widest of all markets we serve. There is hardly a metalworking company in the country that does not have or could not use a Special Widget. Note that when we sell a Special Widget that considerable auxiliary equipment is always sold with it.

B. *Products*

The single item of greatest sales potential is the new Automatic-Automated Widget, to be ready for introduction late this fiscal year.

C. *Buying influences*

A discussion of buying influences in the metalworking market, as applied to our complete line of Widgets, brought out the belief that it is most frequently a group activity.

Purchasing and management-level people are seldom determining factors, except in unique circumstances. These people are involved only in a formal sense; in one case it is preparation of the purchase order, in the other it is the approval of an expenditure. The determining group is composed of process engineers, the plant operations group, and product-development engineers. These titles may vary from plant to plant and include others such as factory superintendent or research engineer.

2. Problems

Since we previously promoted our Numerical Controlled Widget heavily (Machine Tool Show, space advertising) and since have withdrawn further promotion, some uncertainty exists in our field sales organization regarding this unit.

To overcome our problems of product performance and high cost of sales, it is anticipated that engineering will make a number of modifications.

3. Opportunities

Automation is the basis of future growth in the metalworking market.

Use of automation, and particularly numerically controlled equipment such as we manufacture, is growing at a combined rate of almost 70 percent a year. With our reputation for Automated Widgets that really work, we are in a very favorable competitive position.

4. Marketing objectives

To create a market for our Automatic-Automated Widget and sell $2 million worth this fiscal year.

To achieve 10 percent more sales in Modified Widgets.

To double our share of the market for Complete Widget Lines, from $12 million to $24 million.

5. Marketing strategy

Reactivate the technical sales-training courses used so effectively several years ago. Almost one-third of our present field sales force lacks technical competence in selling Automatic-Automated Widgets.

Automation will have to be sold by personal contact for a long time. Sales of automated equipment result in a number of additional sales of supplementary equipment; in fact, sales of some of our Widget controls are directly dependent upon sales of automated equipment.

Promote our unique technical ability to solve customer problems connected with use of Standard Widgets. Rekindle the enthusiasm of the field sales force, as far as the Numerical Controlled Widget is concerned.

6. Communications needs you requested

There is no need, you feel, to change our present theme of being able to provide the *one* right Widget to solve customers' production problems. You feel this should be retained, but that we should also emphasize the excellent reliability of all of our Widgets.

Awareness and comprehension of our products, and of our technical capabilities to solve customers' problems are your foremost communications requirement.

Develop a color-sound 16mm. movie on automation, featuring the Complete Widget Line installed at Doaks Manufacturing Company, Inc. The film would be used by all of our field sales force with their present projection equipment.

7. Communication-strategy concept

Continue to produce current technical sales literature for field distribution.

Continue space advertising in key media.

Feature more case-history material.

Space advertising to create awareness of the new Automatic-Automated Widget.

Develop a new theme for trade shows.

Exhibit at the national trade shows in which we participated last year; also consider feasibility of exhibiting in local or regional shows.

8. Sales forecasts

>Our share of the Widget market will increase to $68 million.

>Sales in the automated area alone will increase to $19 million.

>Automatic-Automated Widgets to be introduced later this year will account for $2 million.

>/s/ Advertising Manager

This data is in the "raw" state, for it has yet to be approved by management. Its accumulation and orderly arrangement make it possible for the ad manager to plan his program with little waste time and motion, particularly if he has responsibility for more than one market, handled by more than one market manager or product manager. Compiled thus, he can compare apples with apples, rather than unlike items.

You cannot finalize advertising objectives while working with such raw data. You can, however, make a machine copy of this memo, and make marginal notes for your future guidance in establishing your department's objectives.

For example, under Section 4, we find an objective, "To create a market for our Automatic-Automated Widget and sell $2 million this fiscal year." Now, your own market knowledge tells you that the automotive market—specifically the Big Three automobile manufacturers—are the prime market for this production tool. Knowing your customers, and that SIC 3711 is the major group they're in, you check the Standard Industrial Classification Manual for other classifications where this product could logically be used effectively. Subclassification 3714, Motor Vehicle Parts and Accessories, is also a likely market.

Make a marginal note—perhaps in red, or whatever memory-jogging device appeals to you most—that to achieve this marketing objective, your advertising objective is *to create awareness of, comprehension of, acceptance of, and demand for, this new product.* It's early to do this, but one thought usually triggers another, so let your mind run on, making note after note. For example, to reach an audience such as this your past experience tells you, you will want to evaluate and consider certain media. Make this note, too, using only publication names, such as these: *Automotive Industries, Iron Age, Production, American Machinist* and *Factory.* And, since the market is small in terms of the numbers of smokestacks you want to reach, make the notation, direct mail; then product publicity, sales literature, technical literature. These are the how-tos, how you will attain your objective, the tools you will use to communicate with those prospects who represent that $2 million.

Farther down the list of marketing objectives is, "To double our share of the market for Complete Widget Lines from $12 million to $24 million." This is an auspicious objective, but if management feels it is attainable, it is up to you to provide the support program which makes it possible. Again, analyze the market; delve into this with the product and marketing people in charge of Complete Widget Lines. Find out where equipment of this type is sold by examining your list of customers and sales; if the firms in these lines of business have been buying this equipment from you, other firms in similar lines of endeavor are prime suspects to buy more. Pick them out by SIC. Analyze media which will reach the key buying influences. Determine how many prospect firms you have to hit if a rifle approach with direct mail, buttressed by a broad and expanded program of space advertising, is to have sufficient impact to do the job. Ask if inquiries are wanted, and find out whether they will be properly followed by the sales force. See if repeat sales to those who have already purchased Complete Widget Lines are likely. If so, target in with direct mail.

Make your marginal notes on this basis, then determine just what communications functions advertising can perform more effectively, more efficiently, and at lower cost than any other activity. Make no attempt to assign to advertising those tasks that it cannot handle. What advertising can—and cannot—do has been summed up by Du Pont as follows:

Advertising *can* do these things:

—Introduce a new product.

—Give information.

—Interest prospects.

—Develop inquiries.

—Create demand.

—Help open new markets.

—Stimulate the trade—agents, distributors, jobbers, jobber salesmen, retailers, and retail salesmen.

—Test sales techniques.

—Test its own various types of appeals.

—Help determine buyer preference.

—Help make a product competitive in the market.

—Support sales programs.

—Open the door to salesmen.

—Reach pin-pointed markets at pennies per reader or listener.

—Reach mass markets at pennies per prospect.

—Reduce selling expense.

—Establish and maintain prestige of company or product or both.

—Build customer relations.

—Speed product acceptance.

Advertising can *not* do these things:

—Sell a bad product—twice.

—Sell an overpriced or otherwise noncompetitive product.

—Sell a poorly distributed product.

—Sell a seasonal product out of season.

—Sell products to persons having no use for them.

—Work overnight.

—Do the selling job alone.

Writing the Advertising Objectives

When writing your advertising objectives, always bear in mind that an unstated objective is to create a frame of mind in the reader of your ads. To do this, write with the *prospect's* viewpoint and desires in mind; determine just what impression you wish to convey to him, and what you want him to think after reading your message; how he should react if you make a request for action. This is another way of saying you'll come out ahead if you are "you-oriented" rather than "me-oriented."

Be specific. If you want to develop a flow of inquiries, say so—and say exactly how many. A definite correlation exists between the number of inquiries advertising produces and the sales volume of many industrial products. This relationship is so constant that it can be expressed as a percentage with perfectly acceptable accuracy. So, if the sale of one piece of equipment results from every 350 inquiries—and this figure is a valid one for many industries—a legitimate advertising objective is to produce as many *well-qualified* inquiries per ad as possible. There are many ways to assure a continuing high level of inquiries, and they will be covered later.

Another advertising objective that is always present but unstated is to produce a positive mental response to the advertising message. This can, and usually does, take the form of a favorable impression of your product and your company.

Objectives necessarily have to be written to comply with any restrictions placed upon advertising by management. For example, if management selects media—and this occurs with distressing frequency, and almost invariably is based primarily upon "political" considerations—then advertising objectives must be written to reflect this. Too, geographic patterns enter into planning at this time because there may well be areas where your company is poorly represented, or where there is so little potential that no effort has ever been made to exploit possibilities of that territory. If this situation exists, consider the advisability of using regional editions of media; this assures satisfactory coverage of the market where adequate sales coverage exists, yet does not waste money trying to reach steel mills in northern Montana.

The Budget Determines

The size of the advertising appropriation naturally influences establishment of and writing of advertising objectives. If the wherewithal isn't there, the ad manager will be forced to settle for less ambitious objectives. As a matter of good practice, make it firm policy always to develop objectives and work out a sound advertising program *before* working up a budget and submitting it to management for approval. Your chances of having a program approved are infinitely better than those of having a budget approved.

Phrasing of advertising objectives is something like writing the Great American Novel—you can't do it carefully enough to please everybody without some revision. Here, as in the phrasing of the marketing plan, everybody must agree with the objectives and how they are stated.

Questions you will want to consider are: Is each objective stated so that each and every person concerned understands it clearly? Is it so stated that everybody agrees with it? Does the agency understand and agree with it? Is enough information given so there will be no possibility of misinterpretation by those who will actually create the advertising and collateral material?

To get meaningful answers to these and other questions, common practice in many companies is for the ad manager to reproduce his advertising objectives and circulate copies to pertinent personnel —the director of marketing, sales manager, marketing managers, product managers and others within the company; also to the account executive, account supervisor, creative director, and art director at the agency. Then, if no question arises, it is safe to assume the objectives are solid and well stated and that they will act as firm direction in all of the subsequent steps.

A trap lurks, though, and it should be avoided like the plague. All too frequently objectives are established whose prime virtues are plausibility and the ease with which the program designed to achieve them may be measured. Questions, serious ones, have been raised as to the advisability of using so extensively the two criteria most frequently used—awareness and comprehension. Many advertising practitioners are firmly convinced that neither objective in itself, nor, for that matter, the two together, are adequate for products which have previously been advertised and sold. When it comes to new products, it's quite a different story, of course, for creation of awareness and comprehension are two advertising strong-points.

Gaining Management Approval

Once your objectives are well stated and everybody's questions have been answered and changes they suggested have been incorporated, the next step is to do any rewriting required and get them approved by management. Approval of advertising objectives by top management, usually the director of marketing and frequently the president, *before* submission of a formal advertising program greatly eases the birth pangs attending the appearance of the completed program.

To present the objectives for approval, it usually works best to write a short, explanatory memo that (1) relates advertising objectives to marketing objectives, as given in the marketing plan, (2) tells how these objectives fit in with those established for the sales force, and (3) spells out in detail how the advertising objectives mesh with those for other product lines, other markets, or other divisions of the company.

When your objectives are finally approved, perhaps with slight modifications by marketing management, the time has then come to prepare the complete advertising program. Your chances of having it accepted intact are immeasurably improved. The risk of having it totally rejected has been reduced almost to the vanishing point. If the program does meet with some disapproval by top management, it usually is not because of any basic disagreement with the program or the thinking that went into it, but with the cost. What must be done then is to rephrase some objectives, setting goals which may be attained with a reduced investment, then eliminating portions of the program until it falls in line with the appropriation which management will accept.

Distributing the Finalized Objectives

Final step in the objectives process is to make copies of the approved objectives and distribute them to those who received the tentative ones. To prevent confusion, state in the covering memo that these are final, that those previously received are to be destroyed.

All concerned are now working toward the same end. Misunderstandings, misinterpretations, and misgivings about directions are eliminated. There's a much better chance of achieving the objectives once they're formal and on paper, and the cost of doing so will be less than under any kind of a hit-or-miss system.

Marketing at Pitney-Bowes

At Pitney-Bowes, originator of the ubiquitous postage meter, a leading manufacturer of machines which automate the mailing of huge volumes of letters and packages, and of sophisticated business machines, the entire marketing operation is planned to the *nth* degree. Nothing is left to chance.

The marketing plan is written in the customary manner, with consideration given to the current situation, competition, new-product introductions, opportunities, anticipated income by product line, gross sales, profitability desired, and the promotional program. Advertising investment is determined by allocation of a predetermined percentage of anticipated sales. Five entire pages of the marketing plan are devoted to problems and opportunities, with firm objectives for each product line.

Sales Matched to SIC Classification

P-B identifies their market through use of a two-digit SIC breakdown of sales; this is watched closely to detect any deviation from traditional patterns. Sales are matched to industry classification. In turn, the reader profiles of various media under consideration are matched to the sales pattern. For the most part key buying influences are determined by querying the field sales force, as well as by field trips by members of the advertising department.

One of Pitney-Bowes' striking four-color ads is shown nearby. It appeared in *U.S. News & World Report,* which was selected to reach top management executives. The striking visual compares and compares fast—it is immediately obvious that using Pitney-Bowes' postage meters saves time, saves money, eliminates stamp-stocking, and results in a much more businesslike package. Copy reads:

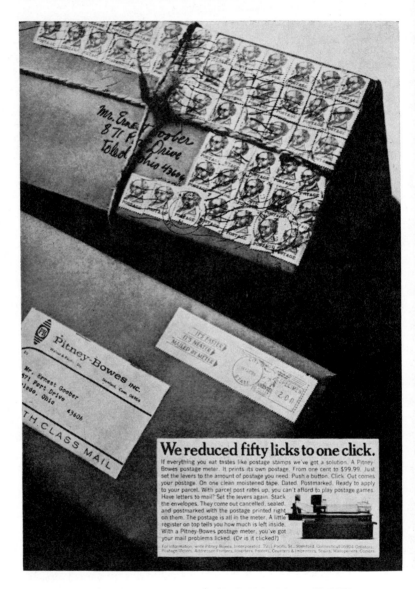

WE REDUCED FIFTY LICKS TO ONE CLICK.

If everything you eat tastes like postage stamps we've got a solution. A Pitney-Bowes postage meter. It prints its own postage. From one cent to $99.99. Just set the levers to the amount of postage you need. Push a button. Click. Out comes your postage. On one clean moistened tape. Dated. Postmarked. Ready to apply to your parcel. With parcel-post rates up, you can't afford to play postage games. Have letters to mail? Set the levers again. Stack the envelopes. They come out canceled, sealed, and postmarked with the postage printed right on them. The postage is all in the meter. A little register on top tells you how much is left inside. With a Pitney-Bowes postage meter, you've got your mail problems licked. (Or is it clicked?)

Interesting, informative, and persuasive—and it reflects the corporate objective of enhancing Pitney-Bowes' position of leadership in metered mail, and the communications objective of creating awareness of and comprehension of the benefits of metered mail. It's easy to see why Pitney-Bowes leads its industry.

Following is a brief condensation of one portion of the Pitney-Bowes marketing plan, that dealing with corporate and communications objectives. The original document contains specific figures, dates, means of attaining objectives and other hard information of a competitive nature.

STATEMENT OF OBJECTIVES

I. *Corporate Objectives:*

Maintain and enhance Pitney-Bowes' position of leadership, as *the* creator and major producer of postage-meter mailing systems. And, in so doing, build an appreciation of, and a desire for, Pitney-Bowes as the source for equipment for the efficient, businesslike handling of mail and other paper.

To broaden Pitney-Bowes' reputation *as a major producer* of office equipment.

Specifically to create a favorable awareness of P-B equipment for:

  a. Mechanical addressing.
  b. Electrostatic copying.
  c. Counting and imprinting.
  d. Folding and inserting.
  e. Weighing mails and parcels.
  f. Related accessories, furniture, attachments, etc.

To enhance Pitney-Bowes' reputation for quality and good service.

To promote Pitney-Bowes' salesmen's morale and involvement with the company as a whole.

To increase Pitney-Bowes' dollar sales over the previous year.

II. *Communications Objectives:*

Enhance the call efficiency of salesmen, thus reducing the cost of selling, and create a favorable climate for the sale.

Create awareness of and comprehension of the major benefits of metered mail, thereby stimulating an awareness of Pitney-Bowes, the originator of metered mail, as an expert source of equipment for office efficiency.

Continue the promotion of the small office market as the best means to develop a broader mass market.

Help develop an interest in and awareness of the relationship of combinations of Pitney-Bowes' equipment among P-B salesmen, their customers, and prospects.

Develop an awareness of and understanding of P-B copiers, SES, Tickometers, folders, and inserters among existing customers.

Maintain Pitney-Bowes' position of dominance in the sale and rental of postage-meter mailing machines.

Improve Pitney-Bowes' position against competition in nonmeter lines such as folders, inserters, scales, and addresser-printers.

Develop inquiries for the sales force.

Simplifying the Planning Process

Setting objectives takes time and it requires thinking. There isn't enough time in the day for most of us to get the administrative work load done right—and thinking is hard work.

The planning job is greatly simplified and handled in less time if it's well organized. That means standardization achieved through well-planned forms which make gathering adequate information easier, and which preclude overlooking important data. Among the best and most complete are those used by Worthington Corporation, one of the leading producers of equipment used for the control and handling of liquids and gases, and for the conversion of energy to useful work. Worthington products include air conditioning, refrigeration equipment, pumps, compressors, locomotives, turbines, valves, controls, motors, and many other industrial items.

Domestic operations include nine divisions and two subsidiaries, organized within five separate groups. Each has a high degree of autonomy and has its own marketing (or sales) personnel. However, a centralized advertising department has responsibility for most of Worthington's advertising and sales-promotion requirements. Headed by the advertising manager, there are account managers for each of the divisions, as well as an account manager for export operations. The account managers must develop and implement promotional plans for all advertising and sales-promotion activities for the product groups which are assigned to them.

The thoroughness with which Worthington plans its promotion programs is shown in the reproductions of various planning forms.

On the first page, or identification sheet of the planning form, space is provided to state either the product line or market area, together with the time period to which the plan applies, and the division or company. Approval of the plan is indicated by the signatures of the division manager and of the advertising and sales-promotion manager; only when both have signed is the plan implemented.

Page 2 of the plan determines immediately whether or not a written marketing plan has been prepared for the product line or market. If not, customer need for this product is stated. Sales goals for the current year, the program year, and two years hence are given, as is a breakdown of sales by industry. Worthington's sales to each of the five industries is estimated, as is the share of this particular market which Worthington can logically expect to secure. Finally, profitability—good, fair, or poor—is stated, again by industry. This facilitates management decision as to the advisability of investing in the promotional plan. The last item is a situation analysis which is merely a recap of the competitive situation.

Page 3 includes in section (b) the account manager's estimate of prospects for the product or market. Additionally, a summary of the advertising and sales promotion of major competitors is given; this includes the type of promotion on which they rely, the theme of their program, and a close estimate of the dollar expenditure which each makes, broken down by business press (including management and news publications).

Page 4 makes it easy—and necessary—for the account manager to list product and service features vital in planning an effective promotion. These are broken down as exclusive and nonexclusive, and the *customer benefits* for each are given. This information is required to develop a copy platform, discussed later.

Plan pages 5 and 6 list "inhibitors" which must be overcome in order to achieve set objectives and sales goals. These inhibitors are the result of experience. Frank answers are a tremendous help in developing a promotional program to overcome hurdles which must be eliminated.

The plan's page 7 defines programs in other Worthington divisions which might influence this specific plan. Comments of the advertising and sales promotion department are summarized, also.

Data on page 8 makes it possible to pinpoint specific areas which need shoring up, and provides a guide to management in allocation of effort and investment in personal selling by salesmen, and by impersonal selling—by advertising and promotion.

Page 9 states both long-range (3 years) marketing goals, and short-range goals (for the program year). Worthington defines a marketing goal as "the total business effect of all efforts to maintain or improve market penetration, reputation, competitive position, sales efficiency, or marketplace profit." The company also says that "specific sales volume figures are not the marketing goal—they are the result of it."

Also stated here are specific sales-promotion objectives which may be the same as short-range marketing goals; if so, this is noted. Final information is required at stages in the sales-promotion program, complete with target dates and a notation as to the individual(s) responsible.

Page 10 lists critically important information—advertising objectives, with emphasis on *auditable* objectives; strategy, with a rationale of how objectives are to be achieved; other support required, with explanation; and, auditing steps, so that it can be determined whether or not objectives were achieved. Worthington's advertising department has a firm policy to audit the degree of achievement wherever this is possible. This usually falls to the account manager.

Page 11 gives a budget breakdown for each plan, separated by fixed budget and variable budget items.

Page 12 summarizes the budget for each plan, and includes various account numbers, budget items, and a monthly and total annual budget figure.

If a number of campaigns are to be run in the same year for different product lines, or to different markets, Worthington prepares a separate plan for each. Forms are usually updated each year, or oftener if changing market conditions warrant.

Worthington management feels, and correctly so, that the importance of gathering and recording basic marketing information cannot be overstressed. The more that is known about the product, the competition, and the market, the easier it is to develop an effective plan and pinpoint communications needs—and fill them with advertising objectives that contribute toward achievement of marketing objectives.

Worthington's planning forms may be somewhat more detailed than the advertising manager of a smaller company needs, but they can readily be altered and adapted to almost any company, for the basic information they record is needed by *all* ad managers.

G-3545
Page 1 of 12

Advertising and Sales Promotion Plan

Product/Market Program _____

Period Covered _____

Division or Company _____

Approved _____ Date _____
(Division Mgr.)

By _____ Date _____
(A&SP)

G-3545
Page 2 of 12

I. Does a product/market plan exist for this product(s)?

Yes _____   No _____

(If "No," complete the remainder of I)
(If "Yes," move on to II)

Customer Need for this Product: _____

_____

_____

_____

_____

_____

_____

_____

_____

_____

SALES GOALS:

Current year:

Program year:

Two years hence:

INDUSTRIES	Estimated % of Total Product Purchased by This Industry	% of Worthington Sales of This Product to This Industry	Estimated Worthington % of Available	Profitability (Good, Fair or Poor)
1.				
2.				
3.				
4.				
5.				

II. a) *Situation Analysis:* Copy from Marketing Plan Facts Section, adding supplementary A&SP comments and analysis.

b) *General Outlook:* Extract from Marketing Plan; supplement as necessary for A&SP purposes.

III. *Competition Advertising:* List below the basic type of program and promotion theme reflected in each competitor's programming. Also, give closest estimate of current annual business paper (including Management and News publications) investment for products such as those covered by this plan. Use same listing as included in marketing plan.

Competitor A _____

_____

_____

Competitor B _____

_____

_____

Competitor C _____

_____

_____

Competitor D _____

_____

_____

Competitor E _____

_____

_____

_____

_____

G-3545

Page 4 of 12

IV. *Product and Service Features:* (Only key points important to promotion programming)

Exclusive:	Customer benefits:
1.	
2.	
3.	
4.	
5.	
6.	
7.	

Nonexclusive:	Customer benefits:
1.	
2.	
3.	
4.	
5.	
6.	
7.	

G-3545
Page 5 of 12

8. What "inhibitors" in this product/market area are at work which must be overcome?

INHIBITORS	Applicable to our area? Yes or No	Explain specific plans to improve in this area
a. Absence of customer-oriented planning		
b. Inadequate marketing objectives		
c. Internal communication failure (Sales, Engineering, Headquarters)		
d. Inadequate distribution		
e. Lack of innovations (product or packaging)		
f. Budget deficiencies in communications		
g. Failure to dominate in external communications media employed		
h. Insufficient knowledge of customer motivation		
i. Too generic an advertising claim or appeal		
j. Inadequate picture of market and customer opinion		
k. Failure to merchandise or "follow-through"		
l. Too much concern with price		

G-3545
Page 6 of 12

INHIBITORS	Applicable to our area? Yes or No	Explain specific plans to improve in this area
m. Poor division communications to salesmen/distributors		
n. Giving advertising jobs it cannot do		
o. Placing management responsibility for communications too high (or low) in organization		
p. Absence of built-in measuring systems in plans and programs		
q. Failure to define and manage the industry/product image		
r. Imbalance between communications . . . space, literature, etc.		
s. Copying competition in communications activities		
t. Failure to update or train marketing organization		
u. Failure to build extra benefits or quality image of product		
v. Internal policy gets in the way of promotion		
w. Inadequate knowledge of competitive strengths		
x. Inadequate sales tools		

G-3545
Page 7 of 12

VI. Multidivision or Market Programs that might influence this area of promotion activity:

VII. Pertinent A&SP Research - Summary:

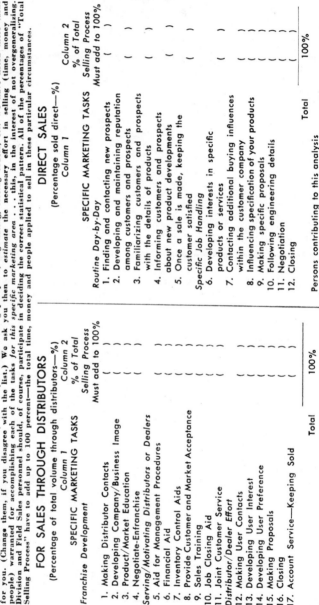

Fill Out This Page to Illustrate Areas of Greatest Promotion Need and Opportunity

VIII. We view *total selling* as the use of personal communications (salesmen) plus mechanized communications (promotion). Selling (or quota achievement) is also conceived as a *series of tasks* which are somehow accomplished in the field. These only involve confirming that previous purchases were satisfactory—or may include finding prospects, negotiating, closing orders, etc. We have listed these tasks for you. (Change them, if you disagree with the list.) We ask you then to *estimate* the necessary effort in selling (time, money and people) warranted for accomplishing each of the tasks *for this specific marketing area* . . . this, in the interest of not overgeneralizing. Division and Field Sales personnel should, of course, participate in deciding the correct statistical pattern. All of the percentages of "Total Selling Process" have to add up to 100 percent—the total time, money and people applied to sell in these particular circumstances.

FOR SALES THROUGH DISTRIBUTORS

(Percentage of total volume through distributors—%)

SPECIFIC MARKETING TASKS	Column 1	Column 2 % of Total Selling Process Must add to 100%
Franchise Development		
1. Making Distributor Contacts		( )
2. Developing Company/Business Image		( )
3. Product/Market Education		( )
4. Negotiate-Enfranchise		( )
Serving/Motivating Distributors or Dealers		
5. Aid for Management Procedures		( )
6. Financial Aid		( )
7. Inventory Control Aids		( )
8. Provide Customer and Market Acceptance		( )
9. Sales Training		( )
10. Job Closing Aid		( )
11. Joint Customer Service		( )
Distributor/Dealer Effort		
12. Making User Contacts		( )
13. Developing User Interest		( )
14. Developing User Preference		( )
15. Making Proposals		( )
16. Closing		( )
17. Account Service—Keeping Sold		( )
Total		100%

DIRECT SALES

(Percentage sold direct—%)

SPECIFIC MARKETING TASKS	Column 1	Column 2 % of Total Selling Process Must add to 100%
Routine Day-by-Day		
1. Finding and contacting new prospects		( )
2. Developing and maintaining reputation among customers and prospects		( )
3. Familiarizing customers and prospects with the details of products		( )
4. Informing customers and prospects about new product developments		( )
5. Once a sale is made, keeping the customer satisfied		( )
Specific Job Handling		
6. Developing interests in specific products or services		( )
7. Contacting additional buying influences within the customer company		( )
8. Influencing specification of your products		( )
9. Making specific proposals		( )
10. Following engineering details		( )
11. Negotiation		( )
12. Closing		( )
Total		100%

Persons contributing to this analysis _____

Division _____ Field Sales _____

IX. *Marketing Goals:* (refer to Product Marketing Plan)

A marketing goal is the *total* business effect of all efforts to maintain or improve market penetration, reputation, competitive position, sales efficiency or marketplace profit. (Specific sales volume figures are not the marketing goal —they are the result of it.)

Long Range: (3 years)

Short Range: (program year)

X. *Sales Promotion Objectives:* (If same as short-range marketing goals, write "same." If "none," so indicate.)

*Sales promotion is the coordinated use of several marketing functions to achieve a relatively short-range result. The effort may be either internal or external . . . and should be noted in the Product Action Plan.

XI. Sales Promotion Program (from Action Plan)

STEPS	DATE	RESPONSIBLE

G-3545
Page 10 of 12

XII. *Advertising Objectives:* State specific and *auditable communications objectives as they relate to previously stated sales promotion program—State the reasoning that led you to decide on these objectives.*

_____

_____

_____

_____

_____

_____

*Who - What - How Much?

XIII. *Strategy:* What is the basic idea behind your proposed communications action, to achieve objectives?

XIV. *Any other support needed* to make this program work? Is it budgeted or agreed?

XV. *Auditing Steps* (what, when, by whom, for how much?)

G-3545
Page 11 of 12

Plan of Action and Budget

Fixed Budget: (Those items which must be produced regardless of promotion programming)

ITEMS	Required by	Cost

Total _____(A)

Variable Budget: Costs directly related to achievement of Promotion Objective)

ITEMS	Required by	Cost

Total _____(B)

Total Direct Cost (A) and (B) _____

Multidivisional Costs _____

Administrative Cost _____

Total A&SP Cost _____

G-3545
Page 12 of 12

Advertising and Sales Promotion Department
Direct Portion Account 49

Promotion Program for Period Covering _____

No.	EXPENSE	Total Monthly Budget	Total Annual Budget
75	Space		
76	Production		
77	Telephone Directory		
78	Bulletin Production Sales Promotion Material		
79	Direct Mail Printing		
80	External House Organs Incl. Postage		
81	Visual and Audio Aids		
82	Postage, Boxing—Shipping Literature Requested		
83	Nonco-op—Distributor Aids and Services		
84	Co-op—Distributor Aids and Services		
85	Photographs—Originals and Prints		
86	Exhibits and Displays		
87	Signs and Maintenance		
88	News Publicity—(Exclusive Photos)		
90	Research Incl. Postage		
91	Calendar—Special Corp. Promotion Projects		
92	Staff Projects		
93	Agency Fees and Supplies		
94	Charged to Other Departments		
	TOTAL		

Chapter 5

COPY—AS A CONCEPT

YOUR prospects are almost as familiar as your next-door neighbor now that you've identified, located, analyzed, and profiled them. You know them, how they think, how they buy, and why they do what they do.

Well and good, because the time has come to stop hiding your light under a bushel. Now's the time to think about saying something to them—something that, hopefully, will exert a positive influence on their future actions as far as your product or service is concerned.

At this time you get together with your advertising agency account executive and discuss copy. Chances are, if the agency is right for you, the agency will do the actual writing. Many industrial ad managers write their own ads however—some from preference, others because of fiendish product complexity, and some only on an emergency basis when the account executive-copywriter is ill, or handling another job. To be able to understand and evaluate and pass judgment on copy, you should have some background information on it, the words in print that your prospects will read. Copy isn't to be considered lightly.

"To think about saying something" isn't a mere phrase, because copy is more than mere words on paper. Copy, good copy, is a concept. It is an abstraction—an idea. The idea may be yours, the sales manager's, or the agency's. That's of little consequence. What is important is to realize that it is a one-of-a-kind inspiration which was conceived to solve a specific communication problem, to communicate one particular piece of intelligence about one certain product to one audience that is meaningful to you, at a time of your choosing.

"Hopefully" because there's more than a kernel of truth in the remark made by Charles F. Adams, executive vice-president of MacManus, John & Adams advertising agency, when he said, "When you sit down to create an ad, the odds are one to three that you will do more damage than good."

Saying something constructive about your product to your prospects doesn't seem hard to do. It should be the simplest thing in the world. After all, you are intimately acquainted with your product, your market, and the buying influences to whom your message is directed. And all of us talk, most of us too much. We have conversations constantly with those around us in business, in our social lives, and with our families. We use words, familiar tools whose use comes easily to us. If there's any one characteristic which can be attributed to every advertising man, it is that he is articulate. Ad men have a unique understanding of, appreciation of, and inordinate fondness for words that are encountered in no other segment of the business world.

Since ad men are such expert word mechanics, it should logically follow that advertising copy (so named almost a hundred years ago by some long-forgotten typesetter to whom every collection of words was "copy") should almost write itself. After all, it's necessary only to shut the door to bar distractions, warm up the typewriter, and whip out an ad destined to become a classic that's oh'd and ah'd over by future generations of advertising neophytes.

Talent Comes From Within

Seldom is it that simple, however. Neither Clio nor Erato—nor any other mythical goddess charged with inspiring budding poets, copywriters, and ad managers—can be depended upon to deliver a massive dose of inspiration on schedule just so you can achieve objectives and meet closing dates. The ability to produce good advertising, sales literature, good sales letters, and a house organ that's a pleasure to read—or any other communication which customarily falls into the advertising manager's bailiwick—comes from within the individual. He must draw upon his own resources.

It is usually understood that there are six essential attributes the successful practitioner of industrial advertising should possess, be he copywriter, ad manager, or a combination of the two as is often found. These are:

1. *Competitive instinct*

The advertising manager-copywriter (or copywriter-advertising manager) must delight in being a keen competitor. He realizes instinctively that he is personally in direct competition with his counterpart in a competitor company, and he acts accordingly. He knows that it is mandatory that he outperform and outproduce this unknown individual to make his company's advertising more effective than that turned out by the competition. He must relish being a key element in the marketing arm of his company and find a large amount of inner satisfaction in helping his company achieve at the expense of the competition. Somebody is going to get a larger share of available business than the others, and the topflight ad man has a burning desire for it to be his company.

2. *Imagination*

The ad manager must be somewhat of a paradox; he has to be practical and level headed, but he must also be imaginative. He should be a source for ideas. He should innovate, experiment, and, as Webster says, "form mental synthesis of new ideas from elements experienced separately." Some decry imagination in advertising when, in truth, imagination liberally used and well seasoned with the salt of practicality results in outstanding advertising that contributes immeasurably to a higher level of economic activity.

3. *Willingness and ability to think*

On the surface, naming this attribute seems trite. But thinking, *really thinking,* requires more effort than many people are willing to exert. Even the good minds subconsciously flinch at the prospect of having to think through a knotty problem, and they go through intricate and tortuous nonproductive motions trying to convince themselves that they are thinking, when in fact they are merely indulging in mental gymnastics. Self-discipline of the highest order is required to think when it is required. There are innumerable ways to avoid thinking—sharpening a pencil, putting a new cartridge in the ballpoint pen, cleaning the typewriter keys, answering the day's mail, phoning a friend, calling the agency about something trivial. Only the perceptive person *knows* when he is really thinking, and only the honest one admits it when he is not. Thinking is basic to good advertising because advertising is largely problem solving. It has been said that, to think a problem through to a solution, it is necessary to do three things: Identify the problem, find out the facts, and, finally, come up with an idea. The experienced ad manager knows when he is using his time well—he knows when it is time to sit back, pull out the sliding leaf on the desk where the internal telephone numbers are taped, prop his feet up and relax—and think. Sound advertising is based on sound thinking.

4. *The ability to write*

Clear thinking results in good writing. Good writing is more than words grammatically arranged, more than ability to compose catchy phrases, or the knack of creating an effect. The ability to write is

THE DARTNELL ADVERTISING HANDBOOK

part intuition, so strong that when a good selling proposition is conceived it is *recognized* instantaneously; it is part discernment, so that the extraneous and the trivial are rejected without wasting time; it is part sound judgment and knowledge of good business practice. And it is, of course, being able to express thoughts so that they interest others, so that others *want* to read what you have written, thus enabling you to implant the idea which you had originally and which you want prospects to retain.

5. *Curiosity*

There is no substitute for curiosity, no stronger words than "I wonder," or "What if . . . ". A mind that probes off the beaten path, that questions, that doubts, that demands to know why, that refuses to accept the easy and the pat and the trite, that tempers known "facts" with a healthy dash of old-fashioned skepticism, that takes the Missouri attitude of "show me"—that is the mind most likely to conceive an entirely new and tremendously effective plan. Reach, ask, reject the obvious, search for something elusive, something that seems unattainable, but which is there in every situation. It can make the difference between acceptable and good, between good and outstanding.

6. *The ability to visualize*

This is an ability that every successful ad man has, and has to spare. It consists of thinking in terms of the whole, rather than segments or component parts. In the case of an advertisement, it means thinking in terms of the complete ad—layout, copy, illustration—rather than considering copy only. Visualizing the end result inevitably results in a better ad, one with more impact, or a better piece of literature. For only by doing this, either consciously or subconsciously, can the mind channel itself in the right creative direction and organize the thought sequence in logical order. A few pencil lines scribbled on a tablet, with copy blocks and the headline roughed in, are an aid in thinking visually, as a whole. The so-called "thumbnail" or "copywriter's rough" doodled out to organize thoughts is more than exercise.

7. *The ability to project*

This is nothing more than being able to identify with those with whom you want to communicate. Fortunately, almost everybody except the self-centered introvert has this ability to some extent. Nurture it, for it is a key to advertising *for* the prospect instead of *at* him. There's a world of difference.

Think as Your Prospects Think

Where many copywriters fumble, where both ad managers and agency men go off onto a tangent, is that they fail to shift mental gears. Nothing else will do except that the man writing the copy must cultivate a certain frame of mind—actually be a quick-change artist with his thought patterns—in order to think from the *prospect's* viewpoint, rather than from his own, or from that of his company or clients.

Stop for a minute when you sit down to write an ad. Do nothing but think. Forget for the time being what you want. Disregard your desires and put the all-important prospect in the center of your thinking. Concentrate. Make the situation real for yourself by making the prospect come alive. Think back on what you've learned about him, where he works, what his habits are when he makes a purchase of a product for his company. Visualize him as a person with normal human wants, needs, and desires. Project yourself right into his mind so that you actually think of your product in terms of what it means to him, of what it will do for him.

Do this and you've become prospect-oriented, reader-oriented—which is exactly what you must accomplish if your advertisements are going to be read. When the typical prospect is reading a trade publication which just happens to contain your ad, he couldn't care less about you, your product, or your company. Perhaps he isn't even aware that they exist. The prospect is concerned exclusively with himself, his company, and his job—and with products or services which he believes can help him upgrade his job performance, or which will solve a problem on his job. Your advertisement must persuade him to believe that your product does exactly this.

McGraw-Hill proved this in a Reader Feedback survey which asked readers to select for extensive comment *one* ad in the issue of the magazine being evaluated. Readers were asked to select an ad which "describes a product or service, or gives information that may be helpful in your work." A high proportion of the top-ranked ads were selected for comment on this basis—a much higher proportion than the difference in readership scores alone would warrant. This shows that top-rated ads spoke to the readers in terms of job interest. Results showed that 61 percent of the top ads were selected for comment as "helpful in your work" as against 11 percent of the bottom ads.

This is so elementary it's scarcely worth mentioning—except that a surprisingly sizable percentage of today's industrial ads fail, and fail miserably, on this score. The reason for this is because the man who wrote them—and the ad manager who approved them (perhaps one and the same individual)—overlooked this basic premise. He had the wrong concept of the tack to take.

Another score on which ads fail is equally inexcusable—they talk product features. This is fine and dandy around the office where everybody regards the product as approximately equal in importance to the arrival of a first son and heir. But talking features is anathema to an ad. Engineers, product managers, draftsmen, and the mail boy enthusiastically discuss features, but advertisements subordinate features to discuss user benefits. Or, they talk features and promptly translate features into benefits. They do if they're successful ads, that is.

What benefits me is what the reader is interested in. He simply doesn't care whether or not the Joseph J. Doaks Company's widget has a shaft of heat-treated chrome-molybdenum steel, $1\frac{1}{2}$ inches by $17\frac{1}{4}$ inches, and that this is the longest, strongest plunger shaft in the entire widget industry, and the only one in the industry made of this expensive alloy.

Instead, tell him in a case-history ad that the heavy-duty plunger in this widget reduced downtime 27 percent for the XYZ Company, saving $57,986 in time and maintenance in only nine months, and you've touched him where he lives. That's a user benefit he can fondly clutch to his heart because he's been having trouble with the plungers in widgets of another manufacture—or he's afraid he might have trouble, or possibly he's farsighted enough to look ahead and plan to protect his continuity of production by installing the widget that will prevent this loss to his company.

Put his interests first and your message will get through. Every time.

Three Kinds of Ads

As every ad manager knows, there are only three kinds of ads:

1. Good ads.

2. Ads which never should have been approved and never should have run.

3. Indifferent ads.

Ads in the first category were conceived and written by competent craftsmen who knew what they were doing, and why they were doing it. Those in the second category were done by incompetents who perhaps should have been apprentice plumbers. Those in the third were done by tired copywriters, copywriters who had only a superficial interest in their jobs, or those who were content to slide by and turn in a perfunctory performance. No ad that is *almost* good should ever get past the copy and layout stage—if it gets that far.

Even poor ads serve a useful purpose, though—as horrible examples. The author has no intention of denigrating or embarrassing any advertiser, so to discuss examples of poor ads objectively the advertisers and their products will, for the most part, be afforded the protection of anonymity. When this is done and the company name must be used, it will be called "Smith." Products, when identifiable, will be Smith Widgets or a variation which is suitably descriptive without being too specific.

Making your ad stand out from the herd so that it will be read is quite an accomplishment when the average businessman is assaulted with more than 1,600 advertising impressions *each day*. To succeed in the face of such odds requires a high degree of ingenuity—of creativity, to use an overworked word. There's a difference between legitimate creativity, however, and merely being offbeat for the sake of offbeatness.

Recently one advertiser confused creativity with being different without a valid reason for doing so. His one-page, two-color ad features illustrations of seven—yes, seven—dancers, including a close-up of a hula dancer's navel. The headline is feature-oriented, written either by or for the manufacturer. It reads: *Even a dancer doesn't have all the moves of Smith's ram & saddle turret lathes.* Let's assume for some unknown reason that this little gem might possibly have stopped a reader and enticed him into pursuing the subject further; perhaps he's a terpsichorean by avocation. However, the body copy continues in the same unrewarding vein: *Ballet or belly. Ballroom or bar. Even a dancer would have trouble keeping up with all the motions possible from Smith's ram & saddle turret lathes.*

That's not reader-benefit copy, reason-why copy; it doesn't involve the reader, it fails to reward him for spending his valuable time with this ad. It's a poor ad in an ill-conceived campaign that should never have seen print. But the sorry aspect is that this campaign cost just as much as one that would have produced positive and tangible results for this advertiser. The basic concept was wrong.

Another, taking the coy approach, features an illustration of an awesomely endowed cutie in a stretch swimsuit leaning indolently against a driftwood stump on a deserted beach. Headline is: *Do ceramic problems have you STUMPED?* (That stump supporting the curvesome cutie had to be explained, apparently.) Body copy is almost a classic example of extreme self-interest; it ignores reader benefits, fails to examine the product from the reader's viewpoint. It goes: *Our products are chosen for quality, uniformity, and speed of delivery. For greatly increased strength and thermal shock resistance in their most economical form, it's easily blended Smith Substance or Smith Stuff. Much less of our products is required to give you the high alumina body content you desire. If it is a ceramic or refractory problem, let Smith Substance correct it. We make shipments in any manner you desire.* End of copy.

One unsupported claim of using less of the product (and the ad *actually* says "our products"), which the reader might possibly infer would result in lower costs, along with the assurance that shipment will go forth by the specified carrier. Not much in those unspecific and uninspired statements to persuade a prospect to use Smith Substance rather than something he's now buying, and it's due to lack of empathy with the prospect. The ad is written from the seller's viewpoint, with the seller's desires in mind. Chances are few got as far as the bottom of the body copy, however, for they're given nothing to make them want to read that far.

Dissection of a complete ad, cliché by cliché, written for Lindberg Hevi-Duty by a former agency, shows how dreary and dull ad copy can be when it's written by somebody who lacks the basic knowledge of what copy should—and can—do. The original version of the ad on semiconductor diffusion furnaces read:

Within easy reach . . . new production records!

Like to set a few production records? Then take a good look at the Lindberg Hevi-Duty Mark III Diffusion furnaces. They're setting all kinds of records every day.

The reason? Three independently controlled, stacked furnaces that fit ever-so-compactly in the floor space of one. Anyone of average height finds even the uppermost furnace within easy reach. Some people say the Mark III conserves valuable floor space like a miser. Two Mark III's can even be placed back to back.

Because each furnace is controlled independently, it's possible to simultaneously set up to three different process temperatures. And operation is simple. Even major temperature changes can be handled by the nontechnician.

The Mark III furnace profiles are guaranteed to ± ½°C over a length of 22", from 800° to 1300°C, with almost incredibly precise repeatability.

Cabinet temperature outside? Remains at a safe-to-touch room temperature. Thanks to double-shell construction, new insulating characteristics, and three-way cooling system.

What's more, the exclusive "Disposa-Core" lets you quickly and economically replace coil-and-insulation sections whenever necessary.

Lindberg Hevi-Duty has the largest coast-to-coast staff of sales and service engineers to assure you of complete installation and start-up service, and to guarantee equipment operation.

Want the complete Mark III story? Write Lindberg Hevi-Duty. (Single- and two-stack furnace models also are available.)

Here are the fatal flaws which would have assured almost no readership of this ad:

Within easy reach . . . new production records! Headline is weak, needlessly verbose.

Like to set a few production records? The rhetorical question is permissible and effective in places, although it shouldn't be overdone.

Take a good look. Nobody is interested in taking a good look at anything just because they have been admonished to do so in an advertisement.

They're setting all kinds of records every day. What kinds?

Where? Even on Sunday and holidays?

The reason? Another rhetorical question.

ever-so-compactly. Precious and cute. And it's even hyphenated.

uppermost. This is a coy way of saying what the copywriter actually meant—top.

Some people. What people? Where do they work? Are they acknowledged experts in this field? Does their word carry weight? Are they respected? This is the phony-testimonial approach and it always sounds the death knell for copy believability.

even. Try reading the sentence without it and see the difference. *Possible to simultaneously.* Adhering slavishly to the rules of grammar is stultifying, but split infinitives grate on many people. Avoid them.

Even major temperature changes can be handled by the nontechnician. This comment is not strictly a critique on copy—but this statement is a technical error and would have been recognized as such by the average reader of this technical journal. The copywriter *must* present his facts correctly.

Cabinet temperature outside? Another rhetorical question.

safe-to-touch. Cute, "addy." People simply do not talk like this, except possibly at an afternoon tea attended by beaming dowagers.

Thanks to. Nobody says "thanks to" in an ad—not since approximately 1920, at least. It's a cliché and reflects a lack of thinking.

double-shell construction. Technical error; should be triple-shell. Facts must be correct. Everybody makes mistakes, but in the marginal agency they're part of the scheme of things.

whenever. Putting on the dog weakens a statement. Be simple and direct.

Lindberg Hevi-Duty has the largest coast-to-coast staff of sales and service engineers to assure you of complete installation and start-up service, and to guarantee equipment operation. Sentence is too long. Too big a mouthful. Also, a manufacturer's field men do not guarantee equipment—the company does. There's a vast difference. Failure to make a correct statement on such an important subject indicates fuzzy thinking. There's no place for it in advertising—particularly in copywriting.

Want the complete Mark III story? Is there no end to the

rhetorical questions? (It can become habit-forming). (Single- and two-stack furnace models also available.) This is known as P.S.-type copy; it is basically feminine and should be avoided in advertising directed to industrial buyers. "Available" is a fine catalog word, but it is a cliché and merely proves the copywriter is either too lazy to select a better way to express himself, or he is incapable of doing so.

For comparison, the ad is illustrated (page 216) as rewritten for a leading electronics magazine. This version, written by the ad manager, shows that an industrial ad can be reader-oriented, can talk user benefits, and can be informative and interesting at the same time.

Note that the headline is stronger—despite use of the rhetorical question! It makes a point and a promise fast. The reader is involved and because a benefit he wants and needs is promised to him, he is lured into reading the body copy. Body copy tells him how to realize the benefit which interests him; no analogies such as "just as" or whatever, no beating around the bush. Reasons why follow immediately.

A few specific comments on the copy:

No need to recruit labor from the Tall Girls' Club. A touch of humor breathes life into a potent sales point. It translates a product feature into a user benefit—easy of operating this diffusion furnace by the average female employee. This is a competitive advantage and users of this equipment are fully aware of it.

As frugal with floor space as a miser is with money. Vivid and highly descriptive. This kind of analogy makes an indelible impression. Also, note there is no vague reference to unknown people, no pretentiousness about using the word "conserves."

You operate the Mark III Diffusitron merely by dialing the temperature you want. It's that easy. This is straight talk. No nonsense, no nontechnician gobbledygook. The simple, declarative sentence is strengthened by a change of pace—the very short sentence.

And the operator doesn't need asbestos gloves . . . cabinet always stays at room temperature. An extremely strong

New production records? Easy to reach!

All you need is Lindberg Hevi-Duty's new Mark III Diffusitron furnace. It has three tubes, each with a separate control to do three different jobs at the same time.

Top tube of the Mark III is only 64¼" from the floor. No need to recruit labor from the Tall Girls' Club.

Lindberg Hevi-Duty's three-stack design is as frugal with floor space as a miser is with money. The Mark III is compact, can be installed back to back. Or flush against a wall, if you want.

You operate the Mark III Diffusitron merely by dialing the temperature you want. It's that easy.

Profiles are guaranteed ± ½°C over a length of 22", from 800° to 1300°C. With precise repeatability.

And the operator doesn't need asbestos gloves with Lindberg Hevi-Duty's Mark III. Cabinet always stays at room temperature. That's due to triple-shell construction, new and better insulation, and a three-way cooling system.

Lindberg Hevi-Duty's exclusive "Disposa-Core" lets you replace coil and insulation sections when necessary. Quickly, easily. No long-drawn-out down time.

Sales and service engineers everywhere give you skilled installation and start-up service. And if you need them, they're there. Want the whole story on the Mark III — or on single- or two-stack furnaces? Drop us a line. You have nothing to gain but profit. Lindberg Hevi-Duty, Watertown, Wisconsin 53094.

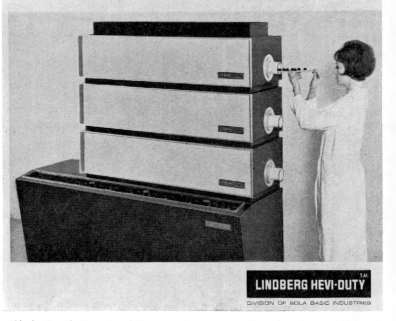

LINDBERG HEVI-DUTY T.M.

DIVISION OF SOLA BASIC INDUSTRIES

This is the Lindberg Hevi-Duty ad that was rewritten and rescheduled by the ad manager after the text had been oriented toward the potential purchaser rather than representing the manufacturer's views. User benefits are stressed in an interesting way, and the reader becomes involved because the benefits promised are bound to be of importance to him in his work.

statement that is believable because the reason why follows immediately afterwards.

. . . exclusive Disposa-Core lets you replace coil and insulation sections when necessary. Quickly, easily. No long drawn-out downtime. That product feature and its user benefit come through loud and clear. It's like money in the bank compared to loss of production. Manufacturers understand this kind of talk because they are vitally interested in equipment reliability.

And if you need them, they're there. Simply stated, vastly reassuring, and convincing.

Drop us a line. You have nothing to gain but profit. A bid for action and a potent promise.

The ad is replete with vivid word pictures, colorful, readable, inherently interesting to those in the business of manufacturing semiconductors and integrated circuits because it is reader-oriented. Copy should read as if it literally flows from the typewriter, even if every word, every phrase, every analogy was practically the result of blood, sweat, and tears. If it's worked on, it will.

The Question of Honesty

Honesty is not the best policy—it is the *only* policy.

The veracity of statements made in ads is not under discussion—being fair and honest with your readers is. The fastest way yet devised to lose a prospect's confidence, perhaps irretrievably, is to trick him into reading your advertisement by traveling under false colors.

There's no disputing the fact that the advertisement must attract the attention of the reader. It must arouse and maintain his interest long enough for him to read and understand the message, otherwise the money invested in production and space is a total waste because the ad failed in its purpose.

But this can be done honestly, everything aboveboard. Fortunately, there's an elemental truth not known to—or believed by—most industrial advertisers. The truth is that the vast majority of all readers of business publications read advertisements *because they want to*. They want to because in these advertisements is information they need, information that is important to them. They are not serving you by reading your ad, they are serving their own self-interest.

Air is cheaper than water

Sure, a ship's freight bill is lower. But indirect and hidden charges can cost you more in the long run. Just look:

TWA compares the cost of a 435 lb. machine parts shipment from Chicago to Zurich.				
Via Surface:	**Time: 20 days**		**Via Air:**	**Time: 15 hours**
Packaging	$ 48.00		Packaging	$ 9.00
Insurance	36.00		Insurance	12.00
Inland freight (Chicago-N.Y.)	22.00		Inland freight	—
Documentation	22.00		Documentation	1.00
Ocean freight	51.15		Air freight	176.12
Customs clearance	20.00		Customs clearance	10.00
Inland freight (Genoa-Zurich)	49.00		Inland freight	—
Interest charges	19.60		Interest charges	—
	Cost: $267.75			**Cost: $208.12**

$59.63 and 19 days saved by air! And that's just the beginning.
You can reduce your inventory and warehousing costs.
Give better customer service.
And increase your sales in time-limited situations.
The speed of air also cuts your investment in goods in transit,
increases capital turnover and holds obsolescence to a minimum.
Get all the details. Call or write
your nearest TWA Air Cargo office.
Nationwide, worldwide...depend on TWA.

A good example is TWA's dramatic all-type ad shown here.

The stark simplicity of the ad in a field where everything is contrived, designed, deliberate, and studied produces an impression of immediacy, importance, and honesty. Invariably it produces results.

And the arresting, provocative headline in big, bold type, the abundance of white space, and an exceptionally clean layout all combine to demand readership by those responsible for specifying the method of shipment of their products—and by management whose main interest is in turning a respectable profit. Tell a management man he's paying too much for a given commodity, in this case surface shipment, and you have a man hanging on every word you say.

TWA itemizes every cost element of both surface and air shipments to lend credence to their statements. By using one specific commodity flown between two given points as a sort of case history, TWA proves that air shipment—supposedly the premium-priced way to move freight—actually costs less when all pertinent factors are taken into consideration. It amounts to $59.63 less, with a bonus of 19 irreplaceable days thrown in for good measure. Time is a pretty difficult item to which to attach a price tag, but in today's competitive economy it is certainly a significant factor in total costs of operation of a business. Then add reduced inventory, lower warehousing costs, lower investment in goods in transit, increased capital turnover, and minimum obsolescence. TWA's proposition is almost irresistible.

According to Lawrence V. Stapleton, vice-president of advertising and sales promotion of Trans World Airlines, "Air Is Cheaper Than Water" has proved to be a superior ad that works very hard for TWA Air Cargo. An Ad-Chart survey of readers of *Iron Age* magazine shows that it scored an outstanding 64.1 percent Noticed, and that 58.3 percent of the interviewees contacted by the rating service stated they found the ad Very Informative. Only a negligible 4.2 percent felt that it was only Somewhat Informative. (Survey terminology is capitalized.)

And a Mills Shepard survey of the ad as run in *Purchasing Week* showed that 64 percent of the sample interviewed Remembered Having Seen the ad, while 38 percent Read Partially, and a full 25 percent Read Thoroughly.

Some verbatim comments made by those interviewed by Mills Shepard follow.

"I discussed this ad with our traffic manager and he sent for more information."

Supervisor, Electronics Buyer

"I sent this ad to our shipping department as a reminder that fast shipments via air freight are practical and the head shipper agreed."

Purchasing Agent
Electronics Company

"We discussed at length the chart shown in the ad and since then we have used TWA for flights."

Purchasing Director
Manufacturer of Brick Block Concrete

"After reading the ad, I sent out a shipment TWA for trial."

General Purchasing Agent
Manufacturer of Crankshafts

"I checked their air rates because of the center of the ad information. I have sent out shipments TWA and was satisfied."

Buyer
Manufacturer of Awnings

One of TWA's most important advertising objectives in air cargo is to communicate the advantages of air versus surface, and to illustrate the cost efficiencies that go even beyond the cost of a specific air freight shipment. Traffic and purchasing people are very important to TWA, and they tell their story in a select list of magazines that reach these buying influences effectively. They add, however, that it is quite possible that top management is actually the single most important group in the long-range development of air freight. The carrier has regular advertising schedules in such management publications as *Fortune, Business Week,* and *The Wall Street Journal.*

United Takes Another Route

Although both companies obviously have the same ultimate goal—to capture a larger share of an expanding air freight market—United Air Lines takes a different approach than TWA. United's striking two-color, two-page-spread ad is illustrated at the left.

The illustration does a good job of showing the product—as much as a service can be shown, at least—and of arresting the attention of readers. Night photographs, with their massive, dominant black areas, always rate near the top of the heap in interest. Perhaps this is because so many millions of people are casual photographers who automatically think of picture-taking in terms of either sunlight or flash. When confronted with a punchy, contrasty night photograph, few can resist giving it a second—or third—glance.

Copy, instead of hitting home at one strong central point as does TWA's, extolls instead the virtues of air freight in general, and United Air Freight secondarily. This adds up to *two* ideas in one ad, when every ad should concentrate on just one. Copy reads:

CEILING
UNLIMITED

Air freight volume will double
in the next three years,
with no end in sight.
Reason: more and more
companies are seeking new ways
to reduce overall distribution
costs or gain a marketing edge.

Not only are more businesses
turning to air freight every year,
but more kinds of businesses.
They're using it more consistently,
shipping bigger loads. One
attraction is the cost saving:
air freight may prove the means
to reduce field inventories, lower
packaging costs, reduce the capital
once tied up in transit. Another
appeal is the marketing edge:
with jet speed delivery
comes greater customer
satisfaction, faster restocking of
distributors, greater flexibility
to explore new markets. United
delivers to more U.S. markets
than any other airline, with the
world's biggest freight lift.
And at United it's always
handle with extra care.

Deft use is made of United's consumer slogan, "Fly the friendly skies of United" by the carrier's air freight arm, for it is transformed into, "The big birds fly the friendly skies of United Air Lines." This provides strong corporate identification and capitalizes on United's position as the industry leader.

In addition, the air freight operation's slogan, "handle with extra care," is the tag line in the copy block, and it also appears prominently in red—the only spot of second color in the spread—in the signature area.

United's marketing objective in the air freight area is almost classically simple: "United hopes to build the air freight market by providing a satisfactory product to the shipper at a profit for United." To do so, United is of the opinion that top management is the single most important group of buying influences to whom they must communicate. The carrier has singled out, through research, the executives—by title—whom they have to reach. They are: President, financial vice-president (or controller), marketing vice-president, sales vice-president, and operations vice-president.

United stated: "We would like to increase both the number of shippers and the kinds of shipments we receive. In order to do this, we address ourselves both to management, *who makes the original decision to try air freight,* and to traffic management who makes the decision as to which carrier to use after the initial decision to ship by air has been made."

United wants to tell management the reasons for making an air freight decision. These include less capital tied up in traffic, less inventory and warehousing, faster shipping during peak selling seasons, and better service to customers.

Current top markets for United Air Freight include automotive parts, perishables such as produce and flowers, aerospace equipment, and, oddly enough, printed matter. Relative importance of these prime markets was determined by market research and an analysis of sales records.

Although there has been no measurable response to this ad, it has been surveyed by Daniel Starch and Staff and placed well into the top-readership quarter of all ads in that issue of *Business Week.*

Other media include *Fortune, Wall Street Journal, U.S. News & World Report,* selected to reach top management, and *Traffic World, Air Transportation, Purchasing, Purchasing Week, Distribution Age, Traffic Management, Pacific Air & Truck Traffic,* and *Transportation & Distribution Management,* these latter to tell purchasing and traffic management executives about United Air Freight.

If Ads Are Good, They Are Read

Powerful though this ad obviously is, nonetheless it lacks something almost intangible—perhaps the persuasiveness, the dollars-and-cents "proof" of TWA's ad. There is little doubt that, of the two ads, TWA's outpulled United's in readership and outproduced it in results. And it did so at far lower cost. TWA's ad required no expensive night photograph which could easily have cost $500— or even double that—no expensive half-tone engraving; it used half as many colors, and half as much space.

That people in industry want to read trade publications and their advertisements is again proved quite conclusively by a study conducted by McGraw-Hill Publishing Company. A survey was made to study the readership of "business, industrial, trade and technical publications." Personal interviews were made by McGraw-Hill Research with 1,330 individuals in the metalworking and chemical processing industries. Principal functions and size of plant groups were proportionately represented in the sample.

Sought to Avoid Bias

In order to avoid bias, the interviews were conducted under a name having no connection with any publishing company or publication. The source of the list of plants was the McGraw-Hill Census which encompasses almost all of industry.

The question, "Are you spending more, less, or about the same time reading such publications as you did three or four years ago?" was answered by two groups—those who had changed jobs and those who did not change.

Fifty percent of those who changed jobs spent more time reading business publications; 20 percent spent less; 30 percent spent the same amount of time reading.

Among those who did not change jobs, the results showed that 27 percent spent more time; 18 percent less time; 55 percent spent the same amount of time.

The conclusion is obvious. In today's highly mobile society where more individuals occupy different positions each year than remain in the same slot, business publication reading is regarded as a necessity. It is so important because it is a part of a continuing educational program which makes it possible to keep pace with technological changes. Even among those who resisted the lure of greener pastures, 82 percent spent either the same amount of time, or more time, on business reading. Knowledgeable executives usually consider the man who does not read business publications as narrow, unambitious, and ill-qualified for advancement.

Interviewers asked the same people another question: "Do you feel you rely on them (business publications) for information more, less, or about the same as you did three or four years ago?"

Among job changers, and this includes those individuals who changed companies as well as those who transferred or were promoted to a more responsible position within their original companies, 49 percent placed more reliance on the business press. A scant 12 percent placed less, while 39 percent relied to the same extent.

Twenty-five percent of those who stayed put relied more, a minimal 8 percent relied less, and 67 percent stated they relied to the same extent as before.

Top Executive Opinion

In a recent newspaper supplement produced for the American Business Press, a number of top executives of major corporations said they "couldn't do without" business publications—for both informative reading and effective advertising.

Russell De Young, board chairman of Goodyear Tire & Rubber Company, said, "Speaking from personal experience, I can say that no person in management could perform his job effectively, or hope to progress, lacking the information and knowledge available to him through well-edited, perceptive business publications." Goodyear subscribes to some 350 different business publications for the benefit of its executives and staff. In addition, many other publications are received directly by Goodyear people.

Robert S. Stevenson, board chairman of Allis-Chalmers Company, is quoted as saying that business publications "serve us in two ways. The first is that they provide authoritative and knowledgeable information relating to a specific business—a type of information just not available from any other source. The second value is that of providing a specific vehicle for us to use in advertising to our customers." Communication is a two-way street.

Noting that his firm does not major in the business of providing goods or services for the general consumer market, Mr. Stevenson added, "It is quite inefficient and overcostly for us to consider advertising in the mass media . . . if we did use those media, we would spray our message over too much territory, wasting our efforts and investment on many who could not possibly be customers, and, of course, the cost per useful contact would be outlandishly high.

"In other words, we would be shooting with a shotgun when we really need a rifle. Business publications provide those rifles and as a result we can buy directed coverage. For that reason we are good customers."

Business publications are read because they are an indispensable tool. Most top managements—particularly in progressive companies which outpace their industries—urge, and many insist, that all of their technical and management personnel read the business publications in their fields. It is an anachronism cherished by those who haven't had an original thought in years that business publications are not read.

And in the right environment—editorial that is essential to their self-interest—97 percent of business publication readers read the advertisements. It's up to you to make your ads so interesting and so informative that they will achieve high readership. And do it without subterfuge.

What You Owe the Reader

Although it's not often considered this way, the plain fact is that you're asking a favor of the recipient of a magazine every time you insert one of your advertisements. This shouldn't be done unilaterally. Your ad, merely by being there, implies an obligation on your part to compensate the reader for what he has freely given you of his own volition—his time. Make his investment worthwhile. Don't waste it.

You owe the reader:

1. *Information*—concise, precise, specific.

2. *Truth*—no puffery, no exaggeration, no playing fast and loose with facts.

3. *Clarity*—no obscurity, no gimmickry.

These three debts you repay to the reader in exchange for his time eliminate the old saw about the trouble with magazine advertising: That people who live in cities don't believe it, and people who live in small towns don't understand it.

Information

If your selling proposition is right and the concept of the man who created it is right, a good industrial ad should exert such a strong appeal that recipients of business publications will want to read it. The illustration specified by the copywriter should pique the reader's imagination. Then, the headline, which must telegraph what you want to say, should arouse enough interest to entice him into the body copy.

Marsteller Inc., the country's largest industrial advertising agency, has this to say about campaigns, ads, and copy. They must have, and do, the following:

1. Campaign identity.

2. Orderly arrangement.

3. One dominating element.

4. Focal point.

5. Identify subject at a glance.

6. Functional layout.

7. Functional color.

8. Be direct.

9. Short, short, short.

10. Simple typography.

11. Single idea.

12. Offer reward.

13. Reader involvement.

14. Don't brag.

15. Buyer language.

16. News, information.

17. Drama.

18. Be specific.

19. Be friendly.

20. Advertiser identification.

The one thing the reader expects from an industrial ad is information. Give it to him in terms of his self-interest, and he'll read. Deprive him of it, or beat around the bush and talk in generalities and he'll do one of two things—skip over your ad entirely, or read part of it and immediately forget it. He has other things to do with his time, such as reading a competitor's ad which *does* reward him for his time.

An example is the ad (see next page) for an industrial degreaser made by a company whose name is not the "Smith" given in the text. The illustration has little inherent interest, and isn't even remotely related to the product. The headline reads: *You can't drive a spike nail with a tack hammer!* The phrase "with a tack hammer" is underlined to emphasize these words, apparently to explain the illustration. Headlines and/or illustrations that have to be explained to readers are woefully weak.

So far, there's not much to lure the prospect into reading the selling message, but things get worse. Body copy continues: *Driving a spike with a tack hammer would be a very tedious, time-consuming, thankless, profitless job.* That's something short of a grabber

Driving a spike with a tack hammer would be a very tedious, time-consuming, thankless, profitless job.

Whatever the task, it is essential that we use the proper tools to achieve the desired result.

For example—some metalworking manufacturers still degrease small parts in old, hand-operated degreasers when they could save a lot of time and money with a new

Thousands and thousands of parts can be degreased at amazingly low costs in this modern, efficient machine. And there is a varied choice of models to fit different production requirements. All machines will handle a wide variety of parts.

Whatever your metal cleaning need—call in the man from the Industrial Division. Chances are he will give you a practical and economical way to make the job much easier and more profitable.

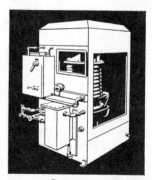

Degreasers are built in four basic sizes with capacities ranging from 1,000 to 12,000 lbs. per hour. Exclusive construction features a spiral trough elevator which carries the parts from vibrating hot solvent bath to controlled vapor spray to pressure steam drying.

DHTPHX
CHEMICAL INDUSTRIES, INC.
P.O. BOX 501, DEPT. MP-666, DETROIT, MICHIGAN 48232

for an opening paragraph, but it does give the reader the idea that continuing to read this ad could well be a very tedious, time-consuming, thankless, profitless project. Then the second paragraph: *What-*

ever the task, it is essential that we use the proper tools to achieve the desired result. Still no concrete information, no news, no dramatic statement, no reader involvement. There is proof of fuzzy thinking on the part of the copywriter. He was—or should have been—aware that if he hasn't offered the reader a benefit in the headline, it is imperative that he does so immediately in the body copy.

Body copy continues: *For example—some metalworking manufacturers still degrease small parts in old, hand-operated degreasers when they could save a lot of time and money with a new Smith Degreaser.*

Thousands and thousands of parts can be degreased at amazingly low costs in this modern, efficient machine. And there is a varied choice of models to fit different production requirements. All Smith machines will handle a wide variety of parts.

Whatever your metal cleaning needs—call in the man from Smith's Industrial Division. Chances are he will give you a practical and economical way to make the job much easier and more profitable.

It's not until the caption under the line drawing of the product that specific information is found. Caption reads: *Smith Degreasers are built in four basic sizes with capacities ranging from 1,000 to 12,000 lbs. per hour. Exclusive construction features a spiral trough elevator which carries the parts from vibrating hot solvent bath to controlled vapor spray to pressure steam drying.* And even then, only product sizes are given, discounting discussion of a product feature without exploiting the user benefit.

The ad is pedantic and condescending in tone, vague and non-specific, self-oriented, and does not reward the reader for his time. It is also a waste of money.

Unfortunately, this ad is typical of far too much industrial advertising seen in the business press. It is a prime reason for management's questioning advertising's effectiveness.

Kimberly-Clark's dramatic ad is in vivid contrast to the pallid generalities in the preceding ad. Kimberly-Clark's bold headline is as shocking as a cold shower to members of a society conditioned to regard cheap as synonymous with worthless or inferior. It tantalizes the reader and few can resist looking at the illustration. When they do, they immediately receive another shock—the incongruity of a 53 cent price tag attached to a dirty, discarded shop towel. This, in turn, leads to the advertiser's provocative statement: *shop towel*

CHEAP

shop towel cost analysis can be a shocker

Have you ever figured out what it costs you when a three-dollar-an-hour worker leaves the job to go get a three-cent shop towel? We call it "walk time," and it can blow up the cost of such a simple item as a shop towel to enormous size.

The answer is an inexpensive disposable wiper that can be dispensed right on the job. Like one of ours. We make a broad line of sturdy, versatile wipers that come bundled, boxed, band-wrapped, or whatever is most efficient. And our distributor salesmen, who have just finished a six-week course in Wiping Analysis, can make sure that you get the right wipe in the right package for the right job. See your Kimberly-Clark man, or write Kimberly-Clark Corporation, Neenah, Wisconsin.

THE KIMBERLY-CLARK FAMILY OF INDUSTRIAL WIPERS

TERI*TOWELS KIMTOWELS* KIMWIPES* KAYDRY* LITHOWIPES*

analysis can be a shocker. The stage has been set. The reader has been lured into reading further.

Body copy immediately involves the reader. *Have you ever figured out what it costs you when a three-dollar-an-hour worker leaves the job to go get a three-cent shop towel? We call it "walk time," and it can blow up the cost of such a simple item as a shop towel to enormous size.*

The answer is an inexpensive disposable wiper that can be dispensed right on the job. Like one of ours. We make a broad line of sturdy, versatile wipers that come bundled, boxed, band-wrapped, or whatever is most efficient. And our distributor salesmen, who have just finished a six-week course in Wiping Analysis, can make sure you get the right wipe in the right package for the right job. See your Kimberly-Clark man, or write Kimberly-Clark Corporation, Neenah, Wisconsin.

The ad is simple and straightforward. It has a strong central idea—a concept. The selling proposition is sound. The ad is informative and rewards the reader for his time. It offers an important user benefit, reduced costs, and it does so believably and logically. And it inspires confidence in the salesman who will call on a sizable number of the readers of this ad, making his job easier, reducing the amount of time he has to spend on each sales call, thus reducing the cost of selling. This Kimberly-Clark ad is a fine example of what industrial advertising should be—and what it should do.

Note that there's a built-in invitation to read. Clean layout, a single idea, helpful information, dramatic presentation, short copy, simple typography, a direct approach that doesn't fritter away the reader's time, and strong advertiser identification.

The layout makes effective use of a proved principle—that a reader's eye is trained to start at the top of a page and proceed downward in a clockwise direction. Thus, each element of the ad follows in logical sequence, aiding assimilation of the advertiser's message.

Lighthearted Information

Although they are physically dissimilar in layout, illustrative technique, typography, and even in the size of space used, Mathatronics' ad (next page) adheres to the principle that an industrial advertisement's reason for being is to give information to the reader. It does so in a deceptively lighthearted way that makes it a pure joy to read.

Headline is: *Can an engineer flunk Fortran and still find happiness?* Body copy, unjustified (uneven margins) left and right, continues with subheads breaking up the copy block—letting in air, as it is called. It reads:

Happiness is

*finding a digital computer with a simple keyboard,
whose language is algebra.*

Happiness is

*having 48 to 88 individually addressable storage registers
plus 5 separate registers for arithmetic manipulations,
480 steps of program memory,
and/or 18 optional prewired programs of 48 steps each,
right in your own department.*

Happiness is

*not spending a million dollars for a digital computer,
or $50,000 or $20,000, or even $10,000.*

Happiness is

*getting 8 or 9 significant digit accuracy
with a 2 digit power of ten exponent,
automatic decimal placement,
paper tape readout,
100 column number capacity.*

Happiness is

*getting intelligent accessories,
like a paper tape punch and reader,
or a page printer.*

Happiness is

*a Mathatron 8-48 plus the new
Auxiliary Program Storage.*

MATHATRONICS, INC.

To the average reader—all of us noncomputer types, that is—the term "Fortran" in the headline might seem not to communicate. But this is the language of the buyer and is common terminology in many scientific disciplines. Fortran is a language which translates human language into computer language. It must be learned in order to communicate with a computer and it is the *last* thing an engineer or scientist is interested in. This would be analogous to a medical student having to learn Latin when his real interest is in medicine.

A major user benefit of the computer offered by Mathatronics is that it requires no machine language such as Fortran. The instrument understands and generates on simple algebraic input which is the established working tool of the engineer.

That the ad *does* provide information of importance to readers is proved by one method of measurement—response. This ad and one similar ran in several electronics, computer, and engineering magazines for a year. Number of insertions varied from six to 12. The two ads consistently pulled an average of 800 inquiries per month, with letterhead inquiries, usually considered of higher caliber than bingo-card response, accounting for at least 10 percent of the total. This ad delivered the message.

Mathatronics' objective is not to generate inquiries, however, for the company actually has more than can be handled effectively. Rather, the advertising goal is to attract attention to a relatively unknown—due to its newness—product, and to a small company which is competing successfully with giants in this market. Mathatronics sells through dealers and representatives, making it virtually impossible to correlate the effect of advertising and sales. However, sales doubled last year, so *something* contributed!

This two-thirds page ad has everything going for it. Given the right concept, the strong central idea, pertinent information of a highly technical nature is fed to readers in a palatable way, in the readers' language. This is another ad that more than paid its way.

Truth

It's unpalatable, but it's a fact of life that a vast number of people —including businessmen—question advertising's truthfulness. This is detrimental to business and detrimental to advertising.

The Advertising Code of American Business, initially developed and distributed by two advertising organizations and now widely disseminated by the Association of American Advertising Agencies, is illustrated.

Point number 1 in the Code, that advertising shall tell the truth, is understood and accepted wholeheartedly by every industrial advertising manager today, almost without exception. Understood, but not as widely accepted, is point number 8 in the Code—that advertising shall avoid the use of exaggerated or unprovable claims, and use of big, bombastic words and phrases. Braggarts are not believed. The day when a gullible public could be talked into buying Old Doctor Janco's Snake Oil as a cure-all for dandruff, gout, and consumption is long gone, and happily so.

THE
ADVERTISING CODE
OF AMERICAN BUSINESS

1. Truth ... Advertising shall tell the truth, and shall reveal significant facts, the concealment of which would mislead the public.

2. Responsibility ... Advertising agencies and advertisers shall be willing to provide substantiation of claims made.

3. Taste and Decency ... Advertising shall be free of statements, illustrations or implications which are offensive to good taste or public decency.

4. Disparagement ... Advertising shall offer merchandise or service on its merits, and refrain from attacking competitors unfairly or disparaging their products, services or methods of doing business.

5. Bait Advertising ... Advertising shall offer only merchandise or services which are readily available for purchase at the advertised price.

6. Guarantees and Warranties ... Advertising of guarantees and warranties shall be explicit. Advertising of any guarantee or warranty shall clearly and conspicuously disclose its nature and extent, the manner in which the guarantor or warrantor will perform and the identity of the guarantor or warrantor.

7. Price Claims ... Advertising shall avoid price or savings claims which are false or misleading, or which do not offer provable bargains or savings.

8. Unprovable Claims ... Advertising shall avoid the use of exaggerated or unprovable claims.

9. Testimonials ... Advertising containing testimonials shall be limited to those of competent witnesses who are reflecting a real and honest choice.

Developed and initially distributed by: the Advertising Federation of America; the Advertising Association of the West; the Association of Better Business Bureaus, Inc.

The sad fact remains, however, that advertising as a whole, and this doesn't exclude industrial advertising where the credibility gap is significantly narrower than in the consumer field, has an unfortunate penchant for exaggeration and manufacturer brag-and-boast. In leafing through a couple of trade publications, these examples were found:

Headline in a one-page, two-color ad for a machine tool: *PROVED PERFORMANCE! THE MOST CONVINCING REASON TO BUY A SMITH AUTOMATIC TURRET LATHE.* Copy then goes: *Time after time the Smith has proved it cuts costs for both long and short production runs.* The statement is not documented in any way, no reason why it might be true is given, it is completely unsupported. Believability suffers.

A different ad, also two-color, one-page, in *Factory* magazine proclaims: *Greater Choice of Lifting Speeds and Drum Capacities . . . That's What Makes the Big Smith Model 3 Hoist Different From Others!* Copy then says: *Take a close look at the clean, functional design of this Smith Hoist. See how the Motor, Drum, and Gear sections are assembled in a "straight line"—not a "box" like some other heavy-duty hoists. Because of this, many drum and motor combinations can be brought together within the basic Smith hoist design to give you the lifting speed and drum capacity that's just right for your handling requirements. That's what makes the Smith different from other heavy-duty hoists!*

Let's start with readership. Readership always goes down when legibility does down, and capitalizing every word in the headline creates a jumpy appearance that repels the eye. Good typography is the least expensive part of advertising. Poor typography, perhaps the most expensive.

As for content, the headline is strictly brag-and-boast, self-serving, and therefore unconvincing. It fails to persuade because of unsupported claims. The reader quite logically interprets this as exaggeration—and thus is created another skeptic who questions all advertising copy.

Body copy proceeds to insult the readers' intelligence by putting quotation marks around terms that the average reader of *Factory* readily understands. Talking down to readers alienates them. Credit readers with having the intelligence to get the message if it's expressed in language familiar to them.

Proceeding, the copy then offers platitudes instead of information, discusses features instead of benefits. It continues for another long paragraph, then closes with an admonition to see the Smith distributor nearest the reader. If anybody read that far, he must have been whiling away the waning hours of a quiet Friday afternoon when his vacation started at 5 o'clock.

Then there's the two-color, one-page ad run by an instrument company. Seemingly it *invites* skepticism, at least from those who are not addicted to a current TV situation comedy. Not everybody is, and those who aren't will skip this ad as fast as they can turn the page. The headline is: *Would You Believe This Steroid Analysis?* Reader reaction to that one is a laconic nope.

And Chevrolet, who should know better, makes a pitch for a larger share of the fleet market with this appeal: *Your company's Chevrolet: easier to own because it's easier to sell. This year, more than ever, Chevrolet's the first-choice car. It's bigger looking. Solid feeling. Better looking, inside and out. There's even more value built in with features like . . .* ad nauseam. Generalities, vague and imprecise, ghost comparisons, no meaty information, and absolutely no feel for the market. Somebody should tell the copywriter that fleet cars are all easy to own because the companies buying them have the wherewithal to pay, and it's a deductible expense. "Easier to sell" may well be true, but who would object to some supporting facts—such as statistics from wholesale used car markets in four geographical areas? Then the time-worn ghost comparison technique —bigger looking than what? Perhaps a Volkswagen? Better looking, inside and out, than what? More value built in than what? Would this bear the scrutiny of a strict value analysis by a corporate purchasing department? This ad, to be persuasive, needs less puffery, less brag-and-boast, and some solid facts. Acceptance of the concept that advertising copy must communicate, must inform, would help a lot.

On the other hand, advertisers with real savvy realize that making a strong statement, then backing it up with proof, makes a powerful presentation of their sales proposition.

IBM provided a good example in a recent spread ad in *Modern Casting*. Left page is in four-color and shows a dramatic photo of white-hot molten metal being poured from the ladle; inset into the upper, dark area is a four-color closeup of the scrap metal that comprised the charge being poured. Headline says: *With the savings from melt charge calculations alone, Georgia Iron Works justifies its computer.* Since calculating the proper proportion of different types of metal for each charge is, after all, a small work load for a modern computer, IBM goes into a straightforward case-history copy approach that carries real conviction. It reads: *Danforth W. Hagler, vice-president of Georgia Iron Works, estimates it would take about 95 man-hours to calculate the least-cost mix for a typical charge. Much too long and expensive to be feasible. But with an IBM 1130 computer, they are now able to perform all of their charge calculations, using less than 1% of the computer's time—and realize enough savings on charge materials to make the 1130 pay its way. This means that the other 99% of the computer's time they get as a bonus.* Typical uses, including shop order reporting, price evaluation, scheduling, production control, cost account and sales analyses and forecasting are then given to illustrate the bonus uses of the computer. Following a paragraph about Georgia Iron Works, IBM adds: *The computer can be an invaluable tool for foundry management. Call your nearest IBM office and learn how. Like Dan Hagler did.*

This is sincerity and believability. There's a refreshing absence of braggadocio and no exaggeration. Just the plain, unvarnished truth. No advertising manager in his right mind quotes a customer and gives the customer's name and company as a reference unless the facts are exactly as stated. It's too easy to pick up a phone.

Diametrically opposed to exaggeration is an extremely effective technique—deliberate understatement. It is actually whispering instead of screaming. An example is Lindberg's Hevi-Duty spread ad on valve aluminizing equipment. Lindberg Hevi-Duty has an unusually strong story to tell here, one that is, perhaps, truly unique. As far as is known, there were only 21 valve aluminizing lines in the entire free world at the time this ad was prepared.

Instead of strutting and chest-thumping and proclaiming how wonderful it is, the company soft-pedaled its position and let the sheer force of quoted numbers tell the story. This was, incidentally, at a time when a would-be competitor was proudly announcing to all and sundry that it had just produced a valve aluminizing line.

On a more prosaic product Lindberg's Hevi-Duty low-key approach could be disastrous. But here the situation is different. The buying influences in the handful of establishments who could possibly be classed as prospects *know* how many installations of this type exist, and who built them. It is a close-knit industry.

Headline of the ad is: *One firm turned us down. But we've learned a thing or two from our 21 other valve aluminizing lines around the world.* Body copy is pithy and succinct and plays it straight: *Like how to get fast production. And control coatings precisely. And most of all, we've acquired a thorough understanding of how to design a valve aluminizing line that keeps producing.*

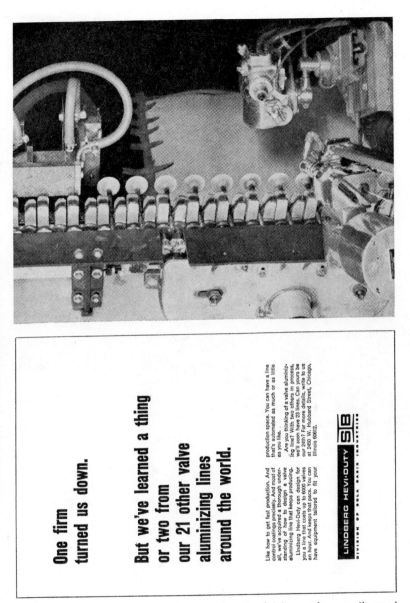

Here is the ad for Lindberg Hevi-Duty valve aluminizing equipment, discussed in detail beginning on the opposite page. The low-key approach is justified by the fact that this is a small and highly specialized industrial area with knowledgeable buyers.

Lindberg Hevi-Duty can design for you a line that coats up to 6,000 valves an hour, and keeps that pace. You can have equipment tailored to fit your production space. You can have a line that's automated as much or as little as you like.

Are you thinking of a valve aluminizing line? With two others in process, we'll soon have 23 lines. Can yours be our 24th? For more details, write us . . .

The full page, closeup illustration of the business end of the aluminizing gun is stark and simple and it's successful in stopping the reader's eye. Layout is clean and free from clutter, it has inviting white space, and the typography is legible and tasteful.

Underplay it, speak softly—and watch your readership ratings soar!

Clarity

Nobody works at ad reading.

The readers of business publications are busy men. They are unwilling to inconvenience themselves to receive your message. They will not invest extra time to interpret or decipher a message that is not immediately clear. Clarity costs nothing; lack of clarity costs everything, for lack of readership, the one essential, accompanies it.

Automation magazine recently quoted Stephen Spender, British poet and thinker, who wrote in *The Saturday Review* that "It seems to be universally recognized that everyone should learn to read and write. Not to be able to do so is illiteracy. Little importance is attached to what you read and how you write. The idea that writing is not just a physical attainment, like using a knife and fork, but is communication—and that everyone should be concerned with it to the degree that he has experience and ideas to express—seems to be regarded as eccentric.

"One has only to look at the essays of most sociologists (and almost all business writing) to realize that writing, the language of communication, is often the last thing people who have very important things to tell about the state of our society have taken trouble about. We enter the era of mass communication when the study of the traditional—and ultimate—means of communication, the English language, is looked at as a matter concerning only literary specialists."

Mr. Spender's comments could be shrugged off, even though, upon reflection, we remember that teen-agers in high school cannot spell, nor can college students write a grammatical essay. The comments may well seem out of context in any discussion of industrial advertising, of advertisements prepared at considerable expense by specialists in the art of communications. Obviously all ads should be so crystal clear that the message is transmitted and absorbed almost instantaneously.

It is little short of amazing, however, how many incredibly vague, ambiguous ads appear in the business press, ads whose message is murkily obscure, whose product is difficult to identify, and even the name of the advertiser must be searched out.

An example of this type of ad appeared in a recent issue of a metalworking book and is reproduced on the following page.

Granted this ad has shock value. Nobody overlooks the large type, the taking-a-swipe-at-management headline which enjoyed a brief burst of popularity. Then there's the cute, simple copy written for cute, simple people—who promptly ignored it. There just wasn't anything there for them. No reader involvement, product identity, product benefits, information, or drama. Even the advertiser identification is weak—there is no logo. Most of all, though, the ad suffers from lack of clarity due to not having a strong, central idea.

Anaconda Aluminum's ad is even shorter, but is a vigorous, striking ad which succeeds on every score where the other failed. The large four-color illustration is dramatically simple, direct, and to the point. Its presentation of the selling message is unusually effective.

The copy, all headline, *This is an ad for Anaconda Aluminum* casually places the company name in the headline without being ostentatious about it. It identifies the product and, combined with the illustration, promotes a major product benefit.

The mental transition of going from the illustration to the headline, then to the thought of "paint wouldn't blister and peel if the siding were of Anaconda Aluminum. Downspouts of Anaconda Aluminum wouldn't rust. Nails of Anaconda Aluminum wouldn't rust, either." Readers, mostly homeowners, easily identify with the situation shown in the ad. It is immediately clear what is being said to them. They can visualize themselves with this problem and, if the product solves the problems in homes, it is logical to assume that it would solve rust and corrosion problems at the readers' companies.

The impression is made quickly, but strongly. This is an ad that enjoyed excellent readership and it is a campaign that, if continued, will exert a strong influence on awareness of Anaconda Aluminum as an excellent company from whom to buy ingot, sheet, and other aluminum products for industry.

Our founder had holes in his head.

Big holes and little holes. Medium holes, round holes, square holes, diamond holes, straight, oblique, and herringbone holes—the best holes in the world.

And we've been making all those holes ever since Eli Hendrick founded us in 1876. If you want the best holes in the world, come to us.

And, if you have holes in your head that even we haven't thought up yet, that's all right. We're very open-minded.

Hendrick Manufacturing Company, Dundaff Street, Carbondale, Pennsylvania

That clarity, or the lack of it, affects readership is unquestioned, but the degree to which it does so is largely open to question and to individual interpretation. A paucity of information exists on the subject. You can determine for yourself how readership nose-dives when clarity is lacking, merely by analyzing any business publication whose readership is measured by Daniel Starch and Staff. The actual study results are sent to the advertiser accompanied by a marked copy of the magazine studied. Each studied ad has affixed to it a number of little stickers. These stickers have percentage figures on them, showing the percent of readers who noticed, in the case of an illustration, or read, in the case of headline or copy or company name, as well as the percentage who noticed the ad at all. Further breakdowns are given and will be discussed later on.

You'll find, in almost every instance, that ads which excel in clarity—those which are well laid out, those which do not contain too many elements, and those which have a strong central idea and are well written—excel in readership.

Research Proves the Point

This is borne out also by an analysis of the results of Ad Chart studies of a large number of business publications. Invariably when an ad is not arranged in an orderly fashion, or when it presents a multiplicity of thoughts with no dominant one, that ad rates poorly. This holds true for analyses of the findings of other readership services as well.

Other factors in addition to copy affect clarity—layout, typography, and illustration chief among them. These will be discussed in subsequent chapters.

McGraw-Hill Publishing Company has done considerable research on the subject of clarity, and in its Laboratory of Advertising Performance the company reports that advertisements with high readership ratings were consistently easier to read than ads with low ratings.

To carry out the survey, 100 one-page advertisements with the highest readership ratings and the 100 ads which rated lowest were selected from all other one-page ads in 10 issues of *Factory* during the period which was studied. Readership ratings were established by McGraw-Hill's Reader Feedback Service.

Ads were analyzed to determine if reading ease of the main copy block differed significantly in the group of high-rated ads, as compared to those which achieved low readership.

McGraw-Hill adapted a formula developed by Dr. Rudolph Flesch and described in his book, *The Art of Readable Writing,* and applied it to each of the ads in the high and low groups. The result was definite: The higher the reading ease score, the higher the readership.

This is an ad for Anaconda Aluminum

This is the Anaconda Aluminum ad analyzed on page 241.

The Flesch Reading Ease Scores of all of the ads were charted to compare them to each other and to editorial material in *Factory* magazine. The 100 top-scoring ads averaged out with a score of 48; the bottom 100 with 39—almost 20 percent difference. Editorial matter in *Factory* scored 51 on the Reading Ease chart, quite close to the 100 best-read ads.

It is interesting to note that McGraw-Hill made a point of the fact that the ads were designed to supply information to managerial, technical, and professional people who read *Factory*—and that most of these readers have a college education or its equivalent. Even with readers of this educational level and position in industry, readership of ads went up when they were clearly written in as simple language as possible to put across the idea the advertiser wanted to convey.

Other research indicates that lack of clarity cripples advertising effectiveness in three ways: (1) use of words which are not easily understood by the average reader of the publication, (2) use of the wrong word, and, (3) fuzzy phraseology that just does not convey the idea properly.

Communication's the Goal

There is no acceptable excuse for any of these shortcomings. The goal of the copywriter is to communicate an idea, not to impress people with the fact that he has an unusually large vocabulary and is an accomplished sesquipedalian. The ad that should require the average reader to consult the dictionary *won't send him there*. It will, however, send him to the next page and a competitor's ad may just happen to be there. In general, it is advisable to use the shortest, commonest, most descriptive word that does the job without sacrificing the color and flavor of the copy. Use of the wrong word is unpardonable. The advertising manager must demand precise thinking on the part of the copywriter—or organize his own thoughts if he does the writing. This will automatically eliminate any fuzzy phraseology.

Research on this subject is all well and good, but it is the consensus that lack of clarity in advertising is the result of not having a strong central idea—and of failing to consider copy as a concept. Leafing through a dozen or more trade publications in each of a half-dozen different fields every month makes this conclusion unavoidable. When ads crop up, in one form or another, like the one for a basic raw material that says: *Sh-h-h . . . Smith Product's part of the process. Many Smith Product users say a lot by not talking*

IT CAN'T BE DONE!

It can't be done! No, sir, it can't be done. You don't get labeled *the action company* by saying maybe, or we'll try, or perhaps, probably or possibly. In other words, no pussyfooting. And, Norplex hasn't! Doesn't! Won't! Norplex acts ... now ... with complete customer service. No maybe about it ... when you want price and grade information ... or research and development action on special grades ... or immediate shipment of standard grades. Norplex has a complete range of over 75 standard grades of industrial laminates ... plus glass and paper epoxy and paper phenolic copper clad grades ... for all kinds of electrical, mechanical and chemical applications ... manufactured to meet or exceed all NEMA and MIL-P specifications.

WRITE TODAY ... for your copy of the complete Norplex Catalog ... sheet sizes and specifications on the complete line of laminates from Norplex.

The Action Company In Laminated Plastics
NORPLEX CORPORATION, LA CROSSE 17, WISCONSIN
Formerly Northern Plastics Corporation

An example of what the author calls "the feline school" of advertising. What makes the technique dubious is that the reader is required to wait for the product benefits until the purpose of the illustration and headline is explained by the word, "pussyfooting." Many readers won't wait.

... and then, in the first paragraph of the body copy, *You almost have to be a Sherlock Holmes to discover how and where Smith Product is being used in many plants these days. Chemical Engineers just won't talk about its application to improve processes or develop new products.* Predictably, the illustration is of two men in hard hats, presumably Chemical Engineers (the advertiser's capitalization), one of whom has his finger to his lips, going sh-h-h to the other.

Intentions of the ad manager or agency copywriter who created this ad were undoubtedly of the best. But can he honestly believe for one minute that readers, as busy as they are and with the number of advertising impressions rising constantly, will take the time to ferret out the process? And what process? Or that readers will exert the extra effort of wading through paragraphs of inanities to find out why they would have to be a Sherlock Holmes—and they may not want to be Sherlock at all—to discover how and where Smith Product is being used in such a manner that it presumably benefits somebody like himself in another company?

Then there is the feline school of advertising, most of which is as hazy as pea-soup fog. Consider the ad with the illustration of a meowing cat, and the headline *IT CAN'T BE DONE!* Copy goes, *It can't be done! No, sir, it can't be done. You don't get labeled the action company by saying maybe, or we'll try, or perhaps, probably, or possibly. In other words, no pussyfooting.* And so on and on and on. But the pussyfooting *did* explain the illustration. See next page.

Another ambiguous feline ad has the headline, *What do cats and waterless sand with Activall* have in common?* This is explained by the subhead saying, *you're right, they both have nine lives!* This startling bit of intelligence leads to the body copy where we learn that: *Don't mess around. Some cats will put anything in a sand pile!* Readership stopped there, of course. And it never was made very clear what that Activall mentioned in the headline is, was it?

Beware the Off-Beat Ad

An abortive effort to be creative is a final hindrance which frequently makes clarity impossible. Some advertising people—on both advertiser and agency sides of the desk—are imbued with the idea that an ad has to be gimmicked up, it has to be off-beat, to succeed. They'll go to almost any lengths to keep from presenting the product story simply and logically, without pretense or phony frills. Little does it matter, apparently, that the resulting ad isn't read—or readable. This precociousness, this immaturity, this grandstand play to

What
do
cats
and
waterless
sand
with
Activall*
have
in
common
?

you're right, they both have nine lives!

Don't mess around. Some cats will put anything in a sand pile! But you don't have to add water or anything like it. Just Activall.* Works so well you can make nine consecutive castings without adding a doggone thing. Saves money, too. Up to 50% on sand costs. You can put the difference in the kitty. Write for details: P.O. Box 6504, Houston, Texas 77005. *Magcobar Activator for Water-less Bentonite-Sand Molding System.

attract the attention of other advertising practitioners costs advertisers vast sums annually in ineffective ads and an incalculable amount in sales which never materialized for this reason. Although not as prevalent in industrial advertising as it is in the consumer field—remember the Renault campaign of a few years ago, in which

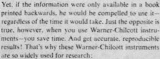

dozens of type faces appeared in one ad?—nonetheless perverted creativity rears its head all too often.

Another attempt to be creative, to be different at any cost—including readership—is the advertiser who had the headline of the ad set backwards. Note that it isn't set so that a fast trip to the washroom where there's a mirror available will help. Nor will holding the page up to the light and reading through the paper, if that's possible. The type is actually set backwards so that it can be read if anybody is willing to spell out each word to himself, writing it down on a handy tablet until the complete three-line headline is transcribed. Headline says: *Can you imagine the time it would take for a researcher to get much-needed information from a textbook printed like this?* Can you imagine the time it would take a reader to flip the page? It's unfortunate, too, because this catalog-type ad is unusually clean and airy for one which shows as many products as it does. It would have done the job, except for that headline.

Be Selective

This is in no sense a suggestion that the genuinely creative idea, the fresh approach, the new and compelling way to state a thought should be discarded. Rather, when writing an ad you should train yourself to be highly selective, to discard the ideas which lack merit because there are plenty more where they came from! Occasionally a gem of an idea is born, as in the case of the fine ad run by Simonds Abrasive Division of Wallace-Murray Corporation.

Some products are inherently easy to dramatize due to their end use or the place in which they are used—such as an item of equipment for pouring molten metal in a foundry, for example. Others, more prosaic, demand more of the writer if he is to present them in an aura of excitement so that readers of business publications will find the ad attractive and want to read it. The grinding wheels manufactured by Simonds Abrasive Division is an example of the latter type of product.

There are few ways to make a snagging wheel—one used for rough grinding operations to remove excessive material from foundry castings—have much visual appeal. They all look alike, and, quite likely, even users have few reasons to prefer Brand X over Brand Y.

The creative platform for Simonds wheels says, in part: "Take a relatively undramatic product—abrasives—and present it in a highly unusual and imaginative way. Each advertisement to be built around an idea so attention-getting and provocative that it will stand out from the mass of competitive ads—and from noncompetitive ads, for they also compete for readers' time. Regardless of what technique or method is used to get the readers' attention, it must be a functional one. It must be something inherent in our product or our message. Not merely a gimmick that has nothing to do with what we're trying to say, or trying to sell."

AT 12,500 S.F.P.M. HERE'S WHAT YOU GET FROM SIMONDS SNAGGING WHEELS.

Metal removal costs drop as much as 60%. Grinding time drops as much as 30%. Wheel life goes up as much as 35%.

These are the kind of reports we get back from customers who give Simonds YA Borolon wheels with fiberglass reinforcing a trial. YA Borolon is a specially developed aluminum oxide abrasive with 40% zirconium oxide additive. It produces the results at high speed. The fiberglass reinforcing makes sure you can do it with safety.

Simonds reinforced High Speed snagging wheels are available for all types of 12,500 S.F.P.M. snagging grinders. Before you standardize . . . try Simonds. See what they can do for you. And see what Simonds Superior Service from a fast, local distributor can do for your grinding room efficiency.

Typical Simonds High Speed Wheel 30" x 2½" x 12" for 12,500 S.F.P.M. floor stand grinders.

SUPERIOR SERVICE THROUGH LOCAL DISTRIBUTORS—TECHNICAL KNOWHOW, FAST DELIVERY

SIMONDS ABRASIVE
Wallace-Murray Corporation
PHILADELPHIA, PA. 19137

West Coast Plant: El Monte, Calif.—Branches: Chicago • Detroit • Los Angeles • Philadelphia • Portland, Ore. • So. San Francisco, Shreveport—In Canada: Grinding Wheel Division, Simonds Canada Saw Co., Ltd., Brockville, Ontario • Abrasive Plant, Arvida, Quebec

The ad pictured here is a stopper. The yellow and black sign is actually the headline, and the basic concept is so forceful, so vivid and compelling that it simply cannot be bypassed. How many signs state the speed limit as 142 miles per hour?

This speed, in miles per hour, is merely the surface feet per minute at which the wheel is rated expressed provocatively so that it stands out from all of the other ads in the book, as the advertiser's copy platform stated.

The sign headline is quickly explained by a subhead that reads: *AT 12,500 S.F.P.M. HERE'S WHAT YOU GET FROM SIMONDS SNAGGING WHEELS.* Body copy is terse, fact-filled and convincing. It starts out *Metal removal costs drop as much as 60%. Grinding time drops as much as 30%. Wheel life goes up as much as 35%.* These aren't figures which Simonds tosses around lightly, for the ad goes on to explain that speed had been increased from 9,500 S.F.P.M. to 12,500 S.F.P.M., and the Simonds wheel could stand the gaff because it has fiber glass reinforcing, a specially developed aluminum oxide abrasive with 40% zirconium oxide additive. That's good writing—giving the user benefits, then building in believability by giving the nuts-and-bolts reasons why.

Simonds had a Starch study made of the ad as run originally with minor copy changes and it scored well. The ad as a whole achieved a 29 percent noted rating, seen-associated 21 percent, and various elements ranging from 29 percent on the sign to a low of 4 percent in the slogan copy across the bottom. A creditable performance due to a good basic idea, and to such clarity that the ad almost telegraphed its message.

Chapter 6

THE COPY PLATFORM

THE COPY platform contains all of the guidelines which the copywriter must have to write effective selling copy. It is concrete, specific, and formal because it is written. Because it is written, there are no vague generalities.

The written platform, or plan, contains among its ingredients all of the many things which it is mandatory to do—slants, approaches, directions. It contains an irreducible number of sacred cows near and dear to the heart of somebody up there in the corner office. A small herd must be included more often than not, if for no other reason than that it's desirable for everybody to hold his job. They can and should be accorded only a once over lightly when used, and as seldom as possible at that.

Also in the platform are clear and firm instructions *not* to discuss certain topics deemed detrimental to the company's competitive position or its image. These verboten topics are usually based on one of several things: A product weakness as compared to similar products in the marketplace, lack of distribution in certain geographic areas, a price disadvantage, unfavorable dealer discount structure, inability to produce the product as quickly as competitive companies can, and, usually, one whim. This last consideration can be considered to carry the most weight when it belongs to top management.

A carefully thought out and clearly written copy platform accomplishes a number of things, all of which are desirable. It makes your work easier. It saves time. It clarifies your thinking. It organizes your thoughts. It enables you to direct your agency more effectively. It is an invaluable reference for agency personnel assigned to your account. And, like a written marketing plan, it *forces* all who work within its framework to be precise. The written copy platform is the antithesis of the half-formed, poorly expressed thought, of the ill-conceived concept. As an instrument to upgrade copy quality, it is in a class by itself.

Furthermore, the written copy platform puts all concerned on record, for it is formal evidence of an agreement as to the purpose and scope of a campaign or an individual advertisement. Depending upon the company, those involved with it may include the advertising manager, the director of marketing, the sales manager, product managers, engineering management—and even the president. Naturally, agency personnel will be involved, including the account executive, account supervisor, group vice-president, copywriter, art director, media director, plans board, or other review group.

Producing a formal copy platform is not "made" work, however, nor is it a bureaucratic exercise merely for the sake of going through motions. With a platform everybody's job is easier. There is a drastic reduction in nonproductive effort. Wheel spinning is largely eliminated. That's because the name of the game—and the rules by which it is to be played—are clearly defined for all to see and understand.

A desirable fringe benefit accrues, for getting entire campaigns (as well as individual ads), approved by the chain of command is greatly simplified.

Finally, and perhaps the most important benefit realized from the copy platform, you'll find development of a campaign is infinitely easier. A campaign, unlike a mishmash of separate ads done one at a time, haphazardly and with little overall planning, is a series of ads with a strong, unifying theme. A campaign is developed to achieve stated objectives. All of the ads in a well-conceived campaign are similar in appearance, of course. They share a basic concept as well as bear a strong family resemblance as far as layout and typography are concerned, and are immediately recognized as individual elements in a campaign.

What the Copy Platform Should Contain

The platform will obviously vary considerably due to differences in the product or service which is to be advertised. This variation shows up most strongly in the sections of the platform dealing with the product or service, while the balance of the platform is equally applicable for a manufacturer of bulldozers, babbitt, or bolts. All companies must accomplish the same basic objectives with their advertising if it is to make a significant contribution to the company's marketing success, for, product and market differences aside, all businesses have similar problems to solve and similar competitive hurdles to overcome.

Essentials for the copy platform are:

1. Objectives of the campaign.

2. Objective for each individual ad.

3. Universe—a brief description of the market and of the buying influences with which the campaign and the individual ads must communicate.

4. Media to be used.

5. Schedule—frequency of advertisement insertion in each medium.

6. Short statement of the company's position in the marketplace and its reputation.

7. Price range of product and comparison with prices of similar competitive products.

8. Channels of distribution, including the number of dealers and/or distributors, their strengths and weaknesses, and how cooperative they are.

9. When the product is purchased, seasonal patterns, historical patterns.

10. How the product is purchased and increments in which it is marketed—gallons, pounds, bales, individual units, and so on.

11. Why the product is purchased.

12. What action the ads are expected to produce.

13. Central idea or theme of the campaign.

14. Slant, or approach, to be taken; this could be problem-and-solution, question-and-answer, case history, testimonial, editorial, narrative, etc.

15. Format; this could range from four-color, multipage inserts down to fractional-page black and white ads, with illustrative techniques described.

16. Product features in order of importance, and features *not* to mention.

17. User benefits which result from the features.

The copy platform is not a duplication of the marketing plan, nor is it a lengthy, verbose document which will repel so rapidly that it's filed away and forgotten fast. It performs a necessary job. Let's see why each of these 17 elements are essential in a solid, complete copy platform.

Objective

A campaign—and an individual ad—must have an objective to accomplish before it has a prayer of a chance of returning one cent of its cost to the advertiser.

Copy is a component of the complete advertisement, just as a caption and the illustration are. However, copy has a different job to perform. Captions and illustrations have as their function the attracting of the reader's attention, of arousing his interest, of stopping him and drawing him into the copy. From then on, the copy carries the complete burden of persuading the prospect to accept the advertiser's viewpoint.

There are many reasons—actually objectives—for which copy is written, but this primary one should be remembered: *It is the primary function of copy to persuade the prospect to accept the advertiser's viewpoint.*

Other functions can be to introduce a new product or a significant improvement in an existing product. Only advertising can spread the word across the nation, or around the world, about a new development quickly and economically to a universe which may encompass hundreds of thousands, even millions, of prospective purchasers. Copy in an advertisement is able to make these prospects aware of the new product and make them understand its significance in terms of what it means to them. Copy can create an awareness of product features and user benefits and how the product should be used to produce these benefits.

If copy is well written, interesting, and informative, it can produce tangible results measured by response from readers of the publications in which the ad appears. Copy can cause people to react as you want them to, people far away with diverse interests and backgrounds.

Different products are introduced successfully into different markets by advertisers with varying objectives; one advertiser, for instance, may want response in terms of inquiries which will be followed up by either his dealer organization or his field sales force. Another may desire only to increase awareness of his company, his trademark, his product, or a radically different process.

When the economy as a whole is volatile and there is an inexorable trend to government-induced inflation, advertising copy can do much to remove the curse from an across-the-board price increase. This is particularly important in a basic raw material, and is an objective of the steel industry, among others. Such nonproduct, nonselling copy in an ad is actually a public relations effort, despite its being in a paid message form.

And, in time of war, even a "limited" one, many products critical to the defense effort are in extremely short supply for the general business community. In these circumstances advertising can do much to help retain the goodwill of industrial buyers, irked at not being able to place an order and get normal delivery, by telling them—reminding, actually—why.

Copy can do a tremendous job of building awareness of a new or expanded warranty policy. When capital equipment is involved, this is an unusually potent sales point and one which, although something of an intangible, is of great importance to the purchaser. Advertising copy did a great job for Dodge trucks in explaining the industry's first long-term warranty on the vehicle's power train, and what this meant to the truck user.

These are a few valid objectives for a campaign or for an individual advertisement. You undoubtedly have others equally good.

When writing an ad, or giving directions to your agency, you'll find it good practice to write down the objective for this specific ad. It's remarkably helpful to write down what you want the ad to accomplish for your company and what you want the prospects to do after having read it. You'll have to bear in mind, of course, that pie in the sky is unattainable, and that no ad can produce for you the world with a white picket fence around it. Be realistic, face facts, and make your objective realistic so that the ad can attain it. This means that your ad cannot be all things to all readers, or even hope to be.

Be specific, stick to a strong central idea and exploit it for all it's worth. You can include a wrap-up, or summary, of additional product features and benefits, of course, but to do so at the expense of weakening the core idea is to welcome failure with open arms. Multiple ideas always result in dilution of copy effectiveness. Magazine editors, hard-nosed and real experts at evaluating copy, have long stressed the fact that a magazine article must be built around one central idea. *One central idea.* They know it is impossible to develop fully two ideas in a single article, even one of 7,500 to 10,000 words. And it's simply beyond the realm of reason to expect to be able to do so in an industrial advertisement considering how few words you're permitted.

Universe

You'll want to include a short statement in the platform about who you want to read your ad. It's an important element of the platform. A condensed personality profile of the individuals to whom the ad should be slanted is desirable. This profile should include titles or job functions of the buying influences, their educational level, whether they specify or recommend specific brands of products and/or specific purveyors, whether they approve purchases, if theirs is the ultimate decision, and the stage in the purchasing process in which they enter the picture. This, of course, will be from Stage 1 through Stage 7, as previously discussed.

Include also a short statement as to the type of company to whom you're most likely to sell. This will probably mean one of a specific size in terms of number of employees and gross dollar volume.

The profile is simplified if it is charted as shown below. This pyramid chart was originally developed by Bramson Publishing Company and is used with their permission. It can be used for any number of products in any number of markets where buying influences might vary; simply check off the appropriate group and include this as an appendix in the copy platform.

President,
Vice-President,
General Management

Plant Manager, Mgr. of Mfg.,
Manager of Manuf. Engineering,
Master Mechanic,
General Superintendent, Chief Engineer

Production and Design Engineers:
(Process, Methods, Industrial, Plant, Product Engineers)

Operating Department Heads, Managers, Supervisors, Foremen

Position of your key buying influences in the pyramid obviously will affect the way the ad is written. A glaring error which will nullify your ad completely is to write an ad slanted toward foremen and supervisors in the same language as one directed toward the president—and vice versa. The two groups won't both read one ad because the appeals would be wrong. User benefits would be different because you'd talk profit to the president and easier production or a similar benefit to first line management. Difference in the level of sophistication also is too great for there to be much reader involvement regardless of the difference in the factors which motivate different echelons of management.

Media

Media in which the ad will appear should also be in the copy platform. Certain publications almost demand a certain slant due to their audience composition. Although it's not always the case, different media usually call for different ads if each is to achieve its greatest potential readership.

Schedule

The schedule—the frequency with which the ad will appear (if it is to run only one time in a publication or is to be repeated in selected media)—and the months of the year in which it runs are important to the copywriter. A short statement with the schedule in tabular form is a good planning tool for the ad manager.

Company Position in the Market

There is no need to go into a lengthy discussion here, but this is a subject which could influence the writing of the ad. It is simple enough to extract a short paragraph from the marketing plan, or condense a section into a few short sentences for the copy platform. Competitive position influences copy approach, and this information should be at the copywriter's fingertips without his having to search through a lengthy dissertation to determine just what it is.

Price

Price of the product being advertised, particularly in comparison to similar products produced by others, is necessary information when an ad is being written. This holds true even if price is not given in the ad. If the price varies considerably depending upon the number of optional features the customer selects, a price *range* should be given and compared to a price *range* of competitive products.

It may well be that your product is priced substantially higher than your competition. If so, there's bound to be a reason which justifies this position and this reason can frequently be turned into an advantage, instead of a disadvantage, in an advertising campaign. Industrial buyers are not gullible; they recognize that getting exactly what you pay for is a fact of business life. They don't expect something for nothing. When giving this information include the dealer or distributor discount structure.

Prices, incidentally, are not company secrets, nor are dealer/distributor discounts. This information is widely circulated and rare indeed is the heads-up manufacturer of relatively expensive equipment who doesn't have a complete catalog and price book of his major competitors' lines. They're easily gotten from friendly dealers, "acquired" at trade shows, or are a fringe benefit which somehow happens to coincide with hiring a salesman or executive from a competitive company.

Distribution

Channels of distribution must be given in the copy platform because they, too, can influence the slant of an ad. From the price section of the platform the person writing the ad can quickly tell if there are advantages in the price or in the discount structure to exploit—since this information is given with comparisons to competitive products.

Discuss the distributive process in a sentence or two, give the size of the field sales force compared to that of competitors. Point out any major geographic strengths or weaknesses.

When Purchases Occur

Most industrial products are purchased all year around. With some, however, there is a strong seasonal pattern. An example is Freon gas sold by Du Pont to automobile manufacturers for use in automotive air conditioners. Auto builders' purchasing departments place blanket orders well in advance of anticipated use, then schedule shipments against the original order. This means that Freon is sold not in the hot summer months, or even in the late spring, but when winter is waning. Construction materials, including structural steel, are traditionally sold around the first of the year for delivery in late March, although the building season varies in different areas of the country.

If there is a historical pattern—such as machine tool orders being preceded by a rise in carloadings—or some other reliable barometer, this information belongs in the copy platform. Every iota of information which helps the man behind the typewriter contributes toward more effective advertising.

How Purchases Are Made

State how the product is purchased, what unit of measure applies, such as gallons, tons, yards, pounds, kegs, or similar units. Give the size of the average sale. Also give the largest and smallest sales over the last 12 months, and the smallest profitable sale. A brief table giving a statistical analysis of the previous year's sales in percentages according to the number of units sold per individual sale is helpful.

Why Purchases Are Made

This is the time to draw upon the sales manager's knowledge of the product and reasons why prospects' decisions are made the way they are—if you feel even slightly unsure of your ground in this area. And even if you *are* sure, a discussion may turn up reasons why your product is purchased that you've never thought of. Communication between various departments and advertising is almost never what it should be. Others do not realize what can help the advertising manager can help them.

Purchases are made for objective reasons, carefully and logically reasoned out by the industrial buyer. The most important are:

1. *Quality.*
2. *Delivery schedule.*
3. *Price.*

That is probably their order of importance too, although this can vary according to the state of the economy and product availability. In times of scarcity of your product, price would definitely come last. On the other hand, in a recession with its buyers' market, price would move up into second place—but not into first under any consideration.

Those are the basic reasons for specifying one make over another, or one purveyor over another, that the buyer *thinks* he is basing his decision on. There may be hidden reasons why he makes the decisions he does, however. These may not even be recognized by the buyer. And even if they are, he may not admit them even to himself. These are decisions made subjectively, emotionally, despite the industrial buyer's lack of personal involvement with the product because he does not consume or use it.

One study in motivation research in industrial buying showed that fear was a factor in a surprisingly high percentage of industrial purchases. This included fear of switching from a familiar supplier with whom the buyer has dealt for some time; fear of changing from a product which he knows from past experience will perform satisfactorily—even if he has every reason to believe the alternate product may be superior—and, underlying all others, fear of making a wrong decision and thus incurring the disapproval of his superiors.

If your product is not very well known, if your company is relatively small and you're bucking giants in the marketplace, your advertising must reassure buyers that when they select your product they're making a wise decision.

Another emotional factor influencing purchases is pride, which is actually the desire to attain personal prestige. This is evidenced by a decision to buy from the largest and best-known source in the industry because that is obviously what the majority of other buyers do. There's safety in numbers.

Ambition motivates many who influence industrial purchases. The desire for self-aggrandizement, to advance within the company, to achieve more than others do, is a potent factor in the makeup of many individuals—most, in fact. It frequently leads to the "safe" decision to avoid mistakes, or the selection of the "best" supplier.

The basic instinct for self-preservation plays a strong role, too, and is similar to the desire for self-aggrandizement; the emotional considerations are almost identical. In both cases it is up to the advertiser to satisfy the emotional yearnings of such individuals, to reassure them that when they buy your product they are acting in their—and their company's—self-interest.

Response

Every industrial ad should close with a request for action, just as every good salesman always asks for the order. Not to do so is a wasted sales call—either in print or in person.

The bid for action should be carefully thought out and a decision made as to what response you want from the readers of your ad. You may, for instance, want a quantity of bingo-card inquiries. If such is the case, have the publication print on the bottom of your ad, *Circle No.000 on the Reader Service Card for more information.* Then, when the cards with the key number assigned to you are returned to the publication, or to the book's inquiry-handling service, you will be notified of the names, companies, and addresses of each inquirer who is interested in your product. This generally produces a sizable volume of inquiries if your selling proposition, the message, and the media are right.

Or, you may want to make an offer—free literature, a pocket calculator of the slide-rule type, a wall chart converting fractions of an inch to decimal equivalents, an actual sample of your product (offers are discussed more fully later on), or a proposal to go into a prospect's plant and analyze his equipment requirements or production processes—at no cost to him, of course. Each of these offers can be counted on to produce a volume of inquiries.

On the other hand, your ad may deliberately be very hard hitting and competitive. It may be written so that it directs the prospect to consider both your product and similar ones produced by other companies—and to compare them in detail. Hopefully, this will be to the detriment of the competition. It will be if the ad is well written and the facts are marshalled correctly.

In any event, the individual ads can be tailored to produce the response that you decide upon. What that will be depends upon your coverage in the field by your sales force, your distribution, availability of your product, production backlog, and many other factors.

Theme

A campaign isn't a campaign without a theme. It can't be. A theme is an absolute essential. It is the theme which transforms a random assortment of individual ads into a cohesive, unified whole, making a neat, logical package.

The theme, however, is *not* the subject of either the campaign or of any individual ad except in rare instances where an advertiser feels his theme needs explaining. And, if it needs explaining the theme is somewhat less than appropriate.

The subject is the product or service which is being advertised, made more desirable by the theme's presenting its user benefits from the viewpoint of the prospect.

A few of the better known campaign themes used by industrial companies follow. Although not all themes are stated, they all refine the selling message and condense it to a few compelling words that are easy to understand and easy to remember. The one central thought each presents runs through all of the ads in the campaign. This thought is repeated time and time again, exerting a progressively stronger effect upon the reader with each repetition.

Almost all currently successful advertising campaigns are built around a strong central idea, or theme. The theme is usually repeated in advertising directed toward consumers, either print or broadcast, if the company markets products directly to consumers. Many industrial companies advertise to both—General Electric, for instance. It appears in sales literature, the theme follows through in sales presentations and audio-visual presentations. It unifies the entire promotional effort.

The most trusted name in electronics
Radio Corporation of America

You expect more from Standard and you get it!
Standard Oil Division, American Oil Company

You can be sure if it's Westinghouse
Westinghouse Electric Company

Hertz rents Fords and other good cars
Hertz Corporation

The airline built for professional travellers
American Airlines

Leader in adhesive technology
H. B. Fuller Company

It pays to do business with the airfreight specialist—
Tiger International

Wherever you look . . . you see Budd
The Budd Company

Machines that make data move
Teletype Corporation

You'll find our brand all over the West
CF&I Steel Corporation

The big birds fly the friendly skies of United Air Lines
United Air Freight

The discovery company
Union Carbide

Standard of the plotting industry
California Computer Products, Inc.

The better ideas are at UOP
Universal Oil Products Company

Tested . . . trusted products since 1868
Eaton Yale & Towne, Inc.

Have you looked at Wheeling lately?
Wheeling Steel Corporation

Progress is our most important product
General Electric Company

Look ahead—look south
Southern Railway System

Going in new directions with new ideas
Boise Cascade Corporation

Serving man's basic needs worldwide
Worthington Corporation

Where the big idea is innovation
United States Steel

Ford has a better idea
Ford Motor Company

We don't stop with paper
Crown Zellerbach

You can take the pulse of progress at
Republic Steel Corporation

Gulf makes things run better!
Gulf Oil Corporation

For companies going places!
Mack Trucks, Inc.

Preferred performance
Sealed Power Corporation

Themes are deceptively simple. They look easy to create. Most, however, came into being only after company marketing people and their agency counterparts racked their brains for countless hours. It's not uncommon for hundreds, even thousands, of ideas to be suggested, carefully written down, and sifted through in the final selection process. Sometimes data is fed into a computer in hopes the output of its semiconductors, integrated circuits, and other electronic hardware will result in the birth of a revolutionary new product name, which, in turn, will lead to development of a theme to end all themes.

Sometimes, though, you can't plan these things. They're like Topsy—they just grow, or just evolve. Once in a while inspiration strikes like a bolt out of the blue and a new theme pops full-blown into someone's mind—probably while he's shaving or reading the paper on the 5:15. And the chances are that this theme will be just exactly right, that it's one that neither people nor computers can top.

How to Bag a Theme

Actually, though, it is not necessary to wait for inspiration to strike. Inspiration can't be scheduled. A suitable theme can be stalked and bagged if you know where to hunt for it. The most logical place to start is with the product itself.

Ask yourself, what makes this product different? What makes it better? What sets it apart from similar products? Why is it more desirable from the prospect's viewpoint? What will it do for him that competitive products won't, or can't, do? What is the one best reason you can think of to buy it?

List your questions on a legal-sized tablet. Rule it off, include as headings your product and similar ones produced by major competitors. Ignore cats and dogs such as regional manufacturers if you have national distribution unless they are unusually tough competition in the area they have staked out. Answer these questions, plus others that will occur to you, for each competitive product— by model number, perhaps—and briefly write down the answer on the pad. Be objective, be honest. This is no time to let emotion and loyalty to good old Ajax company influence you.

If nothing revealing results, go a step further. Chances are you either have, or have access to, detailed analyses of competitive products. Every company has them—or should. They're lovingly compiled and tabulated by a statistician in the market research or sales department, generally carried out to the fourth decimal place, and then distributed to key individuals inside and the entire field sales force. Emphasis is usually placed on specifications of the products;

in the case of mechanical equipment, for example, sizes of various components, capacities, horsepower, and similar methods of comparison are used. Examine these carefully, compare them with your own product. You'll find a number of areas in which yours is definitely superior.

Let's take a hypothetical road grader for the sake of illustration. Now, the fact is that one road grader is very much like another. Rated capacities, power output, size of hydraulic equipment, blade size, cab comfort and what have you are remarkably uniform. Industry doesn't build too many Edsels—of the kind that fly or the kind you drive—and stay in business. Competition serves to assure a remarkably uniform level of high quality.

Our road grader, however, may excel slightly—but only slightly—in several areas. It may, for instance, have an engine with somewhat larger piston displacement; its blade may be an inch or so wider, or deeper; the cab may have a little more elbow room for the driver, or a bit better visibility. Any or all of these product features can be translated into user benefits of real significance to prospective purchasers.

The Rating Game

So, how do we develop a theme? Perhaps by rating, or grading, all competitive road graders. Stress the areas of your grader's superiority. Hammer home the fact that you graded the grader, that you made a thoroughly objective comparison. This can also infer that manufacturers of competitive graders were afraid to do this. Handled properly, you can come up with a catchy, memorable theme that has real impact. Although none of these are such a theme, they do give the general idea of the thought process involved in theme development. *The Grade A Grader. The grader that earned an A grade. The top-graded grader.* Some similar theme can lead to quite a campaign in which the theme—that this grader was graded on features, on performance, on long life, on freedom from maintenance, on high-residual value at trade-in time, and so on—is natural and believable. The old ploy of comparing, in the ad, grader A, B, and C with yours could be employed. Or you could be bitterly competitive and actually name the other graders and give their scores; when writing an ad like this, be absolutely certain that you have your facts right.

In this case, the theme resulted from product superiorities that came to light when the detailed specifications of the hypothetical grader were compared to those of competitive machines. A different tack could have been taken by comparing performance of this grader with others. When products are this expensive, it is common practice for manufacturers of such equipment to go into the market-place and buy a number of competitive units. These are then tested in the company's proving grounds under typical operating conditions, then returned to the manufacturer's research department for disassembly and a thorough study of how they are built. This gives the sales and marketing departments a wealth of competitive information that's almost impossible to come by in any other way. Re-assembled, the equipment brings a good price—almost as much as the manufacturer paid, as a rule—on the used equipment market because it has had so little use.

Such tests quickly point up a difference in performance of your product and those of your competitors. More miles per gallon, more work per hour, bigger loads, faster cycle time, or some other vitally important user benefit usually results. The advertising manager should always be on the list of those receiving reports on such tests.

Where it's not feasible to purchase, test, and disassemble competitive products, a thorough analysis of competitive literature acquired by or through sympathetic dealers or distributors can show where you have a competitive edge. Literature on industrial products is replete with performance data—what the product will do for the purchaser. Compare these statistics with those for your product and you'll probably discover several areas where you have a decided advantage, either in performance or in versatility. This latter can be presented as giving the purchaser more for his money, since if equipment doubles in brass and handles two jobs, there might well be no need to invest in supplementary equipment which might be idle a good part of the time.

Availability As a Benefit

Availability plays a critically important role in the sales picture of many industrial products. In automotive replacement parts, for example, mere availability to the purchaser is credited by many leading companies with exerting a decisive role in a high percentage of purchases. With adequate or better distribution, a manufacturer has a potent sales point—and all the more so if this broad distribution goes hand in hand with better service. International Harvester Company ran a trade campaign for IHC motor trucks a short time ago in which some of the ads ended, *Branches and dealers every-where.* There is simply nothing to be said on the subject which can begin to equal this statement—much less top it. The other builders of heavy-duty trucks must have been envious. Harvester had the final word.

Company capability can result in an effective advertising theme. If the company is the recognized leader in its industry, with a product line bigger and broader than that of its competitors, this can lead to a theme of total capability. This was used with excellent results by Lindberg Hevi-Duty for some time in all of its promotions to five major markets ranging from the semiconductor industry to the foundry field.

Or you could make your product stand out and develop a catchy theme if you do more merchandising to a dealer or distributor group than any of your competitors, thus helping them sell your product to a manufacturer who incorporates it into the end product. This is particularly effective if you market a product which competes vigorously for a market composed of such manufacturers—acetates and other fibers used in clothing, "Corfam" for shoes, chemicals, building materials, and so forth. Many companies run campaigns which are almost institutional, or corporate, in character, yet their primary objective is to stimulate demand by the end manufacturer for their component or their raw material.

No product is so pallid or so deficient in believable superiorities that a memorable advertising theme cannot be developed if all factors are considered. The greatest theme ever developed may not come to you immediately, and you shouldn't expect it. But, with work, a good one will emerge.

Many companies have themes because they are recognized as vitally necessary for continuity and cohesiveness, but they are not actually used in print. Even if one doesn't appear in every industrial ad you notice, you can accept as fact that the campaign has an umbrella theme—if the campaign is a good one.

18 Basic Themes

In its Laboratory of Advertising Performance, McGraw-Hill published data on basic copy themes. To find out what themes were being used most effectively by industrial advertisers, the publishing company made an analysis of the highest ranking ads in 21 different McGraw-Hill publications. Results are:

1. *Corporate:* Including promotion of logotype or trademark, primarily to enhance the company's reputation and aid in its recognition.

2. *Public or Industry Service:* This type of message is essentially noncommercial in nature and is designed to give the reader information which would help him.

3. *Announcement:* This large category includes introduction of new products, services, product features or user benefits.

4. *General Description:* This narrative-style of advertising usually makes a relatively broad statement about the quality of the product.

5. *Unique Product Features:* Unique is the key word here, because this type of ad discusses exclusive features of a product or product line.

6. *Product Line:* A catalog-type ad showing the number of different items produced by the manufacturer.

7. *Catalog:* Similar to the above type of advertisement, but more detailed so as to include sizes, dimensions, materials, specifications, and so on.

8. *Testimonial:* A case-history ad in which a user's good experience with the product is described, usually in his own words.

9. *Specific Problem Solved:* How a product solved a specific problem, usually with emphasis on the company's overall problem-solving ability.

10. *Product Performance Facts:* Features and user benefits of the product.

11. *Suggested Product Application:* Ways in which the product may be used are discussed and illustrated.

12. *Product Test Results:* A graphic representation of the results of using the product.

13. *Safety:* How the product, when used as directed, reduces or eliminates hazards to factory personnel, or to the public as a whole.

14. *Modernization:* How the product prevents obsolescence; keeps an operation competitive with modern equipment.

15. *Savings, Economy, or Profits:* The pocketbook appeal. Ads stress how the product eliminates unnecessary labor or superfluous operations, reduces maintenance costs, amortizes itself quickly.

16. *Teaser:* A campaign that whet's the reader's appetite by arousing his curiosity.

17. *Tie-in:* Relating the product or service to a current event to secure higher readership.

18. *Reader Action:* A campaign designed specifically to produce a desired reaction on the part of the reader. This could be returning a coupon, sending for literature, telephoning for a price quotation, asking for a salesman to call, or a similar response.

Slant

How a campaign is slanted, or how it is aimed, will be determined by the product itself, the audience for the campaign, the type of buying influences who must be communicated with and a number of other factors. Some are inherent in the marketplace.

The slant, or approach, should be stated in the copy platform after careful consideration of campaign identity and advertiser identification. You won't want to slant one ad one way, then switch to an entirely different slant in subsequent ads. To do so sacrifices campaign identity and dilutes identification of your company as the sponsor of the ads.

The decision isn't always an easy one to make—and sometimes, unless the right decision seems very obvious—it's best not to make it immediately. Instead, write some ads and make rough layouts (copywriter's roughs) using different slants. Once something is down on paper, you can then evaluate its effectiveness much more easily. This isn't wasted effort, for it will save time later on.

Most common approach for all business publication ad copy is straight narrative style. This is simply telling your story in a straightforward manner, presenting your facts one after the other as attractively as possible. It is, perhaps, easiest to write and is equally appropriate for new product announcement ads as it is for products which have been on the market for some time. General description, product features, problem-solving ads and many others fall readily into this category. Unless another approach is strongly indicated, the narrative style is probably the best.

There's also the popular problem-and-solution slant which results in excellent reader involvement because *everybody* has problems, and those in industry tend to fall into well-defined patterns. This type of ad usually enjoys high readership, assuming the problem is a universal one.

Another way to involve the reader is to use the time-proved

question-and-answer approach. Similar to the problem-and-solution type of ad, it assures good reader involvement and good readership —if the question(s) is well chosen. Incidentally, the correct form *is* problem, solution—question, answer. It is *not* problem, answer— question, solution. This mistake crops up constantly, even in ads by huge, sophisticated companies. It's extremely bad form.

Case-history ads have been around since the dawn of advertising itself, but they continue to be persuasive and believable—perhaps even more today than in the past. When a firm runs a case-history ad the reader can accept as gospel the statements made about the product. It's common practice—and good practice—to give the name of the firm using the product the location of that company, and usually the name of the individual involved with the product. He'll be the person either specifying it or using it, probably the latter. In a surprising number of cases, the reader does what the ad makes easy for him—he picks up the phone and verifies the statements made in the ad. He does this not because he doesn't believe the advertiser's statements, but because he wants the reassurance of somebody like himself who is presently using the product successfully that he will make a wise decision if he buys it. Since no advertiser would feature anything other than a highly satisfied user of its products, it becomes obvious why generations of ad managers hold the case-history ad in such high esteem.

Testimonial ads are similar to case-history ads, although usually based on either a well-known individual who is making the statement, or on a giant company whose name is a byword. Famous names add authenticity to an advertiser's claims.

An editorial approach is frequently taken, sometimes with the advertisement looking much like editorial material in the medium in which it appears. It's a mistake to make it resemble editorial matter too much, for the reader might get the impression you're trying to deceive him. The editorial ad usually runs to long copy which, in the case of a complex product, is desirable because it gives ample room to explain various features and specifications. Either in spite of the long copy, or because of it, the editorial-type ad invariably rates high in readership.

The newsletter is another highly effective approach—*if* it honestly contains newsworthy material of genuine interest to the reader. If it doesn't, he'll turn the page so fast that even the name of the advertiser may fail to make an impression. An ad of this type is no place for a collection of rehashed publicity releases. The newsletter format, well done, can do a highly effective job for the advertiser over a lengthy period of time. The famous Rockwell Report has proved this over a number of years. This campaign has consistently rated near the top of the book in the publications in which it appears, and has done so ever since it was launched.

Format

Include a brief discussion of the format for the ads in the copy platform, along with a short statement giving the rationale for the selection. For example, the format might be four-color inserts, perhaps multipage; two-color spreads; black and white spreads; black and white pages; or fractional pages. Also note here the illustrative technique which you've decided to use, and say why. Before making a final decision, review once more photography, line drawings, illustrative art, cartoons, and so on.

Product Features

A listing of product features in the copy platform is desirable—unless it results in a document longer than the Oxford Unabridged Dictionary. If such is the case, of if it even comes close, you'll want to consider including only the exclusive features of your product, those which the competition lacks.

Be sure to include a separate short paragraph listing the features which are *not* to be discussed.

User Benefits

Benefits of the features are the real meat of the copy platform. Discuss them factually and fully, but briefly. Think as the prospect thinks, look at the product as he would. Don't attempt to write ads here, but do be constructive and promotional in tone. Explain what your product does for the user, exactly how it saves him money, increases production, reduces maintenance, results in better quality of his end product, eliminates an entire operation, makes possible lower tooling cost, makes his plant secure against fire or theft, or what have you.

Relate user benefits to features, stress those which are unique to your product and nobody else's. Give the copywriter some real meat that he can get his teeth into so that he can create a campaign with the broadest possible appeal—yet one which zeroes in on its target audience.

This section is the one most important part of the copy platform, so think through carefully all of the user benefits that you, sales, marketing, and engineering can come up with. List them in descending order of importance. Don't feel that just because the product has been on the market for some time that everybody knows all about the benefits to be derived from using it. Everybody in your company is familiar with all of them, but those in your universe—all of the countless prospects out there—certainly aren't.

How to Compile Source

"Source," in the lexicon of the advertising manager, is the vast mass of reference material about the product, its production, its price, its distribution and selling that must be on hand before any writing can be done.

Seemingly, there's no end to the amount of source the ad manager, or the agency copywriter, finds he needs before he can sit down and produce the first word of an ad, a piece of sales literature, a film, or any other promotional material. Experience proves this true. It is very difficult to have too much source at hand, and very easy to have too little.

Having insufficient source for ready reference invariably results in padded copy, in puffery replacing hard facts—facts that are highly pertinent from the prospect's point of view. From the advertiser's point of view, it means an ad that is almost certain to fail to do its assigned job.

First thing to do after you've firmed up your copy platform is to plan how you'll line up your source material. Compiling enough applicable information about the product appears to some advertising managers to be a formidable task. It needn't be, however.

You know from your copy platform the type of information that's needed. You know the things you are obliged to include, as well as those which can't be mentioned. The project of compiling source is simplified if you look at it this way:

The logical place to start is with the product. It's something you know—or should know—inside out; it's something you've already analyzed when you were preparing the copy platform. Quite frequently the product itself will suggest a course of action in developing individual ads, or, for that matter, an entire campaign. Most products, especially in the capital equipment field, are rich repositories of ideas for individual advertisements. Exploit this opportunity that is available only to you.

Take a tablet, legal size is best, and rule in three heavy vertical lines with a "squeakie"—a felt marking pen. Head one column "Features," the second, "User benefits," and the third, "Ideas." The ideas, of course, are possible approaches for ads. You'll be surprised how fast they flow.

The Creative Process

List all of the ideas that come readily to mind, even those that seem too offbeat to be used. None should be discarded out of hand. The creative process is unique in all the world, unique with each individual. There's no telling what inapplicable idea can trigger one that is a real gem.

Chances are you'll immediately come up with a number of ideas. Don't force the process. Nobody has an inexhaustable supply of brilliant thoughts—at least, not at any one time. When the flow of ideas dries up, accept it. But leave room on the tablet for additional thoughts which will come to you at unexpected times.

Now that you're organized and this far along, have a shirt-sleeve discussion with the sales manager. Ideally, he should be your equal on the organizational chart and you should establish rapport with him. Also talk with the engineering manager, the man in charge of manufacturing or production, and, perhaps, the top research and development man.

Conserve your time and theirs by drawing up a list of questions to which you need answers. Do it before scheduling the meetings. The list won't be complete by any means, but it can serve to channel the conversation in the direction you want it to take. During the discussions your questions will suggest others to you and to the technical people. Questions stimulate thoughts that may be completely different from any that had occurred to you beforehand, but one of them may be the spark that ignites your thought processes and leads to a new approach as fresh as a bright blue morning after a long wet week.

Explain your problem to these specialists, show them how they fit into the picture. Be frank and open, confide in them. Tell them you need their help, that they are the people who can supply information vital to you so that you, in turn, can help advance the company's entire marketing program. By doing so, you give them a sense of participation and it is one they will derive pleasure from because they will be active in an area which they considered outside their province.

Remember, it is human nature to want to help others if asked properly. And it is a universal truth that people with specialized knowledge take pride in using it, in showing somebody how much they know, if he knows less. They are flattered at having the opportunity and, even if they don't show it, gratified at being able to expound on their favorite subject. Like all the rest of us, they want to be appreciated and want to show others how much they can contribute to the company—particularly outside their primary job function. Your coming to them shows that you recognize their ability.

It is likely that these department heads will delegate some of the more routine portions of these source-gathering sessions to certain key individuals on their staffs—marketing managers, product managers, or engineers, for example—who are close to day-to-day problems.

How to Deal With Technicians

A word of caution here. Be diplomatic when talking with these technical people. *Don't* be condescending. In most instances you'll find technical people are as different from advertising men as day is from night. Their basic thinking process is completely unlike yours. The way they approach a problem, the way they regard the product is foreign to the ad man. Possibly you'll be better off if you draw them out, let them talk about the product in their own language, and at their own pace. This is slower than you think, for these technical people are deliberate and phlegmatic. An advertising man characteristically mentally sorts and discards the relatively irrelevant and concentrates on and retains certain key points, unconsciously, perhaps. But the technical people, certainly those with an engineering background, don't. To them each and every little product feature is a rare jewel to be dwelled upon to the point of belaboring it to death. They are constitutionally unable to skim lightly over minor matters and concentrate on the truly significant. All you can do in such instances is to be courteous, listen, and remember that technical minds work in weird and wondrous ways. And there's always the chance that the engineer to whom you're talking may have conceived the original idea for many of the features he's talking about.

Despite what you may consider—and rightly so—verbosity, rambling, and inability to differentiate between the important and the inconsequential, act interested—*be* interested—in what he's saying. Never by word nor attitude let slip the fact that you feel, as most advertising men do, that these technical people are a breed apart, that they inhabit their own special little dream world where they're out of touch with what happens outside the confines of their laboratories, drafting departments, or blueprint rooms. There'll be times, many of them, when you'll be sorely tempted to end a long-winded, repetitive monolog with a pointed question. Resist it.

Try to talk in his language, not yours. Ask him questions about competitive products. Have him compare them to yours, feature by feature. Although advertising and marketing personnel are in a much better position to evaluate products in terms of their potential and competitive strength in the marketplace, engineers are usually better qualified to do so as regards quality, significant features, overall design, and construction. The fact that their viewpoint is vastly different from yours, and possibly more objective and less emotional, enables them to broaden your outlook and make it possible for you to examine the product from another vantage point.

All the while you're talking with the technical people continue to use your ruled pad of features-benefits-ideas, in addition to taking notes of the gist of the conversations. A small tape recorder, or a portable dictating machine, is invaluable. It frees you from the burden of trying to imitate a court reporter, as well as from having to attempt to decipher your scrawl afterwards. Use a machine now on hand, or get approval to buy one for the advertising department. You'll use it in your own plant, and if it's one of the truly portable ones, it will more than pay for itself when you take it into the field where your product is in use.

When you've established a good working relationship with the technical people, you'll have valuable allies. In addition to supplying you with the source you need, they can prevent embarrassing—and costly—errors from creeping into your copy. Give them the opportunity to review it for technical accuracy before releasing an advertisement for insertion in a publication.

Everyone's an Expert

One thing to bear in mind, however, is that everybody considers himself an advertising expert. Advertising is so simple and easy and deals with such commonplace things as the product and pictures and words that everybody automatically becomes qualified to be a copywriter. And everybody is a copy chief, capable of editing and rewriting your copy—even if they can't write a literate, simple, declarative sentence without becoming entangled with semantic grotesqueries to the point of absurdity. Also, everybody is an art director and a media director.

Resist letting technical people make changes in copy unless there is a technical error. Refuse, in fact, but do so as tactfully as possible. You need these technical experts, so be sure to motivate them to *want* to help you by your being properly appreciative for their contributions. We'll get into how to get ad approvals later on, in greater detail.

Make it standard operating procedure to build goodwill for the advertising department by thanking the technical people for their assistance. Lay it on a bit thick, tell them that without their help the ad, or the sales literature, or whatever is involved couldn't have come to fruition without them. And, to build a checking account upon which you can draw in the future, write a memo of thanks with a carbon to the man's superior.

Ultimately there will come a time when you've just about exhausted the amount of source which can be compiled inside the company—except for incoming reports of activities on the outside. Almost all industrial companies publish an inexpensive rundown of incoming orders, unusual sales activities, or a mere list of equipment sold during the preceding month; this is usually mimeographed or multilithed in the internal reproduction department.

Purpose is to keep the field sales force, dealer organization, or representatives informed as to what is selling where, new applications for a product, and acceptance of new products. Generally this morale-booster is just that because common practice is to describe the product very specifically by model number, describe what it is used for, then give the name of the salesman who closed the order. Everybody dotes on recognition, salesmen to a greater degree than most.

This "Business News," "Sales Bulletin," or whatever it is called is a prime place to secure product source material, especially if you plan a case-history campaign, or one featuring specific applications for a complex product. Keep a file handy of this internal publication. Then, knowing the approximate lead-time your company requires to produce the product from date of sale, you'll know about when shipment should be made to the customer. If you want to get straight product photography while it's still on the production floor, this will trigger action on your part at the appropriate time. Then, once shipment has been made, you can follow up for an application story.

Detailed data on your product's performance on the job can be almost as difficult to come by as your first million dollars. Or, it can be so simple that it is mere routine.

If you've checked off the equipment in which you're most interested—from the listing of new business—you can then contact sales or marketing to be certain that these specific units are of interest to them as far as promotion is concerned. This is wise because it sometimes happens that specials, or modifications, are not something management wants to emphasize.

After that, it's a simple matter to calendarize the products, setting up shipping dates, and then followup dates at which time you can contact the proper field salesman or district office to get customer clearance. Name of the correct individual in the customer establishment for advertising to contact must come from the field. It's then easy to write, phone, or wire to obtain permission to have photos taken and feature their equipment your company manufactured in ads, house organs, publicity releases, and so on. Many customers want to approve copy, many don't. It depends upon the individual and upon his relationship with the salesman or dealer.

Good Customer Relations

Human nature being what it is, many customers want to be featured in case-history or testimonial ads. Psychologically, this is due to their desire to be recognized as experts who want others to realize how astute they are to have selected the equipment which they bought from your company. It is reassuring to them to see their firms, and perhaps themselves personally, in your print advertisements. This is good after-the-sale salesmanship, too, to enable them to enjoy this warm feeling of having made a wise selection. It is not unknown for a case-history ad to influence a repeat purchase!

Field salesmen, district managers, dealers, and distributors recognize this, although they may not have reasoned it out in exactly this manner. They do know, though, that their customers desire recognition, and because the salesmen sold the product to them, they want to see the customer and his equipment publicized. In addition to keeping the customer happy and sold, it gratifies them.

Encourage salesmen to report to you good advertising "suspects." Many companies with which the author is familiar have an established policy of offering a tangible reward for such above-and-beyond-the-call-of-duty efforts by salesmen. This usually is a cash bonus, $25 or $50, a savings bond, or, in one instance, a $100 hat. The hat has a universal appeal to successful and affluent salesmen. Few of us enjoy the luxury of wearing a $100 hat!

Remember, salesmen are salesmen. They are intimately acquainted with the product and its applications, and they are extroverted, personable, and persuasive. Seldom, however, does one happen along who is qualified to develop a good case-history, hire and supervise a top-notch professional photographer, and supply to you all of the background information necessary for creation of an informative, convincing ad.

Salesmen are unable to separate the wheat from the chaff. They are actually emotionally involved with their customers and with the product. They tend frequently to identify themselves more with the customers than with their companies because their livelihood depends, after all, on customers—more than with a sales manager in the home office half a continent away. Too, it's a rare salesman who really understands advertising's functions, much less what is needed to produce an ad.

Don't expect your salesmen to be able to gather advertising source for you—even if they have the time, which is unlikely. You can hire any of a number of photojournalism reporting firms to do the job for you, as will be discussed at greater length later.

Go Out to the Boondocks

Or, you can perform the hat trick. This is best of all, and consists of nothing more or less than getting up out of a comfortable swivel chair, locking the desk, putting on your hat, leaving the air-conditioned office and getting out there in the boondocks. There you'll come face to face with the most important individual you're likely to encounter in your advertising life—the man who specifies, buys, and uses your product.

Be prepared when the salesman introduces you to the customer. Have a checklist with you of all pertinent topics you want to discuss. These might include miles per gallon, weights hauled, material handled, sizes of loads, frequency of trips, feeds and speeds, flow charts, process descriptions, and so on, depending on the type of product. Try to determine what primary benefits the customer enjoys as a result of using your product. These could be cost reduction, decreased maintenance, faster production, improved quality control, reduction of rejects, or similar ones.

The author has developed and worked with many checklists for a variety of industrial products. Because of product differences, none bears much similarity to the others. All have in common the fact that they stress features translated into user benefits, and all have space for direct quotes from the customer.

Take the battery-powered dictating machine or tape recorder with you. This will avoid the traumatic experience of taking brief notes on a complicated operation and getting back to the office only to find you can't rely on your memory quite as much as you'd anticipated. It's always embarrassing to have to phone the customer to have him remind you what you and he discussed. With the handy little machine, you can have your secretary transcribe *exactly* what you want, including comments made in the same sequence as your checklist, direct quotes which can be attributed to the customer, remarks made by maintenance superintendents and others important to you.

Back before the day of the ubiquitous transistor-equipped electronic gadgetry, the author spent many an evening in motel and hotel rooms transcribing the day's notes before the semilegible scrawl transcribed itself into Egyptian hieroglyphics. It's never sport after a hard day.

Final source needed is photography of the product, unless it has been decided to use art. This is a topic all by itself, and will be discussed in the chapter on illustration.

Chapter 7

HEADLINES

SINGLE out one component of an industrial advertisement as the one most important and the headline wins hands down.

It is the illustration, however, which initially attracts the attention of the reader in most instances and stops him for that all-important fleeting moment. If the illustration is compelling enough, if it is pertinent and related to what you have to say, it will accomplish its assignment—*which is to secure readership of the headline.*

That done, your ad then has its first, and perhaps only, opportunity to achieve its ultimate objective. If the headline makes a strong appeal and makes it fast, if it arouses sufficient interest, your prospect will then proceed to read the body copy of the ad, giving it a chance to persuade him to accept your viewpoint about your product or service. The ad will have registered a positive impression and strengthened to some extent the acceptance of your product, thus paving the way for a salesman to make a call and make a sale.

According to Dr. Daniel Starch, pioneer in measurement of advertising readership and effectiveness, the headline is one of the most potent psychological factors which influence readership of an advertisement. And McGraw-Hill, in its Laboratory of Advertising Performance, reports an analysis of several thousand industrial advertisements with different types of headlines. One conclusion was reached immediately: It was strikingly apparent that headlines per se increase readership significantly. Some types of headlines exert a greater positive effect than others, of course, as we shall see.

Indeed, many veteran industrial advertising practitioners are of the considered opinion that the headline constitutes at least *three-quarters* of the benefit the advertiser realizes from running his ad in business publications. A vast mass of research bears them out, for study after study has shown that if an ad is merely "noted," and not "read partially," the headline is the element recalled by almost 75 percent of those interviewed. This means, then, that almost 75 percent of the investment made in producing the ad and in the space it occupies *is made in the headline.*

The say-nothing headline has no place in industrial advertising. The headline couched in vague, general terms, the headline that is unrelated to your product and the story you want to tell about it, should never see type. And the headline that, through borrowed interest or some other illegitimate device, misleads the reader into thinking your ad will interest him—and then fails to do so—does your company a distinct disservice. No industrial advertiser has money enough to waste, and such headlines are just that—waste.

Readers of business publications have no interest in the nondescript, nor do they have time for fuzzy thinking or vague generalities. Generalities are pallid, specifics are vivid and fact-filled; they put color and life and vigor into your headlines by giving information slanted toward the reader's self-interest. And make no mistake about it, readers are vitally interested in facts about products which might help them on the job. They want concrete information about products—yours among many, incidentally. Fail to give them something solid that they can get their teeth into in the headline, or promise to do so, and your ad has fallen flat on its face.

Du Pont says that the headline should:

1. Assist the illustration select the desired audience.

2. Present sales points in terms of reader benefits—clearly, directly and specifically expressed.

3. Induce reader interest and stimulate further reading.

4. Repeat the product story told in the illustration.

5. Appear in display type, upper and lower case.

6. Be isolated from other elements for ease of reading—not overprinted.

7. Avoid: "teasers"; rhyming, double-meaning, coined words; metaphors.

8. Contain *main* appeals.

9. Avoid tricky headline treatment: change in style, size and color of type; wavy or zigzagging headline; printing on tint block.

These salient points represent the viewpoint of just one company, of course, but they are almost all important. And Du Pont has done reasonably well in business by adhering to them.

Classes of Headlines

Headlines come in assorted sizes, shapes, and lengths. They vary in format and in content, as well as in the approach to a problem common to all advertisers. Good headlines share three main characteristics. They are:

  1. Clear   2. Appropriate   3. Interesting

For ease of discussion and illustration, headlines can be grouped into four broad classifications. These are:

  1. Direct   3. Combination

  2. Indirect   4. Virtually useless

Twenty-three basic types of headlines comprise all except a few scattered mavericks within these four major classifications. They are:

A. Direct

  1. Command   5. Reason why   8. Dialog

  2. Specific fact 6. How to   9. Comparison

  3. News   7. Testimonial 10. Prediction

  4. Statistical

B. Indirect

  1. Question   3. Emotional

  2. Teaser   4. Slogan

C. Combination

  1. Cumulative

  2. Headline comprises headline *and* body copy

D. Virtually Useless

  1. Negative   4. Precious   6. Say nothing

  2. Borrowed interest 5. So what? 7. Brag and boast

  3. Irrelevant

Let's discuss these 23 types of easily recognized headlines and look at examples of some of the more important. Then we'll consider why some are inherently stronger than others, where and why they excel, and why other types should be avoided like the plague.

The Direct Headline

Ernest Hemingway is credited with having said, when commenting on the then current literary style—or lack of it—that, "Nobody seems able to write a simple, declarative sentence."

The same statement applies also to present-day industrial advertising. It suffers from a dreary lack of imagination which, in turn, results in appallingly dull fare which enjoys little readership—or from an almost frantic desire to look, sound, and *be* different—primarily, it seems, for difference's sake.

Nowhere is this more evident than in ads in the lesser trade publications. In fairness, they can't be held up as typical of all industrial advertising because of their containing a preponderance of small-budget advertisers who presumably have less know-how than do larger advertisers. All the examples which follow are drawn from major business books, so they *do* typify contemporary industrial advertising.

The direct headline, in all 10 of its sub-types, is simply a headline that is informative. It is informative because it makes believable statements about a product, statements that impart information important to the reader. Following is a critique of each of the 10 in turn, with examples of the more widely used ones.

Command Headlines

Figure that in 15 seconds!
　Friden, Inc.

Stop worker resistance to wearing gloves
　The Wilson Rubber Company

Put power in your hands with Skil
　Skil Corporation

Grab hold of Allflex . . . it handles easier!
　Raybestos-Manhattan, Inc.

Put more power where the power starts with heavy-duty engine parts
　Gould National Batteries, Inc.

Get the facts on Naylor pipe . . . send for this booklet
　Naylor Pipe Company

Drill it with Blue Dragon Power Ring 200
J. K. Smit & Sons, Inc.

Put power flexibility in your plant
Anaconda Wire and Cable Company

Not all great headlines by any means, but each has something in common with countless others of this same general character in magazines serving hundreds of different industries. These command headlines are simple, easily understood, and they have strong reader involvement. Readers feel involved because "you" (the reader) are either the given subject of each headline, or are implied. Then follows an action verb which demands reader response.

If the headline commands the reader to do something that he recognizes as being in his self-interest, you're on solid ground with this type of headline. The reader realizes you're interested in his welfare. But where an ad is obviously self-oriented, as in the Blue Dragon ad, there is better than an even chance that the reader will ignore the admonition completely and turn to somebody else's ad that *is* interested in him.

Skil's fine ad shows a number of high-quality power tools in a wide variety of situations and, combined with the headline, offers the reader a reward for spending his time reading the ad. The transition from reading about and seeing different applications for Skil power tools to considering them for use in his plant is an effortless one for the reader, as it should be.

Gould has a quality story to tell, and tells it well indeed. The ad is convincing enough to warrant use of the command headline. Gould avoids the pitfall of commanding the reader to read his ad, then to take action, and failing to carry out its end of the bargain by not rewarding the reader. Doing so results in a disgruntled prospect who harbors a subconscious resentment toward your company, and loss of readership of subsequent ads in the same campaign—and perhaps longer.

An outstanding example of the command headline—and one which combines the strength of the command with the power to arouse the curiosity of the teaser headline—is the fractional-page ad with the almost unbelievable headline *THINK RATS*. This ad run by Ai-Research Manufacturing Company, a division of The Garrett Corporation, appears to violate the rule that an unappetizing subject is not presented in a headline. In this instance, however, "rats" is an abbreviation—or, rather, the initials—of the company's Ram Air Turbine Systems. Small space is used logically, cleanly, and to

excellent effect. AiResearch men report they initially looked with disfavor on the ad because they felt queasy about the headline, but decided to run it and see what the reaction would be.

Combination of the striking headline in huge display type, highly informative copy, the graph showing performance characteristics of the equipment and the photo produced a flood of inquiries—more than from any other ad the company has ever run. And this from an advertiser that habitually runs full-page ads in a number of media!

Obviously, the headline alone didn't trigger such response. But the shocking command headline *did* produce high readership as proved by reader response. And this is the function of the headline, after all.

Specific Fact Headlines

$28.10/M sliced from the cost of Rival Electric Knives by TRS rivets and riveters
Townsend Company

New Kenloc 5° positive rake insert has 8 cutting edges
Kennametal, Inc.

Blanchard grinds 3½ hours off end-column machining time
The Blanchard Machine Company

Every car in the Indy 500 was Fram equipped . . . your trucks deserve the same protection
Fram Corporation

This Transferline machine is triple-tooled to turn out dozens of different hydraulic brake hose connections at 3,100 an hour
Gilman Engineering & Mfg. Co.

A CL&T Cintimatic slashed the scrap rate on this part from 35% to less than 1%
Cincinnati Lathe and Tool Co.

Each of these headlines attracts *quality* readership because of the specific facts—of interest to those reading the ad—otherwise, they wouldn't be reading it. Readers are qualified prospects because they qualify themselves; this is especially true when the subject which the ad will discuss is mentioned prominently in the headline. Uninterested readers of the book who are not concerned with products of this type will merely pass on to editorial material, or to an advertisement about some product in which they are interested.

Polaroid's specific fact headline, *200X in 10 seconds,* is as specific as can be—even to showing the results the user will obtain in that minute time span. The promise of no more long-drawn-out waiting to see if the photomicrograph turned out well is enough to trigger a call from the metallurgist or other technical expert to the purchasing agent—Polaroid's goal. The ad is clean, the headline packs a lot of punch because of its promise, and the copy fills out the picture interestingly. No wonder Polaroid has grown by leaps and bounds! (See illustration, next page)

News Headlines

New tool for quantitative analysis of the crowded high frequency spectrum
Hewlett Packard

Nexus devises 6 new operational amplifiers . . . each of which may bring a little happiness into the life of a hard-pressed engineer
Nexus—a Teledyne Company

New NDT system checks 250 bars an hour for both surface and internal defects
Automation Industries, Inc.

This modular control center can be assembled, wired and installed in less than 3 days
Allen-Bradley Co.

Methods of carburizing alloy steels
Bethlehem Steel

Polaroid's new close-up camera does all the figuring and focusing for you. Then delivers a perfect close-up in seconds
Polaroid Corporation

New Life Line Globar elements last 50% longer, cost not a penny more
The Carborundum Company

Uniformly coats, but doesn't close the eye of a needle
The Glidden Company

Pittsburgh Corning, the insulation people, announce Celramic-Board, the first roof insulation able to "breathe" without loss of insulating value
Pittsburgh Corning Corporation

POLAR

200X in 10 seconds

With a Polaroid Land camera back and Polaroid Land film, you can see your photomicrographs 10 seconds after you take them.

You are always sure of your picture. If you don't get exactly the picture you want the first time, you'll know immediately, and can take another then and there.

You don't have to waste any time in a darkroom only to find out the picture isn't right—that illumination, or filtration, or focus, or field coverage is not perfect. And you never run the risk of having to repeat a difficult and time-consuming photomicrographic setup at a later date.

Because 10-second photomicrography has proven itself an invaluable laboratory tool, Polaroid Land camera backs (or the Polaroid 4x5 Land Film Holder) are offered as standard equipment with most well known photomicrographic instruments.

Land camera backs are available for our roll or pack film formats. The 4x5 film holder, of course, accepts our 4x5 sheet films.

There are two basic Polaroid Land films for photomicrography, and they are available in all formats. There's a panchromatic black and white film, rated at A.S.A. 3000, which lets you shoot at low light levels with fast shutter speeds, and gives you a finished print in 10 seconds. And there's Polaroid color film which gives you an accurate full-color recording in 60 seconds.

The system is well worth looking into, don't you think? We'll be happy to supply more information. **Polaroid Corporation, Cambridge, Mass.**

To date, 44 Spectrovacs have been ordered by leading metal producers!!
Baird-Atomic

The profusion of news headlines is easily explained. Most new-product ads—accepted even by confirmed skeptics as a desirable function which advertising performs with dispatch and efficiency—fall within this type. So do genuine technological breakthroughs. And new applications for existing products. Improvements made on products which have been on the market for some time. An expanded or revised warranty. A more liberal service guarantee. Easier financing. Lower interest rates. Legitimate announcements made most easily by industrial advertising are probably more numerous than an entire chapter in this book could list. Headlines of the news type always enjoy much higher-than-average readership—unless their effectiveness is diluted by vague language or failure to make the user benefit crystal clear.

Hewlett Packard's headline is the most widely used type for announcements. It starts out with a straight-from-the-shoulder statement that the company has developed a new product, then gives the application for it. Simple, easy to write, no nonsense. This headline is admittedly old hat, but it is not hackneyed. Instead, it exploits fully advertising's unique ability to tell a lot of people about the new tool in a big hurry.

Nexus' fine headline is loaded with reader interest because of a highly technical new product livened up with a delightful light touch seldom seen. This headline communicates with *people*—as well as engineers to whom it was directed, who are, after all people, too. A sure hand on the typewriter produced this headline.

"If it's new to me, it's new" is the way most readers react to industrial advertising. Allen-Bradley's news-type statement about a product which may have been on the market prior to this ad nonetheless gives news of interest to users of control centers. They can see at a glance that this product may solve a perplexing problem for them. Bethlehem's all-text ad falls into this class, also.

You're fortunate indeed when you have a truly interesting announcement to make. A hard-hitting news headline has you halfway home if you make it clear, concrete and informative.

Here's the newest in structural beams: Koppers fiber glass reinforced polyester is the great headline of Koppers' fine ad. Containing the magnetic "newest" in the first line of the headline gets the ad off to a good start, almost assuring readership of the entire headline. Then comes the company name in the headline so the headline is credited to the right firm. Following comes fiber glass, which has assumed almost magic properties in the public mind, as has polyester to a lesser extent. As you'll note in the reproduction nearby, the ad can't miss. Powerful headline, pretty girl convincingly holding the product (which would be heavy, heavy, in a competing material), dress of the newest (newest again!) modern print, and those ultra-modern mesh stockings, clean layout, and lots of white space attract the eye. The complete ad is informative, attractive, tasteful—and it has impact.

This is one of a series of ads Koppers beams to managers in business and industry, each of which is devoted to a single product. Koppers has established through research that its previous communications level was not high enough—prior to this campaign.

Objective of the ad is to launch the new product in very positive terms, to create awareness of the fact that Koppers possesses the capability to manufacture structurals, and to generate interest among business executives and motivate them to "do something" after having read the ad.

Ad Inspired Inquiries

The "something" could take the form of a direct inquiry, a call to a Koppers sales office, clipping and routing the ad to an associate, or placing an order. Koppers says that over-the-transom inquiries for additional information following appearance of this ad is almost three times higher than from other ads in the campaign.

Fiber glass structurals are a completely new product for Koppers, and an ancillary objective of this ad and its companion promotional campaign is to help find and define the market where the product has the most potential. By careful analysis of inquiries (received in the thousands) the company can pinpoint the industries by S.I.C., and the prospects by title and function, as well as some of the end uses for the structurals.

Koppers uses the news headline ad for new-product introduction and future sales followup most effectively.

Statistical Headlines

The man who said, "Who needs a 5-year or 50,000-mile engine and drive train warranty?" never broke his cylinder block, cylinder head, engine internal parts, or his intake manifold, water pump, or his flywheel, flywheel housing, clutch housing, or his torque converter, transmission case or its internal parts, or his transfer case, drive shaft, center bearings, or his universal

Here's the newest in structural beams: Koppers fiber glass reinforced polyester

The 4½-foot I-beam the girl's holding weighs less than 17 pounds, yet it has tensile and compressive strengths (longitudinal) of 20,000 psi. It's eXtren* fiber glass reinforced polyester, and no other structural material can match its combination of corrosion resistance, strength, light weight and electrical insulation. Koppers makes beams, rods, angles, tubes, bars, and sheets. Right now these structural shapes are solving problems in the chemical processing and electrical industries, and they could be the answer to your requirements for a strong, lightweight, corrosion-resistant material. Write Koppers Company, Inc., Room 1424A, Koppers Building, Pittsburgh, Pa. 15219.

*eXtren is a trademark of Universal Moulded Fiber Glass Corp.—a Koppers subsidiary.   C-6

Koppers

joints, driving axle, or differential, or his drive wheel bearings. We hope his luck holds out.
Dodge Division, Chrysler Motors Corporation

Weighs 86, lifts 1600
Sky Climber, Inc.

This one lifts 35-ton loads and travels permit-free—Koehring truck crane is 8' wide, 12'5" high
Koehring Division, Koehring Corporation

This is compaction—49,000 lbs. of dynamic force applied 20 times per second!
Hyster Company

Cleco's new W-1200 will tighten 1¼" A-325 bolts to 71,700 lbs. tension in just 4 seconds
Cleco Division, Reed International, Inc.

Mister, if you want rugged, dependable power to move 3,000 gpm of water; provide 125-cfm, 200-psi air power; pump 40 cu. yds./hr. of concrete 100 ft. up or 500 feet horizontally; automatically slice miles of concrete; then the 60-hp WISCONSIN is your engine
Wisconsin Motor Corporation

Crucible Verasteel slits 10,000 tons of alloy and stainless sheet at a 40% reduction in tool costs
Crucible Steel Company

Maybe the longest, but certainly one of the best statistical headlines is the explanation of its warranty by Dodge. This was an unusually difficult copy problem to solve because warranties traditionally are phrased in legalese and set in 4-point type almost impossible to read except by the eagle-eyed. A crisp, clean layout and fine typography teamed up with this fine headline concept. Of note is the fact that this is a true statistical headline, yet it contains only two references to specific figures.

On the other hand, Wisconsin Motor Corporation's long but informative headline is loaded with statistics in the form of performance figures. The various applications, or jobs, the engine can handle are of interest to contractors on construction jobs. The facts are there, clearly and forcefully put. If only the headline is read, Wisconsin's ad is still a success.

Cleco's headline is shorter, but still fact filled. This is exactly the kind of information a prospective purchaser wants—and needs—to base a purchase decision on.

Shortest of all is Sky Climber's succinct headline. It contains two of the most pertinent statistics about the product, states them fast and unobtrusively, then gets out of the way so the reader can proceed into the body copy for additional facts.

Statistical headlines are inherently interesting. They can do a real job of capsulizing the highlights of your story. Make sure, however, the statistics are those of highest interest to the reader, and that they're also ones which present the product most favorably.

Reason-Why Headlines

Five reasons why more aluminum is held in Tercod Bowls than in any other type
Electro Refractories & Abrasive Corporation

Here's why plant engineers have replaced nearly 200 roofs with corrugated roofing of Crucible stainless steel
Crucible Steel Company

Why name contractors name P&H
Harnischfeger Corporation

Should a miner 67 years old change his name? We did. And here's why.
American Zinc Company

Why do you suppose we keep the ball joint as simple as we can?
TRW Michigan Division, TRW, Inc.

Readers like reason-why headlines because it tells them whether or not the body copy will interest them. It's a timesaver. If the headline indicates that the copy following is of interest, or that it will help them, they'll read further.

For example, every management man in a nonferrous foundry is interested in a bowl that holds more molten aluminum than the ones he is now using. For this reason, Electro Refractories and Abrasives Corporation's ad with the reason-why headline is a well-conceived ad. The headline tells the reader what the body copy will tell him, and promises specific facts—not puffery.

The same holds true for the headline in Crucible Steel Company's powerful ad. No maintenance man with an interest in his job could possibly pass by this ad without reading it. Most likely replacing a leaky or weak roof with one of stainless steel hasn't occurred to the majority of industrial maintenance superintendents, primarily because of the relatively high cost of the material. Crucible's headline causes them to wonder, first of all, just why their counterparts in other companies chose stainless steel. Then it arouses enough interest to assure readership of the balance of the ad.

No Automatic Readership

Just because a headline is of the reason-why type doesn't automatically result in readership so high it warms the cockles of the heart. If the reason why applies to a subject of little inherent interest, the ad will promptly tally up an abysmally poor score. No type of headline can persuade readers to read about something they couldn't care less about.

Harnischfeger's ad couldn't help but suffer for that reason, and American Zinc's received even less readership. Reasons why a firm, even if it *is* 67 years old (and who cares?) changes its name elicit a long, lengthy ho-hum unless the campaign announcing the change is truly outstanding. Few are.

TRW's ad, on the other hand, proceeds to give a convincing product-superiority story, and for that reason the headline contributed to a successful ad.

The Polaroid ad reproduced here is a classic example of a well-thought-out reason-why headline—and ad. *The shots you goof. The best reason for 10-second photography*. As fine a reason why the industrial camera user should use a Polaroid as can be found. And the illustration is a beautiful marriage of headline and illustration. Copy is terse, informative—and mighty convincing.

How-to Headlines

How to make one Sarco "25" valve body do any of 7 different control jobs
Sarco Co., Inc.

To cut heating and cooling costs, and reduce noises, insulate sheet metal ducts with G-B Ultralite
Gustin-Bacon Manufacturing Co.

How to save money and avoid headaches in transformer and inductor design.
Ferroxcube Corporation

The shots you goof.
The best reason
for 10-second photography.

Everybody makes mistakes. But when you're using Polaroid Land photography you don't suffer for them.

Say you're shooting a photomicrograph and the exposure is off. Or the filtration. Or the position of the slide. You'll know it 10 seconds after you snap the shutter—when you see your Polaroid print. You can then make your correction and take a perfect picture right away. While everything is still set up.

This nice advantage comes with all Polaroid Land films. And there are quite a few to choose from. There are black-and-white emulsions rated at A.S.A. 3000, 400, and 200. They're the ones that develop in 10 seconds. There's also a black-and-white film that gives you a positive and a true film negative outside the darkroom in 20 seconds. And, of course, there's Polacolor film which gives you a full-color recording in 60 seconds.

Sorry we can't make you infallible. We can only offer you the next best thing.   "Polaroid" & "Polacolor" ®

Polaroid Corporation, Cambridge, Mass.

Addressed to industrial users, this Polaroid ad goes right to the heart of an industrial photography problem and clearly explains how the product can be of using in overcoming that problem. The illustration is most pertinent.

How to succeed in Higher Profits without really trying on a Cleereman Layout Drilling Machine

Cleereman Machine Tool Corporation

Six ways Addressograph helps keep 700,000 items shaped-up when they're shipped out

Addressograph-Multigraph Corporation

4 ways to view displays with Tektronix Type 564 split-screen storage oscilloscope

Tektronix, Inc.

Four foundry execs tell how their companies saved from 27% to 44% on Workmen's Compensation insurance costs.

American Mutual

The two little words "how to" are among the four or five most powerful words in the English language for use in headlines. Every management man is a part of management for one reason only: He is able to solve problems. Otherwise, he'd be a clerk or a janitor or a draftsman.

When you run a headline of the how-to type, you're promising the reader then and there that you're going to tell him how to solve a problem—hopefully one that's been bothering him—with your product or service. Helping him solve a problem hits him right where he lives in the business world. Assuming your solution, based on your product, is applicable and pertinent, this is a type of headline that comes as close as any to assuring excellent readership.

How to reduce inventory, freeing capital and effecting a savings, is the promise held out in Sarco's headline. After all, if one Sarco "25" valve body is flexible and versatile enough to do seven jobs, it can easily solve inventory, storage, and application problems. Sarco pulled 'em in with this headline.

Cutting costs interests everybody, as does a reduction in noise. Gustin-Bacon's product should be right down the alley of the maintenance man with heating and cooling and noise problems. Note that this is a true how-to headline, but the word "how" isn't used; it isn't essential that it appear, although a headline is stronger with "how" than without it.

Addressograph-Multigraph's headline promises it will tell how to make order out of chaos six ways with its equipment—and with 700,000 items involved, that's quite an order.

Long though it is, American Mutual's headline contains a pocketbook appeal, a testimonial, and is a how-to headline—much more you can't ask for. It has built-in believability and inherent interest.

How to fight
the cost per copy war.

*With all the cost per copy attacks and
counter-attacks it's often pretty hard to know who's
offering you the best way to make your copies.*

*We don't claim to always have the best answer, but
we can make it easier for you to decide who does.*

*Only A.B. Dick offers you all the copying and
duplicating methods. So we're not for (or against)
copiers or mimeographs or offset machines. Or any
of the other ways to make copies.*

*That's why you can depend on us to show you
a true picture of the cost per copy for each method.
And then let your needs decide what's best for you.*

*In the cost per copy war we have the
ultimate weapon:*
Objectivity.

A·B·DICK®

ELECTROSTATIC COPIERS • OFFSET • MIMEOGRAPH • SPIRIT • AZOGRAPH • PHOTOCOPY • VIDEOGRAPH • FOLDERS • PAPER • SUPPLIES
A. B. DICK COMPANY, 5700 WEST TOUHY AVENUE, CHICAGO, ILLINOIS 60648

A. B. Dick's all-type ad with a how-to headline is as fine an example as has come down the pike in many a moon. The office copy machine market is a jungle with dozens and dozens of firms large and small competing for a larger share. Some are giants, like Xerox, others smaller but with products equally satisfactory. Some have a breadth-of-line story to tell, others concentrate on one single type of machine and sell it hard.

The persuasive ad illustrated here hammers hard at the most significant factor in selling a copy machine—cost per copy. For copy machines, like autos, have as the prime consideration not the original cost, but the cost of running the things.

Headline of A. B. Dick's ad is: *How to fight the cost per copy war.* Body copy is so logical, so simple and convincing that the entire text follows.

> *With all the cost per copy attacks and counterattacks it's often pretty hard to know who's offering you the best way to make your copies.*
>
> *We don't claim to always have the best answer, but we can make it easier for you to decide who does.*
>
> *Only A. B. Dick offers you all the copying and duplicating methods. So we're not for (or against) copiers or mimeographs or offset machines. Or any of the other ways to make copies.*
>
> *That's why you can depend on us to show you a true picture of the cost per copy for each method. And then let your needs decide what's best for you.*
>
> *In the cost per copy war we have the ultimate weapon:*
>
> *Objectivity.*

A. B. Dick approached its current advertising campaign with several thoughts in mind. First of all, there exists a great deal of confusion regarding the multiplicity of copiers and duplicators on the market in the minds of prospects—ranging from a one-man dentist's office to the largest corporation in the country. So many manufacturers with so many different machines and different systems make it extremely difficult for a conscientious buyer to be sure that his ultimate selection is the best for his needs.

As a result, A. B. Dick—the only company in the industry to offer all of the major copying and duplicating processes—decided that its unique position gave it a competitive edge nobody else could have: complete objectivity.

With this in mind, the company decided to prepare advertising that was not only very honest, but unusually straightforward in style and presentation. Furthermore, Dick wanted ads that looked different to separate themselves from the herd. Obvious approach was to have the typical pretty blond girl sitting on, leaning on, looking at, or operating a typical machine in a typical office setting. That particular type of ad has been done to death by scores of companies in this and allied fields.

The all-type ad was decided upon as the one best solution to putting across the A. B. Dick story in the strongest possible manner. That the how-to headline and the logical, objective approach had paid off is borne out by readership ratings by Starch and others. In the first issue of *Business Week* in which this ad appeared, it was the sixth best read ad in the book of this same size, and the cost ratio was 225. A measurement by Gallup and Robinson indicated an achievement approximately double the average *for this type of product.*

A sound selling proposition, an outstanding product line, believable copy—preceded by an intriguing how-to headline—is performing well. All are mutually dependent upon the other to some extent, of course.

Testimonial Headlines

"The rotary worktable on our Scharmann horizontal has cut operation setups from three steps to one"
Scharmann Machine Corp.

"Most of the time my 295B's haul just as much dirt as my twin-engine, four-wheel drives. More, altogether, because the 295's haul it faster."
International Harvester Company

"The steering of this machine is excellent . . ."
Manitowoc Engineering Company

"We've had no breakdowns . . . since Torc-Pac's were installed in 1963"
U. S. Industries, Inc.

"Just wish we'd known about the Bobcat sooner!"
Melroe Bobcat

These testimonial headlines are all from case-history ads, of course, and are direct quotations from statements made by individual customers or individuals in customer companies. In each one, except for the U. S. Industries ad, the quotation was identified with a specific person in the ad, along with his title or job function. U. S. Industries chose to quote the company rather than an individual.

Best thing the testimonial headline has going for it is that it is so believable. The advertiser is not making any glowing statements about his product; a third party—theoretically a disinterested one with no ax to grind—does this for him. In this way the headline gains credence. Too, the reader finds it easy to identify with the product user who is making the statement. In many tightly knit industries, he may well know him through the trade association.

When you get a really good direct quote from a customer you'll have a hard-working headline. You may even have to help the customer a bit to make sure his quote is up to par by putting words in his mouth; you can say them, then ask him if that isn't right. When he agrees, he's said it and you can quote him. This is technically honest, but shouldn't be relied upon to any great extent or your ads will all end up sounding like the same man did all of the talking—you.

Frequently after a get-acquainted session with the customer, and perhaps a good long lunch, he's relaxed enough to regard you as a friend and loosen up. Then's when the colorful, colloquial quotes come rolling out—and you'd better be ready to write them down or record them fast. Somehow they always bring to the printed page a sense of immediacy, of hearing the gospel truth, of learning something about a product that should be remembered.

One of the finest, most colorful testimonial headlines in the author's experience was that for a four-color insert ad prepared for the truck fleet publications for the old Diamond T Motor Truck Company. This headline quoted a California dump truck operator who said, without prompting, "These trucks don't owe me a penny." The ad, incidentally, enjoyed excellent readership, partially because it started off with talk that truckers understood.

International Harvester's quote headline is particularly good. Care was taken that it was good, that it understated originally just how good the performance of the machines was—then followed up with the second punch—the fact that these machines actually outperform larger ones. This headline carries great conviction.

All of us can hear somebody say he wished he'd known about something sooner—probably after a less than satisfactory experience with a competitive product. That makes Melroe's headline about its Bobcat unusually effective, with the bonus benefit that there's an implied statement of outstanding performance.

With a major user benefit—freedom from maintenance expense —in the headline, the Hendrickson ad reproduced here is a good example of a fine testimonial headline.

"After 1,800,000 miles of hard use, our nine HENDRICKSON Suspensions are as good as new!" The illustration reinforces the headline, showing as it does, a tractor with rear axles on different

axes due to uneven terrain; mud on the tires and thrown mud on the front fender belong in this type of photograph.

Hendrickson's body copy adheres to a rule from which you should never deviate—when you quote a customer, immediately give his name, firm and address. It starts out: *"We've never had a break-down due to suspensions," states Jim Bobb, owner of the Queen City Grain Company, Cincinnati, Ohio. "In fact, after 200,000 miles each on our nine Hendrickson-equipped Ford tractors, we're still running all the original beam end and center bushings in these suspensions."* Copy continues with facts about Queen City's operation, including weight of payload and so on.

Get a statement like that from a satisfied customer and run it in your testimonial ad and you have something with real credibility. Prospects believe such headlines and ads because they know they *have to be true*—picking up the phone to call Jim Bobb in Cincinnati about his Hendrickson suspensions is the easiest thing imaginable. No advertiser would stick his neck out even a little bit in a testimonial headline.

True, testimonial headlines have been around since shortly after the dawn of time, but they are just as effective now as they were decades ago.

Dialog Headlines

"We're a little short on working capital." "Ever considered reducing your steel inventory and depending more on steel service centers?"
Steel Service Center Institute

"Right, George. We figure now is the time to invest some of our profits in more Aro Automation Tools for our drilling, tapping, and assembly operations. They'll give us a boost in production, improve quality control, and trim our labor costs. Then when business isn't all milk and honey any more, and we have to fight for our orders, those Aro Automation Tools will give us a competitive edge."
The Aro Corporation

As a rule, a fatal flaw is automatically built into the dialog headline. Quoting a "conversation" between two executives rendered in charcoal art imparts an air of unreality to the headline. It's immediately apparent that these are not real people talking, they're make-believe, a figment of the imagination—the advertiser's imagination.

They're suspect. Logical inference is that the situation itself doesn't exist, that the problem posed is fictional, and that the solution is a contrived one to benefit guess-who—certainly not the reader. Steel Service Center people didn't help the cause of service centers with this ad, but there's every reason to believe that their reasoning is right, up to a point. If they take the same premise and find real, live customers who have realized the identical benefits they're talking about by purchasing steel from their Steel Service Center—and then quoting them, and identifying them—they'll have an ad with believability.

And the phone conversation between a nonexistent Arrow Collar-type drawn with phone in hand and an insipid grin on his face as he talks with an equally nebulous George also lacks conviction. This is too, too. Aro invites disbelief, invites readers to flip the page as quickly as possible and does nothing to encourage them to think well of either Aro products or the company. Had its men quoted a similar—but not so verbose—conversation which transpired before purchase of their equipment, then did a followup after the equipment was at work, they'd have had something. Naturally, the individual would have been identified, his company would, and it would have been located. Facts and figures about lower production costs, reduced maintenance and so on would put icing on the cake. The ad would have been believable.

Don't confuse the dialog headline with the testimonial headline just because both use quotation marks. There's a world of difference between them and just as much difference in what they can do for you.

Comparison Headlines

This 988 does the work of two machines . . . cuts handling cost per ton 36%
Caterpillar Tractor Company

One way to increase your frequency range. A better way from Sierra
Sierra Electronic Division of Philco

Motor lamination production upped from 150 to 250 per minute. Speed and productivity increased 66⅔%.
The Minster Machine Company

Half the plies. Twice the service.
B. F. Goodrich Industrial Products Company

Comparing the product—by inference with competitive ones, or with older models of the same product prior to improvements—results in dramatic headlines that press a point home to readers quickly and positively. This holds true if the comparison is a valid one, but not if apples and oranges are compared. An attempt to trick the reader with a phony comparison will surely backfire and reflect adversely on the advertiser; people are pretty sharp. After a new product introduction, for example, a logical followup could be one of comparison of new and old so that improvements, benefits, and features can be incorporated into the headline.

"Does the work of two machines"—Caterpillar's comparing its new model wheel Loader with the older units is about as strong a statement as is possible to make. Run this type of headline and you instantly cause huge dollar signs to flash in front of the eyes of readers using this type of equipment. The benefit of savings in equipment, in labor, and in maintenance comes through loud and clear. The headline leaves the impression that Cat equipment can bump up the profit picture for contractors; if they read nothing but the headline and noticed the signature or logo, the ad has accomplished something positive.

A basic mistake was made by Sierra, though. One illustration in the ad shows a balding tuba player sitting on a stage, ready, apparently, to perform for a large and distinguished audience. The other shows Sierra's wide-range wave analyzer. Comparing the two is not cricket. This attempt to borrow interest from a subject totally unrelated to the problem at hand—and actually comparing them—defeats the ad. Only tuba players, who probably comprise a small percentage of the population, would find the advertisement inherently interesting.

Minster Machine Company's comparison of new equipment and that formerly used by a good customer sells hard, as does B. F. Goodrich's comparison of a new BFG conveyor belt with a competitive one which gave poor service. Naturally, the competitive brand was not named. Used properly, comparisons convince.

Undoubtedly the finest comparison headline—and entire comparison ad—to appear in the business press this year is Firestone's in *Commercial Car Journal,* a leading truck fleet publication.

Headline is: *one Duplex tire and rim replaces . . . 13 dual tire and rim parts.* Our illustration of the spread ad in black and white shows, on one page, the revolutionary new Firestone Duplex truck tire and rim; on the other page is the multiplicity of parts, 13 in all, needed to do the job of the simpler Duplex. Graphic, persuasive, convincing.

Body copy is well written, ties in smoothly with the attention-grabbing headline. It goes:

307

Here's what you do without when you go with Firestone Duplex truck tires: 2 dual tires, 2 tubes, 2 flaps, 2 rim bases, 2 lock rings, 2 side rings, and a spacer band.

Eleven fewer parts to buy and stock. Eleven fewer parts to replace. Multiply that by the number of dual tires you're running now and you'll get an idea of just how much Firestone Duplex tires can be worth to you.

And Firestone Duplex tires have other ways of outdoing duals. Duplex tires provide maximum mobility and flotation —especially in soft, sloppy going. Where duals put down a pair of slim tracks, a Duplex gives you one big, wide, flat "footprint." That's why the Firestone Duplex goes where duals fear to tread.

You make fewer trips to the fuel pumps with Duplex tires. There's less rolling resistance. Your fuel mileage is up as much as 10 percent. There's less wear and tear on brakes, too. Drums have greater air exposure. And they stay cooler. The linings last longer. So does your maintenance budget.

But the Duplex tire does more than just save money for you. It helps you to make more money—by reducing axle weight up to 300 pounds per axle! That, of course, means bigger payloads on every trip, including trips to the bank. And you'll make more trips on Duplex tires with long mileage Sup-R-Tuf rubber.

Ask the tire experts at your nearby Firestone Dealer or store about new Duplex truck tires and the low-cost Duplex Changeover Plan. And remember, always specify Firestone tires, rims, and wheels on new trucks and trailers.

Look at the points Firestone makes—all user benefits: (1) Fewer parts to stock, less investment in parts inventory; (2) better flotation, a potent point for operators of dump trucks, ready-mix trucks or other units which encounter mud and snow off the highway; (3) better fuel mileage; (4) longer brake drum and brake lining life; (5) lower tare weight up to 300 lbs. per axle. This means, for example, that in a tandem-axle trailer pulled by a tandem-axle tractor, that this weight savings could amount to 1,200 lbs. A common rule of thumb in the trucking business is that a pound saved is equal to a dollar a year in increased revenue. Without belaboring the point—admittedly there are variables in the rule which are not always possible to define precisely—Firestone makes it easy for truckers to compute their own extra earnings with Duplex tires; each of them knows how the earnings formula applies to his specific operation; (6) longer tire life with Sup-R-Tuf rubber; (7) a trucker won't run up a bill rivaling the national debt by switching over to Duplex tires, due to Firestone's Duplex Change-over Plan.

All of these benefits are telegraphed in the headline, shown in the two photographic illustrations, then fleshed out in the body copy. This is thoroughly professional, effective industrial advertising.

Prediction Headlines

If your plant electrical system can not be economically expanded Davey Permavane natural gas-driven compressors will solve your compressed air problems
Davey Compressor Co.

Capacity in flat rolled steel will increase 30% at Granite City
Granite City Steel Company

The 1970 trains may ride a little smoother, last longer between maintenance jobs because of the researchers in Building No. 3 in Sandusky, Ohio
New Departure ● Hyatt Bearings
Division of General Motors Corporation

Dictaphone Corporation will save enough on this one part to pay for a new Brown & Sharpe No. 3 Ultramatic within one year
Brown & Sharpe

You'll find a plus in buying raw materials from the company that manufactures its own oxo alcohols
Enjay Chemical Company

More work gets done when your Towmotor truck operator gets "shiftless"
Towmotor Corporation

A fine opportunity exists to get the one most important user benefit into the headline when the prediction headline is used. Believ-ability is its long suit, and it is particularly effective if a logical explanation of why the prediction is made follows immediately in the body copy. If no explanation is forthcoming, or if the explanation itself lacks in the credibility department, all that's been accomplished by the ad is to convince the reader that your company plays foot-loose and fancy-free with the truth.

Predicted user benefit promised in the headline must materialize and you should be able to cite chapter and verse at the drop of a hat on where, when, and how it has benefited others. Do that and the prediction headline will cause readers to regard your product favorably.

Brown & Sharpe's predicted cost reduction, enough to amortize the machine tool within one year, is an excellent example of how this type of headline should be used. Note especially that this prediction is a true prediction, not a vague hope, and that the customer is named. A year after installation of the machine—when it has performed as predicted—a compelling case-history ad, referring back to this ad, and restating the savings realized will have tremendous impact.

Be Positive

Hedging the bet, or in this case the prediction, is basically poor policy. New Departure • Hyatt Bearings' headline would have been considerably stronger if it had substituted "will" for "may" in the headline. As it now reads, there seems to be some uncertainty in the advertiser's mind as to whether or not the prediction will come true. Obviously the same doubt—or more of it—exists in the minds of the readers. Chances are they wonder why the manufacturer isn't sure enough of his product to make a firm statement. Residual impression may well be that if the company isn't sure of itself, that's no place to take one's problems.

The word "will" does not have to appear in a prediction headline. Towmotor's headline is a true prediction type, although it also is a statement of a specific fact. Use of "shiftless" in quotation marks requires no explanation of a labor saver in a society conditioned to expect an automatic transmission in every car; the very fact that this situation exists does much to strengthen Towmotor's claim. Everybody knows that automatic transmissions take work out of driving a car, so it's logical that it would do the same in a lift truck.

Just because a headline contains a prediction doesn't mean that every recipient of a trade publication in which the ad appears will consider it of earth-shattering import. Granite City Steel's headline is weak because it is self-oriented and is of interest primarily to those at Granite City Steel Company. There's no user benefit given, no promise of one, nothing is done to draw the reader into pursuing the copy which follows.

INDIRECT HEADLINES

If you like to live dangerously, use the indirect headline. When you do, you're going for broke.

The direct headline, as we've seen, invariably produces an impression about the product or service. At its most ineffective, if the business reader absorbs only the headline, the ad has been partially successful.

But the sole function of the indirect headline is to induce readers to do one thing: continue reading. You're putting all of your "begs" in one "askit." If your headline is punchy enough to succeed in its purpose, your ad will receive readership far above the average. However, if it fails, you'll probably get next to no readership and you can scratch the number of dollars invested in ad production and space cost.

Sometimes, however, an indirect headline which asks a question can still make a name or brand impression on the reader. He'll at least be aware that he saw the name of your product. This, however, is the exception. Let's take a look at some indirect headlines.

Question Headlines

Which plate size is best for electron micrographs?
RCA Scientific Instruments

How did we get to be Number 2 in integrated circuits?
Motorola Semiconductor Products, Inc.

Looking for a weather-proof, crack-resistant, chemical-resistant stack paint? And an off-shade lemon yellow for the boss's office?
Devoe Paint

Pioneering? You don't have to have someone re-invent the wheel
Micro Switch

What new motor line has the lift-off top?
Allis-Chalmers

Is the d-c unit substation you're considering worth its salt?
I-T-E Circuit Breaker Company

What will make the biggest change on the interchange in '67?
FMC Corporation

What cable jacket material has the toughness Grumman wants for its A6A Intruder? For its E2A Hawkeye?
Pennsalt Chemicals Corporation

Who could keep bringing new efficiency to oil control better than the people who introduced it originally?
Sealed Power Corporation

Each of the above question headlines risks everything on its ability to whet the appetite of the reader, to arouse his curiosity sufficiently to make him read the body copy. Note that the name of the advertiser is not given; the product itself is scarcely mentioned, except in a generic way. And in Micro Switch's ad no hint whatsoever is given of the topic of discussion in the body copy. Others are a bit more specific, but rely mainly on luring the reader into the text. This is risky business.

Following, though, are question headlines in which either the advertiser, the product, or the problem being considered is included in the headline. Despite this, these headlines are indirect.

Why can you depend on MSA for safety eyewear? For the same reasons you depend on MSA for gas detectors.
Mine Safety Appliances Co.

What in the world is Raytheon doing at 50 fathoms?
Raytheon Company

Tire makers use cords of rayon, nylon, polyester, cotton, glass and steel . . . so why do they specify rayon for their new radial tires?
American Viscose Division

When does it pay to purchase a Trackmobile?
Whiting Corporation

Why saddle a $40,000 turret lathe with a job an $18,000 Blanchard grinder can do better . . . and for less?
The Blanchard Machine Company

Question headlines can undoubtedly produce exceptionally high readership, but before deciding upon one, sit back and reflect and consider carefully whether or not you're willing to stake everything on one turn of the card. Perhaps you have too much at stake, too small a budget, or just aren't ready yet for such strong medicine.

On the other hand, it has been conclusively proven time and again that ads which rank at the top of the heap in readership ratings state or imply a user benefit—or ask a question about it which stimulates interest.

Could be the decision-making will be a bit easier if you'll do this. Read each of the above question headlines, plus any ready at hand in trade books, and ask yourself what your response would be if you were a reader-prospect. Very possibly in a number of instances your immediate response will be negative—who knows? I couldn't care less! Why don't they tell me instead of giving me the printed third degree?

If most question headlines cause you to react this way, probably you'd better steer clear of them. But if they intrigue you, if they stimulate a desire to learn more, if they're tantalizing and provocative and they stir the mental corpuscles around, this reaction will be reflected in copy you write, the direction you give to your agency, and your presentation of your product. Should that be the case, a bang-up ad should emerge from your typewriter—at least the odds are in your favor!

Two Outstanding Examples

Jones & Laughlin Steel Corporation uses the question headline with great effectiveness in two separate campaigns, examples of which appear below.

First campaign is to promote J&L Cold Finished Bars to users of this type of steel, and to producers of screw machine parts to whom it is raw material. Objectives of this campaign are to cultivate screw machine parts producers by promoting their interests and the importance of the industry.

Communications objectives are to emphasize the quality of Jones & Laughlin Cold Finished Bars, and to stress the importance of this bar quality in obtaining the best service and reliability from screw machine parts.

For this product, J&L communicates with buying and production influences in the screw machine industry, such as purchasing agents, design, production and quality control engineers and others, within the preselected S.I.C. classifications.

What makes your screw machine parts producer turn gambler? is the provocative headline of this striking four-color spread insert ad. An aura of realism is a strong point of the ad; the facial expression of the "gambler" couldn't be improved upon, the cigar and the glass and the eyeshade belong and nothing is out of character—even

What makes your screw machine parts producer turn gambler?

the screw machine parts fail to strike a jarring note because they, too, belong, due to having been mentioned in the headline. This set the stage for their inclusion in a striking photograph. Complete body copy follows to illustrate a perfect marriage between headline and text.

He's a reliable guy, really.

And he does a great job for his customers who buy screw machine parts.

In fact, that's part of his problem; he does such a great job. He bids as close as possible to his cost for your benefit.

But he runs certain risks in his operations. Risks that his bar stock may not be uniformly machinable. Or that his bar stock is at the lower end of its machinability range instead of at the midpoint or higher.

That's where J&L cold finished bars come into the game. Their reliability and uniformity take the guesswork out of high speed machining.

No one has done as much research in machinability as J&L—research which has achieved uniformity in bar machinability on the high side of the machine range, for

*every grade of bar. There's no gamble on bar uniformity
with J&L cold finished bars.*

This four-color insert appeared in *Steel, Purchasing Week,
American Machinist, Automatic Machining, Production,* and *Automation.* Readership surpassed the competition, held up well when
compared to products with greater and more widespread inherent
interest. *Steel* was discontinued several years ago.

The steelmaker's campaign for its extensive line of stainless steel
also utilizes question headlines with outstanding results. Shown is
another four-color spread, an insert ad which has great impact due
to superb photography and printing, clean layout and typography—
and the question headline.

It reads: *Do you want to reflect the whole truth, or just a glimmer
of it?* Then, the text: *Beautiful stainless steel finishes from J&L
run the gamut from bright annealed JalGLEAM® (left), that
accurately plays back every detail of light, color and form, to non-
reflective Grain Line® (right), that joins in a soft, subtle relationship with its surroundings.* □ *Different as an apple from an orange,
each finish appeals in another way. One excites with its bright,
straight-forward gleam; the other intrigues with the glimmer that is
caught in its fine-line, straight-line pattern.* □ *But these are only
two of the many stainless steel finishes available from J&L.* □ *If*

your product or structure calls for stainless in an alternative mood, call on J&L for that too. J&L has all the answers in practical, care-free, durable—and beautiful—stainless steel.

The sharp, citrus smell and the tangy taste of the Delicious almost exude from the pages. Color fidelity is beyond reproach—this insert is of such superb quality that the Printing Industries of America, Incorporated, presented its coveted Certificate of Award to J&L and its printer.

That's one reason, of course, why the ad did so well when directed to architects, designers, and metalworking buying influences. Jones & Laughlin's communications objective of presenting the company's stainless steels as a modern, clean, durable, corrosive-resistant, and desirable product—and to show the range of reflectivity—were achieved through a question headline that literally *pulled* readers into the ad, by top quality printing, and by persuasive, informative body copy. Just how well it did is shown by the Starch Advertisement Readership Service rating.

Percentage of Readers Who Have

Noted %	Seen-Associated %	Read Most %
65	51	19

Jones & Laughlin's competition rated 5 percent and 9 percent in Read Most in the same issue of *Machinery* in which this study was conducted.

Ad-Gage study of *Machine Design* showed that this insert ad was the best-read ad in the magazine, and it received an Award for Top Performance.

Concept, headline, copy, photography, printing, typography, and layout are all outstanding. And attention to small details resulted in a winning ad that more than paid its way.

Teaser Headlines

Movies in flight: No fighter pilot should be without them.
International Telephone and Telegraph Corporation

Go five miles and turn right
J. Bishop & Co.

Blabbermouth
Consolidated Electrodynamics

The story of the man-made diamond
General Electric

I was a nobody
 United States Steel Corporation

Make us prove it
 Chas. Pfizer & Co., Inc.

The teaser headline is even more nonspecific than the question headline. Complete reliance is placed on its ability to arouse enough interest to secure text readership, and this fails to materialize in most instances. Assess the teaser headline as a stockbroker would if shares in a company were under consideration, and the judgment simply has to be that it is strictly speculative.

If you're having trouble getting rid of all of the money allocated to advertising, if you don't *really* care whether or not your advertising produces results, if you're not held responsible by management for a return on the advertising investment, or if you just don't give a damn, by all means use the teaser headline.

Otherwise, don't touch it with a 10-foot pole.

Blabbermouth—now that's a great headline. No question, it's modern, colloquial, slangy, friendly, in the vernacular, common as an old shoe, and unpretentious. Fact remains, however, that it fails spectacularly to communicate one fact about either the product or the company. When not an iota of information is available, just how is the unwary reader to determine if he might, or might not, be in the market for any electrodynamics—particularly electrodynamics manufactured by Consolidated Electrodynamics? Incidentally, just what is an electrodynamic? Something to hush a blabbermouth with?

Nor does *I was a nobody* present data galore about the specific product U. S. Steel is promoting at the moment, and *Make us prove it* probably elicited a singularly universal response—the turned page.

All might have aroused the curiosity of some readers, but only a mighty tiny percentage of them. Could be that some were intrigued enough to pursue the matter to the bitter end, but, then, some people read dictionaries and telephone books for recreation. There's no accounting for tastes.

Remember, *at best*, teaser headlines are a calculated risk. Objectively evaluated, you have more chance of winning the Irish Sweepstakes every year than you do in producing an effective ad with nothing but teaser headlines on every attempt.

Most of us prefer better odds. So, if the budget is small, if costs keep rising, and you're under pressure to produce, go some other route. Leave the risk-taking to the giants who can afford it.

Martin Marietta Corporation won on such a long shot, because of a teaser headline. Meshing nicely with a striking stop-motion illustration, this layout ties two pages together better than most, and eye-catching white space provides another reason for good readership of the ad illustrated nearby.

Martin Marietta is a major producer of crushed and graded rock for construction. Because rock is solid, a quality construction material for roads, airfields, jetties, and so on, the headline becomes a teaser with relevance.

**For a smooth
ride, put rocks
in the road.**

Almost $7 billion will be spent this year to stretch the U.S. road network to 3.7 million miles. Roads are built up with rock, up to 15,000 tons of it every mile. The Rock Products division of Martin Marietta supplies a good deal of this rock from over a hundred major plants around the country. But rock for roads is just part of the story.

. . . Construction rock is rarely used in the random form in which nature supplies it. It's of such density and hardness that it must be blasted into manageable chunks for processing.

It is then fed into giant crushers, washed and precisely graded for size, and carried through miles of conveyor belts, until it is finally stored in orderly piles waiting for transport.

Martin Marietta has automated many of these operations, so that one man can often push buttons which direct huge and complicated machinery spread over acres of plant.

. . . Martin Marietta divisions produce and market cement and concrete additives as well as rock products. We are, in fact, among the largest producers of these basic construction materials.

As for rock, there's a kind of down-to-earth glamour in digging deep into a $2-billion annual market.

Corporate in nature, although a product ad, this spread establishes Martin Marietta's being in the rock market, and a capability to supply quality rock from more than a hundred shipping points—

For a smooth ride, put rocks in the road.

Almost $7 billion will be spent this year to stretch the U.S. road network to 3.7 million miles. Roads are built with rock, up to 15,000 tons of it every mile. The Rock Products division of Martin Marietta supplies a good deal of this rock from over a hundred major plants around the country. But rock for roads is just part of the story.

People are inclined to take rock for granted, as just something lying around underfoot. Yet commercial-type rock remains one of the most extraordinary materials available to man. Nothing else offers such a combination of strength, durability, hardness and low cost.

That's why rock products now constitute a $3 billion annual market, and have become the solid foundation for practically everything.

In the form of crushed stone, gravel or sand, rock aggregates give concrete and asphalt their mass and bulk.

Rock is the hard rock, too. Rock ballast supports the traffic on highways, sidewalks and airport runways. (What else but rock would take the landing impact of 150-ton jets year in your out.) It's especially early used in the random form in which nature supplies it. Its of such density and hardness that it must be blasted into manageable chunks for processing.

It is then fed into giant crushers, washed and precisely graded for size, and carried through miles of conveyor belts, until it is finally stored in orderly piles waiting for transport.

Martin Marietta has automated many of these operations, so that one man can often push buttons which direct huge and complicated machinery spread over acres of plant.

In the rock business, planning ahead, decades ahead, is a requisite part of marketing strategy. Which section of the country might be having a construction boom twenty years from now? Who will be needing millions of tons of processed rock? Once we've made our predictions, our geologists begin exploration.

Martin Marietta dissolves crushed and smaller cement and concrete additives as well as rock products. We are, in fact, among the largest producers of these basic construction materials.

As to rock there's a kind of down-to-earth glamour in digging deep into a $3 billion annual market.

The second division of Martin Marietta makes specialty chemicals, electronic parts, aluminum wire, aluminum, aerospace systems, housing materials. For more information write: Martin Marietta Corporation, 277 Park Avenue, New York, N.Y.

MARTIN MARIETTA

no small consideration for something as heavy as rock—and the fact that it also produces other allied construction materials.

And there's not one slap at (you'll pardon the word, Martin Marietta) asphalt, nor is there any discussion of the fact that concrete—as most of us know—is the best, longest-lasting material for roads.

Teaser headlines are too risky to rely upon, they shouldn't be used, but occasionally, as in this instance, they come on strong.

Emotional Headlines

Helping people with heart problems to a new lease of life
Hewlett Packard

To your bookkeeper, who may be terrified that we're going to automate her billing department
Friden, Inc.

Till death do us part
Mobil Oil Corporation

Generally accepted is the fact that industrial purchases are the result of a liberal helping of logic and a detailed analysis of all alternative actions. Emotions, so the theory goes, have absolutely no part in the decision making.

Theory is fine and dandy, but frequently it bears little relationship to things as they actually are. Management people in industry who buy for their companies are just that—people. They're just like the rest of us. They are not bloodless robots or three-eyed creatures from outer space, and they don't push a button to turn off their emotions when they walk into the office at nine each morning. Instead, they react emotionally and viscerally. However, the advertising manager cannot overtly appeal to their emotions in an ad. Doing so covertly, however, occasionally leads to exceptionally powerful advertisements.

Hewlett Packard's great spread ad is an excellent example. On one page is a four-color illustration of an appealing 3-year-old boy in a hospital bed—and a small child seriously ill tugs at every heartstring. The headline, combined with the illustration, has a dual appeal—pity and curiosity. Hewlett Packard capitalized on this and proceeded in a full page of copy to tell its product story of how their electrocardiographs, sound amplifiers, vector cardiographs and other instruments enable doctors to perform near miracles and cure, or control, a number of conditions formerly thought hopeless.

Emotional appeal in the headline and illustration handed this advertiser an oversize prescription of readership.

The middle-aged woman bookkeeper in Friden's fine four-color ad *looks* worried, so reinforces the headline. The photograph used was taken in a typical office setting. Principal purpose of the ad is to appeal to the emotions of all business executives because Friden recognizes that displacement of people—especially longtime or middle-aged employees—by machines is probably the most difficult situation which has to be faced when a company automates a portion of its operations. Nothing is more distasteful than to have to terminate employees.

Friden handles the situation logically and persuasively by pointing out that the company's 5010 Computyer doesn't *displace* people—it makes them more productive, thus making it possible for them to find greater job satisfaction.

The message is directed to management, of course, and quite obviously succeeds in its objective of stimulating thought about modernizing the accounting function. Subconsciously, the prospect of having to dispense with old and faithful employees may well have caused postponement of the decision to purchase new equipment to accomplish this objective by many companies. This ad lays to rest that unpleasant prospect—and paves the way for sales of a lot of Friden Computyers.

A Classic in Safety

Classic—and in a class completely by itself—is Mobil's safety-oriented campaign. Designed to communicate with both the industrial buyer and the consumer, the campaign is one of the rare ones of recent years to influence such a broad universe so effectively.

One of the basic communications objectives of the campaign is to project an image of Mobil Oil Corporation as a compassionate, public-spirited company and, in so doing, enhance Mobil's position with present customers and acquire new ones—preferably in large numbers, of course. This applies equally to the suburban housewife ferrying the kids around in the family station wagon and to the fleet operator who buys tens of thousands of gallons of gasoline and diesel fuel at one time, as well as to the plant engineer responsible for purchases of lubricant to keep the machines running and fuel oil to heat the factory.

A theme suitable for such a disparate universe isn't the easiest thing to find, and after considering and rejecting uncounted possibilities Mobil decided upon safety. Safety was chosen due, in part, to the tremendous amount of publicity automotive safety has received as the result of the federal government's intrusion into auto makers' design prerogatives.

That Mobil is genuinely interested in helping its customers help themselves is apparent to all who read its ads. Partly due to the subject matter itself, as well as to the company's sincere desire to help reduce the carnage on the nation's highways, the campaign has produced a massive response.

Mobil has been deluged with requests for permission to reprint this ad in mass media—major consumer magazines, newspapers—and in trade publications, house organs, etc. Permission was happily granted, of course, resulting in Mobil's receiving millions of dollars' worth of additional exposures—including editorial comment—at absolutely no cost to the company.

This great ad is so timely, so well written, and of such intense interest to parents of driving teen-agers that the copy is quoted here in its entirety, while the ad itself is illustrated nearby.

Till death us do part.

It may be beautiful to die for love in a poem.

But it's ugly and stupid to die for love in a car.

Yet how many times have you seen (or been) a couple more interested in passion than in passing? Too involved with living to worry about dying?

As a nation, we are allowing our young to be buried in tons of steel. And not only the reckless lovers—the just plain nice kids as well.

Everyone is alarmed about it. No one really knows what to do. And automobile accidents, believe it or not, continue to be the leading cause of death among young people between 15 and 24 years of age.

Parents are alarmed and hand over the keys to the car anyway.

Insurance companies are alarmed and charge enormous rates which deter no one.

Even statisticians (who don't alarm easily) are alarmed enough to tell us that by 1975, some 15,000 young adults will die in cars each year.

Till death us do part.

It may be beautiful to die for love in a poem.

But it's ugly and stupid to die for love in a car.

Yet how many times have you seen (or been) a couple more interested in passion than in passing? Too involved with living to worry about dying?

As a nation, we are allowing our young to be buried in tons of steel. And not only the reckless lovers - the just plain nice kids as well.

Everyone is alarmed about it. No one really knows what to do. And automobile accidents, believe it or not, continue to be the leading cause of death among young people between 15 and 24 years of age.

Parents are alarmed and hand over the keys to the car anyway.

Insurance companies are alarmed and charge enormous rates which deter no one.

Even statisticians (who don't alarm easily) are alarmed enough to tell us that by 1970, 14,450 young adults will die in cars each year.

(Just to put those 14,450 young lives in perspective: that is far more than the number of young lives we have lost so far in Viet Nam.)

Is it for this that we spent our dimes and dollars to all but wipe out polio? Is it for this that medical science conquered diphtheria and smallpox?

What kind of society is it that keeps its youngsters alive only long enough to sacrifice them on the highway?

Yet that is exactly what's happening. And it's incredible.

Young people should be the best drivers, not the worst.

They have the sharper eyes, the steadier nerves, the quicker reflexes. They probably even have the better understanding of how a car works.

So why?

Are they too dense to learn? Too smart to obey the obvious rules? Too sure of themselves? Too un-sure? Or simply too young and immature?

How can we get them to be old enough to be wise enough before it's too late?

One way is by insisting on better driver training programs in school. Or after school. Or after work. Or during summers.

By having stricter licensing requirements. By rewarding the good drivers instead of merely punishing the bad ones. By having uniform national driving laws (which don't exist today). By having radio and TV and the press deal more with the problem. By getting you to be less complacent.

Above all, by setting a decent example ourselves.

Nobody can stop young people from driving. And nobody should. Quite the contrary. The more exposed they become to sound driving techniques, the better they're going to be. (Doctors and lawyers "practice," why not drivers?)

We at Mobil are not preachers or teachers. We sell gasoline and oil for a living and we want everyone to be a potential customer.

If not today, tomorrow. And we want everyone, young and old, to have his fair share of tomorrow.

Mobil.
We want you to live.

A great corporate image ad by Mobil Oil Corporation.

(Just to put those 15,000 young lives in perspective, that is far more than the number of young lives we have lost so far in Viet Nam.)

Is it for this that we spent our dimes and dollars to all but wipe out polio? Is it for this that medical science conquered diphtheria and smallpox?

What kind of society is it that keeps its youngsters alive only long enough to sacrifice them on the highway?

Yet that is exactly what is happening. And it's incredible.

Young people should be the best drivers, not the worst.

They have the sharper eyes, the steadier nerves, the quicker reflexes. They probably even have the better understanding of how a car works.

So why?

Are they too dense to learn? Too smart to obey the obvious rules? Too sure of themselves? Too unsure? Or simply too young and immature?

How can we get them to be old enough to be wise enough before it's too late?

One way is by insisting on better driver training programs in school. Or after school. Or after work. Or during summers.

By having stricter licensing requirements. By rewarding the good drivers instead of merely punishing the bad ones. By having uniform national driving laws (which don't exist today). By having radio and TV and the press deal more with the problem. By getting you to be less complacent.

Above all, by setting a decent example ourselves.

Nobody can stop young people from driving. And nobody should. Quite the contrary. The more exposed they become to sound driving techniques, the better they're going to be. (Doctors and lawyers "practice"; why not drivers?)

We at Mobil are not preachers or teachers. We sell gasoline and oil for a living and we want everyone to be a potential customer.

If not today, tomorrow. And we want everyone, young and old, to have his fair share of tomorrows.

MOBIL
We want you to live

Create an ad or an entire campaign with emotional headlines that ring true and you can have an all-time great. Beware, however, of the maudlin and the overly sentimental tearjerker. Motives show through. Ads are not opaque—they're far more transparent than many an ad man realizes.

Slogan Headlines

Progress is our most important product
General Electric Company

You can be sure if it's Westinghouse
Westinghouse Electric Corporation

Ford has a better idea
Ford Motor Company

When you care enough to send the very best
Hallmark, Inc.

The quality goes in before the name goes on
Zenith Corporation

These are typical and familiar themes—and occasionally they show up as the headline of an industrial advertisement. None will be quoted here because, even when paraphrased, they're too easily recognizable. In the past several months, however, the author has culled from business publications 14 such ads.

Using a theme or a slogan for a headline is a mistake. Presumably you've already drummed home the slogan into the reader's subconscious, so there's no earthly reason to use it for the headline in an ad. Besides, the typical slogan is too vague and nonspecific to make a really effective headline. It doesn't say anything of interest, and it doesn't promise specific benefits. Resist the temptation to do so, even if such a nonheadline headline would bring smiles of rapture to the faces of the powers that be within your company. Make your advertising money work, make it produce. Repetition of a slogan isn't the way to do it.

COMBINATION HEADLINES

Combination headlines are just what the name implies—combinations of one or more other types of headlines, or headlines that combine separate elements into a different type of headline than any of those previously mentioned. They are currently in vogue.

Cumulative Headlines

Use Nalgene laboratory bottles for just about any application. Every one of them will bounce.
The Nagle Company, Inc.

Knock off 35% of shielding material costs with Hipernom. And stay competitive into the 1970's.
Westinghouse Metals Division

Bans backlash!
 Our new safety shut-off handle protects the operator . . . helps him tighten fasteners securely and uniformly
Gardner-Denver Company

Population explosion.
 Our innovators in switch design have produced more than 200,000 different types. That's a lot of switches.
The Arrow-Hart & Hegeman Electric Co.

The Victor Digital Printer, just $335.
 $335?
Victor Comptometer Corporation

Parts like these produced in ⅓ to 1/6 the previous time.
 Up to 11.5 hours' saving per piece on N/C Omnimil Machining Center at Royal Oak Tool & Machine Co.
Sundstrand Machine Tool

Characteristic of the cumulative headline—or the supplementary headline, or the one-two punch headline, as it's sometimes called—is the fact that the two or more elements of the headline are physically separated from each other in the ad. This is, of course, done by the art director when he lays out the ad, although the copywriter who writes it usually instructs the art director to do so. This device tends to build interest with each segment of the headline, thus drawing the reader bit by bit into the body copy after he completes reading the various elements of the headline.

A cumulative headline enables the copywriter to get more information, news, statistics or benefits into the headline than he would be able to if some other type of headline treatment were used. And the cumulative headline undeniably has great impact, what with the staccato statements hitting the reader one after another in rapid succession.

Use the cumulative headline, by all means, if it enables you to tell your story easier and faster and better.

Headline for Nagle Company's ad is a vigorous combination of a command reinforced with the specific-fact subordinate headline. Effectively used here, you'll note, because the specific fact explains why it is in the reader's self-interest to obey the command.

The Arrow-Hart & Hegeman Electric Co. use a cumulative headline that is composed of a teaser headline followed by a specific-fact headline. In this case use of the teaser is quite permissible since readership of body copy does not depend entirely upon reaction to the teaser.

A specific-fact headline followed by a short question headline is used by Victor Comptometer Corporation to make its point that the Digital Printer isn't inordinately costly. The point is made swiftly and surely, leaving the reader to find out why the unit isn't priced higher.

American Optical Company exploits the possibilities inherent in the cumulative headline to the fullest, as you'll note in the ad shown on the next page.

> *Can you recall these details . . .*
> *when examining these?*

Compare them simultaneously with AO's Duo-Star Microscope.

What could be more natural—or beneficial to American Optical Company—than to ask a question, split into two parts, while illustrating the user benefit derived from the product? The question and the extreme closeups team up to almost force a reader to admit to himself that he can't remember every tiny detail, even if it's important that he do so. The human mind doesn't function that way, and American Optical is astute enough to point it out. And to do it very convincingly.

Then comes the payoff—the statement of specific fact that *you,* the implied subject of the third portion of the cumulative headline, don't have to have a memory like an elephant to avoid making a mistake. American Optical's unique Duo-Star Microscope enables you to avoid guesswork without fiddling around with back-and-forth specimen changes.

Can you recall these details...

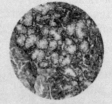

when examining these?

Compare them simultaneously with AO's Duo-Star Microscope.

You view two specimens side by side with the split field of AO's unique Duo-Star Microscope. No guesswork. No back-and-forth specimen changes. No chance of memory playing tricks.

The rugged optical bridge connects two of AO's famous Microstar Laboratory Microscopes. A movable vertical line divides the two images. It is moved transversely so that either field can be viewed individually, or portions of both fields can be viewed simultaneously. You can match, compare and study specific areas of interest.

Either binocular or trinocular bodies can be accommodated. An optional viewing screen fits on the third tube of the trinocular body to facilitate teaching and group observation. Or this third tube will accept an optional camera for photomicrography.

Unless you possess total recall, investigate the Duo-Star Microscope. Just contact your AO Sales Representative or write for more facts.

AMERICAN OPTICAL COMPANY
INSTRUMENT DIVISION ● BUFFALO, NEW YORK 14215

This advertisement by the American Optical Company explores the possibilities of the cumulative ad to the fullest. The copy and illustration set up a problem in microscopic analysis and then systematically supply all the arguments for the superiority of the Duo-Star microscope in dealing with the problem.

Layout is unusually clean, simple and uncluttered. Normally, half-tone illustrations in odd shapes (other than the conventional square or rectangle) are inadvisable. Here, however, because of the product itself, the round shape is exactly right because that is what the user of the product sees. Any other shape would have been wrong.

This ad telegraphs the facts, the user benefits, and what the body copy will contain even faster than a telegram could!

HEADLINE-IS-ALL-OF-THE-COPY HEADLINES

We have a new plan to help you make lube "pros" out of your oilers and cut maintenance costs. It's called Gulf LubeChek '67 and requires practically no effort on your part. Your Gulf Sales Engineer is anxious to tell you about it. Call him at your nearest Gulf office. Or, if you prefer, write us direct for the free brochure which fully explains the plan.
Gulf Oil Corporation

If you process at least 100 tons of steel per month, or 25 tons of aluminum or any other metal—we can provide you with documented proof that you should be using a Warner & Swasey coil conversion system.
Warner & Swasey

Since the mid-60's, the all-headline ad has enjoyed a burst of popularity, and justifiably so. Assume that you have only one or two major points you want to make—such as getting names in response to an offer of literature, or to have the reader pick up the phone to ask a district office for information—this can work well. The most significant user benefit can be communicated to an unusually large universe this way, for these ads usually are well read.

Gulf's ad quoted above is a spread; the left-hand page contains a bleed illustration of a lube "pro" wearing his Gulf button, while the right page is the one which carries the message to Garcia and everybody else. It's all in display type, which has great fascination for the average reader. The only other element in the entire spread is a coupon to be clipped and mailed—if the reader doesn't pick up the phone. The ad does a fine job of getting the message across when the product is of negligible interest, at best.

Although Warner & Swasey's ad contained a keyed schematic drawing and an admonition to write, wire, or phone, the long headline *is* the ad. The machine tool builder carefully qualifies readers by the "if you process" lead-in to make certain that only those who measure up to the criteria established by Warner & Swasey's sales department actually read the ad. These are quality readers, quality prospects, for W&S—the ones it must talk to.

Large type is eye-catching, it's easy to read, and because of its dominance the reader unconsciously infers that the message is of more than ordinary importance. In this way oversize type frequently contributes to better than average readership.

VIRTUALLY USELESS HEADLINES

Incredibly, advertising's role, the contribution it can make to marketing success, and how the individual ad performs its function still are widely misunderstood—or simply not understood at all.

Only possible explanation for this is that hundreds of industrial advertisers habitually waste their money, three-fourths of it at least, by creating and running ads with useless headlines.

Such ineffective ads may be even worse than merely ineffective—they conceivably exert a negative influence. Instead of just failing to make any impression whatsoever on the reader—the prospect, that is—they may, indeed, make a poor impression because the ad presented either the product or the company in a derogatory manner.

Let's look at the six types of headlines that are useless at best, harmful at worst.

Negative Headlines

Your stock is bound to drop
Detroit Diesel Engine Division, General Motors Corporation

The Company that Bought these Furnaces Wanted Its Money Back
Sunbeam Equipment Corporation

Don't don't don't buy a high frequency AC calibration source . . .
Holt Instrument Laboratories

"We have learned through bitter experience that Allen-Bradley resistors are unmatched for reliability"
Allen-Bradley Company

Pssssst. Wanna get some nice cards free?
Brown Company

What They Don't See Can Hurt You!
R. E. Dietz Company

This Ad got us in deep trouble
North American Manufacturing Company

We're not so nutty
Prestole Fasteners

We can really get you into hot water
Lauda Circulators

You'll miss the "whole"
Joslyn Stainless Steels

Finally it's become impossible to describe a new machine in a few words
Link-Belt Speeder

When you pay over a grand for a tire, it better not go up in smoke
UniRoyal

We wouldn't blame you if you never bought another new part from us . . . now that our own brand X is here.
Reliabilt (authorized rebuilt Detroit Diesel parts)

Including a negative word, phrase, or thought in a headline is a perfectly legitimate ploy, but it's a mighty hazardous one. When hurriedly scanning the ad, the reader can easily take with him the negative thought—not the positive one you want to convey.

The Detroit Diesel ad, for example, has a headline that's enough to chill one's soul if he owns so much as a single share of stock in any company. Read the headline and the logo, or signature, and the thought which immediately leaps to mind is that somehow or other if you buy a Detroit Diesel engine your stock will decline in price. You'll lose money. *Your* money. Happy prospect, eh?

Sunbeam's headline is, if possible, even worse. Assuming that all of the countless readership studies have some degree of validity, that headline readership is the *one* thing you can count on getting, and this ad does the advertiser a grave disservice. *The Company that Bought these Furnaces Wanted Its Money Back,* then the signature, Sunbeam—and what impression does the reader retain from having skimmed this ad? That of a company which builds such miserably poor products that its customers clamor for their money back. Steer clear of headlines such as this; they're too easily misinterpreted so as to distort the message.

Poor taste makes Brown Company's headline distinctly negative. *Psssst. Wanna get some nice cards free?* is innocuous in itself, although hardly inspired. Possibly the headline is passable, except that it teams up with the illustration all too well. That shows a seedy, sinister, mustachioed, bearded hippie with hair longer than General Custer's *before* the battle, leering into the camera; his hand is reaching inside his coat for, one gathers, feelthy post cards to peddle. The power of the word "free" is lost completely in this ad—which is a born loser. It's illustrated nearby.

Don't don't don't buy Holt Instruments is the message flashed by the headline and logo in that company's ad. Hardly one they wanted to convey, of course, but the negative used not once, but repeated two more times, is overpowering. It's more than enough to damage Holt, perhaps indefinitely, in the minds of those who skimmed the display type in this ad.

A connotation of deliberate prevarication—or, at the very least, of flirting with the truth—is created by North American Manufacturing's negative headline. Merely stating that *This Ad got us in deep trouble* is distressing enough; nobody is interested in the other fellow's trouble. There isn't sufficient time for a reader to delve into why somebody he doesn't even know has trouble. If there is a sure-fire way to guarantee nonreadership, this headline does it. Then, to top off a futile attempt, "Ad" is capitalized in an effort to lift the headline and the ad out of the realm of the generic and into the exalted status of enduring literature. For some reason, this particular piece of prose didn't quite make it.

Link-Belt Speeder's inability to articulate significant facts about its new machine is touching. However, it leads to the inescapable conclusion that there can't really be much to say about it. Never, never confide to the reader that you're so overcome with emotion when you even think about the new Widget that you're all choked up, that words escape you. Doing this in print isn't a headline or an ad—it's a true confession; if this is what's wanted, follow the old formula of sin, suffer, and repent; type the manuscript neatly on blue-bordered paper and submit it to one of the pulp confession magazines. Possibly a check might accidentally come floating back, computed on the basis of a half-cent a word. Keep the hearts and flowers and hauntingly sad violins out of the business press.

Mistake made by UniRoyal is that its headline talks about an expensive tire going up in smoke caused by friction—and that hurts

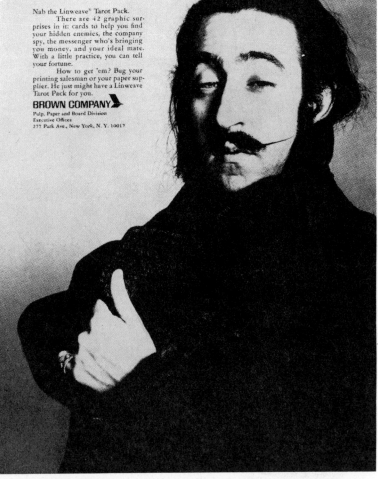

where it *really* hurts, in the pocketbook—and the illustration used ties right in. It shows a tire caught in the very act of destroying itself by—you guessed it—going up in smoke. Now, if the body copy isn't read, and it might not be, UniRoyal has left the impression that its most costly tires are prone to self-destruction. This is not exactly a positive approach to wooing additional customers, or of cementing relationships with present ones.

no! no! Miss K*...
that's not what we mean by **WOOD BLOCK**
factory floor **MAINTENANCE**

Our heroine is "all gummed up" and rightly so because she's being too literal. We have no pat process for removing gum, but we sure know how to keep wood block floors in business for a long, long time. Kreolite End Grain Wood Block Floors are our "babies"... we've been manufacturing, installing and maintaining them for over 55 years (many of the originals are still performing as usual). We know that it's very easy to keep them working for the life of the building, and we'd like to show you how. Old floors that look like new are our best salesmen. So-o-o, let us help you cut costs and improve working conditions.
Call EV 2-3411, or send this coupon for advice and counsel.

We've got a slide film that'll painlessly show you how!

There's absolutely no excuse for letting your wood block factory floor deteriorate...it's just a matter of knowing how to maintain it and that's where we come in. A Jennison-Wright Sales Engineer in your area is ready and willing, in fact, anxious to show you our new enlightening sound strip film "Tender Loving Care for Wood Block Floors." Even if you don't have wood block floors—see this film and we'll give you odds you'll want them.

JENNISON WRIGHT

KREOLITE WOOD BLOCK FLOORS
TOLEDO, OHIO | Inquiries Limited to Continental U.S.A.

Name _____ Company _____ Address _____ City and State _____ Zip Code _____

☐ Please send "Low Cost Maintenance" folder and new area marking formula folder
☐ or better yet, send a factory trained Jennison-Wright Wood Block Flooring Expert

No! No! Miss K* ... *that's not what we mean by WOOD BLOCK factory floor MAINTENANCE* is the headline of Jennison Wright's ad illustrated here. Negative, dangerously so. The man in a hurry can easily read it like this: *No! No! not wood block factory floor* ... *MAINTENANCE.* That's three negatives in a row, followed by the dirty word, maintenance, in capital letters. This implies that it's prudent to avoid wood block factory floors, that if you have one installed all you end up with is a headache caused by excessive maintenance. And even the curvesome cutey in the cartoon can't offset that negative impression.

Borrowed Interest Headlines

up! up! up!
Armour Industrial Chemicals

Bet you didn't know that U. S. Grant & J. S. McCormick were inaugurated together
J. S. McCormick Co.

"Le bain a tout faire"
Gilson Medical Electronics

Just imagine a billion spark plugs
The Prestolite Company

Dead center!
Welch Drill Bushing Company

Come and get it!
American Cyanamid Company

In "The Great Relay Race" you're a winner every time!
Eagle Signal

Et tu, Brute!
Jo-Line Tools, Inc.

The Case of the Flying Stamping
The Crosby Company

If you're a "far sighted" bird, you'll insist on A. O. Smith quality
A. O. Smith Corporation

A lot of fight comes in a small package
Tulsa Products Division

A good decision
The Fremont Flask Co.

For some obscure reason that's difficult to fathom, a few ad managers and copywriters adopt a defensive position about presenting their product to their public. Apparently they feel that readers are not interested in it, making it necessary to disguise what they're up to, what they're going to talk about. They have an urge to make it appear that they're on the verge of discussing something entirely different from the product.

This is the borrowed interest gambit, an exercise in circumlocution—both verbally and visually. Symptoms which make diagnosis of this malady simple are a headline which has little or nothing to do with the matter at hand, usually accompanied by an illustration which is equally inapplicable.

Relying on borrowed interest is a tricky thing; basically, it's dishonest because an attempt is made, consciously or unconsciously, to fool the reader. And there's always a construction job to be done, a bridge to be built between the subject from which interest is borrowed, and the product or service. Most attempts to do this are clumsy and contrived and few readers proceed past this point.

Shortly after World War II, the borrowed interest approach was enthusiastically endorsed by a number of unsophisticated industrial advertisers. Eventually they saw the folly of their way, and the borrowed interest headline fell from favor. Unfortunately, it didn't fall far enough, for it continues to crop up even today.

Let's examine a few ads of this type whose headlines were given above.

up! up! up! Armour's headline is accompanied by an illustration of a cute little four-year-old girl either bouncing on a trampoline or thrown high into the air by her doting father. She's appealing, her expression is appropriately gleeful, and she's quite obviously having fun. And who can deny that four-year-old girls, in common with those 20 years their senior, are of universal interest? The little ones touch the heart and bring a smile to the lips. But Armour isn't selling little girls' dresses, skirts, hair ribbons, or what have you; the body copy following the borrowed interest headline is so boring, so self-serving, so inept that it's a wonder it ever saw the light of print. Copy starts: *We're growing . . . bursting our seams. . . jumping* (see, the little girl was jumping—that explains why she's there at all, particularly up, up, up) *to meet your needs. We are expanding our facilities and all units are working at increased capacity to serve you better. Serving as we do more than 15 basic industries, we have heard often that our line of*—and so on, ad nauseam. Switch names, product lines, and logos and this collection of trite clichés could have been run by any advertiser who wanted only to see his firm name in print. Few readers found any incentive to go past the point in the ad where the quoted copy stops, if they even went that far. And that's debatable.

You know, there's no disputing J. S. McCormick Company's headline. They are absolutely 100 percent right. The author confesses to *not* knowing that J. S. McCormick Company and U. S. Grant were inaugurated together. However, there's some consolation. If we exclude those few people at J. S. McCormick and its agency who chose this desperate approach (complete with a "woodcut" illustration of the late President), chances are those who were aware of this startling bit of intelligence could be counted on the fingers of one hand—with a few fingers to spare. Copy goes: *It's true. U. S. Grant started in Washington about the same time J. S. McCormick Company started in Pittsburgh. So?* So, who got past the "so"? But it turns out that J. S. McC. hedges a bit in the body copy since that says the President and the company were inaugurated *"about the same time."* Now, inaugurated together and at about the same time is a horse of another color. This is reaching far too far. In an attempt to lure a few history buffs or admirers of an heroic general and great President, the ad stretches the truth, then immediately contradicts itself. The number of readers who went on to learn that there was an expansion of Our Plant, and how hard J. S. McCormick Company has worked over the years were few and far between. Who cares?

Consider for a minute, then make a guess. How many buying influences in industry are multilingual? How many, narrowing this down further, read French? With no crystal ball handy, a guess would be 5 percent to the first question, one-fifth of 1 percent to the second. This means, of course, that Gilson automatically beams its headline only to this minute segment of its universe—and despite the illustration of a pert French maid in which there *is* interest—the ad was a waste of money. No illustration of an irrelevant person who has nothing to do with the product can begin to compensate for casting aside three-fourths of the ad's ability to produce an impression.

Reliable estimates place the number of gun owners in this country around the 50-million mark. A tally of hunting licenses sold by all of the states disclosed that some 20 million Americans take to the field each year, gun in hand. Add the serious hobbyists, arms collectors, target shooters, and trap and skeet enthusiasts, and the total is impressive. So Welch Drill Bushing people aren't as far off in their borrowed interest headline as they could be, especially so since the illustration is of one of their small products superimposed in the center of a target with three bullet holes in a typical triangle group, framed by a rendition of a Colt Army Model 1848 cap-and-ball revolver. Welch has going for it the average American's traditional love of guns, plus the cherished right, unique in all the world, guaranteed by the Constitution, that all of us may own and use guns for legitimate purposes. Even so, the bridge between a brief discussion of the antique arm and the product is contrived and pretentious.

Vintage airplane buffs might be attracted to the photograph of the 1911 Cessna after reading about the flying stamping in Crosby's ad, just as ornithologists and random bird-watchers might pore over A. O. Smith's headline and four-color photo of a singularly determined looking eagle. And animal lovers in general might glance at Tulsa Products Division's illustration of the ferocious-looking wolverine seemingly on the verge of attacking something—perhaps a doe and fawn.

All of these headlines and copy approaches are essentially self-defeating because of the basic premise that the product is not of interest to the reader. Or the assumption is made that he doesn't want to read about it because he'd rather read about eagles or wolverines or old Colts. Both are wrong.

Torrington's ad, illustrated nearby, is something of a shock, and it's also out of context. The Torrington Company campaigns have been excellent over the years. Especially noteworthy is the current campaign on the ability to produce small, intricate parts at lower cost than can most end users. It's noteworthy, persuasive, and un-doubtedly effective.

In this ad, however, it takes the borrowed interest tack. *Things are looking up at Torrington* is the headline, with an illustration which appears to be—unless you read as far as the third paragraph of body copy—a rough-looking individual about to do someone bodily harm. In the third paragraph we find that this is not the case. The man shown is an astronaut enduring the stress of 20 to 30 G's, hence his anguished (not threatening) expression.

In addition to borrowing interest which Torrington can never completely make its own, the headline is negative. Implied is that it's high time things look up at Torrington before something terrible happens.

Shy away from the borrowed interest headline. Interest can't be appropriated permanently, there's every chance of losing the reader in the bridge between the nonsubject and the product-subject of the ad, and that you can't afford to do.

Things are looking up at Torrington.

Right up into space!

Because one of the latest and most remarkable Torrington Bearings is helping to condition our Astronauts for their trip "out there" and back.

The Astronaut you see here is whirling around on a contour couch at the end of a fifty-foot arm that revolves around a central pivot and goes so fast it can create pressures of 20 to 30 G's.

It's the centrifuge at the NASA center near Houston. In it, our Astronauts will be readied for the sustained forces that are exerted on a space vehicle when it brakes during re-entry into the earth's atmosphere.

The gondola is gimbal-mounted on four Torrington Spherical Roller Bearings, 18.11" I.D., 24" O.D. by 5.14" wide. Ordered by The Rucker Company which built the centrifuge for NASA, these bearings were specifically designed and made for the job.

But what an assignment!

The extended length of the arm, the unusual strains placed on the bearing, the extreme misalignment and the tremendous speeds generated presented a whole new set of problems and specifications to Torrington.

If your problem is "way out," we'll give it a whirl at our Bearing Divisions, South Bend, Ind. 46621 or Torrington, Conn. 06790.

THE TORRINGTON COMPANY 100TH YEAR

SERVING INDUSTRY EVERYWHERE WITH ANTIFRICTION BEARINGS: METAL SPECIALTIES: SWAGING MACHINES: SEWING MACHINE & KNITTING MACHINE NEEDLES: STITCHING MACHINES.

The Torrington Company, maker of small, intricate parts for industry, has been noted for excellent advertising campaigns for many years. Here, however, difficulties were encountered when the "borrowed interest" technique was tried. The illustration is compelling, but does not go with the body copy beneath.

Irrelevant Headlines

G-Whiz
International Equipment Company

Varoom
Belden Corporation

What's up?
The Mitre Corporation

Happy landings
United Air Freight

Is your wife cold?
National Fuel Oil Institute

Although the number of irrelevant headlines is relatively small, it's not small enough. After reading the above, do you have the faintest idea of what the product or service is?

Headlines must communicate, and those don't. Any valid relationship between headline and product is strictly coincidental.

Take *G-Whiz*, for example—and it's set in huge display type. Supposedly this should interest the reader, at least those prospects for an ultracentrifuge, in one of the gadgets that can "take you into areas of biological research where you've never gone before." Somehow or other, the headline doesn't exactly say that unless there's a highly technical G-Whiz effect on specimens whirled at great speed. International Equipment Company would have fared far better in the battle for readership if a product benefit—or even a hint of one—appeared in the headline.

And Belden just doesn't say anything in the irrelevant headline, *Varoom*. If it were accompanied by an illustration of a slightly blurred Indianapolis racing car flashing down the straightaway in an ad run by the manufacturer for a component part which was subjected to great stress and strain, it might have some relevance. For wire used in magnets, lawnmowers, and material-handling equipment, huh-uh. Not even for the neighbor's threshing machine barbering his lawn at 7:30 a.m. on Sunday.

What's up? could apply to baseballs, airplanes, or arrows, but hardly to a team of engineers who are discussed, not shown, in an all-type ad. And *Happy landings* could be relevant to a relaxed vacationer at the airport, ready to take off for Hawaii; to a businessman, briefcase in hand, hurrying to get into the company jet; or to a fighter pilot taxiing down the strip on a mission. But not to *air freight*. Inanimate objects cannot have either happy landings or unhappy landings since they're incapable of experiencing emotion.

In a class by itself is, *Is your wife cold?* This headline appearing over the signature of National Fuel Oil Institute could have just as easily been run by a dedicated group of psychologists, psychiatrists, and gynecologists dedicated to fighting emotional and physical causes of frigidity through mental therapy or, perhaps, surgery. If such were the case, and if the ad appeared in a medium read almost exclusively by young married adults, it could be both relevant and appropriate. As is, the headline is not relevant—but it *is* vulgar and tasteless and crude. Advertising hinting of the gutter should be refused by media, for it accomplishes only one thing: It hurts advertising in general.

Spend your budget money to talk about user benefits and about the product. Going off onto a tangent and talking about a subject foreign to the one you should discuss is unforgivable.

Precious Headlines

Today, the big deal in construction is the Giesel-powered truck. The what-powered truck?
White Trucks

Time you stopped horsing around?
The Fellows Gear Shaper Company

This boom hoist out boom hoists all other boom hoists!
Northwest Engineering Company

We're not fishing for a compliment . . . we're just "bassking in our glory"
Alloy Metal Abrasive Company

Quit tooling around.
Michigan Tool Company

Don't be "hoodwinked"
Kewaunee Mfg. Co.

What makes SAMI run?
United States Shoe Machinery Corporation

We'd rather freight than switch!
Missouri Pacific-Texas & Pacific

Coined words always require an explanation. Explaining what a coined word means is a fast way to accomplish two things: (1) cause readers not really interested in the coined word to skip over the ad, and (2) encourage nonproductive verbosity through a long-winded explanation which shouldn't have been necessary in the first place.

White Trucks, Division of White Motor Corporation, accomplishes both with one "swell foop." All truck operators and a large segment of the general public are thoroughly familiar with Rudolph Diesel's ultraefficient engine which operates on low-cost fuel oil rather than on more highly refined and more expensive gasoline. The diesel engine has earned an enviable reputation and widespread acceptance because of its cheaper fuel, as well as because of its longer prime of life and greatly reduced maintenance cost. White's attempt to link a new gasoline engine with conventional electrical ignition with the economical diesel which fires from compression is too precious for words.

And it fails to achieve its objective, which obviously is to promote acceptance and demand for the company's new 250-h.p. Mustang gasoline power plant. White could have used the powerful word "new," followed by the name of the engine, its displacement, and a user benefit, and harvested a bumper crop of readers and prospects. For some reason, however, it didn't. More's the pity.

Time you stopped horsing around? in Fellows' headline is followed, predictably enough, by horses pulling a wagon—but the product is plastic. No user benefit, no product feature, but a mighty precious play on words.

This boom hoist out boom hoists all other boom hoists! My, my, we *are* precious, aren't we?

For a manufacturer of fume hoods to demand that readers not be "hoodwinked" is going pretty far. But to then insult their intelligence by putting the term in quotation marks to make sure they understand the little joke is mighty, mighty precious. The same space and the same production investment could have presented a user benefit—and the advertiser's name—at the same cost.

Literary allusions are undesirable because not everyone is familiar with the passage, or the work, referred to. And if they're not, they skip the ad because the headline makes them feel like a clod. Many have read Budd Schulberg's hard-bitten novel, *What Makes Sammy Run?* But more people, many more, haven't. Granted, the headline is cute, primarily because the Semi-Automatic Multiple Inserter abbreviates to SAMI—close to the name of Schulberg's protagonist. Even if the spelling were exact, it's poor policy to allude to fictional characters. Some people might not find them admirable. Some people might find them detestable, in fact, and there was much to detest about Sammy Glick. It's not quite the same thing as tying in a promotion with Santa Claus, for example, or dropping Uncle Sam's name when mentioning customers.

Referring to another product's slogans, as Mo-Pac did when the carrier casually adapted Tareyton cigarettes' campaign theme, can be disastrous. To those unfamiliar with the original slogan, this headline is meaningless. And what conceivable good can accrue from a meaningless headline? When a copywriter is desperate for an idea, when the creative stream has ceased flowing, when the well of ideas has dried up, that's when another product's headline, theme, or slogan is filched. Trying times shouldn't ever be that trying.

United States Shoe Machinery Corporation's headline—a headline that is both headline and body copy is exquisitely precious—so precious, in fact, that it stands alone. It must be quoted in its entirety. It reads:

> *See the turning spindle on the other lathe.*
> *See the tracer slide under the spindle.*
> *See the chips fall and stop the slide.*
>
> *Hear the spindle go PR-R-R-KLONK!*
> *Hear the angry machine fixer.*
> *Hear the boss howl.*
>
> *See the turning spindle on this lathe.*
> *See the tracer slide over the spindle.*
> *See the chips fall free.*
>
> *See the smiling machine fixer.*
> *See the happy boss.*
> *See the profits grow.*
>
> *See DBM.*
>
> *Try a Detroit Tracer Lathe—for better profits.*

See Spot. See Spot run. See Spot run, Dick. See Spot run, Dick and Jane. Color precious ads juvenile.

So-What Headlines

> *This Smith Widget Line adds vigor to a growing industry in a growing country.*
> Smith Precision Widgets, Inc.

The name of the game is Experience
Pittsburgh Steel Company

Magnecraft Relays go industrial
Magnecraft Electric Co.

Supermarket
Turco Products

et cetera, etc., etc.
HPM, Division of Koehring Company

From the shadows of the past . . .
Revere Copper and Brass, Incorporated

When you have work to fasten automatically
Precision Welder & Flexopress Corporation

Safe, efficient paint handling
Cleveland Tramrail Division

Buy job-mated hoists
Shepard Niles

When a headline instantly and automatically evokes a "so what?" response from the reader, it certainly hasn't aroused his interest or done much of a selling job.

. . . adds vigor to a growing industry in a growing country. So what?

The name of the game is Experience. So what? (Not even *what* game?)

Magnecraft Relays go industrial. So what?

The so-what reaction is one you can do without. As the teen-agers would say, and perhaps this sums up the so-what headline as well as any other comment, "Blah."

Try on a headline for size if you're the least bit unsure as to whether or not it's of the so-what variety. Read it to yourself a couple of times, read it aloud, repeat it a few times. Evaluate it objectively, and if it produces a so-what response, waste no time in consigning it to the round file—but don't use it.

An unusually tasteless example is shown. *Dyna-Quip is in a family way,* the headline states. Nothing in the headline to pull a

Dyna-Quip is in a family way

so, we're proudly passing out Free Catalogs of our new, complete fluid power component line! When we gave birth to the first completely new design in pneumatic quick couplings in over 50 years, your enthusiasm for our brain-child encouraged us to try again.

This time, it was a multiple birth . . . a complete line of fluid power components.

By adding "that something extra" to water and steam couplings, hydraulic couplings, hose fittings and adapters, general purpose hose, self-storing hose, ball valves, snap valves, blow guns, filters, regulators and lubricators . . . we feel we have quite a family going for us,

Write for our Free Catalog filled with pregnant ideas on how to improve your fluid power systems.

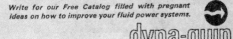

dyna-quip

A DIVISION OF STILE-CRAFT MANUFACTURERS, INC. • 1801 Lilly Ave., St. Louis, Mo. 63110

Author Stansfield's analysis of this ad begins on the opposite page.

reader into the copy, but it's replete with precious little things like *When we gave birth to the first . . . our brain-child . . . multiple birth . . . quite a family going for us . . . our Free Catalog filled with pregnant ideas*—and Dyna-Quip capitalized Free Catalog. This advertiser has managed to transform something joyous and beautiful into locker-room snickers. All for what? A so what!

Say-Nothing Headlines

It's taking the world by storm
General Electric

The shape of things to come
Drake Manufacturing Company

Simple Folks
State of Georgia

If you make automobile trim (or other aluminum products) better make them with HOWMET aluminum
Howmet Corporation

A winning team in the war against downtime!
International Research and Development Corporation

You've got to be an expert to see what TRW makes.
TRW

What would you do without your Authorized SKF Distributor?
SKF Industries, Inc.

Production increases can now be made in the twinkling of an eye
Hobart Brothers Company

Saying something of genuine importance about a product with which a person is intimately acquainted should be the easiest thing in the world. On the other hand, writing a headline that doesn't actually say anything, stringing words together grammatically and logically but without meaning should take a bit more **doing.**

Many advertising managers and so-called copywriters manage this, though, as a perusal of the preceding headlines and riffling through any decent trade publication proves.

For some obscure reason, some copywriters strain to be obtuse. Maybe a deep-seated personality problem enters into it. These individuals may have a feeling of inadequacy, a pressing need to prove

beyond a shadow of doubt that they are more astute, more perceptive, more of everything than all of us in the common herd. Then
again, it could be they merely don't understand advertising; or
they're not cut out to be writers; or they're immature. Too, they
may be searching without success for a sound selling proposition,
or the problem wasn't thoroughly explained to them, or they may
not give three whoops whether the headline is effective or not. You'll
find all of these personality types in the advertising field, working
right beside the real pros.

Regardless of how and why it originated, the say-nothing headline is a flop and a serious mistake in judgment. Comments on a
few of the above say-nothing headlines are:

General Electric's statement that *It's taking the world by storm*
doesn't say anything, doesn't sell anything. It what? Why is it doing
so? No information, no enticement to read further, no strength.
And no headline.

The shape of things to come. What shape? What things? Where
are they? What are they good for? When will they come? What
will they do for the reader? How will they help him in his job? How
do they get here? What price are they? How are they sold—singly,
in pairs, by the pound, by the gallon, in gross lots, or? Drake's
headline leaves a few questions unanswered because it says nothing.
Unanswered, also, is the question of why a reader would read the
advertisement.

And Howmet didn't say *why* you'd better use its aluminum.
There's only the veiled threat that you'd *better* use it, with the
implication that there's an or-else somewhat less than pleasant.

When the clichés go marching in, International Research's say-
nothing headline is bound to be out in the front ranks. "Winning
team," "war against," and similar trite couplings of tired words have
moss on them. Use such worn-out phrases to say nothing and you'll
get exactly that, as far as readership is concerned.

What would you do without your Authorized SKF Distributor?
That's a tough one to answer. The only rejoinder that comes readily
to mind is: "Just exactly what I'm doing right now." Somehow or
other, the author has gotten along in this world all of these years
without ever once having come into contact with an Authorized SKF
Distributor—and seems little the worse for it as far as can be
determined. You can rely upon the average business reader to think
like that, too.

At first glance Brown Company's headline appears to be of the
cumulative variety, composed as it is of two parts. Closer examina-

Our best salesman is an mpty disp ns r.

(The other guy's.)

With some suppliers, it's a toss-up whether you run out of
patience before you run out of towels. With Brown Company's
Service Products distributors you won't run out of either.

The reason? Our men are hand-picked. They're aggressive.
They know your needs. They're committed to the policy
that no order is too tough.

Need NIBROC* towels or tissues fast? Or any other related
products that will make your job easier and more efficient?
Our area distributor will work overtime, if necessary, to deliver
your supplies on time. And in good condition.

You'll find our NIBROC absorbent products top quality—and
our distributor's service unbeatable.

So count on your local Brown Company Service Products
distributor to keep your dispensers full.

He'll do it. We'll do it.

Service Products Division / BROWN COMPANY
Kalamazoo, Michigan 49004 / Executive Offices: 277 Park Avenue, New York, N.Y. 10017

tion of the headline, however, discloses that this headline is actually
a say-nothing headline.

Initially, this was probably a pretty decent ad. Good, that is, until
somebody decided to be ultracreative and illustrate with missing
letters that something missing isn't too desirable.

Only thing, when a headline reads: *Our best salesman is an mpty disp ns r.* the reader won't exert himself enough to fill in the missing letters. Give a reader a puzzle to solve, a task to do, or otherwise make work out of reading an ad—and he doesn't. He'll skip over the ad almost invariably because the business reader doesn't have time for fun and games. Of prime interest to him are ads that telegraph a benefit that will help him. Fail to flag his attention in this way and you've lost him.

Second portion of the headline *(The other guy's),* was probably noticed only by a tiny portion of those exposed to this Brown ad. Too bad, too, because the body copy does a persuasive job of selling Brown's services and its towels. It deserved to be read.

Brag-and-Boast Headlines

We are No. 1 in RF Voltmeters and you better believe it!
  Boonton Electronics Corporation

Ampholine—The New Dimension in Protein Separation
  LKB Instruments, Inc.

For the medical student only the best is good enough
  E. Leitz, Inc.

Tougher products for the surfers—thanks to AMOCO IPA
  Amoco Chemicals Corporation

Miles from nowhere . . . only the best in valves is good enough
  Jenkins Bros.

Thoroughbred products with a winning tradition verify Eaton Yale & Towne capability
  Eaton Yale & Towne, Inc.

Morse means "the most" in cutting tools
  Morse Twist Drill & Machine Co.

At whatever stage of your project you need a cabinet, your most reliable choice is EMCOR
  Ingersoll Products

Wotan Horizontal Boring Mills are setting new standards for accuracy and performance . . .
  Wotan Division of Hunter Douglas International Corporation

Hamilton Standard leads with electron beam machines for all types and conditions of production welding
Hamilton Standard

Brag-and-boast headlines are so patently self-serving that they lack credibility. Readers ignore them in droves. Readers read what appeals to them, and that doesn't include hearing somebody pat himself on the back. As stated before, headlines have appeal for business readers because they find in them a benefit resulting from use of the product. Nobody, but nobody, is the least bit interested in listening to an unknown party brag about how smart he is to have developed such a magnificently superior product, or about how his company—because he's in it, of course—is so infinitely better than any other company. There's always the unseen, but nonetheless present, capitalization in most brag-and-boast headlines where the product appears to be capitalized even if it's not, as if the word were coming down from on high direct from some omniscient being who's letting the reader in on a good thing as a personal favor and with the purest and most unselfish of motives, of course.

We are No. 1 . . . and you better believe it! And just what happens if the reader chooses not to believe it? This is salesmanship in print?

Only the best, only the best. Come, come E. Leitz. Your reputation has been firmly established for more than 30 years; the superb Leica camera, unexcelled optics in microscopes, binoculars, and other instruments have solidified your preeminent position in the industry for you. Superiority of Leitz products is accepted without question. Brag and boast like this ill becomes you. And it's not necessary.

Jenkins Bros. headline would have been far more effective if, instead of merely bragging and boasting, it had said something like this: *Jenkins valves on this oil company's header, 57 miles from the nearest town, have required no maintenance since installation 11 years, 7 months ago.* Some interesting story about Jenkins valves has to be there if they actually are the best—or even nearly that good. Had the company searched out that story and told it factually and interestingly, and with a benefit the reader could visualize as helping him, the ad would have triggered more than yawns and turned pages.

Being customer-oriented rather than self-oriented prevents brag-and-boast headlines from getting farther than the typewriter. Cultivate the mental attitude that causes you to ask yourself, "Now what does the prospect want to know about my product? What benefit will appeal most to him?" Do this and you'll write headlines that do what you want them to—drag the reader into the body copy.

No-Headline Ads

Since the headline accounts for a full 75 percent of the readership of the ad as a whole, on the surface it would seem that no advertiser would run an ad with a virtually useless headline—or (horrors) with no headline at all.

Things are not always as they appear to be on the surface, however, for many advertisers commit the cardinal sin of producing headlineless ads. Why they do this is a moot point. Chances are it's because they think—mistakenly—that their ad, lacking a headline, will stand out from all of the other ads in the book, thus garnering great flocks of readers who might otherwise have passed their ad by. This is a costly fallacy.

Sun Oil Company's two-color spread ad, headlineless, is well written, the selling proposition is sound, there's a story to tell about the product, use of the second color only in the logo is restrained and dignified. As a whole, the ad is well conceived, based as it is on the concept that "a good lubricant's only *half* the story." Sunoco know-how, Sunoco ability to help the customer is the other half of the ad's story.

The device used to attract attention—cutting the pages in half, with white space above the illustration and copy—is legitimate and it accomplished its purpose. The ad does strike you, it has great impact.

Apparently, however, neither the copywriter nor the art director could solve the problem of just how to get a headline in a spread ad which has the top one-third of it consigned to oblivion. A shame, because this ad could have been great with a little more thought and creative time put in on it.

If any one thing can be certain in an uncertain business, it's that ads sans headlines will receive substantially less readership than ads with headlines—even poor ones. Why make it tough on yourself?

Headline Length

There's an old saying to the effect that a man's legs must be long enough to reach the ground. Few are inclined to dispute this. Almost the same thing applies to the headline, although there is opposition to this statement. The headline, too, should be long enough

A no-headline ad by the Sun Oil Company—analyzed on previous page.

to do the job—but should be neither arbitrarily shorter nor unreasonably longer. No reason which will stand up under serious scrutiny exists for anybody to assume a dictatorial attitude about length of the headline, either in favor of short or long.

On the contrary, all available data bears out the contention of most of us that length of the headline has remarkably little to do with how well read it is. Content determines that.

McGraw-Hill reports in its Laboratory of Advertising Performance on a study made by the publisher's Reader Feedback rating service on 4,993 industrial advertisements. Objective was to determine, among other things, whether headlines must be short as a highly vocal group of advertising men proclaim. Exponents of short headlines scored such a hollow victory that not one loud, exultant hurrah echoed from their camp. Results of the study show that headline length influenced readership to this extent.

Words In Headline	Number of Ads	Index of Average Reader Feedback Score
1 - 3	661	127
4 - 10	3,136	126
More than 10	1,130	126
No headline	66	100

So, we see that headlines composed of three words or less collected for themselves the tremendous amount of 1/127th extra readership as compared with headlines of *more than* 10 words—headlines which obviously could contain more information and do a better job of attracting favorable attention of prospective purchasers of the product.

Ignore injunctions against the long headline. This is not to advocate long, rambling, verbose headlines whose outstanding characteristic is that they're long. But if the situation calls for a lengthy headline, don't hesitate to use it.

Factors other than length influence readership of headlines, and of complete ads, as we shall see in subsequent chapters.

Chapter 8

BODY COPY

THE illustration, if it's well conceived, striking, and pertinent, has by now stopped the reader—at least momentarily. Fleeting as this moment is, it's long enough to arouse sufficient interest for him to take the next step. This is the critically important one of reading the headline.

This sequence of events is based, of course, on the premise that you're preparing a conventional ad with illustration, headline, and body copy, rather than an all-copy ad. When using the all-copy approach there's naturally one less step in the process.

At this time, the headline—the single most important element in the ad—is able to build upon interest generated by the illustration and, in turn, perform its job. That is to entice the reader into the body copy. The headline is a good one if it does this, regardless of whether it's deathless prose or not.

Even if the headline *is* the most important element of the ad, we must nonetheless recognize that it gained this distinction due to its dominant position and its unique function, to gain readership of the text which follows. For when all is said and done and the money has been invested and the ad has appeared in publications on schedule, in all except a tiny handful of ads the effectiveness of the ad rests pretty largely upon the readership the body copy received.

We've all heard the old clichés that businessmen are too busy to read ads, and so on. Supposedly, as the pace gets more frantic and more and more demands are made upon our time, we don't read much of anything, much less business publications.

This is dead wrong.

Contrary to uninformed opinion of behind-the-times management of unsophisticated industrial companies (opinion invariably based on personal prejudice and reinforced by lack of exposure to effective industrial advertising and the other marketing services), advertising copy *is* read, and read thoroughly.

There's simply no disputing this. Readership of industrial advertisements has been thoroughly documented, probed, analyzed—and proved—in countless major studies made over the years. Studies were made by publishers and agencies, who admittedly have an ax to grind, as well as by individual advertisers and various independent research organizations. They have no ax to grind. This fact of business life is questioned only by the naive or the incompetent.

The Desire to Achieve

We're lucky. Every industrial advertising man who writes or approves copy has a very potent ally working for him—the fact that the people he wants to talk to read business publications because they consider this a vital part of a continuing educational program to enable them to handle their present job and qualify for a better one. The desire to achieve and to advance is one of the strongest you'll encounter in industry, or, for that matter, in the male of the species wherever he toils.

When we're talking to such readers they are in a businesslike frame of mind. They're in the mood to learn. Furthermore, they have both the need and the desire to acquire information about products which can help them, and they're eager to absorb what you want to tell them about your product if you relate it to their interests, their problems, and their needs.

Our typical prospect is quite receptive, something like the well-heeled individual who wants a new car and enters a dealer showroom *wanting* to be sold. The automobile salesman's job is ridiculously easy when he has a prospect with this mental attitude. And having tens of thousands of prospects with this same outlook makes your job as ad manager—and/or copywriter—simple, too. Industrial advertising, after all, is merely salesmanship in print. This makes the writer the first salesman from his company to contact the prospect with a specific selling proposition. You're halfway home free when your prospect wants to buy. All you have to do is show him why he should buy your product instead of a competitor's.

Oddly, only a small percentage of all industrial advertisers take full advantage of their prospects' desire to be sold. The majority kick opportunity in the teeth. They write and place ads so vague and inept and dull that the impression they make has about as much substance to it as a tendril of fog at dawn.

While it is a marketing function to assign specific, measurable tasks to advertising in support of the written marketing plan, it is advertising's responsibility to handle these assignments with the greatest possible efficiency. The burden, in the final analysis, rests on the advertising manager. He relies on his heavy artillery in the battle for prospects' minds—copy.

This burden isn't a burden in the sense that it weighs heavily or unpleasantly on the industrial advertising manager, however. Exactly the opposite is true because it presents to him the opportunity to solve problems and to express himself with copy that is interesting and informative, lively and logical, pithy and persuasive.

There's a great deal of satisfaction in writing industrial advertising copy. Creating tight copy is rewarding and fulfilling. The writer derives a unique sense of accomplishment from the knowledge that his output is the end product of an orderly, organized mind, of a man who analyzed and solved a problem, and who knows *what* should be done and does it the way it should be done. He realizes also that he alone in the company has the ability to handle this important job.

This ability to adhere closely to a strong core idea, to discard the irrelevant, and to ignore that which is not truly pertinent, sets the advertising man and his copy apart from the product-oriented, engineering-oriented associates around him. Usually they're so bogged down in minor details and unnecessary technicalities about how the widget operates and what it should be used for that they're simply unable to grasp the fact that prospects must be told *what the widget will do for them.*

To produce results, copy must do seven things to and for the reader. These are:

1. Interest him.	5. Convince him.
2. Inform him.	6. Persuade him.
3. Involve him.	7. Induce a response from him.
4. Help him.	

Let's take a look at each of these seven musts and see how they relate to each other—and to an effective ad.

Interest

Ideally, advertising copy should be inherently interesting—interesting, that is, to the average reader of publications in which the ad appears, as well as to those who are your most logical prospects. Face it, though: Just because your company manufactures a valve or turret lathe or a widget doesn't automatically make this fact interesting to the reader who isn't economically or emotionally involved with the product. Your ad about the product isn't intrinsically interesting. It's up to you to make it interesting.

As far as the reader is concerned, you're on the spot. You're on trial—or your ad is—right from the opening sentence in the lead-in paragraph. You remain on trial through the body copy to the signature at the bottom right-hand column of type.

It's here, in this first sentence of body copy, that you have a moral obligation. You must follow through on the promise, express or implied, in both the illustration and the headline. They promised the reader a reward for investing his time in your ad. You've had it if you fail to live up to this promise and do it immediately. The reader remains a reader, but of another ad. Not yours.

For some unknown reason—probably because they've found they can get by with it—only advertising copywriters consistently produce a high proportion of vapid, inane, uninteresting copy. If these same writers wrote material for sale, instead of for a salary, they would be forced to punch up their copy and make it come alive. Any popular magazine offers a number of examples of copy on a wide variety of subjects that are genuinely interesting from the first line of the lead-in paragraph.

Take the opening sentence of an article on the mysterious billionaire, Howard Hughes, in the old *Saturday Evening Post,* for example. It reads:

> *7000 Romain Street is in that part of Los Angeles familiar to readers of Raymond Chandler and Dashiell Hammett: the underside of Hollywood, south of Sunset Boulevard, a middle-class slum of "model studios" and warehouses and two-family bungalows.*

Every mystery story addict, TV watcher, and moviegoer is familiar with Chandler and Hammett. "Underside of Hollywood" is a promising phrase, as is "model studios." You can imagine what goes on in *them.* The neighborhood comes alive with this colorful description, and so does readers' interest. Obviously the editors' did, for the article sold.

Or:

> *Forty minutes after the assassination of President Kennedy, Mrs. Helen Louise Markham left her second-story flat at 328 Ninth Street in the Oak Cliff section of Dallas and walked over to catch a bus.*

This lead sentence from an article in *Esquire* comes as close to guaranteeing readership of an article as any 35 words possibly can. There's an aura of suspense, a feeling that something important is to be disclosed for the first time. The casual reader of *Esquire* is compelled to read on, especially since there are so many unanswered questions about the Kennedy assassination and so much legitimate criticism of the Warren Commission and its report.

Then in *Outdoor Life:*

> *After stalking that bull elk for nearly a mile, we now had him coming toward us.*

Name three sportsmen who could pass that one by! Name two. Even one.

Fortune magazine has a lead-in that goes:

> *The mightiest rocket in the Western world, perhaps in all the world, stands poised to invade the starry seas of space —a rocket whose size and power will unlock fantastic new possibilities in the exploration of the solar system.*

That's topical, taut, downright interesting. The article was read.

But, a distant voice complains, those are professional writers. They have to produce salable material. True enough. They do—or end up with a mailbox full of rejection slips. You don't have to be a full-time author to know how difficult it is to cash rejection slips at the local bank.

Copy Review Important

The obvious question is, why shouldn't the same high standards apply to copy written about an industrial product? Because the product lacks the inherent interest, the drama, the mass appeal of Raymond Chandler, of Howard Hughes who discovered Las Vegas, of elk hunting, the Kennedy assassination, the hippies, or space exploration?

That may be partially true. But never lose sight of the fact that readers of trade magazines (called "books" in the trade), are doing what they're doing because it's in their self-interest. These trade publications are intensely interesting to readers because they affect their ability to handle their jobs. Products advertised in these "books" relate to everyday problems of the readers. They must solve these problems in order to hold their jobs, and to advance. What could have a stronger sense of immediacy? What could be more interesting?

One reason industrial advertising copy isn't better than it is, is because there's nobody to judge whether it's good, bad, or indifferent. Agency copywriters, some of them anyway, submit their output for review—and possible rejection—by an account executive, account supervisor, copy chief, or the creative director. Theoretically this prevents poor, off-target copy from seeing the light of type. This system also acts to prevent the client's learning that all agency wordsmiths are not hypercreative types who exude a steady stream of superlative ideas.

Furthermore, such copy is again reviewed by the advertising manager. Presumably he routes it to the marketing director and/or the sales manager for approval. This, too, should prevent hopelessly inadequate copy from being printed.

In practice, however, many agency account executives write copy for their clients, get it finish typed without submitting it to anybody for their opinion, then blithely trot off to the client to get his okay. And he's the advertising manager who, depending upon the established procedure, or who's out of the office on business travel, or how many upper echelon people are on vacation at the moment, may decide to accept or reject it without consulting anybody.

And if the advertising manager is also the copywriter, as he frequently is in most smaller industrial companies, he'll write, revise, edit, and finally approve his own copy. He then proceeds to have the ad produced 'and placed. No checks, no balances, no outside viewpoint. It's all about as objective as a horseplayer's hunches.

But even if copy is routed to a designated committee of company executives, little likelihood exists that any one of them is qualified by either inclination or training to judge copy. As long as the product is mentioned by name, and the copy doesn't cast aspersions on the product, company, J. Edgar Hoover, or the United States flag, it will receive the benign approval of all involved. Then tally up another collection of worn and weary words worth precious little to anybody, especially the company that pays to see them in printer's ink.

Later on we'll go into how copy *should* be approved.

In the meantime, though, let's look at some lackluster copy and see why it falls flatter than a bride's biscuits:

The International Loadstar dump truck has the strength to move mountains of dirt, rocks, gravel, anything you want to haul. Plus the sure-footed agility to climb over the roughest terrain.

That's the complete lead-in paragraph of the copy in a black-and-white spread ad as run by International Harvester. International dominates the heavy-duty truck market, of course, a fact known to all who are remotely likely to buy a dump truck. Hence International has no need to exaggerate—which, when you get right down to it, is what the reference to moving mountains is. We all know that no dump truck yet built is literally able to move mountains—even one mountain, for that matter. IHC would have been ahead of the game if they'd added interest by stating the cubic yards, or payload weight, the Loadstar can handle. Specifics are interesting, generalities uninteresting.

People aren't hopelessly provincial any more, and most of us have seen terrain that no dump truck, even a Loadstar, could climb. Had International said something like, "easily climbs a 17% grade with a GVW of 72,000 lbs.," they would have aroused sufficient interest to make prospective purchasers of dump trucks want to read further. Perhaps the worst thing about this lead-in paragraph is that it could have been written exactly as it now is—but about *any* make of dump truck.

Mason Color and Chemical Works, Inc. ran an ad with a four-color illustration which was beautifully done. The fine illustration was nullified by body copy which was absolutely devoid of interest. Starting out, it reads:

> *When the quality of your work demands the finest ceramic colors, extra-finely ground for smooth, uniform firing— try our line.*

"Quality" is a word that's so loosely bandied about today that it has become almost meaningless. "Finest" is merely another superlative that readers have trained themselves to ignore. "Extra-finely" —just *how* fine is that? And how smooth, how uniform? The clincher that gives interest the *coup de grace* is that self-serving "try our line."

A two-color, one-page ad of United Transformer Company is far from exciting, starting as it does:

> *Over 30 years of experience in the design and production of special filters have resulted in UTC being a first source for difficult units. Present designs . . .*

Readers are not interested in UTC's—or anybody else's—30 years of experience, or the fact that the company considers itself the first source. Readers want to know what the product or the company will do for them. Chest thumping neither attracts prospects nor motivates them to read dull ads.

Before you decide that your hydraulic power requirements are "special," check Bellows-Valvair's new modular "packaged" power packs. More and more applications can now be handled by these cost-saving units.

This lead-in fails to arouse interest, it fails to create a sense of excitement, it fails to give a reader the feeling that, at long last, here's a product that might bail me out of the trouble I have on Assembly Line No. 3! Not only does it not generate interest, it goes so far as to repeat, almost verbatim, the headline in the first paragraph of copy. Headline is: *More and more applications can be handled by Bellows-Valvair "packaged" power units.*

Instead of senseless repetition, Bellows-Valvair would have been better off to have given two or three dramatic applications of the packaged power units, then told how they upped production, reduced costs, resulted in better quality, or whatever their most important user benefit is. Then readers who probably hadn't even considered whether or not their power requirements were "special" would have read the ad. That way they'd have known that B-V has the product and know-how they need. As is, this doesn't come through.

And from Louden Machinery Company we find:

Transporting the correct batches of dry-bulk ingredients to the proper mixers for a variety of packaged dessert products was a recent problem confronting the engineers of a prominent food processor.

All right, so the customer's name isn't given; we've all encountered obstreperous customers who resolutely refuse to let their company be identified because it's against Company Policy—with upper-case C and P, so it sounds like invoking the name of diety.

That doesn't mean, though, that the first sentence has to be 31 words long. Or that words such as "ingredients" and "confronting" and other three- and four-syllable words must follow each other in relentless succession. This makes for difficult reading; reading that lacks interest, reading that lacks readers.

Had Louden said something on this order, readership would have been substantially higher:

A leading producer of packaged desserts had a sweet little problem. He had to move big batches of dry-bulk ingre-

> *dients to a number of mixers—on schedule and to the right ones, of course. Not much demand for a mixture of butterscotch and chocolate. Here's how we gave him his just desserts . . .*

Specifics were studiously avoided by The Metal Removal Company in a fractional-page, two-color ad on carbide tools. They said:

> *Metal Removal Company solid carbide tool technology offers opportunities for faster, better, and lower cost production with maximum accuracy and using standard machine tools.*

A mouthful, that. And because it doesn't really say anything, doesn't give a solid user benefit that is significant to the reader, it is devoid of interest. How much better the ad would have been if Metal Removal's copy had given some concrete facts; as we all know, carbide tools outwear and outperform tools of alloy steel. Had the copy given some facts on tool life and production rates, then discussed the fact that no modifications need be made on existing machine tools, it would have interested a vast audience of metalworking men who need this product.

> *Centuries ago man ground some earth and mashed some berries and colored his works of art. Color was vital then . . . it is vital today. And because color is important to man, color is important to Harshaw. We've spent more than fifty years making colors.*

The Harshaw Chemical Company may harbor the impression that this copy is interesting prospects, but it's difficult to see just how. Vague generalities and a self-administered pat on the back for having been in business for more than 50 years do not present user benefits of interest. And, somehow or other, the impression persists that color is important to Harshaw because it is important to man— not because Harshaw makes a profit in supplying the material to gratify that urge for color. Surely Harshaw isn't a nonprofit institution.

Grim as these examples of uninteresting copy are, they're happily not typical of all industrial advertising copy. Ad copy can be just as dramatic, just as gripping as a well-written magazine article bylined by a big-name professional.

For instance, consider this:

> *Your guards see a lot, but they miss a lot, too. A guard*

can see only one area at a time. He would like to see more.
Like around corners, behind walls. And be in several places
at one time. Now, with Motorola Closed-Circuit Television,
he can. Here's how.

This lead-in paragraph follows a striking illustration of a close-up
of a factory guard's face, eyes anxiously searching the black night,
and the headline, "If he can't see it, he can't guard it."

With rioting, fire-bombing, and looting the order of the day,
it's an unusual executive in industry who's not deeply concerned
about the security of his plant. Motorola capitalizes on this universal
concern, identifies the problem, and in the first short paragraph
promises a solution. A spot illustration of a guard watching two
closed-circuit television screens shows how the system works, adds
believability to Motorola's description of its product.

In a striking two-color ad Philco-Ford division of the Ford Motor
Company exploits the business community's awareness of what is
rapidly becoming a national problem. Body copy reads:

Problem: 70% of California's water is where 77% of her
people aren't. Solution: Direct the flow from North to
South through rivers, canals, concrete aqueducts, pipelines,
and dams. A $2.6 billion project that's computer controlled.

The problem-solution approach to copy has high interest and is
particularly effective when the problem is universally recognized as
being a serious one. Copy goes on to tell how Philco-Ford produced
a system that is helping alleviate the problem, and that other states
are watching with great interest the progress California is making.
This copy received high readership, and not only from California
residents:

During the Arab-Israeli war, U.S. carrier-based planes
scrambled over the Mediterranean.

Their mission was peaceful, but watching Russians had
no way of knowing this.

Within minutes, though, Soviet Premier Kosygin knew
it. The White House chose to assure him of it over the
Washington-Moscow Hot Line.

It was the first time the Hot Line had ever been used
during a crisis.

International Telephone and Telegraph Corporation, manufacturer of the teleprinter which transmits messages directly from the

White House to the Kremlin, was incredibly lucky in having such a vitally interesting topic to discuss. Once readers were drawn into the ad by the action-packed photograph of a jet fighter being cata-pulted from a carrier deck, and by the headline, "The day the Hot Line got hot," there was no backing out before ITT's story was told.

Few advertisers are blessed with such a spine-tingling situation, but they *can* make their story and their product interesting if the copy is fresh and vivid. There's always a way.

For example, Kaiser Aluminum & Chemical Corporation devel-oped a unique procedure for handling payment of routine invoices, and told about it this way:

> *The idea is to give our suppliers "instant money" instead of endless paperwork. In the past five years we've sent out more than 700,000 signed blank checks—to pay for every-thing from typewriter ribbons to transportation service—without a single instance of misuse!*

Kaiser has much going for them in the lead-in into this skillfully written piece of copy. The thought of instant money is enough to intrigue almost everybody, of course, but the idea of actually mailing signed blank checks is unique in business. Then, when Kaiser says they cut down on the blizzard of paperwork, everybody takes note. All of us desk-bound people take a kindly view toward that.

Then add the fact that Kaiser reinforces our faith in our fellows by pointing out that not once did a heart full of larceny crop up to abuse an honor system, and readers will want the full story. Kaiser gives it to them, explaining how they send a purchase order and a signed blank check in the same envelope. Excellent image-building for Kaiser. Any company that thinks this way is obviously a progres-sive firm, one with which it is desirable to do business.

Specifics arouse interest, and Hyster Company makes the most of this proved principle. Copy in this four-color spread ad begins:

> *Hyster's new C450A Embankment Compactor changes the whole compaction profits picture—by doing a better job faster than ever before. It compacts a full 80-inch swath in a single pass. Compacts to required densities at rates up to 2500 cu./yds./hr. Slams 330 tamping feet into the job with the authority of 330 h.p. twin-diesel power. Snakes around slower equipment at 17 mph. Climbs 35 percent grades. Handles as easily as a compact car.*

A long one, but that's a lead-in paragraph with meat in it. Every contractor who sees the illustration realizes instantly why Hyster's claim of compacting an 80-inch swath *twice* in a single pass is absolute fact, for the new machine has two drums with *twice* as many tamping feet as the traditional single-drum compactor. The succinct, fact-filled copy is interesting because Hyster is reader-oriented, not self-oriented. What the reader wants to know—what the machine can do for him—is right there where it reaches him fast. You could say, it's what's up front that counts.

Copy That Demands Reading

Chromalloy American Corporation's compelling ad is another that *demands* readership. Photography is superb, the headline is exciting and has high interest and strong emotional appeal. The ad, illustrated on the following page, says:

Somewhere in this jungle, there are 19 Viet Cong and a downed American flier

Mission: find the flier, and get him out alive.

How?

The pilot carries a tiny electronic strobelight. Its 25-mile flash guides the helicopter right to him— without tipping off the Viet Cong.

The 'copter swoops down, lowers a chair. And the pilot switches to a miniature two-way radio whose 100-mile power guarantees clear communication with his rescue crew. Fast talk— and skill—will bring him through the trees, limbs and life intact.

The radio, and the strobelight, saved 454 lives in Viet Nam last year.

Both are inventions of Chromalloy American's ACR Electronics Unit.

ACR also devised the first camera to produce films in outer space.

And designed the recovery marker lights for NASA missiles.

Illustration, headline, and copy combine to demand attention.

*And conceived a portable lighting
system that can beacon an airport
runway within 5 minutes of
electrical failure.*

> *And created the rescue light*
> *now required on every commercial*
> *airline life jacket: a 1-inch light,*
> *activated by water, with 2-mile*
> *visibility.*

> *ACR Electronics is one of 24 units*
> *of Chromalloy American.*

> *Inventiveness is something they*
> *all have in common.*

That's an outstanding presentation of an interesting and vitally necessary product, with a smooth transition into a strong corporate story. We'll all read about a product which can save even one life. But one that has already saved 454 young lives in the dark and bloody jungles of strife-torn Viet Nam in just one year can't be ignored.

Chromalloy American tells the story with a fine economy of words, then gets in mentions of other divisional products and indicates the size of the entire corporation. Few readers deserted Chromalloy American before absorbing all that the company wanted to tell them. As a result, Chromalloy American comes off as a vital, vigorous, inventive company with forward-looking management. CA's ad is honestly interesting.

Almost all industrial advertisers present products of genuine merit to readers. They should interest them. That some do and some don't can be attributed to *what* is said about the product and *how* it is said.

How is considerably more important than what—for, in the final analysis—if your ad is uninteresting it will receive mighty little readership. If you simply can't make your ads interesting, you'll be better off to save time and energy and run just one ad. Set it in 32-point type and use an inspirational message such as:

Compliments of Smith Widget Manufacturing Company

At least, this wouldn't bore anybody.

Surprisingly, dull ads aren't easy to write. Skim any number of trade journals and tick off mentally the ads that interest you, even if you're not in the market for the products. Note especially ads from industries which are traditionally dull and dreary—such as the foundry industry or the industrial heating equipment industry.

For the most part, ads for products used in these markets reflect a deep-seated desire to avoid the pertinent in favor of unimportant little details. In the foundry industry, for example, you can almost see the involved workings of the Germanic engineer's mind as he strives mightily to see how he can reject a new concept, to develop valid reasons why a new product or new method described in an ad will not—cannot—work in *his* foundry. He'll do almost anything to justify clinging to the old tried-and-proved ways and things familiar to him, just as they were comfortingly familiar to his predecessors for decades. Writing these innocuous platitudes required just as much research, fact gathering, and effort as would writing something with sparkle.

Writing dull ads for products used in such industries is done because it has always been done—and because backward management will approve them.

Approximately the same expenditure of time and effort is required to develop an effective campaign and write ads that interest people. The main difference you'll find is that writing a dull ad is drudgery. You don't finish the job with a sense of achievement. Put a little—just a little—extra thought into it, however, and you actually impart something of yourself to the ad. You flavor it with your personality, so that it has freshness and vitality and interest.

Who wants to appear pallid and plodding and pedestrian?

Never hesitate to inject colorful thoughts and expressions into your copy. The different—and better—way of saying something is usually interesting. This is what distinguishes Shakespeare from Spillane, what transforms a prosaic monolog into copy that's light and lively.

Invest some extra effort. Any product or service can be made interesting if you'll refuse to let go of an ad until you've found the one approach that's fresh and different, until you've created the spark that ignites the readers' imagination.

Build in interest, then watch the return.

Information

The *one* thing readers of industrial advertisements want above all else is information.

Feed them information that's pertinent, information that relates to their main interest—their jobs—while they're reading trade journals, and your ad stands a better than even chance of being read despite any minor shortcomings it might have.

To business readers, pertinent information is information about a product that can help them solve a work-related problem.

The controller, for example, might find his accounting department bogged down trying to work up the monthly profit-and-loss statement for management. A new system for handling paper work, or a new calculator or adding machine which performs work faster and easier would be a boon to him. And, by the same token, the plant manager might have a bottleneck in the sheet metal shop; a new power shear or cut-off saw which turns out more work in less time would enable him to meet stepped-up production schedules. Give either of these harassed decision makers the information they need in order to specify your product and you've taken the first step in making a sale.

Just what specific information belongs in an ad should be ridiculously easy to decide. After all, there's the copy platform. It contains guidelines. Listed in it are pros, cons, sacred cows, and the things that are never mentioned except in a hushed voice behind a closed office door.

Naturally, not every ad in a campaign can include every iota of information in the copy platform. But the campaign as a whole must include all of it within a specified time, usually a fiscal year.

Pinpointing specific facts which must be communicated to your universe shouldn't entail much effort. But for some reason or other many advertisers—far too many—feed too bland a diet to prospects for the ads to be palatable.

When you're considering what product information you want to put in ad copy, list each feature *and user benefit* you want to talk about. Make the list complete. It's all right if it's as long as a wet week; you can always blue-pencil items which are relatively minor. You'll be sure to include everything that belongs in the list if you mentally analyze your product—and compare it with competitive ones.

Then go a step further. Cultivate an empathic mood—put yourself in the reader's place and try to *anticipate* just what it is that he wants to know and what questions your ad will leave unanswered. If you're thorough and if you're honest with yourself, there'll be questions. Chances are there will be several, one or two of major importance. Remember, your prospects for whom the copy is written are unfamiliar with your product in varying degrees. Some may never have heard of your brand or of your company, and they may even be unaware that either your product or similar competitive ones exist.

Ask yourself exactly what information you—as the reader—must have in order to arrive at a well-reasoned decision to seek more information about your product from a salesman, and how he would justify purchasing it to those in his company. Be meticulously exact in this analysis. Be very specific. At this stage of the game fuzzy thinking cannot be tolerated. It can't help but result in an ad which fails to inform. That way lies lost sales.

Let's look at a few ads currently running, such as Instron Corporation's spread in *Metal Progress.* The first two paragraphs of the body copy go like this:

> *New higher capacity instrument incorporates closed loop control, dynamic response, modular design, advanced programming capability.*

> *Here is a new Universal Testing Instrument with the versatility and precision needed to provide materials researchers with the means for accurately determining basic physical properties, as well as achieving a better understanding of more subtle characteristics—in a wide variety of new and improved materials.*

Now, these high-flown words are fine for engineers who don't really communicate with words if they have access to blueprints or charts or graphs. And the tone is nice, with "higher capacity," "incorporates," "modular design," "advanced programming capability," and "versatility" following hard on the heels of the other.

Copy written in this engineerese is, if you'll stop and analyze it, puffery. It doesn't inform. No actual product superiorities or user benefits are given. No real reason exists for anybody to spend time reading this ad. It is uninteresting and uninformative.

Then there's The C. M. Kemp Manufacturing Company ad:

> *Creative Engineering slanted to the creative engineer concerned about Systems for the generation of Inert Gas, Nitrogen or gas atmospheres. What is Kemp's approach? Simply this: Kemp uses its special product knowledge and unique field experience as a basis for selecting, developing, and combining components into a system that performs at maximum efficiency. This creative engineering can save you up to 75% of your costs. Kemp's record for increasing its customers' product quality and production rates is unmatched in the gas generation field.*

Again, no pertinent information is given to the buying influences the ad is trying to influence. Aside from telling one and all how good Kemp is (and this "information" will be regarded as suspect because it comes from you know who), no information is given to help the reader.

A surefire way to prove this is to substitute Smith Widget Manufacturing Company for The C. M. Kemp Manufacturing Company, then substitute Widgets for Systems, and so on. The ad would have been just as ineffective if written for and run over the signature of any other company in any other industry. This is the way all companies like to think of themselves. But readers couldn't care less.

> *You'll find a plus in buying chemical raw materials from the company that has one of the nation's largest polypropylene plants. Discover all the advantages of doing business with Enjay Chemical Company.*

That's all the copy in this one-page ad except for a tedious listing of products Enjay manufactures—and this includes the headline. It's so sketchy as to information that its effectiveness is open to serious question.

> *If your work involves olefin polymerization, check Stauffer. We have a complete line of titanium and vanadium catalysts —liquids and solids, organic soluble and insoluble, different valence states. We're . . .*

Some information there, of course, because Stauffer managed to state what they have for sale. But there's no information of any kind as to why a reader should have any desire to specify Stauffer, why he'd fare better if he used Stauffer chemicals instead of any other brand.

Another ad in the same vein reads:

> *Extraordinary. That's the word for Witco's Emcol surfactants. Because nearly all of them were formulated for out-of-the-ordinary problems that customers asked us to solve. After 30 years of solving them, it's no wonder you find us with such a wide range of extraordinary Emcols . . .*

. . . and on and on and on. This is another ad that doesn't really give information relevant to the readers' interests. Readers aren't about to wade through several paragraphs of self-praise and recounting how long the firm has been in business to find helpful information.

From Union Carbide comes the next gem of noninteresting non-information. Following is the entire text from a one-page, two-color ad in *Foundry* magazine:

> *This new Ucar graphite symbol assures you that all the skills and experience that created National electrodes will continue to serve foundrymen around the country. Wherever you see this new red and blue design, you can be confident of consistent leadership in product quality and performance. Total product control from raw materials to finished product. Comprehensive carbon and graphite research, development, and manufacturing facilities.*

So who read it? Who was influenced by it, who was motivated to pound on the desk and demand, by George, that the purchasing agent purchase only National electrodes henceforth?

We've already discussed how to identify and define the market for a product and how to pinpoint the various buying influences throughout prospect companies. Baker Division, Otis Elevator Company, a leading manufacturer of lift trucks, has done a noteworthy job in this area for some years now.

When the time came to develop a new advertising campaign, it was only natural that Baker should ponder about what information should be presented to prospects—and how to verify beyond a shadow of doubt that information benefiting both prospects and Baker was included.

Baker decided to find out. Hunches have no place in today's industrial advertising, so Baker's director of advertising went to the people whose opinion means the most—prospective purchasers of Baker lift trucks. A detailed questionnaire was sent to 4,997 known buying influences, who had been identified by name and title earlier, when the company analyzed its market.

The survey was spread over 26 SIC categories. A return of 2,341 questionnaires, for a 46 percent response, in effect gave Baker that same number of assistant advertising managers. This advisory staff prefers the following approaches in Baker ads, which is merely another way of saying how they want information dished out to them. The kind of information desired follows:

33 percent—mechanical details

23 percent—situation ads

16 percent—corporate ads

24 percent—some of each

2 percent—none of above

Baker paid heed to the unpaid assistants. Some ads of the nuts-and-bolts type were prepared, situation ads were produced, as well as combinations of the two.

Not too surprisingly, a number of those who completed the questionnaire appeared to like girls. Feeling that this is no accident and no idiosyncrasy confined to a handful of respondents, Baker decided to feature girls in some of their ads—a radical departure from lift-truck advertising in general, which heretofore had never admitted publicly that there was anything in life sexier than a bright yellow lift truck, even if some of us *do* know better.

Result is a four-color, four-page insert (see pages 374-375). It is chock-full of precise and detailed information a prospect needs to evaluate product quality intelligently. And it makes it easy for him to relate Baker's lift trucks to his operation.

The front page sets the stage for the spread which follows, showing as it does an even half-dozen teaser illustrations, all in full color, as well as a tightly cropped picture of a Tiger Series Baker lift truck. The jewelled open-end wrench and a tool box full of hand tools painted a delicate, feminine pastel, combined with the small picture of an unusually attractive young lady wearing a Baker "B" make this page impossible to pass by. It leads unerringly to the meat of the ad on the inside spread. First-page copy reads:

Follow the track of the cat to quality . . .

Introductory copy in the spread goes:

We make our Tigers by design . . . with the roar left out. The parts that could roar are too carefully made. They tend to purr.

You won't need a wild animal trainer for one. We make them beautifully controllable, but don't leave out any muscle. We kept a ground hugging low profile, because it makes our Tigers both safe and comfortable. We make them fast and powerful, because that's what material movement is all about.

Most of all we make them with quality, because nothing could distress us more than a sick Tiger. In fact, the quality is so high, the reliability of all components so great, the efficiency so unusually good, that most cost analysts think our Tigers are really kittens. From 3,000 to 8,000 pounds capacity, they represent an exceptional breed. By design.

At left, a monotone of the first page of the four-page, full-color ad for Baker lift trucks. Six teaser illustrations lead the reader to turn the page to an inside spread full of information.

At right, the back page of Baker's four-page ad series. Listing the dealers makes it easy for readers to respond to the ad, and also serves to increase the loyalty of Baker dealers.

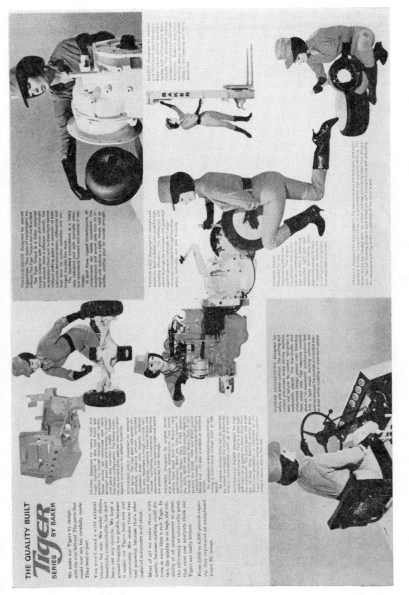

The second and third pages of the Baker lift-truck ad contain specific data about the "Tiger," but the demonstrating "Tiger girl" enlivens the layout.

That intro copy is friendly, low-key, colloquial, and it sells. Following is detailed nuts-and-bolts copy which explains exactly why Baker's Tigers are a different breed of cat. Typical major subheads and copy read as follows:

> *FRAME. Designed for heavy loads and rough treatment. A box-type frame was selected for overall strength and rigidity. Stress points are reinforced with extra strength steel plate and bracing to protect vital parts and maintain a stable, trouble-free frame configuration. The frame is electrically welded, shot-peened, heavily coated against corrosion for added durability.*
>
> *POWER AXLE. Designed for strength and durability. Built to Baker's demands for high-operating efficiency. The differential and wheel bearings are enclosed and gasketed against abrasive materials. All components are accessible through the three-piece, malleable-iron axle housing.*
>
> *BRAKES. Designed for dependability. The service brakes are hydraulic and pedal operated. A brake lining of 125 sq. in. is provided for high-capacity braking. The brake drums are integral with the wheel castings, promoting rapid heat dissipation. Two full floating shoes in each wheel are self-energizing and self-adjusting. An adjustable parking brake is operated at the driver's seat.*

Fact filled and informative, that copy is. And it's just plain intriguing, what with the continuity provided by effective use of "design" and "designed." The eye-catching layout and restrained use of background tint blocks complement the illustrations of the worker assembling a Tiger, each adjacent to the proper copy block. Incidentally, little doubt can exist as to the gender of the mechanic; no real-life production worker ever encountered by the author wore coveralls this fetchingly.

Baker signed off with a concise bit of copy which struck precisely the right note. It says:

> *This is our Tiger. We designed it and built it with care. For you it means the greatest value in the fork lift field. For us it means pride in setting the standard for the industry. Write Baker and we will send you additional information we think you will find valuable. Or call your local dealer listed at right. He'll be pleased to assist you.*

Listing dealers makes it easy for readers to respond to the ad with a phone call, of course.

This ad has consistently earned unusually high readership ratings, frequently standing at the top of the list. The only formula it relied upon to achieve this success is to give the readers the information that Baker thinks they need—and which they say they want. Nothing complicated about that.

Another of Baker's four-color, four-page inserts, this one on the company's electric-powered Bobcat line of lift trucks, is reproduced here. Again the front page does nothing more than arouse reader interest and act as a lead-in for the spread. That's where the solid product information is given.

The Bobcat fork lift truck is dramatized by being pictured in a jungle setting with a snarling Bobcat peering through the foilage. Copy is not as nutsy-and-boltsy, instead stresses the advantages the user realizes with Baker's double guarantee of 180 days or 1,000 hours of operation. This, Baker says, is twice the industry average, hence a potent sales point.

Back page features a four-color photograph of the bottom of the Bobcat—which couldn't have been too easy to take. Again, dealers are listed to trigger response.

In a campaign aimed directly at management, Baker emphasizes that their Bobcats and Tigers are stable and safe. Body copy explains that the fork lifts are:

> . . . *nimble beasts . . . quick as their namesakes and beautifully balanced, with stability unexcelled . . . low center of gravity and wide tread design keep them superbly surefooted, whatever the load . . . driving motions easy and natural, never awkward . . . easy, safe boarding from either side . . . driver visibility is unimpaired . . . positive action controls . . . stability and safety in design.*

All of this is to allay management fears of fork lifts, the materials handling tool that's indispensable but universally considered hazardous. This attitude by top management men could easily swing the purchase decision Baker's way.

Elements unifying the campaigns are repetition of the slogan, "Track of the Cats," continued stressing of the identifying names Bobcat and Tiger, and Baker's beautiful brunette. Nobody objects to *her*.

Just how effective an advertising campaign is as far as sales volume is concerned is a moot point. More on this later. That

Another intriguing o p e n i n g page for a Baker ad features a close-up photo of tracks of a bobcat and tracks of a Baker Bobcat. Again the reader is led deftly into spread pages of the ad.

Again, dealers are listed on the back page of the ad so as to become targets of any inquiries. But the detail photo of the undercarriage of the Bobcat also gives selling points.

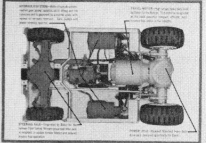

Spread pages this time concentrate on product's user benefits and guarantee.

Baker's advertising is successful is beyond question, however. Since the company first defined its market, then gave qualified prospects the specific information they need to make buying decisions, Baker's sales volume has doubled—then redoubled.

Cull out the unimportant, discard the irrelevant, and present information in your ads that you'd like to see there if you were in the reader's shoes.

Then your advertising campaign can make a contribution to sales success on the order of Baker's.

Involvement

The reader feels a sense of personal involvement with your copy *when it tells him how to solve a specific problem through use of your product or service.*

Involvement occurs because the reader is able to identify with the product or service, or, in some instances, with the selling proposition. Copy which involves the reader does exactly what a well-trained salesman does—it imparts suggestions which the reader recognizes as being in his self-interest.

The one best way to achieve good reader involvement, a must if your copy is to be effective, is for you to take the first step. That's acquiring a feeling of empathy with the prospect.

Note especially that the word is *prospect,* not prospects, plural. Project yourself. Put yourself into this individual's position, mentally seat yourself behind his desk, feel with his feelings as much as it is humanly possible to do so. Use your imagination. Make a determined effort and you'll find that you're automatically beginning to think in terms of what you and your copy can do for Mr. Prospect.

With a little practice, it's easy. You've already identified all of your prospects by name, job function, title, company, location, and SIC classification. This enables you to select a real flesh-and-blood person if that helps you think of him as a living, breathing individual. All of this background information about him gives you some pretty penetrating insights into his needs and his thought processes.

Oversimplifying a bit for the sake of illustration, we know that engineers are, by and large, unimaginative and almost painfully literal. And they almost completely lack the ability to visualize. Copy slanted toward them must of necessity include many more relatively insignificant details than you'd ordinarily want to put in one advertisement. But if all of these little details aren't there, you've left too many unanswered questions. This quickly dilutes involvement because engineers can't make the mental transitions required to fill in minor information gaps.

Since you know your prospect so well, write directly to him—not to some hazy group of faceless beings in a never-never land that exists only on the paper of a circulation statement. And by all means resist the temptation to lecture or preach. There's no place in industrial advertising copy for a soapbox or a pulpit.

Writing to a person, as opposed to writing to people, imposes a certain discipline on the copywriter, one which he willingly accepts because it helps him.

Talk to "You," Not "They"

Imagine, for example, that you're talking to one of your best friends about the product your company manufactures. You're describing it, stressing how it's better than similar competitive ones on the market. You're telling him what it will do for him. Naturally, you're enthusiastic and it shows. You are fully aware of his involvement with your story from his facial expressions, his nods of understanding, his smiles and gestures. Unfortunately, you aren't able to establish this intimate a rapport with your reader prospect, but you can and must feel an affinity with him.

This relationship you've cultivated will help you write copy which involves him both logically and emotionally.

Personal-appeal copy, rather than mass-appeal copy, imparts a special flavor to the ad which heightens the reader's sense of involvement. A hypothetical ad, again using the Widget for the product, might well read this way if the copy is based on mass appeal:

Production men who are responsible for keeping assembly lines humming know the importance of Widgets that work every time. Smith Widgets don't let them down because. . .

On the other hand, personalized copy for the Widget would start out this way:

You can avoid lost production due to faulty Widgets by switching to Smith Widgets. Smith Widgets have oversize, hardened shafts and tapered roller bearings, in contrast to all others which have small, soft shafts and ball bearings. Smith Widgets take the load better, cut your costs, and boost your production.

There's a world of difference. Stray from this concept and copy immediately loses its sense of immediacy and its vitality. Generalities creep in to replace specifics. There's no bite, no vigor.

> *On land, in the air, and on the sea . . . Hitchiner investment castings are proving their value in weight reduction, strength, corrosion resistance, and functional adaptability.*

Certainly there's nothing in that lead-in paragraph of a one-page, two-color ad to cause the reader to feel an overpowering sense of involvement. That's because this is mass-appeal copy, general and nonspecific and not even very interesting.

Some well-done catalog-type copy appears in a two-thirds-page ad by Clarage Fan Company in *Factory* magazine. However, it never really gets off the ground as far as reader involvement is concerned. Body copy is messily executed by the headline and illustration; shown is a frowning, aggressive looking man pointing his finger at the reader, for all the world as if he'd caught you with your finger in the till. Headline reads: "We want you! . . . to order Clarage ventilating equipment"—and, believe it or not, the quotation marks and exclamation point are the advertiser's. Phony involvement is worse than none at all.

Copperweld Steel Company starts a two-color, second-cover ad in *Production* this way:

> *Heavy feeds at high machining speeds require steel that is uniform in cross section. To manufacture cluster gears, the Power Take-Off Division of Dana Corporation specifies Aristoloy 8620H cold-finished bars.*

This is hardly individualized to involve the reader, but it is positive, specific, and it drops a respected name and thus builds in believability. The copy, though, as it continues is pedantic and preachy.

And The Cross Company started its two-color, spread ad by saying:

> *In general terms, this 22-station Transfer-matic is used in the foundry to prepare rough cylinder block castings for the machine shop operations.*

Highly important, highly visible space is thrown away by saying "in general terms." Reader involvement is negligible because there's nothing in which to get involved. Few of us can get all misty-eyed over something that starts out, "in general terms."

However, if Cross had begun the copy something like this, for example, readership—due to reader involvement—would have been much higher.

Are you satisfied with the way you're now preparing rough castings for the machine shop? Is this part of your operation costing more than it should? Here's how you can . . .

And so on to involve the reader right from the start. Never make the fatal mistake of throwing away those critically important first few words. If they don't "pull," your ad is a lost cause.

How AT&T Uses Advertising

Two outstanding ads as far as reader involvement is concerned were created for American Telephone and Telegraph Company. They appeared one after the other.

A particularly knotty problem faced AT&T, whose objective is to induce salesmen, district sales managers, home office sales managers, and marketing directors—and any others responsible for sales volume in industry—to make more long-distance telephone calls.

The company presents a very persuasive picture and advances a hard-headed dollars-and-cents reason why their selling proposition is sound.

The first ad starts with the headline:

They don't call it a waiting room for nothing

The illustration shows a bored salesman resignedly cooling his heels at the end of a long row of chairs in a reception area, obviously at the tag end of a succession of callers.

Body copy continues:

There's a better way to cover small accounts you "can't afford" to see. It's called Long Distance. A planned schedule of calling leaves no sales stone unturned. You can serve small accounts, large ones, and develop new prospects. Think of the waiting you save! Take a new look at Long Distance. Call your Bell Telephone Business Office and ask for a Communications Consultant to get in touch with you.

The "waiting room" ad is reproduced on the following page.

They don't call it
a waiting room for nothing

There's a better way to cover the small accounts you "can't afford" to see. It's called Long Distance. A planned schedule of calling leaves no sales stone unturned. You can serve small accounts, large ones and develop new prospects. Think of the waiting you save!

Take a new look at Long Distance. Call your Bell Telephone Business Office and ask for a Communications Consultant to get in touch with you.

Ah, but there is a way to cover small accounts profitably. It's called Long Distance.

It's the way to give small accounts the importance they deserve at a selling cost you can afford. At the same time, Long Distance enables you to serve the big accounts and cultivate new prospects as well. Call your Bell Telephone Business Office and ask that our Communications Consultant get in touch with you. Take a new look at Long Distance.

As a followup, the second ad shows the same salesman after moving up the interminable row of chairs, still bored, tired, unproductive.

385

Headline of this ad says:

Ah, but there is a way to cover small accounts profitably. It's called Long Distance.

Body copy continues:

> *It's the way to give small accounts the importance they deserve at a selling cost you can afford. At the same time, Long Distance enables you to serve the big accounts and cultivate new prospects as well. Call your Bell Telephone Business Office and ask that our Communications Consultant get in touch with you. Take a new look at Long Distance.*

Everybody who's even remotely connected with sales identifies with this universal problem—that of having a salesman (or a whole staff of them) whose calls cost an average $35.55, sitting idle and unhappy about a situation beyond their control. The problem's a common one, and as field costs inexorably creep up—salaries, fringes, car leasing, commissions, every one of dozens of expenses incurred keeping salesmen out in the territory—it becomes more pressing.

AT&T involves the reader right up to the presidential level, and does so immediately with its expressive visual and its short, persuasive copy. The company follows through by stressing the benefits the phone user derives by covering *all* prospects, small and large, and of developing new prospects by long distance.

Frosting on the cake is AT&T's promise of help by a communications consultant, who is presumably a highly knowledgeable individual when it comes to special telephone plans such as the WATS Line, which gives heavy long-distance users more for their dollar. This bid for action gives AT&T a chance to do some personal selling, something that's not easy to do when the product is already in service, and is as ubiquitous as the telephone.

Reader involvement is built into Friden's two-thirds-page ad in *Space/Aeronautics*. It goes like this:

> *This engineer is winning a $5 bet. Someone gave him the following problem: Find the length of side "a" of the illustrated triangle (dimensions given). He laughingly said he could do it with his hands tied behind his back. Someone bet him $5 he couldn't. He will win the bet in 30 seconds*

*using the new Electronic Calculator by Friden with auto-
matic square root. The Model 132 stores intermediate answers and displays them on a TV screen in four visible
registers. As he works through the problem, these answers
drop into the working register automatically. There's nothing to write down. Square roots are derived with just a
touch of a button.*

The headline about the $5 bet infers something of both personal
and professional interest. Personal because betting involves a challenge and the prospect of personal gain—and it usually isn't done
on company time. Professional interest may be assumed because
the headline talked about engineers. Too, the ad wouldn't be in a
business publication if it didn't concern readers' job interests.

The illustration shows two laughing engineers in shirt-sleeves,
leaning over and timing with a stopwatch as one of their colleagues,
hands tied behind his back and pencil in his mouth, pushes buttons
of a Friden Calculator. It's natural and believable, and accordingly
results in immediate reader involvement. Every engineer is able to
put himself in this situation as he absorbs Friden's product message.

When Bendix Automation announced nine new numerical controls, the body copy of the ad opened with:

*Because one is designed specifically for your kind of ma-
chining. And that puts an end to the compromises and
limitations of numerical controls that try to please everybody. It also means, dollar-for-dollar, you're getting more
control and more machining capability than N/C has ever
offered before.*

In all of industry, is there a harassed production executive who
hasn't at some time or other thought his problems were unique?
Who hasn't moaned about the fact that machine-tool manufacturers
and those who produce numerical controls try to be all things to all
men while they blithely ignore *his* production bottleneck? This ad
recognizes this attitude and this problem, and the copy involves the
reader *with* a problem—and who doesn't have one in this day of
increasingly complex technology?

Both Friden's and Bendix' ads contain two elements which ensure immediate reader involvement: A core idea of interest to the
reader, and product information which promises to solve a problem
for him.

Practically no industry, with the possible exception of the foundry
industry and one or two others, has clung so tenaciously to yester-

day's obsolete approaches in marketing and advertising as have manufacturers of machine tools. These industries, along with the industrial heating equipment industry, just can't seem to abandon the moss-covered concept that their goal in life is to sell hardware, hence their communications objective is to tell their universe that they make hardware.

Advertising managers in these industries undoubtedly realize the weakness of this antiquated concept, and they know full well that it accomplishes one undesirable objective: It makes their company and their industry look backward and outdated to prospects in industries to which they sell.

Realizing this and convincing management of it are two different breeds of cat, though.

A Classic From Cincinnati

It's partially for this reason that The Cincinnati Milling Machine Company's four-page, two-color ad in *Production* magazine is like a breath of spring after a blizzard-filled winter. Primarily, though, it's because this outstanding ad is a classic example of a hardware manufacturer's understanding that selling hardware is almost as much a thing of the past as a quill pen. Today, the company competing well in the capital equipment field is the company that sells solutions to problems. Not hardware.

Considerable courage was required to approve this ad. The entire first page contains no company or product identification, except in a general way. Copy on page one reads:

> *"Sure, your machine cuts metal. But what else can it do for me?" As a production manager, you're probably looking at today's machine tools in a new way. Sure, you know that new machines will turn out more parts per hour to closer tolerances than your old ones can. But you're also looking for solutions to problems like these . . .*

With that tantalizing lead-in, the second page of the ad spells out knotty problems found in almost every metalworking plant in the country. Short, fact-filled body copy then solves each problem directly below each subhead and spot illustration.

> *"We just don't have enough floorspace."*
> *With floorspace at a premium in almost any manufacturing plant, you're looking for single machines that will turn out the work of two or three old ones. Cincinnati's champion*

space saver is probably the TWIN GRIP centerless. If you're doing thrufeed grinding now with a line of three machines, you can probably do that same job with one Twin Grip. That's a 66% reduction in floorspace. Tolerances and production rate are also usually improved.

"I've got to find ways to reduce lead time."
Production men are continually being challenged to shorten the time between design and delivery of a new product. Sometimes the only answer is a whole new machining concept, like numerical control. One manufacturer is combining a dozen different machining operations on propellor control housing with NC, making them three-at-a-time on a Cincinnati 30" NC Hydro-Tel. Setup time is reduced by an average of 60% and machining hours have been cut 65%. His lead time for these operations has been cut by 30%.

"I have to produce a greater variety of parts every year."
As the customer demands more and more product variations, you find yourself doing a lot more job-shop-type work. Lot sizes may be 25-150 with a lot of milling, drilling, tapping, and boring. A Cincinnati Cim-X machining center was designed for this kind of flexibility. Separate heavy-duty milling (7½ hp) and drilling spindles, plus an integral 72-position index table give you the ability to handle most multiple-setup machining jobs in a single setup. Both NC and manual versions available.

That's page two, with three major problems which plague metalworking production men analyzed and solved with Cincinnati products.

Page three continues:

"I simply can't find enough skilled men."
In times when skilled labor is scarce, modern machine tools let semiskilled workers turn out "skilled" work, freeing up your skilled men for more critical jobs. For example, our Hypowermatic belt-type milling machines with Telematic (pegboard) control often combine two or three difficult milling jobs into a single operation. The operator simply loads the part, whether it's a shotgun barrel or crankshaft, and pushes the cycle start button. Telematic then takes the machine through its complete automatic cycle.

Here the first page of a four-page ad for the Cincinnati Milling Machine Co. tackles the tough job of dealing with technical benefits. Note that first page names no company, nor is product identified.

Concluding page of the ad, after disposing of the problem of inventory, suggests, "Let's Talk," then gives phone numbers of field representatives so that interested prospects may call.

"I also have to solve warranty problems."
Profits already made can disappear when warranty costs get out of line. Many Cincinnati's can help prevent excess warranty expense. For example, in a car's automatic transmission is a valve spool smaller than your little finger that meters fluid to change speeds. If it hangs up, the whole unit must be taken apart for repair, perhaps at your expense. Our Centuramatic centerless grinders grind these critical spools to close tolerances (.0003 size, .000050 roundness), assuring smooth operation of your transmission through a great many warranty periods.

Finally, page four gives one more problem and solution:

"Our in-process inventory is a lot bigger than it should be."
Semifinished parts tie up your company's capital and take up floorspace that could be used productively. One tractor manufacturer had to keep large lots of drive housings in process at all times, tying up three milling machines, because there were seven different surfaces to machine on four sides of the part. Now in-process inventory can be reduced at least 25% because all of these operations can be handled in smaller lots on one heavy-duty Cincinnati Vercipower with a rotary table and Telematic control. In the bargain, over-all costs are cut by 18% and quality is improved, since all surfaces are machined in one setup.

Then follows a strong bid for immediate action. It's headed:

Let's talk.

This is punched up with an illustration of a telephone off the hook, all ready for somebody to pick it up and call Cincinnati. Body copy reads:

Manufacturing problems of all types often get solved when your engineers and our engineers get together. The Cincinnati-Heald Engineer in your area is trained to assist you with inventory, floorspace, lead time, skill, flexibility and warranty problems. He can call on reinforcements for additional help on specialized problems. Call your Cincinnati-Heald representative today. One visit could suggest a solution to your toughest production problem.

Cincinnati makes it easy for readers to respond by listing the telephone numbers of their representatives in major cities from

Two pages of spread dealing sympathetically with prospect's problems Cincinnati Milling ad, and offering solutions to each problem discussed.

Boston to Syracuse, complete with the necessary area codes. After all, many prospects in smaller towns would call the Cincinnati representative in the metropolitan center nearest them, which might well be in a different state; the area code would naturally be different from the caller's.

This fine four-page ad makes it obvious that Cincinnati is thoroughly familiar with the various stages in the purchasing process. Some of the problems they cite go all the way back to Stage 1, Increment 1, of the process—origination of the idea to make a purchase. Other problems they use continue on through Stage 4. It's noteworthy that Cincinnati concentrates on problems in Stages 1 through 4, which is where advertising is most effective; and, of course, these are the stages in time when a Cincinnati salesman has probably not yet made contact with most of the buying influences involved in the contemplated purchase.

This is unquestionably a highly effective ad. Cincinnati knows how to achieve strong reader involvement, and they did just that. Nothing was stinted in the manufacture of this ad—deliberation, reflection, or projecting the writer into the prospect's mind. The finished product proves it.

Helping the Reader

There's an old truism to the effect that an effective ad is composed of only two elements, no more, no less.

These are a problem—the reader's—and the solution—which, coincidentally, just happens to be the advertiser's product. It's wonderful how things work out.

And more than a kernel of truth lies in the old saw that all you have to do to build a booming business is to recognize a universal need, then fill it.

Equally true, although cynical enough to have been coined by Malcolm Muggeridge, is the old advertising man's proverb that if you tell the reader you're going to help him, you're well on the way to selling him.

Helping the reader is consanguineous to informing and involving him, of course, but with a subtle little difference. All of these actions depend upon presenting problems and solutions, as well as providing information that's pertinent and interesting to the reader. When you help him by discussing how he can solve his problem through choosing the proper type, model, size, formulation, horsepower, specifications, or other criterion depending on the product, he considers the message a valid one and he'll believe it.

Furthermore, if you proceed to offer additional help by suggesting how he can use your product most efficiently, how it is compatible with his present equipment, how he can maintain it, how he can install it, how he can break it in—then you have a prospect who regards your company and your product favorably. You've helped him. He's appreciative.

Let's see how some advertisers help readers, and how others don't.

One who misses the boat is HPM Division of Koehring Company, whose ad's headline is:

Very big on getting the job done

This startling bit of intelligence is immediately followed by body copy that's of precious little help to anyone. Here's what it says:

> *A special purpose HPM hydraulic press isn't necessarily completely custom. We've built too many. Your special pressure forming problems could be one of the many we've solved for others. You benefit from this wealth of experience in time and engineering costs. HOP gets the job done. In plastics with a broad line of screw injection machines that lead the industry in high-speed production. In die casting of nonferrous metals with the famous . . .* and so on.

This copy doesn't help the reader—it's self-oriented, long on air of elevated temperature and braggadocio.

ACCURACY

Shrieks the headline in type a full 5 inches high in Consolidated Electrodynamics' ad for analytical instruments. It is followed by body copy which does nothing to support the promise shouted by the headline. Complete body copy reads:

> *CEC Direct Reading Emission Spectrometers provide the most accurate information on dynamic background correction, dark current correction, optical interlock and other features which contribute to emission spectrometer accuracy. Call your nearest CEC Field Office, or write to . . .*

There's no help there, only the sketchiest information to trigger a response.

Binks Manufacturing Company's ad in a metalworking book starts the body copy with leaders, like this:

. . . but there is one company—and only one company— which offers you a selection of all systems. That company is Binks.

The copy didn't end there, it brags on and on. That's probably as far as 999 readers out of 1,000 pursued the matter, however. Right from the start the copy made it painfully obvious that there would be little, if any, help toward solving the readers' problems in that ad.

Incidentally, it's not considered good practice to use both leaders (. . .) and dashes(- -) in the same ad, particularly if the copy is relatively short. There's no hard-and-fast rule, but it's a question of taste.

The basic mistake made by Stackpole Carbon Company, Electronic Components Division, is an almost interminable recounting of past triumphs which the company has achieved. Naturally, it immediately evokes a reaction of: "But what have you done for me recently?" Body copy starts out:

In 1965, Stackpole began supplying Automatic Pincushion Correction Cores, a major advance, for color television. 1964 saw the introduction of Stackpole 90° color components including Flyback, Yoke, and Convergence Cores. As far back as 1954, these same components were introduced for the 70⁵ color Deflection Systems. The list of contributions Stackpole engineering and production knowhow has made to the growth of color in television is long and varied . . .

Ancient history is of somewhat less than nominal interest to readers of business papers, and in the electronics industry things that happened last year—or even six months ago—are very old hat indeed. Stackpole wasted expensive space, space that was strategically located in the ad, to talk about dead issues, instead of telling readers something which would help them.

Right on target is Statham Instruments Connector Division's ad for the company's Mini Connector. It wastes no time getting to the point and loses no readers with a long preamble. Body copy gets into the story like this:

Statham's Mini Connector weighs in at a trim 2 grams. Mini boasts a body diameter measurement of 0.290 inch and a total mated height of less than 0.75 inch. Mini is the smallest hermetically sealed high-temperature connector available in 1-, 2-, 3-, and 4-contact configurations. Mini's body and pins are stainless steel. Each pin is individually insulated with Statham's exclusive "Stacer" ceramic. Mini thrives in climates of -320°F to +750°F, and can withstand a thermal shock from the upper to the lower extreme without damage or degradation. Consider these intrinsic features—small size, big performance, closed entry socket, weldability, and hermeticity. Then consider Statham's Mini Connector; the world's lightest heavyweight. For more information . . .

And write to Statham they did, for here is help aplenty for the engineer engaged in miniaturization. Statham's ad manager is fully aware that, as competitive as the electronics market is, the ad had to help the buyer if it was to help Statham.

Standard Pneumatic is frank and open in stressing the fact that its product would help the user. Body copy follows:

Here's an automatic screwdriver designed to help your operators work at top efficiency all day. It's the lightest, handiest, most efficient fractional horsepower screwdriver in the world! Smooth running and quiet, it will deliver as much as 100 in.-oz. torque on only 3.2 CFM of air. You can specify a torque-peak clutch for three torque ranges from 1 to 100 in.-oz. for precise torque control . . . If your assemblers must work with #00 through #6 fasteners, we can help their efficiency. For more information . . .

That's help, a promise that assemblers will be more efficient; any production man quickly translates that into "more production, lower costs," and other benefits.

An unusually effective campaign based on helping the reader is being run by Handy & Harman, a leading manufacturer of brazing alloys. Format is the familiar one of posing a problem, asking a question, then explaining how to solve it through use of Handy & Harman's product. A typical ad is shown nearby. Clean layout, rebus illustrative technique (which will be discussed in a following chapter), attractive typography, and tight, well-written copy combine to make an ad that scored up near the top in readership in the magazines in which it appeared.

A continuing theme sets the stage for the question-type headline.

Problem in production design:

How would you make a part that "can't be made"?

They throw you a curve.

They hand you a sketch of a metal part whose conformation defies normal machining methods. To top it off, they want you to plan production of 50,000 of those parts.

And, as a gentle hint, they suggest that you keep costs down.

Here's what the part is supposed to look like:

Looks simple, doesn't it? And maybe you picture a machinist cutting bar stock to length and turning the diameters on a lathe or screw machine.

But you look once more. You notice there's a rectangular shape, protruding from the smaller diameter. And you realize that no lathe you ever saw could turn that "interrupted" diameter.

Vague thoughts run through your mind. An indexing head operation? Rotary table? No, they eventually run afoul of the same problem—the juxtaposition of two "contradictory" shapes.

Maybe some kind of exotic contouring machine? No good. Even if it could work (and your shop owned one), you'd be in for some fancy tooling. And you're supposed to solve this problem economically.

By now you're beginning to get a little irritated. You take a trip to the water cooler and come back for a fresh look at the problem.

Wait a minute. This miserable part is really *two* parts, isn't it? Look at it this way:

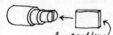

At last you're getting somewhere. You'll make the round part on a lathe and the rectangular part out of flat stock—the natural way.

And you'll join them.

Any problem joining them? None at all. Just mill a slot in the small diameter, push in the flat block—and braze.

Insert and braze

You wind up with a strong metal part, fabricated at the lowest possible cost. The finished assembly would look like this:

Is production brazing practical here? It is. You'd probably have the pre-assembled parts conveyorized past a bank of fixed burners, which would heat the assemblies.

The brazing alloy could be applied on a production basis, probably in the form of metered amounts of brazing paste automatically dispensed to the joint area.

Now, this example is admittedly an oddball. Most metal parts *can* be made by "normal" fabrication methods. But the question is—how economically?

Very often, metal parts can be made better and cheaper as *assemblies* than as monolithic parts. Particularly where the "part" is characterized by widely-differing configurations, thick and thin sections, rounds and flats and so on.

We'd like to pass along to you some ideas on brazing these assemblies. As a leading manufacturer of brazing alloys, we've learned a good deal about the kind of problems brazing can solve.

So we wrote a booklet, "Brazing Ideas," that suggests just where brazing can do a job for you—and where it can't. The booklet is written in plain

English and illustrated with the kind of doodles you make yourself.

If you like ideas, you'll like "Brazing Ideas." Write for a free copy.

HANDY & HARMAN

850 THIRD AVENUE, NEW YORK, N.Y. 10022
OFFICES: CHICAGO, CLEVELAND, DALLAS, DETROIT, LOS ANGELES, PROVIDENCE

Question-type headline is used effectively by Handy & Harman.

Both theme line and headline are given below, just above the body copy which is a pleasure to read.

Problem in production design:

How would you make a part that "can't be made?"

They throw you a curve.

They hand you a sketch of a metal part whose conformation defies normal machining methods. To top it off, they want you to plan production of 50,000 of those parts.

And, as a gentle hint, they suggest that you keep costs down.

Here's what the part is supposed to look like:

(sketch)

Looks simple, doesn't it? And maybe you picture a machinist cutting bar stock to length and turning the diameters on a lathe or screw machine.

But you look once more. You notice there's a rectangular shape protruding from the smaller diameter. And you realize that no lathe you ever saw could turn that "interrupted" diameter.

Vague thoughts run through your mind. An indexing head operation? Rotary table? No, they eventually run afoul of the same problem—the juxtaposition of two "contradictory" shapes.

Maybe some kind of exotic contouring machine? No good. Even if it could work (and your shop owned one), you'd be in for some fancy tooling. And you're supposed to solve this problem economically.

By now you're beginning to get a little irritated. You take a trip to the water cooler and come back for a fresh look at the problem.

Wait a minute. This miserable part is really two parts, isn't it? Look at it this way:

(sketch)

At last you're getting somewhere. You'll make the round part on a lathe and the rectangular part out of flat stock—the natural way.

And you'll join them.

Any problem joining them? None at all. Just mill a slot in the small diameter, push in the flat block—and braze.

(sketch)

You wind up with a strong metal part, fabricated at the lowest possible cost. The finished assembly would look like this:

(halftone)

Is production brazing practical here? It is. You'd probably have the pre-assembled parts conveyorized past a bank of fixed burners, which would heat the assemblies.

The brazing alloy could be applied on a production basis, probably in the form of metered amounts of brazing paste automatically dispensed to the joint area.

Now, this example is admittedly an oddball. Most metal parts can be made by "normal" fabrication methods. But the question is—how economically?

Very often, metal parts can be made better and cheaper as assemblies than as monolithic parts. Particularly where the "part" is characterized by widely differing configurations, thick and thin sections, rounds and flats, and so on.

We'd like to pass along to you some ideas on brazing these assemblies. As a leading manufacturer of brazing alloys, we've learned a good deal about the kind of problems brazing can solve.

So we wrote a booklet, Brazing Ideas, *that suggests just where brazing can do a job for you—and where it can't. The booklet is written in plain*

(sketch)

English and illustrated with the kind of doodles you make yourself.

If you like ideas, you'll like Brazing Ideas. *Write for a free copy.*

According to Starch and other readership surveys, Handy & Harman's ads in this campaign received unusually high readership —and unusually thorough readership.

They were conceived to appeal to the engineer, who delights in any kind of mechanical puzzle or quiz. These production engineers absorbed Handy & Harman's message completely, and responded in large numbers by writing for the cleverly executed booklet, *Brazing Ideas*. Naturally, this provides a constant flow of sales leads for Handy & Harman's sales force, as well as proof of advertising effectiveness in disseminating exactly the information about brazing that Handy & Harman wants prospects to have.

Conviction

Copy must convince the reader that claims made for the product are the truth.

Copy must convince the reader that claims made for the product are the truth.

This point is so essential it bears repetition. In an era of constantly increasing advertising pressure on readers of the business press, convincing them of your veracity sometimes isn't the easiest thing in the world to do. But it *must* be done.

The task is made easier by the fact that business readers want information about products that are new to them, hence they are more than willing to be receptive to the claims you make. Even so, we must recognize that the truth is not what we say it is, but is what readers believe it to be. Thus, when a product claim is advanced it should immediately be supported with proof of truth—proof acceptable to the average reader.

Even then you'll never achieve 100 percent believability, you'll never convince all readers of your truthfulness. Of interest is that some research shows that *no* ad will ever be entirely believed because of its basic purpose—to cause people to change their minds.

Claims should be made—and supported with proof—*within the framework of the reader's past experience.* Every statement you make in your copy, all of the facts, figures, performance data, comparisons with previous models of your product or with current competitive products, should be presented so the reader can sit back and assess your claims from his own personal experience—and from what he readily accepts as truth.

Convictive copy never results from use of "than-what" comparisons. Readers have no reference point when "than-what" comparisons are used. For example, Cleco Pneumatic said in a recent ad:

> *Extra strength in the ratchet parts keeps the tool on the job longer.*

This is a "than-what" comparison. The obvious question in the reader's mind is, *longer than what?*

Winter Brothers Company's ad in *Production* magazine on Skew-Shear taps contains two "than-what" comparisons. It said:

> *In many cases Skew-Shear taps have lasted 2 to 3 times longer. And even greater increases in tap life are not at all uncommon!*

Two or three times longer than what? Even greater than what? Then there's this one:

> *Less worker fatigue, higher productivity, and fewer rejects due to misaligned parts at assembly.*

Less worker fatigue than what? Higher productivity than what?

Fewer rejects than what? Smith Widget Manufacturing Company courts outright disbelief at worst, a condescending ignoring of obvious unsupported puffery at best. Even if the "than-what" comparisons merely resulted in the latter attitude, could the company's advertising manager actually believe that this ad was doing a job for him?

What countless "than-what" comparisons actually accomplish is to lessen the effectiveness of *all* advertising. Don't use them. Don't permit your agency to.

And don't wander afield. Be precise and, above all else, be specific. Use actual instances in your copy—real, honest-to-goodness things, facts, companies, figures, people. They convince readers of the truth of your claims.

For example, Precision Welder & Flexopress Corporation started their ad in *Production* magazine by saying:

Precision Palletron lowers assembly costs.

That's a positive statement, a good claim, and it's a user benefit that every production man would dearly love to see happen on his production lines. Precision Welder & Flexopress quickly followed up with actual figures which prove to one and all the point they make:

This Precision Palletron assembly system for automobile starter motors handles 18 components and subassemblies at 5 manual, 3 semiautomatic, and 8 automatic stations. It can assemble 400 motors an hour.

The illustration complemented the copy, with the end result that PW&FC achieved conviction in their ad—a vitally necessary step toward making a sale of some expensive equipment.

Testimonials are always convincing, especially so when the name, title, firm, and address of the person being quoted is given. Use them freely. If the opportunity arises, quote expert testimony of acknowledged leaders in the field—men whose names are known and respected carry much weight. More often than not they will permit quotations about your products, assuming the product is performing properly, or did what you said it would do for them.

If your product has received official recognition, such as winning a blue ribbon at a design show, receiving approval by the National Association of Electrical Manufacturers, or the blessing of Underwriters' Laboratories, don't be a shrinking violet. Mention this in your ads, and mention it frequently. This carries conviction.

There's the name-dropping technique that's effective if the names you drop are either very big or are newsworthy in themselves at dropping time. Rocket Research Corporation did this quite nicely in a striking four-color ad in *Space/Aeronautics* magazine which said:

> *Twelve Rocket Research monopropellant hydrazine rockets will provide precise attitude control propellant settling, and velocity addition control for the Titan IIIC Transtage. Each employs a blow-down pressurization system providing about 25 lbf thrust . . . Rocket Research has received more than 30 contracts for hydrazine propulsion systems, developed rockets from .02 to 300 lbf; developed, manufactured, qualified, and delivered control rockets to NASA, Navy, Air Force, and industry.*

The fact that Rocket Research Corporation's hardware has met the exacting standards set by some of the most finicky buyers in the world, and that their propulsion system's reliability is so outstanding that a total of 12 of their units will control yaw, roll, pitch, velocity, and other flight characteristics in some of NASA's most important space projects is a real endorsement. And they're sharp enough to parlay this into an ad that's long on conviction.

Addition of "and industry" at the end of the copy adds just the right touch; this could easily encompass every firm in the country from AT&T to Smith Widget Manufacturing Company. Dropping names like these can't help but convince readers that Rocket Research Corporation's statements are true, that it manufactures outstanding products, and that it's a good company to do business with.

The reputation of the advertiser aids in convincing readers of the truthfulness of the statements in an ad. So does calling attention to widespread acceptance of the product, a permissible bit of chest-thumping.

For example, Worthington Corporation ended an ad in *Factory* magazine by saying:

> *. . . in the Worthington line that covers all plant air requirements. And its dependability has made it the most widely accepted name in industrial air supply. Worth remembering when you expand.*

The Worthington name alone lends credence to what has been said in the ad. And when Allen-Bradley tells about the enthusiastic acceptance the company's Modular Control Centers have earned—and supports it with believable statements from eight users who point up different user benefits—that's convincing.

Let's look at two examples of ads which do much to convince the reader that he can rely on statements the ads make.

First is a classically simple, tasteful, black-and-white, one-page ad run in *U.S. News & World* Report by Carrier Air Conditioning Company. The advertiser relies on the headline-is-the-copy technique and on a continuing campaign of succinct, convincing statements based on a premise which the reader has been conditioned all of his life to accept as absolute truth.

Layout is clean, simple, uncluttered and replete with plentiful eye-catching white space. The grace and charm of the Taj Mahal enhance the concept the copy advances—that low bidders usually are low bidders because of product shortcomings. All of us have been familiar all of our adult lives with various cartoons, caricatures, and jokes about the two bums on the park bench, one telling the other how *he* always used to be low bidder.

Carrier makes excellent use of that part of the reader's past experience with highly readable copy that goes:

> *If low bidder had built the Taj Mahal, would it still be a monument to excellence? We suspect not. Craftsmanship, in architecture as in air conditioning, can seldom be short-cut in the name of price. Quality, in the form of craftsmanship, is another reason why more people put their confidence in Carrier than in any other make.*

The ad does double duty with equal effectiveness: It tells Carrier's quality story to the buying influences in business and industry, and it tells it also to these same individuals *as homeowners and consumers.* This fringe benefit of a campaign aimed primarily at business and industry is of significant, if secondary, value to Carrier.

Norton Company's superb four-color spread is just about as convincing as it's possible for an ad to be. Honesty and sincerity come strongly through the copy, as it should in every well-written ad. It reads:

If a wheel fails, we not only know why, we know who.

It isn't easy to be Norton.

When a Norton wheelmaker weighs out and mixes your wheel's abrasive and bond according to its personal prescription, he signs his number on that wheel's traveling

**If low bidder had built
the Taj Mahal,**

would it still be a monument
to excellence? We suspect not.
Craftsmanship, in architecture as in
air conditioning, can seldom be shortcut
in the name of price. Quality, in the form
of craftsmanship, is another reason
why more people put their confidence
in Carrier than in any other make.

Carrier Air Conditioning Company

pedigree form. And the form stays with the wheel through every step, collecting the identity of every man who has a hand in its making.

That way you get the right wheel, made right, every time. But if a wheel isn't right, we know why and who was responsible.

You get that kind of care at Norton whether you order one wheel or a thousand. Although we started the abrasives industry by inventing the first modern grinding wheel in 1877, we've stayed first only because we work at it.

It isn't easy to be Norton.

Coming through unmistakably is Norton's message that Norton is Number One in its industry—that, in fact, Norton *started* the industry. Product quality is superb, the ad implies without actually saying so, because of the unusual degree of personal responsibility assumed by all *who had a hand in its making.*

Norton's story is all the more convincing due to its soft-sell approach which tacitly admits it is possible for a Norton wheel to be other than perfect—although, after reading this ad, it would seem highly unlikely.

The tag line, *It isn't easy to be Norton,* repeating the second half of the headline, is a delightful touch. It does more than its share to convince the reader of the truth of Norton's claims.

Persuasion

Industrial advertising uses print almost to the exclusion of all other media. Consequently, the classic definition of advertising attributed to the late copy great, Claude Hopkins, who coined it before the day of electronic intrusion into our private lives, is perhaps the best one yet stated. According to Mr. Hopkins, "advertising is salesmanship in print."

When we accept this as a valid definition, there's only one conclusion which can be drawn: Advertising's most important function is to do exactly what a skilled salesman does—persuade. Persuade others to accept his ideas, his viewpoint, his advice, his suggestions. Obviously, this is to buy the product.

Any of the seven Type IV headlines, the virtually useless ones discussed in Chapter 7, and the body copy which accompanies them as inevitably as night follows day, is destined to be about as successful as the Edsel or the F-111 jet fighter.

Only copy which is completely committed to furtherance of this primary objective—to present information intriguingly and provocatively so the reader is persuaded to take the action the advertiser desires—merits getting outside the advertising manager's office.

Needless to say, a high percentage of all industrial copy fails to persuade, despite belonging to classifications of copy types which are legitimate and desirable.

This may be because the words "persuade" and "persuasion" are misunderstood, although it's somewhat unlikely. To clear up any misconceptions, let's see what one impeccable source, Webster, has to say on the subject.

"Persuade" means: 1. To induce (one) to believe or do something; to argue into an opinion or procedure. 2. To use persuasion upon; urge.

"Persuasion" means: 1. Act of persuading. 2. Power or quality of persuading. 3. State of being persuaded; induced opinion or conviction. 4. A creed or belief, especially religious. 5. Jocular kind; sort; as, the male persuasion—syn. belief.

From all of that we can cull out something acceptable, such as the first definition of persuade: *To induce one to believe or do something.* This is much to be preferred over the latter half of the first definition. The mere thought of copy presenting information argumentatively is enough to give one the vapors.

As far as persuasion is concerned, the act of persuading is applicable to well-written advertising copy, particularly when it is coupled with inducing an opinion or conviction. This, after all, is the one prime criterion by which copy must be judged: Will it affect the opinion of the reader and cause him to change his attitude enough so that he'll want to purchase the product? All else is secondary.

Whether or not copy is persuasive isn't the easiest thing to judge. For one thing, the decision is frequently—usually, in fact—a subjective one. There are few fixed guideposts, except that copy must, as we've said, interest, inform, involve, help, and convince if it's to achieve its one objective: To persuade.

Viewed in that light, AC Spark Plug Division of General Motors' two-color (red and black) spread ad printed in *Commercial Car Journal* fails to persuade. Let's look at the copy, then see why it doesn't succeed.

AC has nothing to do with downtime

When your fleet is equipped with the Full Time Firepower of AC Fire-Ring Spark Plugs, you'll be minimizing downtime; downtime that costs you money.

Because self-cleaning ACs mean sure performance at all speeds, in all kinds of weather, under all types of driving conditions.

You can cut downtime even more by installing AC ACron Oil Filters, too. They eliminate virtually all engine wear caused by contaminants.

Get AC Spark Plugs and Oil Filters for your fleet. With the complete AC line, you'll really profit by having nothing to do with downtime.

Consider this ad in relation to the attributes effective copy must possess. First, let's take interest. Granted, downtime is the bugaboo that's the bane of every truck operator's life. A truck down is a truck that's not earning its keep, a truck that's increasing costs and cutting into profits. That's elementary.

Every operator is as much opposed to downtime as a man of the cloth is opposed to vice. AC is on firm ground by starting out with a basic premise with which nobody will disagree. That's the gambit known as earning their confidence by making an irrefutable statement, getting 'em on our side by saying things that cause nodding of heads.

Fine and dandy, but the massive disclaimer in the headline is hardly necessary. AC didn't stand in the dock accused of being in cahoots with that wicked old enemy, downtime. The headlined denial is just a little too pious and, at the same time, self-defeating because the immediate reaction to it is, "who says they do?"

Body copy is something less than intensely interesting, even to a man whose livelihood depends on having his trucks pile up mileage, not repair bills. It's pedantic; it preaches as it plods along.

Nothing new is presented, nothing fresh, nothing really solid that the reader can get his teeth into, then sit back, scratch his head, and ponder. As far as factual, helpful information is concerned, there's remarkably little there. In the first paragraph, AC claims truckers minimize downtime if they use their plugs—then they restate the obvious that downtime costs money. This is belaboring the subject to death, but it's probably due to some ivory-tower copywriter just learning that such a thing exists.

AC still doesn't offer any proof; no information is given to support their statement. If somebody happened to read as far as the second paragraph, he'd probably jerk bolt upright in sheer amazement at receiving a piece of information applicable to his job interests—that AC spark plugs are self-cleaning. Even that's not explained, however, evidently on the assumption that the reader knows all about how spark plugs clean themselves. This is taking too much for granted.

Then, stating that AC spark plugs mean sure performance at all speeds, in all kinds of weather, under all types of driving conditions *really* covers the waterfront. However, this doesn't actually *mean* anything except that these trite words are strung together exactly as words in spark plug copy have always been strung together since the advent of the internal combustion engine. They're equally applicable to all brands of spark plugs, of course.

Next, AC informs one and all that you can cut downtime even

more (which is an excellent example of a "than-what" comparison) by installing AC ACron oil filters, too, because they virtually eliminate all engine wear caused by contaminants. This presents just about as much information as the first two paragraphs—next to none.

And precious little information is in the bid for action and the "snapper"—although it *does* clarify the headline (never, *never*, NEVER, *NEVER* feel the need to clarify a headline!) a bit. But does it inform, or does it explain the copywriter's play on words?

Reader involvement? Vapidity never results in deep personal involvement.

What help is there in this ad for the reader? Well, the illustration shows him what a spark plug and an oil filter look like. Although he's presumably in the business of operating a fleet of motor trucks, he might not have known. As far as helping him on his job, huh uh.

Inspire conviction? For obvious reasons we can skip discussion of this vitally important attribute copy must have.

Ah, now comes persuasion. And persuade. Fine, strong words and the prime criterion by which to judge copy. Here again is the definition which we accept for these words, as applied to copy: "To induce one to believe or do something; to induce an opinion or conviction." This copy never comes close to persuading the reader to continue buying AC spark plugs if he now does, or to switch to ACs if he's currently using another brand. He hasn't been told why he should.

Neither an emotional nor a logical reaction is evoked by this copy because it is not firmly committed to persuading the reader to take action by presenting the subject matter so intriguingly and provocatively that he finds it difficult to rationalize doing otherwise. Ineffectual copy like this takes a small but sure toll against all advertising. Bore people long enough and they'll overlook you completely.

The CB&Q Is Convincing

Advertising copy *can* persuade by being informative, helpful, intriguing and provocative. The Chicago, Burlington & Quincy Railroad proves that while promoting a service that's little different than that offered by competitors.

The Burlington and its agency faced one of the facts of business life: That empty freight cars are neither objects of art nor objects of interest—until a shipper needs them right now.

To set itself apart from the herd, the Burlington wisely decided upon a copy approach that gives the railroad a fresh, forward-looking, vigorous image and a distinct personality. Personality automatically accompanies use of names of actual key employees who help shippers get better service, enabling the Burlington freight customers to think of the railroad as people, not tracks and cars and locomotives. This results in good reader involvement and gives the copy a chance to persuade—which it does.

A typical CB&Q ad is shown on the following page. Copy starts with the shocking headline:

Art MacDonald says
this railroad specializes
in empty promises!

Next part of the cumulative headline takes the curse off of the opening teaser and entices the reader further into the ad:

Who does he think he is?

Then, in the final segment of the headline we find:

He's one of the hard-driving wheels
on the Burlington Railroad.

In dialogue form, quoting Art, the body copy says:

"We not only promise empties," Art insists, "we go all out to deliver. That's why we're likely to have more cars on hand when our customers want them."

As Burlington's service and car utilization director, it's Art's job to track down empty cars. To get them right back into service. And to help our customers use these cars most efficiently.

Unloaded cars just sitting around benefit no one.

So Art has set a deadline for their return. As empties begin beating the deadline, he shortens it. And demands even quicker turnaround time.

Tough challenge? Sure. But we've developed a few short-cuts.

Like a computer that tells us instantly which cars are moving and which aren't. Where they're going. What they're carrying. And when they're unloading.

Art MacDonald says this railroad specializes in empty promises!

Who does he think he is?

He's one of the hard-driving wheels on the Burlington Railroad.

"We not only *promise* empties," Art insists, "we go all out to *deliver*. That's why we're likely to have more cars on hand when our customers want them."

As Burlington's service and car utilization director, it's Art's job to track down empty cars. To get them right back into service. And to help our customers use these cars most efficiently.

Unloaded cars just sitting around benefit no one.

So Art has set a deadline for their return. As empties begin beating the deadline, he shortens it. And demands even quicker turn-around time.

Tough challenge? Sure. But we've developed a few shortcuts.

Like a computer that tells us instantly which cars are moving and which aren't. Where they're going. What they're carrying. And when they're unloading.

So instead of cars sitting around on some siding gathering rust, they're out working where they belong.

Art has good reason to boast about faster return of empties. But one thing's certain.

It's no empty boast.

Burlington Lines: Chicago, Burlington & Quincy Railroad; The Colorado and Southern Railway; Fort Worth and Denver Railway.

A dangerous flirtation with a compelling but negative headline works out well for the Chicago, Burlington & Quincy Railroad because the copy quickly recovers a positive approach and talks convincingly of shipper benefits. Negative headlines, however, should be used with the greatest of care.

So instead of cars sitting around on some siding gathering rust, they're out working where they belong.

Art has good reason to boast about faster return of empties. But one thing's certain.

It's no empty boast.

The selling proposition is sound, a user benefit is given in the first paragraph, and it is backed up with good reason-why copy. This is an ad that is believable—and that's persuasive. If you were a manufacturer on one of the Burlington's routes, wouldn't you be inclined to try Burlington facilities because of their approach to giving you faster service?

The Goodyear Tire & Rubber Company's striking four-color spread ad shows how persuasive copy can be for a specialized industrial product. Written in terse, tight style that's almost telegraphic, this fine ad reads:

There are 30,000 ways to cut costs with Goodyear rubber engineering

This is how they cut costs at Lake Okeechobee:

Giant rubber suction hose—business end of world's largest automated dredge—outwears steel 8 to 1. First 600,000 tons of abrasive sand and gravel ruined steel swivel joint. So company switched to flexible 12-ft. length of 31" diameter Goodyear hose. It connects drill head to dredge, pumps 4500 tons an hour nonstop. After 2½ months on world's largest irrigation-flood control job, hose has pumped 5 million tons, now looks good for 22 million more.
Goodyear can help you cut costs: With rubber products engineered to work harder, last longer on little maintenance. And replace more expensive materials. Goodyear has engineered rubber products to meet 30,000 different specifications. The

*right one could cut your costs. Call your Goodyear
Distributor. He's backed by a rubber engineer who
understands your business . . . the G.T.M. (Goodyear
Technical Man). Or write: Goodyear Industrial
Products . . .*

Goodyear wisely relies on the basic pocketbook appeal and gives
valid reasons why users of Goodyear products produce more at
lower cost.

"Business end of the world's largest automated dredge" is colorful, highly descriptive, and just plain interesting. Everybody is curious about almost anything that's in a record class as to size, performance, or what have you.

"Outwears steel 8 to 1" lays the prime user benefit right on the
line. A mathematician of Einstein's genius isn't required to see that
Goodyear's rubber hose which handled 5 million tons and still looks
good for 22 million more, compared to a steel swivel joint that bit
the dust after a mere 600,000 tons, is by far the better buy. Specific
facts are presented provocatively. The copy is designed to convince
and persuade and *sell.*

50 Years For the Same Theme

Goodyear's campaign has been running for more than 50 years.
During this half-century the campaign has been refined, of course,
but it retains its basic approach, founded on research—readership
studies and analyses of creative approaches told Goodyear this was
the tack to take.

The same headline, "There are 30,000 ways to cut costs with
Goodyear rubber engineering," is in its fourth year with no apparent
loss of readership, proving once again the truth of the old saying
that advertisers get tired of their campaigns long before readers do.
In fact, many advertisers discontinue campaigns which are becoming more effective with each advertisement merely because they
have wearied of seeing what are, to them, the same old ads.

Goodyear's campaign consistently appears near the top in any
readership studies performed by the publications. Usually they are
in the top three, and frequently are Number One. In four studied
issues of one national trade magazine, Goodyear recently had the
highest *Noted* score in the book on three ads, the second highest on
the other one.

Success of this campaign hinges on communications objectives

This is how they cut costs at Lake Okeechobee:

Giant rubber suction hose—business end of world's largest automated dredge—outwears steel 8 to 1.

First 600,500 tons of abrasive-sand and gravel rushed steel-swivel-joint. So company switched to flexible 12-ft length of 8"-diameter Goodyear hose. It connects drill head to dredge, pumps 4500 tons an hour nonstop. After 2½ months, on world's largest irrigation-flood control job, hose has pumped 5 million tons, now looks good for 72 million more.

Goodyear can help you cut costs: with rubber products engineered to work harder, last longer, cut down maintenance. And replace more expensive materials. Goodyear has engineered rubber products to meet 30,000 different specifications. The right one could cut your costs. Call your Goodyear Distributor. He's backed by a rubber engineer who knows your business—the Man from Goodyear. Or write: Goodyear Industrial Products, Akron, Ohio 44316.

GOOD/YEAR
INDUSTRIAL PRODUCTS

There are 30,000 ways to cut costs with Goodyear rubber engineering

The Goodyear Tire & Rubber Company is proof that an organization can use the same ad campaign for half a century and still develop creative copy themes. Campaign is planned carefully to appeal to all in Goodyear "universe."

415

which can be realized. Goodyear's case-history campaign is designed to:

1. Create a favorable image so that Goodyear representatives will encounter a favorable selling climate when calling on prospects.

2. Present Goodyear product quality so convincingly and persuasively that prospects will accept the fact that Goodyear products will cost less to use in the service to which they are put.

3. Enhance Goodyear's reputation for leadership among prospective customers, distributors, and their sales staffs.

Among the buying influences in Goodyear's universe are maintenance men, foremen, plant engineers, design engineers, purchasing agents, managers, and top management.

Goodyear reaches this diverse group of influences through several business publications, including *Iron Age, Plant Engineering, Mill & Factory, Purchasing, Business Week,* and several general news publications. Among these are *U.S. News & World Report, Time,* and *Newsweek.*

Inducing a Response

An ad that fails to induce some kind of reader response is worthless.

However, this emphatically does *not* mean that every reader of every industrial advertisement must race through the copy with a mounting sense of excitement, throw the magazine hastily aside and breathlessly place a phone call to the advertiser requesting that a salesman rush to see him immediately to accept a six-figure order which he'll force the salesman to write up.

Things just don't happen that way very often.

Sometimes, though, an advertisement is read by the prospect in just the right climate, at exactly the time when his need is greatest and he *does* respond that way.

An example is the Lindberg Hevi-Duty ad shown nearby. The ad's illustration is a dramatic, extreme close-up of a safety-glassed, hard-hatted engineer in a foundry. A ladle of molten metal is in the background for authenticity. Purpose of this ad is to induce a response—preferably a telephone call.

Perhaps this doesn't appear to be too compelling an ad, at least to those outside the foundry industry. But to the foundry owner or

Give us four hours,

and we'll give you a frank analysis of your best way to melt.

For new foundries or old. And without bias—because we're the only ones who sell all furnace types.

We'll look, we'll ask, and we'll dig. What will you melt now, and five years from now? What charge materials are available, and where'll you store them? What metallurgical properties do you need, and will they change? Our analysis goes on and on.

Then we'll evaluate induction channel, induction coreless, medium frequency, resistance, arc, and fuel-fired furnaces. With no holds barred. And we'll recommend what we think is best.

Let's make a date. Call Roger Hadfield at 312/221 7000. Or write to him at 304 Hart Street, Watertown, Wis. 53094.

LINDBERG HEVI·DUTY   SB
DIVISION OF SOLA BASIC INDUSTRIES

OTHER DIVISIONS: ANCHOR ELECTRIC • ENGINEERED CERAMICS • HEVI-DUTY ELECTRIC • NELSON ELECTRIC • SOLA ELECTRIC

Any good industrial ad should be designed to induce responses—but the right kind of responses from the right persons. The copy in this Lindberg Hevi-Duty ad produced few responses from literature collectors, but many calls and letters from production people with problems Lindberg Hevi-Duty could solve. This is the kind of response that brings in profits.

superintendent in a dilemma about the type of equipment to buy, it is. He knows, through his association with his counterparts in an unusually tight-knit industry, that Lindberg Hevi-Duty *is* the only manufacturer to offer every type of melting furnace, just as the ad says.

To him the ad's logic is unassailable. The advertiser's claim that he can give the foundryman an unbiased evaluation of the one best method for him to use, with consideration given to many factors which influence the decision, such as fuel costs, quality of melt, charge materials, air pollution, and so on, is unquestioned. The ad copy reads as follows:

Give us four hours,

and we'll give you a frank analysis of your best way to melt.

For new foundries or old. And without bias—because we're the only ones who sell all furnace types.

We'll look, we'll ask, and we'll dig. What will you melt now, and five years from now? What charge materials are available, and where'll you store them? What metallurgical properties do you need, and will they change? Our analysis goes on and on.

Then we'll evaluate induction channel, induction coreless, medium frequency, resistance, arc, and fuel-fired furnaces. With no holds barred. And we'll recommend what we think is best.

Let's make a date. Call John Blank at 123/456-7890. Or write to him at . . .

The bid for action is a strong one. There's a sense of immediacy due to giving John Blank's name and phone number. This induced the response the advertiser wanted—written and long-distance-telephone inquiries. Sales engineers from the advertiser's office staff promptly followed up on these inquiries. The ad, which appeared in the primary metals edition of *Iron Age,* and in *Foundry* magazine, *has produced several dozen inquiries from prospects upon whom the advertiser's sales force had not previously called. A number of inquiries have been converted into actual sales—to the tune of several hundred thousand dollars.*

Useful life of this ad is far from over. The advertiser continues to run it, and it is still producing a very gratifying volume of inquiries. It's quite possible that this one ad may unearth hidden prospects to whom a million dollars worth of equipment will be sold—all for the nominal expense of producing a one-page, black-and-white ad, and for a few thousand dollars invested in space. This is yet another example of how advertising lowers the cost of selling.

Naturally, the response induced by an ad must be one that is favorable to the advertiser. Not all industrial advertisements are designed to pull inquiries, though. Some go even further—they're written so that the reader response is to write and mail a check for an item that's within the price range of an impulse purchase—and some items sold to industry are just that.

Much more frequently the response that's wanted is a request for a piece of literature. The advertiser mails this material to the inquirer, and also feeds the respondent's name to the field sales force for a followup sales call.

A good industrial ad, regardless of the response desired, will always include a bid for action. This is similar to a good salesman always asking for the order after making his sales presentation. Fail to do it and you have an ad that's a lost cause.

Reeves Vulcan Division missed this point in a one-page ad in *Commercial Car Journal,* the magazine of fleet management. Copy-cat copy starts with a headline influenced by consumer advertising—also of the "the-the" school which labels the product, preferably in outlandishly oversize display type, with a name which theoretically denotes its function. In this instance the headline is:

The Protector

And the body copy then proceeds to tell us about the tarpaulins Reeves manufactures for "rag-top" trucks and trailers:

You need protection from wet freight claims. And the best protection you can buy is a tarp made of Coverlight. Coverlight is the only tarp material with exclusive Ripstop construction for twice the tear strength of conventional tarp materials.

419

And Coverlight is not affected by soil, solvent, oil, mildew, or dry rot. It's lightweight and permanently waterproof. Available in vinyl, neoprene, Hypalon, and Hypalon/ neoprene combinations. In a wide range of weights and colors.

Smart fleet owners specify Coverlight for open tops, tail curtains, pickup covers, and winter fronts. And The Protector always acts like a hero.

Only in six-point type, way down at the bottom of the ad where it's easily confused with a slug-line, does Reeves indicate that letters or phone calls wouldn't be returned to sender, or be refused. There's no bid for action at the close of the copy; it's far too easy for the reader to infer that nothing is desired from him.

And Cummins Engine Company—whose name doesn't even appear in their black-and-white spread in the same publication—makes the same basic mistake. This ad blunders badly by using a dramatic photograph of a corral full of horses. The saddle stock is milling around, facing all different directions, and a realistic haze of dust hangs over the scene. So far, all this is well and good—but the two-page, bleed illustration of the Western corral never is explained, nor is it really tied in with the copy.

Cummins also committed the unforgivable sin of omitting a headline, thus losing the major portion of the immediate impact on the reader. This also obscures what the product is, what it's used for, or a user benefit, as well as doing a dandy job of hiding the identity of the advertiser. Copy starts right out, in the absence of a headline, this way:

You say 210 horsepower isn't enough? And 220 won't do the job either?

Okay. Cummins closes the horsepower gap. With the NH 230.

Now, you know who Cummins is. And you know all about engines named NH. So we'll skip the usual adjectives.

The news is, if you need 230 horses or so, now you can get them from Cummins. Conveniently harnessed in the most economical package in this horsepower range.

There may well be 230 horses in the illustration, although a diligent tally of horses' heads and horses' other ends leaves some doubt about this. But the advertiser assumes much too much. There undoubtedly are truckers who have used no other power plants except Mack Thermodyne or Maxidyne engines since starting in business, hence are completely unfamiliar with Cummins engines.

Assuming they know Cummins engines are built to develop 210 or 220 horsepower is taking an awful lot for granted. Neither can they be expected to know the horsepower range of competitive engines; this is something of vital interest to the manufacturer who is reaching for a competitive advantage—but not to the reader.

Granted, the name Cummins will undoubtedly be recognized, but recognition is hardly reward enough to justify production cost of the ad, plus some $2,000 worth of space for every insertion.

Only in the final paragraph is it evident that this is an ad written to introduce a new product—a new 230-horsepower engine. Presumably it's a diesel engine, since Cummins concentrates on diesels, although this, too, is left for the reader to assume.

Additional omissions—there is no signature, no company name, no telephone number, no address, no advertiser identification, no headline, no bid for action, no logotype. In all likelihood, no reader response, either.

The copywriter went to great lengths to make his message as obscure as possible, possibly because he's under the impression readers will exert themselves to assimilate information the advertiser wants them to acquire.

He's wrong. They won't do it.

The Concept Is All

Underlying every piece of copy, good or bad, is a concept—the basic idea of what the words in print should convey, and what the ad is designed to achieve. If the concept is good, chances are the copy will be, too.

Let's now look at copy—an entire integrated campaign, in fact—which was conceived to achieve just one critically important objective: To induce reader response.

First, though, before we read copy and examine ads and what accompanies them, a bit of background on the competitive situation faced by the advertiser, Fairchild-Davidson, Division of Fairchild Camera and Instrument Corporation, is in order.

In its industry Fairchild-Davidson is in direct competition with a well-known, well-entrenched competitor who is a giant in the field. This competitor is blessed not only with his long-established position, but with a name that's thoroughly familiar to the majority of his prospects. This meant, of course, that Fairchild-Davidson had to solve the problem of bringing their field salespeople face to face with many more prospects than they were now seeing in order to demonstrate their equipment.

Demonstration is the key to the sale, and Fairchild-Davidson simply was not as well known in the duplicator field as was the competition. This meant that quite often Fairchild-Davidson didn't get an opportunity to demonstrate their product when prospects were in a buying mood.

Apparent to Fairchild-Davidson advertising management was the fact that the only way to receive more opportunities to demonstrate was to issue a challenge—through advertising—that was big and brash and bold. It had to have teeth and claws in it. The buying public, of course, sees such a challenge as a form of dare, so accepts the advertising exactly the way the advertiser wishes him to.

First ad in this great campaign is illustrated. Fine, colloquial, hard-hitting copy is set off to good advantage by clean layout, an amusing spot illustration, and good clean typography. Copy gets right to the point:

The Fairchild-Davidson Gambit: We'll pay you $25 if you see our offset duplicator, and then buy somebody else's.

The quizzical looking individual is saying:

How's that again?

You read it right.

We'll give you our check for $25 toward the purchase of any other offset duplicator you select. Provided you've looked at ours first.

That's not as wacky as it sounds.

It's worth the $25 to us just to get the chance to show you how the Fairchild-Davidson can help you cut costs and boost production.

As things stand now, we don't always get that chance. Because we're relatively new to office duplicating, we're

The Fairchild-Davidson Gambit:

We'll pay you $25 if you see our offset duplicator, and then buy somebody else's.

You read it right.

We'll give you our check for $25 toward the purchase of any other offset duplicator you select. Provided you've looked at ours first.

That's not as wacky as it sounds.

How'd that again?

It's worth the $25 to us, just to get the chance to show you how the Fairchild-Davidson can help you cut costs and boost production.

As things stand now, we don't always get that chance. Because we're relatively new to office duplicating, we're not the first name a businessman thinks of. Sometimes they don't even think of us at all.

But the satisfying fact is, more than 50% of the companies who do see our demonstration, and who buy a press, buy ours.

$25 says you will too.

Look for the Fairchild-Davidson listing under "Duplicating Machines" in the Yellow Pages. Or get in touch direct-

FAIRCHILD DAVIDSON ly with Paul Smith at 123/456-7890.

(He's the one who signs the checks.)

Our great "get-acquainted sale":

$25 off any competitive offset duplicator if you still want one after you've seen the Fairchild-Davidson.

Hurry! Supply of competitive machines is limited! Buy now and save!

Actually this $25 gambit of Fairchild-Davidson's isn't as kooky as it sounds.

Old favorite

You see, we're relatively new to office duplicating. Even though we offer some impressive advantages in the way of increased production and decreased costs, many businessmen still haven't heard of us.

But of those companies who do see our demonstration, and who buy an offset duplicator, more than 50% buy ours.

So what we're really after is your attention.

After we've gotten it, if you can still resist, we'll cheerfully shell out $25 toward your purchase of Brand X.

Look for the Fairchild-Davidson listing under "Duplicating Machines" in the Yellow Pages. Or get in touch direct-

FAIRCHILD DAVIDSON ly with Paul Smith at 123/456-7890.

Our competitors know of this ad.

---

*not the first name a businessman thinks of. Sometimes they
don't even think of us at all.*

But the satisfying thing is, more than 50% of the companies who do see our demonstration, and who buy a press, buy ours.

$25 says you will too.

Look for the Fairchild-Davidson listing under "Duplicating Machines" in the Yellow Pages. Or get in touch directly with Paul Smith at 123/456-7890.

(He's the one who signs the checks.)

Frank, engaging, intriguing and provocative. And it was followed up with equally interesting ads, all of which stress the pocketbook appeal.

The headline of the second ad in the campaign reads:

> **Our great "get-acquainted sale":
> $25 off any competitive offset
> duplicator if you still want one
> after you've seen the
> Fairchild-Davidson.**

423

Caption for the spot illustration of the F-D duplicator is:

Old Irresistible.

And the body copy:

> *Hurry! Supply of competitive machines is limited! Buy now and save!*

> *Actually this $25 gambit of Fairchild-Davidson's isn't as kooky as it sounds.*

> *You see, we're relatively new to office duplicating. Even though we offer some impressive advantages in the way of increased production and decreased costs, many businessmen still haven't heard of us.*

> *But of those companies who do see our demonstration, and who buy an offset duplicator, more than 50% buy ours.*

> *So what we're really after is your attention.*

> *After we've gotten it, if you can still resist, we'll cheerfully shell out $25 toward your purchase of Brand X.*

> *Look for the Fairchild-Davidson listing under "Duplicating Machines" in the Yellow Pages. Or get in touch directly with Paul Smith at 123/456-7890.*

> *Our competitors know of this ad.*

The concept is great, really creative, and the quality of the copy throughout the campaign is uniformly high, as you'll note from the small illustrations of four of the Fairchild-Davidson ads. Each adheres to the "Gambit" theme, of course, with individual approaches and a sure-handed light touch that's a real pleasure to read.

Fairchild-Davidson kicked off the campaign at a national sales meeting, where it received an immediate and enthusiastic response from all of the company's branch managers and field sales distributor supervisors. Concurrent with the sales meeting, kits announcing the new campaign were sent to all branch salesmen and distributors throughout the country.

Included in the merchandising kit was a 33⅓ rpm long-playing record which explained the whole campaign from concept to execution on one side, then requested the listener to flip to the other side and "hear music to gamble $25 by." Also in the kit were ad reprints, samples of the initial direct mail units, "Gambit" certificates in a

We'll contribute $25 to our competitor. In your name.

(And they're not our favorite charity.)

It's something less than lovingkindness which prompts the Fairchild-Davidson $25 gambit.

We're doing it for our health.

Not enough of you businessmen know of the remarkable advantages offered by our offset duplicator. Particularly the way it squeezes more production out of each working day.

(Although more than 50% of the companies who do see our demonstration, and who buy an offset duplicator, buy ours.)

So we hit on the idea of paying you $25 toward your purchase of a competitive machine. Should you still want one. After seeing ours, that is.

That way, if we don't score, it won't be because you never heard of us.

If the spirit moves you, look for the Fairchild-Davidson listing under "Duplicating Machines" in the Yellow Pages. Or get in touch directly with [...]

FAIRCHILD DAVIDSON We have one consolation if we lose.
Our $25 is tax deductible.

This is the largest-selling offset duplicator in the country.

We'll bet you $25 you won't buy it.

No.1

Once you've seen ours, that is.

Take a good look at No. 1 and at the Fairchild-Davidson. Ponder a bit.

Then if you still want to go ahead and buy No. 1, we'll help you. To the tune of $25.

There's a method in our rashness. We're relatively new to office duplicating. So we're not the first name you business people think of.

In fact, some of you never think of us at all.

But it's gratifying to report that more than 50% of the companies who do see our demonstration, and who buy an offset duplicator, buy ours.

We'll wager $25 you're another.

Look for the Fairchild-Davidson listing under "Duplicating Machines" in the Yellow Pages. Or get in touch direct-ly with [...]

FAIRCHILD DAVIDSON (If we get to be No. 1, the whole deal is off.)

Does Avis pay Hertz?

Then what's with this $25 bit of ours?

Fairchild-Davidson is probably the only company in existence that offers to shell out $25 every time it loses a sale to a competitor.

Even Avis doesn't go that far to catch up with No. 1.

It could hurt if our offset duplicator wasn't pretty exceptional.

But it is. And not just on our say-so. More than half the companies who see our demonstration, and who buy an offset machine, buy ours.

Our only problem is that, since we're relatively new in office duplicating, not enough of you businessmen know of us yet.

So to get your attention, we're willing to stick our neck out. See the Fairchild-Davidson. See the others. Then, if you buy one of the others, we'll give you a $25 check toward its purchase.

Look for the Fairchild-Davidson listing under "Duplicating Machines" in the Yellow Pages. Or call [...] at

FAIRCHILD DAVIDSON (If we get to be No. 1, the whole deal is off.)

If you see our offset duplicator and buy it, you get to wear this medal.

Otherwise, we will.

I LOST $25

It's a medal for heroes, sort of.

We'll pin it on ourselves if you buy any other duplicator after you see the Fairchild-Davidson.

Because we'll have handed you $25 toward the purchase of the other fellow's machine. A noble, if carefree, gesture.

But if you buy our machine, you win the medal. To commemorate the way you lost $25 but won the war for flawless duplicating.

What are your chances of being decorated?

Well, look at it this way. More than 50% of the companies who see our demonstration and who buy an offset duplicator, buy ours.

Our only real problem is that, since we're relatively new to office duplicating, not enough businessmen know us. Hence our $25 gambit.

If you aspire, look for the Fairchild-Davidson listing under "Duplicating Machines" in the Yellow Pages. Or get in touch directly with [...]

FAIRCHILD DAVIDSON (If he doesn't answer on the first ring, be patient. He may be busy counting his medals.)

"Gambit" wallet, a complete rationale on the program in black and white, and a comprehensive rundown of the greatly expanded media schedule that would be used throughout the year.

Three mailings were made to support the "Gambit" campaign. The first mailing was simply a letter introducing the "Gambit" concept,

Direct Mail Letter #1
National and Local
(also enclosed is Gambit Reply
Card and Reprint of Ad No. 1)

Dear Sir:

We mean it. We'll send you a check for $25 if, after seeing a demonstration of a Fairchild-Davidson offset duplicator, you decide to buy somebody else's.

Obviously, we believe we've got some pretty top-rate equipment and we're willing to risk $25 to prove it. If you're in the market to buy an offset duplicator, you're probably planning to see several different makes before making a final decision. All we ask is that you come see one of our offset duplicators as well. See what our simultaneous two-sided printing, roll paper conversion, push-button automation can mean in your particular situation. If then, you still buy someone else's, we'll pay $25 toward its purchase.

That's the gambit.

If you'd like to know more about Fairchild-Davidson or our line of duplicators first, that's fine with us. Just check the appropriate box on the reply card and drop it in the mail.

But whatever you do, remember you've nothing to lose and $25 to gain.

Very truly yours,

—Paul H. Till
General Sales Manager

Fairchild-Davidson, a Division of Fairchild Camera and Instrument Corporation, 5004 E. Jericho Turnpike, Commack, L. I., N.Y. 11725

with an ad reprint of the first advertisement, along with Fairchild-Davidson's standard business reply card.

The letters and the entry certificate are shown nearby. The certificate has space for countersigning by appropriate branches or distributors to validate the prospect's having seen a demonstration. To

Direct Mail Letter #2
National Only
(Also enclosed is Gambit
Certificate and Reply Card)

Dear Sir:

As further proof of the sincerity of our offer, enclosed you will find a Fairchild-Davidson $25 Gambit Certificate.

It officially qualifies you to (1) see all the competitive offset duplicating equipment available, (2) see Fairchild-Davidson's, and then (3) decide.

Should you decide to buy ours, like most people who see it in action, we'll be delighted. But if you buy one of theirs, we fork up $25 toward its purchase.

Fair enough?

Look for the Fairchild-Davidson listing under "Duplicating Machines" in your Yellow Pages, or fill out the reply card. When you see the Fairchild-Davidson, the demonstrator will validate your certificate.

Then we'll see what we shall see.

Very truly yours,

Paul H. Till
General Sales Manager

Fairchild-Davidson, a Division of Fairchild Camera and Instrument Corporation, 5004 E. Jericho Turnpike, Commack, L. I., N.Y. 11725

qualify for the $25 check, the winner of the $25 check has to show a valid purchase order for a competitive duplicator—indicating that he wasn't sold by Fairchild-Davidson.

As of this writing only four $25 checks have been issued *nationally*. Fairchild-Davidson's sales staff sells well, apparently.

Subsequent mailings also were sales letters, but the enclosures were fresh and varied. Among them were the little brochure explain-

OFFICIAL ENTRY BLANK

The Great Fairchild-Davidson Gambit Sweepstakes

Simply fill in the information requested below, then check the rules governing "The Great Fairchild-Davidson Gambit Sweepstakes" on your copy of the "Official Entry Blank." It's as simple as that.

NAME_____ TITLE_____

COMPANY_____ PHONE_____

ADDRESS_____

CITY_____ STATE_____

5311

My entry is governed by the rules printed below, and on the reverse side, and is subject to State and local laws.

Interested in:

☐ Dualith 400 ☐ Dualith 600 ☐ Dual-A-Matic 720
☐ Dualith 500 ☐ Dualith 612 ☐ Dual-A-Matic 760
☐ Dual-A-Matic 520 ☐ Dual-A-Matic 620 ☐ Roll Convertor
☐ Dual-A-Matic 560 ☐ Dual-A-Matic 660 ☐ 3000 Collator
☐ Dualith 500 TL ☐ Dualith 700 ☐ Supplies

Comments: _____

_____

_____

_____

(SHOW)_____ (SIGNATURE)_____

Home Office Copy

I LOST $25 FAIRCHILD DAVIDSON

OK

gambit according to Webster:

gam·bit (*gam'bit*), *n.* in chess a strategy in which a pawn or other piece is sacrificed to gain an advantageous position.

gambit according to Fairchild-Davidson:

gam·bit (*gam'bit*), *n.* in offset duplicating, a ploy to demonstrate our machines while risking the loss of a sum of money if the prospect sees our demonstration and buys someone else's. Otherwise known as the Fairchild-Davidson $25 Gambit.

ing what "Gambit" means, according to Webster and according to Fairchild-Davidson. It, along with a miniature chessman with "OK" on a rubber stamp at the bottom, and a button which proclaims "I LOST—FAIRCHILD-DAVIDSON." They're shown nearby. All attracted the attention of prospects.

To supplement the program, Fairchild-Davidson ran a special three-month promotion, "The Great Fairchild-Davidson Gambit Sweepstakes." In the sweepstakes, which broke at the National

The Great Gambit Sweepstakes:

See a demonstration of the Fairchild-Davidson offset duplicator. You could win a snazzy new Jaguar.(Plus $25).

It could be yours.

We're convinced the Fairchild-Davidson duplicator will do a better job for you than any other machine. In the full range of duplicating needs. Reproducing business forms, computer printout, price lists...even printing sales literature in colors.

That's why we are continuing our Gambit offer: $25 toward your purchase of a competing offset machine if you see a demonstration of *ours* and then buy *theirs*. And now adding to it a chance to win a Jaguar.

As an added attraction, we'll show you how to cut paper costs 17% to 34% with our new Roll Converter. And a way to imprint bulky catalogs, wafer-thin envelopes and most everything between with our exclusive top-loading feeder.

Just for seeing a demonstration, your Fairchild-Davidson dealer will enter you in the Gambit Sweepstakes. First Prize is a Jaguar X-KE 2+2 (retail list price $6300). Next 100 prizes: 100 games of "Gambit".

How can you lose? Only by not calling your Fairchild-Davidson dealer for a demonstration. Give him a ring today (he's in the Yellow Pages under "Duplicating Machines").

FAIRCHILD DAVIDSON

Wouldn't that Jaguar look great in your driveway?

(Sweepstakes closes midnight December 8, 1966. Winners will be selected and notified by December 15, 1966. Offer void where prohibited by law. All federal, state and local regulations apply.)

Fairchild-Davidson, a Division of Fairchild Camera and Instrument Corporation, 5004 E. Jericho Turnpike, Commack, L. I., N.Y. 11725.

Association of Photo-Lithographers trade show in Washington, D.C., the advertiser awarded a Jaguar XK-E to the lucky winner. We've all seen useless trinkets and genuinely useful giveaways handed out at trade shows, but a Jaguar!

Certificate No._____

This is the Official Fairchild-Davidson $25 Gambit Certificate.
Once validated at an authorized Fairchild-Davidson Demonstration Center and attached to a bonafide copy of a purchase order for any new competitive offset duplicator, this Certificate is worth $25 of Fairchild-Davidson's hard-earned money, which shall, on demand, be paid by check to the Company hereafter named. This Certificate is valid for a period up to, but not longer, than six months from the date of validation. If, after seeing Our Equipment and what it can do, you buy ours like most Buyers do, this Certificate is worth only the paper we printed it on. Are you game?

_____ Company _____ Branch or Distributor

_____ Date _____ Signature

Space ads, such as the one illustrated, promoted the sweepstakes—and since the Jaguar was illustrated and discussed, whetted the appetite all of us have for something for nothing. Direct mail reinforced the space ads. The Jaguar was shown at all trade shows in which the company exhibited during that three-month period. To say that this created a stir in the industry is an understatement.

Eligibility for both the sweepstakes, as well as for a $25 check, was established by the prospects seeing a qualified demonstration of the Fairchild-Davidson duplicator in a local showroom.

Media used for the space advertising program in a typical month included the following publications: *School Management, Administrative Management, In-Plant Printer, Business Management, Business Automation, Financial Executive, Inland Printer, Modern Office Procedures, The Office, Reproduction Methods, Business Week, Reproductions Review, Dun's Review, Graphic Arts Monthly,* and *Printing Impressions.*

Fairchild-Davidson wanted to induce a response from readers of its ads. To succeed in raising sales, the advertising had to produce.

So what did the "Gambit" campaign actually accomplish?

Just this, in Fairchild-Davidson's words: "To say that the 'Gambit' campaign has been a rousing success would be putting it mildly. The number of telephone inquiries received from all over the country during the first several weeks of the campaign forced us to print a telephone inquiry form that our various sales department employees could use in obtaining the required information to process these leads.

"We have a number of case histories where signed purchase orders for competitive equipment were subsequently torn up and rewritten to specify Fairchild-Davidson equipment.

"The campaign, to date, has been so completely successful that *we are now 40 percent ahead of the sales forecast for this period— and are so completely backlogged on machine orders that we are quoting 90-day delivery on all equipment. Prior to this campaign we were able to make same-day deliveries.*"

Fairchild-Davidson's files show that the company received approximately a 30 percent increase in inquiries compared to the same period a year ago. This is well and good—but the relationship of inquiries compared to conversions to sales jumped dramatically. This is explained in part by the fact that the company received appreciably better cooperation from the distributor sales organization, as far as followup calls on leads were concerned. This is due, of course, to enthusiasm aroused by the entire campaign.

Thought, careful analysis of the sales problem, and creativity produced this copy, this campaign, which achieved exactly what Fairchild-Davidson wanted.

It induced readers to respond—and to buy.

Chapter 9

BODY COPY—STYLE

H ARD-and-fast rules almost always lead to inflexible, hidebound thinking that effectively stifles creativity.

Quite possibly those who believe—or profess to believe—that the fewer the rules the better, as far as copy is concerned, are right in their thinking. The fact remains, though, that there are some elements of style with which you must be familiar if you're to turn out consistently good copy.

Some of them are almost painfully obvious, so much so that it's not really necessary to discuss them. Riffling through the business press proves conclusively that some of these elements of style are not known, or they've been forgotten, or they're ignored. One cause is as bad as another, because any of the three can lead to some gruesome ads.

Style, in this chapter, doesn't mean a definite *type* of copy. Rather, the word is used in the newspaper manner, or in the way in which it's used in journalism schools to tell how something should be done. In this case, style means how copy should be written as far as the following 13 points are concerned:

1. Long copy versus short copy.

2. Copy must be in the vernacular.

3. Organize ideas in logical sequence.

4. Stick to the core idea.

5. Use short words.

6. Use short sentences.

7. Use short paragraphs.

8. Be specific.

9. Avoid participles.

10. Avoid superlatives, avoid exaggeration.

11. Refine your copy.

12. Make copy visually attractive.

13. Make the tone suitable.

Let's look at each element individually, along with some examples.

Long Copy Versus Short Copy

The controversy about copy length rages just as fiercely today as it has at any time during the last half-century.

There's simply no meeting of the minds, no unanimity of thought on the subject. Each viewpoint—that copy *must* be just as short as it's possible to make it, or that it's quite permissible for copy to be as long as is necessary—has its staunch adherents. They resolutely refuse to embrace the opposing philosophy.

The hue and cry about copy length has even involved entire agencies to the extent that the law is laid down as to approximate copy length. Some agencies are known as short-copy agencies, others as long-copy shops.

The scale is tipped, however, in favor of those who believe unreservedly in not skimping on words that explain the product and the user benefits—even if the short-copy cult has increased its membership in recent years. There's one sententious slogan that can't be refuted for advertising in general, and especially for industrial advertising: The more you tell, the more you sell. That little gem has been the watchword for many highly successful industrial advertisers for decades.

We've all encountered our share of doubting Thomases with little or no faith in advertising. They maintain that long copy stands little chance of being read. If you'll poke and prod a bit, these same doubters will admit they don't believe, deep down, that *any* advertising copy receives very much readership. Oddly enough, these nervous Nellie doubters are more often than not practitioners of advertising, in one capacity or another. They're frequently introverts. Their attitude toward advertising copy reflects a negative outlook toward almost everything in life. Advertising just happens to be handy, so it's included in the long and dreary list of things they either question or disparage.

Throughout much of the business world, especially in those industries which are less sophisticated than the more fast-moving ones, and particularly those which have a large proportion of engineers in top management, this doubt permeates the upper echelons.

Sometimes the nuts-and-bolts types are almost pathological on the subject. One president of a well-known industrial company, himself an engineer, is known to have remarked that he "hasn't read a magazine or a book in 20 years." He added, "All I read is my mail."

Now, this gentleman didn't adopt this antiquated attitude just to hear himself sound silly. He actually believes that the business press isn't read, consequently advertisements contained in it are not read, either.

This naiveté was extremely widespread 25 or 30 years ago, but fortunately for industry it has disappeared to some extent as management has become more well rounded, rather than being specialists in one narrow field.

The Rise of Marketing Management

In a recent issue of *Forbes* magazine was a penetrating analysis of the thinking of top management of General Electric Company. The conclusions which may be drawn from this article augur well for advertising managers and agency men beset by engineering-oriented management who seem incapable of understanding advertising—even if they wanted to.

Forbes' study took a long, hard look at the progress the General Electric Company has made since the late '30's. Although it's been long forgotten, in the late '30's giant GE's sales volume was only $300 million. Also buried in the past is the fact that Westinghouse, arch competitor of General Electric, was at one time quite close to GE in total sales. Now General Electric does several times the annual volume that Westinghouse does; GE's sales now top $7 "billion."

Of significance is the fact that General Electric management—in contrast to many competitive companies it outstripped—has been firmly committed to the marketing concept and to all of the marketing services. The company advertised vigorously and continuously, knowing full well that merely having well-engineered products and a sales force that was willing to sell didn't automatically assure sales success.

Furthermore, as *Forbes* emphasized, General Electric top management men have been drawn from the ranks of those who believe in advertising because they know from firsthand experience what it has done for the company.

It's unlikely the implication in this definitive study will be overlooked. This and similar articles presage an accelerating trend for specialists to remain specialists, and for top management to be composed to a larger and larger degree of generalists.

Advertising men, of course, will find it easier to communicate with the generalists than they ever have with the throwbacks to another era. With each passing year ad men should be able to make a greater contribution to the success of their companies' marketing efforts as they are able to work more effectively with top management. The generalists, who have not spent their business lives confined in an unimaginative field like engineering, are people-oriented, rather than thing-oriented.

This makes it easy for them to understand how people react to stimuli, how they can be motivated to accept your viewpoint. On the other hand, the engineering mind just can't conceive of motivating a blueprint or a slide rule. Generalists readily accept the necessity to advertise because they find it easy to understand and appreciate advertising's function and how it accomplishes its objectives to further the marketing program. And copy, which is composed of words carefully chosen to influence people, is understood and accepted by the generalists.

The above is not digression. Getting copy approved by all of those in the chain of command sometimes seems to be an almost insurmountable task in a company which leans heavily toward engineering. The ad manager who is going to achieve *his* objectives must realize the situation exists so that he can lay his plans to overcome the dim view in which advertising is so often viewed.

The uninitiated are wont to deplore long copy. The chant, "It's too long. It won't be read," is a familiar one to most of us. The fact is, however, that many factors influence the readership an ad receives—size, shape, layout, typography, illustration, number of colors—far more than does the length of the copy.

Copy length has remarkably little to do with whether or not the ad is read. After all, *any* copy has to be interesting in order to be read. Short copy that's insufferably dull and unappealing simply won't be read just because it's short. But make the copy interesting and lively and informative and it will receive excellent readership regardless of how long it is.

Long Copy Wins in Readership Study

McGraw-Hill has done extensive research on readership of long copy, as opposed to short copy. A thorough analysis of 4,993 ads in four McGraw-Hill publications made by the publisher's Reader Feedback readership service shows that contrary to what the copy-length alarmists say, long copy receives *better* readership than short copy in business publication advertisements.

Not readership that's just as good, but *better*.

A total of 263 ads with 350 or more words of copy received a Noted score of 109, while 4,730 ads with less than 350 words of copy received a Noted score of only 100 on an index base.

All of these ads were one page, run-of-publication, bleed and nonbleed, black-and-white or two-color. They appeared in 68 issues of four publications. In some instances ads in categories not pertinent to the analysis were omitted—such as ads with no main copy block. McGraw-Hill held more than 6,800 interviews with readers of *American Machinist, Engineering News-Record, Factory,* and *Textile World* to study readership. The question asked to secure the Reader Feedback score was: "Did you read this advertisement?" (By read, we mean read enough to get the main idea.)

Analysis of 1,125 ads in two publications measured by Starch disclosed that 123 ads of more than 350 words received a Noted score of 103, and a Read Most score of 106. This compares to 1,002 ads with less than 350 words which achieved a Noted and Read Most score exactly the same—100.

Daniel Starch and Staff studied ads which were all one page, run-of-publication, bleed and nonbleed, black-and-white and two-color, which appeared in 20 issues of *Power,* and in *Chemical Engineering.* The figures resulted from personal interviews with 100 readers of the publications. The Noted figure represents the percent of readers who remembered, when interviewed, that they had seen the advertisement in the study issue. The Read Most figure is the percent of readers who had read 50 percent or more of the copy in the ad.

Numerous other studies bear out the findings of both McGraw-Hill and Starch. They make it very apparent that long copy does not detract from readership of an ad—but that it actually enhances the chances of your ad's attracting a larger number of readers.

A few percentage points in total readership may not seem to be of earth-shattering importance, but if long copy consistently performs even a *little* bit better than short copy, why handicap yourself by not telling your story as fully as need be to get your message across?

Naturally, there's no hard and fast rule as to how long your copy should be. One truism that can't be ignored, though, is that the copy in every advertisement must present your *complete* selling proposition. You simply cannot rely on having the same readers read every ad in your entire campaign in order to absorb your complete sales message. The chance of that happening is slim indeed.

Make Each Ad Complete

Play it safe and make each ad complete in itself. You may not get a second chance at some of the readers before they buy.

Industrial advertisements are read for information. The more information you present—if you do it interestingly—the greater your chances are of selling your product. This is not an indorsement of long, dull, dreary copy that's been puffed up with a deadly parade of inconsequentials, however. Instead, it is a strong suggestion to use as many words as are necessary to promote your product. The dividing line's pretty fine, but you'll find it if you try.

X-acto Precision Tools Inc. does a marvelous job of presenting its product and telling its story in just 73 well-chosen words in a half-page ad in *Plastics Design & Processing*. The striking layout and illustrative technique make their sales point—instrument versatility—immediately obvious. Copy reads:

X-acto handles your cutting

deburring

carving

etching

hollowing

slicing

sawing

scraping

scribing

skiving

piercing

slitting

stripping

trimming problems.

X-acto has a handle and 28 surgically sharp interchangeable blades to solve all these and many other problems. If your problem isn't listed here, write and tell us what it is. We'll send a free catalog and try to help you select the right X-acto blade for your specific job. Handles shown: #1, #5, #2.

It's a fine ad, and seeing the X-acto knives will be a nostalgic

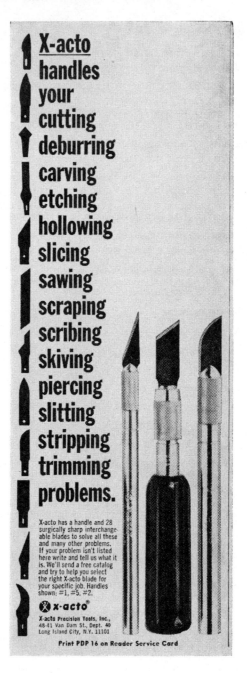

experience for many a reader who can remember this great little tool from decades ago, when making a model airplane out of balsa wood was the major problem occupying his attention.

Poles apart from the X-acto ad, although sharing its excellent craftsmanship in copy, is IBM's clean, lively black-and-white spread on packaging systems.

Despite its being axiomatic that an industrial ad, if it's to be truly effective, should confine itself to a single subject and have one strong core idea, IBM successfully discusses three separate products. The ad "carries" well, however, because all are closely related so the copy doesn't have to wander off onto any tangents.

IBM carefully qualifies its readers right at the start, in the headline. Subject matter of the ad is announced immediately to enable those readers who are not interested in these products to skip over the ad. All who do read it, however, may logically be considered to be excellent prospects for these IBM industrial products.

Of interest is that IBM used a total of 663 words, excluding those in the coupon, in the copy. But the copy isn't padded, isn't blown up, it contains not the slightest bit of puffery. It's well written and tightly edited to eliminate any superfluous words or thoughts, as good copy should be. Each thought follows logically on the heels of the one preceding, leading readers through the copy from start to finish.

Also, there's no hint of the highly stylized, supersuccinct, telegraphic approach which usually manages to sound like a badly wounded English officer, pith helmet askew and with a growing stain on his tunic, giving final orders to his faithful sergeant as the heathens prepare to charge in the final episode of a blood-and-thunder TV epic.

Spot illustrations, a diagram, and a graph break up the copy blocks and add eye appeal to the ad. The prominent coupon in the lower right hand corner (the proper place for a coupon) almost asks aloud for a reader response. Even if most readers take the easy route and use a bingo card, the coupon still serves a worthwhile purpose—it serves fair notice that IBM wants a response and that it will be welcome.

The copy reads, in part:

Packaging cost reductions

Performance Measurements Co., Detroit, Michigan, reports significant savings in packaging their new electronic recording system. The packaging method previously employed

IBM Circuit Design and Packaging Topics

☐ packaging cost reductions
☐ high-speed switching
☐ reed switch application data

☐ packaging cost reductions

Performance Measurements Co., Detroit, Michigan, reports significant savings in packaging their new electronic recording system. The packaging method previously employed required two gates to mount the components in the main console. Now with IBM's modular packaging as pictured below, only one gate is needed. That's because the IBM technique makes the most efficient use of console space with compactly mounted and connected circuit boards, relays and hardware.

Mounting time has been saved too. Pluggable components, low-cost card receptacles and interlocking card guides have so simplified the packaging job, that Performance Measurements now saves 70% on the cost of mounting hardware. Fewer and shorter wires are needed in the compact console—eliminating three feet of 11½-inch cable and shortening a second cable by eight inches. The modular chassis also permits freedom to experiment freely with various mounting configurations. It also permits easy access for servicing and diagnostic analysis.

The same design freedom, plus significant hardware and labor savings are available in many applications.

IBM components and packaging can help you in timing control, digital logic testing, telemetering, process or numerical control.

☐ high-speed switching

IBM wire contact relays were originally designed for data processing use. Now they are being used extensively in machine tool and assembly applications. One of these assembly applications is a numerically-controlled component insertion machine. It sequentially inserts random combinations of up to 24 different types of axial lead resistors and diodes into printed circuit boards. Such machines have been widely used, often on a round-the-clock, three-shift basis, in IBM's electronic assembly operations. Insertion rates range from 3,000 to 4,500 components per hour, depending upon the type of components being inserted.

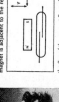

Instructions from an 8-channel punched paper tape provide the logic input to the relay gate. The gate employs three rows of 6- and 12-pole IBM wire contact relays. These relays control the movement of each printed circuit

board through the X and Y axis positioning of the board for each component insertion. They also control the component feed, component insert, and cut-and-clinch cycles for each insertion operation.

IBM wire contact relays can perform in excess of 200 million operations with an operate speed as fast as 4.5 ms, a release time of 5 ms maximum. The product line includes 4-, 6-, and 12-pole Form C relays, 4- and 6-pole latch models, all with compact, solderless, pluggable mountings—with coil-voltages up to 100 VDC.

☐ reed switch application data

Data on the magnetic switching characteristics of miniature dry reed switches is available to design engineers on request. The data was compiled from extensive tests conducted by IBM to help the design engineer use these switches most effectively. It can also help him determine the motion and position of the magnet required.

Simply described, a miniature dry reed switch operates under the influence of a permanent magnet. When the magnet is adjacent to the reed switch,

the flux of the magnet flows through the cantilever beams, as illustrated. While this magnetic flux is being carried by the beams, a polarity exists across the beams. Look at the overlap area of the beams. The north pole of one beam and south pole of the other beam are in proximity. Since unlike poles of a magnet attract each other, when the magnetic force becomes great enough to overcome the physical mass of the beams, they "snap" together, thus switching.

On the graph the X axis represents the displacement (in degrees for rotary motion, inches for lateral motion) of a magnet's center with reference to the center of the reed switch. The Y axis represents displacement (in inches) of the magnet from the outer edge of the

dry reed switch glass envelope. Dimensions shown along both axes represent displacement from the center of the magnet in alignment with the center of the reed switch.

There are some "gray areas" where performance varies due to minor differences in the characteristics of each switch. In these areas the status of each switch is not completely predictable.

Assume the zero point on the X axis is the magnetic center of an IBM reed switch. The magnet is positioned with its center at +.5 on the X axis, and .04 inches above the glass envelope. If the magnet is set in motion along the X axis toward the center of the switch, some reeds will pick when the center of the magnet reaches the point +.12 on the X axis. (The magnet has then reached the "gray area"). If motion is continued toward the center of the switch, all reeds will pick when the center of the magnet reaches the point +.09 on the X axis.

required two gates to mount the components in the main console. Now, with IBM's modular packaging as pictured below, only one gate is needed. That's because the IBM technique makes the most efficient use of console space with compactly mounted and connected circuit boards, relays, and hardware.

Mounting time has been saved, too. Pluggable components, low-cost card receptacles and interlocking card guides have so simplified the packaging job that Performance Measurements now saves 70% on the cost of mounting hardware. Fewer and shorter wires are needed in the compact console—eliminating three feet of 1½-inch cable and shortening a second cable by eight inches. The modular chassis gave designers freedom to experiment freely with various mounting configurations. It also permits easy access for servicing and diagnostic analysis.

The same design freedom, plus significant hardware and labor savings, are available in many applications.

IBM components and packaging can help you in timing control, digital logic testing, telemetering, process, or numerical control.

This clean spread appeared in *Control Engineering, Electronics Design,* and in *Electronics,* one insertion in each "book." Over a three-month period, the ad produced a total of 1,798 inquiries. Of this total, 197 or 12½ percent of the inquiries were coupons.

Readership was predictably excellent. Richard Manville Research, Incorporated, showed that the ad received a Seen score of 57, Read of 33, Read One-Half of 20, an Attitude Change Score of +63, and a Manville Effectiveness Rating of +36. Issue averages were: Seen 41; Read 21; Read One-Half 13; Attitude Change Score +47; Manville Effectiveness Rating +20.

Small space doesn't necessarily mean a small number of words of copy, nor does large space automatically demand copy half a dictionary long. Copy length should be determined by what there is to say, and the one best way of saying it.

Avco Bay State Abrasives Division uses just as much space for its compelling four-color ad as did IBM, but the copy in Avco Bay State's ad contains less than one-fourth as many words.

Superb photography and outstanding color printing result in a

reproduction so razor-sharp you can almost feel the coarseness of the grinding wheel and the texture of the wood chips.

By bleeding the illustration on all four sides (running it off all edges of the page, that is), tremendous impact is achieved. Readership studies show this campaign well up near the top.

Avco Bay State's copy has an important objective—to help the company increase its share of an approximately $250-million market for grinding wheels. Avco Bay State is in third place in the market, trailing Norton Company and Carborundum Company. Principal markets are in metalworking industries—primary metals, machinery, and transportation. Practically speaking, nearly all of the 31,479 metalworking plants in the *Iron Age* census which employ 20 or more people, as well as an additional 12,000 establishments in the stone, clay, and glass industries where grinding wheels are used, are prime prospects for Avco Bay State.

Copy slant is logical for Avco Bay State Division because of the fantastic number of different kinds of grinding wheels the firm manufactures—some 160,000. The number grows larger every year, too. The maker feels that grinding wheels are not actually a commodity in the usual sense, but a product that's infinitely variable for a constantly changing variety of applications.

Accordingly, Avco Bay State has taken a few hints from Theodore Levitt's little booklet, *Industrial Purchasing Behavior,* and is using its advertising dollars to build a generalized reputation for the company and its products.

The number of buying influences that Avco Bay State must reach in more than 40,000 establishments is tremendous; they're found in purchasing, manufacturing, administration, engineering, and other areas. Additionally, industrial distributors and others in the division's distribution channels are important to them.

Copy which builds a good generalized reputation, or an image of quality products and technical competence on the part of the company, achieves Avco Bay State's communication objective. Salesmen are then relied upon to do the specific selling, the nuts-and-bolts communications.

Avco Bay State's analysis of the role that advertising plays in this marketing program is an interesting one. The company's manager of marketing services, who handles the advertising program, says that a black-and-white page in a metalworking publication costs about $35 per thousand readers. A four-color spread in the same book can be bought for about $68 per thousand circulation. Personal sales calls, on the other hand, cost the company at least $66,000 per thousand. If advertising can be relied upon to build the generalized reputation—a vitally important element in the communications package—Avco Bay State is strongly of the opinion that advertising is both economical and essential if an increase in sales is to be achieved.

A Boon to Salesmen

This is an excellent rationale and explanation of how advertising reduces the cost of selling.

Using advertising to create the impression of a quality company, a technically competent company with the know-how to solve customers' problems, also frees salesmen from doing preliminary missionary work. When Avco Bay State's salesmen call, they can get right into the product story without having to recite chapter and verse of company history, who they are, business philosophy, product quality, reputation of the company, financial responsibility, and what have you. This obviously makes the salesmen more productive, both in dollar sales per call and in the number of calls they can make in a given period of time.

A sure hand was at the typewriter when Avco Bay State's copy was written. It has bite, it's tight, it's just right for the company and its product and its objective. It reads:

**Quality control . . .
control . . . control**

**Another way
Avco Bay State
assures you
"the extra edge"**

*Avco Bay State goes all the way with quality control. Even
to checking the size and dryness of the wood chips which
protect our wheels during shipment. "Sawdust" we don't
want. It could work into the wheels. Too much moisture
is bad, too. So we make sure it's kept below 10%.*

*The point is, we pay attention to details like this because
each one is important. More than 300 other raw materials
get an equally thorough going over by the meticulous men
in our quality control lab. They're constantly scooping and
sampling, measuring and testing. Fact is, our quality control specifications fill a 19-volume library that's four feet
thick!*

*A lot of control? Maybe. But it pays off in consistently
top quality . . . another big reason why Avco Bay State
wheels assure you "the extra edge" in grinding productivity.*

Persuasive, when you can tell a prospect that your company insists on wood chips instead of sawdust, then tells him why so
believably he'll find it interesting. Then this fact is deftly topped off
with the statement that moisture content is held to a low 10 percent.
All of which sets the stage quite nicely for the quality control copy
which follows.

Avco Bay States' copy is short, to the point, and is exactly right
for the story the company wants to tell. And all in 154 words.

Copy in the Vernacular

If copy is to communicate its meaning quickly and clearly and
unmistakably, it must be written in the vernacular of the day. There
are no two ways about it.

This means copy must be expressed in the idiom of the group to
whom you're directing your appeal.

Use of stilted style, literary allusions, or pretentious phrases assures next to no readership.

Flee from pedantry, ostentatiousness, formalism, and didacticism.

Just for a fleeting instant give the impression in copy that you're lecturing—like a learned professor in rimless eyeglasses, upraised finger waving in the breeze as he talks down to a captive audience of more or less interested students—and there'll be a mass migration to the next page.

Be superior, condescending, or patronizing, and again you've alienated your readers. They'll not read this ad, perhaps they'll harbor a subconscious resentment which will cause them to ignore future ads in the campaign—and possibly even in other future campaigns for your company.

Readers are like elephants when it comes to memory. They may not remember specifics, but they remember an attitude they've formed. Completely changing an attitude toward a company and its products can be an expensive undertaking, one that can't be done overnight. Don't risk causing resentment—which poor copy can do.

As long as we're being negative at the moment, here's another don't: Don't be coy or cute or precious. And don't force your style. Be natural in your writing and realize that it's inevitable that the personality of the writer will show through in the copy. Let it. If copy lacks the stamp of the writer's personality, chances are it also lacks flavor and vigor and it will read like an annual report—as dry as dust.

The one best way to learn how the buying influences who can give (or withhold) the nod of approval to your product think, feel, and talk, is to do as the author's good friend, Wim van der Graaf, Du Pont ad man, advocates: *Perform the hat trick.*

The hat trick is easy to learn, for it consists of arising from one's posterior, pushing back that comfortable chair behind the desk, crossing the office and putting on your coat and hat—then getting out where the products are bought and used. While you're out there, cultivate people who can make or break your advertising program by deciding what to buy—or what not to buy—including your product.

Ask Questions and Listen

Establish as close a rapport with these readers of your advertising as you can. Loosen up a little, use the expense account, pop for lunches, and encourage those you're entertaining to talk. You *listen.*

Ask questions about the product you're advertising and about competitive products. Use a list which you drew up before putting on your hat. This will help you avoid those uncomfortable silences while you rack your brain trying to think of another intelligent question. The list of questions, or checklist if you will, organizes your work and thought sequences, and enables you to cover all of the ground you need to.

Frequently your prospect won't mind if you make notes of the conversation. Some people, perfectly articulate and expert in their field, freeze up at sight of note taking or tape recording. If this happens to you, resign yourself to the inevitable and try to remember pertinent points; make careful note of them as soon after leaving the prospect as possible.

The Language of Truckers

Many years ago, shortly after joining the old Diamond T Motor Truck Company, the author made a number of field trips to gather case histories, testimonial material, and operating photographs of the company's heavy-duty, custom-built vehicles. Watching, breaking bread with, and talking to members of the trucking industry from drivers and maintenance superintendents to presidents of many Class A common carriers, as well as with numerous individual owner-operators, provided copious notes—and a feeling for the flavor of truck-type conversation.

For example, truckers commonly refer to a tractor-trailer as a "rig." A trailer of the high-cubic-capacity type is a "hi-cube box." A tractor running down the highway without pulling a trailer is "bob-tailing it," a tank-trailer is simply a "tank," which may haul either liquids or "dry bulk flowables" such as flour, dry cement, or chemicals.

In the electronics industry, "IC's" are integrated circuits, the "diffusion process" refers to imparting precisely controlled amounts of impurities into the silicon semiconductor material in a furnace with a carefully controlled heat-time cycle, under a protective atmosphere. And "purple plague" isn't an esoteric serious illness to which our troops in the tropics are likely to succumb, but an unwanted deposit accidentally put on the semiconductor material during the bonding process.

Foundrymen talk of an "acicular structure," which is a microstructure characterized by needle-shaped constituents, or of "black heart," which is American-type malleable iron; the normal fracture shows a velvety black appearance with a mouse-gray rim. "Inverse segregation" has absolutely nothing to do with forcing any segment of our society to live in suburbs; instead, it concerns concentration of certain alloy constituents which have lower melting points, in the region corresponding to that first solidifying; it is caused by inter-dendritic flow of enriched liquid through channels where the pressure drops with the contraction of dendrites. The internal evolution of hydrogen may also give a positive pressure, aiding this flow and causing a liquidated surface or tin sweat. Too, foundrymen talk of a "charge," and this doesn't mean having a ball; it is the collection of material, either pig iron, scrap, or a combination of the two, along with certain alloying materials, which will be melted to produce the finished castings. "Analysis" to them has nothing to do with dissecting an ad, examining a readership study, or taking a good hard look at a market. Instead, it means the chemical composition of the "melt," or molten metal, when it is analyzed prior to the "pour"—actual pouring of the molten metal into ladles, flasks, or carriers.

Use Colloquialisms Correctly

Learn the colloquialisms common in the industry to which you're selling, then use them in copy.

A word of caution, though: The best way in the world to look just plain silly and fall flat on your face is to misuse the colorful, highly descriptive slang and nicknames found in every industry. Check them out with one of the technical people before your copy gets any further than the yellow-paper stage. Don't ask them to approve content or concept, merely the terminology. In a short time you'll be on sure ground and writing as if you'd spent a lifetime in a field about which you actually know little.

Using the vernacular breathes life and flavor and authenticity into your copy. But be careful not to overdo it. You'll find industry slang and nomenclature a highly effective way to set the stage for a straight product story if you use it right.

Two examples from the trade press are just about as far apart as can be when it comes to use of the vernacular. Shown is a full page, black-and-white ad run by Genisco Technology Corporation for the company's Instrumentation Airborne Magnetic Tape Recorder/Reproducer. Naturally, it's one ad from a campaign. The others follow the format and style of this ad, which is illustrated on the following page.

The illustration is an artist's rendering of a nude Eve sitting nonchalantly on a massive apple almost as tall as she is. A serpent is coiled at her feet, head raised to the level of Eve's eyes.

Copy is in dialogue, breezy, slangy and catchy—before the product sell gets under way. It reads:

"So, Eve baby, you act as stocking rep for my new Apple series, jack up sales in the Eden market, and I lay on you Startling Knowledge."

"Well, I do have a prospect in mind. But first how about a sample of this knowledge?"

"O.K. As a starter there's Genisco's Model 10-276A Instrumentation Airborne Magnetic Tape Recorder/Reproducer: just the thing for high accuracy data acquisition for aircraft, helicopters, submarines, etc."

"Fascinating. But will I learn the facts of life?"

"Sure thing. This recorder has a 6-speed, electrically switchable transport with low inertia, motor drive and serv-o control which eliminates pulley-belt changes and minimizes flutter. Not to mention its dual differential capstan drive which provides constant tape tension, gentle tape handling, and eliminates pinch rollers and solenoids."

"Hmmm. I like that part about pinching. You've got a deal, Mr. Serpent."

"Eve, I've got a hunch you'll be a very successful rib."

Here another part of this esoteric ad begins:

OUR EYES ARE ON THE GROUND, BUT OUR FEET ARE ON THE STARS

Something like that. Anyway, our telemetry gear stays on the ground. It's light enough to fly. But it just doesn't feel like it.

The Model A-180 is the world's only completely portable ground station. It will completely de-multiplex any standard FM/FM signal it gets hold of. Operates over any standard IRIG channel. Ideal for checkout of airborne or sledborne radio link telemetering systems.

The Model A-186 is the other world's only completely portable ground station. Has fourteen dirt cheap channels which perform so sweetly it brings tears to your eyes. Receiver is continuously tunable over the 215MC to 260MC band. Frequency stability is 0.001%/°C. Spurious response is greater than 5db below fundamental frequency. Hot stuff, eh?

HERMES TRISMEGISTUS, WON'T YOU PLEASE COME HOME?

Good ol' Herm, as you indubitably know, wrote several books on occult wisdom which were very big in the 17th century. He also invented the hermetic seal. Which is very big in the 20th century.

Each capacitor in our series of power line filters has its very own hermetic seal. Plus its very own separate metal container within the filter enclosure.

Rated from 30 amps to 200 amps, 120 V to 250 V, single or three-phase, the three series are designed for typical circuit breaker panelboards with or without requirements for power line filtering, and for use in shielded rooms and for installations requiring electrical distribution.

If you'd like more information, pulse us a brain wave, or 22 on Reader Service Card.

HOW TO START YOUR OWN THERMONUCLEAR HOLOCAUST

1. *Assemble a warhead and missile.*

2. *Design the electro-explosive device to be armed by RF energy after launch.*

3. *Ignore the possibility of its being armed accidentally by a random bit of radio frequency energy.*

4. *Launch.*

5. *Cower.*

But if you're not particularly in the mood to create a disaster, why not contact Genisco, nationally recognized experts in the field of RF hazard testing? If we don't have in stock the ideal filters or attenuators for your electro-explosive firing circuits, we'll design them for you.

If you're going to proceed without us, we'd appreciate it if you wouldn't fly your missile near our place.

Not every company wants to be that flip, to present that light-hearted an image. For some, their products and markets make this undesirable. For Genisco, however, the author has a sneaking suspicion that this campaign is just what it needs—particularly for a California-based company in electronics.

Copy presents nuts-and-bolts information in an entertaining, highly readable manner, the readers are lured into the ad—and, before they know it—are led through it and then dropped off with a chuckle and an impression that Genisco is really a swinging outfit. Subconsciously they retain a strong impression that Genisco products are of superior quality because they are manufactured by people who are nice guys.

And nobody will quibble about that copy being written in the vernacular—and with a delightfully light touch.

In vivid contrast to Genisco's light-hearted approach is that of Ford Motor Company's recent ad which discusses research. Reversed out of a box in the upper left hand corner, we find:

Recent findings RESEARCH LABORATORIES

Then, the headline:

Ford Motor Company research in radiation crosslinking mechanisms leads to a new paint-curing process

Ah, there's something the author understands! Body copy follows.

Polymerization initiated by high-energy electrons is being explored by Ford Motor Company scientists. The kinetics of the copolymerization of unsaturated esters with styrene show that unusually rapid rate processes occur by mechanisms which do not follow classical concepts. These results reflect the unique mode of interaction between high-intensity, high-energy electrons and organic molecules.

Optimum reaction rates at a given radiation intensity are noted for solutions containing 65% ester (Figure 1). The overall rate depends both on the reactivity of the components and the steric constraints imposed on the system by the rigid network produced. Since the reaction occurs at room temperature, below the glass transition point of the network, the growing chains are not sufficiently mobile to accommodate the configuration predicted by the established copolymerization theory. The structure of the product depends instead on the concentration of double bonds at the instant of radiation.

As the beam intensity becomes greater (Figure 2), the rates increase linearly; network formation occurs within small, isolated volume elements swept out by the incident electrons. At still higher intensities, the volume elements overlap, so that the efficiency of the reaction now is reduced. A consequence of such fundamental studies was the development of a major innovation in paint-curing technology. Chemical structures exhibiting maximum sensitivity to radiation, and with rheological and weathering properties required for optimum performance, were designed and synthesized. The result is a coating that cures in seconds. And at room temperature.

Finally, something else the author understands!

Even the eggheadiest eggheads don't have to be lectured to in that tone, Professor Ford. You'll come out 'way ahead of the game if you'll bear in mind one thing: *Regardless of occupation or discipline, advertising's basic purpose is to communicate with people.* Not to use jargon that only a funny little man in a white lab coat who peers around myopically through lenses like Coke-bottle bottoms would even attempt to decipher. And, after all, they're technicians, not prime buying influences who can initiate purchases. Talk to *all* of the people in your universe, Professor, and see how much more you sell.

Grumman Aircraft Engineering Corporation's dramatic black-and-white spread shown nearby is just about halfway between Ford and Genisco when it comes to copy talking in the vernacular of the day. Copy in this fine image-building spread, which shows some of the esoteric hardware screaming through the frigid blackness of outer space, says:

GRUMMAN'S MOBILE HOME

Way-out work, like this space station, is in Grumman's orbit. Right up our alley, in fact. Our Lunar Module (LM), scheduled to land on the moon in this decade, will be test-orbited soon. Now we're working on the Apollo Telescope Mount (ATM), based on the LM, and have our eye on an Orbiting Space Station for 1975.

> *Space systems are second nature to us. There's a family resemblance in the problems involved. And our scientists have been there before. They may reside on Long Island, but they live in space. Have for years.*

That's the way to communicate with people. This copy is conversational and colloquial. It's in the vernacular. The way people talk. Make it easy to read, so it *is* read.

Idea Sequence

Disjointed, disorderly copy that rambles and is full of random thoughts in no particular sequence is either the product of a copy cub, or of a poorly organized writer. There are a few of them around.

The competent copywriter, however, is one of the best organized individuals in the business world. He has to think through each of his ideas, evaluate them as to relative importance, sort them out, and then present them in logical order so that each is reinforced by the one which follows it.

This results in copy which builds on interest already aroused by the illustration and the headline, copy which moves steadily to a proper climax at the end of the ad.

453

First thing which must be done when writing copy, of course, is to follow through on the promise you made in the headline. Don't let the reader down. To do so is to lose him.

For example, if your headline was a command, tell the reader immediately why he should do as told to do. If you used a question headline, answer the question at once. If you have a news headline, as in a new-product announcement, don't procrastinate—get right into the story of the new product at once. Never mind all of the puffery about how long the company has been in business, how eager it is for more business, or what have you.

Lapp Insulator Company ran an ad in *Electronics* magazine a while back which violated this fundamental rule. The headline read:

Wanted: "big" insulator problems.

And the body copy continued:

> *Solving "big" insulator problems is Lapp's specialty. Wherever insulator requirements call for high strength, special electrical specifications, maximum dependability, and long service . . . Lapp is the company to contact. Lapp has been designing, testing, and making insulators for communications installations for a half century. On many special jobs, our experience provides the basic engineering and design, which enables us to deliver the job quicker and save you money.*

Then after all of that, including a "than-what" comparison which is of little interest to anybody except the powers that be at Lapp Insulator Company—because it doesn't really say anything—the copy goes on:

> *How "big" are the jobs we've done? How about tower base insulators to 9 million lbs. ultimate strength with 500 kv peak wet flashover. Or, compression cone guy insulators to 620 thousand lbs. strength and in strings with grading rings giving wet flashover to 700 kv peak.*

After this paragraph, which finally has some meat in it, Lapp continues to give solid product information about the range of sizes of equipment the company produces. That's all well and good.

Weak point of the ad, though, is that it is primarily a recitation of capacities, puffed up with vague generalities about how you can always rely on good old Lapp.

The copywriter who turned that out would have been better off had he done more doodling and gazing out the window while he organized his thoughts. Then, once the ad assumed shape and was put on paper, if he'd blue-penciled the first two paragraphs and the last brag-and-boast that used space for words without user benefits, he'd have had an ad that probably would have influenced readers.

When it's organized properly, a well-written advertisement can, with complete justification, be compared to any number of other logically constructed works—a song, short story, play, or novel, for instance.

The comparison may be drawn because each adheres to the same basic principles. The songsmith, the writer of fiction, and the advertising copywriter must keep within certain prescribed boundaries imposed by the rules of logic.

Music, for example, is so constructed that it has what amounts to a lead-in paragraph of sound. Its ideas are developed so that each capitalizes on those already developed. And, gradually, the theme is completed so that the only logical thing is to proceed into a crescendo to signify completion of the story, much like an ad's closing sales points and bid for action. Consider Ravel's *Bolero*—or Woody Herman's *Apple Honey*. Play one or both and listen to the headline-introduction, body copy-melody, and the bid for action-crescendo. You'll see the analogy is a legitimate one.

Orderly arrangement is an integral part of the scheme of things. It is accepted without question. Deeply ingrained in all of us is the subconscious expectation that everything we listen to, everything we read—including advertisements—will be orderly and rational and logical, with a distinct, readily apparent beginning, middle, and end.

Build on Basic Premise

It's neither good advertising writing, nor good writing of any kind, to put what obviously is a concluding thought or argument at the beginning of an ad. The correct way is first to establish a basic premise, then build on it. Trot out product advantages, marshal features and user benefits—particularly benefits—one after the other. Reach a peak with such irrefutable logic that the bid for action *belongs* there, so that without it the reader would sense an incompleteness.

Just as undesirable as peaking without a bid for action is to put the bid at the start of the ad. It's out of place, illogical. It doesn't belong there because there has been no build-up, no valid reasons have been advanced to justify asking the reader to do as you want him to.

Sterling National Industries, Inc., makes this basic mistake in an ad in *Foundry* magazine. The headline doesn't actually say anything, but it exhorts readers to do something without having told them why it's in their interest to do it. It reads:

For the ultimate in flasks, buy Sterling.

Short, bulleted body copy says:

World's leading producer of flasks for all types of molding facilities. Unequaled engineering and manufacturing capabilities. Highest quality workmanship—your assurance of consistent dependability.

Now, those are grand words—ultimate, unequaled capabilities, highest quality. Undoubtedly they pleased the president of the company. But to the reader they don't evoke a strong, positive mental image. Actually, they're so nebulous they don't evoke *any* image. Readers have been assaulted for too long by far too many brag-and-boast ads which don't say anything. They've conditioned themselves to skip such ads without even skimming them for possible benefits to themselves. The amount of good which accrued to Sterling from this ad probably was scanty.

And the headline in Standard Tool & Manufacturing Company's two-color, spread ad in *Tooling & Production* magazine says:

Present conditions demand better products . . . at lower cost . . . through better methods . . . consider your position . . . send us your inquiry.

All of this *preceded* two cluttered pages of self-oriented copy that talked features, features, features. The bid for action—send us your inquiry—should have been at the end of the ad, after the ad convinced the reader it was in his self-interest to do this. As is, it's out of place and will probably be ignored.

In the same issue of this magazine, N. A. Woodworth's ad is an example of ideas arranged in the proper sequence to tell the story the way it should be told—but the story's the wrong one for the advertiser. It reads:

FAMOUS FIRSTS

Sir Edmond Hillary reaches the top of Mt. Everest, May 29, 1953.

Mountains are there and men must climb them. And none more than Everest, the giant of the Himalayas, had so unceasingly challenged and rebuffed those who would scale her gargantuan mass of earth, rock, and snow. But Everest was beaten 14 years ago when Edmond Hillary, together with Nepalese mountain climber Tensing Norkay, reached the summit. They achieved the near-legendary kind of feat which somehow moves other men to look to the best in themselves—to be the first, perhaps, to scale their own Everests.

In 1957 Woodworth climbed its own Everest and produced for industry a Famous First, the "Ball-Lok" Power Chuck.

Production of this ad cost a pretty penny. The illustration is four-color art, printed ROP—run of paper—by the offset process. Although the author is a dedicated mountain lover and would rather climb than eat, this isn't everyone's cup of tea. Most people are odd. They can take mountains or leave them. For such eccentrics—and they happen to be the majority of all readers—it's all too easy to leave this attractive ad.

The point is, the ideas are well organized and the copy is readable enough and interesting—intensely so to a minority of the magazine's readers. But there's no bid for action, which is akin to a salesman not asking for the order at the end of his sales presentation. And the product plug is soft-sell carried to an extreme. There are no user benefits, not even a listing of product features to arouse interest. It's a shame, too, because the mountains are beautiful!

Use Copy Platform as Guide

Your copy platform is the guideline as to what ideas you'll want to discuss, of course. Keep it handy. Refer to it, then simply list the ideas—topics, that is—you want to discuss in any given ad. No need to write a lengthy outline, just a one- or two-word heading for each idea is sufficient. Arrange them in numerical sequence, or a-b-c-d.

When an ad is organized in this manner *before it's written*, there's little likelihood that the copy will wander off on a tangent or have the ideas in illogical sequence.

Note in The Torrington Company's striking ad reproduced on page 459 the simple, orderly presentation of ideas which build upon interest aroused by the dramatic close-up photo. Copy reads:

Are you still
making small
precision
parts (like these)
yourself?

Pity. It's really a shame. Especially when you consider that Torrington can supply you with shafts, spindles, pivots, dowels, and taper pins—virtually any cylindrical part you need. In any shape or hardness, with diameters ranging from .375" down to .010". And tolerances tailored to your needs, too—even as close as ± .000015"!

We will make these for you in multithousands or multimillion lots. And we'll do it faster, cheaper, and easier than you can do it yourself. You see, we have all the facilities for the production of these parts—the tooling, the grinding, the hardening, the micropolishing—all under one roof. Each operation is automated and quality carefully checked. As a result, we can give you a superior product at a surprising low price.

If that's what you're after, send a drawing or a blueprint of the part or parts you want made plus quantities used—to: (address)

Stick to the Core Idea

Only one core idea, call it a central theme or a basic premise if you like, can be communicated effectively by a single piece of advertising copy.

One, just one.

Naturally enough, this means that you have a decision to make before writing copy for an ad. Crystal-clear in your own mind must be the core idea, which is the most important thing about the product —or your selling proposition—you want to implant in the minds of those who read your ad.

A single piece of advertising copy can't be all things to all men, nor can it even come within shouting distance of attaining the non-attainable. This includes your audience, readers of the publications in which your ad will appear, as well as product managers, market managers, the sales manager and others within your company—including top management.

The importance of clinging to the core idea in an industrial advertisement isn't generally appreciated—or understood—in industry.

Are you still
making small
precision
parts (like these)
yourself?

Pity. It's really a shame. Especially when you consider that Torrington can supply you with shafts, spindles, pivots, dowel and taper pins – virtually any cylindrical part you need. In any shape or hardness, with diameters ranging from .375" down to .010". And tolerances tailored to your needs, too—even as close as ± .000015"!

We will make these for you in multithousands or multimillion lots. And we'll do it faster, cheaper and easier than you can do it yourself. You see, we have all the facilities for the production of these parts—the tooling, the grinding, the hardening, the micropolishing—all under one roof. Each operation is automated and quality carefully checked. As a result, we can give you a superior product at a surprisingly low price.

If that's what you're after, send a drawing or a blueprint of the part or parts you want made plus quantities used—to: Specialties Division, The Torrington Company, Torrington, Conn. 06790.

THE TORRINGTON COMPANY
100TH YEAR

SERVING INDUSTRY EVERYWHERE WITH METAL SPECIALTIES; ANTIFRICTION BEARINGS; SWAGING MACHINES; SEWING MACHINE & KNITTING MACHINE NEEDLES; STITCHING MACHINES

Torrington told them they shouldn't dilute their efforts doing the job of a specialist, told how good Torrington parts are, why they're good, why they're priced right—and ended up with a bid for action that resulted in action. The ad is persuasive, convincing, and logical. Hard combination to beat.

More often than not, the pressure to touch all bases, to cover every conceivable sales point, to list features galore and include everything in the ad from trivia to a lengthy dissertation on *A History of How This Widget Is Engineered, And Why,* comes from within the ad manager's company.

If you cave in and accede to the blandishments of the nonadvertising professionals who seemingly *always* want to emasculate copy by rewriting it in engineerese to make it "more general" or "more universally applicable," you can be absolutely certain of accomplishing one thing: You'll end up with a vague bunch of generalities, couched in clichés, and a diluted selling proposition which has neither impact nor interest.

Avoid destruction of good copy. Avoid failure to reap the benefits good copy can produce for your product in the marketplace *by selling sound copy.*

Explain it. Believe in and rely upon repetition, just as you do in advertising, to gain acceptance of what is to many a unique new concept—that an advertisement can communicate just one core idea. Go over this again and again and again, each time you present copy to be checked for technical accuracy, for review, or for approval.

Without launching into a lengthy harangue or an intricate explanation of advertising theory, tell your people how the copy adheres to sound advertising practice. Briefly explain what it is and the reason for it. Then stand up on your hind legs and defend your copy, refuse to let it be chopped to pieces.

Inland Steel Company apparently couldn't make up its mind upon what specific idea it wanted to discuss in a four-color spread ad in the business press. As a bit of background, the Inland Steel Building is a beautiful functional structure which bids fair to acquire reputation as a modern classic. But it's been standing so long in Chicago's Loop that it has almost become a landmark. Yet the ad-maker was either told to reassure readers of Inland's continuing occupancy of its own building, or else he felt it was desirable for some reason which doesn't explain itself. After this decision was made, somebody else wanted to get in the idea that Inland Steel produces a wide range of steel; another person—or perhaps a committee—decided he should say what fine people work at Inland . . . anyway, the copy reads:

We're doing business
at the same old stand

Outside, the building is modern. All shining steel and glass.

Inside, procedures are equally modern—streamlined and automated to speed service to customers. Yet you'll find the same "first name" top management people who have always made dealing with Inland a pleasant experience—people pleased to see and talk with you any time. Each personally dedicated to the quality of Inland products. Each concerned with customer needs. Each always available for consultation and no-waiting decisions. We are the one major steel company headquartered in the Midwest. Producers of a comprehensive range of sheets, bars, plates, and shapes. In our nearly 75 years we've grown tremendously. We're big. Big enough to meet all your steel requirements. But complete customer satisfaction—your satisfaction—is still our primary concern. We want your business.

On the plus side, there's the fact that the Inland Steel Building was illustrated. And Inland's name was seen, their logo was displayed. But the ad is far from memorable. The message is simply not important to the reader. That's because the copywriter didn't start with a single strong core idea, and he didn't develop a straight-through, logical sequence of ideas culminating with a distinctive selling proposition. And there's no bid for action that moves people. "We want your business" is pallid and you-know-who oriented.

Once in a while an ad crops up that is distinctive, striking, highly readable and, upon initial consideration at least, nearly perfect. An example is the attractive black-and-white spread ad run by Xerox in the media it selected to reach management men. Layout is stark and simple, the headline is intriguing, but the body copy lacks a core idea. It reads:

The day a Xerox Analyst had to recommend Brand X

He almost bit his tongue.

Our Analyst had been analyzing a customer's business and he found a problem he couldn't solve.

The purchasing department needed a fast copier. But they didn't have any space. So they needed a machine that would fit on a desk.

*What they needed, we didn't
make. Our 813 desktop copier
wasn't fast enough, and our 720
wouldn't fit on the desk.*

*So our Analyst gritted his
teeth and recommended Brand X.
It wasn't exactly right, but it was
closer than anything we had.*

*(We promise our customers we'll
put the right machine in the
right place. If we don't happen
to make the right machine,
that's our tough luck.)*

*But our Analyst didn't take
it lying down.*

*He complained to the
Branch Manager. The Branch
Manager complained to the
Zone Manager. The Zone Manager
complained to the . . . etc., etc.*

*Research and Engineering
took it from there. And now we
introduce the new 660. The fast,
fast desktop copier.*

*The new Xerox 660 makes 660
copies an hour directly from the
original. At the push of a button.
You get exact full-size copies of
everything that's on the original.
And that's all. 11 copies a minute.
Perfect black and white copies on
ordinary paper.*

*And the 660 is small enough
to fit in the corner of a desk.
Or the corner of a corner.*

*Now if Brand X is as honest as
we are, they'll have to recommend us.*

The day a Xerox Analyst had to recommend brand X.

He almost bit his tongue.

Our Analyst had been analyzing a customer's business and he found a problem he couldn't solve.

The purchasing department needed a fast copier. But they didn't have any space. So they needed a machine that would fit on a desk.

What they needed, we didn't make. Our 813 desktop copier wasn't fast enough, and our 720 wouldn't fit on a desk.

So our Analyst gritted his teeth and recommended brand X. It wasn't exactly right, but it was closer than anything we had.

(We promise our customers we'll put the right machine in the right place. If we don't happen to make the right machine, that's our tough luck.)

But our Analyst didn't take it lying down.

He complained to the Branch Manager. The Branch Manager complained to the Zone Manager. The Zone Manager complained to the... etc., etc.

Research and Engineering took it from there. And now we introduce the new 660. The fast, fast desktop copier.

The new Xerox 660 makes 660 copies an hour directly from the original. At the push of a button. You get exact full-size copies of everything that's on the the original. And that's all. 11 copies a minute. Perfect black and white copies on ordinary paper.

And the 660 is small enough to fit in the corner of a desk. Or the corner of a corner.

Now if brand X is as honest as we are, they'll have to recommend us.

XEROX

You'll be struck immediately with the fact that this ad can't make up its mind as to its purpose. Actually, it has *two* core ideas: (1) That Xerox makes all types of copiers which will fit into just about any old space that happens to be available in the office, and (2) that Xerox is now producing a new desktop copier called the 660 which makes 660 copies an hour on ordinary paper.

This comment is not to cast aspersions on the typical breadth-of-line ad that's so ubiquitous throughout the business press. The *We-Make-All-Types-Of-Widgets* message is a perfectly legitimate one for advertising to disseminate, and a thoroughly acceptable core idea—assuming this is the type of message which will achieve the communications objective of the advertiser at that particular time.

However, in this ad Xerox combined the breadth-of-line idea with a second core idea—which was to announce a new product.

The fundamental weakness of this advertisement is that *neither* core idea is dominant. Neither is hit as hard in the copy as it would have been had the ad had just one basic premise. Granted, the two ideas complement each other, but neither strengthens the other appreciably.

Readership studies prove that in most instances only one basic idea will be retained by the overwhelming majority of readers. In this case, it is logical to assume that most readers will retain the thought that Xerox makes all sizes and types of copiers.

This can't harm Xerox, of course. But the dollars allocated won't work nearly as effectively as they would have if the copy had come through loud and clear that Xerox has a new product, that Xerox has developed a great new copier that almost obsoletes competitive units. This is far and away the more important of the two ideas, and if the readers fail to remember it when they're considering purchasing a new copier, the ad hasn't even come close to doing its job.

Polaroid's campaign to sell the company's film and photograph equipment to industry is so excellent that it's nothing short of industrial advertising's equivalent of Volkswagen's classic consumer campaign.

In the ad shown here, Polaroid shows us exactly how a headline

Design a new circuit? It only takes 10 seconds to find out that maybe you didn't.

Polaroid Land film for oscillography is as quick to point out a mistake as it is to point out a success.

You never have to wait for darkroom development only to find out that your new breadboard needs more work.

You get your results in 10 seconds flat. And it's always a sharply detailed, high-contrast trace recording.

You can study it, attach it to a report, send it as a test record along with a product shipment, or file it for future use.

Choice of films? Yes. There are four different films for oscilloscope recording in pack, roll, and 4 x 5 formats.

The standard film speed has an ASA equivalent rating of 3000.

If you want to take a picture of a trace so fast you can't even see it, we've got a

special film called Polaroid PolaScope Land film with an ASA equivalent rating of 10,000. It's the fastest film around. It will actually record a scintillation pulse with a rise time of less than 3 nanoseconds.

To use these films on your scope, you need a camera with a Polaroid Land Camera Back. Most manufacturers have them (Annlab, BNK Associates, Coleman Engineering, EG & G, Fairchild, General Atronics, Hewlett-Packard, Tektronix).

You can get complete details from one of these manufacturers, or by writing to Polaroid Corporation, Technical Sales, Dept. 30, Cambridge, Massachusetts 02139.

Polaroid Land Film for Oscilloscope Trace Recording

and body copy should relate to the illustration, then how both should relate to the body copy. And you'll see there's just one core idea behind this copy—that Polaroid film and equipment assure fast, precise results in making a critical evaluation of electronic instruments. Copy reads:

**Design a new circuit?
It takes only 10 seconds
to find out that
maybe you didn't.**

Polaroid Land film for oscillography is as quick to point out a mistake as it is to point out a success.

You never have to wait for darkroom development only to find out that your new breadboard needs more work.

You get your results in 10 seconds flat. And it's always a sharply detailed, high-contrast trace recording.

You can study it, attach it to a report, send it as a test record along with a product shipment, or file it for future use.

Choice of films? Yes. There are four different films for oscilloscope recording in pack, roll, and 4x5 formats.

The standard film speed has an ASA equivalent rating of 3000.

If you want to take a picture of a trace so fast you can't even see it, we've got a special film called Polaroid Pola-Scope Land film with an ASA equivalent rating of 10,000. It's the fastest film around. It will actually record a scintillation pulse with a rise time of less than 3 nanoseconds.

To use these films on your scope, you need a camera with a Polaroid Land Camera Back. Most manufacturers have them (Analab, BNK Associates, Coleman Engineering, EG&G, Fairchild, General Atronics, Hewlett-Packard, Tektronix).

You can get complete details from one of these manufacturers, or by writing to Polaroid Corporation . . .

Polaroid Land Film for Oscilloscope Trace Recording

That copy sells hard. Polaroid does a fine job of anticipating readers' questions by explaining clearly and quickly how their film works, by telling them about the high film speed, various sizes available, and the formats that are offered. Furthermore, Polaroid counters any possible objections to using Polaroid film by name-dropping, mentioning the various manufacturers of electronic test equipment whose units accommodate Polaroid Land film and camera attachments. Using these manufacturers' names also provides Polaroid with an implied endorsement, which never hurts.

Polaroid gives facts and figures which support the claims it makes, advances a sound selling proposition, and presents its story simply and logically and persuasively. All without wasting a word or a thought.

Many things go into creation of an outstanding ad, but a fundamental which cannot be ignored is that a good ad results from having *only one* core idea. Have more than one and you have two strikes against you; it'll be next to impossible to turn out a really top-notch piece of copy.

Use Short Words

When you're writing copy, resist the temptation to be a sesquipedalian. Sesquipedals invariably distract many readers and frequently alienate a large number of others.

A sesquipedalian, of course, is a hapless individual with an unconquerable penchant for using long words, and a sesquipedal is one of the tongue-twisters with which he's enamored.

Oddly enough, many industrial copywriters exhibit the same weakness which makes much business writing an impenetrable morass. They write, but they don't communicate.

For some obscure reason, a feeling of insufficiency, perhaps, they feel compelled to prove their erudition by organizing an awesome parade of formidable words and trotting them all out for all to see. They give the impression that *they're* under the impression that use of multisyllable words will overwhelm the reader and persuade him to accept what the writer says as gospel truth, or else they will browbeat him into believing.

But there's not a chance.

We in industrial advertising like to fancy ourselves professional communicators. As such, we must realize that the average person to whom we're writing is more intelligent, better educated, and better equipped to understand what we're writing than is the average American.

That's because we're directing our message to technical and management people in industry who have the advantage of more education and a broader experience than the factory worker or cab driver.

The fact remains, though, that these people, for the most part, are relatively unskilled with words. Technical people—chemists, engineers, research scientists, metallurgists, and so on—are simply not involved with words to the extent that the advertising man is. They think, talk, and write in a jargon peculiar to their specialty in order to communicate with their colleagues and business associates.

Maybe they *do* communicate. But the tortured thought processes which result in the semi-incomprehensible technical papers presented in an endless succession of annual meetings of various technical societies is indeed weird and wondrous.

The intellectual fare of the technical people is composed of gobbledygook disguised to look like writing, done, for the most part, by their counterparts in other companies. It is published in the technical journals they dote on. These journals usually are dull in both content and format, have very few illustrations, and a dreadful gray sameness in page after page of solid type. They thrive because they publish these pseudointellectual exercises in obscuring the meaning of what the technical man turned "writer" is trying to say. And this takes a bit of doing, but this material is presented with an impeccable editorial deadpan expression. Another reason these publications thrive is because advertising managers and agencies cannot read them to evaluate them, so assume that just because *they* can translate the gibberish only with extreme difficulty that the technical people *can*—hence their advertising belongs where it will be read by the technical types they want to talk to.

One thing too many ad men overlook is that even technical people are people. And this is still an English-speaking country. Well-written English communicates even to the far-out eggheads who consider a sliderule thrilling reading.

Let's look at a couple of pieces of copy chosen at random from one of the leading chemical books. One ad says (and this is verbatim except for changing the firm name):

If you're looking for a more efficient emulsifier with the right hydrophilic/lipophilic balance, Smith arylates may be your answer. Phenylstearic acid and its quaternary or ethoxylated derivatives are useful in synthetic latices, as mineral oil emulsifiers, and in invert systems—separately or in combination. Their greater efficiency permits lower use-concentration.

This is no diatribe against necessary technical terms, for they're often the only way to express an exact meaning. There's no quarrel with hydrophilic/lipophilic balance, for example. Nor with the other chemical names. But that last sentence could have communicated much better if it had said:

Smith arylates are more efficient. So you use less. At lower cost, of course.

Something on that order would have made the point easier, faster, more pointed. As is, the copy is pedantic, pretentious, and pseudo-intellectual. This is a form of snobbery, of course. Few of us can work up much of a feeling of affinity for a snob.

Further on in the same issue of the same book we find this:

Smith 6752-C Bis (hydroxethyl) Azelate (GFUYB) is a new polymer-grade intermediate designed primarily for modification of high molecular weight polyesters. It may be used directly in polyester polymerization processes as a commonomer for production of copolyesters suitable for adhesives, specialty film, and fiber applications. The hydroxyl functionality also suggests investigation as a co-reactant with isocyanates for urethane elastomer and fiber applications.

Again, there's no quibbling with use of chemical names of substances and processes. But to say *functionality also suggests investigation,* and do it with a perfectly straight face, is blind refusal to admit that this is imitation academicism. No copywriter worth his salt writes like that unless he's an out-and-out phony who's dishonest enough to take the course of least resistance and continue to turn out cliché-ridden gibberish just because it's been traditional in many technical fields to do so for decades.

Interestingly—and the copywriter himself bears out what the author said above—the ad closes with this bid for action:

Use coupon below to request evaluation sample and data sheet.

That's straightforward, written in English, and to the point, sans all pretense of being written so as to try to obscure what's really meant. The bid for action is in writing that says something, as opposed to writing that doesn't really convey any meaning.

Short words put your message across better, even if you're not writing to the technical man. Top management in industry is different, some ad men think, from the technical men who report to them. But look around you in your own company. Chances are if your firm manufactures a highly engineered product, or one that is made for a specialty market, you'll find the same type of people in all of the paneled offices right up to the corner one with four windows. Executives who head industrial companies are usually ex-technical men themselves, or ex-accountants who graduated to controller, then moved up the ladder to the top spot.

The nontechnical men have a broader outlook and more diversified experience, of course, but the fact remains that they're little, if any, more word-oriented than they were when they started in business. As we've discussed, however, the trend in industry is for top management to be composed of generalists, so there's hope that advertising can contribute more each year.

When you keep the words short you're helping your advertising copy do its job.

Ways to Measure Reading Ease

Research has proved that ads relatively easy to read receive higher readership than those which are more difficult. In its Laboratory of Advertising Performance, McGraw-Hill reports that the 100 one-page ads with the highest readership ratings—and the 100 with the lowest—were selected from among all similar advertisements in 10 issues of *Factory* magazine. Readership ratings were those determined by McGraw-Hill's Reader Feedback Service.

These ads were analyzed to determine if ease of reading of the main copy block differed significantly in the high-scoring group, compared to the low-scoring group. The reading ease formula developed by Dr. Rudolph Flesch, which appears in his book, *The Art of Readable Writing*, was applied to the main copy block in each ad in the 100-ad sample of high and low scoring ads. The result was as expected: The higher the reading ease score of an advertisement, the easier it is to read.

The 100 best read ads averaged a numerical score of 48 on a scale which ranges from zero (very difficult), to 100 (very easy). The 48 score of the best read ads was about halfway between the two extremes, in the area about midway between "fairly difficult" and "fairly easy."

The 100 ads which had the poorest readership averaged a score of 39, which is "fairly difficult."

Dr. Flesch's formula is based on the average length of sentences and the number of syllables per 100 words.

Only 8 percent of the high rated ads fell toward the difficult end of the scale (21 to 30 in score), while 22 percent of the poorly read ads were in that group. Toward the easier-to-read end of the scale (61 to 70 score) 12 percent of the high rated ads appeared, while only 1 percent of the poorly read ads were found there.

Except for ease of reading, the two groups of ads were comparable. The ads didn't differ significantly in the number of words in the main copy blocks, so copy length definitely wasn't a factor which influenced readership ratings.

Interestingly, the principal editorial material in a typical issue of *Factory* was checked for reading ease, using the same formula. Thirteen articles averaged a Flesch Reading Ease Score of 51, quite close to the 48 averaged by the best read ads.

Any number of formulas have been devised to classify advertising copy (and other written matter) as to form, content, and the ease with which it may be understood. If you'll familiarize yourself with one or two of these formulas, then use them to analyze and evaluate your copy, you'll find it will help you produce copy that conveys its meaning quicker and with less chance of its not being understood— or not being read.

Formal structure of written material is analyzed, in a broad sense, by the frequency with which frequently used, readily understood words appear. Of all words in the English language, only a tiny fraction are used in daily conversation and in writing which communicates instantaneously, as an advertisement must.

Dale-Chall and Hass Formulas

The Dale-Chall Formula is one of the best known methods of determining how easily writing is understood. This formula is based on a list of approximately 3,000 words in common usage, and on the average length of the sentences. The formula was developed according to the educational level necessary for comprehension of the written material. It is considered reasonably satisfactory, although its shortcoming of being based on a static list of words is recognized. English is a vital, dynamic language which is in a constant state of flux. Think of how many words you can call to mind which didn't even exist a few years ago.

Another widely used method of determining how easily a piece of prose may be read was developed by C. R. Hass. Hass compared literary works, advertising copy, and telegrams. Immediately apparent was the tightness of advertising writing, the precise selection of words, and the succinct style—almost telegraphic.

His next step was to develop a ratio so that he could assign a numerical score on a scale, with literature at one end and telegrams at the other. He laid down definite rules of how main words and subsidiary words were to be distinguished, with instructions on how to apply his formula of Ratio of Main Words to Subsidiary Words. Hass' index makes it relatively easy to analyze one important characteristic of advertising copy—its "density" of content. Hass stresses that the most important part of the message be told in as few words as possible for best comprehension.

Dr. Flesch's Reading Ease Score, which McGraw-Hill used, is certainly one of the best ways to analyze and evaluate copy. It is based on length of the average sentence in number of words, and on length of the average word by number of syllables, in 100 words.

This means that Dr. Flesch makes use of the two most important factors in studying copy to determine its comprehensibility—word length, which also involves frequency of use of words, and sentence length, upon which clarity hinges.

Many conscientious advertising managers routinely check out their copy—not all of it, of course, but some of it—or copy for which they are responsible. Also, a number of newspapers and magazines make periodic surveys to determine that the readability of their output remains up to their standards. Periodicals have proved beyond question with the split-run technique that easily read copy achieves far higher readership than copy which is reasonably difficult to read.

Gunning Fog Index Good

Similar to Flesch's Reading Ease Score is the Gunning Fog Index. This evaluation procedure is based upon sentence length and the ratio of words of three or more syllables to shorter words. Actually, a percentage is used in calculating the Fog Index, or the fog level as it's commonly called in advertising. In addition to providing a guideline for the advertising manager, Gunning indicates the number of years of formal education required to comprehend typical writing, with scores based on his percentage figures.

Using typical examples, you can easily determine the complexity of writing which will be readily comprehended by the buying influences to whom your copy is directed. Gunning recommends that you don't write over the heads of those with 12 years of education. You may prefer Gunning's method because it is somewhat easier to apply than Flesch's. The Gunning method is explained in *How to Take the Fog Out of Writing* (Dartnell).

Flesch also devised a terribly complicated formula for determining the amount of human interest in any particular piece of copy. This is so involved that it is almost useless for the advertising manager who wants to do just one thing: Tell, as closely as possible, whether his ad's content contains sufficient meat that it will appeal to most readers.

A better way, and one that's much easier to apply, to analyze the content of copy is Bernard Berelson's Content Analysis method. It is particularly appropriate for use with advertising copy.

Content Analysis involves determining the frequency with which certain elements—words, sentences, symbols, for example—occur, then computing their dependence upon each other. In this way, according to Berelson, you can make an objective breakdown of the copy and arrive at an accurate evaluation of its probable effectiveness. Many advertising agencies habitually use the Content Analysis method of evaluating copy to find out if it measures up.

When it comes to determining how easy it is to comprehend the entire piece of copy, two methods are most widely used. Most common is the recall and feedback technique, in which readers are interviewed and asked if they remember having noticed or read advertisements in the issue of the publication being studied.

Chilton's Ad-Chart, largest and perhaps the most useful of the readership evaluation services, Starch, McGraw-Hill's Reader Feedback and similar services rely on interviews and interpretation of the information readers give them. Professional measurers have made evaluation of readership a fairly precise science, and with a relatively small sample are able to project it over the entire circulation of a magazine which goes to, say, 85,000 individuals in the business world. Results are statistically correct, and if you interpret what the survey says, you'll find yourself in possession of information that's most useful.

Another method in general use for measuring how easily copy can be understood is one devised by W. L. Taylor, who called it the Cloze procedure.

Taylor examines the way copy is structured, as well as its content. The Cloze procedure has extra appeal to many because it is equally effective when used on copy as it comes from the typewriter—*before* one penny is invested in production, art, space, or what have you— as it is upon ads which have already appeared in print. This can be a money saver.

On the surface, the Cloze procedure seems pretty esoteric, involving as it does the actual copy which is being tested—with every *nth* word, fourth, fifth, or sixth, for example—deleted. Persons assisting in the copy evaluation are asked to complete the copy by filling in all of the missing words so that the copy reads the way the writer intended it to. Naturally, those tested should be familiar with the product, market, process, and so on, in order to make the test valid.

It's even possible to test several versions of a piece of copy to tell which one communicates best. The rub is, in order to produce results which stand up under critical analysis, a rather large sample is required; it goes without saying that the more individuals tested, interviewed, and asked for assistance, the higher the cost of the project. Few ad budgets are unlimited.

To many of you advertising managers and agency men, research on words, reading ease, comprehensibility, construction, and content of copy is useless spinning of wheels. If so, well and good. Presumably you're morally certain your copy is easily read and easily understood. If there's any doubt, however, even a slight one, by all means investigate these methods of copy evaluation.

Check with your local library, the A.I.A., A.A.A.A., or your local advertising club for literature on the subject. Buy a good book for your departmental library, study it, then study your copy. There's no telling how much more effective you might be able to make it. It's worth the effort.

The "Nonword" Phenomenon

Speaking of using short words, one pitfall into which many of us fall almost as a matter of routine is that of using nonwords. The nonword isn't a figment of anybody's disordered imagination. It occurs with dismaying frequency in industrial advertising (which may have fathered it).

Nonwords are the brainchildren of frustrated technical people, for the most part, people who feel a faint stirring somewhere deep within themselves to prove that they're creative. This unfamiliar urge is welcomed with broad smiles as they gleefully tack fancy names, usually nonwords composed of segments of two or three honest-to-gosh words, glued together so they delight the eye and ear of their originators—and are utterly incomprehensible to readers, and even to those perfectly familiar with the product.

There's no intent to arouse the populace to take up arms and march in righteous indignation against those who want to assign a perfectly acceptable name to a product. After all, there's precedent aplenty for naming products—all the way from the ubiquitous

Parker Jotter to the Rolls Royce Silver Cloud you ride in if you're doing a little bit better than the average ad man.

Well-chosen names are catchy, memorable, easily written, and easily understood. They actually say something positive to the prospect. And they make promoting a product easier for the ad man and make choosing it easier for the buyer.

What you don't want to do, however, is make the mistake made by so many companies—letting the engineers assign a coined, nonword name to the product or some feature of it. This frequently happens when the product is being designed or engineered—and the name sticks to it all the way from the drawing board, through the tool room, during prototype production, and on up into the upstairs offices where marketing planning goes on.

By that time the nonword name which doesn't say anything to anybody adheres to the new product with leech-like tenacity. It's an oversized albatross around the ad manager's neck. Usually it's deliberately misspelled, cutely so, if an actual word is used.

Examples of Nonsense Words

Riffling through a few current trade books turns up these examples of warped creativity, each of which inflicted upon some perfectly innocent ad manager a gobbledygook name which would require the entire copy block to explain—if it could *be* explained. In practice, most ad managers suffer silently with the product names foisted off onto them and use them grimly until death do them part —unless this occurs sooner due to development of a superimproved, revolutionary new Mark IIVXMVIX version of the same product, then there's the fun and games of having the nonword name *plus* the beloved "Mark" followed by a plethora of Roman numerals. Explain that one to the readers!

Some of the nonsense, nonword names follow:

> *Diffusitron, Treet-All, COMPACT, Electroverb, HYEN, Acehi, Fluidic, Dialatron, NuCon, "Ball-Lok," Monomatic, Centalign, Ultraversamatic, Grindomatic, Versofab, Palletron, Centroservo, Gageometer, HYEX, HiPowerMatic, and so on and on and on . . .*

There's no end to the nonsense. If a name remotely approaches making some semblance of sense, the would-be creative types can be depended upon to either capitalize it in its entirety, or put it in quotation marks. This serves only to insult the intelligence of the reader.

Get enough of it into one ad and you can end up with one that reads like the first sentence and part of the second in an ad in *Automation:*

> *Strippit has scored a technical knockout in the metalworking field with its new Strippit C/C* Computer Control.***
>
> *Working as a part of a Strippit Fabramatic* Hole Punching and Notching System, the Strippit C/C* Computer Control** now makes . . . etc.*

In that brief bit of copy the reader is forced to go through the mental gymnastics required to translate the precious little trick names into simple, everyday English that those of us who are not Strippit engineers can understand.

Once that's done, though, the reader is still forced to look down to the bottom of the ad every time he encounters a * or a ** to find out that * means trademark of the manufacturer, and ** means patent applied for. Seems as if a plain, simple, little old footnote in tiny italics at the tag end of the ad would have provided sufficient legal protection without keeping the reader at the ragged end of his tether from jumping back and forth from a * to the bottom of the book, then back up to **, then to the bottom again. And all of the time there's the gnawing worry that he might, just might, encounter a ***. *That* would be enough to really shake him.

Strip away the nonsense and the gibberish, Strippit, and find yourself with many more readers.

Use nonsense names and you can be pretty sure of three things:

1. The ad's harder to read.

2. It's more difficult to comprehend.

3. Fewer people will read it.

Shy away from nonsense names and nonwords.

Far better to use a generic name or a model number—we're all familiar with Boeing's 707, 720, and 727, with Douglas' DC-8, and with 33 rpm. These model numbers and numbers describing how something operates are descriptive, pleasant, memorable. They say something to the businessman. After all, a name has only one function when applied to a product—to communicate a thought or benefit, or to identify it beyond the possibility of confusion. Who wants to buy a Dialatron or a Diffusitron? And what if some misguided soul named a new four-engine jetliner a Jetatron or a Jetamatic? Make you want to entrust your life to it?

Write Readable Copy

Knowing how reading ease can be measured and analyzed is helpful, but the fact remains that you must *write* readable copy. If we eliminate the nonsense names and nonwords there shouldn't be any problem. Right?

Wrong.

Far too much industrial advertising copy sounds exactly like an interoffice memo from the land of the sliderules and blueprints to marketing management. It's stilted, pretentious, and literally teems with big words.

For example, a sentence from an ad in *Metal Progress* says:

> *The annealer utilizes radiant tubes to heat strip to . . .*

There's a concentration of three three- and four-syllable words in a row. That's too many. And it's not even necessary, because the sentence could have said exactly the same thing and been easier to read and easier to comprehend, if it had said:

> *The annealer uses radiant tubes to heat strip to . . .*

After all, according to Webster, "utilizes" means "uses." Why not say what is meant—uses—in the first place and make it easy for the reader to get the message? Deliberately slowing him down can result in losing him.

And, in the same publication, we find this one:

> *Precise location of the edge of a conductive material can be reliably determined. Permits accurate measurements of horizontal displacements of the probe with respect to many edge or symmetrical geometrics. Automatic control signals can be furnished directly from the differential analyzer for many critical alignment procedures that are carried on in the fabrication of welded products and structural members.*

The fog level's pretty high there. Out of 59 words, 12 have two syllables, 11 have three syllables, and 8 have 4 syllables—and one even has 5 syllables! That's a total of 32 multisyllable words in that one paragraph. Substantially too many if the copy is to be understood.

This book isn't intended as a short course in rewriting somebody else's copy in ads that have already appeared. But reread that paragraph, then compare it with the following one which says the same

thing and even includes some real mouthfuls that couldn't be avoided
—at least when unfamiliar with the product and its applications:

> *It's easy to find the exact edge of a conductive material
> with the new Smith Widget. You can measure exactly how
> much the probe is off horizontally. Then compare this to
> many edge or symmetrical geometrics. You can have auto-
> matic control signals that go right from the differential
> analyzer. This makes them ideal for many jobs where close
> alignment is important—such as fabricating welded prod-
> ucts and structural members.*

That's 69 words—but if we deduct the five extra ones that do the
important job of getting the name of the product up front where it
counts (as some ads say), we're left with only 64. And words could
still be cut from the copy if absolutely necessary, because "easy"
and "you" and "this makes them ideal" could be deleted, as could
"new." But these small words and the important personal touch add
sell to the ad. It lacked in that respect before.

Speaking of "in that respect," note that this clumsy verbiage has
been consigned to the round file. "Can be furnished," for example, is
archaic, superfluous, and undesirable. Almost anything in life can
be furnished for a price—even an unfurnished apartment. And
"with respect to" is pedestrian. People don't talk that way unless
they're engineers—and even *they* don't usually talk that way unless
they're discussing products.

Of the 69 words, we find an even dozen that now have two
syllables—the same as in the original, hard-to-read copy; six now
have three syllables, which is five less than before; seven have four
syllables, for a gain of one; and the same word, "horizontally," with
all five of its syllables, is retained. Familiarity with the product
might well make it possible to clean up even this rewritten copy,
enabling readers to absorb it faster and better. The rewritten version
is a big step in the right direction, though. You can prove this to
yourself by reading both versions against a stopwatch. And then
reading at the same pace for comprehension, and timing that reading.

In *Foundry* magazine we find the following little gem which bids
to become an all-time classic:

> *Components of Smith Widgets are custom-engineered and
> meticulously manufactured to unusually precise tolerances
> to facilitate rapid replacement when the necessity arises
> without impairing operating efficiency or accuracy.*

It's a crying shame there aren't prepositions and conjunctions with five syllables. Then we'd have a piece of copy that would *really* have impressed the technical troops!

For a moment let's be 100 percent negative. Let's take a look at a few important don'ts.

Don't say "incorporates," say "has." Never use "facilitate," instead substitute "makes it easy," or "makes it easy to," or a similar expression. "Components" is a mouthful and is applicable, usually, only when referring to major components of a complex mechanical product—such as engines, transmissions, and axles are components of a motorized vehicle; or electrical components are actually complete subassemblies used in a product.

"When the necessity arises" is clumsy, stilted, and hard to read. Instead, say "when you have to," or "when it's time to," or even "when necessary." "Simultaneous" is a mouthful, "at the same time" is longer, but easier to read.

You can think of scores of long clichés that you should avoid, and skimming the trade magazines will unearth scores more. Eliminate them and you shorten your copy, make it easier to read, and breathe life into it at the same time. You don't do it simultaneously, not in an ad, anyhow.

> *Continuing fundamental research; nationwide technical coverage; revolutionary technological developments; diversified distributive pattern; maximum dependability; adjustable feature eliminates expensive alterations; revolutionary productivity concept; confirmed maximum material utilization; original installation quotation; economically eliminated multiple machining operations; automatically compensate; consistent and continuous innovation; technological breakthrough; unvarying structural uniformity; obsolescence-eliminating sequential operation.*

Those are phrases, or possibly even thoughts if anybody could think like that, taken from various ads in the same issue of *Foundry*. Repeat—ads. Ads should be easier to read than editorial. The ones containing this gobbledygook were infinitely more difficult to read than *Foundry's* editorial material, for it's very professional. But shouldn't ads be?

Even after reading some of these ads, it's not really very apparent what a "confirmed maximum material utilization" was, although with some hard work it's possible to interpret this as meaning that use of the product by a certain customer results in less waste of raw material and more finished product from the same, or less, raw material. Gunning would have had a tough time determining what educational level was necessary to comprehend that one.

The trouble is, it's actually darned hard work to write like that. Some writers work harder making their job hard than they do at the job itself. Their companies, clients, and agencies get short-changed.

And "economically eliminated multiple machining operations" could have been said, "did the job a new way . . . with less machine time, at lower cost." Which communicates?

Enough of the things not to do. Short words are powerful words, and some of the most potent ones you can use—should use—whenever the opportunity arises are these:

Free	*Cut*	*Facts*	*Here*
New	*Compare*	*End*	*Find*
How to	*You*	*Stop*	*Now*
Easy	*Your*	*Put*	*Try*
Fast	*Learn*	*Wanted*	*Check*
Quick	*Earn*	*Improved*	*Gain*
Offer	*Plug*	*Get*	*Profit*

Power words aren't all one syllable, but they're commonplace, easily understood words that never slow down reading. Greatest grabbers of attention for headlines are the first two—*free* and *new*. Both give a promise in one short word—something for nothing, to which none of us is the least bit averse, and the implication that the something new is actually something better, something that will help the reader. The others are promise-words, action-words, motivating-words that produce a response. Use them well and wisely and they'll produce for you.

Short Sentences

The average person in industry is addicted to using long sentences.

We've already touched briefly on the fact that long sentences make copy difficult to read, just as long words do. As a rule, when you encounter one you'll find the other, because both are cherished by the same type of writer.

A good rule is that a sentence should never be longer than 15 words. Sentences of 15 words or less enable a writer to say exactly what he means. Succinct writing helps the reader. He finds it simple and easy to read, so he reads it.

Adhering slavishly to the 15-word rule isn't a panacea. It's not a secret formula for success. In fact, it's a pitfall. Follow it religiously, make every sentence 14, 15, or 16 words long, and you'll have copy so unbelievably monotonous there's an odds-on chance it'll put you to sleep while you're writing it. People in droves will skip it, even if they won't stop to reason why.

Just for the fun of it, write a short piece of copy on any subject or product that pops into your mind, even a hobby or favorite sport. Write about 10 or 12 sentences and deliberately make them all approximately the same length, about 15 words. This may require a bit of doing. But when you're finished, read what you've written and see how stilted it sounds and how incredibly dull it is. You'll notice immediately that it's completely lacking in the spark that would make a total stranger want to read past the first three or four sentences.

There's no question that short sentences are desirable in advertising copy. To overcome the monotony of sameness, vary the length. One short, one long—but not alternated so often that you create *another* pattern which repels the mind and eye.

Also, it's desirable to alter the basic structure of your sentences. You'll find, for example, it's best to have a number of simple sentences one after the other. Then break the pattern by inserting a complex sentence and follow it with several simple ones. A compound-complex sentence relieves tedium, and, if followed with an extremely short sentence, is immensely effective. An extremely short sentence is visually attractive. It telegraphs a single thought. It punctuates. It creates a bridge. The short sentence channels thoughts straight into the next sequence of ideas, and emphasizes the most important. Use it.

Almost all of the ads illustrated and quoted as good examples of how copy should read use short words, short sentences. And they have varied sentence length and structure to avoid a humdrum sameness.

In a way, copy is much like music. Copy should have a definite beat, a rhythm that you can almost feel. Many people are under the impression that only poetry has rhythm. This isn't so.

On the contrary, good copy should have a beat, a bounce, a cadence that can be felt. One way to write copy that moves rhythmically is to tap it out on your desk with a pencil, just as if you were a drummer in a jazz band.

An example of rhythm in copy is a headline for an old ad for Diamond T trucks. Use your hand and drum it out on the desk. *Feel* the beat.

Diamond T diesels meter the minutes for Motor Cargo's Midnight Chief.

That's a long headline. And to those not familiar with highway freight hauling, it's an obscure one. But to those in the know who are aware that diesel engines have fuel metered to them by an intricate fuel pump which corresponds to a car's carburetor, it says something. It says even more to truckers who delight in reading and talking about hot operations on a tight timetable. This carrier's Midnight Chief run is known, respected and admired. Motor Cargo's Diamond T diesels tallied up a thousand miles a day, 350,000 miles a year, on that haul. Engines were shut off four hours a month for preventive maintenance, otherwise the rigs ran 'round the clock with shifts of drivers. As tightly knit as the trucking industry is, word about equipment performance on that operation circulated fast. The ad was unusually well read, due in part to a rhythmic headline with short words, and copy with short sentences that said something of interest to the readers.

Short Paragraphs

Sparkling copy with everything going for it can be killed deader than the Edsel by improper paragraphing.

Paragraphing doesn't even have to be improper in a sense that's ungrammatical, or that the breaks come at just the wrong times in the sequence of thoughts. Merely having the paragraphs too long can ruin an ad. Readership goes down fast as paragraph length goes up.

Overly long paragraphs are as grim and forbidding as a Mexican jail. They never fail to give the impression that their contents will require vast effort and grim, single-minded concentration by the reader if he's to wade through and assimilate the information they contain. As the art directors and typographers are fond of saying, long paragraphs look "soggy."

By this they mean there's so much type with so little "air"—or open white space left by the paragraph breaks—that the type seems to be set solid. Type set solid represents hard work. It's reminiscent of a textbook on a dull subject, or of some impossibly tedious memorandum from the engineers about product features.

You can avoid having ads that cause readers to beat a hasty retreat to the sanctuary of more easily read ads by writing short paragraphs.

Short paragraphs open up a copy block.

They make it inviting.

When judiciously mixed, short and long, the copy looks as if it would be fun to read.

And read it is, read by almost 17 percent more readers than is soggy, visually unattractive copy. Numerous studies over the years have left no doubt on this score.

Let's look at a few examples.

Of course, we can skip the example preceding this sentence—where the copy on the page of this book was deliberately opened up with short paragraphs and plenty of white space—and look only at ads.

Here's the entire first paragraph of a one-page, two-color ad in the current issue of *Commercial Car Journal,* the magazine of fleet management.

> *Unique Victocor "200" gaskets help compensate for mating surface defects automatically. That's because they have "soft-sealing" faces made of a special asbestos-rubber compound packing that is permanently bonded to a thin steel core with continuous tangs penetrating each surface. This exclusive construction gives the compressibility, resiliency, and stability to seal even irregular heads correctly.*

The fog swirls in, dank and dense and impenetrable in that opening paragraph. It's too long, it contains far too many multisyllable words, and it's devoid of the spark which breathes life and interest into copy. Throw in the fact that the copywriter couldn't resist the temptation to lapse into latter-20th-century businessese—that compressibility bit—and you have a piece of copy that's in an ad that cost around $800 to produce, one that occupies a page in the leading fleet book at a cost of approximately $1,000—and mighty few readers read it.

Too long, too soggy, too many four-dollar words. Gaskets aren't sold to doctors of philosophy, or even to presidents of giant trucking companies. They're sold to maintenance superintendents, foremen, and head mechanics. Educational background of these prime buying influences hasn't prepared them to absorb *rapidly* and *easily* copy of this fog level. And if they can't absorb it rapidly and easily, they'll flip. To another ad, that is. As mentioned before, nobody *works* at ad reading.

Here's a rewrite of this ad. Granted, it probably isn't the best that could be done—but it was rewritten only once. The first whack around follows, with no polishing, no intense effort. But read it for content, then notice how the short paragraphs open up the copy, let in some air, and impart visual appeal.

> *Only Victocor "200" gaskets make mating surfaces mate perfectly. Every time.*
>
> *They do it automatically and easily. Surface defects don't matter. Forget them.*
>
> *These gaskets are in a class by themselves. They have soft-sealing faces. And they're made of our special asbestos-rubber compound packing.*
>
> *It really stands the gaff.*
>
> *The compound is bonded for life to a strong, thin steel core. A row of tangs all around the gasket penetrates each surface.*
>
> *Wild horses couldn't pull 'em apart.*
>
> *Yet the gaskets compress easily, are resilient and stable so they seal right every time—even with irregular heads.*

Or consider this one, also from *CCJ*, which starts with leaders (...):

> *. . . just name your holding device—from simple, carburetor-holding legs through diesel engine stands capable of handling a V-16 engine—chances are, Kent-Moore supplies it. This includes such items as differential repair stands, piston and valve racks, transmission mounting brackets. Also transmission holding fixtures for bench work, differential carrier holders and transmission jacks. And, of course, diesel engine parts racks.*

This (whew!) lead-in paragraph, which is supposed to clutch the reader by stating a premise with which he'd automatically agree, then launch into the selling message, is a flop. It falls flat. It's preceded by an illustration of a pair of suspenders and the headline: *This is about the only holding device Kent-Moore doesn't supply.* In itself, this headline is hardly enough to cause lightheadedness.

Long, dull, and advertiser-oriented, a long recitation of a list of products the manufacturer supplies. And nary a hint of a user benefit to lure the reader into reading past the first paragraph—if, indeed, he read even a third of it.

Now, let's look at an advertisement that doesn't suffer from long-paragraphitis, hence is appealing and attractive and downright inviting. Naturally, a typewriter is somewhat removed from transmission mounting brackets, but it's still a tool used by business and industry. And it must do the same thing as any other tool—be used to produce a profit.

And, when all is said and done, it must be sold to buying influences who are somewhat similar. Remarkably few office managers, chief accountants, or controllers, who seem to get involved in purchases of almost every mechanical thing used in offices, are noted for being particularly eleemosynary.

Royal Typewriter's ad reflects the growing influence of consumer advertising on industrial advertising. This striking four-color ad appeared in *Business Week* and in *Business Management,* media selected to reach the executive level in business and industry. The ad is clean, attractive, and it sells hard. It's highly competitive. After all, Royal has a giant competitor who has long dominated this field. Copy reads:

If you want the best of today's leading electrics . . . COMPARE ALL TWO

That's right. All two.

There are just two leaders in the office typewriter field. Royal is one of them. (Most people know the other company by its initials.)

You see one of the reasons for this leadership here. The Royal 660. The all-new 660 is Royal's first office electric since we joined Litton Industries. There's a lot here to see—and to compare.

The keyboard of the 660 might look the same as the typewriter with three initials, but it's way ahead in performance. It's designed to make your secretary more efficient.

If you want the best of today's leading electrics...

Compare all two

That's right. All two.

There are just two leaders in the office typewriter field. Royal is one of them. (Most people know the other company by its initials.)

You see one of the reasons for this leadership here. The Royal 660. The all-new 660 is Royal's first office electric since we joined Litton Industries. There's a lot here to see—and to compare.

The keyboard of the 660 might look the same as the typewriter with three initials, but it's way ahead in performance. It's designed to make your secretary more efficient.

Instead of six, there are eight repeat control functions for greater speed. And if she should make a mistake, we've added a half-forward spacer for fast corrections.

Then compare the printwork. Originals are never punctured and you get clear, readable copies every time. That's because the 660 automatically computes the number of carbons fed into it, then automatically adjusts itself for perfect impact.

Have your secretary compare the Royal 660 with the brand that used to be best.

Royal will show her something better.

ROYAL ⊞ ROYAL TYPEWRITER COMPANY, INC.
A DIVISION OF LITTON INDUSTRIES

Instead of six, there are eight repeat control functions for greater speed. And if she should make a mistake, we've added a half-forward spacer for fast correction.

> *Then compare the printwork. Originals are never punc-
> tured and you get clear, readable copies every time. That's
> because the 660 automatically computes the number of
> carbons fed into it, then automatically adjusts itself for
> perfect impact.*
>
> *Have your secretary compare the Royal 660 with the
> brand that used to be best.*
>
> *Royal will show her something better.*

This copyriter knew what he wanted to say and he said it effectively. Note how quickly he translated features into believable
benefits. For example, "eight repeat control functions for greater
speed." The busy executive can make a fast mental translation of
that into higher productivity, more work done per day. And "we've
added a half-forward spacer for fast corrections." That creates a
mental image of no wasted time, more letters turned out in less
time—and letters that look better, too.

Short words, short sentences, short paragraphs—and highly
readable copy. And none of this "...............ibility" nonsense which
pervades industry, cherished by engineers and technical men because
it gives them the capability of exploiting the "obscuribility" of the
language they're using since they're unable to say it simply.

Be Specific

Generalities in copy are like dead mackerel in the moonlight. They
glitter, but they also smell.

Vague, half-though-out ideas and a school of nonspecifics waft
toward the reader an unprepossessing aroma of something he instinctively realizes he'll want to avoid because there's nothing he
wants in it for him.

A number of times we've touched briefly on the importance of
being specific. This can't be stressed too hard. Nonspecifics say
nothing of any interest to anybody except the advertiser. And there
are many ways he can talk to himself without paying for the
privilege.

Just one or two examples prove the point so thoroughly that even
the most hard-bitten doubter from Missouri won't have to be shown
more than these to become a true believer.

One example is a second-cover, two-color ad in *Precision Metal*
magazine, placed by Aluminum Smelting & Refining Co., Inc. The
copy—all of it—reads:

Uniform quality ingots

Rigid alloy control through use of the quantometer as a production tool . . . personnel with years of know-how real pride in our product—all these factors assure you uniform quality aluminum ingots.

These modern production methods assure continuous precision production in your plant.

Ingot after ingot . . . bundle after bundle . . . shipment after shipment—you will always find the same uniform quality.

Your confidence in the use of a uniform quality ingot has made our continuous expansion possible.

There's remarkably little specific information in that copy, there's little or nothing to pique the imagination, nothing to arouse curiosity, nothing in the nature of a reward for the reader if for some unknown reason he should happen to read this copy. And all of those leaders and dashes clash madly with each other; give the impression that this copy isn't actually copy, but an unrelated collection of generalities that bear little relationship to each other.

Then, Alloys and Chemicals Corporation, in a four-color ad in the same book, says in its copy:

When time is a factor and quality is a must . . .

Centuries of accuracy from the fleur-de-lis-clock; years of dependable service from Alloys and Chemicals; yet our industry demands something more . . . prompt Delivery and Consistent Quality . . .

. . . only part of our Service . . . in both aluminum and zinc at Alloys and Chemicals. Round the clock production backed by the industries' most modern warehouse enables you to receive our product to your quality specification and your production requirements.

The rest . . . take a minute to call . . . our sales engineers and technical staff are available for consultation.

Vaguewise, as advertising men are supposed to say, that ad stands above all others. That's the entire body copy, headline, and all of the information offered to the reader. Immediate reaction, of course, is why read it? It's hard to understand just how copy like that could help the reader on his job.

As if it's not ineffective enough because it's so nonspecific, the copy-writer felt compelled for some obscure reason to clutter up the copy with leaders at the drop of a hat—or, perhaps, even at the *thought* of the drop of a hat. Too, for some obscure reason that's impossible to fathom, he felt he had to capitalize "Delivery, Consistent Quality, and Service." Add the fact that "industries'" should have been "industry's," singular, and it's a pathetic situation. The dollars spent on this ad aren't working for Alloys and Chemicals Corporation.

The problem isn't new, however. Nonspecific copy has been around about as long as advertising itself.

A classic example of copy that doesn't actually say anything is Ned Jordan's ad, "Somewhere West of Laramie." Many will throw up their hands in horror and cry loudly that this is little short of heresy, for this is a famous ad, acclaimed as one of the greatest ever written. But it gives not one iota of information about the automobile it's talking about. The copy is composed of vague generalities, pretty word-pictures, imaginative analogies and overworked clichés.

Perhaps there's no real need to discuss the car's engine—cubic inches of displacement, horsepower, the reduction each gear of the transmission provides, rear axle ratio, foot-pounds of torque at the rear wheels, or the steering geometry. Even if this is the case, however, wouldn't the ad have been infinitely stronger if it had given readers information—real, solid information they could think about and retain and use for comparing the car with competitive ones? As is, the ad relies entirely on emotional appeal, and that's not enough for a big-ticket item.

Judge for yourself. Headline and body copy follow.

SOMEWHERE WEST OF LARAMIE

Somewhere west of Laramie there's a bronco-busting, steer-roping girl who knows what I'm talking about. She can tell what a sassy pony, that's a cross between greased lightning and the place where it hits, can do with eleven hundred pounds of steel and action when he's going high, wide and handsome.

The truth is—the Playboy was built for her.

Built for the lass whose face is brown with the sun when day is done of revel and romp and race.

She loves the cross of the wild and the tame.

There's a savor of links about that car—of laughter and lilt and light—a hint of old loves—and saddle and quirt. It's a brawny thing—yet a graceful thing for the sweep o' the Avenue.

Step into the Playboy when the hour grows dull with things gone dead and stale.

Then start for the land of real living with the spirit of the lass who rides, lean and rangy, into the red horizon of a Wyoming twilight.

Now let's read a piece of copy that *is* specific, that *does* give the reader helpful information. It's an unusually attractive one-page, black-and-white ad run by Dana Corporation in *Automotive Industries*. The illustration combines a bird's eye view of a happy little girl merrily playing hopscotch with an extreme closeup of a brawny hand holding the shift lever of a heavy-duty truck transmission. Copy, starting with the headline, goes:

Spicer makes child's play of 16 speed shifting

New single-stick shift for 8500 series transmissions shifts with almost "light truck" ease. Now your drivers can shift through normal sequences from start to top speed with only four moves of one shift lever. They make all other shifts by merely flicking the splitter air control to the next position, then releasing and reengaging the clutch.

Drivers will also appreciate the added control they have over their vehicles, regardless of road and traffic conditions. They can downshift from top road speed to 35 mph without moving the shift lever. They can keep one hand on the steering wheel at all times, keep their full attention on the road, with no need to reach for a second lever.

You will enjoy the benefits of reduced maintenance and repair downtime, too. There are no complicated rear-unit mechanical shift controls to adjust, and the air shift controls will help eliminate driver errors.

For further information about this new "single-stick"

compound transmission, and other fine Spicer driveline components, write . . .

To the uninitiated, this isn't real nuts-and-bolts copy, but to the fleet operator there's plenty of food for thought there. Shifting, especially with two shift levers, is enough to try the patience of a saint—and enough to sap the energy of the hardiest truck jockey.

Obviously the less shifting that's required, the less physical energy the driver must expend. A reduction of physical labor results in drivers who are more productive, and, because they're less tired, drivers who are more alert and who drive more safely.

Dana Corporation has something good going for them here. Benefits are illustrated, described, and then the promise of less maintenance is dangled enticingly like the icing on a cake. This is giving the reader specifics that are important to him.

Copy can contain specifics and still not do a job if it's full of puffery, if it's dull and uninspired, if it plods and preaches. An example of such copy written for Lindberg Hevi-Duty by a former agency follows:

Machine-gun speeds for die and wire bonding

It's revolutionary. You get up to 800 eutectic die bonds an hour or 4000 wire bonds an hour with these new Lindberg Hevi-Duty die- and wire-bonding systems. One reason . . . an exclusive belt-and-cartridge transport system.

More than this, bonding is uniquely rapid and reliable. There's not another machine that can touch it in performance. Bonding force, temperature, and protective atmosphere gas-flow are all controlled automatically. A binocular microscope keeps work clearly in view at all times through a mirror linked to needle movement that tracks the action.

Modular design permits fast optional changeover between pilot line and laboratory use. For complete information see your Lindberg Hevi-Duty sales engineer. Or write . . .

At the start specifics are overshadowed by the headline that exaggerates the speed with which the equipment operates. Cyclic rate of a heavy machine gun is on the order of 600 rounds a minute, far in excess of the rate at which this equipment turns out work. Exaggeration doesn't convince. Then, there's the opening sentence

Fastest bond anywhere. Even faster than 007!

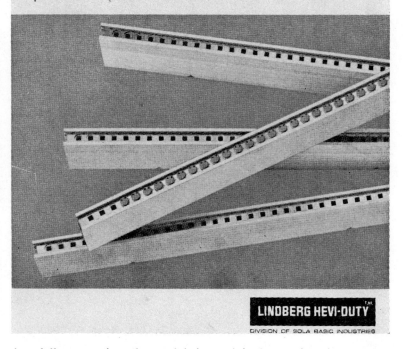

Take your pick. 800 eutectic die bonds an hour. Or 4000 wire bonds. That's what you get with Lindberg Hevi-Duty's new die- and wire-bonding systems.

Lindberg Hevi-Duty's exclusive belt-and-cartridge system makes this speed possible. Feeds work through like a belt of ammo going through a machine gun. And you get this trouble-free transport system only from Lindberg Hevi-Duty.

You can rely on bonds this system produces. They're right. No other machine even comes close to the performance Lindberg Hevi-Duty builds into this one. Bonding force, temperature and protective atmos-phere gas-flow are all controlled automatically.

A high-quality binocular microscope shows the work razor sharp. It's always in view. Through a mirror linked to needle movement, the 'scope tracks the action.

Lindberg Hevi-Duty's modular design takes the time and trouble out of converting to pilot line or lab use, if you'd like.

If you want a bond so fast that James looks slow, get it. Install Lindberg Hevi-Duty's die- and wire-bonding system.

The full story's in Bulletin 94122. It's yours for the asking. Lindberg Hevi-Duty, Watertown, Wis. 53094.

LINDBERG HEVI-DUTY T.M.

DIVISION OF SOLA BASIC INDUSTRIES

that falls somewhat short of being original—or, for that matter, specific, convincing or believable.

Copy in the Lindberg Hevi-Duty ad above was written by the advertising manager. It says essentially the same thing, but with

491

sparkle, style, and a lighter touch to captivate readers, not clobber them, and to intrigue them into reading and remembering.

That this was a successful ad is beyond doubt. Product people for this line of equipment reported, somewhat defensively at first, that "everybody's talking about that James Bond ad." When it was pointed out that people talked about it because they read it and remembered it, proving it made a definite impression, the attitude changed to one of enthusiasm. It's interesting to note that ads are remembered far longer than seems possible in some instances. After this ad was run for the last time, customers and prospects brought it up in conversation with manufacturer salesmen for almost a year. This ad worked hard. Copy follows:

Fastest bond anywhere. Even faster than 007!

Take your pick. 800 eutectic die bonds an hour. Or 4000 wire bonds. That's what you get with Lindberg Hevi-Duty's new die- and wire-bonding systems.

Lindberg Hevi-Duty's exclusive belt-and-cartridge system makes this speed possible. Feeds work through like a belt of ammo going through a machine gun. And you get this trouble-free transport system only from Lindberg Hevi-Duty.

You can rely on bonds this system produces. They're right. No other machine even comes close to the performance Lindberg Hevi-Duty builds into this one. Bonding force, temperature, and protective atmosphere gas-flow are all controlled automatically.

A high-quality binocular microscope shows the work razor sharp. It's always in view. Through a mirror linked to needle movement, the 'scope tracks the action.

Lindberg Hevi-Duty's modular design takes the time and trouble out of converting to pilot line or lab use, if you'd like.

If you want a bond so fast that James looks slow, get it. Install Lindberg Hevi-Duty's die- and wire-bonding system.

The full story's in Bulletin 12345. It's yours for the asking.

The headline and the next to last paragraph made the ad memorable.

Be specific and you're helping the reader. Help him and he reads, remembers, and is partially sold by the ad. It's that simple.

Avoid Participles

Participial writing is weak writing.

A participle, according to Webster, is a word that partakes of the nature of both a verb and an adjective. An English verb has two participles—(1) the present, in which words end in *ing,* as in writing, talking, analyzing, and evaluating, and, (2) the past, or perfect, variation of the word; usually this version ends in *ed, d, t, en,* or *n,* as in posted, worked, proved, kept, written, proven, taken.

One major indictment which can be laid at the door of the participle is that when participles are used, verbs are not. Without verbs, writing is wishy-washy, weak, drab, and passive.

Verbs are action words. They are inherently strong and masculine. They connote doing something, taking a course of action, making decisions, moving, giving the heave-ho to the status quo. Verbs strengthen copy. They impart a sense of immediacy, heighten interest, arouse curiosity to see what is going to *happen* next. Verbs impel people to react to your copy—to do what you want them to.

Let's look at a few participles and participle-filled ads and see why the copy is weak and without vigor or bite.

In *Foundry* magazine The Fremont Flask Company starts an ad:

> *Foundrymen are discovering that this newly developed Guide is reducing scrap from shifts as much as 40% on perennial difficult jobs.*

Style is mass-appeal, impersonal, short on reader involvement; there's no *you* in the first sentence of the copy, only the all-inclusive foundrymen. Also, "are discovering" and "is reducing" is weak writing. How much more impact the copy would have had if it had started:

> *You'll find this new Guide is a money-maker. It reduces scrap from shifts up to 40%—even on the tough jobs.*

Or we can go a step farther and improve it still more. Compare this version with the pallid original:

> *You can reduce scrap from shifts up to 40% with this new Guide.*

Verbosity is out. Instead of 21 words, there are 13. And the opening sentence says the same thing, but says what the advertiser *wanted* to say, not to be confused with what he *thought* he'd said.

Furthermore, the copy is punchier, more direct, and more easily understood. That's because those participles aren't there to becloud the issue in a haze of foggy prose that doesn't say anything.

With the opening set right, all that remains to be done is to explain why this new Guide reduces scrap. That done, the copy will be believed and the ad will score points with readers.

Here's a stray sentence from an ad in the same book, this one in an ad run by International and Hough:

> *Their busy foundry keeps six Pay Loaders working full time, handling sand, loading coke, charging hoppers—even snow removal.*

There's information there, and since this is from a testimonial ad, it's sure to carry conviction. But effectiveness of the ad would have been greatly increased if the copy had been rewritten somewhat along this line:

> *Their busy foundry works six Pay Loaders full time. The Hough Pay Loaders do 'most everything—handle sand, load coke, charge hoppers—even remove snow.*

This sentence has a greater sense of immediacy. It's stronger because the verbs are there to impart a sense of action and accomplishment to what is said about the equipment. No "working, handling, loading, or charging"—instead, the foundry *works* the machines; they *handle* sand, *load* coke, *charge* hoppers, *remove* snow. This copy makes the equipment look busy, it shows it's being used constantly on various jobs, in contrast to the participle-filled copy that didn't give that impression nearly as strongly.

And the superfluous participle weakens a statement; forgo this construction. Add the extra participle and you lengthen copy, slow down reading, use the limited space in the ad to detract from your copy instead of strengthening it. Trade books are full of horrible examples. There's little use in belaboring the point to death, for one or two examples will suffice. Here's one from *Precision Metal* magazine:

> *Today . . . right now . . . more castings are being handled on MAY-FRAN hinged-steel conveyors than on all similar types of equipment added together.*

Eliminate the one word "being"—just eliminate it and leave the copy as it is then—and see how much stronger the sentence is. It gains a sense of immediacy and gains strength because the verb "handled" stands on its own feet without a qualifier.

Today . . . right now . . . more castings are handled on MAY-FRAN hinged-steel conveyors than on all similar types of equipment added together.

And this one here may establish new standards for unnecessary use of participles:

Now . . . handling of deburring and finishing operations by providing processing flexibility . . .

There's no need to continue. The *ings* are seemingly without end.

In vivid contrast is Sealed Power Corporation's fine two-color ad which ran in the automotive aftermarket trade books. It's short, punchy, filled with verbs to give the reader a feeling of action. The copy concentrates on the first indication the motorist has that something's not quite up to snuff in his car's power plant—the fact that the engine throws out a cloud of blue smoke due to oil consumption. Copy then tells how the product, Sealed Power stainless-steel piston rings, solves it. The copy reads:

Stop smoking *right now!*

It's easy.

Install a Sealed Power KromeX ring set. With Stainless Steel oil rings. The job's done right. You've stopped smoking, stopped oil consumption.

And this ring job lasts. Stainless Steel doesn't pit or etch due to acids and gases. It stays smooth, doesn't collect carbon, resists plugging.

Sealed Power uses a special process—electro-polishing— to remove tiny burrs, smooth out rough spots. Deposits don't have a chance to build up.

And Stainless Steel, in Sealed Power's proven design, retains its original tension at operating temperatures. Fit lasts, side-sealing lasts, oil control lasts. Who could ask for more?

Product benefits the service station owner, auto dealer, or independent repair-garage owner can expect his customer—the car owner—to derive from use of Sealed Power Stainless Steel oil rings are spelled out right down the line. They're logical, believable, and convincing. Copy is easy to read, and since there are no hordes of participles to weaken it and to slow the reader's absorption of the message.

Although the author wrote this ad some years ago, it's still satisfying.

The Cult of the Superlative

Face it: Everything your company manufactures is *not* unequalled, revolutionary, unexcelled, unique, the world's best, finest yet, the most outstanding, sensational, fantastic, unbelievable, amazing, or the absolute living end.

It's very possible the product you're talking about in your copy simply doesn't qualify for even one of these overworked superlatives. But even if it honestly does—in your opinion—can you convince readers of this? If not, you've lost ground by making a claim that, to the reader, is sheer puffery.

For far too many years now we've all been assaulted by a barrage of superlatives and exaggerated claims for everything from typewriter ribbons to putty knives. Far too few claims were ever proven to the satisfaction of the objective reader—and he's the guy who *wants* to be sold.

If the claim concerns something outside the personal experience of the reader, if it's made about a product with which he's unfamiliar, if it's blatantly obvious that the claim is made to benefit the advertiser, or if the copywriter simply threw in superlatives to "strengthen" the ad, it's a lost cause you have on your hands. Reconcile yourself to it.

As the late, great jazz trombonist Jack Teagarden sang in one of his classic recordings back in the '30's, ". . . don't start lying, I never cared for fiction . . . speak real clear, don't want no friction with your diction."

No reputable company would dream of deliberately misrepresenting its product in an advertisement or in sales literature. However, excessive use of superlatives and/or gross exaggeration certainly *looks* like unmitigated prevarication to the reader, so the result is about the same. Tax his credulity and you've probably lost him as a potential customer. The business world is made up of well-informed, well-read individuals who have a vast experience with almost every product on the market, even with those very similar to the revolutionary, supersensational, all-new Widget of Tomorrow that's being introduced today just to give the lucky customer a break.

The business-press readers can't be snowed. This is not 1890.

Superlatives don't have to be expressed as such; for example, use of too many superlatives starts in the headline of Hathaway Instruments' two-color ad in *Electronic Packaging & Production* maga-. zine. It reads:

> *Whatever the switching assignment . . . Hathaway Form "C" miniature Drireed relays can do it!*

Even knowing precious little about just what it is that Form "C" miniature Drireed relays can do, this claim is just too much to swallow. "Whatever the assignment" is too all-encompassing. Some-where, somebody surely has to have an assignment that *no* existing piece of equipment, electronic or otherwise, will handle. Technology changes too fast for such sweeping claims. All they can accomplish is to encourage disbelief of legitimate user benefits of the product.

Body copy of Hathaway's ad is short, but it doesn't offer proof to back up the claim made in the headline; it consists of bulleted generalities, and reads:

> *Problems with your small form "C" reed relays?*
>
> *Hathaway's true form "C" Drireed relay is your answer!*
>
> - *High reliability*
> - *Consistent contact resistance*
> - *Operating speeds up to 500 Hz.*
> - *True break before make*
> - *Short bounce characteristics on normally closed contact*
> - *Uniform long life*

Some advertisers who claim too much, and thus run the risk of having their copy considered exaggerations have said in recent ads:

> *Ulano is the leading manufacturer of screen process stencil film . . . any kind!*

Undoubtedly this is a statement of fact. Ulano probably does pace the pack, but this headline in lieu of an illustration fails to impart believability to the claim. Body copy does nothing to reinforce or prove to the reader that the claim is a valid one, nor does it present to him a user benefit he can retain after he's through reading the ad. Entire body copy follows:

> *In screen processing of complex printed circuitry . . .
> there's no margin for error! That's why Ulano offers a
> complete line of Screen Process Stencil Films especially
> designed for the Electronics Industry.*

The entire copy, headline and all, for Universal Engineering
Company's full-page ad in *Metalworking* states:

> *Universal has the most complete selection of precision-
> made jig and fixture components in the United States.*

Granted, this may very well represent a valid communications
objective—to establish acceptance of Universal as the biggest single
source for jigs and fixture components. If so, and if the objective *is*
valid, then the copy does a job. However, if the ad is other than
part of a well-planned campaign created to achieve specific objectives, the copy is pure brag and boast and is distressingly advertiser-
oriented at that.

Incidentally, when using an absolute term or a very specific item
of information in an ad, you must be certain that it is correct. Many
an industrial advertising manager has found to his regret that use
of such terminology opens a Pandora's box of messy ills in the
form of possible legal action by a dissatisfied purchaser of the
product. This character can be depended upon to triumphantly
produce the very ad that *promised* in print exactly what he feels he
didn't get.

Be particularly careful about use of words like these:

Never	*Certain*
Foolproof	*Positive*
Fail-safe	*Always*
Can't fail	*Invariably*
Impossible	*Will*

Refer to the instruction manual, descriptive plates giving rated
capacities, engineering drawings, and other reference sources that
are beyond question for your information. Even then, check it out
with the technical people for accuracy.

Even a tiny connotation of something undesirable can set the
legal eagles loose to pounce upon an innocent, unsuspecting advertising manager, even though he is pure in heart as all ad managers
are.

Several years ago the author hired a photographer in another city by long-distance phone to photograph a new heavy-duty motor truck. The truck was delayed several weeks in production because a photograph was needed for a new-product advertisement to run in a number of fleet publications; if the picture hadn't been urgently needed, the truck would have been produced on schedule. This is known as Stansfield's law, a variation on Murphy's law that when time is a critical factor anything that *can* go wrong *will* go wrong. It usually enters the picture when deadlines are either at hand, or else when you're on an extension from publications in which the ad will run.

Anyhow, this photographer followed instructions. And he did the job immediately. He made sure the proud new owner's name, ICC permit numbers, gross weight, tire size and other necessary data were lettered appropriately on the driver's door, and that the tractor and trailer were both washed immaculately clean—at a cost of $45.00 for the wash job alone.

He then led the owner-driver out to a picturesque spot on a local road at the edge of the city and took a well-lighted, well-composed picture. Huge, spreading elm trees (without Dutch elm disease) formed a pleasing background. All in all, the picture was quite satisfactory. The rig looked like it was running down the road, busily working. So it was put into production without delay; copy had been written, checked, cleared, and approved beforehand, the type had been set, so no time was lost on that score.

The ad was effective. It induced a highly satisfactory volume of reader response and 11 known sales were traced to it—nine tractors and two straight trucks for a total selling price of something over $135,000.

Only one insignificant thing went wrong. In one corner of the background behind the parked tractor-trailer, shaded by those magnificent elm trees, was a portion of a cemetery. This was noticed at the time, but was not considered objectionable because it was far from being a dominant element in the picture. In fact, the cemetery was hardly visible. And, after all, cemeteries *do* exist and we all know what they're used for.

The owner-driver of the new rig had a soul filled with larceny. He thought he saw a golden opportunity to turn a fast buck without working for it, so he retained an attorney to sue the company. The company was protected with a signed, witnessed model release giving it permission to use the photograph of the tractor-trailer and/ or any driver or other person connected with its operation for any legitimate advertising, sales promotion, public relations, or other use—as is customary. The photographer had gotten the release signed, as instructed to do, had given the driver the traditional dollar remuneration for signing, and had the signature witnessed by a nearby owner of a service station. But the owner-driver's attorney claimed that his client was held up to ridicule due to the cemetery's being in the picture, that the connotation was so negative that the poor, hapless, helpless individual stood to lose untold huge sums of money from revenue lost because he drove a "cemetery truck."

Attorneys for the manufacturer ran a strong bluff and convinced the attorney for the plaintiff that they were perfectly willing to make a major investment in time and money to win the case. So, as it turned out, the hungry trucker received nothing except a bill from an attorney who was willing to press a case for which there was little hope in the first place.

Moral of the story is you can't be too careful about what you say and show in an ad—and always have model releases—*always*—and have *written* clearance from customers whom you quote in an ad, or whose equipment or place of business you illustrate. A slip here could be very costly in money and deucedly damaging to the ad manager's reputation.

Here, incidentally, is a model release form that will hold up in court and protect your company and your good name as a professional in the business.

Date..

MODEL RELEASE

It is hereby mutually agreed between (individual's name), for compensation received and acknowledged, hereafter referred to as the undersigned, and Smith Widget Manufacturing Company may do as follows:

1. Smith Widget Manufacturing Company, its agents, representatives, or assigns may take or have taken still photographs and/or moving pictures of the undersigned while he or she is at work, connected with the operation

   of Smith equipment, or on the premises owned or operated by ....

   ....

2. Smith Widget Manufacturing Company may use, publish, reproduce, retouch, or declare the photographs and/or moving pictures for any legitimate purpose without restriction.

_____

(individual's signature)

_____

(signature of witness)

Another superlative—maximum—doesn't really say anything to anybody, but it does encourage disbelief and skipping over the ad to one that doesn't strain the reader's credulity.

Rockford Machine Tool Company claims in a headline:

Rockford Mills provide maximum capability

That headline isn't a grabber because the superlative has been worked to death for so many years it no longer communicates anything of significance. The headline would have received far higher readership, as would the body copy that follows, if it had given some specific fact which would benefit the reader. It could have claimed essentially the same thing, of course.

And just what is maximum capability? Was it ever measured? Has it ever been achieved? How can it be recognized if it is? Do you know? Does Rockford Machine Tool Company know?

Pompous eloquence and bombastic prose reach the height of absurdity in today's automobile advertising. Apparently the impression is harbored in Detroit that the average American is a full-sized person with the intellectual attainments of a not-too-bright second-grader. Superlatives abound, unsupported claims run rampant. If they were mad dogs in a city, it would panic. The assumption is made that every reader is completely aware of every feature of a car just because there have been ads on these features for periods ranging from a week to several years. 'Tain't so, Detroit.

A headline that really strains the imagination was run by Pontiac in one of the big, expensive consumer books. It proudly proclaimed that:

Learn the great American sport of Wide-Tracking
in a great American sports car

The car maker *must* be firmly convinced that every prospective purchaser is aware that Pontiac's front axle is a whisker wider than that on most of the competition, hence the car leaves a wide track. After all, the company's backing it with big money.

You really have to reach, though, to consider Wide-Tracking as a great American sport—on a par, say, with golf, trap, tennis, skeet, skiing, or hunting. Have you ever heard this question put to a group: "Wide-Tracking, anyone"? And to consider the typical Detroit convertible in the tradition of such great road machines as Jaguar, Mercedes 300SL, Allard, Ferrari, and Maserati wreaks sheer havoc with the imagination. Face it, Detroit: Pontiacs are as scarce at Le Mans and Sebring as boll-weevil boosters at the Cotton Growers' Ball.

Body copy abounds with superlatives and pretentious clichés which, it would seem, are supposed to communicate with a mass audience. It reads:

> *Wide-Tracking isn't hard to catch onto, once you've got the right equipment. And five of the most magnificent pieces of equipment around this year are those bearing the Pontiac Firebird emblem. All five models sport such new excellences as smoother riding rear suspension, upper-level ventilation system (eliminating the need for vent windows), and new stuff under the hood. But, if you think Wide-Tracking is just a rich man's sport, you'll learn a thing or two by taking a look at some of our magnificently demure price tags. You can choose anything from a 175-hp Firebird to a 330-hp Firebird 400, each with a bevy of new safety equipment (like padded armrests, front and rear side marker lights) that makes Wide-Tracking more secure than ever. Front-wheel disc brakes, 4-speed shift, mag-style wheels and stereo tape are among the decisions you'll have to make. But the first thing to learn is which one of the Magnificent Five Firebirds is for you. Drive one . . . it's a very educational experience.*

Nowhere is Wide-Tracking explained, although it's apparently regarded by the manufacturer as a prime user benefit. The word magnificent is hardly underplayed, and Pontiac actually *said* excellences. Honest to gosh.

The power of understatement isn't generally appreciated in the advertising world, more's the pity. Some of the strongest ads written don't come within shouting distance of superlatives, unsupported claims, or exaggerations which cause readers to cast a jaundiced eye at the copy—and the company. One of the better examples is shown (page 504), a fractional-page, black-and-white ad by Jones & Lamson, Division of Waterbury Farrel, a Textron Company—and even that impossibly long signature is handled tastefully in the small space. The copy says:

516 Crazy Holes to Control
. . . a J&L Optical Comparator does it
in 5 minutes. It used to take 3 days!

> *This gear is the heart of a Pitney-Bowes postage meter's "accounting system." Its accuracy is vital and must be*

spot-checked regularly for dimension drift, or tooth-form breakdown.

Pitney-Bowes, Inc. solved this production control nightmare —eliminated a serious bottleneck—with a Jones & Lamson Optical Comparator. Here's how they do it.

A gaging head contains two probes. One is the work probe that contacts the gear in the staging fixture. The other is the dummy probe which indicates position of the work probe and whose shadow is projected onto a special comparator chart. The position of this shadow provides the means to check the radial position and form of the gear teeth.

Inspection is accomplished in minutes instead of days! The entire production operation is monitored and kept on schedule.

For more information call your nearest Jones & Lamson office, or write us direct.

Jones & Lamson played it smart. The copy is without frills, it's simple and direct and filled with facts and user benefits. The advertising manager is obviously aware that neither superlatives, nor exaggerations, nor hysterical flag waving for the good old company makes an impression—other than a negative one—on knowledgeable readers. And knowledgeable readers are exactly whom you're talking to in copy in ads in business publications.

Purple prose repels. It's a standing invitation not to believe. And, even worse, its effect lasts and lasts. Even today you don't find too many of the country's best cranberry salesmen mentioning Aminotriazole. *That* happened years ago. Negative impressions have a nasty habit of sticking in people's minds long after logic tells you they should have been forgotten or replaced by a positive attitude.

Refine, Hone, Polish Your Copy

All of the really competent copywriters—whether agency men or members of an industrial advertising department—have one thing in common: They are unabashed users of very large wastebaskets. And at the end of a typical day's writing, these wastebaskets are filled to overflowing, so there's a small mountain of crumpled yellow paper in the corner of the office behind the typewriter stand.

This is because the human mind, though a magnificent mechanism, is far from perfect. Thought processes leave much to be desired, as

516 Crazy Holes to Control

... a J&L Optical Comparator does it in 5 minutes. It used to take 3 days!

This gear is the heart of a Pitney-Bowes postage meter's "accounting system". Its accuracy is vital and must be spot checked regularly for dimension drift, or tooth-form breakdown.

Pitney-Bowes, Inc. solved this production control nightmare — eliminated a serious bottleneck — with a Jones & Lamson Optical Comparator. Here's how they do it:

A gaging head contains two probes. One is the work probe that contacts the gear in the staging fixture. The other is the dummy probe which indicates position of the work probe and whose shadow is projected onto a special comparator chart. The position of this shadow provides the means to check the radial position and form of the gear teeth.

Inspection is accomplished in minutes instead of days! *The entire production operation is monitored and kept on schedule:*

For more information call your nearest Jones & Lamson office, or write us direct.

JONES & LAMSON
DIVISION OF WATERBURY FARREL

Author Stansfield has selected this Jones & Lamson ad as a good example of the power of understatement. The simple and direct copy is packed with facts and benefits to the user. Addressed to knowledgeable trade-press readers, the ad contains neither superlatives nor exaggerated claims. There is nothing here that the most sophisticated reader would find difficult to believe.

do powers of concentration. The copywriter doesn't live who hasn't found—on far more accasions than most like to admit—that his mind wanders and little things distract him so he's unable to concentrate on the task at hand. Rough copy, which is the copy in its raw state before being worked over, reflects this human failing.

It rambles. It's verbose. The message isn't compressed into the tightest, most concise statements the writer can put down on paper. Organization of the copy leaves much to be desired. Sequence of thoughts isn't the most logical, nor does the copy progress smoothly with well-ordered precision from one point to the next, building and heightening interest as the time for the bid for action approaches. And frequently the fog level's high, words are impossibly long, paragraphs are only a whisker shorter than these in *War and Peace,* and gobbledygook that doesn't really say anything to anybody has crept in.

Few writers are able to concentrate enough to "write on the white." Writing on the white is merely writing carefully polished, finished copy on paper that'll be used to submit the copy to the powers that be for comment and approval. The mind refuses to discipline itself enough to make this possible.

Writing "On the White"

After almost two decades in the advertising business, and after working with scores of copywriters, some very gifted indeed, the author knows only *one* who can write on the white consistently. Dick Perry, copywriter, playwright, scriptwriter, novelist, author of numerous articles and short stories written for the mass media, with whom the author worked some years ago in a Chicago agency that's now a thing of the past, enjoyed this rare gift. Perry was a prolific producer. He pondered, paced, and planned, then pecked at incredible speed with two fingers. His copy required virtually no rewriting, no deletions, and no revisions.

And J. Woolsey Stanton, marketing genius in package products as well as items sold to sportsmen, and sometime author of tales for the fish-catching and coon-chasing books, is also blessed with being able to write and not rewrite. Stanton, one-time publisher's representative, claims to be able to think a piece of copy through from start to finish and then type it off—not write it—as conceived with every word, every thought in apple-pie order. The author has seen much of his writing, and it's fresh and sprightly and inventive.

However, we ordinary mortals usually find it necessary to doodle out a plan for each piece of copy. Naturally, this involves determining the core idea that is to be conveyed to the reader, then casting about with the aid of various and varied incantations, rituals, and sorcery just this side of voodooism for the *one* best way to express it to the individual who influences the purchase of the product. Again, note that it's individual, *not* individuals. Remember, too, you're not selling the product or its features, you're selling what it can do for the buyer and his company. You're trying to bring prospect and product together so that a purchase results.

Next step, then, is to write a rough draft following the outline you've prepared and including all of the information you've determined is advisable to put in the copy. It follows, of course, you're bearing in mind the concept of the entire ad—illustration, headline, copy, and rough layout as well as the media in which the ad will appear.

Incidentally, it is the copywriter's responsibility to specify the illustration; he alone is able to determine what it should be because he is the individual who's creating the ad, who's responsible for its success or failure.

Welcome Good Ideas

Often, however, the art director, account executive, or some other person involved in your advertising program will contribute a worthwhile suggestion that will improve upon the original idea. After all, rewriting and expanding upon what's already been done comes considerably easier than does creation of an entire ad right from scratch.

Good copy being as difficult to get on paper as most of us find it is, an idea is welcome from any source. Nobody has a corner on them. The one criterion for assessing ideas is that they must be good. Creativity by committee seldom results in copy with vitality and bite, though, so don't learn to lean on a crutch. Copywriting is a lonely job and it's hard work. It's accomplished without benefit of communal fun and games. When all's said and done, copy is the distillation and refinement of ideas of one person charged with writing it.

In the rough draft try to be as fresh and original as possible in wording and phrasing your thoughts about why the prospect will want the product. Never for an instant lose sight of the fact that you have no inalienable right to bore the reader. He won't stand for it.

On the other hand, you have a moral obligation to your company *and* to the reader to feed him information in a form that's palatable and acceptable to him. This doesn't mean your copy must entertain him. If you set out to entertain, all's lost. Copy that only entertains may produce a pleased little smile here and there, but it certainly won't produce a lasting impression about—or desire for—the product.

There are many mechanical techniques for copywriting. An Ivory-soap-like percentage—roughly 99 44/100—of all advertising men who put words on paper do so with a typewriter. This includes presidents of major agencies, creative directors, and directors of advertising who administer multimillion dollar budgets. Those who don't type handicap themselves needlessly.

Touch-Typing Gives Advantage

The writer who types, preferably touch-types (it can be learned at any age, in business school in just one or two nights a week for a few months) has a distinct edge on those who don't. He's equipped to retain those fast-flowing thoughts which race through the creative man's head, to get them on paper fast. Ideas and figures of speech are transitory things at best, and many with charm and vigor and impact are lost irrevocably because they weren't captured and put on paper before they got away in the unexplored recesses of the mind.

Learn to type. Your copy will improve measurably in both quantity and quality. And you don't have to be writing all of your company's space advertisements to benefit from typing. The average industrial advertising manager communicates on paper constantly—internally with product managers and marketing people, externally with a dealer or distributor organization and field sales force. Almost everything that leaves the advertising department is in written form and the better the writing the more effective a job is being done.

Naturally, you won't want to type your own letters. They're better dictated if only for the sake of time saved. Usually they're fairly routine, but occasionally a very important letter comes along that you'll want to rough out on the typewriter, then polish with a pen before giving it to your secretary for finish typing. You'll find this letter far more precise in wording and feeling than if you'd dictated it.

Too, when you type you'll find your work easier. The sheer physical job of writing by hand with a quill pen, or even something as relatively up to date as the centuries-old pencil, is laborious. Tediously putting down one word after another, instead of capturing entire phrases, analogies, thoughts, concepts smoothly and quickly with a typewriter, stifles creative thinking. An advertising manager who relies on a pencil reduces himself to little more than a clerk. It is almost enough to preclude producing sparkling copy for all but a few highly individualistic, unorthodox copywriters who make a fetish of belonging to the feet-on-the-desk, Turkish-water-pipe, aren't-I-brilliant-because-I-don't-cut-my-hair schools of what is, to them, apparently an art form for the ultrasophisticated urbanite.

A scant few copywriters think clearly enough to dictate, almost invariably to a dictating machine to avoid the distraction of having another person watch them struggle for expression. Their secretaries then type a rough draft for them, triple-spaced to allow room for blue-pencilling and revising. This procedure wastes time, however, for it ties up two people to do the work of one, and can be depended upon to complicate the task and cool the flow of ideas as time is wasted waiting for transcriptions.

Revision and editing of the rough draft is the next step. Shortening, tightening, and honing is the primary task; the advertising copy must be shortened in almost every instance to reduce it to the bare essentials. Excess verbiage wastes critically important space, wastes the advertiser's money on inconsequentials, and wastes the reader's time—if he'll give it to you under such circumstances. All of these wastes have to be avoided, the last one most of all. Readers will not fritter away time on witless wanderings in copy. To retain their interest, copy has to be concise.

Weigh Each Word

As discussed, copy length *per se* is seldom of critical importance. Both short and lengthy copy can be equally effective if properly written. What is essential, however, is that every single word of copy carries its weight, that it have a legitimate reason for being. There never is room for extraneous words for which there exists no real need.

A classic example of exquisitely honed copy is Lincoln's Gettysburg Address. In just 272 emotion-filled words of quiet dignity and lasting beauty, Lincoln expressed the hopes and aspirations of a bitterly divided nation in its hour of agony. Perhaps never again will so few words make so indelible an impression.

Each sentence should be studied, each word weighed to consider just how much it contributes to the total effect of the copy. Consider synonyms, keeping in mind there's a delicate and subtle nuance of thought between most of them. Choose the one that's precisely right to reflect the exact thought you want to convey. For example, the Grand Tetons are not beautiful—they're majestic. The Black

Canyon of the Gunnison isn't striking—it's magnificent, awe-inspiring, breathtaking. A product may not be strong or husky or large, but it may well be massive. Choose words with great care.

Experiment to see if one carefully considered word can't be made to do the work of several; if so, there's no doubt it will be vastly more effective. One word communicates more clearly and puts across the meaning much faster. Be sure to use power words.

Often you'll find that one rewritten sentence can replace two; one paragraph, after tightening and revising, can replace two or even three. Experienced copywriters have said for years that it's almost always a good idea to discard the first paragraph of copy because, unless the writer is unusually adept, it usually consists of generalities or at best an introduction to what the writer really wants to say. Space is too expensive for such luxuries.

Once copy is shortened and tightened as much as possible, sit back and read it. Read it slowly and carefully for both context and for tone. Check all facts and figures. Make sure you're right. Good copy is spare and lean with no superfluous words, but it *doesn't* read as if the copywriter had strict instructions not to use a single unessential word, much as though he was personally paying for a transoceanic cablegram at a horrendous word rate. If it's too terse, too telegraphic, the flavor isn't right and the reader is repelled because he gets the impression somebody's forcing something on him.

Copy that tight is too tight. But relieving the feeling of being hammered at by an overwhelming procession of facts aimed menacingly at the reader is accomplished merely by reintroducing some of the words which personalize copy—*you* and *yours,* for example, and by adding a few transitional words in carefully chosen places. We'll look at some examples shortly.

Now that you're editing the rough draft, make sure there's no possibility of confusing the reader. Copy must be clear and definite and specific. Any hint of vagueness or ambiguity should be eliminated by rewriting and rephrasing. Consider also whether the words used will be readily understood; advertising copy is no place to impress the reader with the extent of your vocabulary. You're familiar enough with the reader to whom you're writing that you know his vocabulary limitations, of course. Govern your copy accordingly.

Copy must relate to the reader's interests—and, as we've discussed, this boils down to a simple matter of economics in most cases. If the copy proves it will be to the reader's advantage to buy the product, probably because it has been economically justified, you have a reader who's pretty well persuaded that your product is for him. You must be thoroughly familiar with prospects' interests, needs, and problems, of course, in order to produce copy which relates to them and which will convince them.

Check, too, for interest. Be as detached and dispassionate as possible. Read the copy to make absolutely sure that it looks at the product from the reader's point of view. Make certain the reader's interest is first and foremost—not the advertiser's. Above all, though, try to make it friendly and inviting and rewarding to read. Interpret product benefits so the reader finds it easy to identify with them and *desire* them.

Although tightening copy by shortening it has been stressed, *never* cut copy to fit a layout. Layouts are made after copy is written —copy written to an arbitrary length merely to fit into a preselected space stultifies itself almost without exception.

Let's look at two excellent ads written for the farm industry. They show how copy can be short and tight, but still appeal to the reader's interest. The ads appeared in *Successful Farming* magazine.

The end to your manure handling problem

2 COMPLETE CLAY LIQUID MANURE SYSTEMS

One man hauls 2-months' manure from 400 hogs, or 1-month's manure from 80 cows in less than one day! Conserves fertilizer value of manure; reduces fly problem; haul once a month or as weather and your schedule permit.

"Honey Wagon" has pump in tank which provides vacuum to load from pit; pressure to spread load in field in 7 minutes or less.

Auger Agitator chops up big solids and straw in pits; homogenizes liquids and solids for fast, easy spreading

Trailer-Mounted Chopper-Agitator-Pump loads top-loading "Slurry Surrey," chops up straw and solids in pit.

NEW CATALOG—FREE PIT PLANS FOR HOG, BEEF, DAIRY SET-UPS

(coupon)

That's a hard-working one-third-page ad. There's not a single wasted word in the copy, not an excess thought. User benefits come through with no danger of being misinterpreted—and the bid for action makes an offer to induce reader response, as it should. Clay Equipment Company without doubt receives a gratifying volume of inquiries from this fractional-page ad.

Ralston Purina Company's powerful four-color spread ad, shown below, also ran in *Successful Farming*. The dramatic close-up of the well-groomed, healthy-looking young pig busily engaged in his favorite pastime—which involves the advertiser's product, happily enough—is appealing to farmers and nonfarmers alike.

On the face of it, this seems like an odd statement. However, the author is assured by James Wettersten, General Electric market research executive to whom he is indebted for a number of thoughts on this marketing service, that there is an unorganized but very active group of pig buffs in the country. Frequently they band together to pursue their hobby of pig-watching, just as binocular-equipped bird-watchers traipse through the countryside in the spring of the year indulging their interest. In the spring, pig buffs can be seen leaning on fences intently watching young pigs eat; so there's every reason to assume the photo would appeal to them, as well as to farmers in general. Many pig buffs get pass-along copies of farm books. They'll read Purina's ad, and although they don't buy pig chow, many are dog owners—and Purina also makes a very fine dog chow. This is a minor residual benefit from the ad for Purina, of course, but not one to be written off as of no value.

Purina takes full advantage of the power words with the most impact to get every bit of benefit from the ad. The most powerful word that can be used, "free," appears only slightly smaller than a barn, spread as it is entirely across the page containing the copy. Note, too, the positive, image-evoking power words skillfully sprinkled through the copy: *offer, present you with, at no extra cost, take advantage, learn, pays off,* and, again, *free.*

Probably not one reader who read this issue of *Successful Farming* thoroughly failed to notice this ad if he opened these two pages; if he riffled through the book and didn't separate them, naturally he missed the ad. Body copy is well written and enjoyed good readership. It reads:

Start your next litter

FREE

Special March offer at your Purina dealer's

From March 6th through March 18th only your Purina dealer can present you with your choice of a 50-pound bag of Purina Baby Pig Chow or Purina Early Weaning Chow Free, with your order of ONE TON of any Purina Hog Chow products for delivery within that period. If you order two tons you get two 50-lb. bags of Purina pig starter at no extra cost, and so on.

Take advantage of Purina's pig starting offer! Learn what so many folks have already found out. Purina starters give pigs grow-and-go power. High fortification for disease protection and high nutritional levels provide "built-in" livability. Pigs go for them, too. Cost is low—about ½-cent per pig per day from the time pigs are one week to three weeks old . . . that's the critical period when extra disease protection and a high nutritional level really pays off.

This offer is available to participating Purina dealers everywhere. Place your order now *for delivery between March*

6th and March 18th . . . and start your next litter FREE
. . . on Purina. See for yourself how your pigs thrive and
grow!

Purina's selling proposition is simple and easily understood and
will be accepted by the reader as being in his interest. This copy
was refined until there's not a waste word, not a thought that doesn't
belong. It's an excellent example of lean, spare copy that exploits
to the fullest Purina's offer. The company got it's money's worth
from this ad—and then some.

The advertiser received quite a bit of recognition among farm
advertising groups. In the national N.A.A.M.A. awards contest in
1967 Purina captured:

1. Regional Award of Merit for the hog campaign in color.

2. Regional Award of Merit for the hog campaign in black-
   and-white.

3. Regional First Prize for a single ad in color, up to spreads.

4. Award of Merit as runner-up to the national winner in
   Chicago in single ads in color, up to and including spreads.

That's quite a few "bingles" for one ball game.

Make the Copy Visually Attractive

Appearance of the completed industrial advertisement depends
largely upon the man who wrote it.

Let's back off a bit and admit there's no denying that most ads
consist of an illustration, copy, and a layout that brings order into
chaos. Also that art or photography has to be purchased, type has
to be specified (specced), and the ad has to go through a rather
involved production process. Everybody concerned contributes.

But there are those even in good agencies and well-run advertising
departments who feel the writer's job is to write, period. They're
of the opinion that the writer has no business "intruding" in other
areas once his part of the job of manufacturing an ad has been
completed.

This attitude is extremely shortsighted. It can easily result in
weakened, watered-down ads that have little of the freshness and
vitality of the original concept.

When all's said and done, the copywriter, be he advertising manager, account executive, or a writer in an agency copy pool, *is*
intimately involved in the appearance of the finished ad. It's the

writer who determines the illustration, the format, number of colors, and size of space for the ad—within a prescribed overall cost, of course. In a forthcoming chapter will be a discussion of just how illustrative techniques are selected and how specific layouts are arrived at.

Right now, though, the main concern is to produce a visually attractive piece of copy.

The first thing the writer does when he settles himself at the typewriter is to outline the ad he's going to write. That's basic. This will indicate to him approximately how much space will be required for what he is going to say. Depending upon the budget and upon communications objectives for both the campaign as a whole and for this individual ad in particular, he may specify a fractional page, full page, spread, special pull-out insert, gatefold, or perhaps a multipage insert—possibly perforated so it can easily be torn out and retained for reference if the reader is so inclined.

One thing is as certain as rising space costs: If copy is visually unattractive, readership plummets.

Be Concerned About Type

Of course, the copywriter usually doesn't specify what type face is to be used, the point size of the type, or the leading between lines —that is, he doesn't "spec" the type, as this is called. However, the experienced writer with good business sense (and the good ones *do* have it) is often more of a both-feet-on-the-ground type of person than is an agency art director or an artist in an independent studio which the advertising manager may use. So he is vitally interested in the appearance of the ad—which he, perhaps more than anybody else involved in producing it, considers to be *his*.

A purely selfish reason exists for this concern, in addition to the writer's professional concern. If the ad receives poor readership, the man who conceived it and wrote it is the ultimate recipient of the buck that is passed. He can't deny fathering the ad, and nobody enjoys having his judgment or ability questioned.

In many smaller companies the advertising manager is a complete one-man department and advertising agency. He conceives, writes, lays out and produces ads from start to finish. This ad manager is especially concerned that his output measures up to high standards.

Always, though, the writer provides either graphic or written direction to the artist to guide him in reflecting the writer's concept of the ad. Later we'll see how this is done, but right now let's consider what it is that makes copy visually attractive or unattractive.

SOUTH POLE GUINEA PIG

Testing in the cryogenic climate of the South Pole is a simple thing for the Penguin tribe. They have an ideal "guinea pig." If Penguins suspect the presence of sharks or killer whales in the ocean they take a quick vote, then push one of their number into the water. If he survives, it's safe for the rest of the group to go swimming. It's a simple, ingenious, foolproof test—and costly. Testing your components, sub-systems and systems can be done far more inexpensively and in a much more sophisticated manner by the Test Department of Brown Engineering. The Brown Test Department is engaged in reliability, qualification, and research and development testing for government and private industry. We have three main functions, each of which encompasses many specialized capabilities: (1) The engineering function provides component and system evaluation applicable to testing requirements; test planning and direction; data analysis and reports. (2) The fluids and dynamics function encompasses hydraulics to 75,000 psig with flow to 128 gpm; pneumatics to 30,000 psig with flow to 80,000 scfm; liquid nitrogen, oxygen and hydrogen under static conditions; acceleration to 31,000 g's; vibration to 22,000 force pounds; and mechanical shock to 150,000 force pounds. (3) The environmental function provides testing to military and NASA specifications in the environments of RFI, sand and dust, rain, humidity, temperature, salt fog, altitude, fungus, dielectric strength, resistance to arc, ozone and explosion. Our specialists enable us to manage and perform programs varying in size and complexity from the individual component, such as a hydraulic hose, to complete systems, such as the engine gimbal system of various stages of the Saturn missile. Our specialists are backed up by a failure analysis team which performs "tear down" and internal investigation of electrical, electronic, hydraulic, pneumatic and mechanical components. Program control is assured by program managers who perform technical consultation, program definition and control activities. Our testing specialists, our failure analysts and our program managers combine skills to develop unique approaches to difficult problems. Write today for a brochure detailing the capabilities of our Test Department. Contact: Test Department, Brown Engineering Company, Inc., Mail Stop 33, Research Park, Huntsville, Alabama 35805, Attn: B. D. Speer. Telephone (205) 532-1641. TWX 510-579-2103.

✳BROWN

*"Expanding man's knowledge
. . . extending man's reach"*

A clean and crisp layout with lots of good white space is marred by a long block of copy without paragraphs and set in too wide a measure for easy reading. Many typographers also frown on the use of an unserifed type for such an imposing block of reading matter.

515

We've briefly discussed word length, sentence length, and paragraph length. And we've touched upon how they influence the ease with which the copy may be read. Type set solid with few widows—short lines at the end of a paragraph—with little or no leading, and with long paragraphs repel the eye. People instinctively avoid such copy as either uninteresting or difficult to read.

Prove this to yourself by analyzing your reaction to the Brown Engineering Company's ad shown on page 515. Actually, this is an excellent ad. Layout is nice and clean, there's lots of appealing white space to attract the eye. The illustration is surrealistic, different and has considerable inherent interest. Combined with the curiosity-arousing headline, it does a fine job of delivering the reader into the body copy. And the copy is well written. It reads, in part:

> *Testing in the cryogenic climate of the South Pole is a simple thing for the Penguin tribe. They have an ideal "guinea pig." If Penguins suspect the presence of sharks or killer whales in the ocean they take a quick vote, then push one of their number into the water. If he survives, it's safe for the rest of the group to go swimming. It's a simple, ingenious, foolproof test—and costly. Testing your components, subsystems, and systems can be done far more inexpensively and in a much more sophisticated manner by the Test Department of Brown Engineering. The Brown Test Department is engaged in reliability, qualification, and research and development testing for government and private industry. We have three main functions, each of which encompasses many specialized capabilities . . .*

That's an intriguing lead-in for a company-capability story, and the Brown Engineering Company people have an excellent story to tell. They tell it persuasively and convincingly and with a fine flair. This is a well-conceived ad, and it would have enjoyed excellent readership except for one fault—and unfortunately it's a major one—the ad is almost illegible. This is due to setting type for the body copy in such wide measure—all the way across the page—and setting it in just one copy block, sans paragraphs. Result is it's soggy, difficult to read, and people don't *want* to read it.

In this case the advertiser discouraged receiving the one thing he wanted most, readership. Studies have shown that readership falls off as much as 42 percent when copy is set solid in one copy block with no relief provided by columns of type and paragraphs. This is a stiff price to pay for smart appearance.

How does the Playboy Club handle billing inquiries 50% faster?

The key is a 3M Microfilm Cartridge System.

The Playboy Club needed a system to make record keeping as fast and accurate as possible, and provide billing protection for over 550,000 cardholders. That's when they discovered a 3M Microfilm Cartridge System.

Now up to 15,000 bills, applications and other correspondence can be reduced to one 16mm microfilm roll.

Each roll is housed in a compact cartridge, indexed for immediate retrieval. Questions and other billing problems can be solved in minutes by looking up records and making copies in a 3M Microfilm Reader-Printer. Bar and food checks are never lost or misplaced. And file space is reduced up to 96%.

Many different types of businesses are solving paperwork problems with a 3M Microfilm System. Now it's your turn.

For more information see your 3M Business Products Center or write to 3M Microfilm Systems, Dept. FCR-17, St. Paul, Minn. 55119.

LOOK TO 3M FOR IMAGINATION IN IMAGE-MAKING!

3M COMPANY

3M Company doesn't have quite as much to say, but they, too, relied on borrowed interest in an ad which is unusually effective because it is so easy to read. The ad appeared in *International Science & Technology* magazine. It is shown above.

Where Brown Engineering used penguins as a hook to haul in readers, 3M uses Bunnies—which are, perhaps, of even more universal interest.

A bit of research on these two ads among business associates showed that a lopsided majority, 26 out of 27 interviewees, preferred the illustration of two Bunnies to the illustration of one penguin. Although this is supposition, it seems only logical to assume that the results of the survey were not materially affected merely because *two* Bunnies were shown and just *one* penguin was illustrated. The research proved conclusively that 100 percent of all who notice an ad will definitely not prefer one illustration, or one illustrative technique over another. After all, the secretary of one of the author's friends *did* prefer the penguin, as did his own secretary. This proves, too, there's no accounting for tastes.

The illustrative technique 3M uses accomplishes two objectives. It is attention-arresting and it makes effective use of a "human interest" illustration *and* a rather sterile, static straight product photo. Too, it is a perfect way to break up an 18-word headline of the question-and-answer type. Copy reads:

How does the Playboy Club handle billing inquiries 50% faster?

The key is a 3M Microfilm Cartridge System

The Playboy Club needed a system to make record keeping as fast and accurate as possible, and provide billing protection for over 550,000 cardholders. That's when they discovered a 3M Microfilm Cartridge System.

Now up to 15,000 bills, applications and other correspondence can be reduced to one 16mm microfilm roll.

Each roll is housed in a compact cartridge, indexed for immediate retrieval. Questions and other billing problems can be solved in minutes by looking up records and making copies in a 3M Microfilm Reader-Printer.

*Bar and food checks are never
lost or misplaced. And file space
is reduced up to 96%.*

*Many different types of businesses
are solving paperwork problems
with a 3M Microfilm System.
Now it's your turn.*

*For more information see your
3M Business Products Center or
write . . .*

*LOOK TO 3M FOR IMAGINATION
IN IMAGE-MAKING!*

According to 3M's advertising/merchandising manager, the ad pulled Noted and Read Most scores of over 200 in a Starched issue of *Business Week.* That it performed this well is due only in part to having the copy broken up in nice, appetizing little bites—headline presented in segments, body copy well paragraphed and broken into easy-to-read columns. All elements contributed to the success of this ad. One thing is certain, though: If the copy had been visually unattractive the ad would never have tallied up the readership it did—Bunnies or no Bunnies. It would have rated high in Noted, of course, but assuredly not in Read Most.

Another example of visually unattractive copy, but for an entirely different reason than the other ad we looked at, is the full-page bleed ad run by Olin *POW-R-QUIK,* Associated Products Operation, a part of Olin Mathieson Chemical Corporation. It is shown nearby.

Illustration is bleed, that is it runs off the page, in this instance on all four sides, and shows an International tilt-cab diesel tractor in the midst of a baby blizzard. The cab is tilted, so there's the connotation of something being wrong with it.

The headline doesn't really explain itself, nor does it have great mass appeal. Mentioning death in a headline is just about as negative as it's possible to be; death is neither widely popular nor in great demand. Research bears this out. Talking about it in display type can cause readers to flee as a bird to the sanctuary of safer pages. It reads:

The life
after death system.

Body copy, fortunately, does explain the headline immediately—

although headlines should never, *but never*, require explanation. Copy says:

> *It can start a dead diesel in the freezing cold.*
>
> *One of your biggest problems is no longer one of your biggest problems.*
>
> *Olin has developed an all-weather starter that works every time—in normal weather, and in sub-zero cold.*
>
> *It's a dual system—a conventional air system, engineered to include a unique new starter cartridge.*
>
> *In nice weather, use the air system. In freezing cold, use the cartridge.*
>
> *It'll not only keep you out in the cold, it'll do it cheaper.*
>
> *It can save truckers at least $2 per cold weather start. And literally thousands of dollars in total investment.*
>
> *It requires a smaller air tank (20 gallons as opposed to the conventional 60 gallons).*
>
> *It weighs less, 200 pounds less than electrical starter systems.*
>
> *It's easy to install. You can adjust it to any position, instead of the usual 90 degree increment.*
>
> *And it's called Pow-R-Quick®, the only real all-weather starter. Buy it and quit stalling.*

Not only does the ad start out by talking about a virtual unmentionable in advertisements (the subject is even skirted in ads in *The American Cemetery* magazine), but copy mentions it again in a bold-face subhead at the start of the body copy. Then, throw in the precious little paragraph that's number one, right at the top, and chances are readership was nearly nil. Olin would have been better off to delete the first paragraph of body copy and get right into the product story, which is well told.

What really kills (that thought's contagious) this ad, though, is the fact that it's almost impossible to read. The dark background of the uneven gray snow is so confusing and distracting that reading the body copy becomes a real chore. Few readers *work* at ad reading.

If the ad had had an illustration running about 8¼ inches in depth, bleeding on three sides—top, right, and left—and then had the customary white space for copy, it would have been vastly im-

The life after death system.

It can start a dead diesel in the freezing cold.

One of your biggest problems is no longer one of your biggest problems.

Olin has developed an all-weather starter that works *every time*—in normal weather, and in sub-zero cold.

It's a dual system—a conventional air system, engineered to include a unique new starter cartridge.

In nice weather, use the air system. In freezing cold, use the cartridge.

It'll not only keep you out in the cold, it'll do it cheaper.

It can save truckers at least $2 per cold weather start. And literally thousands of dollars in total investment.

It requires a smaller air tank (70 gallons as opposed to the conventional 60 gallons).

It weighs less, 200 pounds less than electrical starter systems.

It's easy to install. You can adjust it to any position, instead of the usual 90 degree increment.

And it's called Pow-R-Quik, the only real all-weather starter. Buy it and quit stalling.

Olin *POW R QUIK*

For full details, circle 112 on reply card

Author Stansfield has these comments about the ad shown above: Death is a negative topic; the headline must be explained; the dark tones of the snow foreground make the type extremely difficult to read. As a general rule, type should always run in otherwise white space in order to make the reader's job as easy as is possible.

proved. Copy then would have received considerably more readership than it did.

Final example of visually attractive copy is that in Ingersoll Milling Machine Company's whimsical four-color spread, shown below.

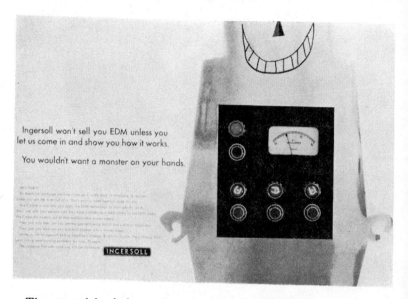

The spread is tied together nicely by having a slice of the illustration carry over on the page containing the copy. The illustration itself is delightfully light touch; it's nice to see an industrial advertiser who doesn't take himself so seriously he's positively grim about the whole thing.

Headline starts out in a light vein, but has some hard sell in it, too, reading as it does:

**Ingersoll won't sell you EDM unless you
let us come in and show you how it works.
You wouldn't want a monster on your hands.**

Good psychology, that. The headline contains the advertiser's name; the much-used observation that if they read *only* the headline they'll receive an impression about company and product has much merit. It also contains the abbreviation for the product—electrical discharge machine; the fact that the advertiser wants to help the reader (good word) who's a prospective purchaser of the equipment; and the fact that it's complex enough to warrant this extra service. People tend to relate complexity with omniscience, or with an almost uncanny ability to accomplish the near-impossible. Sometimes this is all for the best.

Body copy reads:

> *Let's face it.*
>
> *An electrical discharge machine could be a costly blob of hardware. A monster. Unless you get the most out of it. That's exactly what Ingersoll does for you.*
>
> *We'll come in and help you apply the EDM technology to your specific work. We'll live with your people until they have confidence in their ability to use EDM wisely. We'll take the mystery out of that sophisticated power supply.*
>
> *Then and only then can you get the best efficiency out of that piece of machinery.*
>
> *Then and only then can you turn that monster into a money-maker.*
>
> *Write us. Write Ingersoll Milling Machine Company, Rockford, Illinois. The company that's been licking metal-working problems for over 70 years.*
>
> *The company that sells solutions, not just hardware.*

That's mighty potent copy. It's readable because it's good copy, first of all, but also because it's visually attractive. Note how much leading—or line spacing—there is. And short paragraphs make it light and airy. And how the copy fits logically and neatly into a vast area of white space. This spread was designed to be read, and it received one of the highest readership ratings in the book.

All of us like attractive things. Make your copy visually attractive and you'll show readership heels to competitive ads that don't measure up to yours.

Make the Tone Suitable

Tone is a nebulous thing.

It's hard to put a precise definition on the word. When it's applied to a sound, either vocal or one made by a musical instrument, tone refers to pitch or quality. In the spoken word it can refer to pitch or accent. But when we mention tone in a discussion of writing —copywriting—tone refers to a style or manner of expression.

Actually, that's narrowing it down a bit too much. Tone, as used here, refers also to the character of the copy. To its mood, to the feel of it. And it can also apply to how the copy is slanted, how it attacks the problem of communicating with the reader and telling him the essential information he has to have to make a rational decision as to whether he's interested in buying the product.

Tone also, by inference at least, refers to the way in which appeals are made—whether they're cold-blooded, logical, and dispassionate. In copy this could well mean a dry-as-dust presentation of charts and graphs and a tabulation of how the product can be used in 1,478 different ways to do a given job. Now, this may all be very helpful to the reader. If he reads it.

Appeals to the reader can just as well be based on emotion, perhaps more effectively so. We've seen how Mobil Oil Corporation's great ad tugs at the heart strings because it appeals largely to the emotions, and how Chromalloy American's emotion-charged copy enthralls the reader so he's perfectly willing to read the body copy to absorb information the advertiser wants him to have—even after the appeal to his emotions is past.

Tone means not only the rhythm with which you march your words across the page, the sentence length, symmetry, paragraph length, or other specific factors. Tone of the copy, if it's right, breathes life and feeling and human warmth into company and product and gives both personality. It hits the reader right where he lives, it involves him so that he feels an affinity for the advertiser and the product. Temporarily, at least, he feels a kinship with the advertiser.

No One Approach Best

No tone is better than any other for all advertisements written to all audiences at all times. Nothing can be all things to all men. The skilled copywriter varies his tone to suit the circumstances. Actually, at any time the writer has a wide choice of tones; with complete justification he can adopt a modest, unassuming attitude which will completely disarm the reader and smooth the way for him to accept everything the ad says as truth, absolute truth.

Avis, for example, doesn't really want to convey the message that it is only Number 2 in the car rental field. What it wants readers to remember is that if they go to Avis, chances are they'll receive a car that's cleaner, in better mechanical condition than cars rented from its giant competitor, and that the car will be full of gas and oil. Also, that Avis people try harder so that when you go to Avis you can reasonably expect to receive better service—with less waiting, less red tape, less chance of being disappointed.

At other times the writer is perfectly justified in taking an authoritative tone. If, for example, a company has a unique selling proposition, if it leads the industry, the situation may be exactly right for assuming the position of *the* authority, the leader to whom customers and prospects should rightly look for the final word on the subject. Naturally, this doesn't mean to brag and boast and send up meaningless smoke signals all over the sales hills; that avails the advertiser nothing. A total capability story, for example, if it's true in the most literal sense of the word—and if the universe is at least partially aware that it's true—can provide an extremely effective podium for the advertiser to talk from.

What copy says is important, there's no disputing that.

But how it says it is equally important.

On the surface, it is difficult to understand why all industrial ads are not interesting. They should be. After all, two competent advertising men can be given the same products, same universe, and the same selling proposition. Both are accustomed to thinking objectively, to analyzing the problems involved in promoting the product, and in developing logical, workable solutions to them.

Given an ad to write, or a campaign to develop, one will retire to his office, close the door, and ultimately emerge with platitudes that don't hurt anybody's feelings, but which fall lamentably short of arousing any real interest in the company or its products.

The other, though, quite likely will put forth about the same amount of effort and in approximately the same amount of time or words will produce copy with bite and impact and an oversize measure of reader interest. The difference is in the tone.

Both may have said essentially the same things about the product. But the second man was able to impart freshness and vitality and sparkle to his copy through some mental process which hasn't yet been isolated, analyzed, and labeled by the psychologists. *How* he expressed his thoughts made the difference between wishy-washy words and vibrant, lively copy bound to succeed.

Many tones, many styles, slants or whatever you want to call the approach to copy can be right for many different advertisers. The one cardinal sin is to have such a complete absence of tone that the copy is flat and flavorless and devoid of any personality which separates it from other people's copy for other products.

Let's look at some examples of tone—good, bad, indifferent—and of types of tone that succeed and types that fail.

The flat and flavorless, when combined with a contrived, slightly unrealistic tone is typified by NVP Company's two-color, one-page ad in *Factory* magazine. Although it's clean, well planned, and has ample white space, the copy sounds the alarm clearly and unmistakably: This ad falls flat. It reads:

New Dimensions in Materials Handling Ideas
. . . ready for your use

These thermoformed containers are typical of current NVF production. A month from now the array will be substantially different . . . because each is custom-engineered to satisfy a specific customer need.

Uses for NVF containers range from handling in-process parts, to inter-plant transport, to storage or shipping. In each instance, they offer the money-saving advantage of reusability . . . over and over and over again.

NVF thermoformed containers are uncommonly durable though light in weight. They are attractive, available in popular colors, and surprisingly easy to maintain. Normally, they nest and stack in very little space when not in use. In short, they are an excellent choice for an infinite number of handling jobs.

When you need special help in solving your materials handling problems, come to the source where containers come in all dimensions . . . including those that will meet your special requirements. Write for our new Thermoformed Products brochure on more Creative Container Ideas.

It's high time that both business and the advertising community faced up to a fact of life: Readers are simply not interested in New Dimensions in Widgets, New Dimensions in This, That, or The Other. Even when capitalized.

Ponder this for a minute. Just what's in it for the reader when he's struck with two words in display type in the headline that proudly proclaim to one and all: New Dimensions? What's he to think? How's he to react? Just what in those two words—apparently magic, they're so overworked—is supposed to motivate him to

want to read further? And he must *want* to read further if he's
to do so. If he doesn't why bother putting copy in an ad—just put
New Dimensions in the headline, or even NEW DIMENSIONS,
big, *big*, BIG, *BIG;* run a picture of the product and sign off with
the admonition to write for information, put in the company name,
address, Zip Code, and logo. Also big, of course.

New Dimensions. Does anybody really know what NVF is
talking about? Does NVF? Does anybody care? Does the advertiser
honestly believe that this sort of thing will make any kind of dent—
even a little, tiny one—in industry's vast apathy to what concerns
NVF?

New Dimensions. This is antiphrasis, a malapropos malapropism.
Better it is to communicate. Come right out and *say* what you want
to say. Readers have no desire to guess what you mean.

There's no real need to critique the copy for overall tone; the
headline pretty well establishes that. Noticeable, though, is that it's
"ady"—full of words people don't use, that "copywriters" fondle
lovingly under the misguided impression they communicate. Substantially, reusability, uncommonly light in weight, surprisingly,
have no real place in copy about a product—at least not as used
here. And when a copywriter has to say "in short," it's a tacit admission he's been verbose and nonspecific. Why?

How often lately have you and your wife discussed the "reusability" of anything around the house? Try looking up reusability
in the dictionary and see how far you get. Nonwords *don't* communicate more often than they do.

Don't Be Coy

Avoid the elaborate, pretentious, coy, and cute. Cultivate an ear
for copy to see how it sounds to the reader. Rely on your ear, then
use it. There's no substitute for seasoned judgment.

West Penn Power's headline in a two-thirds page ad in *Factory*
magazine is:

financeability

And Carter-Day Company's headline in a two-color, one-page
ad in *Factory* says:

ideability

Of course, *this* headline has a seagull, hawk, jet airplane, glider,
or Unidentified Flying Object just swooping over it; this is no part
of the logo, nor of the conveyor systems the company manufactures.
Body copy of the ad then says:

*Single unit or complete conveying
system . . . check Carter-Day
for better ideas on
keeping your products moving!*

They're ideas based on 86 years of designing, manufacturing, and installing equipment to fit countless dry bulk product conveying applications . . . frequently combined with dust control systems. Carter-Day has the engineering ability to put better conveying ideas to work for you. Plant layout, loading and unloading methods, storage facilities, capital investment, and equipment layout are just a few of the areas which must be considered. You need the right answers—the right equipment—to insure an efficient, trouble-free, cost-cutting system. Highly sophisticated, many conveying innovations are available only from Carter-Day. Complete systems. Special equipment. A full line of accessories. To get detailed information, write for bulletins C-65 and M-362.

That's all one paragraph, set in what appears to be 6-point type, approximately 30 picas (5 inches) wide. Naturally, the copy's hard to read, but the tone is one of self-satisfied approbation, much as if the writer sat at his typewriter beaming ecstatically about Carter-Day's past glories. The reader could care less.

An attractive four-color spread ad in *Construction Methods and Equipment* magazine on the Koehring Hoe, a tracked monster that trenches, also leaves much to be desired. Let's look at the copy to see why.

For the competitive edge . . . dig with the big Koehring Hydraulics

There's an awful lot of ground to cover to bring in a bid profitably today. So your hoe better cover a lot of ground. That's why the Koehring Hydraulics are pulling away with the tough contracts from coast to coast. They give a contractor the edge . . . an edge in production, versatility and availability. Look here . . .

Big Production—*Koehring hydraulic power eliminates time wasting pull-through. Take your bite, roll back the* *dipper and you have a heaped load. Independent traction keeps you moving faster, too.*

Hot on the spot—*Truck loading is easier. You have better control of heaped loads. You can load into a truck body without breaking dumping.*

Great in a box—*Trench shield work is never a problem. The power, control, wrist action combination enables a Koehring to dig deep in short-radius arcs.*

Peel rock and frost—*Big down pressure and crowd force is a winning combination in rock and frost. Wrist action gives you the pry force you need to unseat boulders.*

Set pipe on the go—*Big reach, lift power, and precision control make pipe handling and spotting a snap. Saves time. No need to follow up with an extra crane.*

Clean up under laterals—*Precision digging control lets you dig under laterals and leave them high, dry, and intact. Saves time consuming and costly handwork.*

Drive sheeting home—*Positive down pressure helps you pressure sheeting in place in soft digging conditions.*

TAKE YOUR CHOICE OF KOEHRING'S FULL LINE OF HYDRAULIC HOES . . . SEE YOUR DISTRIBUTOR SOON

The unhappy thing is that Koehring is an outstanding company, and Koehring products are excellent. But the reader doesn't get that impression from reading this ad. The impression he *does* get, and it's unfortunate, is that Koehring Company doesn't have much to say about its equipment.

Read the copy again if you need to. It's general, nonspecific, full of "than-what" comparisons, with no solid facts the prospect for heavy equipment needs to know in order to arrive at a decision as to what make of equipment he wants to evaluate—to look at on a distributor's lot. This is where this copy fails. It doesn't give the reader necessary information he requires.

For example, the lead-in paragraph—all of it—is composed of high-flying generalities. Clichés common to construction are trotted forth, then reiterated, apparently in hopes they'll persuade or convince, or, at the very least, mollify a prospect who might possibly be anti-Koehring for some reason or other.

Then come the "than-what" comparisons—*keeps you moving faster, too.* Faster than what? *Truck loading is easier.* Easier than what? *You have better control.* Better than what? (Two of them in one sentence there.)

Questions come to mind that are never answered. For example, Koehring hydraulic power eliminates time wasting pull-through. Fine. But just *how much* time does it save on an average job? And if no job is really average, why not quote a typical time-saving? That's a user benefit that would interest readers.

. . . *enables a Koehring to dig deep in short-radius arcs.* All right, just *how deep* and *how short* are the radii of the arcs? Everybody with any experience with heavy equipment realizes that it's par for the course for job sites to be crowded with other equipment, natural obstacles are naturally in the way, and mountains of material are stacked so they're always hampering workers' efforts. So this is important information, but here again it's stated in such general terms that the reader isn't ready to accept the statement as solid fact.

Saves time-consuming and costly handwork. How much time is saved, and how much handwork—at what cost—is eliminated, again quoting statistics from an actual job on which Koehring equipment turned in a laudable performance? *That's* information. This copy is puffery. There's no comparison. The tone of puffery is comparable to that of a used car salesman's spiel.

Also in *Construction Methods and Equipment* is a two-color spread of Massey-Ferguson's MF Industrial and Construction Machinery division. Its copy follows in the same footsteps, has an unappealing tone due to the same deficiencies. It says:

Gutsy

MF 2244 Crawler looks small.

Works big. Moves in fast . . . moves out faster. Easy to handle.

Hard to beat.

This MF 2244 Crawler is a "never say die" machine. The kind a construction man needs around the job.

In tight spots, around projections, down gullies, over and through debris . . . the MF 2244 does the job. And it does it fast. You'll find it hard to believe that a compact crawler can do so much work.

One reason is visibility. The operator works confidently because he sees both edges of blade or bucket without moving from the seat. And pedals, controls, and instruments are easy to reach—easy to use.

Unique power balance makes each grouser bite full for maximum traction. You doze or load faster—recover faster.

You need the ruggedness and reliability that MF builds into all its crawlers—proved with over 10,000 in use. Call your MF dealer and arrange to try the MF 2244. You'll be amazed at the power and productivity.

The big JOBMatched line

Gasoline or diesel power? How many horsepower? What about accessories? What is rated capacity when loading? How large a load, in weight, will it doze? What is the space between treads? What is tread length? How is the blade or bucket actuated—electrically, mechanically, or hydraulically? What does the 2244 weigh? What is its maximum angle of lift? Maximum angle of depression? Turning radius? Overall length of the unit? Overall height? Ground clearance? Overall width?

Massey-Ferguson's ad doesn't *say* anything. The tone is wrong because it's almost impossible to write copy without saying anything and sound sincere. Lack of sincerity can result in the reader's having a negative reaction to an ad, and it can't be disguised. George Orwell said, "The great enemy of clear language is insincerity."

"Than-what" comparisons make a big buildup that's not justified *in the reader's mind* because claims are never proved, and unsupported statements work against the advertiser, not for him.

There's the two-color spread run by The Ridge Tool Company in *Factory*. It has much impact, with a red-and-black tractor-trailer racing down the road with the speed made evident by "speed lines" the artist has put in. Copy is short, and says:

*Another load of pipe . . .
just to test our dies.*

*Your guarantee
of perfect threads
every time.*

*Now that's what's known as Rigid Quality
Control.*

Again, this copy doesn't say anything, unless the reader pauses to interpret it. If he'll take the time to do that, and it's doubtful, he might receive, perhaps osmotically, the impression the Ridge Tool Company maintains consistent high standards for its products through the efforts of a busy quality control department. The inference is there that this benefits the reader, as a prospective user of Ridge tools, but there's an awful lot of assuming to do to convince yourself the message comes through loud and clear. And it should with copy so short it's almost a poster, instead of an ad.

Artwork, type, keyline, two-color plates, two pages of space—all probably add up to around $4,000 for one insertion in this one publication. Ridge really put all of its begs in one askit, and didn't ask clearly enough to be understood.

None of us like to be lectured to or preached at in advertising copy, yet many advertisers make this basic mistake. They unwittingly reduce the effectiveness of their ads to an extent that's impossible to determine because these same advertisers, for the most part, never test copy appeals, never pretest or posttest copy to learn what type of copy is best for them.

Frederic B. Stevens Division, The Udylite Corporation, preaches at the readers of *Foundry* magazine, rather than talking to them in a one-page, two-color ad. It reads:

Proved by user demand
Stevens Foundry Facings

Foundrymen like yourselves prove the many benefits of Stevens Foundry Facings by the number of orders they submit every year for these products. Very frequently these thousands of individual orders run into tremendous tonnages. They keep the Stevens plant facilities humming day-in and day-out to meet ever-growing needs.

Stevens also conducts a full-scale research and control program to develop new products, new foundry techniques and methods. It's sole aim is to help you produce more and better castings at lower cost. More than seventy-five years of continuing efforts like these have made Stevens the No. 1 manufacturer of facings in the industry today . .

Not only does Frederic B. Stevens Division put itself on a pedestal and preach down to all of the mere mortals expected to read the ad, the firm also blunders in numerous other ways.

Copy that starts out "foundrymen like yourselves" is mass-appeal copy, not personal appeal. The copywriter envisions a great white blob of faces out in some far-off intangible place called the marketplace; he doesn't write to a prospect with whom he's familiar, so doesn't give this *individual* information and facts *of interest to him.*

It's a peculiar type of reader indeed who would have even the wispiest spark of interest in how many orders his peers "submit" to Frederic B. Stevens Division every year. Why should this matter to him? And why should he give three whoops whether or not these individual orders run into tremendous tonnages? Or that they keep the Stevens plant facilities humming? Keeping the plant humming is Stevens' problem—not the reader's. And readers ignore all of the brags and boasts about how a company is No. 1, too.

One last thing: Why do "foundrymen like yourselves" have to "submit" orders to Frederic B. Stevens Division? Are they submitted for approval, or for acceptance? Who approves them? Who gives the thumbs-up or thumbs-down sign? Are they submitted with bated breath by foundrymen like yourselves who are on pins and needles, hoping against hope the gods will smile on them so Frederic B. Stevens will accept their order? Seems unlikely on the face of it.

Ten pages later in the same issue of *Foundry,* we find another two-color ad, this one a spread run by Herman Pneumatic Machine Company. It reads, in part.

Herman has had a proud, busy year . . . introducing new, revolutionary high pressure molding machines to the industry.

Yes, indeed, we've been busy. Our design, engineering, and manufacturing people have burned a lot of midnight oil to bring these molding machines to the point of reality. They are proven machines, operating successfully in hundreds of foundries here and abroad.

HERMAN'S basic principle of high pressure molding is part and parcel of our Moldmaster Jobber, Matchmaster, and Matchmaster Jobber. All were introduced during this year, and they have been widely accepted as efficient, dependable, cost-reducing units.

Herman then gives one line of nuts-and-bolts information, including dimensions, then breathlessly gets back on the sanctimonious path again with this holier-than-thou paragraph:

We will bring other machines to your attention as they are developed, since we are pledged to a continuous philosophy of developmental work to aid foundrymen.

Now isn't that ducky! A brochure is offered in the closing paragraph. Chances are they're still wondering at Herman why so few readers responded by asking for the brochure. Copy written in that tone will do just one thing: It will assure a plentiful supply of brochures on the storeroom shelves. It certainly won't pull inquiries because it won't be read.

Joy Manufacturing Company, Conveyor Products, starts out its body copy in a two-color, one-page ad in *Foundry* in a ponderous, pedantic tone which quickly changes to lofty omniscience. It says:

Time is an expensive commodity these days. And when you use this valuable commodity to keep your conveyor system operating smoothly and efficiently, you want to stretch your investment as far as you can.

Make it a firm policy never to tell the reader what he wants to do. The reader resents this. It alienates him. He *knows* what he wants to do. Advertisers who assume an omniscient tone in copy are advertisers who aren't very anxious to have their ads read.

Then there's a question of taste in the tone of copy. G. W. Smith & Sons, Inc., ran a one-page, black-and-white ad in *Precision Metal* magazine recently which had as the illustration a very comical drawing of two factory hands attempting to pull a stuck die from a die-casting machine with a plumber's plunger. A bit farfetched, but pertinent to the problem because castings and dies do stick and cause lost time.

The copy, though, causes considerable mental reservation. It reads:

Sucker for stuck castings?

If stuck die castings are clogging your production, Die Slick compounds can get things flowing smoothly again. Die Slick positively ends sticking, scoring, staining, soldering, and buildup. And it thins with up to 100 parts of water (kerosene or solvent if you prefer); you'll be flush with money saved on lube bills. Don't be sucked in by confusing claims about die casting lubes. Die Slick has been the choice of knowledgeable die casters for years. Write for a trial quantity telling about your alloy and your operation. If it doesn't do a plumb good job, pull the chain on the bill.

All of that's set solid in one paragraph which makes it difficult to read. A question of ethics arises when the advertiser says, "don't be sucked in by confusing claims about die casting lubes," for all the world as if competitive lubricant manufacturers were out to deliberately deceive gullible, trusting, dewey-eyed die casters.

Too, the copy is too cute in tone, and it's toilet-oriented. There's the plunger in the illustration; the word "flush," then "plumb" and, finally, "pull the chain on the bill." Best avoid connotations like that. They offend many people. The dividing line between humor and tastelessness is exceedingly fine.

A delightful light touch distinguishes Republic Steel Corporation's campaign in behalf of Steel Service Centers. The illustration is in four-color, the page containing the copy in black-and-white. The decision was made to employ a spread, one page four-color, the other black-and-white due to budget limitations. With a given number of dollars Republic could run more insertions doing it this way than if both pages were printed in four-color. The four-color page was used, though, because it would get much more attention.

The campaign was developed by Republic and its agency, Meldrum and Fewsmith, Inc. One of the first ads in this great campaign is illustrated nearby. Copy reads:

The Frustration of Searching

Our friend also has a search problem at his metal fabricating plant. The steel sheets his production line needs "right now" are often buried under other steel. The bar stock is hidden behind the angles. And so on and so on and so on.

If he'd only make a simple management decision! Stop carrying so much steel in his own already-paid-for inventory. Start buying more from the local steel service center that carries complete inventories of carbon, ENDURO® Stainless, and alloy steels made by Republic Steel.

He would solve his steel storage overcrowding problem. Could eliminate production delays caused by digging out needed items from his own inventory. Could reduce costly and inefficient "making-do" with steel he happens to have on hand. Would eliminate the ever-growing cost of possession factor on steel held overlong in storage. And even rid himself of "dogs" . . . the overage, outdated forms and grades of steel that accumulate through over buying, model changes, and order cancellations.

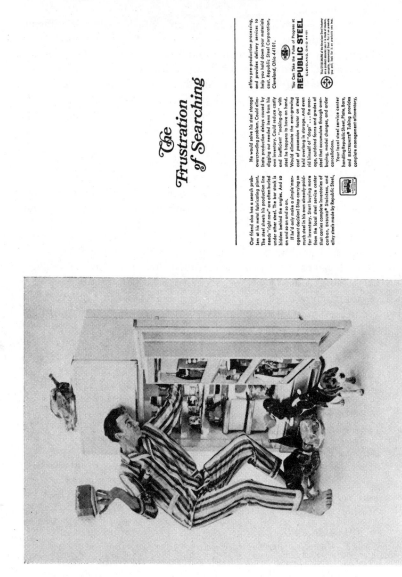

The Frustration of Searching

Our friend also has a search problem at his metal fabricating plant. The steel sheets his production line needs "right now" are often buried under other steel. The bar stock is hidden behind the angles. And so on and so on and so on.

If he'd only make a simple management decision! Stop carrying so much steel in his own already-paid-for inventory. Start buying more from the local steel service center that carries complete inventories of carbon, ENDURO® Stainless, and alloy steels made by Republic Steel,

He would solve his steel storage-overcrowding problem. Could eliminate production delays caused by digging out needed items from his own inventory. Could reduce costly and inefficient "makingdo" with steel he happens to have on hand. Would eliminate the ever-growing cost of possession factor on steel held overlong in storage. And even rid himself of "dogs" . . . the overage, outdated forms and grades of steel that accumulate through over-buying, model changes, and order cancellations.

Your local steel service center handling Republic Sheet, Plate, Bars, and ELECTRUNITE® Tubing provides complete management of inventory.

offers pre-production processing, and provides delivery services to help you hold down your materials cost. Republic Steel Corporation, Cleveland, Ohio 44101.

You Can Take the Pulse of Progress at

REPUBLIC STEEL
CLEVELAND, OHIO 44101

Your local steel service center handling Republic Sheet, Plate, Bars, and ELECTRUNITE® Tubing provides complete management of inventory, offers preproduction processing, and provides delivery services to help you hold down your materials cost.

Since this was a kickoff ad for a new campaign, Republic merchandised it vigorously to its own sales force, prospective customers, and to steel service center management. Copy in brackets in the upper right hand corner reads—in only the merchandised copies, of course:

First of a *new series* of ads . . .

Being run to *help you* and your steel service center . . .

To help you sell *more steel* . . . More *Republic Steel* steel . . .

By telling the *advantages* of buying *Republic Steel* steel . . . from service centers like yours . . . From salesmen like *you* . . .

These ads are telling this story to the *decision-makers* you don't have time to see . . .

Or who are sometimes too busy to see you . . .

But these full-color 2-page ads *get* to these busy men . . . even at *odd hours* . . .

As they read "Fortune," "U.S. News & World Report," "Business Week," "Steel," "Iron Age," "Purchasing," Purchasing Week," and (in black and white) "Wall Street Journal" and "American Metal Market."

Ads like these help convince them that buying from *your steel service center* is *good* business.

Since steel service centers are a major factor in the distribution of steel to end users, Republic conducts an advertising campaign in their behalf each year. The basic message of the campaign is: Buy your steel requirements from your independent steel service center. The ads attempt to promote good will for Republic among steel service center management.

Approach of this campaign was determined by research among top metalworking management personnel. Research, conducted by Republic's agency, showed that top metalworking managements—and heavy mill buyers in particular—need educating as to the benefits of purchasing all or some of their steel requirements from a steel service center.

Research revealed that most executives in metalworking management looked to service centers only in emergencies, or for small quantities, special sizes, and for items not regularly carried in their own steel inventory. Also disclosed by research is that the most important advertising theme is the cost of possession story. Specifically, this is to bring to the attention of metalworking management the hidden costs incurred by warehousing or possessing steel of their own.

Cost of possession includes nonproductive floor space; searching for steel when it is needed, tying up personnel needed elsewhere; overstocking or understocking; scrap, damaged, outdated steel; insurance costs. All of these hidden costs can be eliminated by purchasing from steel service centers.

With this background information, the campaign was developed to dramatize—with as much impact as possible, and as memorably as possible, of course—the dollars-and-cents economic meaning of the cost of possession proposition. Each ad was developed around one central idea, of course. Illustrations were rooted in humor, while the handling and body copy drove home the main idea of the ad.

Republic marketing objectives in this area are very simple—to expand the market for steel service centers, and thus sell a larger percentage of Republic's products through this source.

Communications objectives of the campaign are:

1. To promote the vital role of the Steel Service Centers in the efficient distribution of steel products to the metal-working industry. This is to be accomplished by spelling out the economic and time-saving advantages to metalworking management of ordering more of their requirements from a steel service center.

2. To capture the attention and gain the favor of executives in the steel service centers through Republic's advertising in their behalf.

3. To identify Republic as a major supplier of carbon stainless, and alloy steel, to steel service centers.

The great ad illustrated nearby is also from early in the series. It reads:

The Relativity of Space

When you're squeezed for room, it's time to do something about the bulky stuff and the "dogs."

You can probably pick up a surprising amount of much-needed floor space for profitable production by reducing your own overlarge bought-and-paid-for inventory of steel. And by cleaning out the "dogs"—crop ends, odd lots, obsolete items from canceled orders.

Only a phone call away from you there's a fully stocked,

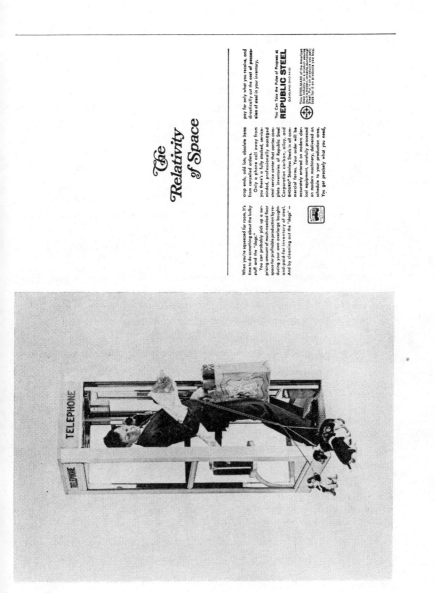

you receive, and drastically cut the COST OF POSSESSION *of steel in your inventory.*

Republic based its objectives on research, of course, but it also follows the thinking that goes into an industry promotion effort. That is, to emphasize first of all the industry's message to its customers—i.e., the service center's message to metalworking management—and, secondly, tie in with Republic's products and services.

This campaign aims at a vast market. The ads are directed primarily at metalworking management in all S.I.C.'s where steel is used, and to a lesser extent at management of steel service centers. The steel service center market itself is huge, since it consists of some 1,700 centers which ship more than 13 million tons of steel each year.

Buying influences to be reached were validated by research. They include top business management, production and purchasing executives in all of metalworking. In the service centers themselves, the key people are top management and purchasing executives.

Soundness of the campaign is borne out by readership ratings. Here is a tabulation of ratings of specific ads in various media.

MAGAZINE	NOTED	READ MOST	NOTED RANK	PRODUCT CATEGORY NOTED RANK	SERVICE
Steel (Frustration of Searching)	50	9	2nd of 82 ads	2nd of 19 ads	Starch
Iron Age (Frustration of Searching)	71	5	10th of 52 ads	2nd of 8 ads	Ad-Chart
Business Week (Frustration of Searching)	42	8	11th of 52 ads	4th of 14 ads	Starch
Purchasing (Frustration of Searching)	53	13	2nd of 82 ads	1st of 24 ads	Starch
Fortune (Frustration of Searching)	61	12	6th of 78 ads	————	Mills Shepard
Business Week (Annoyance of Crowding)	62	7	6th of 112 ads	1st of 17 ads	Starch
Purchasing (Importance of Timing)	37	8	8th of 84 ads	2nd of 22 ads	Starch

The Annoyance of Crowding

Metal fabricators have crowding problems, too. Steel storage areas may be jammed with "dogs"... steel bought for models no longer in production or for products whose specs have been changed...or steel that was overbought to get a volume price.

Steel service centers handling Republic steels can solve your steel storage crowding problem. Buy more of your Republic carbon, stainless, and alloy steels from the steel service center. Re-

duce your own crowded, space-blocking inventory. Save money — when you figure all the costs of possession for your own slow-moving, bought-and-paid-for steel inventory.

Steel service centers also offer savings in (a) Time... prompt delivery to meet your schedules, (b) Availability... precisely the grade, type, and size of Republic sheets, bars, angles, and tubing you need, and (c) Utility... elimination of excessive scrap, idle stocks, and damaged or outdated steel.

Call your local steel service center that stocks steels produced by Republic Steel Corporation and can do much of the pre-production

processing for you. It is run by professional managers of steel inventories who help you save money, time, headaches, and scrap. Republic Steel Corporation, Cleveland, Ohio 44101.

You Can Take the Pulse of Progress at

REPUBLIC STEEL
CLEVELAND, OHIO 44101

Naturally, Republic Steel is something more than glad to receive such excellent readership of the ads in this campaign—particularly when they're compared to all ads in the studied issues. Even more important, however, is that this campaign holds up so well in relation to Republic's competitors. In the Product Category Noted

Rank, Republic has two firsts, three seconds, and a fourth. Good going indeed.

Average Noted score for these seven studies is a healthy 53, average Read Most is 9, which is very good. And when compared to every ad in the book, Republic earned a respectable rating, even though steel has little inherent interest.

As a rule it's hard to point to specific results from an industrial advertising campaign—much to the advertising manager's regret. In this respect, though, Republic has something to talk about.

Evidence of the campaign's effectiveness is the tremendous amount of interest and excitement the campaign has generated. This has been fed back to Republic in personal conversations, and in a substantial flow of unsolicited letters.

Because the ads are lighthearted, the tone is happy and forthright. They're colorful, and contain practical messages of genuine interest to the universe. They are being noticed and commented upon by steel service center executives. And, just as important, they're also being used as a sales tool by steel service center salesmen in their work.

To assist the service center salesmen, the ads were made into imprinted promotional direct mail pieces. Service centers have requested more than 80,000 of these direct mail pieces for distribution to their customers and prospects. This promotion is a welcome fringe benefit for Republic.

Following are a few excerpts—quoted verbatim—from letters Republic has received. They bear out the fact that the campaign is highly regarded by service center executives.

> "Your numerous SSCI Advertising Awards in the past— and I am sure of many more in the future—are certainly well deserved, with the pattern of supporting advertising you have introduced."
>
> *President*

> "It may be of interest to you that Republic Steel moved into the Number One supplier position of our company."
>
> *President*

> "We deeply appreciate the efforts that Republic Steel Corporation is making on behalf of those of us in the steel distributing business and certainly want to take advantage of this opportunity to express our thanks."
>
> *District Manager*

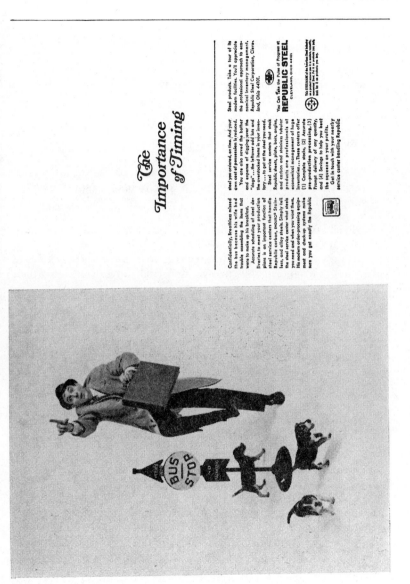

"The steel service centers are a part of the producer's sales, local storage and credit department and we need and appreciate your help like this. This type of advertising is raising our image in the eyes of the consumer." *President*

> "The layouts are most attractive, humorous, and point-getting—what more could be said!" *Vice-President, Sales*

> "Republic is to be complimented for an unusually fine job which should greatly benefit all of us."
>
> *Executive Vice-President*

> "Good advertising like this is certainly mutually beneficial and we are thankful for your interest." *President*

> "Next to pretty girls, I think puppies attract a lot of attention. I am sure that everybody in our industry appreciates support like this." *President*

Feedback from Republic's field sales personnel is one of enthusiasm for the campaign. This is an essential, of course, for one of advertising's most important functions is to enthuse the sales force. This isn't recognized by many industrial advertisers—to their detriment.

Getting just the right tone into your copy takes skill—which can be acquired by practice and more practice, plus the willingness to evaluate copy analytically and objectively. Also, you must be willing to fill the round file full if copy falls short of what you know it should be.

Avoid tone which is pedantic, preachy, and smug. Also avoid the pseudoscientific, the professorial, and the holier-than-thou. Make the tone of your copy straight from the shoulder, sincere, honest, objective, and fair. Then your ads will be read and they'll persuade, which is what you're after.

Incidentally, if your agency writes the copy, *never*—repeat, *never* —ask for "alternate suggestions." You have no need for a group of alternates to any communications problem. Instead, ask for and insist upon getting the one best approach the agency is capable of producing. State for the record you want only its best thinking, not ideas that have been rejected as being too poor to show you. All of us have a plentiful supply of those, and they're best forgotten.

Some years ago the author had a client company which was well managed, and had products that were equal to or maybe a bit better than those produced by a giant competitor that dominated this field. One of the communications problems that was almost insoluble was that this company's advertising manager invariably requested several alternate suggestions when a new ad was under discussion.

Writing an ad that measured up to agency standards—and to the author's standards—and which stood a better than even chance of achieving the stated communications objective was a waste of time. This ad manager wanted to see at least three or four layouts and pieces of copy, then choose what he thought was "best."

This wasted his time and put the agency to unwarranted expense.

The author solved this one by writing one good ad, which was duly blessed by the copy chief and by the creative director, then whacking out three other ads as fast as paper could be run through the typewriter. No time was wasted in layouts for these "alternate suggestions" because the art director was made aware of the situation and he, too, gave his portion of the job a fast lick and a promise. But nobody relishes writing ads that he *knows* are destined for the scrap heap.

Relations with the client went smoothly for some months. The ad manager duly approved the "best" ad each time several were presented, and the campaign resulted in acquisition of a number of additional distributors, thus boosting sales most satisfactorily. Eventually, however, the advertising manager started to complain, "Why is it you fellows seem to have just one good idea at a time lately, and so many poor ones?"

That was when the facts of life were gone into bluntly and frankly over a long lunch one day. The economics of the agency business were explained—as was the fact that account executives were fellow businessmen and professionals in their field, not servants to cater to every whim. Those words were used.

Then the fact was mentioned quite candidly that this alternate-suggestion demand was a waste of everybody's time and money, that it actually prevented the client from receiving all of the agency thinking he was entitled to because he demanded something that was inimical to his and his company's best interests. Then, immediately after this conversation, it was steered to a discussion of the views of the vice-president—marketing's philosophy on writing and advertising—and the message was sent, received, and retained.

This advertising manager wasn't deliberately trying to be obstreperous, nor was he knowingly trying to chisel something for nothing out of the agency. He merely lacked experience. Once the matter was settled he got far better thinking than before, of course, and the agency went all out to produce the very best work possible. His successful campaign became even better, and it became more productive than ever. Inquiries increased, conversions into sales did too, and his company got additional distributors.

Types of Advertisements

The industrial advertising man isn't usually concerned with advertising that is arbitrarily broken down into classifications according to the medium in which it appears—outdoor, radio, transit, television, and mail order. (Direct mail advertising, as opposed to mail order advertising, *is* of interest to the industrial advertising practitioner and will be discussed separately.)

Attempt to classify advertisements and the first thing that's apparent is that the classifications overlap. However, if the hybrids and other ads that are anomalous are disregarded as representing only a minute fraction of all industrial advertisements, there remain only 14 basic types of print ads you encounter with any degree of frequency. All others are offshoots. Naturally, this is excluding corporate ads, which are a breed apart and will be covered in a separate chapter.

The workhorse types of industrial ads are:

1. New product
2. Product description
3. Product performance
4. Product line
5. Problem solving
6. Case history
7. Testimonial
8. Inquiry
9. Catalog offer
10. Newsletter
11. How to do it
12. Trade ads
13. Institutional
14. Comic strip and cartoon

Copy will vary quite considerably from one type of ad to another, of course, because each ad is created to do one specific job. Each job, or communications objective, differs radically from some of the others. Some types of ads may call for unusually lengthy copy —for example, to introduce a complex new product for which the reader will expect a complete technical description and detailed construction specifications. Other copy may be very short; most will fall somewhere between the two extremes.

Let's look now at each type of industrial ad and consider its strengths and weaknesses and the job it does best.

New Product Ads

Here's a little exercise just for the fun of it: Pick any new product that's just been developed, either by your company or one you're familiar with. Look it over carefully, analyze what it has to offer to buyers, consider the price, competition, and all of the other factors you can dream up. Then hazard a guess as to what degree of success the new product will achieve in the marketplace when it's introduced.

Without even knowing what the product is, or to what market it's going to be sold, one thing is morally certain: It stands less than a 50-50 chance of living out a normal life expectancy.

More than half of all new products developed by American industry lose money and languish away while anguished progenitors in the companies who had a hand in fathering them wonder just what happened, and why.

Answers are as many and as varied as are the companies that go through this painful experience. Far too many firms conceive of a Great Idea, pull out all stops and burn the midnight oil to develop a new product for a silly reason—such as having something new to show at a trade show, for instance.

There's too little thought given to what is going to be done with the product once it becomes an actuality and just how it is going to be marketed. In the majority of cases little or no attempt has been made to research the market for the product to see if a real need for it exists, to determine what similar products it will have to compete against, to learn prices of those competitive products, how they are distributed, their share of the market, and whether the total market for the product is growing, stable, or declining.

A Great Little "What's It"

One company did this recently, with an open, childlike faith that things would work out. It proceeded to develop an amazingly intricate and sophisticated little piece of equipment to do highly specialized research work for metallurgical laboratories. Giving credit where credit is due, the product is an excellent one, and it is unique.

The innocent soul in charge of its development very properly went all of the way and hired a capable industrial designer to design the exterior shell, rightfully feeling that it should be first class in appearance so it would have every chance of succeeding. The designer did an outstanding job and the finished unit is a joy to the eye.

The only flaw was this—the product people and the engineers became so wrapped up in their pet project and so enamored with glowing thoughts of how the new Widget would enhance the company's image that they overlooked one relatively minor thing. Nobody stopped to figure out what the product would be used for—specifically, that is.

In due time it was completed with much overtime and double-time in the shop and then rushed to the company's booth at the National Metal Show and Exposition. There it was proudly displayed, powered, ready to operate, and with one of the engineers from an outlying plant where the product was developed on hand at all times to explain all about the fascinating new Widget. The dewey-eyed product man charged with responsibility for the new product had given the engineer instructions to sound out attendees of the show to see if *they* could figure out an application for it.

He did—they couldn't.

After the show was torn down the product was lovingly crated and shipped back to the satellite plant where the product people have their offices. There it sat, undergoing tests and more tests and more tests. Everything worked perfectly, there was never a malfunction of any kind. Everybody was tremendously proud of the product and a gleam of ecstasy appeared in their eyes whenever it was mentioned. This was their esoteric baby.

They even entered photographs and a description of the product, along with a few guesses at some of the fantastic things it could do, in a "design" contest held by one of the trade publications. And, wonder of wonders, the product was one of a hundred or so winners in the contest, thus showering great honor upon its developers. The contest was primarily to promote the publication, however, not the "winning" products.

Fifteen months after its introduction to those who supposedly constituted the universe for the product, it still remained in all of its pristine beauty in the research and development area of the plant where it was born. Nobody quite knows what to do with it. Some unfeeling individuals have been heard to mutter that it is in their way. Others had to dust it. Still others tripped over it.

However, it was finally decided that it might not be a bad idea to see if someone could find out just what applications the product was suited for—and to determine if a market for it actually existed. At last, real marketing thinking!

Accordingly, a graduate student attending a nearby university was hired to "research the market" for the product. He willingly accepted this subsidy out of the blue and there the matter rests—many months later. It's assumed that sooner or later the student will submit a report and recommendations for marketing the product—unless he first acquires the advanced degree upon which he's working and departs for parts unknown.

In the meantime, back in the product manager's office, all is not at a standstill as far as marketing the product is concerned. He has selected media in which to advertise it! Now, if the prospective purchasers of the Widget just happen to be in markets reached by the media given the product manager's stamp of approval, the product might eventually get off the ground.

This story is all too familiar, although not many companies are as inept as this one.

The New-Product Path

Back before Johannes Gutenberg invented movable type some time between 1435 and 1445, disseminating information to widespread audiences was almost impossible. In that era a new product was discussed by individuals, and if the tailor with an improved waistcoat wished to announce his revolutionary method of manufacture, or style, he wrote an announcement with a quill pen on a piece of parchment and put it in the window of his shop—sans benefit of Scotch Tape. Thus passersby could read the notice—at least, those who could read *could* read it—and the word was spread in this fashion.

To try to introduce a new product to industry today in this way, or in any way except paid space advertising, is next to impossible. To be sure, the staunch disbelievers in advertising can develop a better Widget and wait for the world to beat a path to their plant door. But the wait may be a bit long.

Also, the fantastic, revolutionary, sensational, precedent-shattering new Widget can be developed, then the entire field sales force of 71 men can be called in for a special rah-rah-rah sales meeting to hear the virtues of the Widget extolled to them for long, boring hours. Then they can be given a hearty pat on the back and sent forth with instructions to sell, sell, sell.

Of course, a dollar or two is invested in bringing all 71 bodies in from widely scattered locations, the company loses sales while the salesmen are not covering their territories and the home office staff devotes its time and energies to planning and handling the meeting, ignoring routine duties which make money for the company.

Then, if this sales force bears any resemblance to other companies' sales forces selling capital equipment similar to the new Widget, they will make approximately 400 sales calls per salesman per year. This figures out to 28,400 total calls by all 71 of the salesmen in the course of a year.

If this sales force is selling to the metalworking market, for example, with some 33,000 establishments with 20 or more employees, they could spread the word about the new Widget to all of these establishments in only 14 months. They'd see only one buying influence per establishment, for the most part, but we could assume that at least half of these influences might logically be expected to discuss the new Widget that Smith Widget Manufacturing Company has developed with at least one other influence.

Weak part of this anticipated reaction, however, is that we know for a fact that when capital equipment is concerned, a minimum of *five* buying influences are involved in a purchase—and usually more. The frustrating thing is that our salesmen can't get in to see these other influences. So what do we do without space advertising?

The Message Can Get Through

That's simple. We'll use direct mail. We can make up a mailing list composed of names supplied by the field sales force, to start with. But wait—isn't it barely possible they'll give us names of people upon whom they call? And this we don't need. So we can go to D&B, or to a list broker, and get additional names. But even then there's no assurance that we'll reach even a fraction of the decision makers who can make or break sales for the new Widget. It's a physical impossibility to identify them without a lengthy research project designed for this one specific purpose. And the company can't afford to wait that long for sales of the new Widget, not if the sales forecast is to be achieved—and management is sticky on *that* subject no matter what the company's name is and what it makes.

But if we advertise our great new Widget to the metalworking market, suddenly many scores of thousands of buying influences know all about it over night. People in prospect companies from chairman of the board and president and vice-president of manufacturing, works manager, master mechanic—all of them know about it in a relatively short span of time.

It's quite true that each and every one of these people who are important to the Widget's future won't read the announcement advertisement. Every recipient of the media used won't read every issue. A certain percentage of them—perhaps as high as 25 percent —might skip this issue for one reason or another. But if you use more than one book, or if you prove your perspicacity by maintaining continuity of advertising and repeating the announcement ad, those who missed the most important thing to you in the business world will receive your message when the next issues come out.

If you're concerned that all of the influences you want to reach won't receive *any* business publications, relax. Almost all magazines enjoy a pass-along readership—usually around three per copy—within companies that receive them. This is a bonus the advertiser doesn't pay for, but it's one that's important to him nonetheless.

Only space advertising can carry a message to a widespread and diverse market so that businessmen throughout industry all know almost simultaneously what information about your product you feel they should have. It can't be done by smoke signals, by riders on horseback, by skywriting, by mail, or any other method at a price industry can afford to pay.

Another thing: A product is new more than once. It's new many, many times. That's because, while those who live with the product day by day think of it as old hat, untold thousands of prospective purchasers in the marketplace don't know of its existence. They may not realize that any such product has been produced by any company, or they may have an inkling that such a product is on the market but not be aware that your company manufactures it.

A Market Changes Constantly

This is not contradicting what was just said about advertising's ability to announce a product to the majority of your buying influences simultaneously. On the contrary, it merely points out that the marketplace is fluid, in a constant state of flux. Buying influences who can give the nod to your Widget were with another company just yesterday, or they've just been advanced and have new responsibility—including specifying or approving purchases. These influences are not static. They change constantly, up to 40-50 percent a year due to death, retirement, promotions, job changes, mergers, and what not. The marketplace is dynamic. To maintain your position in it—or to better it—you must communicate constantly. Nothing is more true than the old saying, "Out of sight, out of mind."

Then again, the product may well be new to people even if you advertise it consistently, month in and month out. People who read your ads *think* they are about new products. This is known as the if-it-is-new-to-me reaction, or the if-I-had-only-known response, or the I-buy-from-them-but-I-didn't-know-they-made-Widgets statement.

This last frequently happens to multidivision companies when a certain group of buying influences have long been accustomed to specifying the product of one division, but are completely unaware that a sister division produces a product that's complementary to the one they use. They've been going to a different corporation entirely for their requirements of that product. Advertising can do much to increase a corporation's penetration in a given market with products of another division that are not well established there.

Research shows the new product announcement is one of the best-read types of advertising. The word "new" is a potent one. There's the connotation of something improved, vastly better than any product that's ever preceded it, one that will go far toward solving whatever problem it's applied to. And readers of the business press, like all other humans, have their fair share of curiosity. Something new is something all of us want to read about, whether it's something that will help us on our jobs, or something that will make leisure activities more fun.

Run a new-product-announcement advertisement and you're off to a good start at getting more than your pro-rata share of readership, other things being relatively equal. The other things naturally include copy that's provocative in approach and tone; a stopper of an illustration that refuses point blank to let the reader give it short shrift; a fresh layout that piques the imagination; and, of course, media that are right so your message reaches those people who are most important to you.

A new-product-announcement ad run by Clark Equipment Company, Construction Machinery Division, measures up to all of those criteria and then some. This great ad, actually a multipage insert, introduces the company's new Michigan tractor shovels with great impact. The ad was produced by Clark's agency, Marsteller Inc.

Objectives of the ad were:

1. To introduce the new Series III Tractor shovels as high-speed, high-production equipment for heavy construction.

2. Reinforce the prestige of Clark-Michigan as the leader in the tractor shovel field.

3. Arouse interest in the new tractor shovels among Clark-Michigan distributors and prospects with aggressive, new, headline-copy technique.

Let's look at the ad, then go into the rationale of making the announcement this way, the media used, and results produced.

First we see a teaser ad, but not merely a teaser designed only to tease. Shown in the four-color illustration of the full page ad is the business end of a Michigan tractor shovel, digging, flying dirt providing a dramatic sense of motion, of things happening fast and furious. Copy reads:

DIG

The new Michigans dig like no tractor shovels ever built before.

On the next right-hand page in publications carrying the ad, we see another four-color page. Illustration is of the Michigan's Bonus Bucket heaped full, *really* full, of a mixture of rock and dirt. It's a heavy load and it looks like it. Copy reads:

HEAP

The new Michigans heap like no tractor shovels ever built before.

On the next right-hand page of the books we find a closeup of the bucket loading a dump truck. Mechanical details of the hydraulic pistons and lifting mechanism are shown to good advantage. Copy reads:

LOAD

The new Michigans load like no tractor shovels ever built before.

Then, on the next right hand page is another four-color illustration of an obviously bustling Michigan tractor shovel slightly blurred by motion, disappearing to hunt up some more work to do. Big, fat tires kick up dust so the speed of the unit is apparent to the reader. Copy reads:

GO

The new Michigans go like no tractor shovels ever built before.

When the reader flips the page after this terrific build-up, he finds the wrap-up, a great color photograph of a new Michigan loading a tractor-dump trailer in some scenic country. Even the little things are correct here. For instance, the truck driver was undoubtedly fascinated by the preparations of the photographer; truck drivers always are. But here he's looking at the action, the loading, *not* at the camera. This is relatively inconsequential, considering how small he appears in the completed illustration, but it's a detail that contributes its small share to complete authenticity.

Headline of this fine spread naturally continues with the established theme; it says:

The new Michigans work like no tractor shovels ever built before.

And the body copy also builds on the interest generated by the single-page inserts, because the key words—dig, heap, load, and go —are in upper-case letters, boldface type, and break the copy naturally where these key user benefits are discussed. It says:

This is the Michigan—5 new rigid-frame and 2 new articulated models from 1⅝ to 7 yds—designed and "task-matched" to fit your loading jobs. And one thing's certain: you've never seen anything like the way they go after these jobs.

DIG Ever see material explode into a bucket? That's how Michigan Bonus Buckets load—maximum bucket speed and rollback angle with "straight-up digging action" **throws** material in.

HEAP 45° rollback from ground to carry—and in less than a second. Result: one quick pass heaps a bucketful in as little as 4 sec. And Michigans **hold** that load—over rough ground.

LOAD New hydraulics zip the bucket to full height up to 53% faster—as fast as 6 sec. The bucket's up long **before** the Michigan reaches the side of the truck —and back down again before you return to the pile. And Michigan's controlled dumping can be as fast as 1.2 seconds!

GO The new Michigans are rock-stable because wheelbase and weight distribution balance perfectly. They operate as easily as your car. And visibility is great—you can even see **behind** the bucket when it's on the ground.

See the new Michigans. You've never seen anything like them before.

Incidentally, this campaign is a radical departure from long-copy case histories Clark has traditionally run. Clark decided to use this striking consecutive-page technique to get the impact it was felt the ads must produce in order to assure a successful introduction of the new line of equipment.

Prime-user benefits—the superior digging ability, loading ability, load-gathering ability (heaping), and stable mobility of the new tractor shovels were naturals for the individual inserts. In fact, these four major benefits suggested the format. And the advertiser had the opportunity in the wrap-up to get into some specifics—solid nuts-and-bolts information and performance data.

Consecutive right-hand pages (rather than left-hand pages) were chosen because it's traditional in the advertising field to believe

The new Michigans dig like no tractor shovels ever built before.

First right-hand insert.

The new Michigans heap like no tractor shovels ever built before.

Second right-hand insert.

The new Michigans load like no tractor shovels ever built before.

Third right-hand insert.

The new Michigans go like no tractor shovels ever built before.

Fourth right-hand insert.

Above are the first four right-hand, four-color inserts of the Clark-Michigan advertisement. The conclusion was a four-color spread, illustrated on the following page.

that right-hand pages receive higher readership than do left-hand ones. Perhaps they do. This will be discussed later.

The announcement ad ran in the following 17 trade magazines:

Engineering News-Record

Western Construction

Pit & Quarry

Contractors & Engineers

Rock Products

Construction

Construction Bulletin

Construction Digest

Construction News

Constructioneer

Dixie Contractor

Michigan Contractor & Builder

New England Construction

Pacific Builder & Engineer

Rocky Mountain Construction

Texas Contractor

Western Builder

The decision to use consecutive right-hand-page inserts and a wrap-up spread was made purely on the basis of grabbing the full, undivided attention of readers of those key books. This is an extremely competitive market for the sale of equipment, and for advertising advantages as well. Most of Clark's competitors use four-page inserts in just about the same media listed above. To make Clark's ad stand out, something more than a four-page, four-color insert was called for.

In any event, the ads received some of the highest readership ratings ever achieved in the construction equipment field. Studies made by John T. Fosdick Associates of the ad that appeared in *Contractors & Engineers* showed that it received noted scores of 58 percent one time, and 62 percent for another insertion.

Ad-Gage readership surveys of *Pit & Quarry* magazine reported scores of 31 (3rd highest) in one issue; 29 (highest) in another;

26 (6th highest) in another; and 34 (highest) in appearances the ad made in that book.

In studies made by McGraw-Hil's Reader Feedback Service in *Engineering News-Record,* the following scores and comments resulted:

> 56 Percent Saw—"I think that he is trying to present the fact that this equipment substitutes for a power dragline or shovel and is less costly." *Engineer, Government Agency*

> "It's like the TV ads. You think 'loader' and then Michigan 175 comes to mind." *Project Superintendent*

> "It's a good ad. The picture is attractive, and you can't help but stop to look at it." *Superintendent*

> 62 Percent Saw—"This ad gives a description of what their machinery will do—in less time, at less cost. The loader here is one that might be particularly suited to what I would want on my jobs." *Superintendent, Construction Company*

> 60 Percent Saw—"The ad has a good picture; it tells the message. Those of us in this business know exactly what it's saying." *Supervisor, Area and Utility Engineering*

> "I noticed that this equipment is larger. With this Clark equipment, I can get the job done faster."
>
> *President, Road and Sewer Construction Company*

Readers—*prospects*—saw and read this fine ad in unprecedented numbers. And, perhaps almost as important, Clark dealers were highly enthusiastic about the kick-off for the new tractor shovels. They reported many customers' mentioning it to them, indication that the ad made a strong and lasting impression. At least it lasted long enough for them to remember to comment on it to the dealer the next time they met. This may have been days, weeks, or even months since they read the ad.

Isn't this what a new product announcement ad *should* do?

Product Description Ads

The average industrial prospect isn't some kind of a fearsome monster lurking in a murky lair somewhere. Nor is he a robot or some kind of a way-out kook.

He's a flesh-and-blood person with perfectly normal feelings and interests and his share of curiosity. One thing he shares with the prospect for any kind of merchandise—industrial or consumer—is that he's interested first and foremost in himself. Uppermost in his mind is what the product will do for him and his company.

Unquestionably these industrial prospects for your product use more cold-blooded logic when they evaluate a product than does a consumer. And they customarily make a hard-headed analysis of the product, comparing it point by point with competitive ones. For this reason, when you're describing your product in copy for an industrial advertisement it pays to give all of the facts and figures and nuts-and-bolts information the reader will need.

Despite this attitude of the industrial prospect, it doesn't pay to confine your ad to a colorless presentation of a mass of cold statistics. Remember you're talking to a human, not a computer, and you'll find he reacts to emotional appeals, to a clean layout, punchy headlines, first-rate photography, attractive typography, and copy that sits up and sings. Give him these in good measure and you'll have an ad that does a real job for you.

Naturally, the ad should counter the negative influences working against the sale. In a survey McGraw-Hill made among salesmen selling to industry it was determined that the sales resistances most frequently encountered are:

Price 63%

Lack of familiarity with the product 26%

Resistance to change 24%

Competition 18%

All other resistances were far down the scale in comparison to the four listed above, and they were relatively unimportant.

A good product description ad can do much to counter every one of these objections. Offhand, price would seem to be an insurmountable obstacle for an advertisement to overcome. After all, no amount of advertising can produce an immediate effect on price—but a well-written product ad can describe the product in such a way, and from the reader's viewpoint, and can make the user benefits so desirable that price becomes a minor consideration. By and large, industrial buyers are far more concerned with quality, service, delivery, and reputation of the seller than they are with price. This is assuming, of course, that the price is within reason and that superior quality of the product justifies charging it.

Lack of familiarity with the product is a pathetic reason for a salesman's difficulty in making a sale—or for his losing it. Certainly this is an area in which advertising can lay to rest this sales resistance effectively and economically. Describe your product and tell what it will do for the buyer—time and time and time again—and this stumbling block will disappear to a large extent.

Everybody is more or less bound by inertia. People don't willingly change direction or do things differently unless they're acted upon by an outside force. There's this to consider, too, when thinking about prospects' resistance to making a change: Your prime prospects may now be buying a product very similar to yours, but one that is actually inferior. Your product may well have more features, better construction, superior materials, a better finish, better engineering, and it may produce more for the user at lower cost.

On the face of it, this would seem to be an ideal situation. When it exists, all your sales force has to do is march into buyers' offices, explain the facts, whip out an order form and pen, then sit back and watch the commission checks roll in.

Unfortunately, life isn't that simple. There's a great deal of doubt about what *really* motivates people in industry who have the authority to make a buying decision. Pocketbook appeal is vitally important, of course, as is the ability of the product to solve a specific problem such as increased production, less maintenance, using less floor space, and so on. All are perfectly valid reasons to buy a product, or not to buy it if it doesn't measure up to the company's requirements in some respect.

But isn't the prime motivation, once a decision to buy has been made, one to buy the *safe, known product?* Specifying the safe product would not subject the buyer to criticism in the event something unforseen should go wrong, or if the product didn't work out as well as anticipated for some reason. The buyer who specifies the product with which all concerned in the purchase are familiar has, in effect, played the old Army game. He has passed the buck as far as accepting responsibility for his decision is concerned. He has delegated a pro-rata share of the responsibility to all who participated in making the decision.

Here advertising can contribute immeasurably by making the advertiser's products and company name known, familiar, accepted, and safe. Advertising can make a massive contribution by helping achieve acceptance for the product, so that it will never be considered unsafe, something to be avoided, something dangerous, and so be ruled out of consideration when a purchase is contemplated.

Industry would be amazed if the dollar volume of sales lost because products weren't considered "safe" could be measured. Nonbelievers in advertising would have conniptions.

Every advertisement puts the advertiser's best foot forward—or it should. But an informative, tightly written product description can stress the product's strong points, concentrate on those which are exclusive with this product, and create desire for it by making apparent its superiority over competitive ones. In this way advertising counters the competition and helps lay to rest the influence competitors wield with prospects, making it much easier for salesmen to book more orders, and do it in less calls.

The fine product description ad run by Vickers Instruments, Inc. in *Metal Progress* magazine does an excellent job of describing product features and construction of a complicated piece of equipment. It is reproduced nearby.

Small captions identifying key points are reversed out of the black background, and matched up with appropriate features of the metallograph to point them out to the reader. Copy is short and bulleted and to the point. It reads:

The Vickers fifty-five metallograph gives you these exclusive performance features:

- *MICROPLAN FLAT FIELD OBJECTIVE LENSES*

- *AUTOMATIC INTEGRATING PHOTOGRAPHIC TIMER actuates motorized focal plane shutter to expose film up to 5" x 7" (Speeds 5 ASA to 3200 ASA)*

- *MOTORIZED 35MM CAMERA actuated by Timer Unit for fully automatic film operation.*

- *OPTICAL BELLOWS gives continuous variation of screen magnification from 24X to 2800X without changing eyepiece or moving screen.*

- *MAGNIFICATION INDICATOR — semiautomatic read-out of total screen magnification.*

- *COMBINATION MOVEMENT ROTATING STAGE with both gliding top plate and micrometer actuated traverse motions.*

- *PNEUMATIC LOADING MICRO-HARDNESS TESTER—desired load automatically applied at correct rate for load selected.*

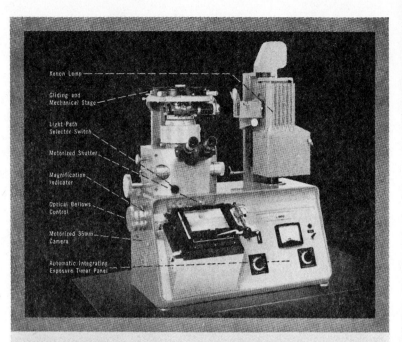

*PLUS UNIVERSAL HIGH-PERFORMANCE OP-
TICAL CAPABILITY—Microscopy of all types—
incident, mixed, and transmitted light—bright field, dark
field, oblique—polarized light—phase contrast—macro
examination and photography 5X, 10X, 15X.*

That copy certainly familiarizes the prospect with features of the Vickers machine.

Product Performance Ads

Quality and performance of the product is the single most important factor in selling to industry.

An excellent opportunity is provided in the product performance-type ad to tell the reader a rousing quality story. You can impress upon him the superiority of the product and the characteristics which make it excel, with no chest-thumping, no boasting.

Furthermore, you appeal to his primary interest—himself—by telling him what the product will do for him. Product performance ads appeal to the reader's self interest, hence enjoy better than average readership. And they automatically enable you to produce reader-oriented copy.

There's high inherent interest in this type of ad because readers of the business press are educating themselves, and they have a lively interest in products and processes which might help them solve a problem confronting them in their company—or which might prevent one from cropping up.

Copy for a product performance ad may discuss features of the product, of course. But it also, and more important, tells what the product does, how it does it, how well it performs its functions, its operating speeds or other characteristics, reliability, maintenance requirements, installation procedure, and other information peculiar to the individual product. All of this is necessary to present it in a favorable light and to give the reader enough information on which to base a tentative buying decision, or to induce a response such as having him write for literature or request a salesman to call.

Just because copy must give nuts-and-bolts information doesn't mean it has to be as dull and unimaginative as a seed catalog. Selecting the *right* information that will appeal most to the reader's needs and interests makes it easy to write an advertisement that's interesting and highly readable. Product differences dictate to a large extent how technical copy should be, although distribution pattern, size of field sales force, and other factors also enter in.

Let's look at three typical product performance ads—three because each varies from the other in the amount of information given to support claims made.

118 lbs. (2 oz.)

Charlene is a telephone operator (from Kansas City. Mo.)—she had to be shown. That's why she took her PPI headset home and weighed it... sure enough, two ounces exactly! Just like we've been saying all along.

But the lightweight headset has a lot of other things going for it too. It's as tough as a hickory bar under rough handling—and gentle as a kitten on Charlene's hair. As if this weren't enough to make PPI headsets the most popular in use today (which they're fast becoming)—they deliver perfect fidelity in voice transmission year after year.

Let's shower girls like Charlene with the things they love—PPI headsets!

PACIFIC PLANTRONICS, INC. 111 Josephine St., Santa Cruz, California

Distributed by: *AUTOMATIC ELECTRIC CO* ● *GRAYBAR* Electric Co., or Contact Your Local Telephone Co. Business Office.

Licensee: S. G. Brown Ltd., Watford, Eng. — a Hawker Siddeley Co.

First is Pacific Plantronics, Inc.'s appealing ad from *Dun's Review*—appealing because who can resist stopping and looking at an illustration of a lovely young miss, hair tucked up, clad only in a large towel, fresh from her shower? Mighty few indeed, and most of these are ready to retire so you can forget about their influencing purchases for very long. The ad is shown above.

Copy of this fine ad strikes just the right tone. It reads:

118 lbs. (2 oz.)

*Charlene is a telephone operator (from Kansas City, Mo.)
—she had to be shown. That's why she took her PPI headset home and weighed it . . . sure enough, two ounces
exactly! Just like we've been saying all along.*

*But the lightweight headset has a lot of other things going
for it too. It's as tough as a hickory bar under rough handling—and gentle as a kitten on Charlene's hair. As if this
weren't enough to make PPI headsets the most popular in
use today (which they're fast becoming)—they deliver
perfect fidelity in voice transmission year after year. Let's
shower girls like Charlene with the things they love—PPI
headsets!*

Illustration and copy are tied together logically and attractively.
First paragraph explains why the illustration is a towel-clad Charlene and establishes a climate of believability for a major product
benefit all at one time. Other benefits follow in the second paragraph
—lightness of the headset is hit again, the fact that the headset is
not fragile, that switchboard operators like it because it doesn't muss
their hair (as tough as good employees are to get today, keeping
them happy is vitally important), and that they deliver superb
fidelity over a long prime of life. Final paragraph is a delightfully
light touch and gets in one more appeal, one more plug to buy the
product.

The spot illustration shows the entire product, including the parts
that don't go on the girl's head. It reinforces the copy and makes
the product come alive.

Another excellent ad with a touch of whimsy is illustrated nearby.
Reynolds Metals Company's two-color ad appeared in *Factory*
magazine. The second color, naturally, is aluminum. It's metallic and
reflects the light just as aluminum paint does.

Again, copy and illustration work closely together; the headline
instantly explains what an otherwise hard-working painter is doing
drawing a jack-o-lantern. Copy reads:

Scare away roof problems

Apply a coat of tough, long-lasting aluminum paint

Even in smoky, corrosive atmospheres, roofs protected with

Scare away roof problems

Apply a coat of tough, long-lasting aluminum paint

Even in smoky, corrosive atmospheres, roofs protected with a coat of aluminum paint stay bright and clean longer. Particles of Reynolds Aluminum Pigment lock together on the painted surface to form a metal shield that resists weathering and corrosion, that will never rust.

Whether your roof is of metal or composition materials, an aluminum shield brushed or sprayed over it will also reflect the sun's radiant heat, and keep your building cooler. Paints made with Reynolds Aluminum Pigment are available in colors and natural aluminum.

To be sure the aluminum paint you're using is the best, be sure it's made with Reynolds Aluminum Pigment. We'll be happy to send you the names of the quality paints that are. Just write Reynolds Metals Company, P.O. Box 2346-PL, Richmond, Virginia 23218.

GIVE THE TOUGH JOBS TO ALUMINUM PAINT

a coat of aluminum paint stay bright and clean longer. Particles of Reynolds Aluminum Pigment lock together on the painted surface to form a metal shield that resists weathering and corrosion, that will never rust.

Whether your roof is of metal or composition materials, an aluminum shield brushed or sprayed over it will also reflect the sun's radiant heat, and keep your building cooler. Paints made with Reynolds Aluminum Pigment are available in colors and natural aluminum.

To be sure the aluminum paint you're using is the best, be sure it's made with Reynolds Aluminum Pigment. We'll be happy to send you the names of the quality paints that are. Just write . . .

Pretty convincing stuff. Roofs that stay bright and clean obviously don't corrode. A metal shield sounds like a husky item to protect a plant. And reflecting the sun's rays to keep the plant cool is certainly a boon that can easily increase employee productivity during the summer months as every manufacturing man knows. This is the kind of copy that whets the appetite for the benefits paints made with Reynolds Aluminum can provide. And Reynolds was astute enough in the bid for action to promise to send the names of *brands* of paints made with its product—thus avoiding the pitfall of advertising to create demand for just any aluminum paint, or plugging a generic name.

Federal Product Performance

Final example of a product performance ad is the exceptionally strong ad run by Federal Products Corporation for the company's Federal Gages. This black-and-white ad appeared in *Production* magazine. It is shown on the following page.

Although it comes quite close to being either a testimonial ad, or a case history ad, it is nonetheless a true product performance ad. Federal's ad falls into this classification because no customer name is mentioned, no customer company is quoted, and the plant in which the machine is installed is not identified.

Copy states what the equipment has done and is doing, making it very easy for the reader to come to the conclusion that Federal Gages can do fully as much for him on his operation.

Federal's multiple headline technique is unusual, but highly effective. It arouses lots of reader interest and creates a strong sense of excitement. The headline sums up the impressive record this piece of equipment has tallied up over the last 10 years.

Body copy is frank and open and believable. The minor maintenance requirements are discussed and documented. The reader instantly senses that Federal would have liked to identify the customer

had that firm's company policy permitted. This is a common problem throughout industry; one with which most people are familiar and understand. It is implied that Federal would be willing to name the customer plant in conversation—and that prospects could then

check with the user of the equipment if they were so inclined. This fine ad reads:

inspected over 2,500,000 engine blocks

20 DIMENSIONS SIMULTANEOUSLY

80 hours per week for more than 10 years

DOWNTIME 0.25%

7 years before cleaning

Chances are, the Federal Automatic Gage in this engine block line has established a new record for high performance and low maintenance. Installed in 1957, it has been working 80 hours a week ever since. It has inspected 2½ million engine blocks, simultaneously checking 20 dimensions and instantly stamping the proper camshaft bore classification on each block that it determines acceptable.

In all that time it has been cleaned just once —in 1964. Parts replacement has averaged one air-electric meter unit per year—one set of air plugs every two years. Total downtime has averaged 10 hours per year—or one quarter of one percent of operating time. Even in the automotive industry, which expects (and gets) the ultimate from its equipment, this is an impressive record!

An example of how the Federal system approach to gaging, integrated into highly automated production equipment, meets the industry's demand for efficient, accurate, trouble-free inspection. Why not get the whole story before you tool up? Write . . .

Federal has an unusually strong story to tell here, and it made the most of it. This copy is down to earth; it talks in the language of the prospect, stresses the benefits he wants in equipment. It carries real conviction.

Incidentally, wouldn't it be great to get reliability in household appliances like Federal Products Corporation builds into its industrial products?

Product Line Ads

There comes a time in the life of every industrial advertising man when it seems he doesn't have much of anything to say. There's a lull in activity. He has no sensational new products to announce. Products he's been advertising have been on the market for some time. So long, in fact, he's just about milked them dry as far as different copy appeals are concerned. This is a logical time to consider preparing a product line ad.

Product line ads serve many useful purposes. First of all, they create an awareness in the reader's mind that the company manufactures an unusually broad line of products, ranging from the smallest shown in the ad up to the largest. A broad range can be impressive.

Many a reader might not have been aware of this range. He may have turned to the company to buy one or two items in the line, but remained blissfully—but unprofitably—unaware that the company also produced items he was buying from another source.

For a customer with a long and satisfactory experience with one product from the company, considerable brand loyalty has been built up. Other things being equal, chances are this satisfied customer would like to buy related items from the company *if he knew it produced them.* One product strengthens the sales of another.

In addition, the product line ad creates an awareness of the company as one with the capability to engineer and produce a complete line. A broad product line gives a company stature. Although the "image" business may be overworked and an image actually be a nebulous thing, don't discount it entirely. A company's reputation as a leader, as one with know-how in depth, as a thoroughly reliable source, is second in importance only to product quality and performance when it comes to selling to industry. Anything that enhances the company's reputation is like money in the bank. Remind an industry from time to time that your company offers every type of widget in existence and the payoff comes in additional sales.

RCA Electronic Components and Devices, a division of Radio Corporation of America, realizes this. RCA did an exceptionally fine job with its two-color spread ad which appeared in *Electronics* magazine; it is reproduced here with RCA's permission.

The second color, red, is used functionally and tastefully. The headline is in red, as is RCA's logo in the lower right-hand corner of the right page. Use of the second color in these two places accomplishes two things: it secures higher readership of the headline

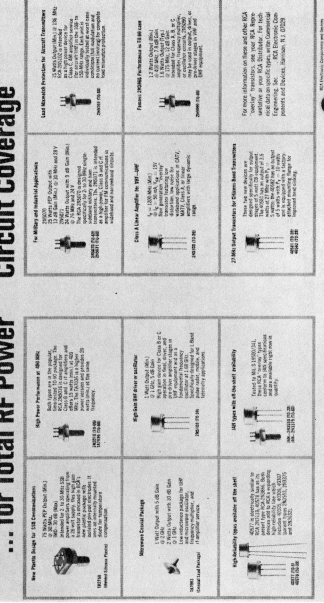

A fine showing of RCA electronic components and devices.

than if it were in black, and it provides very strong advertiser identification.

Too few advertisers exercise restraint when they use a second color; far too many spread the second color around with reckless abandon, apparently under the impression that if they're going to pay for color, they're going to *use* color. This is self-defeating. Overly lavish use of a second color inhibits readership because the ad is invariably so cluttered the reader just can't begin to tell where he's to start reading. The reader won't stop and try to solve little puzzles like this. Instead, he goes on to somebody else's ad.

Organized and Tidy

Despite having 11 different transistors shown, complete with technical descriptions and suggested applications, there's nothing cluttered or junky looking about RCA's ad. The screened boxes organize the copy blocks and illustrations and keep things as neat and tidy as a white picket fence around a vine-covered cottage.

Headline points out that RCA produces the right transistor for each use and the company's broad line makes it a single-source supplier. This is desirable from both the advertiser's and the reader's point of view.

Headline and typical copy blocks read:

RCA "overlay" Transistors
. . . for Total RF Power
Circuit Coverage

New Plastic Design for SSB Communications
75 Watts PEP Output (Min.)
@30 MHz,
IMD—30 dB (Max.)
intended for 2- to 30-MHz SSB
power amplifiers operating from
a 28-volt supply, this high gain
transistor is encased in RCA's
new plastic package with
isolated pin-pad electrodes. It
uses an internally mounted
diode for temperature
compensation.

(Caption)   TA 2758

(Molded Silicone Plastic)

For Military and Industrial Applications
2N5070
25 Watts PEP Output with
13 dB Gain (Min.) @30 MHz and 28 V
2N5071
24 Watts Output with 9 dB Gain (Min.)
@76 MHz and 24 V
The RCA 2N5070 is designed
specifically for 2- to 30-MHz single-
sideband military and ham
transmitters. The 2N5071 is intended
as a high-power, Class B and C rf
amplifier for FM communications in
wideband and narrowband circuits.

(Caption) 2N5070 (TO-60)

2N5071 (TO-60)

Product line ads in regular issues of media normally used in reaching the industrial universe usually do an effective job. They are especially effective in annual issues—so called "Buyer's Guide" issues—and in directories such as *Thomas Register of American Manufacturers, MacRae's Blue Book,* and the various publications of trade associations. In directories the ad gives basic product information which remains "alive" until the next edition of the directory, usually a year.

Problem-Solving Ads

Everybody in industry who has any responsibility has problems connected with his job, and everybody wants to solve them.

Extend a helping hand in an ad—hold out a promise of solving a problem that's bothering the reader and he'll pore over every word you have to say. He'll read and reread what you say about the problem, about your product, then he'll evaluate it based on his past experience.

The approach is an excellent one. You should, however, be sure to give yourself every break by selecting a problem that's relatively commonplace so that a high percentage of readers can identify with it. If you choose some far-out problem your product can solve, one that won't be encountered again until the year 2,000, the "hooker" is too hypothetical and the average reader won't give your ad a second glance. Your sales manager knows what problems prospects encounter regularly; this is fed back to him by the field salesmen.

The problem-solution approach is a time-tested one that's just as potent today and just as interesting as it was when the first industrial advertisement appeared a half-century or so ago.

Identify and describe a problem with which the reader is familiar, then show him how use of your product will enable him to solve it, and he's psychologically conditioned to accept as truth everything you say from that point on. One follows the other just as naturally as night follows day. Base your case on a problem that's pertinent and timely, make it one the reader either has encountered or is likely to, then show your familiarity with it in the copy. Then you're on solid ground.

Readership of a well-done problem-solution ad is usually several percentage points higher than a straight product description ad.

The Dow Chemical Company has an entire campaign based on problem solving; two of the ads are illustrated above. They appeared in *Reinforced Plastics, International Science and Technology,* and in *Materials in Design Engineering* magazines.

Headline is the same for all ads; the subhead varies with specific applications for Dow's line of epoxy resins in order to stress its prime user benefit.

Let's look at the copy of one of these ads:

If we knew about your problem, one of our epoxies might be able to solve it.

The fire-retardant one, maybe.

It's a brominated epoxy resin with high physical and electrical properties. And if that won't do your job, maybe one of our other unique epoxies will. Like our extremely pure one with a viscosity of 4,000—5,500 cps. and 20 ALPHA color max. Or our epoxy novolac resin with unusually high chemical resistance as well as temperature stability. Or our extremely flexible resin.

These are just a few examples. We make a full line of standard resins, too. All are tough, hard, dimensionally stable, chemical resistant, solvent resistant. And one of them just might solve your problem. If you'll let us know about it.

The Dow Chemical Company has developed an unusually good line of epoxy resins which include most of the standard "commodity-type" epoxies plus several others with unique properties. The market for standard epoxies is fairly well known. However, the unique-property epoxies have yet to establish themselves into well-defined market patterns—so this campaign was developed.

There are three primary objectives for the campaign:

1. To increase awareness of Dow's total line of epoxy resins with emphasis on the unique-property resins.

2. Increase awareness of specific properties of Dow's unique-property resins.

3. Produce inquiries to help determine the degree of interest that exists in various segments of the market.

The campaign has been a success. It has produced hundreds of inquiries to be followed up by Dow's field sales force. The sales force is enthusiastic about the campaign and feels it is completely compatible with selling efforts.

Unfortunately, Dow has the same problem most industrial advertising managers have—establishing a positive correlation between the advertising campaign and sales growth. Dow *has* seen significant sales growth in the epoxy area, but cannot attribute any specific percentage to advertising. The advertising has disclosed that one of the largest and most fertile markets for Dow epoxies appears to be among molders of reinforced plastics, so future advertising programs will put more emphasis in media directed to that market.

Micom also poses a problem in the headline, although the word "problem" doesn't appear. It doesn't have to, of course, if it's immediately obvious a problem is to be posed and discussed. This attractive two-color ad is reproduced as it appeared in *Electronics* magazine.

Copy doesn't waste time. It gets right into the heart of the matter in the headline which identifies the problem, then the subhead tells how to solve it. Body copy supports claims and explains exactly how Micom flutter meters eliminate an undesirable situation. The ad says:

How much trouble are you having with flutter and drift?

Here's the only *sure* way to find out:

The Micom solid-state flutter meter provides direct drift and flutter measurement with constant ±2% accuracy . . . an accuracy never before available. Measurements are read out simultaneously on separate front-panel meters, drift from ±0.03% to ±10% and flutter from 0.01% to 10%.

Models are available for use with both instrumentation recording equipment and audio equipment. The 8200 meets or exceeds IRIG Standards; the 8100 measures to NAB and DIN Standards.

These instruments are automatically self-calibrating, making them trouble-free and easy to use. The operator just selects the range and reads the measurement. Their sensitivity is accurate enough for precise lab work yet easy enough to use on the production line.

Why not put these meters to work for you . . . on your tape transport, phonograph turntable, motion picture equipment . . . any rotational apparatus. Write Micom for complete information.

That's a nice package. The problem is posed, the solution is given, then Micom backs up the claim with solid facts. In addition, the copy suggests a number of applications for the flutter meter

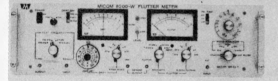

and makes it obvious a graduate engineer isn't needed to operate it. That squelches another sales objection. All in all, a well-done ad that does a job for the advertiser.

Case History Ads

Case history ads give you a double-barreled bonus: They receive higher readership than the average product advertisement, and they are believed implicitly. A combination like that is hard to top.

The reader feels an affinity toward the advertiser and the product featured in a case history advertisement because it is an easy matter for him to project himself and his company into the situation that's illustrated and described. Only a simple mental step is required for him to visualize a piece of equipment in his plant, doing the same job for him that it does for the firm described in the ad.

Chances are the reader has virtually the same problem in his plant (if you've selected it to make sure it's a universal one) and it takes no budding genius to deduce that if a certain product solved a particularly knotty problem at one factory, it surely can in another.

Then, too, there's a theory that many industrial advertising men have shared for a long, long time. No research study has been done to confirm it—or to disprove it, for that matter—but the feeling is too widespread to believe it's altogether lacking in credence. This is that the reader derives a certain sense of satisfaction out of reading that his counterpart in another company has experienced difficulty. He finds this comforting and reassuring. It inflates his ego and contributes to his sense of well being. Naturally, he goes on to read how the problem was solved just in case he ever encounters it, and so absorbs the product message.

It's human nature for one to have a deep interest in reading about the trials and tribulations of others, and to find out how they overcame their troubles and solved their problems. After all, this is the basic raw material from which all fiction is constructed, be it a play, short story, novel, movie, or TV epic. Retain this inherent interest in a case history advertisement where you can show the reader a solid, dollars-and-cents reason why he should use your product, and you will have him hanging on each and every word as if they were sparkling gems, too precious to take a chance on losing.

The reader is perfectly willing to accept the case history ad at face value. It has a ring of sincerity that can't be faked. Statements in the copy are presented to him by somebody with whom he can identify, and in a frame of reference he finds acceptable. And it isn't the advertiser who's making the claims.

Instead of having some unknown advertising manager or agency copywriter trying to force-feed him information which he may or may not want, the reader realizes that copy in a case history ad is a report of the facts; it is based on an unbiased individual's experience with the advertiser's product. Furthermore, the reader knows that verification of the facts is merely a matter of picking up the phone. He is fully aware that no advertiser in his right mind would dream of stretching the truth in a case history ad because the customer's name and company is given.

Built-in believability of the case history ad makes it terrifically potent. If more advertisers were aware ôf its greater impact and greater readership—which means greater effectiveness, of course—there would be far more case history advertisements in the business press than we now see.

Have Copy Verified

When you're writing copy for a case history ad, try to retain the flavor of the remarks the customer made. After all, you're quoting him and putting his reputation on the line. Send the copy to him, asking him to read it for content and accuracy; have him check facts, figures, performance data, production rates, maintenance costs, and other technical material to be sure it is absolutely correct. When you write him, word your letter so that he'll realize you don't want the copy rewritten. You don't want his approval of how you write—merely *what* you write.

You can do this tactfully without ruffling his feelings. Then, when he is satisfied that the copy is "correct," ask him to initial and date a carbon or Xerox copy of it and return it to you with a covering letter stating that it meets with his approval, and that your company has his permission to use it in advertising.

This is a formality in most instances, but should anything ever arise of a legal nature, your company attorneys will regard you as a hero—as will your management. When an ad is being prepared there's no telling whether the equipment may explode in use, or disintegrate, catch fire, injure workmen, or what have you; having copy initialed and formal, written permission to print it can be of utmost importance in such event.

It's always a good idea to show a picture of the customer who's being quoted in the ad. This increases believability and helps the reader by making it immediately apparent this is not a hypothetical story, the copy is talking about a real flesh-and-blood person and company. A fringe benefit is that all of us have a certain amount of vanity and we like to see our names and pictures in print. *Always* have a signed, witnessed model release from any recognizable people in your pictures. Pay the customary dollar for the signature to assure its legality, and make sure the signers are of legal age.

Speaking of pictures, think back for a minute to a group picture in which you appeared. When it was shown to you for the first time, what was your immediate reaction? You looked for yourself. Or, if a group photo was taken in which a friend or customer appeared and you gave them their copy of the photo, didn't they remark at once, "This is good of me," or, "This isn't too good of me." Almost everybody is self-centered to the extent they enjoy seeing themselves in pictures. Customers are no different.

You'll find, if you develop a case history campaign, that you have a bit of difficulty at first in securing enough material—information and photographs. After awhile, however, when the campaign has been running for six months or a year customers will volunteer, perhaps through your field sales force or your dealer organization, to let you feature themselves and their equipment in your ads.

Case history ads accomplish another very desirable objective, too. They firmly cement a good relationship between customer and company. When a customer has been featured in one of your ads, he'll usually become one your hardest-working unofficial salesmen. He identifies with your company and takes great pleasure in telling others in his line of business how good your product is, based on his favorable experience with it. There's no way to measure this residual benefit from a case history campaign, but it's there and it's giving your company advertising that money couldn't buy.

A typical case history advertisement is illustrated nearby. This ad of Lindberg Hevi-Duty's was written by the author. It received a distinguished award, a large and impressive walnut plaque suitably inscribed, from *Ceramic Industries* magazine because this ad received the highest readership of any ad in the magazine for the calendar year in which it appeared, as shown by Cahners Publishing Company's Ad-Ed Audit readership study.

The ad is built on a sound foundation. Uniformity of ceramic products as they are removed from the kiln after firing is a major problem for most manufacturers in that field. If the temperature of the kiln is not completely stable and uniform, product size and quality varies and reject rates shoot up—and profits nose-dive. That the firm featured in the ad fired alumina ceramic pieces within $\pm.003$ (that's three thousands) of an inch, consistently, seven days a week, month in and month out, speaks well for the equipment.

Added authenticity and human interest is built into the ad through use of a small spot illustration of the president of the customer-

Meet a man who fires alumina ceramic pieces within a ± .003 inch tolerance...

He's D. M. Roberts, president of Roberts Engineering & Mfg. Company, Corpus Christi, Texas. He manufactures high explosive "grenades" used to perforate oil wells.

The two halves of the ceramic grenade must fit together *perfectly* to protect the explosive charge until it is detonated. Maximum as-fired tolerance on critical dimensions is ± .003 of an inch.

Alumina ceramic is the ideal material for these sophisticated grenades. Under explosive force it reduces to sand and does not impede oil flow.

Mr. Roberts must have a kiln he can rely on — one with dependable temperature stability and uniformity.

He gets just that with his Lindberg Hevi-Duty Gas-Fired high temperature Car Tunnel kiln. It's been in service three years now, and it works 7 days a week, 24 hours a day. Reject rate of grenades is insignificant.

Lindberg Hevi-Duty has *total capability* in supplying heat to industry. Chances are that Lindberg Hevi-Duty has already solved your problem — or can, and quickly.

For kilns for firing ferrites, electronic ceramics, whiteware, refractories or what have you, write us. Let us study your needs. The address is Lindberg Hevi-Duty, 2450 W. Hubbard Street, Chicago, Illinois 60612. Department Cl351.

LINDBERG HEVI-DUTY SB

company and his plant superintendent. Pictures with people in them always attract more readers than illustrations without people.

Copy is believable because it tells the story from the customer's viewpoint, rather than from the advertiser's. It reads:

Meet a man who fires alumina ceramic pieces within a ±.003 inch tolerance . . .

He's D. M. Roberts, president of Roberts Engineering & Mfg. Company, Corpus Christi, Texas. He manufactures high explosive "grenades" used to perforate oil wells.

The two halves of the ceramic grenade must fit together perfectly *to protect the explosive charge until it is detonated. Maximum as-fired tolerance on critical dimensions is ±.003 of an inch.*

Alumina ceramic is the ideal material for these sophisticated grenades. Under explosive force it reduces to sand and does not impede oil flow.

Mr. Roberts must have a kiln he can rely on—one with dependable temperature stability and uniformity. He gets just that with his Lindberg Hevi-Duty Gas-Fired high temperature Car Tunnel kiln. It's been in service three years now, and it works 7 days a week, 24 hours a day. Reject rate of grenades is insignificant.

Lindberg Hevi-Duty has total capability *in supplying heat to industry. Chances are that Lindberg Hevi-Duty has already solved your problem—or can, and quickly.*

For kilns for firing ferrites, electronic ceramics, whiteware, refractories or what have you, write us. Let us study your needs. The address is . . .

This case history ad is typical of the type in that it gives the name of the individual whose experience is being talked about, his firm name, and the city the customer company is located in. This proves to the reader's satisfaction that the facts are exactly as stated.

This was a highly effective ad. When an ad tops all other advertisements in a book in readership over a year's time, it *has* to have something going for it.

Testimonial Ads

The testimonial ad is a kissing cousin of the case history ad.

And the testimonial ad shares the strengths of the case history ad—excellent readership and believability. Major difference between the two is that in the testimonial ad the customer or user of the product is doing the talking, rather than being quoted.

In actual practice the advertising manager or agency copywriter frequently "helps out a little" by strengthening the customer's remarks, or by making them more grammatical. Often it's necessary to rewrite what the customer said, almost entirely. This is permissible and it's often desirable as long as there is no distortion, no deviation from what the customer actually said.

Many people freeze up when they realize they're going to be quoted. They find it next to impossible to utter more than a monosyllabic grunt, or at most a deadpan yes or no. For some reason or other, the reaction is much the same as the one that occurs when a person unused to having his picture taken sits for a formal portrait, or has a professional photographer take a head-and-shoulder closeup for use in an advertisement. He freezes, becomes extremely self-conscious and his mental processes almost grind to a screeching halt.

If this happens to you when you're gathering background material for a testimonial ad, you're going to have to put words in the customer's mouth. This isn't as dishonest as it might appear. You're undoubtedly thoroughly familiar with the customer's operation, having heard about it from the sales manager, district sales manager, or dealer. What you need now is for the customer to commit himself that the facts *are* the facts—and give you permission to use them over his name.

Ask questions, plenty of questions. When the customer nods yes, or shakes his head no, probe a bit and find out why your supposition is true or untrue. Generally you can count on people unfreezing if you'll be considerate and friendly and genuinely interested in what they're doing. Then the little gems will come trickling forth, the direct quotes in regional colloquialisms that add flavor and color to the copy. Get them down on the tape recorder just as the customer says them—either in his voice or in yours. But get them.

Not all customers are shrinking violets, of course. Many, particularly Southerners, are so loquacious your major effort will be to sort out the wheat from the chaff when you write the ad. It's always preferable to have too much source material than too little, though, so never dry up the fountain that's providing you with the wherewithal for your copy. Encourage him to talk and keep talking, all through lunch, for as long as you consider it necessary to secure sufficient material.

Again, before you set type on copy, be sure to clear it with the customer—and in the case of a large corporation, with the public relations people or whoever has this responsibility assigned to them.

When you're quoting somebody directly a mistake is a serious thing and can be embarrassing for all concerned. Having written clearance and copy approval in the file is something like life insurance; it can't be overdone.

A typical testimonial ad run by Baldwin-Lima-Hamilton, is shown as it appeared in *Materials Handling Engineering, Modern Materials Handling, Factory,* and *Transporte Moderno.*

Interestingly, the headline doesn't quote the customer, although all of the body copy except the bid for action does. And the customer's name, title, company, city, and photograph appear prominently. Copy reads:

Fast, mobile
BLH Austin-Western
hydraulic cranes move
massive loads with ease

"We build gondolas, hopper, and flat cars for railroads and industries at the rate of 2½ new cars per day—plus repairing 5 to 10 cars per week. And our three BLH Austin-Western hydraulic cranes (one 12½-ton 410 Senior, two 7-ton Model 210s) play an important role in keeping things moving—regardless of the weather.

"The A-Ws were picked because of their speed and mobility to handle all kinds of loads in tight spots, even under ice, snow or off-road conditions. Precision hydraulic controls were a big factor, too, because we often must position loads and hold them in place exactly while they are welded. A typical example? An 85-foot-long, 4-ton fabricated steel section of a railroad car. In our book, a crane which can handle a load like that is a useful, versatile machine."

Call your BLH Austin-Western distributor or write us for more details on all nine BLH Austin-Western hydraulic cranes (self-propelled and stationary, boom lengths to 75 ft., capacities to 20 tons).

(Caption)   Certified by Gerry
                    Schmidt, Asst. Supt.
                    Ortner Freight Car Co.
                    Covington, Ky.

Fast, mobile BLH Austin-Western hydraulic cranes move massive loads with ease

Certified by Gerry
Schmidt, Asst. Supt.
Ortner Freight Car Co.
Covington, Ky.

"We build gondolas, hopper and flat cars for railroads and industries at the rate of 2½ new cars per day—plus repairing 5 to 10 cars per week. And our three BLH Austin-Western hydraulic cranes (one 12½-ton 410 Senior, two 7-ton Model 210s) play an important role in keeping things moving—regardless of the weather.

"The A-Ws were picked because of their speed and mobility to handle all kinds of loads in tight spots, even under ice, snow or off-road conditions. Precision hydraulic controls were a big factor, too, because we often must position loads and hold them in place exactly while they are welded. A typical example? An 85-foot-long, 4-ton fabricated steel section of a railroad car. In our book, a crane which can handle a load like that is a useful, versatile machine."

Call your BLH Austin-Western distributor or write us for more details on all nine BLH Austin-Western hydraulic cranes (self-propelled and stationary, boom lengths to 75 ft., capacities to 20 tons). Baldwin-Lima-Hamilton, Austin-Western Plant, Aurora, Ill. 60507.

BALDWIN·LIMA·HAMILTON
A subsidiary of Armour and Company

Copy is convincing because the customer is obviously a responsible individual who knows what he's talking about. He speaks authoritatively.

Both case history and testimonial ads carry great conviction, as is proved by the example pictured above.

585

Inquiry Ads

Far too many industrial advertisers judge the effectiveness of their advertising programs solely by one criterion—how many inquiries are produced.

This is a mistake. It's unfortunate for advertising and unfortunate for the advertiser. Although there's invariably a signature and address at the close of the copy in the ad (except for the Cummins ad discussed recently), and usually a bid for action, most industrial ads are not designed specifically to produce inquiries. Probably nowhere in advertising is there more misunderstanding than there is on this score.

Readers respond to an advertisement—they inquire, as it's put—primarily because they want additional information about a product they feel might be useful to them. Or they inquire because they've been assigned the responsibility of collecting information on all similar products prior to having somebody upstairs making a purchasing decision. Or they want literature to enable them to compare products themselves.

Or they're inveterate literature collectors.

Literature collectors are the bane of an advertising manager's life. One time 10 years or so ago when the author was at the old Diamond T Motor Truck Company, there occurred an encounter with one of the most avid collectors extant. It was like this.

As a matter of policy, all incoming inquiries from space advertising, sales promotion, public relations, shows and so on were carefully and systematically screened. A naturally competitive spirit and a hunger for sales combined with a well-developed sixth sense and much practice made it possible to sense with some degree of accuracy those inquiries which were probably the hottest. No claim whatsoever is made for anything approaching perfection, nor for being able to weed out the out-and-out nixies.

One morning just before 9:30 coffee, while still not fully awake, a particular inquiry rang a mental bell most clamorously. The name of the inquirer was familiar! This was, without doubt, one of the hottest prospects to come down the pike of recent moons. The inquiry was carefully put aside for immediate action—immediate as soon as the rest of the inquiries were screened and coffee break was over.

Then, heavens to Betsy, what should show up in the balance of the day's inquiries except *eight* more inquiries from this same worthy gentleman! Two came from publicity and the others from space ads in six different books; somehow one book duplicated, it seemed.

All of the inquiries were concerned with three different models of motor trucks. In itself this wasn't unusual because all were quite similar and could easily have been used for the same application.

Obviously these inquiries had to be handled right then and there.

The customary snap-out inquiry form wasn't good enough for this prospect. He was too hot. It was too easy to sit there (before coffee) and visualize him sitting in *his* office (also before coffee, of course) just panting in his eagerness to give the company's local dealer an order for an entire fleet of trucks. And the models he was interested in were very near the top of the line. This could be a *really* big sale.

Visions of a large and highly profitable sale directly attributable to advertising danced through the author's head. Nothing would do except to dictate a special letter—and an extremely cordial one at that—to the inquirer, send it and appropriate sales literature by airmail, with blind carbon copies to the district manager and the local dealer to whom the inquirer was referred.

Then all that remained to be done was sit back, take care of routine and anxiously await the long distance call—or an airmail letter at the very least—from the happy dealer thanking the good old advertising department for the lucrative lead.

But nothing happened, nothing at all.

Finally, consumed with curiosity, a memo went out to the district manager. It should have evoked an immediate response, since it was a little bit plaintive. No reply, so the only possibility to be considered was that the district manager was making a lengthy swing around his territory and wasn't up to date on happenings in this particular city.

Nothing from the dealer either, so, consumed by curiosity, a call was made to the dealer. He laughingly thanked advertising for helping him, then explained the inquiries had all come from a 12-year-old whose father was a mechanic at a competitive dealership down the road a mile or so. Out of curiosity, the dealer traced down the whys and wherefores and found the mechanic was in the habit of taking home back issues of trucking publications when the office staff finished with them. His young son was enamored with trucks and soon found out that mailing bingo cards with his home address and a fictitious firm name swamped him with pretty literature. When his father found out that salesmen were wasting their time, he put a stop to it.

This isn't to denigrate inquiries. Inquiries are a valuable source of high quality sales leads. Handling inquiries is a subject all in itself and will be discussed in a forthcoming chapter.

In the meantime, let's look at three distinct types of inquiry ads. Each was produced to perform two functions—give readers a reasonable amount of information about the products and the companies, and to induce them to respond to the ad by filling out and returning a bingo card, or writing to the company directly.

Reichhold Chemicals Inc. does it up big and bold in its one-page, black-and-white ad illustrated nearby. Actually, the ad is composed mostly of coupon, making it more than obvious that Reichhold wants a response from the reader.

Again, the pulling power of the word "sample" is relied upon to help induce a response, and again a free sample of the product is offered—although this fact is not headlined. Instead, the headline makes use of the potent word "new" to stimulate readership, while the actual offer is buried in the body copy. Theoretically this cuts down on the number of inquiries, but raises their quality because, thinking has it, only those deeply interested in the product will have read far enough into the ad to discover the free offer.

Copy of Reichhold's ad reads:

Hydrocarbon Resins:
get filled in on something new.

What's new is Reichhold as a source for your petroleum hydrocarbon resins. We have a new plant now producing several families of high quality, high purity resins for floor tiles, adhesives, paints, rubber and many other applications. Bring yourself up-to-date on these new RCI hydrocarbon resins. Reichhold is one of the oldest developer-manufacturers in resins, with 40 years experience.

Get filled in on what's new from Reichhold. Samples are available upon request. For data sheets and a catalog of all our petroleum hydrocarbon resins, use this coupon.

Inquiry producing ads don't have to be spreads, or even full pages. If the appeal is right and the copy gets right to the nub of the situation, a fractional page can do a job.

An outstanding example is a one-third page ad run by Industrial Electronic Engineers, Inc. This powerful little ad uses one of the most productive headlines possible to devise. The word "free" is probably the biggest puller in the dictionary, and when combined with another power word, "samples," proves almost irresistible.

Hydrocarbon Resins:
get filled in on something new.

What's new is Reichhold as a source for your petroleum hydrocarbon resins. We have a new plant now producing several families of high quality, high purity resins for floor tiles, adhesives, paints, rubber and many other applications. Bring yourself up-to-date on these new RCI hydrocarbon resins.

Reichhold is one of the oldest developer-manufacturers in resins, with 40 years experience.

Get filled in on what's new from Reichhold. Samples are available upon request. For data sheets and a catalog of all our petroleum hydrocarbon resins, use this coupon.

Reichhold Chemicals, Inc.
RCI Building, White Plains, N. Y. 10602

Send me your new bulletin on petroleum hydrocarbon resins and data sheets on your resins for
☐ floor tile ☐ adhesives ☐ paints ☐ rubber ☐ (other application)_____

Name_____

Firm_____

Address_____

City_____ State_____ Zip_____

REICHHOLD [RCI]

This is the most common type of ad seeking a response. Lots of room is given the coupon on which readers may request informational literature. Other response-oriented ads may feature a free gift or invite participation in a contest.

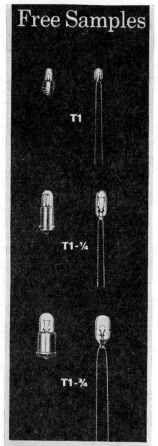
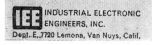
Response was exceptional to this Industrial Electronics Engineers ad, and for *quality* of the inquiries. This ad produced inquirers who were ready to buy.

Copy of this little powerhouse reads:

Free Samples
Miniature Lamps

Our miniature lamp prices are so low—about one-half the cost of competitive lamps—people sometimes wonder about their performance. So we're giving away samples to prove they are top quality, in spite of the low cost. In fact, most of our aged and selected lamps are priced lower than competitive lamps that are not aged and selected.

Simply drop us a line on your company letterhead, describing your application, and we'll send you a sample box of 10 IEE lamps. You select the lamp numbers. We'll do the rest.

We have a wide selection available in stock right now. So drop us a line and we'll send you some. Free.

That's a proposition that's pretty hard to discourage. The thought of getting equal quality at lower cost is enough to tug at one's heart strings.

And this fine ad proves the truth in an old adage: Make an offer and you'll get a response.

The ubiquitous coupon is another surefire way to assure a satisfactory flow of inquiries, as well as to gain a slight increase in readership.

Reversed out of the bold black area, and with the six different free samples shown in the illustrative area, the ad really pulled 'em in.

According to Industrial Electronic Engineers, the primary objective of the ad was to cultivate pertinent information on potential lamp customers. The company sends an evaluation form to each inquirer; when it's returned an analysis of the information will give the company a profile on actual customer requirements, applications, and so on. Names of inquirers will be compiled into a lamp mailing list, and also will be forwarded to representatives for follow-up sales calls.

The hydrocarbon resins are a new product with Reichhold Chemicals Inc. Primary purpose of the ad was to tell the chemical processing industry that Reichhold is very much in the hydrocarbon resin business, and that RCI wants potential customers to have samples of its resins. The ads ran in *Chemical & Engineering News* and in *Chemical Week*.

And the copy in the coupon reads:

> *Send me your new bulletin on petroleum hydrocarbon resins and data sheets on your resins for* ☐ *floor tile* ☐ *adhesives* ☐ *paints* ☐ *rubber* ☐ *(other application)*........

In three months, RCI received 153 inquiries from the two books from the ad shown, 43 inquiries from editorial mention—publicity releases—and 17 letterhead inquiries, for a total of 213.

Names of inquirers were forwarded to the company's field sales force, of course, and if the lead proves promising the inquirer's name is added to RCI's mailing list.

Since RCI started from ground zero with this program, the only way the company can go is up. This will make it relatively easy to evaluate the advertising program by doing a bench-mark recognition study after the ads have run for a year.

A different type of ad—although still of the inquiry variety—is an ad created for Microdot, Inc., West Coast manufacturer of high quality connectors for the electronics industry.

This highly successful campaign was developed to involve the reader and to induce a response from him. Let's look at the copy of the ad, then at the rationale for this type of campaign. It reads:

THE CONNECTOR THING

A periodical periodical designed to further the sales of Mi-

crodot Inc. connectors and cables. Published entirely in the interest of profit.

DICK TRUMMER WINS MICRODOT

You've thrilled to the fabled romance of Damon and Pythias, Pyramus and Thisbe, Proctor and Gamble. Now, grab a hankie and read the tale of Trummer and Microdot.

BOY MEETS CONNECTOR

Once upon a time, as they say, there was a young Wisconsin lad with two compelling interests—space technology and rowing. Richard Owen Trummer pursued both interests at the University of Wisconsin, where he received his B.S.M.E. and coached the rowing team. Later, as a components engineer at AC Electronics, part of his job was to recommend the right components for inertial guidance systems. But an equally important part of the job was helping the people who make those components to do a better job for AC.

One component category of concern to Dick was connectors. That's how Dick Trummer came to know of Microdot. But wait! Even more breathtaking is the saga of how Microdot came to know Trummer.

ALL-TIME CHAMPION CONTEST WINNER!

Our current series of ads is now more than two years old; and almost every ad offers an opportunity to enter some sort of contest. For example, our very first ad in the series asked readers to compete in assembling our Microcrimp connectors in record time. Winners received prizes such as a Honda, a Schwinn bike, and an Irish Mail.

That's when we first heard of Dick Trummer. His speed in assembling our Microcrimp connector beat out all but two other contestants—and made him the proud owner of an Irish Mail. The fact that Dick didn't even know what an Irish Mail was gave birth to a second contest in which

THE CONNECTOR THING

A periodical periodical, designed to further the sales of Microdot Inc. connectors and cables. Published entirely in the interest of profit.

DICK TRUMMER WINS MICRODOT

You've thrilled to the fabled romances of Damon and Pythias, Pyramus and Thisbe, Procter and Gamble. Now, grab a hankie and read the tale of Trummer and Microdot.

BOY MEETS CONNECTOR

Once upon a time, as they say, there was a young Wisconsin lad with two compelling interests — space technology and rowing. Richard Owen Trummer pursued both interests at the University of Wisconsin, where he received his B.S.M.E. and coached the rowing team. Later, as a components engineer at AC Electronics, part of his job was to recommend the right components for inertial guidance systems. But an equally important part of the job was helping the people who make those components to do a better job for AC.

One component category of concern to Dick was connectors. That's how Dick Trummer came to know of Microdot. But wait! Even more breathtaking is the saga of how Microdot came to know Trummer.

ALL-TIME CHAMPION CONTEST WINNER!

Our current series of ads is now more than two years old; and almost every ad offers an opportunity to enter some sort of contest. For example, our very first ad in the series asked readers to compete in assembling our Microcrimp connectors in record time. Winners received prizes such as a Honda, a Schwinn bike and an Irish Mail.

That's when we first heard of Dick Trummer. His speed in assembling our Microcrimp connector beat out all but two other contestants — and made him the proud owner of an Irish Mail. The fact that Dick didn't

TRUMMER'S NEW WINNER: THE HIGH DENSITY MULTI-PIN MARC 53

Here's why Dick Trummer considers MARC 53 a winner: It's the smallest and most flexible high density multi-pin on the market. It meets MIL-C-38300 Rev. A (USAF) and is NASA approved for manned space flight applications. It features "Posilock", the finest blind mating coupling mechanism ever devised, and "Posiseal"—the best environmental seal. (Ask Dick what we mean by the floating interfacial seal concept.) Contacts are completely scuff-proof. Our new MARC 53 RMD gives you a genuinely field serviceable version that takes mass-produced pre-crimped wires and requires neither insertion nor extraction tools for assembly. A color-sound film that tells you all about the assembly of MARC 53 is now available.

even know what an Irish Mail was, gave birth to a second contest in which we awarded lapel buttons reading "I know what an Irish Mail is."*

After that, Trummer was hooked. In a way, so was Microdot. Every contest brought a Trummer entry. Most of them were excellent. And since we're honest folk, we had to judge without partiality. Result: Trummer also won a whole stack of Capitol record albums for a new idea on what to do with our Twist/Con concept. And by June of this year, the word was out among our loyal readers and contest entrants: GET TRUMMER!

And that's what we did.

As of September 1, Richard Owen Trummer has been appointed Military Products Manager of Microdot's Connector and Cable Products. In this capacity, Dick will act as technical liaison man between Microdot and many of its most important customers. *(For one of Dick's new winners, see box on this page.)*

Most important benefit: as a bona fide permanent employee of Microdot Inc., Dick Trummer is now *ineligible* to enter any of our "Connector Thing" contests. Once again, there's room at the top! So take pen in hand with renewed hope. With Trummer out of the way, anything is possible. Who knows. If you win enough contests, we may hire you.

RECENT CONTEST WINNERS (Other than Dick Trummer)

CARY A. MATUSZAK, R&D Technician at the Republic Division of Rockwell Mfg. Co., is the winner of our "Great American Cable" Contest. Happy viewing on your new Sony TV.**

WINNERS of our "Let Microdot Take You To The Movies" contest:
1. **Grand Prize:** ROBERT H. AILOR, NASA Redstone Arsenal
2. **Runner Up:** MARVIN SENTER, Litcom Division, Litton Industries
Honorable mention awards in the form of imitation "Oscars" go to— R. H. KLEMM (Bethpage, N.Y.), G. E. FOGLEMAN (Washington, D.C.), PAUL KURLAND (Lansdale, Pa.), R. R. RIEBSAMEN (W. Palm Beach, Fla.), P. W. LANCASTER (Philadelphia), and — guess who— yep—RICHARD OWEN TRUMMER, *formerly* of Wisconsin. (That's it, Dick.)

*If you know, please write. We still have some buttons left.

**Winning slogan: "Microdot cable withstands the test of time."

MICRODOT INC.

220 Pasadena Ave., S. Pasadena, Calif. 91030

---

*we awarded lapel buttons reading "I know what an Irish Mail is."**

**If you know, please write. We still have some buttons left.*

After that, Trummer was hooked. In a way, so was Microdot. Every contest brought a Trummer entry. Most of them were excellent. And since we're honest folk, we had to judge without partiality. Result: Trummer also won a whole stack of Capitol record albums for a new idea on what to do with our Twist/Con concept. And by June of this year, the word was out among our loyal readers and contest entrants: GET TRUMMER!

And that's what we did.

As of September 1, Richard Owen Trummer has been appointed Military Products Manager of Microdot's Connector and Cable Products. In this capacity, Dick will act as technical liaison man between Microdot and many of its most important customers. (For one of Dick's new winners, see box on this page.)

Most important benefit: as a bona fide permanent employee of Microdot Inc., Dick Trummer is now ineligible to enter any of our "Connector Thing" contests. Once again, there's room at the top! So take pen in hand with renewed hope. With Trummer out of the way, anything is possible. Who knows. If you win enough contests, we may hire you.

RECENT CONTEST WINNERS
(Other than Dick Trummer)

Cary A. Matuszak, R&D Technician at the Republic Division of Rockwell Mfg. Co., is the winner of our "Great American Cable" Contest. Happy viewing on your new Sony TV.**

WINNERS of our *"Let Microdot Take You To The Movies"* contest:

1. *Grand Prize:* Robert H. Ailor, NASA Redstone Arsenal.

2. *Runner Up:* Marvin Senter, Litcom Division, Litton Industries.

Honorable Mention awards in the form of imitation "Oscars" go to— R. H. Klemm (Bethpage, N. Y.), G. E. Fogleman (Washington, D. C.), Paul Kurland (Lansdale, Pa.), R. R. Riebsamen (W. Palm Beach, Fla.), P. W. Lancaster (Philadelphia), and—guess who— yep—RICHARD OWEN TRUMMER, *formerly* of Wisconsin. (That's it, Dick.)

***Winning slogan: "Microdot cable withstands the test of time."*

TRUMMER'S NEW WINNER:
THE HIGH DENSITY MULTI-PIN
MARC 53

Here's why Dick Trummer considers MARC 53 a winner: It's the smallest and most flexible high density multi-pin on the market. It meets MIL-C 38300 Rev.A (USAF) and is NASA approved for manned space flight applications. It features "Posilock," the finest blind mating coupling mechanism ever devised, and "Posiseal"—the best environmental seal. (Ask Dick what we mean by the floating interfacial seal concept.) Contacts are completely scuffproof. Our new MARC 53 RMD gives you a genuinely field serviceable version that takes mass-produced pre-crimped wires and requires neither insertion nor extraction tools for assembly. A color-sound film that tells you all about the assembly of MARC 53 is now available.

As for the rationale of the campaign, thinking was at Microdot's advertising agency, "Who cares about connectors?"

This is a fact of life faced up to by too few advertisers. In some products there simply is very little inherent interest. It's up to the advertiser to *make* the product interesting.

When Microdot and its agency sat back and considered the question objectively, they came to an inescapable conclusion. To solve the problems of promoting a multiproduct connector line to the electronics industry, you address yourself to the question asked above. Who cares about connectors? And the answer is, "nobody."

At least not very much.

The reason doesn't lie in the rarity of the product's application. To the contrary. Virtually every designer of electrical/electronic systems, devices, and assemblies must specify connectors—at least once in a while. But studies show that the amount of thought he devotes to this problem is something less than awe inspiring.

To understand the reason, pick up any current electronics publication and pretend for a few minutes you're a design engineer. In both editorial and advertising pages, you'll find exciting news about the latest integrated circuits, miniaturized digital computers, planar transistors, new measuring instruments, electrostatically focused klystrons, and so forth and so on.

You'll also see a lot of ads on connectors—most of them as dull as an all-thumbs handyman's tools.

And even if they're not dull, why should you read about connectors, when you can bring yourself up-to-date on all those other little goodies?

The very large connector manufacturers (Amphenol, ITT Cannon, Bendix, Sprague and so on) overcome this low reader interest with what could be called "tonnage"—they run almost tons of ads and spend a lot of money. Presumably, they can afford to.

Microdot cannot. Microdot is a pioneer in electronic connectors and offers one of the broadest lines in the industry, but the company has traditionally concentrated on high-quality, high-performance requirements. Sales volume has grown steadily, but is still much smaller than the competitors just mentioned.

Further—for a number of reasons—the company had been a sporadic advertiser of its connector lines for at least two years. New developments needed to be announced and promoted.

On the positive side, Microdot has good marketing management, one of the best networks of representatives in the industry, good distributor coverage, and excellent customer acceptance. And some mighty fine products.

"Involvement" Was Needed

What was required from advertising can be summed up in one word—involvement. The dictionary says the word "involve" means to "draw in as a participant." That's what Microdot felt should be done with the company sales force, representatives, distributors—and customers and prospects. It needed to be done on a continuing basis and at relatively low cost.

The answer turned out to be an approach born from several sound principles of mass consumer advertising too rarely applied to technical communications. First, humor; second, direct participation contests; and third, clever "give-aways" to reward the reader for involving himself in the product messages.

Probably the reason these techniques are so seldom applied to technical advertising is that they are dangerous. A rather deft touch is required, tempered with sensitive judgment. Unless you have both the touch and the judgement it's much safer to go the route of the straightforward product exposition.

In this case, though, both the advertiser and the agency had the courage to do something unorthodox, so reaped benefits quite outsize to the dollars expended.

The first of these weird looking ads ran a little over a year ago in several electronics magazines. It looked like a "one-page newspaper put together by a team of drunken typesetters and layout

men"—as Microdot put it. It called itself "The Connector Thing"—
and in contemporary hip language it was a "connector happening."

The first contest asked the customer to participate in a race for
the world record at assembling Microdot's solderless "Microcrimp"
connector. (Ease of assembly is this connector's main selling feature.) Readers had to send in a coupon. A Microdot representative
would then call on them, show them how to assemble the connector,
give them 10 minutes to practice, and then time their attempt to
win the contest.

For the winner—a Honda; second prize—a Schwinn bicycle; third
prize—an Irish Mail. (Later Microdot ran a followup contest for
people who actually knew what an Irish Mail is). Do you?

In the same ad the company listed all of the trade names of its
connector lines (from Micro/Con, Lepra/Con and Twist/Con to
Golden Crimp and Microcrimp) and pointed out that it was time
readers organized against the ad men who perpetrated these das-
tardly crimes. Microdot then offered a free poster entitled "Help
Stamp Out Advertising Men" to anyone who filled in a coupon.

(If that ploy doesn't line up the engineers in solid ranks, what
will? In the author's opinion, it is a pusillanimous thing to do because ad men were not given equal time—or space—for a rebuttal.
Selling us out, right down the river, and to *engineers,* at that!)

In the next ad the advertiser introduced a new ultraminiature
connector; it was written about extensively and the question was
then put to readers—how many of these mighty midgets would fit
into a Smirnoff bottle—or a Jack Daniels bottle—or a J&B Scotch
bottle. Winners, of course, received a case of the booze of their
choice.

Patience and Persistence

Meantime, the success of the first contest caused Microdot
to hold it over for the next two ads. In between contests there were
offers of lapel buttons, bumper stickers and—actually—pictures of
pretty girls like Miss Twist/Con. And, of course, catalogs and
technical literature. This program wasn't developed for the sake
of charity.

Success didn't come overnight. There was a steady trickle of
coupons that created opportunities for new customer contacts. But
along about the fourth month, the dam broke. Readers had caught
on and the response coupons were coming in by the *hundreds.* Not
bingo cards, but filled-in coupons and attached letters from readers
whose sense of humor combined with genuine product interest had

caused them to climb on Microdot's bandwagon. As the direct response increased, so did the readership ratings of the ads. Today, "The Connector Thing" places in the top 5 to 10 percentile of virtually every readership study run on books in which one of the ads appears.

Perhaps one of the toughest groups of pros from which to evoke enthusiasm about an advertising campaign are the independent representatives. They are constantly under pressure from sales managers to follow through on essentially meaningless "leads" from ads. They are bombarded by their principals' memos on ads; and they get pretty jaded about the whole thing.

Therefore, when Microdot advertising people appeared before a national meeting of Microdot representatives and received unsolicited testimonials from a majority of those present, they really knew "The Connector Thing" was doing a job.

It was and is doing a job because it melds a warm, human tone with a sincere interest in good products. Incidentally, the success of these ads proved to Microdot that—

1. Even engineers will respond to an emotional appeal provided it is backed by solid information to satisfy their technical "need to know."

2. Engineers don't always act like squares. Given a chance to join in something goofy, they'll let their hair down and act almost like the rest of us.

3. There's no need to be afraid of long body copy if it appeals to both emotional and intellectual appetites. "The Connector Thing" ads contain copy that runs well over 500 words. And they get read. Microdot has checked this out by hiding offers in the last paragraph of body copy (with no coupon) and has drawn hundreds of responses.

This campaign has been outstandingly effective in producing high-quality inquiries. According to Leon Levitt, manager of advertising and public relations for Microdot at the time, each of the ads has averaged about 1,000 inquiries; the offer of a 1967½ calendar (just before midyear) drew 3,400 requests.

Obviously with this volume of inquiries it's a pretty difficult thing to track down each one to determine if it resulted in a sale. Microdot hasn't made such an attempt. But one thing is as certain as rising taxes: This flood of inquiries represents far more than paper shuffling.

Connector sales at Microdot are up sharply—very sharply—since this campaign was launched. Nobody at the company maintains that advertising is solely responsible for this surge in sales, but the company still has the same fine marketing management, the same representatives, the same distributors and the same fine products.

The element in the picture that's different is the advertising.

It speaks for itself.

Catalog Offer Ads

The catalog offer ad is essentially an inquiry ad. Inquiries are just as welcome and they're followed up by the advertiser's sales force just as assiduously as if the ad were designed specifically to elicit a response.

Important difference, though, between the two types is that the advertiser who uses the catalog offer is primarily interested in having information about his product in the hands of his prospects. He wants them to be aware of his product so that when they decide to buy—presumably at some time in the future—they will refer to it.

As a rule, catalogs that are offered in ads are "complete line" catalogs. They're packed with such a wealth of information, data, and specifications on such a wide variety of models that it would be a physicial impossibility to mention even a fraction of them in an ad—perhaps even in an entire year's campaign. Back tables and shelves behind the purchasing agents' desks are crammed with thick, bulky, highly informative catalogs to which they refer constantly in the course of a day's work. Merely having the catalogs available is analogous to having merchandise on display in a department store.

Objective of the ad is to announce availability of the catalog, create additional awareness of the company, and to make certain that a group of buying influences—determined by the media selected —*wants* the catalog and *requests* it.

Then, when the field sales force follows up and a sale doesn't result immediately, nobody's surprised or disappointed. But the advertisement has nonetheless achieved its objective because the catalog is where the advertiser wants it to be. And chances are good it will stay right there until it is superceded by a new issue of the catalog, and that it will be "working" all the while.

Rust-Oleum Corporation's half-page ad shown nearby does dual duty in this way. It appeared in *Iron Age, Steel, Industrial Engineering News, New Equipment Digest,* and *Purchasing Week. Steel* and *Purchasing Week* no longer exist as such. Copy reads:

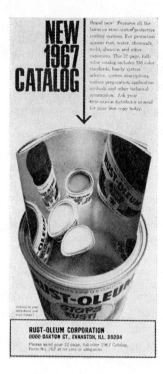

NEW 1967 CATALOG

Brand new! Features all the latest on RUST-OLEUM protective coating systems. For protection against rust, water, chemicals, mold, abrasion, and other exposures. This 32-page, full-color catalog includes 180 color standards, handy system selector, system descriptions, surface preparation, application methods and other technical information. Ask your RUST-OLEUM distributor or send for your free copy today.

Then, in five-point type just to the right of the bucket, in parenthesis, is a nice touch to increase response—instruction is given to clip out the address at the bottom of the ad and attach it to a letterhead. This makes it remarkably easy to reply with no coupon, no bingo card, no having a busy secretary write one more letter.

Rust-Oleum has been running around 100 inquiries a month, with 90 to 95 percent of those representing "good sales potential." One thing is sure, though, even if the inquirers don't buy immediately— they have a rust problem, they're interested in solving it, and with the Rust-Oleum catalog in their possession the chances are good they'll buy the Rust-Oleum brand.

A second catalog offer, this one a two-color spread—with the only spot of second color being a rusty-looking red in the words "stops rust!" in the lower right hand corner of the spread—is being used by Rust-Oleum. This ad also stresses the breadth of line of company products and again offers the new catalog.

Universe, determined by media, is entirely different in this ad, as is the slant. This spread ran in *Industrial Distribution* magazine and has as its objective the broadening of Rust-Oleum's distribution— signing up new distributors for Rust-Oleum products. Copy says:

New 1967
Rust-Oleum
Protective
Coating
Systems
Catalog

Where the action is . . . that's where this great, new sales tool will be! Right on your customers' desks. And Rust-Oleum is going all out to put it there. With national advertising (many ads in full color) in Newsweek, Business Week, *and leading industrial magazines. With direct mail campaigns custom-tailored for each participating Rust-Oleum distributor. And with news releases to the nation's business press.*

The story: 32 pages with full color cover-to-cover. 180 actual color standards. A unique System Selector that pinpoints recommended surface preparation methods and Rust-Oleum coating systems for specific exposures and conditions.

This unique new catalog highlights a complete sales program designed to build more sales for Rust-Oleum distributors.

The advertiser relies on the good old pocketbook appeal and on telling the distributors how much advertising-merchandising support they'll be provided with. A standard approach, but the one that interests this audience most.

Many advertisers customarily offer a less elaborate piece of literature to solicit inquiries in different types of ads. Others offer catalogs—expensive to produce, handle, and mail—on a highly selective basis on the theory that the product must have exposure and this is one way of getting it. Seldom does it pay to run an ad offering a piece of literature on a single new product; just as many inquiries—if not more—will result from using publicity to do this job. Other methods of getting additional mileage from literature will be gone into in the chapter on that subject.

Newsletter Ads

Newsletter ads average around 25 percent higher readership than ads that are more ad-like.

Near relatives of newsletter ads—advertisements which closely resemble editorial matter in publications in which they appear—can be counted on to garner higher readership, also. In the business press this edge in readership is generally considered to be around 5 percent, although some studies have indicated it to be considerably higher; in mass consumer media it has been found that editorial-type advertisements receive as much as 50 percent more readership than obvious paid ads.

This is not to infer there's a dislike for, or rejection of, advertising by readers of business publications. On the contrary, good business paper advertising is read thoroughly, and even poor advertising is read. It's just that newsletter ads are eye catchers. They stop the reader right in his tracks with a strong implied promise that if he'll but take the time to read the ad he'll receive an abundance of interesting and helpful information. Actually, the reader is more inclined to read than he is to pass by. Newsletter ads, by their very nature, have a strong sense of immediacy, of containing something timely and fresh. They have the ability to involve the reader very rapidly.

Newsletter ads excel in being readily adaptable to either corporate or product advertising, and to fit into almost any given situation. All that's required is subject matter that's honestly interesting to those to whom you want to talk. And this is important: *The subject matter must be of genuine interest to those to whom you want to talk.*

Semiconductor Report

ABOUT SPACE-SAVING MICRO-T TRANSISTORS FOR OPTIMUM DESIGN FLEXIBILITY

NEW MICRO-T TRANSISTORS SOLVE HIGH-DENSITY PACKAGING PROBLEMS

Motorola's Micro-T° molded Unibloc° plastic transistors now provide the ultra-small devices you've needed to make those high-density, miniaturized equipment designs a practical reality. The new Micro-T is only about one-tenth the volume of standard plastic or TO-18 packages. Handling problems disappear too . . . because the leads of the Micro-T radiate from the center, making it particularly well-suited to "drop-in" PC-board mounting.

The Micro-T is "at home" anywhere high-density packaging is required . . . electronic watches, hearing aids, satellites, high-frequency instruments and many, many more. In short, the Micro-T lets you design circuits that provide *discrete device* performance and design flexibility; while, at the same time, achieve the component densities and space reductions approaching that of integrated circuits. For example, it makes an ideal device for use in thick-film and unitized circuit assemblies.

COMPLEMENTARY SWITCHING AND AMPLIFIER TYPES FIRST MICRO-T's AVAILABLE

MMT3903-04 (NPN) and MMT-3905-06 (PNP) Micro-T transistors boast a host of premium specs for general purpose switching and amplifier applications, as well as for complementary circuitry. In fact, the specifications are identical to those of their standard (TO-92) plastic-packaged counterparts—2N3903-06. Yet, you gain the added advantages of space-saving and handling-ease—available only with Motorola's Micro-T!

Here are the specs that make these Micro-T types an "evaluation must":

CHARACTERISTICS	TYPES			
	NPN		PNP	
	MMT3903	MMT3904	MMT3905	MMT3906
BV$_{ceo}$	40 V	40 V	40 V	40 V
C$_{obo}$	4 pf	4 pf	4 pf	4 pf
P$_D$ @ T$_A$ = 25°C	225 mW	225 mW	225 mW	225 mW
h$_{fe}$ @ V$_{CE}$ = 1.0 Vdc, I$_C$ = 10.0 A	70 (min)	40 (min)	30 (min)	80 (min)
f$_T$ = 10 mA	50-150	100-300	50-150	100-300

Operating and storage junction temperature range, —55° to +135°C

Prices are moderate *too* — only $1.45 for the MMT3903 and MMT-3905; $1.80 for the MMT3904 and MMT3906 (1000-up). Production quantities are immediately available.

CHIP FROM FAMED 2N2369 SWITCH ALSO IN MICRO-T

For several years, the 2N2369 has been "a standard of the industry" for high-speed, low-current switching applications . . . *except* in microminiature equipment.

Today, the MMT2369 *is* "the standard of the industry." Period!

Now, in the reliable, space-saving Micro-T, Unibloc plastic package, you can have all the advantages you always had — plus! Plus what? Plus the cost-savings on layout, assembly, and even P.C. boards . . . It's also ideal for thick-film digital circuit applications.

In case you've forgotten, here are some of the specs that made the 2N2369 great and make the MMT-2369 even greater now:

CHARACTERISTIC	SYMBOL	MIN	MAX	UNIT
Collector-Emitter Breakdown Voltage	B$_{VCEO}$	15	—	Vdc
Collector Cutoff Current	I$_{CBO}$	—	100	nAdc
DC Current Gain	h$_{FE}$	40	120	
Current-Gain Bandwidth Prod.	f$_T$	500		Mc/c
Turn-on Time	t$_{on}$	—	12	ns
Turn-off Time	t$_{off}$	—	18	ns

Immediately available in production quantities, the MMT2369 is moderately priced at $.97 (1000-up). For complete details, send for the data sheet. Write P.O. Box 955, Phoenix, Arizona 85001.

Circle 310 on readers service card

Circle 309 on readers service card

MOTOROLA Semiconductors
— where the priceless ingredient is care!

*Trademark of Motorola Inc.

This newsletter ad by Motorola is crammed with information of interest to users and potential users of space-saving transistor semiconductors. In breezy newsletter style, the copy is bound to attract readership among the many buying influences in an industrial market.

Fill a newsletter ad with glowing accounts of how ground was broken for your new plant, internal promotions, how great business is, how much sales are up over the comparable period last year, installation of a gigantic new gizmo machine in Plant No. 1, and so on and on, and you'll have a newsletter ad that will lull even a seasoned insomniac to sleep, but fast.

On the other hand, make it sprightly and brisk and write with the reader in mind and your newsletter ad will perform a service *for the reader* as well as for the advertiser. The reader recognizes this, which is why he's willing to invest his time reading what you have to say. He believes he'll receive information he needs from the ad or he wouldn't be "in" it.

One thing, though: Be sure to identify your advertisement as an advertisement, or the Federal Government's watchdogs will be baying at your heels. It's considered by the bureacratic types to be a "deceptive practice" not to identify ads as ads, if there's any possible doubt about it.

A good example of a newsletter-type ad that does right by both the reader and the advertiser is found on page 603. This one-page, black-and-white ad run by Motorola Semiconductors flags the attention of readers of *Electronics* magazine immediately with the magic word, "report." It would be next to impossible for anybody seriously interested in semiconductors to skip over this ad, particularly so since Motorola Semiconductors is one of the most respected names in the industry. When an industry leader makes a report, it's read.

Motorola Semiconductors crams an amazing amount of information into a one-page ad; the ad contains 408 words, plus two halftones, plus two tables. And this word count doesn't include the caption under the table in the center column of type.

Let's see how Motorola helps the reader by giving him information he can put to good use, and how this type of ad involves him immediately. Copy reads:

Semiconductor Report

ABOUT SPACE-SAVING MICRO-T TRANSISTORS FOR OPTIMUM DESIGN FLEXIBILITY

NEW MICRO-T
TRANSISTORS SOLVE
HIGH-DENSITY
PACKAGING PROBLEMS

(half-tone)

Motorola's Micro-T molded Unibloc plastic transistors now provide the ultra-small devices you've needed to make those high-density, miniaturized equipment designs a practical reality. The new Micro-T is only about one-tenth the volume of standard plastic or TO-18 packages. Handling problems disappear too . . . because the leads of the Micro-T radiate from the center, making it particularly well-suited to "drop-in" PC-board mounting.

The Micro-T is "at home" anywhere high-density packaging is required . . . electronic watches, hearing aids, satellites, high-frequency instruments and many, many more. In short, the Micro-T lets you design circuits that provide discrete device *performance and design flexibility; while, at the same time, achieve the component densities and space reductions approaching that of integrated circuits. For example, it makes an ideal device for use in thick-film and unitized circuit assemblies.*

(half-tone)

*COMPLEMENTARY
SWITCHING AND
AMPLIFIER TYPES
FIRST MICRO-T's AVAILABLE*

MMT3903-04 (NPN) and MMT-3905-06 (PNP) Micro-T transistors boast a host of premium specs for general purpose switching and amplifier applications, as well as for complementary circuitry. In fact, the specifications are identical to those of their standard (TO-92) plastic-packaged counterparts—2N3903-06. Yet, you gain the added advantages of space-saving and handling ease—available only with Motorola's Micro-T!

Here are the specs that make these Micro-T types an "evaluation must":

(table)

Prices are moderate too—*only $1.45 for the MMT3903 and MMT-3905; $1.80 for the MMT3904 and MMT3906 (1000-up) Production quantities are immediately available.*

*CHIP FROM FAMED
2N2369 SWITCH
ALSO IN MICRO-T*

> *For several years, the 2N2369 has been a "standard of the industry" for high-speed, low-current switching applications . . . except in micro-miniature equipment.*
>
> *Today, the MMT2369 is "the standard of the industry." Period!*
>
> *Now, in the reliable, space-saving Micro-T Unibloc plastic package, you can have all the advantages you always had—plus! Plus what? Plus the cost-savings on layout, assembly, and even P.C. boards . . . It's also ideal for thick-film digital circuit applications.*
>
> *In case you've forgotten, here are some of the specs that made the 2N2369 great and make the MMT-2369 even greater now:*
>
> (table)
>
> *Immediately available in production quantities, the MMT2369 is moderately priced at $.97 (1000-up). For complete details, send for the data sheet. Write . . .*

Those electronics people talk a language all of their own. For instance, when they discuss a discrete device, even a discreet author reels at that one.

Copy was skillfully written, though. In the subhead under the main headline, Semiconductor Report, Motorola tells the reader what he's going to be told. This qualifies the reader immediately. If he's not professionally interested in semiconductors (he might be in some other phase of the electronics business), he can skip the ad. Those who *do* read it, however, are prime prospects for Motorola Semiconductors.

Then, in the subhead in the left column, the first word is "new." Powerful. And following this is a promise that this new product will solve a problem that's common throughout the industry. How to assure readership of body copy in one easy lesson.

Graphics are excellent; the illustration of the electronic device in the thimble with a needle sticking out of it instantly communicates with the reader. He needn't be a great visualizer to recognize instantly the relative size of the device. (Incidentally, the product the ad is talking about is scattered around on the "ground" at the base of the thimble.)

Body copy explains product features and user benefits, then proceeds to suggest typical applications. Quality of the product is brought home to the reader by tabular matter in which the precise performance of the new transistors are measured against recognized standards. This is nuts-and-bolts information presented in a frame of reference with which the reader is thoroughly familiar. It carries great conviction for that reason.

Motorola clinches its presentation of the new product by quoting prices and by stating that it isn't something to come in the future, but is an off-the-shelf item that's available immediately.

Readership of an ad is always higher when the price of the product is given than when it is conveniently ignored, apparently for fear the price will scare prospects into headlong, panic-stricken flight.

And the bid for action contains an offer of a technical data sheet for those who want more detailed information; it pulls inquiries for sales followup also.

This entire ad is attractive and the presentation of the information is palatable. No exaggerations, no unsupported claims, no brag and boast. The newsletter ad is believable and it achieves better than average readership. Many advertisers would benefit from using it.

How to Do It Ads

Few things in advertising arouse as intense interest—and do it as quickly—as telling the reader you're going to tell him how to do something.

This applies equally to the reader as a member of the business community and as an individual human being. "How to" are magic words. They're semaphoric. Run them up in display type and it's like running up a brightly colored signal flag. They inform the reader in no uncertain terms that this advertisement is going to show him a new way of doing something, and chances are it's a lot better than the way he's been doing it all along. His automatic reaction is to assume you'll tell him a better way to do it so he'll produce more, save more, or reap some other desirable benefit. Otherwise, why spend money on it?

By this time the reader's curiosity is aroused and he's mentally prepared to accept as absolute fact the product story that follows. At the very least, he'll listen to it with an open mind.

The how-to-do-it approach is particularly effective with engineers and technical people, who are constantly searching for ways to improve the product or production process. After all, their primary job responsibility is to find better ways to accomplish specific tasks. When you show them you can help them, you're almost home free.

The how-to-do-it ad is very similar to the problem-solution ad; however, the problem-solution approach is generally broader. How-to ads zero right in on a narrow, well-defined target. They're limited, as a rule, to describing how use of the product for a specific purpose will achieve a desired result.

Waldes Kohinoor, Inc.'s excellent two-color ad, illustrated nearby, is a true how-to-do-it ad, even though the "how to" words are not used as such; the headline instead starts out "how *do*."

This is an ad that has just about everything going for it. The technical people are shown cut-away drawings, closeups showing how the retaining rings are installed eliminate any question in that area. And the copy is nutsy-and-boltsy enough to endear it to even the most literal engineer who questions everything he encounters in life. Copy reads, in part:

How do you lock shaft components under spring pressure?

TRUARC PRONG-LOCK retaining rings simplify design, eliminate costly parts and machining, speed assembly!

(Illustrations)

Locks positively on shaft, serves as spring and shoulder.

The Truarc Series 5139 Prong-Lock is a radially-assembled retaining ring which serves as both a spring and a positive-locking fastener. It derives its name from two prongs on the inner circumference of the open end. Before the ring can be installed, it must be flattened to permit the prongs to enter a groove on the shaft. When the prongs clear the groove, the ring springs back to its bowed form and the prongs lock around the shaft. The ring must be flattened again before it can be removed.

The Series 5139 can be used to replace nuts and lock washers, cotter pins, rivets, screws, and other fasteners. It eliminates springs and bowed washers and can be installed on grooved shafts which do not require costly drilling or threading. The ring has high thrust-load capacity and, because of its positive-locking qualities, can be utilized as a shoulder against rotating parts. The bowed design provides resilient end-play take-up and compensates for tolerances in the assembly.

The Series 5139 is available in nine sizes for shafts .090" to .441" dia. It can be installed and removed quickly

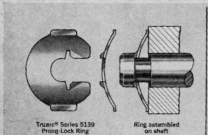

with the Truarc applicator shown above or with a screw driver. The dispenser illustrated—used with stacked rings— is designed for high-speed assembly.

Also shown are two typical uses for Waldes Kohinoor's retaining rings, and a wrap-up offers a free copy of a new 128-page *Truarc Technical Manual.* The advertiser does what many more industrial advertisers should do, but don't—it calls attention to the company's Yellow Pages listings, and to the fact that the complete catalog is in *Thomas Micro-Catalogs.* This is a separate subject, and will be covered in the chapter on media.

An "Anti-Ad" Ad

Sooner or later somebody was going to do it, and Snelling and Snelling did! Snelling and Snelling, the world's largest professional employment service, ran a fine two-color two-thirds page ad that's professional in every respect—yet proves pretty conclusively that advertising is not necessary! It's not in this one case, at least. Let's look at the copy of the ad shown below, at the left. This most unusual ad reads as follows:

How to find
good people
in a tight
employment
market.

Advertise like crazy in the classified pages.

Interview dozens of candidates to find one good employee.

Recruit on major campuses for weeks at a time.

Enlist radio, television, billboards, and vertical trade publications to spread your recruiting story.

Expensive and time-consuming, isn't it?

Why not find your people the easy, efficient way—through a Professional Employment Service.

*The good people today are finding jobs the
professional way. And why not? With more
than 300 offices coast to coast, Snelling
and Snelling offers job seekers greater
opportunities for advancement, greater
mobility, more fine companies to talk
to, and easier job finding.*

*If your company is caught in the new
employee-finding cost squeeze, make the
decision today to call your nearest
Snelling and Snelling office
listed in the white pages.*

*We have the nose for finding
the people
you need.*

Appropriately enough, the illustration—a duotone of brown and black—is of a bloodhound. After all, what else except a bloodhound (and Snelling and Snelling) are experts at finding people?

This is a hard-hitting how-to-do-it ad, one that was very effective for the advertiser. Copy is pithy, punchy and to the point.

Trade Ads

Major objective of so-called trade ads is to gain greater distribution of the product—more outlets, greater acceptance on the part of those who resell the product.

This is usually a dog-eat-dog field. Most advertising designed to increase distribution is pretty strident and hard-sell copy. Restraint is just about an unknown word, for everybody strives to shout a little louder than the next advertiser.

An unusually well-conceived campaign, and one that has been outstandingly effective in the terms all advertisers want—increased sales—was developed by Marsteller Inc. for the Residential Lighting Division, Thomas Industries, Inc.

This company sells home lighting fixtures. Largest and most lucrative segment of the market for its Moe Light fixtures are new homes. Back in the 1950's the bulk of the company's sales consisted of low-priced fixtures that were easily installed. Moe Light had widespread distribution and enjoyed excellent acceptance with electrical contractors; the contractors at that time usually selected the brand of light they wanted to install and home builders were content to accept that fact.

Unit sale—fixtures per house—was low, but the company had an acceptable portion of the market, and it was a rising market. Home building was booming and every year it went up, Moe's sales rose.

Then, in the late 50's, tastes changed. Home buyers were no longer content to accept nondescript styling. What's more, this change in taste coincided with a sharp drop in new home starts and the market for Moe fixtures shrunk. Moe Light couldn't anticipate a rising sales volume merely because the total of new houses kept rising.

At this time style came to the forefront, with price and ease of installation relegated to the sidelines. Also at this time the home builder decided he'd better start making buying decisions to make it easier to sell his customers.

Moe Light's sales edged up, but were well off the boom rate management had become fond of. As far as share of market was concerned, Moe held its own; but that was little consolation in a declining market.

Agency Gets the Problem

The problem was put to the Marsteller Inc., the agency: What could be done to reverse the trend toward a lower dollar volume, and to break Moe Light away from sales fluctuations caused by the size of the total market? After all, a company with plenty of marketing savvy should be able to *increase* its sales in a declining market, rather than sit glumly around resigned to taking it on the chin with a vague hope that things would get better.

Marginal companies should take the brunt of an industry slump, leaving the leader, or leaders, relatively unhurt—or in even better position than before the downturn.

First thing Marsteller recommended was a research project to find out exactly what attitude builders in general had toward Moe Light. This was vitally necessary if meaningful marketing objectives were to be established and a communications program developed to achieve them. If the foundation isn't right, there's little likelihood anything built upon it will be, either.

The study was made and Moe Light was rated a poor second in three important areas: (1) product quality, (2) product development, and (3) product style. Both client and agency evaluated the results of the study objectively and both agreed that it was undoubtedly correct. Moe Light *did* lag.

Then, working together, Moe Light and Marsteller set four marketing objectives:

1. To improve styling and increase the price range.

2. To develop a special sales group to handle sales to the residential lighting market.

3. To do everything possible to gain the favor of the home builder.

4. To get increased distribution in lighting fixture showrooms.

Improving the styling of the entire product line was a time-consuming job, and a great deal of money was poured into the project. The line was also broadened to enable Moe Light to compete in areas where the company had previously not been represented. Poor designs were discarded; poor sellers were scrapped.

Ready for Action

With the product restyled, with fixtures for every price range, and with an eager, beefed-up sales force, the company was ready to exploit all of its efforts. At this time firm communications objectives were developed. They were simple, but were what the company needed. Objectives were:

1. To build greater awareness of Moe Light as a brand.

2. To create an image of Moe Light as the industry style leader in the residential field within 36 months.

3. To give salesmen the backing they needed to enable them to contact builders with an effective presentation.

To help turn the tide that first crucial year, Moe Light's space advertising campaign had as a theme "two ways to win a woman," naturally using the redesigned and greater choice in fixtures to show the builder he'd gain a competitive advantage with Moe Light. Media chosen were three magazines for builders, all monthly publications. One book had 10 spreads; the others ran the same spreads on an every-other-month basis.

Moe Light dominated the market, as far as advertising was concerned, with those 44 pages in four-color. One of the four-color spreads from that first year's campaign is illustrated nearby.

Photography is superb, the mood is one of grace and charm, and the tone of the copy is just right. It reads:

TWO WAYS TO WIN A WOMAN: **VINTAGE RIGHT...**

...OR MOE LIGHT

Moe Light colonial lanterns give her something special to remember about your houses. For more ideas on how to win a woman with lighting, write to Moe Light Division, Thomas Industries Inc., 207 E. Broadway, Louisville, Ky.

TWO WAYS TO WIN A WOMAN: VINTAGE RIGHT . . . OR MOE LIGHT

Moe Light colonial lanterns give her something special to remember about your houses. For more ideas on how to win a woman with lighting, write to Moe Light Division . . .

Where men clamber around in an attic nodding sagely as they pound roof joists with their clenched fists, women notice and remember little touches that contribute so much to a gracious appearance. Moe Light is on firm ground with this appeal.

At the end of a year this campaign had helped Moe Light, but not enough. Attitude of builders, as determined by another study, still showed Moe in second place in two of the three areas, but by not nearly as much. And in one important area—new product development—Moe was tied with its major competitor due primarily to stressing new fixtures in the advertising campaign. Solid progress had been made.

Again the product line was overhauled, revamped, and upgraded. Moe retained the same communications objectives for the next year, and the ads preserved continuity by retaining the same basic format. This year, however, the theme changed slightly and famous women of history were used. The excellent photography and quality four-color reproduction continued to be used. One of the ads in that campaign, featuring Queen Isabella, reads:

If Queen Isabella were here today...   She'd want Moe Light in her library

If Queen Isabella were here today . . .
She'd want Moe Light in her library

A Moe Light pulldown adds a touch of royalty to dining rooms and living rooms too . . . gives modern-day queens something special to remember about your homes. For more ways to add extra appeal with lighting, write to Moe Light . . .

A followup survey was taken after this campaign had been running for a year; Moe Light was solidly established in builders' minds as the leader in product quality, product development, and in product style!

A four-color, spread ad from the current campaign—which still retains the same successful format—also is shown.

Sell the fashionable homemaker
with fashionable Moe Light

She's as style-conscious of decor as she is of clothing. She'll decide whether to take a second look at your model home. So give her something special to remember: a Moe Light chain-hung styling with brilliant suede blue shade and black-silver finish.

For more ideas on how to sell the fashionable homemaker, write to Residential Lighting Division . . .

Sell the fashionable homemaker   with fashionable Moe Light

This is a near-classic example of what can be accomplished with carefully planned market research to establish very specific communications objectives. They, in turn, were the groundwork for a spectacularly effective advertising campaign that exerted a tremendous effect on sales and profits.

There was no head-in-the-sand groping or hoping here. Moe Light and its agency faced up to facts—which many advertisers steadfastly refuse to do—then determined exactly what was needed to reverse a trend and put the advertiser out in front in its market. This they proceeded to do with never a misstep.

Incidentally, here again is proof that a market can be "bought" with advertising, and at not very great expense. Once you have the "trade" solidly sold, increased distribution automatically follows and sales don't merely go up—they zoom!

The author is indebted to Lee Bartlett, recently creative director of Marsteller Inc., and to that fine agency for background material on this case history.

Institutional Ads

Institutional ads that are run in the trade press are *not* corporate advertisements. Instead, they are a weak and wishy-washy form of industrial advertising.

Copy appeal in the typical institutional ad is basically wrong. The premise on which it is based is faulty. The thinking that went into the ad probably was fuzzy. Copy, which should be based on telling the reader reasons why he should buy the product—in terms of features translated into user benefits—goes off onto a tangent. It's vague and nonspecific, and usually of mighty little interest to the reader because there's nothing in it for him.

The institutional approach isn't to be damned in total, however. There may very well be perfectly valid reasons for using it. For example, it's quite conceivable that if a company dominates an industry its primary communications objective may be to keep reminding readers of this pleasant little fact.

Does the Customer Care?

If that's the case, the inference may be drawn that the company achieved this position of dominance for a good reason—product superiority. After all, no company becomes a leader and stays in the number one spot unless it has something nobody else has.

A danger, though, is that ads may harp continuously on product attributes that are meaningless to the customer. They may not really say anything to him. Quality, dependability, productivity, performance, purity, consistency, uniformity, full strength, strict quality control, and other equally nebulous words appear in ads of this type—and they've been so overworked they were ready for retirement on a pension a half-century ago.

Another danger is that it's so infernally easy to fall into the trap of bragging and boasting. Armour Abrasives Company in a recent ad illustrated a roll of belts of abrasive paper in a bank vault; the headline proclaimed: *On the surface, all abrasives look alike. But Armour gives you what your customer demands . . . consistent finish. It cost us $3,000,000.*

Customers don't care about this.

Moreover, if you take the institutional approach there's the ever-present temptation to hold yourself up as the knight in shining armor, a sort of metal-clad Jack Armstrong whose motives are unsullied. A dirty word like profit would never pass his lips.

And even worse, you could be a (ugh) bore. Being cruel to one's aged mother, beating one's wife, starving one's children—even kicking one's dog—could, if the perpetrator were suitably and sincerely sorry, be forgiven. But in advertising the unforgivable sin is to be a bore. It can't be swept under the rug, ignored, simply not discussed, or forgiven. Ever.

One sure way to bore the reader so that he shudders and turns the page for succor is to run an ad with a picture of Our Factory—unless it's for sale, of course. This applies equally whether it's a new factory, or an old one. Worse yet is to show an addition to Our Factory. Our Factory is of interest only to the powers that be who own the place. Period.

The reader doesn't really care one whit if the product is produced in a pup tent, a cave once inhabited by prehistoric man, or in the lair of a purple people-eater. This simply does not concern him.

Yet another way that's guaranteed to cause the reader to flee in panic is to run a picture of Our Founder in an ad. Now, there's surely a place for such a portrait. Generally this gentleman was a hard-bitten, rugged individualist of the old school who forged ahead despite some pretty trying times. He carved out a sizable empire under adverse circumstances when the dollar amounted to something—before the advent of mini-money that's not backed by anything other than a politician's promise. You know what *that's* worth. Give Our Founder credit. He didn't turn pleadingly to Washington (D. C., not George), hand out, begging for a handout. Back in the days when many of today's well-known businesses were struggling little companies whose owners wondered if they'd be able to meet the week's payroll, the man who founded one believed in self-reliance; he had no thought of appropriating the next generation's income which had been confiscated from the present generation to be squandered by an all-powerful bureaucracy—even if it had existed then.

Place for such portraits is in the company conference room, the president's office, or even in the reception area. There it's appropriate and speaks well for the stability of the company and its ability to change with the times. It provides recognition for an unusually dynamic man.

In an ad such as the one illustrated nearby, run by Transue & Williams, the portraits are out of place. They're out of place because they're of interest only to Transue & Williams management. To the reader, they're a relic of a by-gone era; he's interested in the here and now.

Transue & Williams' ad is in two-color—brown and black. The advertiser takes some of the curse off of the approach by showing the company's products beneath the pictures of the gentlemen who founded the company. But the headline and the portraits must have scared off readers in vast herds.

It's a shame, too. The company has a good story to tell and tells

Wonder what our founders would say if they could see what their company is doing now.

For one thing, they would be pretty excited about the recently installed new automatic heat-treat facilities and the new building which houses the equipment. Additionally, they would concur with the streamlining of other important operations. They'd like the new machines we've been adding, plus those on order, to continue our reputation for keeping pace with industries' needs. Our founders might ask, "Why more expansion and process upgrading?" The answer is very simple. It's because our program as a supplier is to continue to serve our customer needs better and better, and do it even more competitively than in the past.

TRANSUE & WILLIAMS
Division of Standard Alliance Industries, Inc.
ALLIANCE, OHIO 44601
Commercial Producers of Drop and Upset Forgings • Deep Drawn Stampings

it well. If it weren't so unceasingly self-oriented, the institutional ad might have done a first-rate selling job. Copy, which is set in too wide measure for reading ease, reads:

Wonder what our founders would say if they could see what their company is doing now.

For one thing, they would be pretty excited about the recently installed new automatic heat-treat facilities and the new building which houses the equipment. Additionally, they would concur with the streamlining of other important operations. They'd like the new machines we've been adding, plus those on order, to continue our reputation for keeping pace with industries' needs. Our founders might ask, "Why more expansion and process upgrading?" The answer is very simple. It's because our program as a supplier is to continue to serve our customer needs better and better, and do it even more competitively than in the past.

Body copy makes it obvious the company is progressive, and it's a company that's well equipped to do a fine job for present and future customers. It's a little too pat and self-serving to come off, though, as far as the reader is concerned.

Spicer's bleed, black-and-white ad, illustrated nearby, appeared in *Commercial Car Journal* magazine. It, too, is institutional in approach, but the whimsy and delightful light touch carries the day. Copy reads:

How do I know you're Spicer?

Show me your identification!

It's written all over me!

Don't be taken in by look-alikes. Only genuine Spicer brand U-Joint Kits are branded "Spicer U.S.A."

Many different brands of U-Joints copy the cross-and-bearing design pioneered by Spicer. So if you're paying for Spicer brand U-Joint Kits, be sure you get them. It's easy to tell if it's the genuine article. Just look for "SPICER U.S.A." on the journal cross assembly and bearing caps.

You probably pay as much for other *brands, but Spicer U-Joint Kits are the favorite choice of auto and truck manufacturers—and they should be yours. Get the right*

How do I know you're Spicer?
Show me your identification!

It's written all over me!

Don't be taken in by look-alikes. Only genuine Spicer®
brand U-Joint Kits are branded "Spicer U.S.A."

Many different brands of U-Joints copy the cross-and-bearing design pioneered by
Spicer. So if you're paying for Spicer brand U-Joint Kits, be sure you get them. It's
easy to tell if it's the genuine article. Just look for "SPICER U.S.A." on the journal
cross assembly and bearing caps.

You probably pay as much for *other* brands, but Spicer brand U-Joint Kits are
the favorite choice of auto and truck manufacturers—and they should be yours. Get
the right ones. The ones branded "SPICER U.S.A." For complete information, write
Dana Corporation, Dept. 86, Toledo, Ohio 43601.

SPICER · CON-VEL · PARISH · PERFECT CIRCLE · VICTOR

*ones. The ones branded "SPICER U.S.A." For complete
information, write Dana Corporation . . .*

Spicer, a division of Dana Corporation, makes no bones about
its interest in selling universal joint kits. Its interest in profit is
something for which the company makes no apology. The ad

strongly promotes Spicer's reputation for industry leadership and pioneering of better automotive products. Also, it counters the flood of low-quality, low-priced automotive replacement parts which can easily victimize the unwary.

Copy gains credibility because it stresses that Spicer brand universal joint kits are the favorite of auto and truck manufacturers—a fact well known to fleet men. Take a known fact, build from it, and copy achieves a quality that causes the reader mentally to nod in agreement with what's being said.

It's quite possible that Spicer would have had a stronger ad if copy had gone into nuts-and-bolts reasons *why* Spicer U-Joint Kits are better, and what this means to the reader. Be that as it may, this is still a strong ad and one that strengthens the brand image. If continued as a campaign, for U-joint kits, transmissions, power take-offs and other components in the manufacturer's broad line, this type of ad cannot help but influence prospective purchasers of such transportation hardware.

Comic Strip or Cartoon Ads

Favorite reading fare of the *majority* of the people in this country is the ubiquitous comic strip.

Whether he's a fan of 'Lil Abner, Dick Tracy, or Terry, the average American regularly reads the comics with mingled amusement and affection. Most people have a favorite character whose activities they follow with great interest.

Life, Time, Fortune, and any number of other literate magazines edited for literate people have run lengthy feature articles on comic strips and comic strip characters. *Life* had a multipage article on good old Charlie Brown, Snoopy, Lucy, Linus, and their cohorts in *Peanuts* and, incidentally, on the philosophy of Charles M. Schulz, creator of these beloved, vividly real little characters.

Indeed, Charlie Brown graced the cover of *Life*—in color. And Charlie and his beagle, Snoopy, who regularly battles the bloody Red Baron in a flimsy Sopwith Camel, and who has the most vivid imagination in the entire animal world, are nationwide favorites of all ages. They appear on sweat-shirts worn by teenagers, college students, and authors.

In a previous article, *Life* came to the conclusion that the comic strip constitutes the most significant body of literature that's read by an overwhelming majority of the American people. Kids and blue-collar workers and advertising men and other executives—even Presidents—read the comics.

On the surface, it would seem that an advertisement that adopted the format of the comic strip would have a decided advantage over others when it comes to securing readership. You can't argue with acceptance. Look how popular sex is.

This is quite true in consumer advertising when the ad appears in broad media reaching great masses of people. Here the comic strip format comes into its own. It's known and accepted by countless millions in Sunday supplements and in the comic sections of the newspapers.

Effectiveness of the comic strip format in industrial advertising depends to a large extent on the company running the ad, the product advertised, and the universe.

McGraw-Hill's Laboratory of Advertising Performance takes a very dim view of comic strip-type advertisements in business publications. It reports a survey made for two industrial advertisements run by The Perkin-Elmer Corporation in *Aviation Week*. One ad was a conventional ad with a large illustration occupying approximately two-thirds of the page, two copy blocks, and the logo centered beneath the copy. The other was a comic-strip-type ad. In all fairness, however, it should be mentioned that this comic strip ad lacked something in layout. It was cluttered, busy, and looked difficult to read.

McGraw-Hill mailed a letter and reprints of the two ads to 1,000 subscribers to *Aviation Week*. Subscribers were asked if they had read either of the two ads, and which one of the two gave them the clearest idea of what Perkin-Elmer did or manufactured.

Of 216 respondents—22 percent—20 percent remembered having seen the comic strip ad, while 38 percent remembered having seen the conventional ad.

When it comes to having read the advertisement, only 10 percent reported they had read the comic strip ad, while 26 percent said they had read the conventional ad. This *is* a difference.

Then, for the question of which ad gave the reader the clearest idea of what Perkin-Elmer did or made, 10 percent chose the comic strip ad, while 83 percent said the conventional ad gave them the clearer idea.

However, the comments which accompanied the returns were most revealing. Typical comments mentioned that comics are useful to sell toothpaste and cereal, but not scientific apparatus; another respondent said he was an engineer, and the conventional ad was "more at his level"; another comment was that the comic strip ad was an "insult to the average engineer"—and that engineers were not interested in comics, but prefer something good and clear and concise and right to the point.

In this connection it's interesting to note that studies place the percentage of adults who regularly read at least one favorite comic strip all the way from 60 to as high as 86 percent. No study the author has seen went below the 60 percent mark. Perhaps this does not include *any* engineers.

United States Steel's fine comic strip, illustrated nearby, is from a highly successful campaign. The one-page ad was in two-color, with the second color (red) reserved only for the advertiser's USS logo and the product, Alloy Steel Bars.

This ad was written with a deft touch and a sure hand. There's just a hint of a gentle spoof, of a good-natured bit of leg pulling, yet the copy in each of the comic strip boxes is down to earth and presents solid user-benefit information about the product. It reads:

Emily . . .
take a letter.

Yes, Daddy.

Dear U.S. Steel . . . your technical
service representative called as
promised, and looked into the
alloy bar grades we were using.
Very pleasant, capable fellow.

He proposed a Carilloy FC grade
that will probably save us $16,000
a year on sprocket and gear
machining.

And he proposed a way that will
enable us to standardize on
just two alloy bar grades for our
entire pinion operation.

Speaking of proposals,
I wonder if he would be
interested in marrying
my daughter . . .

Then, in the lower right-hand box, United States Steel really packs in product information. A very strong bid for action is made by assuring the reader a U.S. Steel technical representative is as close as a phone—and that he is a trained problem-solver who's

A comic strip ad for the United States Steel Corporation not only tells an amusing, warmly whimsical story, but also manages to pack a lot of good product information about alloy steel bars into the space.

ready, willing, and able to put his specialized knowledge to work for the reader. This copy block reads:

> *Call a U.S. Steel technical service representative about your use of standard and specialty alloy bar steels. He may be able to save you money: for example, with a Carilloy FC grade for heavily stressed machine parts. USS Carilloy FC Bars give up to three times the tool life and 50% better machinability than standard steels with comparable hardness. Whatever your needs, you'll find that U.S. Steel can furnish a complete range of alloy steel bars—AISI and SAE standard grades as well as nonstandard grades and other steels with special properties; such as USS "T-1" Steels, maraging steels, 9% nickel and other quenched and tempered steels. U.S. Steel's modern heat-treating facilities for rounds and flats closely control heating and quenching to insure proper structure, hardness, and related properties required by subsequent machining, forming, or service applications. USS Alloy Bars can also be furnished ultra-clean through both the open hearth and the electric furnace VCD processes.*
>
> *Get all the advantages: quality alloy steel bars; competent metallurgical and technical service; the industry's most extensive research and development program; and conveniently located service and production facilities . . .*

USS ran this ad in *Iron Age, Production, Materials in Design Engineering, Purchasing,* and in *Machine Design.*

Well read, believable and informative, this campaign is doing a great job for United States Steel. It's possible that a comic strip ad directed solely to engineers and egg-head scientists might lay an egg, but a good comic strip campaign directed at the right segment of management in industry can do an effective job.

Chapter 10

ILLUSTRATION

PEOPLE like illustrations. They find them interesting. They enjoy looking at pictures. There's something about looking at pictures that enables people to dream and yearn and project themselves into another time, place, or situation. Pictures appeal to the romantic hidden away in all of us.

This fascination with pictures is due, in part, to their being so easily understood. Pictures communicate ideas quickly and easily, so there's almost no chance of misinterpretation of the thought behind them. Partially because of this, pictures have been an integral part of every culture and society since time began.

You can remember fine art from ancient Egypt, from the Ming Dynasty of China, and you're aware that in Europe caverns have recently been found whose walls are lavishly decorated with lively animal portraits painted by skilled Magdalenian artists who worked 10,000 years before the birth of Christ. Theory has it that these ancients produced art so profusely for two reasons: A desire to beautify their quarters, a feeling that's inherent in the human animal, and to propitiate the spirits of animals they painted. This was, perhaps, done to cast a spell, or weave some magic that would enable the painters to achieve victory in the hunt. Colors were carefully blended of mineral oxides and charcoal, and animal fat was blended in to serve as a binder.

Many intriguing examples of similar artistic efforts of Cro-Magnon man painted some 25,000 years ago are in an excellent state of preservation.

A few years ago the author and his family took a fascinating trip back into antiquity, although of a later era, by browsing through a number of cliff dwellings in the colorful canyon country of the Southwest. On the stone walls of many of these long-abandoned homes, beautifully preserved by the high, dry desert air, are illustrations—not mere drawings, but wonderfully detailed and skillfully executed illustrations—of scenes from the contemporary life of the Pueblo artists. Animals long since extinct, exotic tribal customs, and curious religious ceremonies are depicted with charm and precision.

These priceless paintings, part of our national heritage, were done long before Columbus—or was it Leif Ericson?—discovered America, yet this Indian art is as vivid and fresh as if it had been done just yesterday. They give us an enthralling glimpse into life as it was lived a thousand years or more ago.

Pictures exert an even greater attraction for people today than in the past merely because there are so many more of them— pictures as well as people, that is. Through the years as printing and other reproduction processes improved, it has become increasingly easy for the great mass of people to enjoy pictures. For many centuries art was found almost exclusively in churches and in the castles and mansions of the very rich.

The Trend Toward Illustration

However, the printed page, the ubiquitous camera in the hands of the tourist, movies, and the electronic monster that mesmerizes people with pictures of sorts, all combine to make our society picture-conscious and picture-oriented to a degree scarcely possible to foresee.

In advertising an occasional all-type ad sans illustration scores a resounding success in readership and reader response. TWA's ad that we looked at in a previous chapter was an excellent example. If the advertiser's selling proposition is unusually clear-cut and so well defined there's no possibility of its being misunderstood by anybody with anything approaching average intelligence, all's well and good, as far as the all-type ad is concerned.

On the other hand, there's no questioning whether or not there should be an illustration in your advertisement. Incidentally, in the advertising field the illustration is always referred to as the "illustration"—not as the "picture."

The illustration works in harmony with the headline and the body copy to communicate your message. Key word here is that the illustration *works*—it doesn't merely occupy expensive space on the page. An appropriate illustration with real impact hammers home your idea a lot faster than anything else that's ever been devised. If the illustration isn't appropriate, and if it doesn't have real impact, what is it doing in the ad?

When it comes to catching the reader's eye and attracting his attention in that crucial instant when his glance flashes across your ad, the illustration has no competition.

There's no reason to believe that The Sterling Remedy Company's all-type ad, illustrated above, didn't receive good readership, or that reader response wasn't up to the advertiser's expectations.

This classic, circa 1892, appears in *Those Were the Good Old Days*— a "happy look at American advertising, 1880-1930." It was published by Simon and Schuster, and this ad and the two following are reproduced by permission of the author, Edgar R. Jones.

Sterling's ad was written too soon to capitalize on the public's growing awareness of the link between lung cancer and cigarette smoking, so the ad had to do all of the selling job for the product, aided only by an intuitive knowledge that the habit is harmful.

The headline says:

DON'T { TOBACCO SPIT
AND SMOKE YOUR LIFE AWAY!

Subhead following is designed to intrigue the reader, to make him want to know more, thus assuring good readership of the body copy. It says:

IS THE TRUTHFUL, STARTLING TITLE OF A LITTLE
BOOK THAT TELLS ALL ABOUT NO-TO-BAC

Body copy starts out:

> *The ONLY GUARANTEED, HARMLESS, ECO-*
> *NOMICAL CURE for the Tobacco Habit in the world;*
> *not for the REASON it makes Tobacco Taste Bad, but*
> *because it ACTS DIRECTLY ON THE NERVE CEN-*
> *TERS, DESTROYING THE NERVE-CRAVING DE-*
> *SIRE, preparing the way for DISCONTINUANCE*
> *WITHOUT INCONVENIENCE. NO-TO-BAC builds*
> *up and improves the entire nervous system. Many report*
> *a gain of TEN POUNDS in as many days. Get book at*
> *your drug store or write for it—today. DRUGGISTS*
> *GENERALLY SELL NO-TO-BAC. If YOU are a to-*
> *bacco user take time to read the following TRUTHFUL*
> *TESTIMONIALS, a few of many thousands from No-To-*
> *Bac users, printed to show how No-To-Bac works. THEY*
> *ARE THE TRUTH, PURE AND SIMPLE. We know*
> *this, and back them by a reward of $5,000.00 to anyone*
> *who can prove the testimonials false, and that we have*
> *knowingly printed testimonials that do not, so far as we*
> *know, represent the honest opinion of the writers. You*
> *don't have to buy No-To-Bac on testimonial endorsement.*
> *NO-TO-BAC is positively guaranteed to cure or money*
> *refunded. We give good agents exclusive territory and*
> *liberal terms. Many agents make $10 a day.*

Testimonials and case histories were recognized effective as far back as the 1890's when this ad appeared, for the advertiser devoted almost one-third of the space in this ad to five testimonials. A typical one follows:

CURED THREE YEARS AGO—USED LESS THAN A BOX OF NO-TO-BAC

Mt. Carmel, Ill. Oct. 10, 1892—Gentlemen: I purchased one box of your No-To-Bac three years ago. Took about three-quarters of the box, which completely destroyed my appetite for tobacco. I had used tobacco since nine years of age. I had tried to quit of my own accord and found it impossible, but now I am completely cured and do not have the least craving for tobacco. I hope others will use your treatment.

ROLLO G. BLOOD

Then comes a money-back guarantee that's straightforward and apparently made in good faith. In the bid for action there's a kicker, though, because The Sterling Remedy Company says:

READ THIS

Where to Buy
and How to Order
No-To-Bac

It is sold by Druggists generally and sent by mail . . . the Treasurer is Mr. H. L. Kramer, one of the owners of the famous Indiana Mineral Springs, Indiana, the only place in the world where magnetic mineral mud baths are given for the cure of rheumatism. Write to him for a book about the mud baths.

Even the publisher of the newspaper in which the ad ran got into the act; included in the ad is a box with copy that says:

PUBLISHERS:

We, the publishers
of this paper, know
the S.R. Co. to be
reliable and will do
as they agree. This
we
    GUARANTEE

That's hard sell so hard that diamonds are soft in comparison.

Of interest is the business proposition—"many agents make $10 a day." Now *that* might well beat the advertising business!

The copy, as hard sell and apparently effective as it is, speaks in a muted whisper compared to the all-type ad which follows. First, however, the question that's bound to occur to everybody is: Did The Sterling Remedy Company market a product with merit? Did it work? Is the user benefit valid?

These things are sometimes a bit difficult to check out after 76 years, although the author *did* verify that Rollo G. Blood did *not* smoke at the time of his death, nor did he for several years before. A long distance phone call to Mt. Carmel, Illinois, put the author in touch with a Mrs. Marguerite H. Stansfield, and through her a Miss Mabel Jacquess; although neither of these ladies is a professional investigator, both are life-long residents of Mt. Carmel. They talked with friends and acquaintances of the late Mr. Blood and found that he stopped smoking once and for all in 1892, as the ad stated. Mr. Blood was well known in the city, having lived across the street and several houses south of the hospital; his family owned and operated a brickyard just north of their home, and in digging clay for bricks dug what became "Blood's Pond" where local children ice skated.

Since this testimonial was legitimate, it's safe to assume the others were too. It's inspiring to know that truthfulness in advertising prevailed that long ago.

In 1895 The Brandreth Company ran an ad, illustrated nearby, that promises the moon with a chain-link fence around it. It reads:

Salva-cea!
What are its uses?

SALVA-CEA will cure Bruises and Contusions—Daniel Thomas, of Sing Sing, N. Y., had the third finger of his right hand crushed by a heavy log falling on it; the nail was torn off and the end of the finger was reduced almost to a pulp. Salva-cea was applied, and not only did the pain, which was intense, quickly subside, but the finger healed perfectly.

SALVA-CEA will cure Eczema—A child of Victor Savage, of Monroe, Mich., was covered with sores on one side of the body, and had been in that condition for a year. It was an unusually bad case of eczema, yet in one month's time was perfectly cured by Salva-cea.

SALVA-CEA will cure Earache—Peter Venior, also of Monroe, Mich., says that his children have in the past suffered greatly from this painful complaint. He tried Salva-cea, putting a small quantity in the ear and covering it with cotton. The result was instant relief, and now the moment the children are threatened with a return of the pain they come to him, sure of immediate cure.

SALVA-CEA will cure Piles—Testimonials from many persons show that Salva-cea is a specific for this almost universal complaint. Itching piles are immediately relieved and quickly cured.

SALVA-CEA will cure Colds and Rheumatism—A small quantity occasionally snuffed up the nostrils will cure a cold in the head in less time than anything yet discovered. A gentleman to whom it had been recommended for a cold,

Salva-cea!

(TRADE-MARK.)

What are its uses?

SALVA-CEA will cure Bruises and Contusions.—Daniel Thomas, of Sing Sing, N. Y., had the third finger of his right hand crushed by a heavy log falling on it; the nail was torn off and the end of the finger reduced almost to a pulp. Salva cea was applied, and not only did the pain, which was intense, quickly subside, but the finger healed perfectly.

SALVA-CEA will cure Eczema.—A child of Victor Savage, of Monroe, Mich., was covered with sores on one side of the body, and had been in that condition for a year. It was an unusually bad case of eczema, yet in one month's time was perfectly cured by the use of Salva-cea.

SALVA-CEA will cure Earache.—Peter Venior, also of Monroe, Mich., says that his children have in the past suffered greatly from this painful complaint. He tried Salva-cea, putting a small quantity in the ear and covering it with cotton. The result was instant relief, and now the moment the children are threatened with a return of the pain they come to him, sure of immediate cure.

SALVA-CEA will cure Piles.—Testimonials from many persons show that Salva-cea is a specific for this almost universal complaint. Itching piles are immediately relieved and quickly cured.

SALVA-CEA will cure Colds and Rheumatism.—A small quantity occasionally snuffed up the nostrils will cure a cold in the head in less time than anything yet discovered. A gentleman to whom it had been recommended for a cold, when asked if it did him any good, answered, "To tell the truth, I did not use it for my cold, but look at that!" at the same time holding his hand over his head. He went on to say that for three months he had been troubled with rheumatism in his shoulder, so that he could not put on his coat without assistance, yet six applications of Salva-cea, well rubbed in, had given him complete relief.

SALVA-CEA will cure Chilblains, Neuralgia, Headache, all Itching, Chafing, Coughs, and Fever Sores, and is, in fact, a universal external remedy. One great advantage is its speedy action. Only a few applications are needed in order to bring both relief and cure.

SALVA-CEA will come into general use as soon as its value becomes known. It will, in fact, be considered a household necessity, and the only regret of those who ascertain its merit will be that they did not know of it before.

Price, 25 and 50 cents per box. At druggists, or by mail.
THE BRANDRETH CO., 274 Canal St., New York.

[1895]

---

when asked if it did him any good, answered, "To tell the truth, I did not use it for my cold, but look at that!" at the same time holding his hand over his head. He went on to say that for three months he had been troubled with rheumatism in his shoulder, so that he could not put on his coat without assistance, yet six applications of Salva-cea, well rubbed in, had given him complete relief.

SALVA-CEA will cure Chilblains, Neuralgia, Headache, all Itching, Chafing, Coughs, and Fever Sores, and is, in fact, a universal external remedy. One great advantage is its speedy action. Only a few applications are needed in order to bring both relief and cure.

SALVA-CEA will come into general use as soon as its value becomes known. It will, in fact, be considered a household necessity, and the only regret of those who ascertain its merit will be that they did not know of it before.

Price, 25 and 50 cents per box.
druggists, or by mail.

Chuck out that penicillin, discard all of the numerous............................. myacins, stop production of sulfa, give the heave-ho to the wondrous array of wonder drugs. Your doctor can prescribe and bring on the Salva-cea! At last, a cure for the common cold that's also pure magic on those common aches and pains that beset and bedevil the hard-working advertising man!

A question comes to mind, though: Where, oh where, was the Food and Drug bureaucracy?

There's no disputing that The Brandreth Company sells Salva-cea mighty hard, and does it without benefit of an illustration in the ad. What kind of illustration would they have used, though—a before-and-after photo of that wildly inventive chap who used a cold remedy for rheumatism, leaping into the air and kicking his heels while he chortles with glee at being able to put on his coat unaided? Now, *that* would be an illustration!

Usefulness of the illustration was recognized by forward-looking, aggressive advertisers of that era, though, as Schiele & Company proves with their ad shown nearby.

There, flying gracefully around in a moon-drenched sky, are a pair of the most angelic looking angels to appear in anybody's ad before or since. Of course, there's reason to believe there's an ulterior motive for invoking the aid of assistants to Diety. It so happens the angels are wearing such rapturous expressions because they are proudly holding one of Madam Dean's Spinal Supporting Corsets for some reason or other—perhaps because the corset is the advertiser's product.

Copy hits just about as hard as in the two illustration-less ads. It reads:

MADAM DEAN'S SPINAL SUPPORTING CORSETS

They support the Spine, relieve the muscles of the back, brace the shoulders in a natural and easy manner, imparting graceful carriage to the wearer without discomfort, expanding the chest, thereby giving full action to the lungs, and health and comfort to the body. Take the place of the ORDINARY CORSET in every respect, and are made of fine Contil, in the best manner, in various styles and sold by agents everywhere at popular prices. Mrs. Wm. Papes, Keota, Iowa, says:—I have been an invalid for six years, have travelled extensively for health, yet never received as much benefit as I have in a few weeks wear, of your MADAM DEAN'S CORSET. I am gaining strength all the time, and could not do without it. It has proven to me a godsend.

FREE—Our new book entitled: "Dress Reform for

Ad illustrations of the 1800's were wood engravings like this.

Ladies" with elegant wood engraving and Biography of **Worth, the King of Fashion,** Paris: also our **New Illustrated Catalogue** sent free to any address on receipt of two 2-cent stamps to pay postage and packing.

Agents Wanted for these **celebrated Corsets.** No experience required. Four orders per day give the agent **$150 monthly.** Our agents report from four to twenty sales daily. **$3.00 Outfit Free.** Send for terms and full particulars.

Schiele & Co.

Those are claims that are claims. Boldface type pops out the major user benefits—support the spine; brace the shoulders; graceful carriage; expanding the chest; full action to the lungs; health; comfort; popular prices. Hard to fault those without coming out strong against Flag and Motherhood.

Mrs. Wm. Papes explains the illustration, although it's not an appropriate illustration that requires explaining in the testimonial. Her statement that the corset has proven a *godsend* to her obviously caused the copywriter to pause and reflect on his choice of an illustration. His conclusion: Who can top God? So, we have angels because we all know what *they* look like.

Here again—and back in 1895, at that—is the tried and proved formula for triggering a response: Offer a piece of literature about the product or about how it will benefit the reader. Then sit back and convert the inquiries to sales.

Distribution might have been better for Madam Dean's Supporting Corsets, as evidenced by the offer of lucrative territories for agents—complete with a $3 outfit given to new agents absolutely free. And who could sneeze at congenial work with congenial customers?

But selling 20 corsets a day!

Since the late 1800's a higher percentage of advertisements—both consumer and industrial—use illustrations each year. The ad without an illustration is the exception today, possibly accounting for the effectiveness of certain individual ads or campaigns that go the all-type route.

The Writer Specifies the Illustration

At first, at least, the new advertisement is practically the sole property of the advertising manager and the copywriter—unless they're one and the same individual.

The writer lives with his baby. He meditates, cogitates, and usually procrastinates during its incubative period, waiting for the germ of an idea to flower into a complete creative concept instead of merely knowing that he's under the gun to produce a new ad about the new Widget in time to get it produced and placed before deadline.

Usually the process works two ways, depending upon the individual and his background. The ad man who's mostly writer is strongly word-oriented; he tends to think of ideas in terms of headline and copy approaches. Frequently, when doodling and mulling over random thoughts while getting ready to write an ad, the writer receives a complete ad in close to final form as far as concept is concerned—and this includes headline and body copy—almost from out of the blue.

This is probably a slight exaggeration, of course, but it often seems that way on the surface because the writer's subconscious takes a number of different approaches into consideration, tries them on for size and rejects those that are unsuitable. This process of trial and error continues, sometimes for a period of days, until exactly the right approach is found. Suddenly, there's the ad!

There's the ad in word form, that is. Headline. Copy approach. Slant. Tone. It's all there except for one essential ingredient—the illustrative idea. That's where the rub comes in with many writers and advertising managers. Skim through a number of trade publications serving any market and make note of the illustrative ideas that *really* come on strong. Chances are you'll be able to number those from a half-dozen books on the fingers of your two hands—and maybe on one of them if you're fairly critical.

However, if the same product, selling proposition, and marketing problems are presented to an art-oriented advertising practitioner to solve—an art director, for example, or an account executive whose background lies in the art end of the business—exactly the opposite is true, as a rule.

This art-oriented ad man generally comes up with compelling illustrative ideas, ideas that often are highly creative and original, ideas that are completely fresh and new in this particular market. And maybe new in any market, for that matter. Mostly they're good ideas, too, although some will naturally be discarded as unfeasible or so far out they can't be used.

The point is, though, that his ideas are thoughts on the ways to *show* the reader the advertiser's message, rather than *tell* him. Not that the art-oriented ad man is wrong—he's not. But he's only half right. He's developed only half of an ad because he simply hasn't thought through the problem in its entirety, at least as far as the copy is concerned, although he's probably developed a headline idea. For the most part, it isn't in useable form because it's only a basic idea—not words that have been refined and rewritten and reworked.

Infrequently does the ability to create with equal facility in both copy and in illustration occur in one individual. Most seasoned advertising men do both very well, but not equally well. One's more work than the other.

The fact remains that the ad is initially the copywriter's. It's his responsibility and it's up to him to specify the illustration.

If you're the advertising manager and you're writing the ad, you're not expected to be an accomplished artist or a top-flight illustrative photographer. However, you should direct the agency account executive, or the studio with which you work, by telling exactly what the illustration should consist of.

Note that "exactly" was used. This is because you can't leave room for guesses or stabs in the dark. Spell out in detail precisely what it is that you want to see in the ad, then forget the details. You can't dictate nuts-and-bolts mechanics of how the illustration is to be created, physically created. The subject in the illustration far overshadows in importance how it's portrayed.

The Deadly "Dry Spell"

Sometimes the writer gets stuck. Absolutely stuck. There's an awful and inexplicable dearth of illustrative ideas. The creative well seems to have run as dry as the Sahara.

Once, when the author was considerably younger and working as a copywriter with an old-line, 4A agency, a dry spell occurred. This was the first one. I was distressed and disturbed; nothing seemed to go right. Words wouldn't come, much less scintillating, sparkling, shining illustrative ideas. The first afternoon passed with no output; even staring fixedly out the window at the ants a couple of dozen stories below didn't help. No ads.

The next day, after a good night's sleep, the well was still dry. Ideas refused to come. That was when panic came close to setting in. Could it be possible that a copywriter couldn't come up with anything new and different? Couldn't words be strung together interestingly enough to keep from boring the guy who strung them? Could it be?

Well, that was Thursday. The obvious thing to do was be sick on Friday, to relax completely, go out to the rifle range and happily punch holes in small groups at 200 yards until a sore shoulder showed the fun was at an end for the weekend.

Next Monday output was 16 ads—in one day. All complete, all with provocative illustrative ideas, all proofread on the yellow and ready for finished typing. Every one of those ads hit print just as written.

Speed with which a writer works is a highly individual matter. Some writers are prolific. Thoughts and ideas flow fast, seemingly without end. Others take more time—they're deliberate, they procrastinate more, interruptions cause them to lose a train of thought more easily. But all have the same problems and getting stuck at times is one of them.

Don't let it worry you too much when it happens—and it *will* happen. When it does, walk around the office for a while. Go to the water cooler and have a drink. Take a stroll to the company cafeteria and have a leisurely cup. Kid your secretary. Bother your assistant. Check up on your clerk. If some or all of this doesn't help visualize a terrific illustration, let your subconscious take over.

Don't take your plight too seriously. Remind yourself that, after all, the illustration is only a vehicle to convey the appeal you want to make in the ad. It's not a life-or-death matter; there's no law on the books that says it has to spring full-blown to mind, all in vivid, glowing color, complete down to the last little detail.

You're after a picture of something, nothing more nor less. That something may be the product, a benefit realized by using the product, details of construction of the product, a reason for buying the product, or something similar to convey the basic idea of the advertisement as a whole. The illustration should complement the headline and body copy, of course, but it doesn't have to parrot either one.

Chances are if you're stuck for an idea you can talk your way out of it. Talk with others about the problem, that is. Discuss it with your account executive, the art director, a layout artist—even with your secretary. There's no telling where the bit of help you need to nudge your mental processes will come from.

Advertising, whether in an agency or in an industrial advertising department, tends to attract highly articulate visual thinkers, people who are considerably more imaginative than run-of-the-mill employees working in other capacities. Don't overlook them—use them. They'll be glad to listen to you, and you, in turn, should listen to their suggestions. Don't discard anything out of hand. Even if an idea isn't the greatest that ever came down the pike, there's always the possibility that it will trigger one that is.

Purpose of the Illustration

Business has always been competitive, but it's becoming more bitterly competitive each year.

As this trend continues, advertising pressure on readers of business publications has increased steadily and relentlessly. There are no signs of its diminishing. In fact, just the opposite holds true. As the level of marketing sophistication rises, more and more industrial companies are becoming increasingly aware of the major contribution advertising can make to their overall marketing activities.

Consequently, each individual ad has more pressure on *it*. Each ad has a bigger job cut out for it. Each advertisement must work harder, must produce more than ever before. This means, of course, that the components going into each ad have to be of higher quality —illustration, headline, body copy.

Each of these elements depends upon the other. Each is a link in the chain of reader reaction to the ad. Sequence of ad reading is: (1) Looking at the illustration, (2) reading the headline, and, (3) reading the body copy. Let just one element fall down and the ad suffers; it lacks credibility in the reader's mind as he realizes instinctively that something's amiss—even though he can't quite put his finger on just what it is. Lacking credibility, the ad has failed to convince the reader of the validity of the advertiser's claims. This means the ad has failed to make a *sales* call in print; it merely made a call, an incomplete one, one that borders on being futile.

Most of the burden is carried by the illustration. If it doesn't stop the reader long enough to cause him to read the headline, all's lost. Get out the white flag and wave it. Little will it matter if the headline is the greatest ever written, if it's loaded with user benefits and promises the reader everything he's ever desired in his wildest imaginings.

Your illustration must contribute to the strength of the ad as a whole. It can't freeload. To justify itself, the illustration must do one or more of the following:

1. Capture the attention of the reader.

2. Identify the subject of the advertisement.

3. Qualify readers by stopping those who are legitimate prospects, letting others skip over your ad if they are so inclined.

4. Arouse interest in reading the headline.

5. Create a favorable impression of product or advertiser.

6. Clarify claims made by the copy.

7. Help convince the reader of the truth of claims made in the copy.

8. Emphasize unique features of the product.

9. Provide continuity for all advertisements in the campaign through use of the same illustrative technique in each individual ad.

No one illustration is going to do all of those, but every illustration must do one or more.

Types of Illustrations

A real fun experience if you approach it with an objective in mind is to leaf through a dozen leading trade publications, preferably from a number of different fields. Ignore the editorial material and concentrate on the ads.

Amazing is the only word that comes readily to mind—or even comes close to describing the inventiveness of the advertising people who conceived, created, and produced the ads. Simply amazing.

What makes the experience memorable, rather than an academic exercise, is not merely looking at the illustrations in the ads, but taking a few seconds—or, in some cases, minutes—to try to re-create the mental processes of the copywriter at the moment the illustrative idea occurred to him. Try this and you'll find yourself thinking in ways you never dreamed of. The sensation is an odd one.

Illustrations run the gamut from those that are downright ridiculous to some that are little short of sublime. When you're flipping through the magazines haphazardly there appears to be neither rhyme nor reason for many of the illustrations.

And something else that immediately comes to mind is that the subjects of the illustrations are almost limitless; they defy hasty attempts to categorize them into neat little groups or classifications, all neatly labeled. This holds true unless each individual illustration is regarded *not* as an illustration complete in itself, but as a *type* of illustration—one that has many kissing cousins in other advertisers' ads.

Twenty-one basic types of illustrations just about wrap up those used most commonly in industrial advertisements. In various forms they appear and reappear year after year. If treated imaginatively and with good taste, each type of illustration can be effective indefinitely. Let's look at the classifications, then at examples of each. Types of illustrations are:

1. Package containing the product.

2. Product alone.

3. Product in use.

4. Product feature(s).

5. Explanation of feature(s).

6. User benefit.

7. Comparison of products.

8. How to use the product.

9. Storytelling.

10. Implication.

11. Humor.

12. Borrowed interest.

13. Contrast.

14. Curiosity arousing.

15. Charts and graphs.

16. Cutaway or cross section.

17. Symbolism.

18. Negative appeal.

19. Make-believe figures.

20. Abstraction.

21. Rebus.

Package Illustration

Sometimes it's just as important to the advertiser to illustrate the package in which his product is sold as it is to show the product itself. This is particularly true in highly competitive fields where the difference between competing products is either slight, or when it's difficult to convince prospects that the difference that does exist is significant.

In the automotive aftermarket, for example, this situation is frequently encountered. This is due to the distribution system of the industry; manufacturers don't sell direct. Manufacturers sell to warehouse distributors; these WDs then sell to jobbers; the jobbers, in turn, sell to dealers; dealers, as the term is used in this industry, are actually automobile dealers, repair garages, fleets, and so on. Each performs a service, each has salesmen out on the street selling to those next in line in the chain.

Competition for salesmen's time—and to motivate them to push one manufacturer's line at the expense of another—is intense, to say the least. At the warehouse distributor level there's relative indifference about brands and manufacturers. The WD will buy anything he's reasonably confident his salesmen can move at a profit. Brand loyalty is a foreign concept to him. On down the ladder, though, manufacturer salesmen are increasingly preoccupied with development of brand loyalty and constantly engage in "missionary work" to help jobber salesmen on calls to dealers. It is here, on the lowest level, that a product either catches fire or fails miserably.

For some years Sealed Power Corporation emphasized its package for the company's line of stainless steel piston rings. This was done in all advertising directed toward jobbers. "Look for the familiar red box," Sealed Power said in every ad—and the box was illustrated big and bold and in red, its actual color.

The War for Shelf Space

Competition for shelf space in an automotive jobber's place of business is also pretty rugged. When a dealer or garageman comes in to buy parts for a particular vehicle he's working on, he frequently has no preference as to what specific brand he'll buy. Often he's inclined to accept the recommendation of the counterman—the inside salesman. This individual as often as not tallies up a tidy little income on the side in the form of "spifs"—which are nothing more nor less than bribes from a manufacturer to push *his* brand of parts at the expense of others. In the case of a set of automotive valves, for instance, the counterman might be paid 75 cents per set to push the brand made by Smith Valve Company, Inc.

One way to counter competition's spifs is to offer bigger and better spifs yourself. This tactic can become costly indeed as the war escalates. Only so much can be given away without a jump in selling price, which is an additional competitive disadvantage. Or the manufacturer can, through advertising and strong selling, create brand preference and brand loyalty.

To the mechanic—or the garage's errand boy—visualizing a set of automotive valves is the easiest thing possible. That's because he doesn't see the shiny new valves in all of their pristine beauty floating in a cloud-filled sky; *he sees the package the valves come in.* Maybe it's red or blue or brown or black. But whatever the colors or the shape, this buyer visualizes the package. The package is the product to him.

When he enters a jobber's establishment he may well be undecided about what brand of valve to buy. The only thing he's sure of is that it's for a 289 cu. in. Ford V-8 engine. While he's waiting to be waited on, he lets his eye idly roam the shelves laden with neatly stacked fast-moving items handy and up front where the countermen can grab them quickly to speed customer turnover.

This is when the moment of truth arrives for many a manufacturer. Smart marketers faced with similar conditions have distinctive boxes. The manufacturer's name is prominent, it's in type large enough to be read from the customer side of the counter. It has the logo big and bold enough for all to see and identify.

The Timken Roller Bearing Company's fine four-color spread ad illustrated above is basically a package illustration. It is from *Commercial Car Journal* magazine. The copy approach is from the safety angle with the left page devoted to a testimonial given by the president of a large trucking company that consistently wins awards for an excellent safety record. The trucker uses Timken Roller Bearings in his vehicles with outstanding success in terms of bearing life—which can be translated into cost per mile, and in freedom from accidents caused by bearing failure.

The stark, simple right page of the spread has a hand—a greasy, mechanic's hand—holding the package in which he receives Timken bearings. This is the package he sees on the jobber's shelf, this is what he visualizes when he thinks of wheel bearings.

Timken capitalized on the high interest everybody has in highway safety to gain readership, then strengthened product identification and brand recognition with the illustration of the box. A well-done ad.

Need to promote the package was also recognized by Holo-Krome Company, whose delightfully tongue-in-cheek two-color ad is shown on page 647.

The light touch in the illustration was deliberately chosen to draw reader attention to the ad—which it does admirably. It's very easy to chuckle at Holo-Krome's illustration, then proceed into the headline and body copy. Copy is serious and sells hard Holo-Krome's ability to ship more than 98 percent of all orders for its socket screw products the day the order is received. Here again, the illustration works well with the headline and copy.

Product Alone

Time was when an industrial advertising manager, faced with having to show the product in a new ad, invariably specified that it be shown in use. This was done without question, without second thought.

After all, it was a time-honored tenet that the product was *never* shown all by its lonesome in an illustration unless it was for a catalog or a piece of sales literature. It was unthinkable to show the product alone in an ad. It bordered on blasphemy. Thinking was, if just the product was shown the illustration couldn't help but be trite, static, and boring. Nobody but nobody in industry would condescend to give it a second glance, and probably not even a first one, either.

A bulldozer, for example, obviously should be shown gouging out a cut for a new interstate highway; a transverse profilometer would naturally be trailing a test vehicle; an electric typewriter or an electronic calculator might be illustrated in a typical office setting. All of this was done in the name of realism with an uppercase "R."

Nobody wanted to give the impression he was being crass enough to show his product. That would be gauché.

Product-in-use illustrations are effective, there's no denying that.

However, there are times when it's advisable to show only the product—all alone, sans background, without benefit of a sexy model or carefully constructed set that simulates a working atmosphere. With no background or other elements in the illustration, there's nothing to distract the reader by diverting his eye from the product.

The spring illustrated nearby almost jumps out of the page at you because it's so stark, simple, and alone. Photo is by the author.

Consider the new product ad, for instance. The reader is not familiar with the product because he's never seen it before. He doesn't know what it looks like. He doesn't know how it differs in appearance from the old model it replaced. He doesn't know how it appears compared to competitive products. And he has no mental impression of the product to enable him to form an opinion or attitude toward it.

Show an illustration of the product alone and it instantly telegraphs to the reader what the ad's all about, and what the product looks like. Until recent years, the external appearance of an industrial product was considered relatively inconsequential. If the thing worked, what did it matter what it looked like?

A Change in Thinking

Now, however, that thinking has fallen by the wayside. It is generally accepted that appearance of the product is highly important. Despite the fact that buying decisions are theoretically based on value analysis and are made logically and unemotionally, appearance can be the decisive factor in a sale—to a much greater extent than most buyers will admit. Other things being even close to equal, it's an odd sort of individual who won't choose a product whose appearance is esthetically pleasing over one that's unprepossessing. If the product is genuinely pleasing in appearance—and many of today's machine tools and control panels and electronic instruments are beautiful due to growing reliance on competent industrial designers—the smart manufacturer exploits this advantage for all it's worth. And it's worth plenty.

When you have a smart-looking piece of equipment, a simple, straightforward picture of the product all by itself conveys the impression you want the reader to get faster than almost any other type of illustration.